BTEC national

2nd Edition

Information Technology Practitioners

Book 1

Series editor: Jenny Lawson

KT-569-030

www.harcourt.co.uk

✓ Free online support
✓ Useful weblinks
✓ 24 hour online ordering

01865 888118

Heinemann

Heinemann is an imprint of Harcourt Education Limited, a company incorporated in England and Wales, having its registered office: Halley Court, Jordan Hill, Oxford OX2 8EJ. Registered company number: 3099304

www.harcourt.co.uk

Heinemann is the registered trademark of Harcourt Education Limited

Text © Karen Anderson, Peter Blundell, Alan Jarvis, Allen Kaye, Jenny Lawson, Jenny Phillips and Andrew Smith 2007

First published 2007

12 11 10 09 08 07
10 9 8 7 6 5 4 3 2 1

British Library Cataloguing in Publication Data is available from the British Library on request.

ISBN 978 0 435465 49 0

Typeset by Wearset Ltd
Illustrated by Tek-Art
Original illustrations © Harcourt Education Limited 2007
Picture research by Zooid
Cover photo © Alamy/A1 Pix
Printed and bound at Scotprint, East Lothian, Scotland

Websites
Please note that the examples of websites suggested in this book were up to date at the time of writing. It is essential for tutors to preview each site before using it to ensure that the URL is still accurate and the content is appropriate. We suggest that tutors bookmark useful sites and consider enabling students to access them through the school or college intranet.

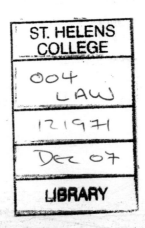

Contents

Acknowledgements

The authors and publisher are grateful to all those who have given permission to reproduce material. Every effort has been made to contact copyright holders of material reproduced in this book. Any omissions will be rectified in subsequent printings if notice is given to the publisher.

Photo credits

Alamy / ACE STOCK LIMITED – pages 80–81, 101–103

Alamy / Alex Segre - page 200

Alamy / Chris Pearsall – page 188

Alamy / David Pearson – page 231

Alamy / ImagePix – page 187

Alamy / ImageState – page 93

Alamy / Photofusion Picture Library – page 186

Alamy / uk retail Alan King – page 96

Alamy Images / Helene Rogers – page 252

Corbis – pages 110, 112, 118

Corbis / Bettmann – page 384

Corbis / Lwa- Jdc – page 211

Corbis / Tony West – page 389

Dreamstime / Natalia Siverina – page 156

Dreamstime.com / Andrzej Tokarski – page 155

Eyewire – page 285

Gareth Boden – pages 45, 49, 50, 329 (×2), 332

Getty Images / Barros & Barros – pages 316–317

Getty Images / Photodisc – pages 11, 73, 242–243

Getty Images / Stockdisc – pages 124–125

Harcourt Ltd / Gareth Boden – pages 153, 280–281

iStockPhoto / Alyda De Villers – page 397

iStockPhoto / Scrambled – page 59

Martyn F. Chillmaid – pages 40–41, 52

Memorysolution GMBH – page 59

NASA / Kennedy Space Center – pages 208–209

Photos.com – pages 292, 300

Reed International Books Australia Pty Ltd / Lindsay Edwards Photography. With thanks to Lort Smith Animal Hospital, North Melbourne, Victoria – pages 2–3

Reproduction of Microsoft Products Courtesy of Microsoft Corporation/Microsoft Deutschland GmbH – page 386

Research in Motion Ltd – pages 382–383

Rex Features / Image Source – page 18

Rex Features / Image Source/Rex Features – page 89

Rex Features / Jonathan Hordle – page 385

Rex Features / Nigel R. Barklie – page 353

Rex Features / Peter Lomas – page 16

Richard Philpott/Zooid Pictures – pages 170–171

Science Photo Library / Jerry Mason – page 385

Science Photo Library / Tek Image – page 53, 254

Topfoto / David Wimsett / Uppa.co.uk – pages 350–351

Zooid Pictures – pages 319, 366, 368

Zooid Pictures / Richard Philpott – 270

Introduction

Welcome to this BTEC National IT Practitioners course book, specifically designed to support students on the following programmes:

- BTEC National Award in National IT Practitioners
- BTEC National Certificate in National IT Practitioners
- BTEC National Diploma in National IT Practitioners.

The table opposite shows how each unit covered in this book fits within the different pathways of the BTEC National IT Practitioners qualification at Award, Certificate and Diploma level. Units marked 'M' are mandatory for the pathway; units marked 'O' are optional for the pathway. Please note that some units are optional at Certificate level, but mandatory at Diploma level.

The aim of this book is to provide a comprehensive source of information for your course. It follows the BTEC specification closely, so that you can easily see what you have covered and quickly find the information you need. Every grading criterion for each unit listed above is covered in the tasks, and a grading grid, showing Edexcel's grading criteria mapped against each task, is available from the Harcourt website.

Examples and case studies from IT are used to bring your course to life and make it enjoyable to study. We hope you will be encouraged to find your own examples of current practice too.

Unit	IT & Business	Network	Software Development	Systems Support	Award/Cert/Dip
1: Communication and Employability Skills for IT	M	M	M	M	A/C/D
2: Computer Systems	M	M	M	M	A/C/D
3: Information Systems	M	O	M	M	A/C/D
7: Systems Analysis and Design	O	O	O (C) M (D)	O	A/C/D
8: Communication Technologies	O	M	O	O	A/C/D
15: Organisational Systems Security	O (C) M (D)	O (C) M (D)	O	O (C) M (D)	A/C/D
18: Principles of Software Design and Development	O	O	M	O	A/C/D
27: Principles of Computer Networks	O	M	O	O	A/C/D
28: IT Technical Support	O	O	O	M	A/C/D
29: IT Troubleshooting and Repair	O	O	O	O (C) M (D)	A/C/D
34: e-Commerce	O (C) M (D)	O	O	O	A/C/D
35: Impact of the Use of IT on Business Systems	M	O	O	O	A/C/D

M mandatory unit
O optional unit
A award
C certificate
D diploma

Guide to learning and assessment features

This book has a number of features to help you relate theory to practice and reinforce your learning. It also aims to help you gather evidence for assessment. You will find the features identified below in each unit.

Your teacher or tutor should check that you have completed enough activities to meet all the assessment criteria for the unit, whether from this book or from other tasks.

Teachers/tutors and students should refer to the BTEC standards for the qualification for the full BTEC grading criteria for each unit (www.edexcel.org.uk).

Assessment features

Activities

Activities are provided throughout each unit. These are linked to real situations and case studies and they can be used for practice before tackling the preparation for assessment. Alternatively, some can contribute to your unit assessment if you choose to do these instead of the preparation for assessment at the end of each unit.

Grading icons

In some activities and case studies throughout the book you will see the **p**, **m** and **d** icons. These show you where the tasks fit in with the grading criteria. If you do these tasks you will be building up your evidence to achieve your desired qualification. If you are aiming for a Merit, in the specification make sure you complete all the Pass **p** and Merit **m** tasks. If you are aiming for a Distinction, you will also need to complete all the

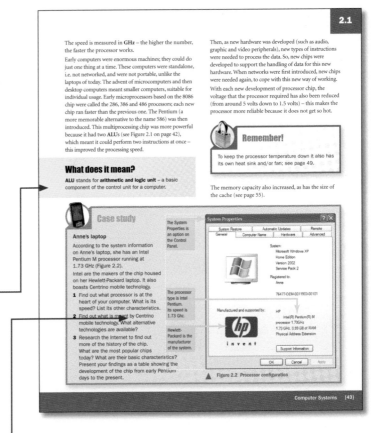

▲ Figure 2.2 Processor configuration

Distinction **d** tasks. **p** means the first of the Pass criteria listed, **m** the first of the Merit criteria, **d** the first of the Distinction criteria, and so on.

Preparation for assessment

Each unit concludes with a full unit assessment, which taken as a whole fulfils the unit requirements from Pass to Distinction. Each task is matched to the relevant criteria in the specification.

Learning features

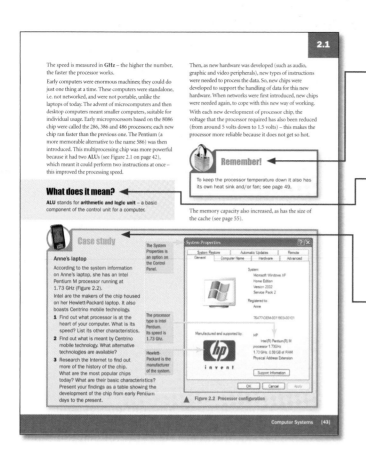

2.1

The speed is measured in **GHz** – the higher the number, the faster the processor works.

Early computers were enormous machines; they could do just one thing at a time. These computers were standalone, i.e. not networked, and were not portable, unlike the laptops of today. The advent of microcomputers and then desktop computers meant smaller computers, suitable for individual usage. Early microprocessors based on the 8086 chip were called the 286, 386 and 486 processors; each new chip ran faster than the previous one. The Pentium (a more memorable alternative to the name 586) was then introduced. This multiprocessing chip was more powerful because it had two ALUs (see Figure 2.1 on page 42), which meant it could perform two instructions at once – this improved the processing speed.

What does it mean?

ALU stands for **arithmetic and logic unit** – a basic component of the control unit for a computer.

Case study

Anne's laptop

According to the system information on Anne's laptop, she has an Intel Pentium M processor running at 1.73 GHz (Figure 2.2).

Intel are the makers of the chip housed on her Hewlett-Packard laptop. It also boasts Centrino mobile technology.

1 Find out what processor is at the heart of your computer. What is its speed? List its other characteristics.

2 Find out what is meant by Centrino mobile technology. What alternative technologies are available?

3 Research the Internet to find out more of the history of the chip. What are the most popular chips today? What are their basic characteristics? Present your findings as a table showing the development of the chip from early Pentium days to the present.

Then, as new hardware was developed (such as audio, graphic and video peripherals), new types of instructions were needed to process the data. So, new chips were developed to support the handling of data for this new hardware. When networks were first introduced, new chips were needed again, to cope with this new way of working. With each new development of processor chip, the voltage that the processor required has also been reduced (from around 5 volts down to 1.5 volts) – this makes the processor more reliable because it does not get so hot.

Remember!

To keep the processor temperature down it also has its own heat sink and/or fan; see page 49.

The memory capacity also increased, as has the size of the cache (see page 55).

The System Properties is an option on the Control Panel.

The processor type is Intel Pentium. Its speed is 1.73 Ghz.

Hewlett-Packard is the manufacturer of the system.

System Properties
System Restore | Automatic Updates | Remote
General | Computer Name | Hardware | Advanced

System:
Microsoft Windows XP
Home Edition
Version 2002
Service Pack 2

Registered to:
Anne

76477-OEM-0011903-00101

Manufactured and supported by:
HP
Intel(R) Pentium(R) M
processor 1.73GHz
1.73 GHz, 0.99 GB of RAM
Physical Address Extension

▲ Figure 2.2 Processor configuration

Computer Systems [43]

Remember!

Important details that you need to keep in mind are under these headings. They will help identify particularly vital information.

What does it mean?

Terms that you need to be aware of are summarised under these headings. They will help you check your knowledge as you learn, and will prove to be a useful quick-reference tool.

Case studies

Interesting examples of real situations or companies are described in case studies that link theory to practice. They will show you how the topics you are studying affect real people and businesses.

Test your knowledge

At the end of each section is a set of quick questions to test your knowledge of the information you have been studying. Use these to check your progress, and also as a revision tool.

Watch out!

Issues you need to be aware of are highlighted under these headings. They will help to ensure good working practice.

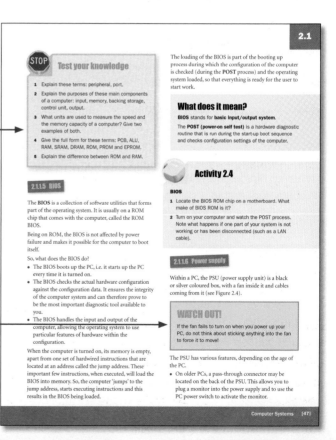

2.1

STOP Test your knowledge

1 Explain these terms: peripheral, port.

2 Explain the purposes of these main components of a computer: input, memory, backing storage, control unit, output.

3 What units are used to measure the speed and the memory capacity of a computer? Give two examples of both.

4 Give the full form for these terms: PCB, ALU, RAM, SRAM, DRAM, ROM, PROM and EPROM.

5 Explain the difference between ROM and RAM.

2.1.1.5 BIOS

The **BIOS** is a collection of software utilities that forms part of the operating system. It is usually on a ROM chip that comes with the computer, called the ROM BIOS.

Being on ROM, the BIOS is not affected by power failure and makes it possible for the computer to boot itself.

So, what does the BIOS do?

• The BIOS boots up the PC, i.e. it starts up the PC every time it is turned on.

• The BIOS checks the actual hardware configuration against the configuration data. It ensures the integrity of the computer system and can therefore prove to be the most important diagnostic tool available to you.

• The BIOS handles the input and output of the computer, allowing the operating system to use particular features of hardware within the configuration.

When the computer is turned on, its memory is empty, apart from one set of hardwired instructions that are located at an address called the jump address. These important few instructions, when executed, will load the BIOS into memory. So, the computer 'jumps' to the jump address, starts executing instructions and this results in the BIOS being loaded.

The loading of the BIOS is part of the booting up process during which the configuration of the computer is checked (during the **POST** process) and the operating system loaded, so that everything is ready for the user to start work.

What does it mean?

BIOS stands for **basic input/output system**.

The **POST (power-on self test)** is a hardware diagnostic routine that is run during the start-up boot sequence and checks configuration settings of the computer.

Activity 2.4

BIOS

1 Locate the BIOS ROM chip on a motherboard. What make of BIOS ROM is it?

2 Turn on your computer and watch the POST process. Note what happens if one part of your system is not working or has been disconnected (such as a LAN cable).

2.1.1.6 Power supply

Within a PC, the PSU (power supply unit) is a black or silver coloured box, with a fan inside it and cables coming from it (see Figure 2.4).

WATCH OUT!

If the fan fails to turn on when you power up your PC, do not think about sticking anything into the fan to force it to move!

The PSU has various features, depending on the age of the PC.

• On older PCs, a pass-through connector may be located on the back of the PSU. This allows you to plug a monitor into the power supply and to use the PC power switch to activate the monitor.

Computer Systems [47]

Communication and Employability Skills for IT

Introduction

As well as the technical skills and knowledge required for specific jobs in ICT, you will need a range of non-technical skills and attitudes that are considered essential to employability. So that you achieve this, Unit 1 focuses on what are called **soft skills**.

What does it mean?

Soft skills influence how people interact with each other. Examples of soft skills are: analytical thinking, creativity, diplomacy, effective communication, flexibility, leadership, listening skills, problem solving, team building and a readiness for change.

One very important set of soft skills relates to communication, which is why communication is included in the title of this unit and why you are required to study the principles of effective communication. You may already possess some or all of these soft skills – and by the end of this unit, you will have identified your own strengths (and weaknesses) and, where necessary, improved the skills needed to make you an effective employee.

ICT provides tools (such as word processing software) with features (such as spell checkers) to assist you to communicate accurately and therefore effectively. In studying this unit, you will learn how to improve your general communication skills by exploiting certain application packages and tools.

Continual self-development is recognised as essential for all employees. The rapidly changing nature of ICT makes this particularly relevant for those who work, or aspire to work, in the ICT industry. While working on this unit, you will create and use a personal development plan (PDP) to capture and track your training needs and the accumulation of new skills and knowledge. This will make you familiar with the self-development process.

After completing this unit, you should be able to achieve these outcomes:

- Understand the attributes of employees that are valued by employers
- Understand the principles of effective communication
- Be able to exploit ICT to communicate effectively
- Be able to identify personal development needs and the ways of addressing them.

Thinking points

This unit should help you to understand what employers seek in their prospective employees, and to recognise the soft skills and non-technical knowledge expected of an effective employee. It focuses on personal behaviour and communication skills and provides you with an opportunity to examine your own strengths and weaknesses.

This sensitive topic may make you feel uncomfortable. Thinking about and admitting to your personal plus points may embarrass you, and considering aspects of your behaviour that might need to be worked on may be even more embarrassing. Your teacher will guide you through this topic and, hopefully, it will help you to become more confident of your value as an employee.

Although you are studying ICT, many of the skills you learn in this unit also apply to employment in other industries, such as retail or banking. This is because the way you behave with people is important, whatever job you do.

If you understand the attributes of employees that are most valued by employers, you will be better able to present yourself to a prospective employer and have a better chance of success in your job search.

Some attributes are specific to a given job but many apply to all jobs. Some attributes relate to you as a person, while others relate to the type of organisation that you hope to join. Each of these types of attributes will now be considered in turn.

1.1.1 Job-related attributes

This section focuses on the attributes that relate directly to the job.

1.1.1.1 Technical knowledge

For any given job, a variety of technical skills might be considered necessary. For example, the level of qualifications required, as well as other skills specific to that job, such as being able to cook or to swim.

- A sales representative needs to be able to drive and to have a clean driving licence. The employer may provide a company car, but some jobs may demand that you have your own means of transport.
- It is courteous for airline employees to respond to passengers in the same language that the passengers have used. So, airlines may demand language skills of some of their employees, such as cabin crew.
- An IT technician who fixes hardware faults needs to have the ability to use hand tools such as screwdrivers, but also be skilled in using electronic testing equipment such as a multimeter.

If a technical skill is essential to an advertised job, it should be made clear to all prospective employees. This will deter candidates without the requisite skills and avoid employers wasting time interviewing applicants who are unsuited to the post.

1.1.1.2 Working procedures and systems

Some jobs involve working procedures and systems which might suit some applicants but deter others. Shift work that involves working at night or at the weekends can appeal to some people but might not be practical for others. Antisocial hours can mean a worker doesn't have 'normal' free time with family and friends but might also attract a higher rate of pay. For people with dependent children, shift work may only be possible if crèche facilities are offered or if the earnings are high enough to cover the costs of paying for child care.

Some jobs involve a level of risk and health and safety issues, which might excite some prospective employees but could also deter others. For example, people planning to join the fire service may have courage and a sense of duty, but should be aware of the personal danger of attending to fires.

Activity 1.1

Job-related technical skills

1. Research the Internet to find out what child care facilities employers are expected to provide so that employees with dependants can have access to the same jobs as those without dependants.

2. Working in groups of three or four, search the local and national papers for examples of job adverts that specify the technical skills needed for particular ICT vacancies. List the attributes that employers seem to be seeking in a prospective employee.

3. Make a list of the technical skills that you have. Compare your list with others in your group and add any to your own list that you had forgotten. Within your group, compile a comprehensive list of technical skills that one or more of you have. For each skill, grade yourself according to your own level of competence.

1.1.2 Universal attributes

Regardless of the job and its particular requirements, there are some skills that everyone is expected to have, to some extent. Having these skills will mean you are better able to carry out the tasks for any job. The more competent you are in these universal skills, the more attractive you will seem to a prospective employer.

This subsection looks in particular at planning and organisational skills, time management, team working, verbal and written communication skills, numeracy skills and other skills such as creativity.

1.1.2.1 Planning and organisational skills

Planning skills are not the same as organisational skills but they do tend to go hand in hand.

- **Planning** involves thinking ahead to decide what you need to do to achieve a goal within a given timescale. You might not need to write a plan, but thinking about it and what could go wrong helps to ensure a measure of success in whatever you set out to do.
- **Organisational skills** involve having a system or routine so that you complete everyday tasks as efficiently as possible. For example, organising your workspace includes having the things you need most (pens or pencils, your calculator, a stapler, etc.) within arm's reach and then keeping everything tidily in its place. Around your workspace, you might have books or folders arranged neatly on a shelf and files arranged alphabetically in a hanging drawer. You might have an address book with all your contact lists and a diary showing your appointments.

If you are good at organising things, you might also have good planning skills. If you lack these skills, try to improve them – they are both essential. Planning skills *can* be learnt, and then you just need practice.

The process of planning – establishing goals, deciding on strategy, setting objectives and then matching your performance against your objectives – is a way of measuring your success. If you fail in some respect, this can also help you: to plan better in the future.

■ HOW TO PLAN

1. First, establish your **goal**. Your goal should reflect how you see the present situation (its shortfalls) and your future needs. Decide on a goal that can be effectively pursued. You might write down your goal. Some organisations frame their goals in a mission statement.
2. The next step is to decide on your **strategy**. Consider what might happen if you take a particular line of action, and make sure you take everything into account: the people involved and any constraints such as timescale and your resources.
3. Your strategy will guide you as to how you are going to achieve your goals and this will lead you to a list of **objectives**.

What does it mean?

A **goal** provides general purpose and direction. It is the end result towards which your effort will be directed.

A **strategy** is a systematic plan of action.

Objectives are like goals except that goals are broad and objectives are narrower. Goals express general intentions while objectives are precise. Goals are intangible (like improving your general fitness) while objectives are tangible (like practising until you can do 20 press-ups in one go).

Planning may involve just you. For example, you might write yourself a 'to do' list with the tasks prioritised, and then check your progress on a regular basis. You may choose to review progress every Monday morning and write a fresh 'to do' list, showing all the tasks to complete by the end of the working day on Friday.

As the week progresses, you could tick off the things that you have done and think about the remaining things on the list. It may prove impossible to complete all the tasks by the Friday deadline, but prioritising tasks should mean that you complete the most important tasks first. It should also help you to make more realistic plans: not trying to fit too much into your day or promising to complete work that will prove impossible given your time and resources.

You might find it more helpful to rewrite the 'to do' list every day – some tasks may have become irrelevant, while other tasks may become more urgent. However, your day should be spent doing tasks, rather than thinking about what to do. So, the administration of your 'to do' list must not become a major task in itself!

Microsoft Outlook's Tasks feature can help you to maintain your list and prioritise your work (see Figure 1.1). Outlook Tasks also offers a reminder feature so tasks that crop up on a regular basis automatically reappear on the list.

Planning can also involve a team of people, each member of the team agreeing to complete their own tasks within a given time frame so that the entire team achieves its objectives. The organisational skills in managing a team are more complex and require more sophisticated tools. If a project involves lots of people and many interrelated tasks, the person managing the project might use a planning tool such as a Gantt chart (see Figure 1.2).

Organisational skills can also be learnt. First, focus on what it is that you want to organise (your workspace, your books, your CDs, your wardrobe, etc.) and then consider the purpose of organising and set yourself a target:

- A receptionist might write: 'I need to organise my workspace so that whenever someone asks me a question I can easily and quickly locate the information I need to answer. This will make me a more reliable source of information.'

- A librarian might write: 'I need to organise my books so that I can find a particular book quickly. This will be appreciated by those who visit my library.'

Then, ask yourself what options you have. In your own workspace, you could arrange your books by type, putting fiction on one shelf and the technical manuals on another shelf. By segregating the books, you reduce the number of books you need to search through to find the one you want. Libraries arrange books according to the Dewey system and, within that, titles are arranged in alphabetical order of author.

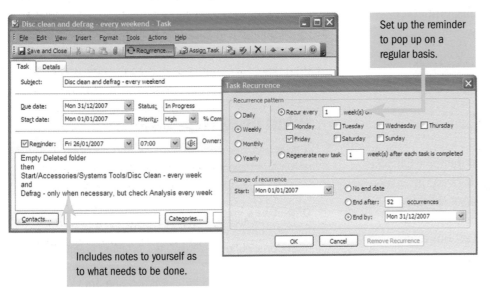

Set up the reminder to pop up on a regular basis.

Includes notes to yourself as to what needs to be done.

▲ **Figure 1.1 Outlook Tasks**

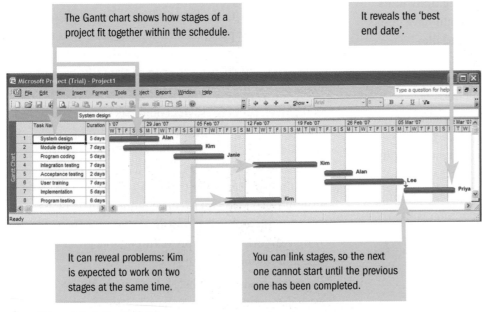

The Gantt chart shows how stages of a project fit together within the schedule.

It reveals the 'best end date'.

It can reveal problems: Kim is expected to work on two stages at the same time.

You can link stages, so the next one cannot start until the previous one has been completed.

▲ **Figure 1.2 A Gantt chart**

Activity 1.2

Organising a workspace

1 Examine your workspace. If you close your eyes, can you say where everything is or should be? Does everything have its own place? Sketch your workspace, showing where the things you use most are kept.

2 Compare the sketch of your workspace with those of others around you. Discuss the pros and cons of the positioning of commonly used items such as your pens, a pair of scissors or a box of tissues. Look for patterns in your and your colleagues' ways of arranging things.

3 Examine other examples of storing things: in your kitchen, in your wardrobe, inside the bathroom cabinet. To what extent are the contents stored in a systematic way? Choose one situation where it might be important to store something in a given place, so that the item could be found very quickly. Sketch how you would organise things in your chosen situation.

4 Some people are almost proud of their untidiness. Within your group, discuss the benefits that untidiness may bring. Draw up a list of pros and cons of being tidy.

1.1.2.2 Time management

To make the best use of your time, you need to manage it effectively. Consider aids to time management, such as diaries or calendars. There are also techniques that you can adopt to make sure that you do not waste time.

Having somewhere to keep track of appointments (whether on a wall chart, in a handwritten diary or using an electronic calendar) will help you to see what will be happening in the next day, week or year. It should help you to avoid double booking your time. It could also remind you to set aside time between appointments so that you can prepare properly for each event. As long as you refer to your diary or calendar each morning, you should never forget an appointment or arrive late (see Figure 1.3).

Handwritten diaries have the advantage of (usually) being small enough to carry with you everywhere. They provide a written record of how you have spent your time, and what will be on your agenda in the future. Electronic diaries are particularly useful in a

▼ Figure 1.3 Who do you think will make the best use of their time?

working environment. For example, Microsoft Outlook has a calendar feature (see Figure 1.4).

Within an organisation, online diaries make setting up a meeting easier – you can see who is free and when, and choose a convenient time. You can send the meeting agenda via email and each attendee's Outlook calendar will be updated automatically.

Calendar features on a mobile phone and **PDAs** such as a Blackberry can be synchronised with electronic diaries such as Outlook.

Many PDAs, such as the Blackberry, are also portable communications devices using wireless mobile phone technology to provide email, telephone, text messaging and web browsing services. So, someone who travels a lot can use their PDA/mobile phone when offline, but synchronise as soon as they have access to a computer, e.g. via their laptop in a hotel room, or at an **Internet café**.

What does it mean?

PDA stands for portable data assistant.

What does it mean?

An **Internet café** is a small informal coffee shop where you can pay to use the Internet. You can use the computers there or, with some Internet cafés, link to their network using your own laptop.

Note that, if you are in an Internet café, to synchronise with your home computer assumes that you have the facility to access your home computer remotely.

Time management also involves using available time in the most efficient way. This means using strategies to prevent events that might result in a waste of your time.

Interruptions can disrupt your work, and these can take many forms, such as emails, phone calls or people. Handling interruptions efficiently is an important aspect of time management.

Studies have shown that on-screen interruptions announcing a new email can seriously disrupt a person's workflow. It takes time to read and respond to each email, but it also takes time to recover the momentum that was in effect before the interruption. Since the emails have to be processed at some point and other work completed too, the best strategy is to batch the interruptions.

Instead of having an announcement arrive on-screen as soon as a new email arrives, you can check your inbox at regular intervals, e.g. once an hour. You can clear all the important emails and then resume other work, resisting checking the in-tray again for at least another hour. The time spent responding to emails is not reduced, but the quality of time spent on other tasks is improved. This is obviously a better use of the available time. Batching emails means there may be a longer delay in responding to any one email, so apply a priority system: deal with the most important emails first.

You can block your time for meetings and other fixed events such as dental appointments.

If the appointment is recurring, the calendar can set aside time for the subsequent meetings automatically.

Figure 1.4 Outlook calendar

Case study

Incoming emails

Heinemann recommends that its employees check their inbox four times a day: on arrival in the office, late morning, early afternoon and late afternoon.

1 Monitor the arrival of emails into your inbox. You could do this by looking at the date/time received of each email (see Figure 1.5).

2 Estimate the time it takes to respond to these emails and work out how regularly you ought to check your inbox, so as to minimise the response time for the most urgent emails.

3 Find out how to identify emails that come from people who are important enough to require almost immediate attention. Look for an automated procedure to do this for you.

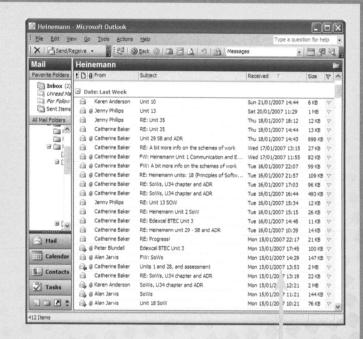

The received dates of emails – shown here for just one project – reveal the volume of correspondence in one week.

Figure 1.5 Arrival pattern of emails

Similarly, if you have a number of telephone calls to make today, it may be better to list them, making sure you have all the details to hand (person you are going to call, their telephone number, any paperwork that you want to discuss with them, your diary, etc.) and then to work through them in one sitting. While you are on the phone, incoming callers may leave messages on your voicemail. So, when you finish making all your outgoing calls, check your voicemail and decide which messages need actioning when you might need to call back and whether you can email a response to better effect. If you let yourself be distracted, you might not complete your list of calls today. Interruptions, such as a voicemail left while you were on the phone, have to be weighed against your current list of objectives.

If people constantly interrupt you, it can be impossible to complete a single task efficiently. Some people resort to arriving at the office an hour before anyone else and staying late. If this happens on a daily basis, there is not enough time for rest and relaxation – an essential part of everyone's day. So, it is important to handle interruptions in a way that does not offend anyone and yet allows you to complete your work during normal office hours.

If you have your own office, closing the door may be enough to deter casual interruptions. If you have an assistant, you might tell the assistant to field all interruptions, leaving you in peace for a specified period. Some organisations encourage workers to work from home occasionally; this cuts out commuting time and helps to ensure quality working time.

The scheduling of meetings and how these meetings are conducted also requires careful planning to make the most effective use of the attendees' time. An agenda should be drawn up so that everyone knows what is to be discussed. Any papers should be circulated beforehand so that everyone can fully brief themselves ahead of the meeting.

Even the process of handling incoming correspondence (paperwork or electronic mail) can be organised so that you do not waste time. An in-tray can be a physical tray for paperwork, or an electronic inbox such as that provided by email software like Outlook. Your in-tray might hold letters from customers or suppliers, reports from colleagues, or sample designs for products that you need to look at. Allocate time to look at this material – but only long enough to identify each item's content and to establish the urgency of any action you might need to take.

- Material that requires no further action should either be binned (moved to the Deleted Items folder in Outlook or shredded if it is paper-based correspondence including sensitive personal details) or filed (electronically in a folder or physically in a filing cabinet). Do not leave it in the in-tray! If you often don't have time to file material immediately, at least create a file called 'filing' and put the item in there, under the correct alphabetical letter. This will speed up the eventual filing process and will allow you to find things that you have not yet filed in the meantime.

- Material that does require time and thought and maybe some other action should be given some priority and/or allocated a time slot. Add it to your 'to do' list and put the paperwork somewhere you will easily find it – in your briefcase if you plan to read it on the journey home or in a pending tray, or the electronic folder called My Briefcase. Do not leave it in your in-tray!

Allocating a short time each day to process incoming mail should stop you overlooking anything important. It will prevent material piling up in your in-tray and reduce the amount of time spent thinking about what to do with a particular item. It should also save time – you will not find yourself hunting through the in-tray looking for something.

'Do it once and do it right' is a simple adage to use that avoids duplication of effort.

1.1.2.3 Team working

Some people work in isolation, but most people work as part of a team. Being a member of a team brings responsibilities. You need to report to others in the team about what you are doing and to keep up to date with what they are doing. This flow of communication helps to prevent the 'left hand not knowing what the right hand is doing' syndrome.

Every team has a team leader and others in the team may have specific roles to play. It is important that everyone understands exactly what roles are undertaken by which team members, and that everyone co-operates. Team spirit, once established, is a motivating force that can help everyone in the team to perform better.

During your course, you will work sometimes on your own and sometimes within a group. Your success will depend on your own input, but you may need to rely on other team members too. The success of the team is a joint responsibility and cause for joint celebration when it occurs.

■ HOW TO WORK WELL WITHIN A TEAM

1 Make sure you understand your contribution to the team effort. You might be given a written brief. If not, write down what you believe to be your role and check this with the team leader.

Activity 1.3

Time management

1 Review your use of a diary or calendar. Explore the software options open to you and find out what others in your group use. Aim to collate your information in one place or maybe use a handwritten diary backed up by an electronic calendar – whichever works best for you. If you do not currently use a diary, test run one for a period of time. How much more effective does it make you?

2 Examine how you process incoming mail. Make notes on how you handle mail. Where do you put it? When do you take action on items that need a response? Share your experiences with others in your group.

3 For a period of one week, monitor the amount of mail (including email and text messages) that you process. Log the time that you spend reading mail, deciding how to respond to it, actioning the mail and filing. Analyse your use of time and compare it with others in your group. Could you manage your time more effectively?

2 Find out who else is in the team and what role they have to play. If you need help, this will allow you to approach the right person straightaway, and reduce unnecessary interruptions for others in the team.

3 Respect the working space of others in your team. If they need peace and quiet to think, make sure you do not invade that space.

4 If you have special requirements, make sure these are known to others. If these are sensitive issues, consult the team leader. He/she should know the rest of the team well enough to know how to handle any tricky situation.

5 If you have a problem concerning another member of the team, try to overcome this by reconsidering your own behaviour as well as that of the other person. You could mention your problem to your team leader, but be aware that others may also have a problem with you. It works both ways!

6 The team leader needs your support. If you have concerns about his/her leadership style, discuss it with him/her. There may be facts unknown to you which result in decisions that may seem strange to you. The team leader may be able to explain why a course of action has been taken – but you may just have to accept that your team leader knows best. Do not discuss your concerns with other team members or try to undermine the team leader.

You need to report to others in the team about what you are doing and to keep up to date with what they are doing

1.1.2.4 Verbal and written communication skills

Communication within a team and within an organisation is essential for the flow of information. This communication may be verbal (within a meeting or a one-on-one discussion) or written (an emailed memo or the minutes of a meeting).

Effective communication relies on verbal and written communication skills. Throughout this unit, you will be set tasks to stretch your verbal and written communication skills.

1.1.2.5 Numeric skills

Although most jobs do not require a high degree of mathematical skills, all jobs require some numeric skills. If you need to do calculations, you must be able to do them accurately. You should be able to use a calculator and know how to check your working by estimating the answer.

During this course, there will occasions when you need to analyse data and then your numeric skills will be put to the test.

1.1.2.6 Creativity

Creativity is needed in all lines of work, not just those involving some artistic output. Employees who can dream up ideas and are able to think laterally and 'out of the box' can make major contributions to the success of an organisation. Some companies have a suggestions box – if you make a suggestion that helps the company to improve productivity, reduce waste or make the customers happier, you may be rewarded for your creativity.

Creativity involves original thought and, for this, your mind needs space to let these ideas flow. Artists – writers, painters, musicians – have rituals that they use to prepare themselves for creative activity. Often, because they are freelancers, they can choose the time and place, e.g. going to a desert island or locking themselves away in a studio. Some writers work best first thing in the morning but spend time sharpening pencils before they write the first word of the day. Some need to fuel their creativity with fine wine or have loud music playing in the background. Each has his/her own way.

In a working environment, creativity has to be channelled within an office full of people, with background noise of machinery and conversation. To allow ideas to come through, you might need to create your own space within this busy environment, and find a place where you can think clearly. You may be able to spark off ideas in a team environment, as in a brainstorming session. The creative process requires discipline and practice.

Activity 1.4

Creativity

1 Set aside five minutes for this activity. On a clean sheet of paper, write down a problem that you have in a single sentence. Close your eyes and for three minutes think about how you might solve your problem. Let all the obvious solutions run through your mind and then wait until your time is up. Other solutions may occur to you. Open your eyes and write down all the possible solutions.

2 Set aside 20 minutes for this activity. Working in a group of six to eight people, appoint one person as chair (to control proceedings) and one as scribe (to record everything that is said). Using a flip chart or whiteboard that everyone can see, brainstorm ideas for how you can improve creativity. Be sure to adhere to the rules of brainstorming: taking it in turns to speak, passing if you have nothing new to offer, accepting that all ideas are good and making no comment on any suggestions made so far. When the time is up, review your collective ideas and select the top five ideas that would work for you.

1.1.3 Personal attitudes

Some skills can be learned, such as the universal skills mentioned already. Other 'skills' (such as determination, independence, tolerance, integrity, dependability, problem solving and others) are part and parcel of a person's temperament.

As each day passes, your attitudes may change.

- This may be brought about by greater understanding of a social situation. You may come into contact with people from different backgrounds and, by interaction with them, learn more about the motivations of others. This may give you a greater tolerance but it may harden your existing attitudes too.

- You may find yourself giving way to peer pressure. Within any group, norms are established regarding acceptable ways of behaviour. What people wear and how they speak to each other can be influenced by peer pressure.

- You may just see things differently as you grow older. It is difficult to think in the same way as a 60-year-old when you are only 30 and, to a teenager, people over 30 may seem ancient and old-fashioned in their thinking. It is only as the years pass that people change their attitudes to certain situations, simply because they are older – and maybe wiser.

The attitudes an employer expects depend very much on the job specification and conditions of working. They also depend on the people already employed – a new employee needs to fit in.

Activity 1.5

Personal attitudes

1 This section considers a variety of personal attitudes. Before you read on, write ten adjectives that describe you. Choose five that you would call plus points and five that are minus points.

2 Focusing on a particular friend, and working as a pair with them, write ten adjectives that describe the other person: five good points and five not-so-good points. When you have both written your lists, swap them. Between you, discuss any aspects that need clarification.

3 Compare your friend's description of you with your own. Do you see yourself as others see you? Do they see a side of you that you would rather they did not see? Are there positive attributes that you need to promote?

1.1.3.1 Determination

Personal attitudes are difficult to learn. Instead, if you consider yourself to be lacking in some respect, you can try hard to overcome your natural inclinations. For many attitudes, there is a spectrum ranging from 'very much so' to 'hardly at all' that might describe you. Determination is one such attitude. How determined are you? Are you so laid back that you are happy to go along with whatever anyone else suggests? Or are you so determined that you cannot see anyone else's point of view and simply railroad through objections?

Neither extreme is to be recommended. However, employers might prefer to have someone who is keen to see a job through, with the determination to overcome difficulties on the way.

1.1.3.2 Independence

An employer might seek someone who can think for themselves and is not totally dependent on being told what to do next. However, they do not want someone who acts without checking first or consulting others as to what is normally done. Instead, common sense and a degree of flexibility are preferred.

1.1.3.3 Integrity

Integrity is essential for most jobs. Honesty is important when handling money, for example. However, in some jobs, you might be more successful if you can blur the truth sometimes, put a spin on things and say what people want to hear, rather than tell them the complete truth. This is particularly true in a management role: a mixture of kindness and sensitivity may be needed, especially when telling employees unpalatable news such as the impending closure of a workplace.

1.1.3.4 Tolerance

Tolerance might be considered essential in all walks of life. To accept that each person has his or her own way of doing things, and that some are more (or less) successful

What does it mean?

Someone who has **independence** is able to act without depending on others – e.g. for financial support, approval or assistance in completing a task.

Tolerance, in engineering terms, describes how far off 'perfect' will be classed as acceptable.

than others in meeting targets, shows a level of tolerance that might be summed up as 'live and let live'. This is especially important in team working situations.

However, in positions of authority, you cannot always be tolerant and you might be expected to show no tolerance at all in certain circumstances. For example, someone who behaves in a way that might present a hazard to others must be stopped from doing so, and someone who fails to hit a deadline may be jeopardising the jobs of fellow workers.

1.1.3.5 Reliability

Reliability is a measure of how dependable you are. Most employers would welcome a worker who is reliable, always turns up for work on time, does

Activity 1.6

Self-assessment

1 Complete a self assessment, creating a profile of your own attitudes. File this in your personal development plan. **p7** (partial evidence)

2 Share your profile with a friend and consider what each of you could do to make yourselves more attractive to a potential employer. Make notes in your personal development plan.

3 Set yourself a target to change your attitudes in some way – to improve your chances of fitting in better with a team environment or to land the job of your dreams. Make notes of these in your personal development plan also.

what is expected and makes no waves. But in some circumstances, a 'loose cannon' (someone who can act as a catalyst, stirring up others) might be exactly what is needed and can prove useful to an employer who wants to introduce change.

1.1.3.6 Problem solving

Presented with a given situation, some people see only the problems they face and are weighed down by them. Others may be quick, perhaps too quick, to see a solution. They may not appreciate the full extent of the problem. Having an open mind plus an optimistic attitude can be helpful when problem solving. If you assume that something is impossible, nine times out of ten you might be right. Similarly, if you take the attitude that nothing is impossible and are keen to look for a solution that works, you are likely to find one.

■ HOW TO SOLVE PROBLEMS

1 Identify the problem. Write down the current situation and what is wrong. Note also what is good about the current situation – your solution must try to preserve the best aspects of the situation.
2 Identify what you are trying to achieve with the solution. This may be a long-term goal and you may need to set some intermediary targets.
3 Think of all the things you could do and what their effects might be. Will they help or hinder progress?
4 Consider known methods of solving this problem that you have seen work before. If these seem to be suitable, you might adopt them, but first set aside time to consider alternative solutions.
5 Having established the choices, measure each in terms of some cost. This could be time, effort, inconvenience to others, etc.
6 Review your options again, taking into account the pros and cons of each.
7 Make a decision and carry it through as planned.
8 Review the results of your decision and note any situation that surprised you or any unexpected positive or negative outcome. Keep this review for future reference.

Activity 1.7

Problem solving

1 During this course, you will be set many problems. In tackling them, be conscious of your approach and your personal attitude to the work you are asked to do. Review your personal profile of attitudes and check that your behaviour during problem solving matches this profile.

2 For one particular problem-solving activity, note exactly how you tackle it. Document every step of the process. Discuss this with others in your group and establish how you might improve any aspects of your problem-solving technique.

1.1.3.7 Leadership

Everyone is a potential leader and opportunities for leadership occur daily. However, many people lack confidence or leadership experience – they doubt that they can lead and so do not even try. Learning how to lead includes learning how to follow, so recognising the roles and responsibilities of leaders and followers is a must for those who work within a team.

To lead well, you need to be aware of your own strengths and weaknesses. For others to respect you as their leader, you need also to respect yourself. You must understand people, so that you can identify what motivates them, what rewards and values matter to them and how, as team leader, you can inspire them with the vision of what the team can achieve.

Activity 1.8

Leadership traits

1 Research the Internet to find out the personal traits of two leaders. Compare your findings with others in your group. Do leaders have common traits?

2 With others in your group, discuss what motivates you. If you were all in one team, what could a leader do to win your support? Make a list of what you expect of a leader.

1.1.3.8 Confidence

If you lack confidence, your approach to problem solving may be too cautious – you may not have the courage to try the best strategy. Confidence that you have abilities to meet the challenges you face can help you to achieve your goals. How confident others are in you can also make a difference to how your ideas are accepted.

However, over-confidence or arrogance might result in you not thinking things through carefully enough while planning your strategy. You may miss a vital clue or skim over an important aspect, resulting in problems at some point. So, confidence is important but needs to be based on genuine skill levels.

Activity 1.9

Confidence

1 Review your personal profile. Where do you come on the confidence scale? If you feel you lack confidence, what can you do to improve the situation?

2 Within a group of six to eight, grade the others according to how confident you think they are in a particular aspect of their lives. (You will probably think of different things for different people.) Share your findings. Set yourself tasks to address any issues that you uncover.

1.1.3.9 Self-motivation

Some people are described as self-starters – they do not need anyone else to motivate them to do something as they have their own internal drive. People who are not self-motivated either do very little or use up their team mates' precious energy to keep them going. Such people are not welcome in a team.

Activity 1.10

Trait improvement

1 Refer to your personal development plan. From your analysis of yourself, and from comments made by your friends, identify one aspect of your personality that you think needs addressing. Do some research to discover what you might do to 'correct' your attitude.

2 Share your findings with others in your team. Your goal is to work better as a team. How can you achieve this? Make notes in your personal development plan.

3 What do you consider to be your best trait? Ask yourself how you can help others to behave in a similar way. Share your ideas with others in your team.

 (partial evidence)

1.1.4 Organisational aims and objectives

Within an organisation, jobs exist at all levels. The top person needs a different skill set from those who work for him/her. Some need to lead, others need to follow.

However, there are some attitudes that all employees should share. The most important of these is a loyalty to the organisation and a sense of ownership of the products or services it provides.

There needs to be a level of pride in working for an organisation which will be evident to any visitor and will serve to promote the organisation to people who come into contact with its employees. Organisations which subscribe to this philosophy may aim to provide a happy and safe working environment. Some aspire to earn the Investors in People standard, a standard introduced in 1990 by the National Training Task Force, in partnership with leading business, personnel, professional and employees' organisations.

Case study

McDonald's

McDonald's is an employer that places importance on staff development – many prospective staff are attracted by their award-winning training and rapid management progression.

If you visit a McDonald's restaurant as a customer, you might think that the job of manager is all about motivating the staff and hurrying the process of serving customers along. In fact, running a McDonald's restaurant involves a lot of commercial management as well. The restaurants have a very high turnover and employ huge teams of staff. Managing such a business involves financial, marketing and operational know-how, as well as a talent for team building.

The McDonald's restaurant managers set targets, plan budgets, control stock and recruit, train and inspire their team of staff. They also create and drive marketing campaigns and try to build bridges with the local community. The ideas, initiative and personality of McDonald's managers help shape the restaurants they run.

1 Visit the McDonald's website and find out more about their training programme. What qualities are they seeking in their restaurant managers, and why?

 (partial evidence)

2 Identify five local organisations, either through the local phone book or local newspaper. Aim for a range of large and small organisations, as well as local, national and international organisations.

Research the Internet to find out more about your chosen organisations. Are any of them 'Investors in People'? You can find out more about this by visiting the Investors in People website: go to www.heinemann.co.uk/hotlinks and enter the express code 2315P.

3 Find out what training opportunities exist within one of your chosen organisations.

Test your knowledge

1 Give three examples of soft skills.

2 Explain the difference between planning and organising.

3 Explain these terms: goal, objective, strategy.

4 Describe what a PDA can do.

5 What is an Internet café?

6 Give five examples of behaviour that can help you to work well within a team.

7 Describe a strategy for problem solving.

This section looks first at general communication skills but then focuses on interpersonal skills and how best to communicate in writing.

1.2.1 General communication skills

This subsection looks at aspects of communication which you need to take into account: your audience, your message and techniques that you can use to make sure you are successful in communicating your message to your audience.

1.2.1.1 Your audience

For communication to take place, there must be an audience for the message. Who that audience is will determine the type of language you use, the way you put the words together and how you deliver the message.

For example, the age of the audience can impact on the way communication happens. You may need to vary your voice to maintain the interest of your audience. You may need to be very selective in your choice of terminology, to make sure everyone in your audience understands your message. You may decide to present your message in a particular format, e.g. using rhyme or music, or to deliver it electronically.

There may also be cultural differences that need to be addressed. Some words or signs that are acceptable in one language or culture may be misunderstood or considered offensive in another. You might therefore choose to use different words from the ones you would usually use.

1.2.1.2 Your message: facts versus opinions

Having adapted the content and style to meet the expectations or needs of your audience, you should next focus on the message that you are trying to convey. To win the hearts and minds of an audience, you may be

Activity 1.11

Meeting an audience's needs

1 Imagine you are going to give a talk on how to integrate images into a document. Consider how your approach might be different when giving your talk to:
   a) a group of primary school children as opposed to a group of adult IT practitioners
   b) a group in the UK as opposed to a group in another country.
   Discuss this with others in your group and make notes on what the main differences would be.

2 Plan a small part of your talk (e.g. locating the source of an image) and explain the differences in language or terminology that you might apply to the different audiences. Take into account style and format, including any technology you would use to enhance your talk. Explain why you made these choices.

tempted to stretch the truth or to make emotive statements to whip up feelings for or against some political or social issue. For some audiences, these tactics may work; but you would be best advised to stick to the truth and to include only facts in your message. Otherwise, you risk being shown to be a liar and losing credibility. Once that happens, no one will listen to you – no matter how conscientious you claim to be.

When aiming to provide accurate information, you need to differentiate between facts and opinions.

- **Facts** can be proved – they are either true or false. Data can be collected and hypotheses tested.
- **Opinions** are more complex – they vary from one person to the next and can change within the same person from one day to the next. Opinions can be strong or weak – they may be influenced by knowledge, or the lack of it, of relevant facts.

Much day-to-day decision making tends to be based on opinions, so it is important to make sure you are fully informed before making decisions, especially important ones and those that affect other people as well as yourself.

Activity 1.12

Facts and opinions

1. Food is an emotive topic. Newspapers report famine in the Third World and obesity in the developed world. So what, and how much, should you eat? Research the Internet on one aspect of eating habits so that you can make an informed decision about your own eating habits. Make a presentation to your class with the aim of changing the opinion of your audience and directing their eating behaviour toward healthier eating.

2. Conduct a review of how political messages are conveyed, e.g. by studying a TV programme such as *Question Time* and by reading newspaper articles. How easy is it to identify facts? How do politicians convey their message so as to generate a reaction in their audience or readership? Do they answer the questions they are asked? Write notes on how best to answer questions within an interview while still getting your message across to the viewer.

1.2.1.3 Techniques for engaging audience interest

To maintain the interest levels of your audience, whether they are reading a report you have written or listening to a presentation, you need to apply some techniques.

Imagine listening to a speaker whose voice never varied in tone – it would soon put you to sleep! When delivering your message, written or oral, make sure that you vary your tone.

In an oral presentation, you can create interest by pausing from time to time – long enough to let the audience take in what you have said, but not so long that they think you have forgotten what you were going to say next.

In a face-to-face situation, to keep the audience's eyes from wandering to their surroundings, you might use multimedia to hold their interest: e.g. show presentation slides, play music or hold up an object to illustrate a point. You might say that, at the end of your talk, there will be an opportunity to ask questions. This may help some of your audience to keep up their interest, thinking about what they might like to ask. Question and answer sessions are particularly useful for clarifying points that you might have skimmed over in your presentation.

As with written communications where diagrams and pictures can be used to good effect, in a presentation, use of animation can enliven the slideshow, but you need to apply caution. Too much activity can detract from your message. Similarly, staying completely still while delivering your message may unsettle an audience, but if you pace up and down, this too can be distracting. A balance is needed.

Activity 1.13

Attention-seeking techniques

1. Look again at how a politician presents his/her message on TV. How do they maintain the audience's interest? Watch for facial expressions, hand gestures, intonation and the way they phrase their words. Watch for breathing spaces or lack of them. Watch for how they link their reply to whatever the questioner asked. Ask yourself again: did the politician answer the question? Review and revise the notes you made for question 2 of Activity 1.12.

2. Watch the news on TV and compare it with how a newspaper presents the same information. Look for devices that they use: headlines, sound bites, photos, cartoons, interviews, etc. Create a poster showing examples of the devices that seem to work best.

3. For a TV interview, make notes on the dramatic devices used by the director to maintain the interest of the viewer: the setting, the different camera angles, etc.

There are many ways to enliven a presentation

1.2.2 Interpersonal skills

This section considers a variety of options for how to communicate your message to an audience and then looks at possible barriers to communication.

1.2.2.1 Communicating interpersonally

For communication to happen, two or more people are involved. One person expresses a message through words (spoken or written), signs, signals, facial and bodily expressions or even silence. The other person uses his/her senses (mostly sight and hearing) to gather aspects of the message.

Someone who is unsighted, or at the end of a telephone line, doesn't have the extra dimension that body language offers during face-to-face communication. This person can still hear pauses though, and will identify any emotion conveyed through intonation.

Someone who is deaf cannot hear your words and may rely on lip reading. The recognised signing system also acts as an aid for communication with the deaf.

To express emotion in verbal communications, some change of tone is needed: a raised voice can indicate anger or impatience; a lowered voice can show fear or insecurity. In face-to-face discussions, the tone of voice may be accompanied by some body language: a fist being thumped on the table conveys more force than hands that are held together as if in prayer or hanging meekly at the speaker's side; folded arms across the chest may show indifference or obstinacy.

In written communications, especially text messages or emails, capitalisation is taken to mean shouting, and is therefore to be avoided, unless you intend to shout. Smileys – also called emoticons (see Figure 1.6) – can be used to express a frame of mind.

Communication doesn't just happen when you are speaking. While the other person speaks, you can communicate in several ways. By paying attention and reacting to what the other person is saying, e.g. with a nod or a frown, you are communicating that you hear what is being said and that you are taking note. Your facial expressions will convey whether your reaction is positive or negative. If you decide not to react and remain impassive, this also communicates a clear message to the speaker that you are bored and have no intention of listening.

It is possible to cut in while the other person is speaking. Depending on how you do this, it may convey enthusiasm or it may be antagonistic. If you make a habit of finishing someone's sentences, this can be irritating and may indicate insensitivity.

Once the other person has finished speaking, they may signal that you are expected to respond in a variety of ways. They might end with a question, e.g. 'Don't you agree?' They might use body language to indicate that it is your turn to contribute to the conversation, by turning their body or inclining their head towards you. You can confirm your understanding of what has just been said by summarising it, before going on to make your own comments.

1.2.2.2 Barriers to communication

Communication only takes place if the person on the receiving end understands the input of the person sending the message. The receiver doesn't have to like or agree with the message – simply receiving the message means that communication has taken place.

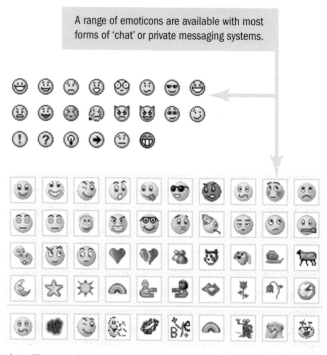

A range of emoticons are available with most forms of 'chat' or private messaging systems.

▲ Figure 1.6 Examples of emoticons

Activity 1.14

Using sight and hearing

1 Listen to a conversation between two or more people, e.g. on the radio. Listen for cues that signal the end of one person's contribution. Listen for pauses especially. Are there any awkward moments? Make notes on the do's and don'ts of verbal communication.

2 Watch an interview on TV with the sound turned off and focus on the body language being used. Then play the interview again, listening but not watching this time. Make notes on the do's and don'ts of non-verbal communication.

3 In pairs, role play a difficult conversation where one person wants the other to see their point of view and the other is reluctant to do so. Take it in turns to be the person who is trying to persuade the other, and video your role play. What persuasive communication techniques did you each use, and why? What other techniques might increase your effectiveness?

There are barriers to communication. To communicate effectively, you should aim to prevent or reduce the effect of barriers as much as possible. For example, for an audience to hear, the spoken voice should be clear and loud enough, without any distortion or interference. So, it is important not to position the mouthpiece of a telephone under your chin and, in direct communications, you should face your audience.

Distractions (such as someone walking into a meeting late or leaving unexpectedly, the tea trolley arriving or a mobile phone beeping) can interrupt the flow of thought of an audience and, momentarily, they could stop listening. As soon as that happens, communication falters and the speaker may feel the need to repeat part of the message.

Background noise should not be underestimated. Even a slight continuous noise, such as the humming of an air conditioning unit, can distract an audience.

It is important to maintain **concentration levels** despite any distractions. The length of a conversation or communication is important – the recipient can only take in so much information at a time. Anything beyond that is counter productive. For example, a short verbal

rebuke might prove useful but, if this turns into a lecture on behaviour, the recipient is likely to lose concentration.

It is the same for written communications. If you can convey your message on one page of A4, then do so. The recipient of a two-page letter will have lower concentrations levels when they turn the page. You also need to match the terminology you use to the experience of the audience.

Body language that indicates a negative attitude can act as a barrier to communication. For example, you are unlikely to persuade someone to open up and communicate with you frankly if you use closed body language and an aggressive stance.

1.2.2.3 Types of questions

Communication is not just two people speaking in turn. There needs to be a link between the people and questions can help to create such a link.

- An **open question** is an invitation to the other person to pick up the conversation and take control. For example, if you ask 'How are you today?' there are a multitude of possible responses. The conventional response is 'I'm fine, thanks. And how are you?' whether or not this is true. During a debate on an issue, a constructive open question might be 'What do you think about this?' This invites the other person to express their views.

- **Closed questions** are expressed in such a way that the options for a reply are limited, perhaps only to yes or no. 'Would you like a cup of tea?' is a closed question. The question can be made less specific: 'Would you like something to drink?' but this may still only result in a yes/no answer. To find out exactly what is required, you would need a follow-up question: 'What would you like to drink?'

Either form of question is acceptable during most conversations. With open questions, sometimes you don't find out what you want to know. You then need to follow up with additional questions – called **probing questions** – to extract the information you want. In personal conversations such questions might be considered unacceptable because they delve too deeply into a person's private space. In some circumstances, repeating questions can be effective, but also runs the risk of being considered aggressive or impolite.

Even closed questions can be threatening if used during an argument. 'You agree with me, don't you?' expects a yes or no answer and makes the other person declare his or her position. A cautious response that shows diplomacy might be 'yes and no' with some explanation about the points of agreement or disagreement.

Questions can be answered in a number of ways: quickly and maybe with passion, slowly after what looks like consideration of all the issues, something in between or not at all. Answering a question with a question is a delaying tactic that is often used in discussions. Repeating the question back to the questioner is another delaying tactic that sometimes works.

Activity 1.15

Questions, questions, questions

1 Listen to a radio programme such as *Today* on Radio 4 with John Humphries, or an interview by a TV presenter such as Jeremy Paxman. Notice what questions they ask and how these questions are phrased. Notice the response that is given, for example, by a prominent politician. Is the question answered? If not, how does the politician dodge the question? How does the interviewer press on? Review and revise the notes you made for question 2 of Activity 1.12 (page 18). Write further notes, this time about the techniques used by the interviewer.

2 Make notes on how an ICT technician might question an end user who has telephoned to complain about a fault with a computer system. What types of questions might the technician use? When might they use open questions? When might they use probing questions?

3 Describe the potential barriers to communication when a technician is talking:
   a) on the phone
   b) in person to a customer.
   Explain ways in which these barriers could be avoided. **p**₂ **m**₂

1.2.3 Communicating in writing

Written communication is fundamentally different from other forms of communication. It requires special skills in the construction of the message – not least, the ability to handwrite or type. It also requires sufficient knowledge of a language, e.g. English, so that the written word conveys the intended message to your audience. You cannot use visual cues such as body language or aural cues such as tone of voice.

Writing something can seem very easy, but effective written communication is another matter.

This section focuses on how best to communicate in writing and considers constraints that might be imposed by your working conditions. It suggests how to use the tools at your disposal to communicate the message to your audience, minimising the risk of misunderstandings.

1.2.3.1 Organisational guidelines and procedures

As an employee, you will be expected to follow organisational guidelines and procedures. You will be allocated space in which to work, and you will be given notice of the times you should attend the office and/or be available for others to contact you. You will be supplied with equipment that you need in your day-to-day work, such as a computer, a telephone and stationery, and you may be given access to other essential materials such as a shared fax facility.

There may be guidelines on the ways computer equipment can be used. There may be templates that you are required to use for your written communications, with style sheets that determine the look of any document. For example, in emails you may be required to use a standard footer with the company name and your job title, or there may be a standard disclaimer. There may be guidelines relating to the use of fax machines and the type of information that can be sent by fax (for reasons of confidentiality).

1.2.3.2 Key messages

Whatever form a written communication takes – report, letter, fax or email – there will be a key message to be conveyed. Within a letter, this may be flagged by the inclusion of a heading, immediately after the salutation (see Figure 1.7), while electronic faxes and emails use a subject line to convey the key message (see Figure 1.8).

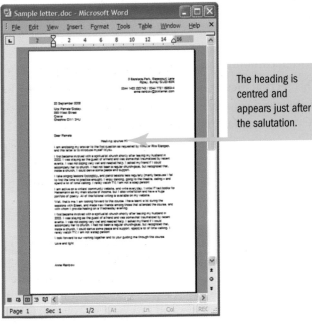

> The heading is centred and appears just after the salutation.

▲ Figure 1.7 Using a heading in a letter

1.2.3.3 Grammar and spelling

The body of a report, letter, fax or email will add substance to the key message. It may provide an explanation or apology. It may contain further information, such as directions or an itinerary, or it may request action. Whatever the content of the communication, it is important that it is written using correct grammar and spelling. Mistakes convey an unprofessional image to the reader. They can also create confusion if they make it difficult to understand what you have written. So, use the grammar checker options available with your word processing software (see Figure 1.15 on page 32).

1.2.3.4 Structure

If the message is more than a line or two, make sure you structure it in a way that aids the reader's understanding. A logical framework will help the reader to take in the information. An illogical framework will mean that the reader has to try to interpret your meaning, and this could result in misunderstandings.

> The Subject column indicates what the email is about.

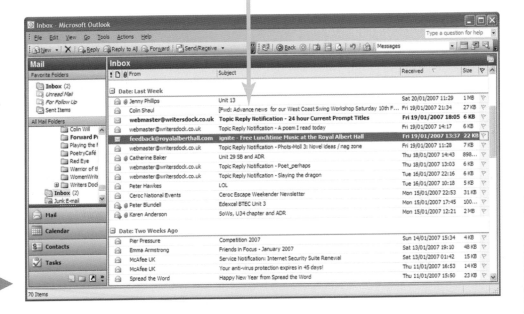

Figure 1.8 Using the subject line to convey the key message ▶

You may be presented with templates for letters and emails, with standard wording that you are expected to adapt for specific communications with suppliers, customers and colleagues. If not, it is a good idea to reuse and adapt communications that you have used previously to convey a similar message.

WATCH OUT!

If reusing a letter to save you writing from scratch, be sure to proofread (see page 24) the text and change any words that refer to the recipient or other details such as dates.

Figure 1.9 Setting up a standard signature for an email

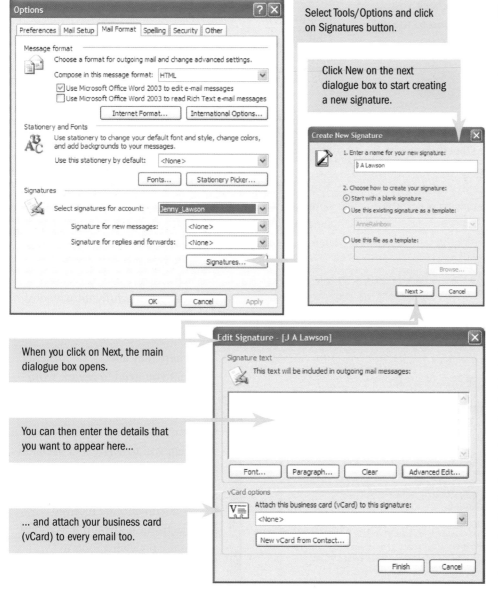

Select Tools/Options and click on Signatures button.

Click New on the next dialogue box to start creating a new signature.

When you click on Next, the main dialogue box opens.

You can then enter the details that you want to appear here...

... and attach your business card (vCard) to every email too.

1.2.3.5 Relevant information

When reading your report, letter or email, the recipient will try to identify relevant information within it. In a structured message, this task is made easier. However, if you have hidden relevant information within a mass of other details, the reader may miss important facts.

Underlining or emboldening important relevant information – such as the date of a meeting – is one way of ensuring that such facts are not missed. However, pruning the message so that it contains only relevant information is even more helpful to the reader.

There may be a standard way of signing off a letter that includes your official title and full contact details, e.g. telephone number, email address and/or postal address. If not, adopt your own standard way (see Figure 1.9) which makes it clear the communication is from you.

1.2.3.6 Reviewing and proofreading own written work

Before you send a written communication such as a report, text message, email or letter, it is essential to review and check your work for accuracy. In the early stages of creating a written communication, the document is called a draft. Each time you redraft the wording, you should **proofread** the text to check you have not introduced errors. This is in addition to the use of tools such as a spell checker (see page 32).

1.2.3.7 Conveying alternative viewpoints

Some documents are used to present alternative viewpoints, e.g. a report or letter. The structure needs to make clear where one viewpoint starts and ends. The structure may include an introduction to explain the purpose of the document and a summary to préçis the main points covered.

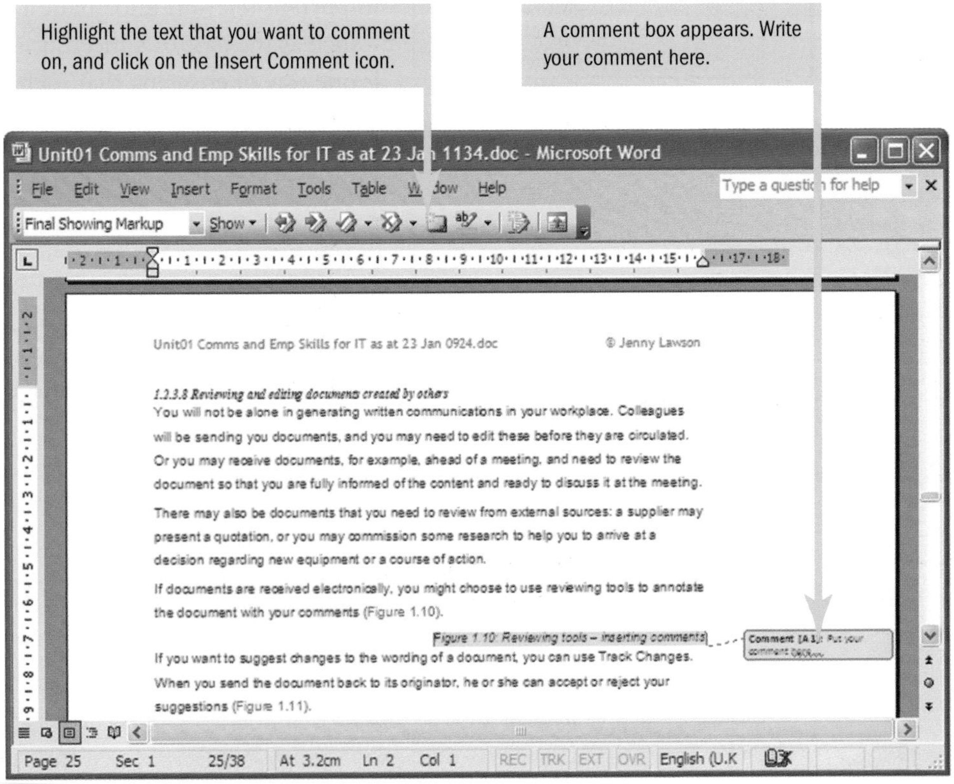

What does it mean?

Proofreading is a checking process, looking for errors within a written piece of text.

For example, a report may consider the effects of two different courses of action – a table may prove useful in presenting the pros and cons of each situation and graphs may help to show alternative results.

Choosing how best to present data is an essential communication skill. See page 32 for examples of when it is a good idea to present data graphically.

1.2.3.8 Reviewing and editing documents created by others

You will not be alone in generating written communications in your workplace. Colleagues will be sending you documents. You may need to edit these before they are circulated, or you may receive a document before a meeting which you need to review so that you are fully informed of the content and ready to discuss it at the meeting.

There may also be documents that you need to review from external sources: a supplier may present a quotation or you may commission some research to help you to arrive at a decision regarding new equipment or a course of action.

If documents are received electronically, you might choose to use reviewing tools to annotate the document with your comments (see Figure 1.10).

Highlight the text that you want to comment on, and click on the Insert Comment icon.

A comment box appears. Write your comment here.

Figure 1.10 Reviewing tools – inserting comments

If you want to suggest changes to a Word document, you can use Track Changes. When you send the document back to its originator, he/she can accept or reject your suggestions (see Figure 1.11).

1.2.3.9 Note taking

While reviewing a communication, you may find it helps to take notes. This is especially helpful when the communication is long and contains a lot of information.

Note taking may involve:

- handwriting key points on a new sheet of paper
- annotating a hard copy of the message: writing in the margin, underlining key phrases or using a highlighter pen for important facts, dates or times
- inserting comments into an electronic document.

What does it mean?

Note taking involves summarising a communication.

▼ Figure 1.11 Using Track Changes

Toggle the Track Changes icon on the Reviewing toolbar to start tracking changes.

Deleted text appears in a bubble in the right-hand margin.

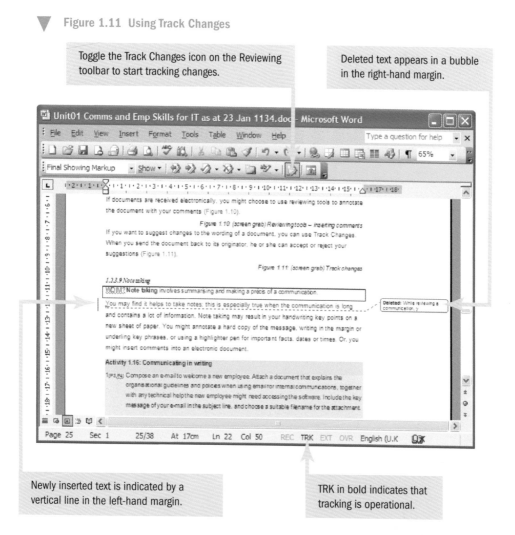

Newly inserted text is indicated by a vertical line in the left-hand margin.

TRK in bold indicates that tracking is operational.

Activity 1.16

Communicating in writing

1 Compose an email to welcome a new employee. Attach a document that explains the organisational guidelines and policies when using email for internal communications, together with any technical help the new employee might need to access the software. Include the key message of your email in the subject line, and choose a suitable filename for the attachment. **p**3 (partial evidence) **p**4 (partial evidence)

2 Proofread both the email and the attached document to ensure there are no spelling, punctuation or grammatical errors within them. **m**3 (in conjunction with 4 and 5)

3 Send your email to another student in your group, making sure that your signature gives contact details so they can reply by email or telephone.

4 You will receive an email from another student. Check the content and the attachment for relevant information. Review the attached document and add comments and suggestions for redrafting, using Track Changes. Save the revised document with a suitable name in an appropriate folder. Compose a response to the email confirming its safe receipt and attach your revised version of the document. **m**3 (in conjunction with 2 and 5)

5 You will receive comments about the document you sent to another student. Read the comments and make notes of the changes you might make to your document. Review the changes suggested and accept or reject these changes as you see fit. Make any additional changes that you consider necessary. Print out one copy of the final document. **m**3 (in conjunction with 2 and 4)

Test your knowledge

1 Explain the difference between facts and opinions.

2 Give three examples of how you might maintain the interest of an audience.

3 Give three examples of how communication can take place.

4 Give three examples of barriers to communication.

5 Explain the difference between open and closed questions. Give an example of each.

6 Give an example of a probing question, and give three ways of avoiding answering it.

7 What is a key message? How can you draw attention to it?

8 Explain the purpose of proofreading. How else can you ensure accuracy of written text?

You will have used ICT for a variety purposes: e.g. to set up a budget, to conduct research on the Internet or to create a drawing. In this unit, you will learn how to exploit ICT to communicate more effectively. This section focuses on the options for communication channels. It then considers the software involved in communicating through them and the tools you can use to ensure the accuracy of your messages.

1.3.1 Communications channels

A number of communication channels are available, each one suited to particular types of message (see Table 1.1).

Activity 1.17

Blogs, vlogs and podcasts

1 Research the Internet to discover some blogs and find out how to set up your own blog. Write notes so that a complete novice would know what to do to set up their own blog. **p₄** **(in conjunction with Task 1, Activity 1.16)**

2 Research the Internet to discover some vlogs. Create a presentation to explain how blogs differ from vlogs. **p₅**

3 Visit the BBC website and download a podcast. What are the benefits of podcasts? How might they be used in the future? **m₄**

1.3.2 Software

This subsection reviews three types of standard software that you will need to be able to use to communicate your message: word processing, presentation packages and email software. It also considers specialist software designed for the visually impaired.

1.3.2.1 Word processing

Word processing software provides a tool with which you can enter, edit, format, save and print out text-based documents. Text can be entered via the keyboard and you can also adapt materials from secondary sources: you could copy and paste text from another document or from a webpage or scan in text and convert it into a Word document.

Editing involves inserting, amending or deleting text to reword the document. It is achieved by inserting new text (keying it in or pasting it into place from elsewhere), amending the text (typing over it while using Overtype mode or pasting over existing material) or deleting text.

Text can be formatted on one of two levels: character formatting or paragraph formatting.

- **Character formatting** affects only those characters selected and can be used to highlight individual words. For example, to make important material stand out, you could change the font colour or present the material in italic, bold or underlined.
- **Paragraph formatting** affects the entire paragraph and is used to control the spacing of lines within, before and after the paragraph. It sets the basic look of the text (font style and size) and may be incorporated into a style sheet or template.

The fact that word processing software lets you save your work means that you can start a letter or report now and then work on it again at some later date. You can retrieve the finished document at an even later date and use it to create another document. For example, an annual report has the same basic structure each year; it is just the

Remember!

Proofreading is a checking process, looking for errors within a written piece of text.

Communication channel	Description/Examples	Benefits	Disadvantages
Word processed documents	• Presented on paper and/or on screen • Can include text, tables and still images • Reports, business letters, newspapers and magazines	• Hard copy is portable: you don't need to have access to a computer • Hard copy can form a permanent record (e.g. for minutes of a meeting that need to be authorised as true) • With on-screen documents, you can use search option to locate particular information within the document	• For a hard copy, the document has to be printed, which uses costly resources: paper and ink • Need a computer to view the document on screen • Some people find navigating through an electronic document more difficult – they cannot memorise where on a page something was
Presentations	• A slide show • Can be viewed with or without a presenter being there	• Usually short and snappy way of conveying key points, especially when used to illustrate a verbal presentation	• Requires presentation hardware: a computer screen, whiteboard and a projector
Web pages	• Can include audio and moving images • Written in HTML code and/or scripting language such as Java	• Available online to all Internet users • Interactivity may be provided, giving the visitor to the site a more rewarding experience while accessing the information • Updating a website can be achieved very quickly, compared to the time it might take to republish, say, a book	• Requires skill in creating the elements of the web page and knitting them together to form a coherent, user-friendly website • Computer with Internet access needed to upload updated web pages
Email	• Electronic message • Can include attachments such as a Word document	• Can be sent to more than one recipient at the same time • Speedier than snail mail	• Sender and recipient both need to subscribe to an email service • Need access to the Internet while sending/receiving emails
Blogs	• An online journal, displaying frequent and chronological comments and thoughts for all to see	• Same benefits as a web page, plus gives insight into one person's view of life • Individuals access a worldwide readership without going through the medium of a publisher or the complexities of setting up a website	• Same disadvantages as web pages except software available to help the blogger
Vlogs	• A medium for distributing video content • Usually accompanied by text, image and metadata to provide a context or overview for the video	• Same benefits as a web page • Opens the door for individuals with little web development experience to air their views on the Internet	• Same disadvantages as web pages
Podcasts	• A method of publishing files (especially large audio files) to the Internet	• Subscribers receive new files automatically • Allows subscribers to decide what they hear and/or watch and when	• Internet access is necessary for downloading files • Users need to subscribe to a feed
Video conferencing	• A way for many people, located in different places, to communicate 'face-to-face' without actually leaving their desk	• Saves travelling time • Costs of setting up and maintaining video conferencing are more than recouped by savings in travel and subsistence costs of delegates	• Requires technical expertise to set up the audio and video links

Table 1.1 Communication channels

What does it mean?

Blog stands for weblog.

A **vlog** is a blog which uses video as its primary presentation format.

A **podcast** is a media file distributed over the Internet for playback on portable media players and personal computers. The term originates from Apple's iPod and the word broadcasting.

Activity 1.18

Word processing features

1 Word processing software provides facilities to create styles. Produce a one-page word processed document explaining the usefulness of setting up a style sheet, aimed at expert IT users. **p₄ p₅**

2 Choose one other feature of word processing software and create a word processed document to explain to a novice user how it works. **p₄ p₅**

details that change. Having set up a report in the required style, the following year's report should take less time to produce.

A word processed document is prepared using word processing software and can then be printed. One benefit of the software is that you can preview the document before you print it. So, you can proofread the document without wasting paper. You can also fine tune the settings for margins and horizontal/vertical spacing to create the best visual effect on the page.

1.3.2.2 Presentation package

A presentation package provides templates for a range of slides. It facilitates the construction of a sequence of slides, in the order you want to display them, with notes. The templates offer a variety of layouts, so that you can incorporate bullet lists, tables and images. You can also

incorporate other media (sound and video) and animation (see Figure 1.12).

The presentation package then offers ways of running the presentation. You might:

- set up the presentation to be shown on a whiteboard, with you controlling the transition from one slide to the next while you talk
- set up the slide show to run continuously at a pace that would suit most viewers, and without you needing to be present during the viewing
- create interactivity to allow the viewer to decide when to view the next slide in the sequence.

1.3.2.3 Email software

Email software is provided by ISPs who offer email as part of the Internet connection deal. You can also install an email client on your computer, such as Microsoft Outlook, which – while you are online – downloads incoming emails into your Inbox and uploads outgoing emails from your Outbox.

Whichever version of software you use, there are functions for composing a new email, replying to an incoming email and forwarding an incoming email. Having set up the email you can attach documents to it and send it to one or more people (see Figure 1.13).

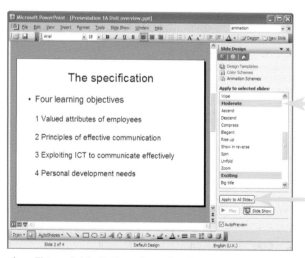

PowerPoint animation options are divided into Subtle, Moderate and Exciting

Animation can be applied to one slide – or to all slides.

▲ **Figure 1.12** Options for animation

Activity 1.19

Presentation software features

1 Create a slide show including a variety of the templates that your presentation software offers.

2 Incorporate sound and some animation into a slide show, and compose notes explaining to a novice user how you achieved this effect. Set up the slide show to run continuously. **P5**

You can set up an address book to hold the email addresses of people you want to send emails to. You can set this up using data which arrives with the email (the email includes the address of the person who sent it). You can also set up distribution lists of groups of people to whom you might frequently want to send the same email.

Activity 1.20

Email software features

1 Check that you are fully competent with all features of your email software. Spend time checking every menu and exploring all the options.

2 Invent questions to ask of others in your group. For example: how might they send an email to a group of friends without revealing any of the email addresses to anyone else on the list? Share your questions and discuss the answers to them.

1.3.2.4 Specialist software for the visually impaired

You might think that the visually impaired cannot see the screen or a hard copy of a document. However, visual impairment covers a whole spectrum of sight problems: some individuals are only slightly affected,

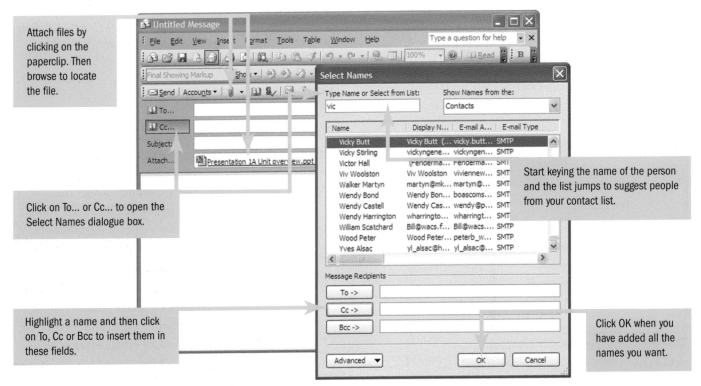

Attach files by clicking on the paperclip. Then browse to locate the file.

Click on To... or Cc... to open the Select Names dialogue box.

Highlight a name and then click on To, Cc or Bcc to insert them in these fields.

Start keying the name of the person and the list jumps to suggest people from your contact list.

Click OK when you have added all the names you want.

Figure 1.13 Sending an email to more than one person

while others are totally blind and cannot distinguish light from dark. Most people are affected by deteriorating vision with advancing age. Some people lose their sight through trauma, as a result of war or through disease. Whether visual impairment comes about quickly or over time, ICT can offer solutions to those who need help.

Specialist software is available for the visually impaired so that they can make use of ICT for effective communication. Text readers (see page 32), for example, can be used to read aloud material that has arrived in text form (by email or as an attached document).

Hardware has also been developed to help: a Braille printer has an embosser that punches dots on to paper rather than printing characters in ink. Braille printers connect to the computer in the same way as text printers, using a serial or parallel port. You can also buy Braille translation software that translates printed text into Braille.

Activity 1.21

Software for the visually impaired

1 Research the Internet for software that has been developed to assist the visually impaired.

2 Extend your research to software that has been designed for other groups of people with disabilities or specific/special needs.

1.3.3 Software tools

Software tools such as the thesaurus and the spell checker offer quick ways of checking your communication. This section looks at these tools and others that can be used to present your message more effectively.

1.3.3.1 Proofing tools

One of the challenges in written communication is to use a varied and rich vocabulary, one that will be understood by your audience – no jargon! – and yet uses the best possible words to convey your message. To provide a variety of vocabulary, you might use a **thesaurus** (see Figure 1.14).

To make sure that you spell all the words correctly, you might use a **spell checker** (see Figure 1.15) which will flag a mistake like 'hwere' instead of 'where'.

▼ Figure 1.14 Thesaurus

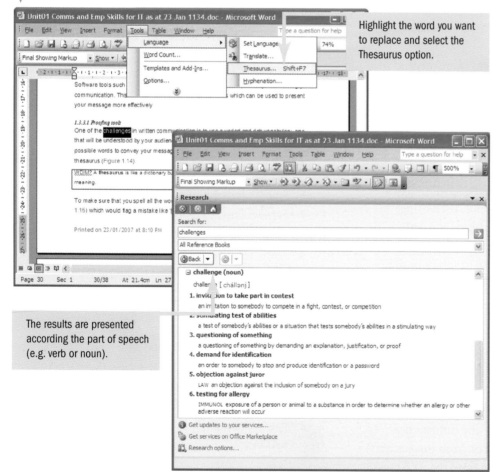

Highlight the word you want to replace and select the Thesaurus option.

The results are presented according the part of speech (e.g. verb or noun).

What does it mean?

A **thesaurus** is like a dictionary but, instead of giving meanings, it lists words with the same meaning.

A **spell checker** compares your words with those listed in a dictionary.

To specify the type of checks you want done, select Tools/Spelling and Grammar.

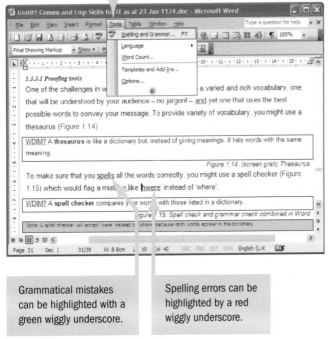

Grammatical mistakes can be highlighted with a green wiggly underscore.

Spelling errors can be highlighted by a red wiggly underscore.

▲ Figure 1.15 Spell check and grammar check combined in Word

But note that a spell checker will accept 'were' instead of 'where' because both words appear in the dictionary.

1.3.3.2 Conversion of tabular information to graphics

Large amounts of numerical data can be hard to digest. Trends, in particular, are difficult to spot. Presenting such data graphically, however, can convey relevant information at a glance. Spreadsheet software can be used to convert tabular information to graphics in the form of pie charts, bar charts and line graphs.

1.3.3.3 Text readers

A text reader provides an aural output which matches the text. For images on websites, the text that accompanies an image is stored in the ALT tag.

Visually impaired users cannot glean any information from the layout or formatting of text or from images on the screen. So, the wording of the text (and the ALT tags) must convey the message in as few words as possible. Special care needs to be taken, therefore, with the language and vocabulary used.

Activity 1.22

Using software tools

1 Write a piece of text of approximately 250 words to describe yourself. Identify all the adjectives, and use a thesaurus to find alternative words. Spell check the document. Swap your 250-word description with a friend. Identify all their adjectives, and use the thesaurus to find any alternative words that you consider to be more accurate.

2 Use spreadsheet software to hold some numerical data. Convert this data to a graphical format. Make notes to explain to a novice user how to do this. **P**₄

3 Visit a website and run the cursor across an image to reveal its ALT text. Is it helpful for someone who cannot see the image clearly? Experiment with using a text reader – do this with your eyes shut. How effective is the text reader feature for a visually impaired user? Make notes. **P**₅

STOP Test your knowledge

1 Explain these terms: blog, vlog and podcast.

2 Explain the difference between character formatting and paragraph formatting.

3 Using slide show software, you could prepare overhead transparencies to deliver a presentation. Give three other examples of how you might set up and deliver a presentation.

4 In the context of emailing, explain these terms: address book, distribution list.

5 Give three examples of software that have been developed to help users with specific needs, such as people with visual impairment.

6 Explain these terms: thesaurus, spell checker, text reader.

Personal development means building on your strengths and managing your weaknesses. When you are in full-time employment, it is quite likely that you will be expected to take part in an appraisal system that monitors your progress and reviews it formally on a regular basis. Often, salary increments are dependent on successful reviews.

This section introduces the concept of personal development needs. It looks at how you might identify and record your needs. It then considers how these needs might be addressed. It also looks at learning styles so that you have an opportunity to identify your own learning style and appreciate how it might differ from the styles of those around you.

1.4.1 Identification of need

Development needs are, by their very nature, personal – they apply to a single individual and each individual may have completely different development needs from his/her neighbour. To discover your personal development needs, the first step is self-assessment. This section also considers assessment by others, e.g. a formal report from a line manager, customer feedback and other performance data that an employer may choose to collect.

1.4.1.1 Self-assessment

During this course, you will have had opportunities to consider your own strengths and weaknesses, your best and worst traits, and those of others in your group. There should also have been opportunities for others to express their opinion of you and for you to assess others and tell them what you think of them.

What others see in you tends to be what you choose to reveal about yourself. You have the option to hide certain traits and to promote the ones that you want others to recognise in you. The same goes for other people. So, in assessing someone else, you should be aware that you are only seeing what that person chooses to reveal. They may have hidden qualities that are only revealed at certain times – perhaps in times of stress or when that person has the confidence to be more honest with you.

Case study

New Year resolutions

At the close of each year, many people decide their New Year's resolutions. Some hope to eradicate a bad habit, e.g. cutting down or giving up smoking. Some hope to improve their health, e.g. joining a gym and starting a fitness plan and/or joining a slimming club. Some people decide to change their lifestyle in a more dramatic way, e.g. joining a club so they can meet more people, or starting a class so they can learn new skills, such as a new language with the intention of travelling more. At the end of the year, when thinking about next year's resolutions, the success or otherwise of last year's resolutions tells you a lot about yourself.

1 What resolutions have you set yourself in the past?

2 How successful have you been in keeping to your resolutions?

3 Discuss the merits of this traditional method of self-assessment with others in your group.

1.4.1.2 Formal reports

Formal reports provide an employer with an opportunity to record your progress within the organisation. A properly conducted appraisal, and the notes recorded from this, can be a powerful tool to help people progress in their job and make improvements in their work, adding to increased self-esteem and job satisfaction. The report can list any decisions that are made to train you or to redirect your energies through promotion, demotion or sideways moves. If your behaviour is less than satisfactory, this may be recorded also, together with targets that you are expected to achieve and that you have agreed to meet.

1.4.1.3 Customer feedback

Some organisations encourage customers to provide feedback about employees. A hotel chain, for example, can ask all guests to complete a questionnaire about the levels of service they have experienced during their stay. This can reflect well or badly on specific groups of employees, such as the receptionist team, the housekeeping team or the bar/restaurant staff. Similarly, a help desk (see *Unit 28: IT Technical Support*, page 282) may invite users to comment on the helpfulness of the guidance they received.

1.4.1.4 Performance data

Some organisations can collect data to record the performance of individual employees. A supermarket, for example, can record how quickly a checkout worker scans products, how many customers they serve during their shift and what turnover they take.

Each of these measures, taken in isolation, may not seem very fair. One customer might buy a lot of low-priced items, all of which are bulk, resulting in a slower scanning process. Another might find that an egg has broken and the completion of the transaction is delayed while a fresh box is fetched.

As with any statistical analysis, for the data to prove useful, it needs to be taken from a large enough sample so that the entire population can be assumed to be represented by the sample. So, over a long enough period of time, one checkout operator can be compared against another.

1.4.2 Records

This section reviews two types of records: personal development plans and appraisal records.

During the course of completing this unit, you should have created and maintained a personal development plan (PDP). The process of thinking about your future and your plans (and setting short-term, medium-term and long-term goals) should have given you an insight into how useful PDPs can be. It is essential to think about what to do and plan how you will achieve your

Activity 1.23

Personal development needs

1 Research the Internet to find out the process that an employer has to follow in order to dismiss an employee without offering compensation. What records need to be kept to prove that the employee failed to meet the terms of his/her contract? Make notes.

2 Look for examples on the Internet of how organisations seek out feedback from customers. What questions are asked? How might the organisations analyse this data to provide useful information?

3 Research the Internet for information on how supermarkets assess the performance of their staff. Look for other examples of performance data collection by large organisations.

goals. It is also important to record these goals and any objectives that you establish, as well as noting the progress that you make, if only to help you to set more realistic targets in future.

For an employer, appraisal records are important as a way of recording what you and your manager plan for the coming year. They are useful for recording work and training goals and for identifying any areas for improvement. See also the section on Formal reports on page 33.

Activity 1.24

Records

1 Review the information in your personal development plan. What else could you have recorded? Discuss the content of a personal development plan with others in your group.

2 Interview someone who is in full-time employment. Ask them to describe the appraisal system used by their employer. What good comes from the appraisal meetings? Are there any downsides to appraisal, from your interviewee's point of view? Make notes.

1.4.3 Methods of addressing needs

There are a range of options open to an individual to address needs that have been identified during an assessment process.

1.4.3.1 Job shadowing

Job shadowing is particularly useful for work experience, when you are trying to decide what career path to follow. It involves being with someone, watching what they are doing every minute of their working day. It provides useful insight into the stresses and strains of the job and how the person doing it copes with the workload and any interruptions.

If there is time, the person who is being shadowed can give a running commentary on what is happening. Sometimes, though, this is not practical, especially if other people could overhear what is being said, such as a customer or supplier during some delicate negotiation. If this is the case, a debriefing session can be used afterwards to explain what was going on.

1.4.3.2 Formal courses

If your job requires knowledge and skills that you don't yet have, you may be asked to attend a formal course. The course may be delivered within your organisation or you may be sent off-site for external training. The training may lead to qualifications for which you have to pass an examination. Examinations, such as those taken by bankers and those in insurance, are set to establish a standard of knowledge and performance expected of those within the industry. Within the ICT industry, Microsoft offers a number of certifications that can confirm your understanding of one or more of their products. Holding such a certificate can prove your level of expertise.

1.4.3.3 Meetings and events

Some learning comes from talking with colleagues and watching them at work. This can happen during team meetings or by attending events outside of the organisation such as conferences. Most industries hold annual events in which people in the same trade or profession gather at some central venue. These events provide an important opportunity to catch up on the latest developments, to share expertise and to find out what your competitors are doing.

Activity 1.25

Meeting needs

1 Review your PDP. How might you address your needs? What courses could you attend? What further qualifications might help you to further your career plans? Identify two different ways in which one of your personal development needs could be addressed – analyse these and decide which would be the most effective way of meeting that need. **p**₆ **p**₇ **d**₂

2 Research the Internet for conferences being held for an industry of interest to you. Where will it be held? Who will be exhibiting? When and how often does this event take place?

STOP Test your knowledge

1 Explain these terms: self-assessment, personal development plan, appraisal, job shadowing.

2 Give three examples of performance data.

1.4.4 Learning styles

Learning styles vary from one person to the next. No two people learn in the same way. However, studies of groups of individuals and learning styles have resulted in terms being coined to describe different types of learners, such as: active/reflective, sensory/intuitive, visual/verbal, sequential/global.

- **Active learners** enjoy working in groups and learn to figure out problems by trying. They prefer to handle objects and to do physical experiments.

- **Reflective learners** prefer to figure out a problem on their own. They think things through, evaluate the various options, and learn by analysis.
- **Sensory learners** look first for facts and prefer concrete, practical and procedural information.
- **Intuitive learners** look for meaning and prefer conceptual, innovative and theoretical information.
- **Visual learners** understand drawings (e.g. a spider diagram) that represent information.
- **Verbal learners** like to hear or read information and understand best explanations that use words.
- **Sequential learners** need information in a linear and orderly manner. They piece together the details to understand the bigger picture.
- **Global learners** see the big picture first and then fill in the details systematically. This is called a holistic approach to learning.

A number of models have been developed as to how people study: how they perceive information, how they process it and then how they organise and present what they have learnt.

The perception stage relies on:
- sight (the **visual** cues)
- hearing (the **auditory** cues)
- other sensations, including touch, temperature and movement (the **kinaesthetic** cues).

Each of these three types of cue (visual, auditory and kinaesthetic) appeals to some people but not to others, so how information is presented can affect how people perceive it.
- An **auditory** learner, for example, is most comfortable absorbing information that they have heard or discussed.
- A **kinaesthetic** learner prefers to learn through practical classes and hands-on activities, rather than by reading books and listening to lectures.

Most people can learn using a mixture of visual, auditory and kinaesthetic cues.

Having acquired information, how you process it mentally (by thinking about it and memorising it) can also vary. When grasping facts, you might prefer to deal with concrete, practical examples or you might be happier with abstract concepts and generalisations.

In ordering information, some people prefer to receive facts in a logical, sequential way so that they can build up a picture one step at a time. Others prefer an overview straightaway, so they look for the big picture first and can then focus on the details. Some people engage with the information they have gathered by active experimentation, while others prefer to let things sink in through reflective observation.

In organising what you know, you may adopt a holistic overview or engage in detailed and logical analysis. When presenting information to share it with others, you might tend to give verbal explanations, while someone else might use images.

1.4.4.1 Identification of preferred style

A number of quiz-type analyses have been devised to help people to identify their preferred learning style. Your answers to a number of seemingly simple questions build a profile of you and you can then be given feedback as to what learning styles suit you best.

1.4.4.2 How to benefit from knowing your learning style

Teachers are trained to recognise learning styles – they should present information to their classes in a variety of ways so that all students benefit, regardless of their preferred learning style. However, if you find it difficult to grasp a subject or find a lesson boring, it may be that you need to adapt your way of listening or note taking so as to make the best of the lesson. For example, if your teacher presents you with a handout that you find hard to understand, you could try transferring the facts into a tabular format or a spider diagram, or some other way of representing the data that makes it clearer to you.

The onus is on you to make the most of whatever your teacher presents, but giving feedback to the teacher may help them to shape the way that they teach. Ask questions if anything is not clear. Offer the teacher your version of the data – your teacher may suggest giving a copy of what you have produced to other students. Similarly, you might learn from how others take notes or represent the information they get from the teacher.

1.4.4.3 The impact of learning style on team working

Because each individual has his/her own preferred learning style, the way a team of people learns can be quite complex. Presented with a brief, such as an A4 sheet of written instructions, some of the team will very quickly grasp the facts of the problem to be solved. Others will need it explained differently, perhaps using a diagram or perhaps by talking it through.

So long as each person understands what is expected before work commences, the team should prove effective. However, any communications between team members needs to take into account variations in preferred learning style. Otherwise, misunderstandings can occur which can hinder progress.

Activity 1.26

Learning styles

1 Research the Internet to discover at least two different models of learning styles. Make notes on each to show how they agree and how they differ.

2 Find out, through the Internet or otherwise, how the following terms relate to the models you discovered in question 1: active/reflective, sensory/intuitive, visual/verbal, sequential/global.

3 Complete an online questionnaire to discover your own preferred learning style. What works for you? What is not likely to work for you? Compare your findings with others in your group.

Preparation for assessment

The assessment tasks in this unit are based on the following scenario.

RAINBOW is a small charity that supports clients who have problems with their sight and need help in using ICT. RAINBOW employs five people, but relies on volunteers to carry out a lot of the work with clients. Some volunteers help to create 'talking books' which are saved on CD and then loaned to clients. Others visit the clients and show them how to load and listen to the CDs. Your role is to work alongside the person who selects, interviews and manages the team of volunteers. She maintains a database of clients and a schedule of volunteers and the work they are expected to do.

Task 1 (P7, D2)

While working for RAINBOW, you are expected to create and maintain a personal development plan. Think about your strengths and weaknesses in terms of the knowledge and skills you will need to manage the team of volunteers who create the 'talking books'. What would you need to learn about the software that is used to record the stories on to a master CD? What about the software used to print the CD inserts listing the tracks and the software used to make copies of the master CD? Identify one personal development need you have in each of these areas and plan how you can meet it.

Task 2 (P1)

Explain, using a table or otherwise, why employers value particular employee attributes. Give two examples of attributes that might be expected of the full-time staff at RAINBOW and identify the personal attributes that might be expected of a volunteer.

Task 3 (P4, D1, M3)

Prepare a presentation to show that you can effectively communicate technical information to a specified audience. Your audience is newly recruited volunteers and the technical information should involve the use of ICT to help the visually impaired.

Having watched other people's presentations, write a brief report analysing the interpersonal and written communications of at least two other people, criticising or justifying particular techniques used. Proofread, review and amend both your own and other people's draft reports to produce final versions.

Task 4 (P3, P2, M2)

Working in pairs, role play the interview process for taking on a new volunteer. Demonstrate effective communication-related interpersonal skills, in the role of both interviewer and interviewee.

Prepare a slide show to explain to volunteers the potential barriers to effective communication and the mechanisms available to reduce the impact of communication barriers, focusing particularly on communicating with ICT users who are visually impaired.

Using ICT tools, create a portfolio of examples to show how, as an employee of RAINBOW, you might use ICT tools effectively to aid communications both with volunteers and with visually impaired clients.

Choose one particular specialist ICT communication channel, such as email, and explain how you use it in your day-to-day work at RAINBOW. Explain the techniques you might employ to use it most effectively. Your explanation may be written or verbal or a combination of both.

Your manager's preferred learning style is verbal/sequential, and she has asked you to give your opinion on how best to manage the volunteers. For example, do you think a formal appraisal system is appropriate, since the workers are volunteers rather than employees? Should the process be optional? Should it be less formal?

You have also been asked to produce a human resources booklet suitable for a new volunteer, describing ways of identifying and meeting their development needs. Include an introduction to explain how knowing their preferred learning style can improve their effectiveness in developing new skills or understanding, and also sample questions from a quiz that could reveal the learning style.

Make sure that your report suits your manager's preferred learning style and that your booklet meets the needs of an audience of people with a variety of different learning styles.

Computer Systems

Introduction

A computer system comprises both hardware and software and these two basic elements need to work in harmony.

Operating systems software is needed to run the computer. This unit looks at the Microsoft operating systems which currently dominate the market, but you will also look at other operating systems and explore at least one other in some detail. The operating system, together with essential utilities, provides the programs needed to manage a computer system. This unit looks at the options available for essential utilities such as anti-virus software, which is often pre-installed but might be purchased from a third party.

Manufacturers of hardware offer a wide range of models, each with its own specification. This unit reviews the many hardware components of a computer system and how they interact, so that you can set up, use, customise and maintain a computer system. Although this unit does not cover fault finding and repair (covered in Units 28 and 29), it does explain the basic maintenance skills that would normally be expected of most computer users.

After completing this unit, you should be able to achieve these outcomes:

- Understand the hardware components of computer systems
- Understand the software components of computer systems
- Be able to undertake routine computer maintenance.

Thinking points

Choosing the right hardware to support the software that you intend to use is essential; a system that cannot cope, one whose performance is unacceptable, will not meet the needs of the intended user. If you could buy any computer, with an unlimited budget, which one would you choose? How would you decide which specification was best for you? What factors would you take into account?

If a friend planned to buy a computer for a particular purpose, could you explain what peripherals would be needed and give advice as to the best specification of hardware to purchase? Would you be able to decide which particular model would be most appropriate?

Do you understand all the terminology that is used in advertisements for computer systems? Could you explain the jargon to someone who knows very little about computers?

This unit provides the background knowledge to help you to make informed choices and to advise others on the best configuration of computer hardware and software to meet a particular need.

The hardware of a computer system – the main components and the **peripherals** – can be found either within the processor box or attached to the computer by some cabling.

There are also peripherals which do not need cabling and which rely on wireless or infrared to transmit data between processor and peripheral, and vice versa. For each type of peripheral, there is a **port** on the processor to which it is connected, either through a cable or via a wireless link.

This section focuses on the system unit components and then looks in particular at backing storage devices and data transmission. It also identifies what you might need to take into account when selecting a new computer system.

What does it mean?

A **peripheral** is any device, such as a printer, attached to a computer so as to expand its functionality.

Ports provide the link between peripherals and the CPU (central processing unit).

2.1.1 System unit components

This section looks at what is inside the box and what options you might have when purchasing a new computer system. It also looks at the peripherals you might decide to attach and the specialised cards you might decide to install.

2.1.1.1 Processors and options

The processor is a chip housed on the motherboard (see Figure 2.3 on page 45) and is the 'heart' of a computer system – it controls everything. It contains the circuitry which processes the instructions in the computer programs by interpreting them into actual movements of bits of data within the computer memory (Figure 2.1).

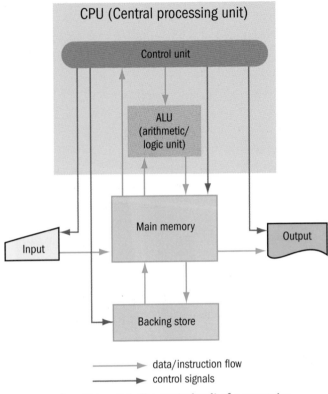

Figure 2.1 The control unit of a computer

The control circuitry pulls data in via the various ports, directs it along data buses (see page 60), stores it within the memory, performs calculations on it and sends the results of processing to a VDU screen, to a printer or to a secondary storage device for more processing at a later date.

Computer manufacturers constantly seek to improve the processor by increasing its capabilities (i.e. the types of instructions that it can process) and its speed.

What does it mean?

GHz stands for **gigahertz**. **Hertz** are named after Heinrich Rudolf Hertz (1857–1894), a German physicist who studied electromagnetic radiation. Hertz are a measurement of frequency in cycles per second: 1 hertz is one cycle per second. **Giga** means one billion – when measuring computer data, it means 230 (= 1,073,741,824), which is the power of 2 closest to one billion.

The speed is measured in **GHz** – the higher the number, the faster the processor works.

Early computers were enormous machines; they could do just one thing at a time. These computers were standalone, i.e. not networked, and were not portable, unlike the laptops of today. The advent of microcomputers and then desktop computers meant smaller computers, suitable for individual usage. Early microprocessors based on the 8086 chip were called the 286, 386 and 486 processors; each new chip ran faster than the previous one. The Pentium (a more memorable alternative to the name 586) was then introduced. This multiprocessing chip was more powerful because it had two **ALU**s (see Figure 2.1 on page 42), which meant it could perform two instructions at once – this improved the processing speed.

What does it mean?

ALU stands for **arithmetic and logic unit** – a basic component of the control unit for a computer.

Then, as new hardware was developed (such as audio, graphic and video peripherals), new types of instructions were needed to process the data. So, new chips were developed to support the handling of data for this new hardware. When networks were first introduced, new chips were needed again, to cope with this new way of working.

With each new development of processor chip, the voltage that the processor required has also been reduced (from around 5 volts down to 1.5 volts) – this makes the processor more reliable because it does not get so hot.

Remember!

To keep the processor temperature down it also has its own heat sink and/or fan; see page 49.

The memory capacity also increased, as has the size of the cache (see page 55).

Case study

Anne's laptop

According to the system information on Anne's laptop, she has an Intel Pentium M processor running at 1.73 GHz (Figure 2.2).

Intel are the makers of the chip housed on her Hewlett-Packard laptop. It also boasts Centrino mobile technology.

1 Find out what processor is at the heart of your computer. What is its speed? List its other characteristics.

2 Find out what is meant by Centrino mobile technology. What alternative technologies are available?

3 Research the Internet to find out more of the history of the chip. What are the most popular chips today? What are their basic characteristics? Present your findings as a table showing the development of the chip from early Pentium days to the present.

The System Properties is an option on the Control Panel.

The processor type is Intel Pentium. Its speed is 1.73 Ghz.

Hewlett-Packard is the manufacturer of the system.

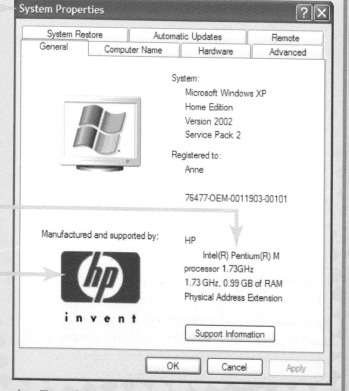

▲ **Figure 2.2 Processor configuration**

2.1.1.2 Motherboards

The motherboard – sometimes called the 'mobo' for short – is the most important component within a PC system. It is a **PCB** that houses many of the essential parts of the PC and all connections between the PC and peripheral go through it.

Although there are a number of different manufacturers of computers (Dell, Hewlett-Packard, Toshiba, etc.) and hence of the motherboards that go within them, there are a limited number of **form factors**. The form factor defines whereabouts the components are positioned on the motherboard (see Figure 2.3) and how it is mounted within the chassis.

What does it mean?

PCB stands for **printed circuit board**.

The **form factor** defines the shape and size of the motherboard.

There are families of motherboard:

- A **motherboard-style mainboard** puts all a PC's primary components on a single PCB – being on a single PCB makes it 'motherboard' style.
- A **backplane mainboard** provides a number of card slots into which other cards (called daughterboards) can be fitted – this allows processors and memory circuit cards to be put together to create particular capability.

There are two types of backplane mainboard:

- A **passive backplane** provides a simple bus structure and limited data buffering – this allows the daughterboards to interconnect.
- An **active backplane** is more complex, and provides extra 'intelligence' to help the daughterboards.

Motherboards may also be integrated or non-integrated:

- An **integrated motherboard** provides nearly everything on the one PCB – this includes items which would otherwise be added using expansion cards, such as video and disk controllers.
- A **non-integrated motherboard** requires all the extra facilities to be achieved using expansion boards.

Activity 2.1

Motherboards

1   Find out what type of motherboard you have installed on your computer.

2   Identify the main components on a motherboard. Draw a diagram to show the position of the processor chip, the BIOS chip, the battery, the power supply connector, the memory slots, the expansion slots, the ports and other important components.

3   Look at how components are slotted into place. Research the Internet to find out what a ZIF arm is used for.

Integrated motherboards seem a good idea as everything is in one place. That works fine until something goes wrong, when the whole motherboard has to be replaced, not just one expansion card. However, the norm is now for integrated motherboards.

2.1.1.3 RAM

Within the processor box, **RAM** memory chips provide a form of memory that offers the same access time for allocations within it (hence the term 'random access'). It is volatile memory, which means you can write to it and read from it, but it loses its data when the power is turned off. So, for example, when your computer crashes and you have to turn it off and restart it, whatever changes you made to a document since it was last saved (either by you or using an autosave function) are lost.

RAM, like other memory, is measured in bytes or, more likely, GB (gigabytes).

Programs that are written and stored in RAM are called software – the instructions can be overwritten. To preserve data and/or program instructions for use later, these have to be stored either on ROM (see next section) or to a secondary storage device such as a hard disk (see page 58).

What does it mean?

RAM stands for random access memory.

(a)

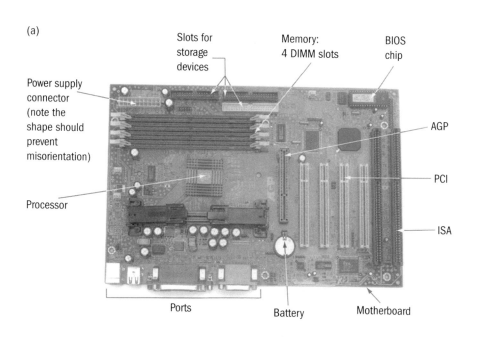

Slots for storage devices

Memory: 4 DIMM slots

BIOS chip

Power supply connector (note the shape should prevent misorientation)

Processor

AGP

PCI

ISA

Ports

Battery

Motherboard

Figure 2.3
(a) AT form factor
(b) ATX form factor

(b)

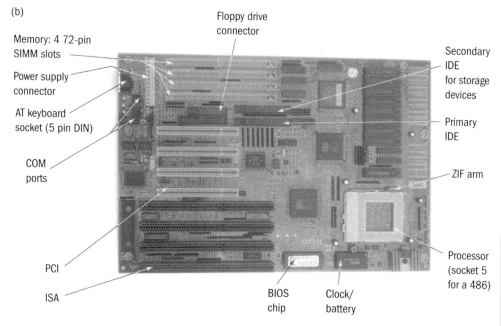

Floppy drive connector

Memory: 4 72-pin SIMM slots

Power supply connector

AT keyboard socket (5 pin DIN)

COM ports

Secondary IDE for storage devices

Primary IDE

ZIF arm

Processor (socket 5 for a 486)

PCI

ISA

BIOS chip

Clock/ battery

What does it mean?

SRAM stands for **static RAM**.

DRAM stands for **dynamic RAM**.

The time it takes to fetch a program instruction affects the speed at which an application can run. For optimum performance, the 'page' of code that is being executed is brought from the backing storage location (e.g. on the hard disk) into RAM. When these instructions have been executed, the next page is swapped into position. Having a greater amount of RAM results in there being space for more instructions that can be held close to the processor at any one time, and this reduces the amount of time spent swapping pages into and out of RAM.

A 'crash' can result when the processor spends its time swapping pages rather than executing the instructions – this can happen if you try to run too many applications at the same time, each of them needing its own page space in RAM.

When adding (or removing) memory, to increase (or decrease) the capacity of a PC, you need to decide what type of RAM to add (or remove): **SRAM** (static RAM) or **DRAM** (dynamic RAM).

The transistors in SRAM, unlike the capacitors which make up DRAM, do not need to be refreshed so frequently. SRAM is very fast but relatively expensive (many times more than DRAM) and takes up valuable space, so it tends to be used for cache memory (see page 55) rather than primary memory.

Activity 2.2

RAM

1 Figure 2.2 on page 43 shows Anne's laptop as having 0.99 GB of RAM. How many GB of RAM (SRAM and DRAM) are installed in your computer?

2 There are also other types of RAM – such as VRAM (video RAM), SGRAM (synchronous graphics RAM) and WRAM (Windows RAM) – each of which serves a specific purpose within the computer. Research the Internet to find out when VRAM, SGRAM and WRAM were introduced, and details of any other types of RAM, such as DDR (double data RAM).

2.1.1.4 ROM

The RO in ROM stands for 'read only' but, depending on the type of ROM, you may or may not be able to write to it (see Table 2.1).

ROM is non-volatile memory. It does not lose its data when the power supply is off, so it can be used to store data and/or instructions (called **firmware**) that are needed when you next turn on, e.g. for the BIOS chip.

Of the two types of memory, RAM is the quicker for the CPU to access. So, to improve performance during the boot process, the BIOS instructions (held on ROM) may be copied on to RAM – this process is called shadowing.

What does it mean?

ROM stands for **read only memory**.

Firmware is the name given to the instructions encoded onto ROM chips – unlike software, once written it cannot be changed.

Activity 2.3

ROM

1 Find out what ROM is installed in your computer.

2 In older computers, to speed up the boot process, a technique called ROM shadowing was used. In groups, research the Internet to discover more about this process.

Type of ROM		Notes
PROM	Programmable ROM	A PROM is a blank ROM chip – all bits are set to 1 initially. A PROM burner can be used to change the binary 1s into binary 0s, so as to store data and/or instructions on the PROM. This process cannot be reversed; once 'burnt', the 0s cannot be turned back into 1s. WYBIWYG = what you burn is what you get.
EPROM	Erasable PROM	An EPROM (pronounced e-prom) is the same as a PROM but with a quartz crystal window. This allows the circuitry to be accessed with UV (ultraviolet) light to turn the 0s back into 1s. The EPROM has to be removed from the PC for reprogramming.
EEPROM	Electronically erasable PROM	An EEPROM (pronounced e-e-prom) is the same as an EPROM except you do not need to remove it to reprogram it. This makes it very easy to upgrade. The reprogramming – using a software utility available from the chip manufacturer – is called **flashing** and the chip is called **flash ROM**.

Table 2.1 Different types of ROM

2.1.1.5 BIOS

The **BIOS** is a collection of software utilities that forms part of the operating system. It is usually on a ROM chip that comes with the computer, called the ROM BIOS.

Being on ROM, the BIOS is not affected by power failure and makes it possible for the computer to boot itself.

So, what does the BIOS do?

- The BIOS boots up the PC, i.e. it starts up the PC every time it is turned on.
- The BIOS checks the actual hardware configuration against the configuration data. It ensures the integrity of the computer system and can therefore prove to be the most important diagnostic tool available to you.
- The BIOS handles the input and output of the computer, allowing the operating system to use particular features of hardware within the configuration.

When the computer is turned on, its memory is empty, apart from one set of hardwired instructions that are located at an address called the jump address. These important few instructions, when executed, will load the BIOS into memory. So, the computer 'jumps' to the jump address, starts executing instructions and this results in the BIOS being loaded.

The loading of the BIOS is part of the booting up process during which the configuration of the computer is checked (during the **POST** process) and the operating system loaded, so that everything is ready for the user to start work.

What does it mean?

BIOS stands for **basic input/output system**.

The **POST (power-on self test)** is a hardware diagnostic routine that is run during the start-up boot sequence and checks configuration settings of the computer.

Activity 2.4

BIOS

1 Locate the BIOS ROM chip on a motherboard. What make of BIOS ROM is it?

2 Turn on your computer and watch the POST process. Note what happens if one part of your system is not working or has been disconnected (such as a LAN cable).

2.1.1.6 Power supply

Within a PC, the PSU (power supply unit) is a black or silver coloured box, with a fan inside it and cables coming from it (see Figure 2.4).

WATCH OUT!

If the fan fails to turn on when you power up your PC, do not think about sticking anything into the fan to force it to move!

The PSU has various features, depending on the age of the PC.

- On older PCs, a pass-through connector may be located on the back of the PSU. This allows you to plug a monitor into the power supply and to use the PC power switch to activate the monitor.

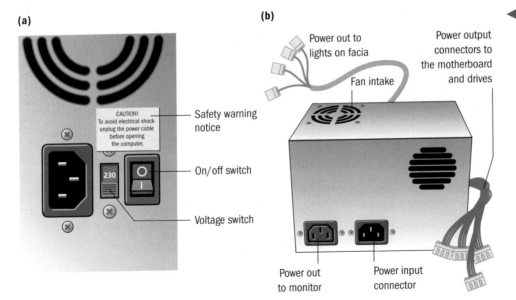

(a)

CAUTION!
To avoid electrical shock
unplug the power cable
before opening
the computer.

230

— Safety warning notice

— On/off switch

— Voltage switch

(b)

Power out to lights on facia

Fan intake

Power output connectors to the motherboard and drives

Power out to monitor

Power input connector

Figure 2.4 The power supply for a PC: (a) connections on the case; (b) the PSU

- A power switch may extend through the case wall of the PSU to a back corner of the PC, or more recently to the front of the PC. On more modern PCs, the on/off switch is electronic (rather than manual) and is attached directly to the motherboard, which then connects to the PSU.
- For PCs that may be used worldwide, there may be a 110/220V selector switch.

The main job of the PSU is to supply power to the various components of the PC. There are two types of power: internal and external.

- The external power via the socket provides **AC** of 110–115V.
- The internal power needed by the various components within the PC is either 5V or 12V of **DC**.

Since PC components work on DC and the power from the wall socket supplies AC, the PSU has to convert AC to DC. So, the PSU converts the incoming supply of power to one that is needed: the right type and at the required voltage.

What does it mean?

AC (alternating current) is a type of electricity. The direction of the current alternates (very quickly), providing an efficient way of supplying power over long distances.

DC (direct current) is a different type of electricity. The power runs from negative charge to positive charge, always in the same direction. This works fine for battery-powered devices where the power has only a short distance to travel.

Activity 2.5

PSU

1 Locate the PSU within your desktop computer's processor box. Note the leads that run from the PSU to other devices. Draw a diagram to illustrate the connections.

2 Find out what voltages different peripherals (such as a monitor, printer and mouse) require. How are these devices powered?

3 Check the type and power of the battery that is located on the motherboard. What is this battery used to power?

4 Find out how a laptop is powered when there is no connection to the mains supply.

2.1.1.7 Fan and heat sink

The airflow and cooling system may seem a minor design point but, like a car engine, if the chips within the PC become overheated, they may fail. Some components generate a lot of heat (3D video cards, multiple hard drives, etc.) and these can affect other chips close to them. So, the placement of essential chips (like the CPU!) has to be carefully decided, all within a limited amount of space on the motherboard.

Early PCs (before the 486) were cooled by airflow within the case created by a fan in the PSU. This type of cooling relied on cool air being sucked into the case by the fan. For later models of PC, a heat sink (see Figure 2.5) or processor cooling fan (or both) were attached to the CPU.

To make the system even more efficient, the PSU fan was reversed so that it acted as an extractor, pulling hot air out of the PC case.

Modern chips, such as the Pentium processor, present special problems: they become much hotter than previous designs of chip and so need a careful heat dissipation system. Otherwise, they can overheat and fail. The heat sink and/or fan is moulded onto the chip and attached with **thermal grease**.

WATCH OUT!

Thermal grease may be mercury-based, so avoid its contact with your skin.

Fins on heat sinks allow heat to pass to air efficiently

▲ **Figure 2.5 A heat sink**

Remember!

Notice that the heat sink has lots of fins so that its surface area is maximised and the heat transfer is maximised.

What does it mean?

Thermal grease is also known as thermal gunk, compound, goo and heatsink jelly. It is a special kind of gel that improves heat conductivity between the two materials that it joins.

Activity 2.6

Airflow and cooling

1 Locate the processor on a motherboard. What cooling device is used?

2 Research the Internet for data on heat sinks. What materials might these be made from?

3 Research the Internet to find out what happens (and at what temperature) if the fan stops working on a PC, or the heat sink is removed or not connected properly to the processor chip.

STOP ## Test your knowledge

1 Give the full form of these terms: BIOS, POST and PSU.

2 Where is the BIOS stored?

3 What purpose is served by the POST?

4 What functions does the PSU serve?

5 Explain the difference between AC and DC.

2.1.1.8 Hard drive configuration and controllers

The hard drive for a computer – together with drives for CDs and DVDs – is usually located within the processor box. However, an external hard drive can provide additional secondary storage and may also be used as a backup device.

Hard drives, wherever they are located, are **IDE** devices, controlled by an IDE controller.

There are two types of IDE controller: a primary IDE controller and a secondary IDE controller – see Figure 2.3 on page 45. The hard drive is normally attached to the primary IDE controller (the IDE1 connector) using an IDE 40-pin 80-conductor ribbon data cable.

> ## WATCH OUT!
>
> The 40-pin 80-conductor ribbon data cable is similar to the CD cable but each conductor has a ground wire and hence there are 80 instead of 40 conductors. If you use the wrong cable, the hard drive will not work properly.

A CD drive (or another hard drive) can then be attached to the secondary channel (the IDE2 connector) on the motherboard using an IDE 40-pin 40-conductor ribbon data cable.

> ## Remember!
>
> The CD drive is also attached via an audio cable. (Audio cables are usually notched to help you to plug them in the correct way. If you connect one the wrong way around, you may hear no sound at all when you power up.)

What does it mean?

IDE stands for **integrated drive electronics**. It is a standard electronic interface between a computer motherboard's data paths (or buses) and the computer's disk storage devices, based on the IBM PC ISA (Industry Standard Architecture) 16-bit bus standard.

An enhanced version called **EIDE** (enhanced IDE) is used in most new computers and an IDE controller is often built into the motherboard.

Each IDE ribbon, attached to either one of these controllers, can support two drives. To know which data relates to which drive, each drive is identified as either the master drive or the slave drive.

- The master drive handles all the traffic on the IDE cable. Its controller retains its own data and passes on data to the slave drive.
- The slave drive sees only the data that is passed to it by the master drive. (N.B. There does not have to be a slave drive if there is only one drive attached to the cable.)

Assigning master/slave to the primary and secondary drives is achieved through jumper settings (see Figure 2.6).

To identify the drives as master or slave, you need to set the jumpers for each drive, from one of four options: single, master, slave or cable select.

- If you only have one drive, then, although it is referred to as the master, you should opt for the **single** jumper setting. This may also be the factory set default option.

Hard disk drive   Jumpers (set as master)

IDE socket

IDE connector   Power connector

Data cable

Jumper settings:

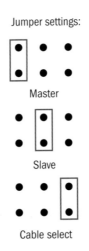

Figure 2.6 A hard drive with jumper settings

Master

Slave

Cable select

- If you have two drives, one is designated as **master** and the other as **slave**.
- The **cable select** option is responsible for the decision making regarding which drive is master and which is slave to the cabling that you attach. You need special cabling for this (a cable-select cable, recognised by having a small hole in it) and it does not work with all drives! The drive nearest the motherboard becomes the master drive and the other the slave drive.

The drive label may tell you exactly how to set the jumpers. Otherwise, you should refer to the documentation provided by the manufacturer or go to the manufacturer's website for details.

Activity 2.7

Hard drives

1 Locate the hard drive within your PC. Check which IDE channel is being used for it. Check the master/ slave settings.

2 Identify any other backing storage devices attached to your computer. Which are internal? Which are external? How are they connected to the processor?

2.1.1.9 Ports

Ports provide the link between peripherals and the CPU. Not all peripherals need a cable to link them to the port; some use wireless or infrared technology (see Figure 2.7).

Remember!

For infrared, the input device has to be in line of sight with the transceiver. There must be no obstruction between the two.

A variety of ports are available so that a range of peripherals, each with differing needs, may be attached to the processor (see Figure 2.8).

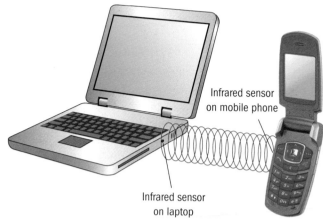

Figure 2.7 Transfer of data from wireless device to PC via infrared transceiver

Figure 2.8 Ports and connectors

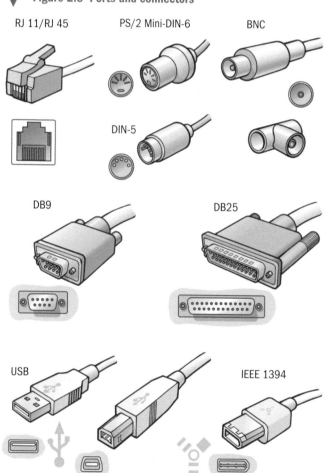

For example, if cabling is used, the transfer of data to and from the peripheral will be one of two types.

- Serial transmission is 1 bit at a time and the cable is usually circular in cross-section.

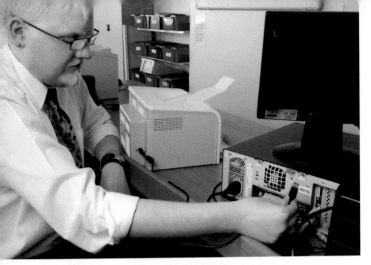

Connecting up a computer system using USB ports

- Parallel transmission is 1 byte (8 bits) at a time. This cabling looks like a ribbon, the wires being laid side by side.

Some devices are so simple they only need serial connection: mouse and keyboard. Others, such as printers, benefit from the two-way communication of parallel connections. However, nowadays, you are more likely to see a printer connected via a fast serial port using a USB connector, this being a faster option than the old ribbon connection.

The serial and parallel ports on the PC are very different, as are the connectors that fit into them (see Figure 2.9).

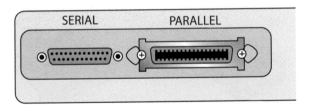

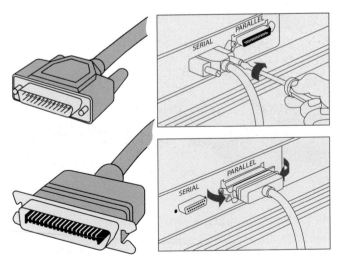

▲ **Figure 2.9 Serial and parallel connections**

- The serial port conforms to the **RS-232c** standard. It requires a 25-pin male port, but PCs only use 9 of these pins so it can be, and often is, replaced by a 9-pin male port.
- The parallel port on the PC, e.g. for a printer, offers a female 25-pin DB (databus) connector. A male 25-pin DB connector on one end of the printer ribbon cable will clip or screw into place. At the other end of the cable, at the printer end, is the 36-pin Centronics connector.

USB is a relatively recent invention designed to make the installation of slow peripherals, such as the mouse, joystick, keyboard and scanners – and other devices, such as printers, digital cameras and digital telephones – as easy as possible.

On most motherboards, the USB host controller is included in the chipset. This host controller recognises when you plug a device into a USB port and allows **hot swapping** of devices. Having recognised the device, the USB controller assigns an **IRQ**.

There may be as many as four USB ports supported by a motherboard (see Figure 2.10).

It is also possible to link the devices in a 'daisy chain' so that the PC may have many more devices attached – each device provides the USB port to the next device in the chain. Another option is to have a USB hub, into which devices can be plugged (see Figure 2.11).

For a wireless mouse (see Figure 2.12), a connector (called a notebook receiver) may be attached to a USB port – the mouse is then battery-operated.

What does it mean?

RS-232c stands for Reference Standard 232 revision c.

USB (universal serial bus) is a higher-speed serial connection standard that supports low-speed devices (e.g. mice, keyboards, scanners) and higher-speed devices (e.g. digital cameras).

Hot swapping means connecting (or disconnecting) a peripheral while the PC is turned on.

IRQ stands for interrupt request.

Generally, transmission via a serial port is a slow, inexpensive method of data transfer. USB is faster than standard serial and an optical serial connection may transfer at an even faster rate, faster than a parallel connection. So, parallel transmission is usually, but not always, faster than serial.

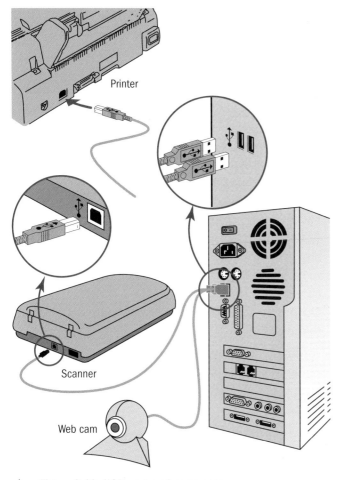

▲ Figure 2.10 USB port and connector

▲ Figure 2.12 Using a wireless mouse is increasingly common

Figure 2.11 Hub options ▶

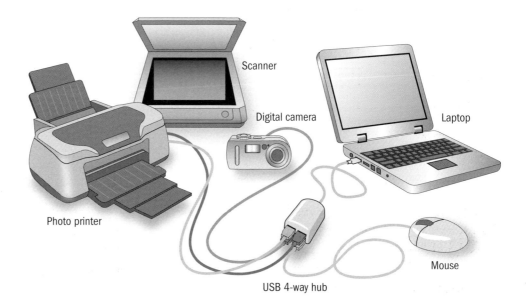

Case study

Anne's laptop

Anne's laptop has an IEEE 1394 host controller (see Figure 2.13). FireWire (IEEE 1394) was developed by Apple and is ideal for connecting devices such as digital cameras, digital video cameras and external hard disks which need to transfer large files. It is similar to USB in many ways, but it is much faster, running at up to 400 Mbps.

1 Check the ports available on your computer. List them and the devices that can be attached to them.

2 Research the Internet for information on devices that could be connected via the IEEE 1394 port.

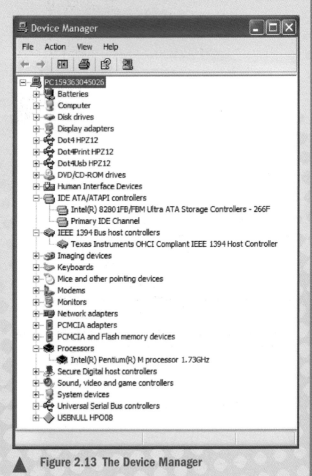

▲ **Figure 2.13 The Device Manager**

2.1.1.10 Peripherals

Peripherals fall into three groups.

- **Input devices** provide a way for the user to put data into the processor (e.g. through the keyboard or a secondary storage device like a CD) and to give commands (e.g. a pointing device like a mouse to click on the application you want to open, or to select an option from a menu).
- **I/O devices** – also known as storage devices or the backing store – provide a place, other than the RAM or ROM memory within the PC, to store data. They also provide portability, allowing data (and software) to be transferred from one PC to another, e.g. on a CD-ROM.
- **Output devices** present the results of any processing to the user.

According to their type (serial or parallel), they need to be connected to the processor using an appropriate cable to an appropriate port (see page 42); or configured as wireless devices.

What does it mean?

I/O stands for input/output.

2.1.1.11 Internal memory (RAM, ROM, cache)

Internal memory is used for two main purposes:

- to store programs that are being run
- to store the data that the program works on.

Although programs (i.e. software) may seem different from data, they are treated in exactly the same way – the computer executes a program, instruction by instruction. These instructions are the 'data' of the fundamental program cycle: fetch the next instruction, decode it and execute it. Then the next program cycle starts to process the next instruction. Even the address of the next instruction to be fetched is just data. So, everything in a computer's memory is data.

Activity 2.8

Peripherals

1 Table 2.2 lists examples of input, output and I/O devices. Copy and extend this table to include more peripherals that are currently available.

2 Research the Internet to find out when the mouse was first introduced. Prepare a presentation to show the development of technologies for pointing devices from then until the present day.

3 Research the Internet to discover how CDs work, and how the technology has advanced to the current DVD technology. Make notes on how different storage media are described – for example, their capacity.

4 There are a variety of printers and often these are combined with photocopiers, fax machines and scanners. Research the Internet to discover various categories of printer such as impact printers, line printers and plotters. Find out what consumables (such as ink cartridges) are needed for these printers.

Input	I/O (input/output)	Output
Keyboard	Hard disk drive	Screen/monitor/VDU
Mouse	CD-ROM drive	Printer
Tracker ball	Zip drive	Loudspeaker
Joystick		Actuator, e.g. a motor that powers a device, such as the wheels of a turtle
Scanner		
Barcode reader		
Digital camera		
Microphone		

Table 2.2 Examples of input, I/O and output devices

There are two main types of memory within the PC: the volatile RAM (see page 44) and non-volatile ROM (see page 46). This section focuses on another type of memory: a fast memory that is used as a data buffer between the CPU and RAM called the **cache memory**.

Cache memory may be internal or external:

- **internal cache** is located inside the CPU chip – also called **primary cache** or **on-die cache**
- **external cache** is also on the motherboard but not within the CPU chip – also called **secondary cache**.

Cache memory can also be categorised according to it closeness (proximity) to the CPU:

- **level 1 (L1) cache** is closest to the CPU and, like internal cache, is housed within the CPU chip
- **level 2 (L2) cache** is not so close – it may also be on the CPU chip (just behind the L1 cache) or it may be external cache.

Remember!

L1 cache cannot be upgraded without changing the CPU. L2 cache can be upgraded; on some motherboards the modules plug into special mounts or expansion sockets on the motherboard.

■ Why is cache memory needed?

Central to the operation of a PC is the communication between the CPU and RAM. These two components (like many others in a computer) work at differing speeds.

- The CPU works in megahertz (millionths of seconds).
- The RAM works in **nanoseconds** (billionths of seconds).

Even though the RAM is so much quicker, it takes time to find the data that is needed and bring it via the data bus to the CPU for processing. To aid the process, the CPU interacts with the RAM by having a series of **wait states** – it actually pauses for a while to allow the data that it wants to be transferred from RAM into the registers within the CPU. Data may be coming from far away, e.g. from a hard disk, and so it has to be transferred from the disk to RAM and then from RAM to the CPU. So, extra wait states may be necessary.

Even when the data is within RAM, there is a delay in transferring data within the PC called **latency**. Wherever the data is, the CPU has to wait – and an idle CPU is not acceptable!

The cache memory is there to solve this problem. It acts as a buffer, and holds data that the CPU will need, e.g. things that are used a lot. Like a printer buffer, the cache memory makes up for the mismatch between the speeds of the CPU and RAM.

Caching involves some guesswork by the system which has to decide what the CPU will need next.

- A good guess for the disk cache is that it will be whatever comes next on the disk.
- For the internal cache, a good guess would be whatever lies in the next section of RAM.

This guesswork uses the principle of **locality of reference**. Most of the time, it is a good guess – and so the net effect is a more effective use of CPU time.

Cache memory is often a small SRAM. This form of RAM offers access speeds of 2ns or faster. Adding more cache memory (at L1 or L2) can increase the speed, but the time it takes the CPU to keep the cache filled can decrease the performance overall. So, a balance is needed: enough to keep the CPU supplied, but not so big that the CPU spends all its time guessing what it will need next. For example, adding 256 KB of L2 might increase the speed, but the next 256 KB added to L2 may adversely affect performance.

What does it mean?

The length of time that RAM takes to write data (or to read it) once the request has been received from the processor is called the access time. This is measured in **nanoseconds** (ns): the fewer ns, the faster the RAM.

A **wait state** is a time of inactivity for the CPU to allow other devices to catch up with it.

Latency is a time delay that could be better used, e.g. for processing.

What does it mean?

There are three basic types of **locality of reference** (also called the principle of locality).

Temporal locality assumes that if a resource (such as a program instruction or an item of data) is referenced now, then it will be referenced again soon.

Spatial locality recognises that most program instructions are to be found in routines and that these routines are usually close together; also that data fields are close together. It assumes that the likelihood of referencing a resource is higher if a resource near it has been referenced.

Sequential locality assumes that memory will be accessed sequentially.

Remember!

There may also be a **disk cache** to compensate for the speed difference between the hard disk and RAM. This will be either in RAM or on the disk controller.

Activity 2.9

Internal memory – cache memory

1 What types of internal memory are being used in your computer? How much is installed?

2 Research the Internet to find out how much cache memory is used in a number of PCs with different specifications.

STOP Test your knowledge

1 List all the terms used as measures of time, with an explanation for each.

2 Explain the meaning of these terms: wait state, latency.

2.1.1.12 Specialised cards

Expansion slots allow the life of a computer to be extended, since new technology can be added as it becomes available. They allow you to add various specialised cards to your PC, e.g. for a modem, a sound card and/or a **NIC**.

What does it mean?

NIC stands for **network interface card**.

The expansion slots are long, thin socket connections located on a motherboard and connected to buses which carry the data to and from the CPU (see Figure 2.2 on page 43).

- The black slots are **ISA slots**. These are connected to ISA buses that move data at the slowest rate, between 3 MHz and 12 MHz, and are used for older and/or slower devices.
- The white slots are **PCI slots** and, because the PCI bus speed can be as fast as 66 MHz, these are used for high-speed I/O devices.

- The grey/brown slot is the **AGP slot** for a video card – its bus runs at about the same speed as the system bus.

Each slot has two rows of metal springs to guide the expansion card connectors into place.

Remember!

On an ATX motherboard, the expansion slots run parallel to the short edge of the motherboard. On an AT motherboard, the expansion slots are parallel to the long edge of the motherboard.

Activity 2.10

Specialised cards

1 Locate the expansion slots within your PC, and list the expansion cards already in the slots.

2 Repeat this activity on other PCs, noting differences between the form factors of the motherboards and the cards that are present in the slots.

3 For one video card, visit the manufacturer's site and find out as much as you can about the card. Compare notes with others in your group.

4 Research the Internet to find out about video adapter card standards: MDA, CGA, EGA, VGA and AVGA. Discover what resolution they support and how many colours they can display.

STOP Test your knowledge

1 Explain the purpose of an expansion slot and give three examples of cards found in one.

2 How can you distinguish between the different types of slots: AGP, PCI and ISA?

3 What does NIC stand for?

Case study

Nina the novice

Nina is nine years old and has just been given a new PC as a birthday present. It has a wireless mouse and an inkjet printer. She has been reading the manual that came with the PC and does not understand some of the terminology – such as backing store, memory and wireless. She does not need a detailed understanding. In fact, she does not need to know very much at all to use her PC, but she has asked you to explain things simply to her.

1 Draw a diagram for Nina, showing the main system unit components. **P₁**

2 Plan a presentation for Nina. In it, you will explain the main functions of each component and how they communicate with each other and with her. **P₁**

Remember!

How you explain things to a nine-year-old might differ from how you might talk to an adult.

2.1.2 Backing store

The memory within a computer is relatively small, located within the computer and the majority of it is lost when the computer is switched off.

- To create a more permanent store for data (including software), a **secondary storage device** or **backing store** is needed.
- To create a portable store for data, offline storage devices are needed: CD-ROMs, DVDs, memory sticks, etc. These are sometimes referred to as **tertiary storage**.

There are a variety of types of backing store now available to the PC user: magnetic and optical and the newer pen drives and flash memory cards.

Magnetic storage uses different patterns of magnetisation on a magnetically coated surface to store information in a non-volatile form. The data is accessed using one or more read/write heads. Magnetic disks are available in external hard drives (for offline storage) or internal hard drives (for secondary online storage).

Optical devices use tiny pits etched on the surface of a circular disc to store data in a non-volatile form. The data is read by illuminating the surface with a laser diode and observing the reflection. Examples are:

- CD, CD-ROM, DVD (for read-only storage, used for mass distribution of digital information such as music, video and computer programs)
- CD-R, DVD-R, DVD+R (for write-once storage, used for tertiary and offline storage)
- CD-RW, DVD-RW, DVD+RW, RVD-RAM (for slow-write/fast-read storage, used for tertiary and offline storage)
- **Blu-ray Disc** and **HD DVD**.

What does it mean?

Primary storage is the memory of the computer; **secondary storage** is a backing store that remains with the computer and provides a greater capacity than the processor can offer; **tertiary storage** is destined for transfer to another computer or archiving and needs to be on a portable medium.

Blu-ray Disc is named after the blue-violet (405 nm) laser used to read and write this type of disk, as opposed to the red (650 nm) laser used on other DVDs. The shorter wavelength (nm stands for nanometre) allows substantially more data to be stored and, as a result, a Blu-ray Disc can store 25 GB on each layer, whereas a DVD is limited to 4.7 GB.

Blu-Ray is a rival technology to the **HD DVD** (high definition DVD), a fairly recent technology developed for the release of movies on DVD.

Pen drives (see Figure 2.14) are small devices that can be used to transfer files between USB-compatible systems and provide a high-capacity alternative to CD-ROMs. They are plugged directly into the USB port and need no batteries for power.

Flash memory cards are a portable medium for data. Commonly used in digital cameras, they can hold your photos until you upload them to your computer or output them to a photo printer. They evolved from the EPROMs and the process called flashing, which involves overwriting what was once considered to be a write-once medium.

 Figure 2.14 A pen drive

Figure 2.15 A memory card reader

A card reader is plugged into the USB port and the card is slotted into the reader. Because there are lots of different shapes and sizes of flash memory card and each one needs a reader of the right shape before the data can be transferred, there is also a range of readers available (see Figure 12.15). There are also some readers available which accept more than one size of card – these have several slots. Laptops invariably have a memory slot and this will take a Type II memory card.

2.1.2.2 Portable and fixed drives

In the design of early computers, the drives (i.e. the readers) were located within the casing. Hard disks were fixed within the casing but other media formats (such as magnetic tape and floppy disks) provided portable ways of storing data. More recently, external hard drives have been developed and this has brought with it the option to move a hard drive (and the hard disk within it) from one computer to another. Similarly, pen drives and card readers, both of which plug into the USB port, provide a portable solution to data storage – with the increased capacity and compact format of these devices, it is now possible to enjoy portability for large amounts of data.

2.1.2.3 Performance factors

When deciding what storage device to use, a number of factors need to be taken into account.

- How much data will the device hold? What is its maximum capacity?
- How fast can the data be stored on (written to) the device?
- How fast can the data be retrieved (read) from the device?

Case study

Pen drive

One manufacturer of pen drives offers a product called PenDrive USB 2.0. It is available with capacities from 64 MB up to 8 GB and claims to have the fastest ever read/write speeds from a USB 2.0 memory stick: 20 MBps. They also offer a Bluetooth version with a range of up to 300 m. It requires no external power and is shock resistant up to 1000 G.

1 Investigate the market for pen drive products. Produce a table to show their promised performance factors and include costings. Compare your findings with others in your group.

2 Research the Internet for data on flash memory cards. Find out which reader(s) is/are compatible with the cards, and compare their performance factors, e.g. transmission speeds.

2.1.3 Data transmission

Data transmission (serial or parallel) is the movement of bits of information from one place to another. A stream of bits or bytes is transferred from one location to another using one of a number of technologies: copper wire, optical fibre, laser, radio or infrared light.

- With **serial transmission**, bits are sent over a single wire individually, one bit at a time. High-speed transfer rates are possible and it can be done with accuracy over long distances, providing a security system such as a check digit or parity bit is sent with it.
- With **parallel transmission**, more than one wire is used and the bits are transmitted simultaneously. This is much faster than serial transmission because more bits travel at the same time. However, interference between the wires means errors can happen and security checks need to be done to ensure the integrity of data.

Parallel transmission is used within the computer, for example, the internal buses, and sometimes also externally, e.g. for printers.

When sending a message, the transmission can be asynchronous or synchronous.

- With **asynchronous transmission**, start and stop bits signify the beginning and end of a transmission. This incurs an overhead of bits (that is, additional bits to those needed for the actual data) but is acceptable when data is to be sent intermittently as opposed to a solid stream.
- With **synchronous transmission**, there are no start or stop bits. The transmission is synchronised by both receiving and sending ends using **clock signals** built into each component. Data is sent, very quickly, in a continual stream between the two nodes. If the clock signals become out of sync, some bits could be 'lost' and the data corrupted. However, using check digits

(which incurs an overhead) to spot this problem and re-synchronising the clocks ensures that the data is correctly interpreted and received.

2.1.3.1 Communication paths

Data travels along communication paths. Outside of a computer, these are the serial cables or parallel ribbons that connect peripherals to the processor. Inside the computer, the communication paths are called **buses**.

Some buses carry data, while others carry control signals or clock signals and some carry a combination of the two.

What does it mean?

Clock signals are controls signals generated by the processor, like someone tapping in time with music. The devices then work to the same timeframe.

A **data bus** connects different parts of a circuit and comprises a group of parallel wires, each one carrying a different logic signal.

Case study

SPI

The **SPI (serial port interface)** is a four-wire serial synchronous interface for communication between chips. The SPI protocol is hierarchical, so one chip on the bus acts as the 'master' and governs the clock and transmission schedule. The other three wires on the SPI are the MOSI (master output slave input), MISO (master input slave output) and CS or STE (chip select). Data from the master to the slave travels on the MOSI line. Data from the slave to the master travels on the MISO line. The STE line is only enabled during communication and is used to wake the slave device.

1   Locate the databuses inside a computer. Map where they travel to and from. Compare them with the diagram given in Figure 2.1 (page 42).

2   Another example of a data bus is the I2C (inter-integrated circuit control). Research the Internet to find out how many wires this uses. Write brief notes on this.

2.1.3.2 Modems

A modem, which can be internal or external, links the PC to other computers via a communications link, e.g. a telephone line (see Unit 8 for other communication links and how modems are used with them):

- an **external modem** has its own box with a power cord and is connected to the PC via a COM port (the serial port or the USB port)
- an **internal modem** is an expansion board fitted into a slot on the motherboard. It may have its own speaker so that you can hear when it is dialling up.

What does it mean?

A **modem** (from **mod**ulator-**dem**odulator) converts digital signals generated by the PC into an analogue signal which can be sent along an analogue telephone line. In addition, a modem converts analogue telephone signals received into digital data that can be processed by the PC.

Figure 2.16(a) shows the connections needed to position a modem between the PC and the telephone line – the RJ-11 connector (see Figure 2.8 on page 51) is used to link the phone line to the modem and then, for an external modem, the modem to the PC. Figure 2.16(b) shows how this is achieved more simply using an internal modem.

A modem needs to both send and receive data, preferably at the same time. Communication that can be done in both directions, but not at the same time, is called **half-duplex** transmission. If communications can be sent and received simultaneously, this is called **full duplex** transmission.

When the modem first dials up, the sounds you can hear indicate that 'handshaking' is taking place.

- When a modem answers an incoming call, it sends a **guard tone** to indicate to the caller that connection has been made with a modem and not with a human.
- If the caller is another modem, it responds by sending a **carrier signal**.
- Having agreed that both ends of the line are modems, the next stage involves much buzzing to establish the quality of the line and an attempt to compensate for any noise.
- Then the speed at which transfer will happen is agreed between the two modems.

So, during the initial handshaking stage, the two computers exchange 'rules' or 'protocols' that determine how they communicate: at what speed the transfer of data will take place, how data might be compressed and what error checks might be incorporated.

The speed at which the communication happens depends on the speed of the modem (in bits per second), on the amount of noise on the line and what route the data is to take. If the route includes a slower patch, then the best speed will be the speed across that slower link.

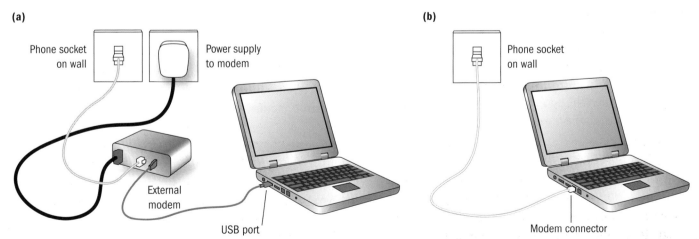

(a)

Phone socket on wall

Power supply to modem

External modem

USB port

(b)

Phone socket on wall

Modem connector

▲ **Figure 2.16 How to connect link line and phone jacks: (a) for an external modem, (b) for an internal modem**

2.1.3.3 Processor speed

The faster the processor speed, the more instructions can be completed within a given time and the more powerful the computer appears to the user. The speed of the CPU is sometimes called the **clock rate**. In cycles per second, measured in hertz, this measures how quickly a computer can perform the simplest of operations such as adding two numbers together or storing the result in a data store. Although different chips on the motherboard may have different clock rates, the term 'clock rate' is reserved for the speed of the CPU.

Clock rates are only useful as a measure when comparing computers using the same processor family. For computers with different processors, some other software benchmark is needed. Clock rates can be very misleading because the amount of work computer chips can do in one cycle varies between makes of computer. For example, a CPU that supports only simple instructions will need to perform more instructions to achieve the same end result, whereas a more sophisticated CPU may have higher clock rates but achieves more in a shorter time overall.

When trying to increase the performance of a computer, some users practise **overclocking**. This forces a component to run at a higher clock rate than it was designed for. However, applying a higher voltage to make the component work faster risks blowing the component. Running at a higher speed can also result in overheating, so additional cooling may be needed.

2.1.3.4 RAM speed

The length of time that RAM takes to write data (or to read it) once the request has been received from the processor is called the **access time**. This is measured in nanoseconds (ns): the fewer ns, the faster the RAM.

2.1.3.5 Impact of transmission media

There are different types of transmission media: twisted pair wire (normal electrical wire), coaxial cable (the type of cable used for cable television) and fibre optic cable (cable made out of glass). There are then options to transmit data by broadcasting through the air: using infrared or microwave signals, for example.

Each transmission medium has its pros and cons, related to speed of data transfer and likelihood of corruption of the data while travelling along the cable. For example, what length of cabling works without data being lost or corrupted by noise and is there a need for line of sight (the transmitter and receiver being in sight of each other)? With reference to security aspects, it is also important to consider how easy it is to overhear the signal. See *Unit 8: Communication Technologies* (page 133) for more information on transmission media.

Activity 2.11

Data transmission

1 Identify the modem(s) on your own computer. Note the settings for speed.

2 Research the Internet for details of internal and external modems. Find out about different modem standards and how these apply to data compression and error correction.

3 Research the Internet to find out more about the practice of overclocking. Prepare a presentation explaining how it is done and what risks it involves.

2.1.4 Considerations for selection

When deciding what computer to purchase (which make and model) and the configuration to construct (how much memory, which peripherals), you need to consider various factors.

2.1.4.1 Cost

Cost is usually a deciding factor in any purchase, not just computers: you need to buy the best specification within your budget. Computers are constantly being developed (faster memories, larger capacity, new and exciting

Test your knowledge

1 Explain these terms: serial transmission, parallel transmission, synchronous transmission, asynchronous transmission.

2 What is a databus? What signals does it carry?

3 What does modem stand for?

4 What is an RJ-11 connector used for?

5 Explain the difference between half-duplex and full duplex transmission.

6 Explain the purpose of handshaking, the guard tone and the carrier signal.

7 Explain these terms: processor speed, clock rate, access time.

8 Give three examples of transmission media that involve cabling, and two examples that do not involve cabling.

peripherals), so to buy something that ignores the latest technologies will mean that your system is out of date as soon as you have bought it.

Savings can be made by buying from a company that offers lower prices, but these have to be judged against intangible considerations, such as whether the kit is going to prove reliable and whether there will be any backup support after you have completed the sale.

2.1.4.2 User requirements

The primary consideration is fitness for purpose. The computer system must meet the needs of the user: the right mix of software, adequate support for the user (more so for a new user), the necessary hardware to integrate with other systems (e.g. home entertainment) and enough processing power and storage to create a usable, fast-moving system.

2.1.4.3 Accessibility for disabled users

Some users have special needs.

• Visually impaired people may need to rely on their sense of hearing and the computer system will need to be set up to produce voice output as appropriate.

• Users with some physical disability may need special peripherals to replace the conventional mouse and/or keyboard.

Activity 2.12

Selection considerations

1 Think of a particular user who needs a new computer system. Identify what they need and write a list of requirements.

2 Use the Internet to research possible configurations that might meet your user's needs and put forward three possible solutions, each within a broad cost bracket.

3 Evaluate your three solutions and write a recommendation for one of your three chosen configurations, explaining why you think it suits your user's needs best. **d**

Having considered a possible hardware configuration to meet the needs of a user, before you place an order the second stage is to decide on the software components.

Applications software is installed so that the user can perform the tasks that he or she wants to do on the computer: e.g. writing letters or reports using word processing, doing design work using painting and drawing packages, processing financial data using spreadsheets or maintaining records using a database.

Often a computer vendor 'bundles' application software with the hardware, trying to make the complete system attractive to a wider market of potential purchasers. These packaged systems may be targeted towards business users, while others might be described as home entertainment systems. Within the bundle, there will be essential software, but also possibly some software for which the user has no need.

You will need to ascertain exactly what is on offer, whether it will meet the user's needs and what extra software might need to be purchased (incurring additional cost).

2.2.1 Operating system software

At the very heart of any computer system is the operating system software. There are three main operating systems on offer:

- Windows: developed by Microsoft and sold under licence; used on IBM-compatible PCs
- Apple MAC OS: a parallel system of software for those users who choose not to follow the IBM-PC hardware route
- LINUX: a Unix-type operating system originally created by Linus Torvalds with the assistance of developers around the world; the source code for Linux is freely available to anyone with Internet access.

2.2.1.2 Command line and GUI operating systems

Prior to the introduction of the **WIMP** environment, early computers relied on command line interpreters.

What does it mean?

WIMP stands for **windows**, **icons**, **menu**, **pointer**.

The operating system (e.g. DOS, which stands for disk operating system) responded to individual commands keyed in by the user. When it had finished doing whatever was asked of it, the user was presented with the command line prompt (usually including a > symbol) and the computer then waited for the next instruction. The user needed to have a high level of knowledge, particularly in how to give the commands in the DOS language.

When windows-based operating systems were introduced, instead of entering a command, the user now indicated their selection or decision by clicking on an option in a menu, pressing a button or completing boxes on a form. The interface became far more user-friendly and it opened up the use of computers to people who had not learnt how to program a computer.

2.2.1.3 Operating system functions and services

The operating system includes a number of accessory programs which offer machine and peripheral management, security and file management. For example, Disk Cleanup and Disk Defragmenter both provide ways of tidying up your disk space (see page 71).

2.2.1.4 Device drivers

For each peripheral device, a device driver is needed to interface between the processor and the peripheral. The driver acts as a decoder, so the data is interpreted correctly. Installing device drivers is necessary when new hardware is installed (see page 75).

Activity 2.13

Software components

1 Research the Internet to discover more about the Linux operating system. Prepare a short presentation to describe its purpose, the main features and its functions.

2 Repeat Question 1 for one other operating system.

3 Write a brief report comparing the purpose, features and functions of two different operating systems.

2.2.2 Software utilities

This section focuses on a limited range of software utilities: virus protection, firewalls, cleanup tools and drive formatting.

2.2.2.1 Virus protection

PCs can be attacked by **viruses**, **worms** and **trojans** arriving with emails or during access to the Internet.

Almost as soon as virus writers invent new viruses, so do anti-virus software vendors produce updated versions of their software. There is a variety of products available.

- The most common form is **virus scanner software** – when using this, the scan is initiated by the user.
- **Start-up virus scanner software** runs each time the PC is booted up – it checks only for boot sector viruses.
- **Memory-resident virus scanner software** checks incoming emails and browser documents and so automatically checks the operating environment of your PC.
- **A behaviour-based detector** is a form of memory-resident virus scanner software that watches for behaviour that would indicate the presence of a virus.

Anti-virus software checks for intruders. It attempts to trace viruses by spotting the **virus signature**. Meanwhile, virus writers adopt cloaking techniques such as **polymorphing**.

The anti-virus software vendors maintain a database of information about viruses: a DAT file of their profiles and signatures. Users who subscribe to an online anti-virus protection service may have this database downloaded to their PC automatically each time an update is released. Other users may receive an email telling them that an update is available.

Having the most up-to-date DAT file, scanning regularly and avoiding opening emails that may contain viruses is the best advice. The main defence against viruses is to subscribe to a reliable software vendor's virus protection service. If the software detects a virus, a pop-up screen may offer options: to quarantine the file (i.e. move it so it can do no harm), to repair the file (i.e. delete the virus but retain the file) or to delete the file.

Anti-virus software vendors may offer to create a **rescue disk** – a bootable disk that also contains anti-virus software. If a virus-infected system won't boot, a rescue disk may solve the problem. Write-protecting the disk may prevent it from becoming infected with a virus.

What does it mean?

Viruses (so-called because they spread by replicating themselves) can erase data and corrupt files.

Worms can forward emails (and the worm) to all your contacts using data from your address book.

Trojans are programs that hide by pretending to be a file or program which is usually present (and harmless) on your PC.

The **virus signature** is a sequence of characters which the anti-virus software gleans by analysing the virus code.

Polymorphing: just as cells in a diseased human mutate, a virus can be designed to change its appearance, size and signature each time it infects another PC, thus making it harder for anti-virus software to recognise it.

2.2.2.2 Firewalls

Firewalls build a protective barrier around computers that are connected to a network, so that only authorised programs can access data on a particular workstation.

The user can control exactly which software is allowed to pass data in and out of the system (see Figure 2.17). For example, automatic updates might be allowed for some installed software.

▼ Figure 2.17 McAfee's PersonalFirewallPlus service

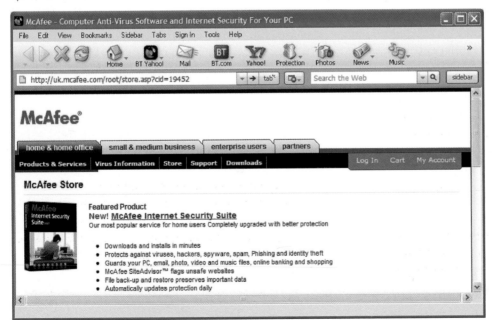

Various vendors vie for the market and may offer other services, such as virus protection, as part of the package.

2.2.2.3 Cleanup tools

Over a period of time, a PC becomes cluttered with data that you do not need.

- Each time you visit a new website and register so that you can receive newsletter updates or make a purchase, a cookie may be left on your PC. This lets the site recognise you the next time you visit. These cookies can be useful as they save you entering your details again. However, you may have cookies for websites that you never intend to visit again, so you might decide you would prefer to remove them from your system.
- Each time you request a page on the Internet, a copy of that page is retained in the Temporary Internet Files folder. This is useful because when you use the Back and Forward buttons, the web page does not need to be downloaded afresh. However, the space taken up by these pages can quickly accumulate.
- Each time you save a file, the space on your hard disk begins to fill. When files are deleted, some space becomes available, which appears as 'gaps' on the map of the disk. There may come a time when a file you want to save will not fit into an available gap. The system copes with this by fragmenting the file and storing the fragments wherever it can and additional space is taken up noting the whereabouts of the fragments. Before long, the organisation of files on the disk is a mess!

Cleanup tools can be used to solve this problem: Disk Cleanup scans a drive and presents a list of files you might like to delete (see Figure 2.18), while Disk Defragmenter (see page 71) rearranges files so that the gaps are used up systematically, leaving available space in contiguous (i.e. connecting) strings.

2.2.2.4 Drive formatting

Before a disk can be used to store data files, it has to be formatted. There are two levels of formatting.

- **Physical (low-level) formatting** creates the cylinders, tracks and sectors on a hard disk. (For floppy disks, there were only tracks and sectors to create.) This involves scanning the surface for imperfections and setting aside those sectors that cannot be used.
- **Logical (high-level) formatting** prepares the disk for files by creating the operating system's file system and management tables and files.

Formatting procedures for the PC user depend on the type of disk.

- There were two levels of formatting needed for a floppy disk, and this was done using a single FORMAT command available with the PC's operating system. If you needed to reformat a floppy disk, you could opt for a quick format which simply redid the high-level formatting.
- Low-level formatting of a hard disk is done at the factory, so only the logical formatting is done using a utility on your PC. However, the hard disk has to be partitioned (if at all) prior to high-level formatting.
- With a CD-R disk, the formatting is done automatically when you write to the disk, so you don't have to worry about it beforehand.

MS-DOS and Windows operating systems format disks to have 512 data bytes per sector. Each sector also has some header information to identify it and trailer information which shows the operating system where the data for that sector ends. The raw capacity of a disk is therefore reduced during formatting due to this overhead of data in each sector.

The high-level formatting process writes material to allow the operating system to interact with the disk: the boot sector, the **root directory** table and the **FAT** table.

The boot sector, near the centre of the disk, is set aside to hold data about how data is organised on the disk, such

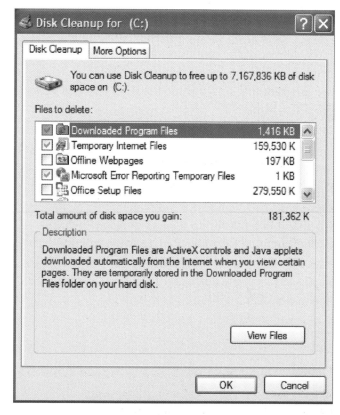

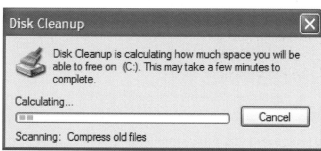

▲ Figure 2.18 Disk Cleanup

What does it mean?

The **root directory** table has an entry for each file on the disk: the name of the file and the file extension, the file attribute, the date and time that the file was created or last updated, the position where the start of this file is to be found on the disk (cluster number) and the length of the file.

FAT stands for file allocation table.

as the number of sectors, the number of sectors per track, the number of bytes per sector, the number of FATs, the size of the root directory and the program needed to load the operating system. (This last item is the program that searches and loads files needed to boot the disk – if these files are missing, the disk is unbootable.)

Since the clusters are too short to store whole files of data, a file will be stored in a number of clusters and these need not be consecutive on the disk. The file is then called fragmented. Keeping track of the many fragments of a file falls to the FAT. It records which clusters are used for which files. Defragmentation (see page 71) is a process which tidies up the disk, reusing the disk space more efficiently after some files have been deleted.

Activity 2.14

Software utilities

1 Identify two different providers of anti-virus software. Do they also provide firewall protection?

2 For one provider of firewall protection, find out what is available for the user. Make notes.

3 Use the Disk Cleanup tool to rid your PC of unwanted files.

4 Find out how to format disks on your PC. Make notes.

Test your knowledge

1 Explain the difference between low-level formatting and high-level formatting.

2 What is a quick format?

3 Distinguish between the purposes of the root directory table and the FAT.

Case study

Nina (2)

Nina now wants to understand a bit about the utilities on her computer. Remember that she is only nine years old.

1 Identify the range of software utilities available on your computer and describe this in terms that will be understandable for Nina. **P₄**

2 Select two different software utilities and prepare a demonstration of their use. Prepare brief notes to explain to Nina how to make the best use of these two utilities. **P₃**

Maintenance is an essential part of running a computer system. Its aim is to prevent problems arising and to save time when diagnosing and fixing faults. It can also extend the life of your PC. This section considers the maintenance of software and hardware, as well as managing files.

Just how regularly the maintenance tasks are performed depends on the task – maintenance could be daily, weekly, monthly or annually, or whenever necessary, as suggested in Table 2.3. If the air in which the PC operates is dusty or smoky, even more frequent cleaning will be necessary.

For some routine maintenance tasks, the computer *can* remain powered up (e.g. cleaning the mouse) or *must* be powered up (e.g. to do a virus check). For others, it is necessary to power down, i.e. switch off the computer (e.g. when cleaning the monitor). As soon as you have completed the maintenance task, make sure that the PC still works!

Remember!

Keep a record of the maintenance you have done, any faults found and what you have done to fix these faults.

▼ **Figure 2.19 Defragmentation is best carried out after a disk cleanup**

Frequency	Maintenance task
Daily	Virus scan of memory and your hard disk Take backup of changed data files
Weekly	Clean mouse (ball and rollers) and check for wear Clean keyboard, checking for stuck keys Clean monitor screen Clean printer Delete temporary files (Disk Cleanup) Defragment hard disk and recover lost clusters
Monthly	Clean outside of case Take complete backup of data files
Annually	Check motherboard: reseat chips if necessary Clean adapter card contacts with contact cleaner and reseat
As required	Record and back up CMOS setup configuration Keep written record of hardware and software configuration

Table 2.3 Preventive maintenance schedule

Some hardware can – and needs to be – cleaned (casings, mouse rollers, etc.) but some hardware is sealed so your maintenance is restricted to 'cleaning' using software (e.g. deleting temporary files off the hard disk).

2.3.1 Software maintenance

Some maintenance of hardware is done using software (such as Disk Cleanup, see page 66), but maintenance also includes looking after the software as well as the hardware.

2.3.1.1 Upgrade software

Software is only as up to date as it was on the day you installed it. Software, such as virus protection, relies on up-to-date data and so you should update this type of software regularly. Anti-virus software vendors tend to offer an automatic update option, so you are never caught unawares.

Vendors of other software may also offer upgrades as the software is further enhanced. These may be free of charge, especially if they relate to the operating system that you have installed on your PC. Some are presented as new 'improved' releases of the software, and you are expected to pay a sum for the privilege of downloading them. Most software vendors offer a licence purchase price for new purchasers and a reduced rate for those who are upgrading.

2.3.1.2 Installation of patches

Software is often released for sale under licence before it has been tested enough to find all the bugs that are caused by logical errors made by the programmers. Once these bugs are found, and the fault found, a **patch** is one immediate solution that can be provided to users as a download from the software manufacturer's website.

The vendor may also identify shortcomings in the design of the software – defects that only emerge through use, perhaps because the design did not (and probably could not) anticipate all the expectations of users or all the silly things a user might try to do.

Some patches become necessary in response to new functionality in the operating system or utilities. For example, downloading Internet Explorer 7 resulted in 'clashes' with software already installed and the software vendors then needed to work out how to solve these problems for their existing users.

See *Unit 28: IT Technical Support* (page 296) for more information on patches.

What does it mean?

A **patch** (or **fix**) is a quick repair job for a piece of code which is found to be faulty after its release to the market. It is usually made available as a replacement for, or an insertion in, compiled code (that is, in a binary file or object module).

2.3.1.3 Scheduling of maintenance tasks

It is possible to use software to remind you when to carry out essential maintenance tasks. Software such as Microsoft Outlook offers a feature where you can set up a task and reminders at times to suit you (see Figure 2.20).

If you prefer, you can schedule the task to happen automatically. This is advisable for essential tasks such as making backups (see Figure 2.21).

The details of the task (what has to be backed up) can be set once, rather than every time you decide to do a backup.

▼ Figure 2.20 Using Outlook – reminders for maintenance tasks

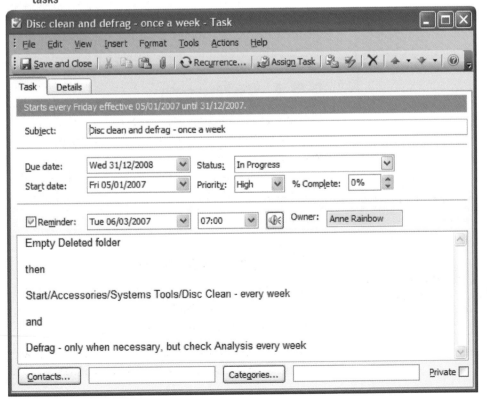

Figure 2.21 A scheduled backup

■ HOW TO DEFRAGMENT A DISK

1 Select Start/All Programs/Accessories/System Tools/ Disk Defragmenter. Alternatively, access this utility through the Control Panel, within the Computer Management folder (see Figure 2.22).
2 Click on the Analyze button. The utility will then estimate the disk usage after defragmentation and make a recommendation: either to defragment your disk or not to, at this time.
3 If you are recommended to defragment your disk, click on the Defragment button. Defragmentation will take several minutes, so you are advised to leave the PC and spend the time doing something useful!

Another utility that you might use for software maintenance is a system **profiler**. The profiler generates a **trace** or a statistical summary of the events that have been observed (hence the term 'profile'). Data is collected through, for example, performance counters.

Microsoft offer a performance monitor (see Figure 2.22) within the Computer Management utility.

2.3.1.4 Utility software aimed at users

Some maintenance, such as disk cleaning and defragmentation, ought to be done by the user, rather than relying on technical support.

Remember!

The defragmentation process tidies up the disk, reusing the space more efficiently after files have been deleted.

Defragmentation is best carried out after a disk cleanup, so that all the unneeded files have been deleted before the tidying up process is done.

2.3.1.5 Other third party utility software

There are many other utilities. This section looks at just two: compression utilities and spyware removal.

When data is transmitted, the volume of data and the speed at which it can be transmitted affect the time it takes for the transfer to be completed. Very large files can take a long time to upload or download. To reduce this time, it makes sense to try to make the files smaller, especially if the link is particularly slow. Various **compression** techniques have been developed for different applications according to the general types of data that are to be transferred.

What does it mean?

A **profiler** is a performance analysis tool that measures the behaviour of a program while it is running.

A **trace** is a stream of recorded events.

Compression involves reducing the size of the file by coding it more efficiently into fewer bits of data.

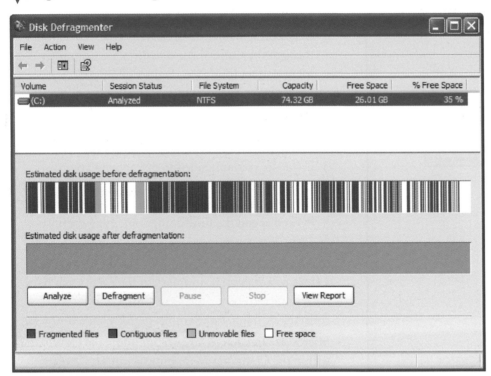

▼ Figure 2.22 Disk Defragmenter

Compression utilities, such as WinZip, can be used to reduce the size of files and to package them together with a utility which allows the receiver to unzip the files.

Spyware software collects personal information about you without you having given your consent.

What does it mean?

Spyware is software that spies on your online activities.

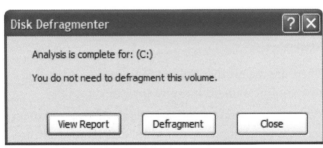

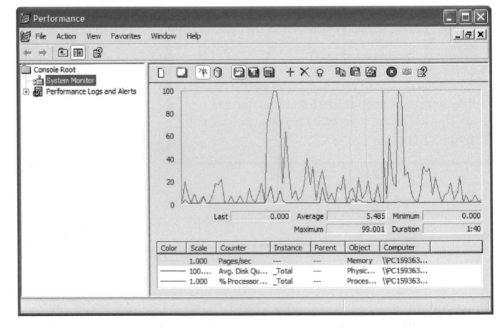

▼ Figure 2.23 Performance profile

BTEC National | Information Technology Practitioners

Spyware uses techniques such as logging keystrokes and scanning documents on your hard disk with the intention of stealing your passwords and financial details. It may also involve recording the URLs of your Internet browsing history so that you might become the target of advertising. Anti-spyware software offers to check your computer to see if spyware software has infiltrated your system and to remove it for you.

Activity 2.15

Software maintenance

1 Establish a routine of software maintenance for your own PC. Utilise software such as Outlook to set up reminders for yourself. **p**₅

2 Set up a scheduled task for some aspect of your software maintenance, e.g. a daily backup.

3 For one item of software, check the Internet for the availability of an upgrade. How much will it cost? And what will the download involve you doing?

4 With the permission of the owner of your PC, install one item of free software. Document the installation.

5 Check whether a hard disk requires defragmentation and, if it does, choose the option to complete the defragmentation. Take screenshots of the disk usage before and after defragmentation to show the effect.

6 Research the Internet for compression software. Identify one such utility and experiment with compressing files. Which files are reduced in size the most?

7 Research the Internet for anti-spyware software. Make notes on what it offers.

Case study

Nina (3)

Nina now has lots more applications on her computer and complains that it is running too slowly for her liking.

1 Show Nina how to use a profiler. Show her how it changes when you perform certain events. Explain the effect of the software maintenance activities carried out on the performance of a computer system. **m**₃

2 Nina wants you to help her to persuade her parents to upgrade her computer for a more powerful one. Write an email to Nina, explaining to her under what circumstances she could justify the upgrade of her existing computer system. Write a report which expands on your explanation to include other types of users and other scenarios, and attach this report to the email. **d**₂

2.3.2 Hardware maintenance

Like any machine, a PC needs some attention on a regular basis, if only to keep it clean. Computers attract a lot of dust: if dust settles on the outside, it soon forms a grimy layer of dirt which is unsightly; if it settles on the inside, it can block airways, preventing the cooling mechanism from working properly. Overheated components may then fail.

2.3.2.1 Cleaning equipment

When choosing cleaning equipment, you should be wary of potential health risks to you in using these products, as well as selecting the right type of product for the task in hand. For example, many of the chemical solvents are poisonous and may need special handling.

With any chemical product that you buy, you should be given a material safety data sheet (MSDS) – or something similar, e.g. as part of the label. This lists important advice to help you to handle and use the product correctly and safely: its toxicity, any health effects, first aid measures (e.g. if you were to ingest some accidentally), how to store the product, how to dispose of it and what to do if the chemical is spilt. Information about the hazards of chemical cleaners is also available on the Internet.

The cheapest liquid cleaning compound is water. Used carefully, it can be used to clean cases, but you must be sure not to wet the electronic parts of the PC.

WATCH OUT!

Water conducts electricity so water on a circuit board can cause a short circuit.

Water can be mixed with a general purpose cleaner, and this may be necessary if the casing has not been cleaned for some time and dirt has built up.

The most expensive option, but the safest for your PC, is isopropyl alcohol. This chemical can be used to clean the PC case, the keyboard case and keys and any other similar casing on your PC. It removes dirt and then evaporates so the equipment does not become wet. It can harm you, though, so be sure to read the instructions carefully – and follow them!

A variety of cleaning equipment is needed.

- A **soft lint-free cloth** can be used for cleaning glass and plastic surfaces of components.
- **Paper towels** may also be useful, especially to mop up any spillages.
- **Cotton buds** or swabs might be useful, e.g. for cleaning the contact points inside a mouse, but take care they do not leave deposits.
- A **non-static brush** or probe and/or a small flat-bladed screwdriver can be used to dislodge stubborn bits of dirt, e.g. on the mouse rollers.
- **Compressed air** comes in an aerosol can and may be used to clean fans and grills or keyboards. To direct the air more precisely, use the long thin plastic tube, taking care to blow the air in a direction that will take the dust away from the PC.

WATCH OUT!

Compressed air is very, very cold, so do not direct it on to your skin.

Vacuuming the inside of a PC can remove a lot of the dust that collects. Some small cleaners include brush heads ideal for the purpose. However, it is important to use non-static vacuum cleaners.

WATCH OUT!

Do not use a vacuum cleaner to try to clean a laser printer. The toner would clog the vacuum, unless it has been specifically designed to handle toner.

Activity 2.16

Hardware maintenance – cleaning

1 Research the Internet to discover what dangers are involved in using **isopropyl alcohol**.

2 In this task, you will give a PC a spring clean and time how long it takes you to do this.

   a) First, examine the PC to see what you think needs cleaning. Make a list of the tasks you intend to do and obtain approval from your teacher before starting.

   b) Assemble the cleaning materials that you plan to use. Also check these with your teacher.

   c) Clean each component separately and then check that the PC still works before moving on to clean the next component.

   d) Tick each item on your task list, noting how long it took you to do.

   e) When you have finished, draw up a maintenance list for future cleaning of this PC. Estimate how much time per week will be needed.

2.3.2.2 Install and configure new peripherals

Nowadays, the installation of new peripherals is relatively straightforward. The vendors supply all the items that you need: the device, any connectors, a CD with the setup software and any drivers that you might need. They normally also provide step-by-step instructions that you should follow carefully.

The usual method is to install relevant software first and then to attach the hardware, which will then be recognised. However, modern operating systems are sophisticated enough to spot when you have attached a new device. You may be led through a series of dialogue boxes which ask questions such as 'Were you supplied with a disk?' and then guide you to install relevant drivers; a search for appropriate drivers on the Internet may even be carried out for you.

Having installed the device, you may need to do some customisation to make it suit the user. For example:

- for a printer, you might want to make it the default printer (see Figure 2.24)
- for a mouse, you might want to set the speed of response or perhaps make it usable for a left-handed operator.

Figure 2.24 Ways of making a printer the default printer

Case study

Nina (4)

Nina has been given some new peripherals and needs help installing and customising them.

1 For one new peripheral, such as a printer or a wireless mouse, study the instructions that are supplied with the product. Explain the instructions to Nina and check that she fully understands the procedure and that she has everything to hand. Demonstrate to Nina the completion of the installation and then test that the new device works. **m**

2 Nina is left-handed. Show her how to customise a mouse so that it works for her. **m**

3 For another device, such as a webcam, show Nina how to research the Internet for help in installing the device. Write brief notes on how you would explain to her how to install and configure it. **m**

The installation of internal components requires a little more expertise than is needed to install a peripheral. You also need to take more care, as accessing the inside of a processor box carries a risk, both to you and to the computer.

Some devices, such as the hard drive, have to be connected to the motherboard and PSU using cabling – this makes installation similar to an external peripheral, the only difference being that they are housed within the box.

Other devices, such as the cards available for graphics and networking, have to be fitted into the appropriate slot. Figure 2.3 on page 45 shows the range of slots available for use.

The Control Panel includes an option to Add Hardware (see Figure 2.25). This software will then guide you through the process of configuration.

■ HOW TO INSTALL A HARD DRIVE

1 Set the jumpers.

WATCH OUT!

If installing a second drive, check the settings for the first drive. Do they need to change from 'single' to 'master'?

2 Put the drive into the bay. You may need to screw the drive into place, or there may be mounting rails that fasten to the side of the drive so that you can click the drive into place.

3 Connect the drive to the motherboard using the ribbon cable.

   a) You need to select the correct cable: 40-wire or 80-wire, depending on the specification of the hard drive. They are the same width and both fit into the same connector!

   b) The cable has two ends: one for the motherboard and one for the drive. There is also a connector midway which you might need to use for another device. However, if you are installing a second IDE device and the second IDE connector is available on the motherboard, use that – you may achieve better performance if the two devices are not sharing a cable.

   c) The end that is furthest from the midway connection belongs in the motherboard.

   d) Be sure to orient the cable correctly: the red stripe along the edge of the cable indicates wire 1, and this needs to match pin 1 on the connector. The connector may have a '1' or a small triangle to show which end is pin 1.

WATCH OUT!

Be careful to connect the correct end of the cable to the motherboard and to connect it the right way round.

4 Connect the drive to the PSU. This is more straightforward! Select a free connector from the PSU and plug it into the drive. The orientation should not be a problem: the connector is rounded on the top edge so it will only fit one way.

Your BIOS should automatically update itself when you next switch on the PC. However, you may decide to partition the hard disk, in which case you will need to format it.

 Figure 2.25 The Add Hardware Wizard

■ HOW TO ADD/REMOVE A VIDEO CARD

1 Check that you know which slot you are going to use, and that you have the correct board for your PC.
2 Be careful to handle the card by its non-connecting edges. Otherwise, you may leave traces of grease and/or dirt from your fingers.
3 Gently place the video card into the slot and press it into place.
4 To remove a card, release the locking mechanism and then slide the card gently out of its slot.

STOP Test your knowledge

1 List five tasks that might be included in a maintenance schedule.

2 What is a software patch?

3 What is the purpose of the defragmentation utility?

4 Explain these terms: profiler, trace, compression, spyware.

5 What do the letters MSDS stand for? What information does an MSDS provide?

6 Under what circumstances should you use water while cleaning your computer?

7 Explain these terms: ionise, default.

Activity 2.17

Installing and configuring additional devices

1 Install an internal device such as a hard drive. Write notes to explain what you did.

2 Install at least one card, such as a graphics card, a sound card or a network interface card.

WATCH OUT!

ESD is a hazard when working on the innards of a PC, so wear an ESD wrist strap. See page 329 of *Unit 29: IT Systems Troubleshooting and Repair*.

2.3.3 File management

This section looks at strategies that can help a user to maintain control over the data stored on a computer.

2.3.3.1 Create folders

Maintaining the hardware and software so that you have a fully functioning computer system is essential, but your file management is also important in order to be able to find your documents.

Microsoft offers some standard folders to encourage users to be systematic when saving files. For example, the My Pictures folder is for your images and photos. Within the My Pictures folder, you would be advised to set up additional folders, perhaps according to the subject of the photos or the date on which they were taken. Otherwise, you will soon find you cannot track down a particular shot without trawling through every photo you have ever taken.

You could put all your documents in the My Documents folder. If you save more than 40 files in any one place, there will be too many to view in one dialogue box, so to select a file you will have to scroll up and down to find it. For this reason, it makes more sense to create folders within the My Documents folder. No two users will have the same arrangement, but you should use logic when organising your folder structure: a logic that makes sense to you.

Many people use their computers partly for work and partly for pleasure. If a computer is used for work purposes, a sensible way of organising files could be to have one folder per client. If there are many clients, it might help to group the clients in some way and to create folders within folders. In this way, a hierarchy of folders can be built up and you can browse through the hierarchy to locate the client and then the particular file that you want to work on.

2.3.3.2 Backup procedures

Having worked on documents and filed them in appropriate folders, if disaster were to hit your system – a power surge which blows components, a house fire or a flood – how would you pick up from where you left off? You should have a system of backing up important documents and data, so that you can recover from such a disaster.

Some operating systems incorporate a backup utility; others are available from third party suppliers.

The scheduling of backups needs to match the relative importance of the data being backed up. If something rarely changes, it only needs to be backed up infrequently; but if something changes by the minute, it probably needs backing up daily or even more frequently.

Backups are considered in other units: see page 93 in *Unit 3: Information Systems*; page 179 in *Unit 15: Organisational Systems Security*; page 348 in *Unit 29: IT Systems Troubleshooting and Repair*; and in Book 2 *Unit 22: Network Management*.

2.3.3.3 Housekeeping

There is a limit to how much you can store on one computer. You could resort to storing data on external drives, but you should ask yourself questions such as: 'Do I really need an electronic copy of a letter I wrote to a client eight years ago?'

Old data could be archived for a period, just in case it is needed at a later date, but eventually some files should be deleted.

When files are first deleted, they go to the Recycle Bin – they are not actually deleted from your computer. It is only when the Recycle Bin is emptied that the space they take up is freed for other files.

Remember!

Emptying the Recycle Bin is one of the things offered in a Disk Cleanup (see page 66).

Until the Recycle Bin is emptied, you have the option to retrieve the file, so you can change your mind!

Activity 2.18

File management

1 Review the structure of folders on your computer. Does it make sense to you? Is it easy for you to find documents?

2 Review the ages of files stored on your computer. Should you delete some files to free up space?

Preparation for assessment

The assessment tasks in this unit are based on the following scenario.

Sam knows very little about computers. They were invented after he left school and his work never brought him into contact with these 'new-fangled machines'. Now that he has retired, his children and grandchildren are encouraging him to buy one. Sam is a keen photographer and wants to share his photos with relatives who live all over the world. His daughter tells him that by using email and the Internet it will be possible for Sam to write to family and friends and to send photos too. As a pensioner, he cannot afford to spend much and has set aside £1000 to buy whatever he needs to become a 'silver surfer'.

Task 1 (P1, P2, M2)

(a) During a visit to the local computer store with his daughter and grandson, Sam is confused by all the terminology, such as 'RAM', 'ROM' and other forms of memory. Produce a diagram with clear supporting notes to explain the function of the system unit components and how they communicate.

(b) Sam's daughter recommends that he buys a Microsoft laptop with the latest Vista operating system. Sam's grandson's advice is to get an Apple. Sam has asked you to explain what all this means. Describe the purposes, features and functions of these two different operating systems. Then compare the features and functions of the two operating systems, summarising their respective strengths and weaknesses. Recommend the one that you think would best suit Sam.

Task 2 (P3, P4, D1)

(a) Sam's grandson says Sam needs utility software as well as the 'normal' software such as word processing. Create a table describing at least four subcategories of utility software, and giving at least one example of each. Using your own computer, demonstrate to Sam the operation of two different software utilities, explaining what each one does.

(b) Evaluate at least three specifications for commercially available computer systems and justify the one most suitable for Sam.

Task 3 (P5, M3)

Sam has had his computer now for over a month and is making good progress. He appreciates that he needs to maintain the hardware and software, but does not know where to begin. Explain the effect of the software maintenance activities carried out on the performance of a computer system. Carry out some routine maintenance tasks for Sam and demonstrate how these improve the performance of his system.

Task 4 (M1)

Sam is ready to use his computer to store the photos captured on his digital camera. Explain and implement the installation and configuration of this additional device.

Task 5 (D2)

Sam is really enjoying using his computer and is now thinking about installing advanced graphics software and a better-quality printer to print his photos. He wonders if he needs more memory or any special upgrades. He is willing to spend another £500. Make recommendations to Sam and justify the considerations for selection in the upgrade of an existing computer system.

Information systems

Introduction

Organisations can exploit information to do better at planning, monitoring and controlling their business activity. However, it is easy to drown in a sea of data. People can best understand and use information when it is organised and presented in the ways that are most useful to them. Powerful PCs, servers and networks provide new tools and systems to process information. This improves how people can run their businesses and plan their activities.

Information systems consist of software, hardware and communication networks. They collect, organise and distribute information. Good decision making comes when this information is reliable and is presented usefully. Information systems can also provide a competitive advantage and also promote efficiency.

After completing this unit, you should be able to achieve these outcomes:

- Know the source and characteristics of business information

- Understand how organisations use business information

- Understand the issues and constraints in relation to the use of information in organisations

- Know the features and functions of information systems.

Thinking points

People need to become skilled manipulators and users of information to ensure that organisations become more efficient and succeed in achieving their aims and objectives. To understand how organisations use information, you need to appreciate how businesses operate and the functional areas into which they can be divided. The former requires analytical skills. The latter needs business, organisational and people skills. What trade-offs might be needed here?

This unit explores the formal ways that internal and external information flows can be represented. You must know of the constraints that impact the use of information in organisations. This includes data protection and other legislation. What might organisations do if there were no constraints on use of information? What impact could even stronger constraints have on organisations?

3.1.1 Characteristics

3.1.1.1 Distinction between data and information

Data is what a business or organisation records about its operations as part of its normal activity. For example, a supermarket might record that it sold two 454g tins of its own-brand beans for a price of 37p per tin to a customer at a specific time on a particular date. This raw data is the input to any computer or manual record keeping system for that shop.

Information is what comes out of the computer or manual system to help people to run a business or organisation. In the same supermarket example, useful information from the system might be the total sales in the shop by hour and the daily sales of tinned groceries. A more complex example is the supermarket's stock control system, which might look at the sales of products to decide when more stock should be ordered from the supplier or warehouse.

Figure 3.1 shows another example of how data is used to create information. In a census taken in April 2001, Jane's age was recorded as 17 years. That is **data**. A simple calculation gives the **information** that Jane was born in 1983 or 1984.

Census Data

Census Year	Name	Age
2001	Jane	17

Processing

Census Information

Name	Date of Birth
Jane	1983 or 1984

▲ **Figure 3.1 Diagram showing data in and information out**

3.1.1.2 Types of information

Two main types of data are considered here: **qualitative** data and **quantitative** data.

What does it mean?

Qualitative data is personal and subjective.

Quantitative data is factual data obtained through well-defined processes. It gives unbiased facts about a subject.

Case study

Fast food customer satisfaction survey

Diana works for a company that runs customer satisfaction surveys for a fast food chain. She visits their stores and carries out surveys with customers. She records their responses, which are used by the store and company management to make improvements.

Here are some of the questions that Diana asks customers. For each question, decide whether the information obtained will be qualitative or quantitative. The first two have been done for you to get you started. Add some more questions of your own and do the same for these questions.

1 How long did you wait to place your order? – quantitative

2 Was your server friendly? – qualitative

3 Was your server well-groomed?

4 How long did you wait for your order to be delivered?

5 How clean was the store?

6 Was your server wearing a name badge?

7 How tasty was your food?

3.1.1.3 Primary data

Primary data is data that you collect yourself. You may do this by direct observation, surveys, interviews or logs. You should be able to rely on primary data because you know where it came from. You also know what you have done to the data to process it.

3.1.1.4 Secondary data

Secondary data is data that you collect from external sources. These might be:

- Internet
- television
- written articles in journals, magazines and newspapers
- stories told to you verbally.

You should rely less on secondary data because you cannot be certain how accurate it is. It may also have bias because of a point its author was trying to make.

Primary data is often expensive and difficult to get hold of. However, you can trust it. Secondary data is usually cheaper and easier to collect, but you may not be certain of its accuracy or scope.

3.1.1.5 Characteristics of good information

Information is of the most use if it has the following characteristics.

- **Valid:** It should be unbiased, representative and verifiable.
- **Reliable:** How well does it fit in with other facts you already know? How well do you trust this source of data?
- **Timely:** Information should be available when it is needed for decision making and not sometime afterwards.
- **Fit for purpose:** Was this information provided for the purpose it is now being used for? For example, a monthly budget prepared six months before the start of the year may not be of much use to forecast the remaining spend for the last two months of the year.

- **Accessible:** You must be able to do calculations with the data. For example, a printed report may be valuable but if it contains a lot of data you would not want to have to key it all in again in order to perform calculations.
- **Cost-effective:** The cost of capturing and producing the data should be very much less than the value of the decisions made on that data. It is said that the cost to business of government laws to capture data is often more than the benefit from these laws.
- **Sufficiently accurate:** Information needs to be accurate enough but not necessarily completely exact. If you are calculating whether you can afford to buy a car, you will need to know how much capital you have available and how much you can spend per month. You will also need to know the expected monthly total running costs and the cost of the car. However, these costs do not need to be exact as there will be some flexibility – e.g. you could reduce your monthly mileage to reduce your monthly costs or buy a cheaper car to reduce the monthly loan repayment cost.
- **Relevant:** There is no point in capturing information if it is not relevant to the decisions you want to make from it.
- **Having the right level of detail:** You need to capture enough detail for the purpose that is required, but no more. If you manage your household accounts, it is unlikely that you will record every postage stamp purchased or every item in your shopping basket. You are more likely to record just the totals.
- **From a source in which the user has confidence:** You need to know how believable it is. For a news item, you are more likely to accept a story reported in several national newspapers rather than one on an individual's web page.
- **Understandable by the user:** It must be at the user's level. For example, share buying advice in a weekend newspaper for the general public might have one paragraph for each share. At the other extreme, financial analysts advising pension funds with billions of pounds of assets would give much more detailed recommendations.

Case study

Retail sales information systems

Two competing retail chains developed sales information systems to help their management have the right stock in their stores at the right prices.

- One captured detailed data from the till systems of every store every night. It provided detailed sales figures for local and regional management by 07:00 the following morning. This gave them an excellent way to manage sales, though it was not completely accurate as it didn't account for returns or exchanges.

- The second system tracked all goods from ordering from a supplier through to customer delivery and possible return. Its main purpose was to provide the company's monthly financial accounts. This was however less successful as a sales information system than the first system as it was several days, and often weeks, before sales information was available in a suitable form for management to take sales decisions.

1 List the advantages to the retail chain of the first system.

2 List the advantages to the retail chain of the second system.

3 List the types of retail store that would prefer the first system and those that would prefer the second system.

3.1.1.6 Transformation of data into information

There are five stages to turning data into information (see Figure 3.2).

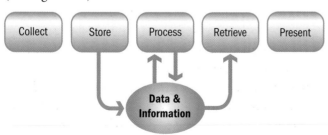

Figure 3.2 Turning data into information

1 **Collection:** Data is taken from where it is generated or available and is checked or validated to make sure that it is as accurate, consistent and complete as it needs to be.

2 **Storage:** The data is kept for the longer term. It is often on disk, either on a personal computer or on a server. It may be on a magnetic card, a flash drive, a CD-ROM, a DVD, magnetic tape or other electronic device. Prior to the widespread use of computers, paper was the most common form of data storage and paper is still in use for small manual systems.

3 **Processing and manipulation:** At this stage the input data is turned into information ready for output. At its simplest, this may just involve producing totals or averages. At its most complex, more than 90 per cent of the complexity of a system may be in this stage.

4 **Retrieval:** The required information from the processing and manipulation stage, with support from the input, is brought back into the computer from storage.

5 **Presentation:** The information is output or presented in the way that the user wants to see it. It can have graphics or text or both. It will most likely be presented on a screen or monitor, or sent to a printer or to another output device.

 Test your knowledge

1 What is the difference between primary and secondary data?

2 What are the possible disadvantages of using secondary data?

3 What is the difference between data and information?

3.1.2 Sources of information

This section distinguishes between internal and external sources of information.

3.1.2.1 Internal sources

Within a business, each department produces information which is of value to other departments (see Figure 3.3).

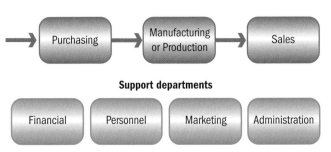

Support departments

▲ **Figure 3.3 Diagram of a manufacturing company, showing each department and flow**

Often, putting this information together right across the business gives valuable insights to the senior management of the company. Below are some examples of information that different departments in an organisation might produce.

- **Financial:** The finance department usually provides information about revenues or income, costs or expenditure, assets or capital items, liabilities or known future costs and investments. The department is often split into financial accounting and management accounting. Financial accounting is usually the source of most financial data (see section 3.2.2 on page 87).
- **Personnel:** The human resources or personnel department provides information about the people that the organisation employs. Typical information would be their contact details, jobs, grades and skills.
- **Marketing:** The marketing team could provide information on the organisation's customers, either individually or grouped by category of customer. They may also be responsible for the definition and description of the products and how these are grouped as brands.

- **Purchasing:** The purchasing department records who supplies which products to the organisation, how often and for what price. This information will come from the purchase order. They may also be responsible for defining these input products.
- **Sales:** This is the 'opposite' function to purchasing. The sales team records to whom the organisation has sold its products, when and for what price they were sold. This data will come from the sales order. They may also be responsible for defining these output products.
- **Manufacturing:** The manufacturing department records what resources were used and the timescales in which input products are turned into output products.
- **Administration:** In some organisations, some or all of the data production tasks mentioned above are done and/or stored by a central administration department.

3.1.2.2 External sources

There is also a lot of information available externally to an organisation that can help their decision making. Below are some examples.

- **Government:** Many governments, both central and local, require organisations to provide them with a great deal of data. Once the government has processed and summarised this data, the information can often be reused. However, as it is produced primarily for government purposes, this is not always timely or detailed enough for other uses.
- **Trade groupings:** Almost all trades have formed groupings of businesses in that trade to influence others for the benefit of their trade.
- **Commercially provided databases:** Many information businesses take publicly available data, add in their knowledge of an industry and process that information to provide information. A simple example is in newspaper publishing. Most newspapers make their current content available free on the Internet. They can profit from the archives by adding powerful search functions and then charging to search for groups of historic stories.
- **Research:** Many consultants with a deep knowledge of a particular industry know exactly where to look and whom to contact to find needed information. Organisations can use this external research to find advice or information to improve their decisions.

Case study

Trade groupings

A good example of a trade grouping is IATA (International Air Transport Association) which is the trade grouping for the airline industry. Its aims are summarised as follows.

- IATA simplifies travel processes for passengers.
- IATA allows airlines to operate safely, securely, efficiently and economically.
- IATA serves as an intermediary between airlines and passengers.
- A large network of suppliers gathered by IATA provides solid expertise to airlines in a variety of industry solutions.
- IATA informs governments about the complexities of the aviation industry to ensure better long-term decisions.

1 What information might IATA supply to its member airlines?

2 What information might IATA supply to passengers?

3 What information might IATA supply to governments?

Activity 3.1

Organisations and information

Consider several organisations of your choice. These could be, for example, your local council, a college, a shop, or a restaurant.

1 What types of information is each organisation likely to need? **p**

2 Where could each organisation get the necessary information from? **p**

3 In each organisation, which departments are involved in collecting and processing the different types of information? **p**

4 What are the similarities and differences in information needs between the organisations you have selected? **p**

3.2 How organisations use business information

This section focuses on the purposes of business information, which functional areas use the information and how it flows through and around an organisation.

3.2.1 Purposes

Organisations use business information in many ways to help them become more effective. Four of the most important ways are operational support, analysis, decision making and gaining advantage. This section explains each of these terms and gives examples of how a business might use them.

3.2.1.1 Operational support

A business can make immediate use of the information from its operational support system to make its minute-by-minute or hour-by-hour decisions – e.g. when monitoring and controlling its activities. For a restaurant, although some of their products are freshly prepared, some products are cooked in batches or need time to defrost. If customer orders are recorded on an **EPOS** system, then an operational support system can alert the restaurant management as to when they need to cook or defrost more bulk products.

What does it mean?

EPOS stands for **electronic point of sale**. It is an automated till system used in many shops and restaurants.

3.2.1.2 Analysis

Analysis is where the business regularly does the same or similar analysis of its information. This is typically to identify patterns or trends and to monitor the business. A business might produce a weekly sales and costs report. This would show a trend of whether profits were increasing or decreasing and whether increased sales drive up costs.

For example, a restaurant chain might use analysis to compare the performance of similar restaurants, to compare one restaurant against the regional or national average or to identify the impact of a promotion on sales and costs. Analysis may also be used to identify patterns such as the increase in sales at Christmas or Easter.

3.2.1.3 Decision making

Information systems support decision making when a problem or issue arises and management needs to take action to resolve it. This is typically done on an ad hoc basis as problems arise. Management can take these decisions at various levels: operational, tactical or strategic.

For example, the management of the restaurant chain might want to reduce costs. They might decide to do this by a reduction in the hours that some of their restaurants are open. They could decide when to close the restaurants by looking at information on sales and costs by hour of the day, by day of the week and by branch. They could open later or close earlier if sales less direct costs were low. This could be operational (for one branch), tactical (for a group of branches) or strategic (for a region or nationally).

3.2.1.4 Gaining advantage

This is the opposite to resolving a problem in that it is about taking advantage of external or internal events. It is done on an ad hoc basis as and when opportunities arise. It is also used to identify patterns or trends, this time with the aim of making decisions to benefit from these events.

For example, how should the restaurant respond when the local football team gains promotion to the premier league? Should management employ more staff or open longer on match days? Should they advertise more at the club ground? Or should they do special promotions?

Another example is if a competing chain goes out of business. What actions should the restaurants near to their former competitor take? What might be the effect of taking these actions?

3.2.2 Functional areas

As well as being sources of information, parts of a business want to gain a good understanding of how they perform. They want to use this information to help them to perform better. This section gives examples of the sorts of things they might do. It builds on section 3.1.2 (on page 85) on sources of information.

3.2.2.1 Sales

The sales department is interested in what products they have sold, whom they sold them to and for how much. Sales analyses are of great use to the sales department. These could include data on sales organised by:

- product and product group
- store, location or outlet and various groupings by geography, store size and organisation hierarchy
- salesperson, for bonus purposes
- customer and customer type.

Each of these might be organised by time of day or day of week, or as a comparison against the previous week, month or year.

3.2.2.2 Purchasing

The purchasing department is interested mainly in how their suppliers perform. They would analyse them by price, by lead-time, by fewest problems and by product availability. The best supplier would have one of the cheapest prices, deliver quickly and reliably, not give problems with product quality or paperwork and always have the products needed available.

3.2.2.3 Manufacturing

The manufacturing department wants to show how efficient they are. This means that they analyse how well they use their staff and machinery, how well they produce the most successful products, how they minimise wastage and how well they can react to changing demands.

3.2.2.4 Marketing

The marketing team is interested in analysing the customers and competitors. Like sales, they are interested in sales by customer and customer type. They may well have segmented the customers into types such as 'wealthy pensioners' and 'trendy teenagers'. They may also have segmented their addresses into groups such as 'rural farming' and 'affluent suburbs'.

They are interested in which products sell best to which customer type, for advertising and promotional purposes. They will also do external competitor analyses. These may focus on what competitors are doing to attract the most profitable customers.

3.2.2.5 Finance

The information from the finance department is often split. Financial accounting is concerned with *what* money the organisation has: its income and expenditure. Management accounting is concerned with *how* the money is spent. For example, the management accounts of a college would say how much money each subject department has spent: ICT, Business Studies, etc.

3.2.2.6 Personnel

The human resources or personnel department analyses information about the people that the organisation employs. They will monitor staff turnover, average staff wages, average days off sick and hours worked in order to comply with labour laws and staff agreements.

3.2.2.7 Administration

If there is a central administration department, they may prepare reports that apply to the whole organisation. They may also prepare and use some of the departmental reports.

Test your knowledge

1 What is an internal source of information?

2 What is an external source of information?

3 List four ways in which organisations might use information to make them more effective.

4 For an organisation of your choice, give an example of how it might use each of those four ways.

5 For an organisation of your choice, list how each major department might use information systems.

3.2.3 Information flows

Information flow is the movement of information relevant to the business, from where it is produced to where it can be actioned. For any organisation, speedy, efficient information flow is very important to its success.

3.2.3.1 Internal information flows

Within most organisations, there are three types of information flow.

- **Downwards:** Senior management informs the rest of the organisation about decisions taken and the direction of the company.

Information needs to be shared within the organisation

- **Upwards:** The staff of the organisation report to management on their progress and on any successes and problems that management need to address.
- **Across:** Information is passed between different parts of the organisation so that they can work together to achieve their common goals.

For example, an IT department has information flows to and from the parts of the organisation for which it develops or maintains systems. It maintains a help desk to record and resolve day-to-day problems with systems used by other departments. The management of the IT department holds a weekly meeting with departments that use ICT services in order to report on progress and identify trends.

3.2.3.2 Information flows to external bodies

Information also flows out of an organisation. Almost all organisations will provide information to their customers. This may be targeted to individual customers (such as a bank statement or utility bill), to a group of customers (such as a council's report on its performance) or to all customers (such as a public company's annual report). In the past, this information would always have been delivered in printed form, but is now increasingly likely to be delivered via the Internet.

Information also flows to suppliers and many organisations are also legally required to send large amounts of information to government bodies.

3.2.3.3 Information flow diagrams

An information flow diagram shows the steps involved in data flow – it includes where data is originally produced, where it is turned into information and where decisions are made on that data.

Figure 3.5 shows the steps involved in an information system today, turning aircraft movement data into aircraft punctuality information.

1 Aircraft movement (data)
2 Time and other movement details entered into local computer
3 External body records aircraft movement data
4 Movement data validated, processed into information, sorted and stored centrally
5 Screens and reports produced analysing movements in many ways
6 Analysts take action on information

▲ **Figure 3.4 Information flow – airline punctuality management long ago**

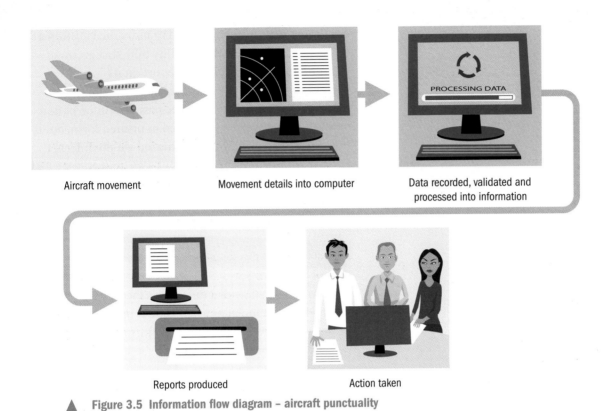

Aircraft movement   Movement details into computer   Data recorded, validated and processed into information

Reports produced   Action taken

▲ **Figure 3.5 Information flow diagram – aircraft punctuality**

Activity 3.2

Information flows

Choose an organisation to research. This might be a local store or other business, your college or another business to which you have access.

1 Find out how your chosen organisation uses information and describe what information is needed, how it is collected and how it is used. **p₂**

2 Find out and describe how the information flows between different departments in your chosen organisation. **p₃**

3 Find out and explain why specific sorts of information are of importance to your organisation. What are the benefits to the organisation of ensuring that the collection, processing and use of information are handled efficiently? **m₁**

4 Make some recommendations for how your chosen organisation could improve the quality of its business information and explain the benefits of each recommendation. **d₁**

3.3.1 Legal issues

There are many laws that affect the use of information. Three of these are the Data Protection Act 1998, the Freedom of Information Act 2000 and the Computer Misuse Act 1990.

3.3.1.1 Data protection legislation

The **Data Protection Act 1998** provides a framework to ensure that personal information is handled properly. It also gives individuals the right to know what information is held about them.

The Act works in two ways. Anyone who processes personal information must comply with eight principles. These make sure that personal information is:

- fairly and lawfully processed
- processed for limited purposes
- adequate, relevant and not excessive
- accurate and up to date
- not kept for longer than is necessary
- processed in line with your rights
- secure
- not transferred to other countries without adequate protection.

The Act also provides individuals with important rights. These include the right to find out what personal information is held on computer and most paper records.

The **Freedom of Information Act 2000** deals with access to official information. It gives individuals or organisations the right to ask for information from any public authority, including central and local government, the police, the NHS and colleges and schools. They then have 20 days to provide the information requested. They may refuse if the information is exempt from the Act. Examples of exemption are if releasing the information could prejudice national security or damage commercial interests.

3.3.1.2 Other relevant legislation

The **Computer Misuse Act 1990** details three offences:

- unauthorised access to any computer program or data – the most common form of this is using someone else's user ID and password
- unauthorised access with intent to commit a serious crime
- unauthorised modification of computer contents. This means impairing the operation of a computer, a program or the reliability of data. It also includes preventing access to any program or data. Examples of this are the introduction of a virus, modifying or destroying another user's files or changing financial or administrative data.

Some minor changes to tighten up this Act were introduced as a small part of the Police and Justice Act 2006. This made denial of service attacks on a server illegal.

Test your knowledge

1 What are the eight principles of the Data Protection Act 1998?

2 What right does the Freedom of Information Act 2000 provide?

3 What are the three offence of the Computer Misuse Act 1990?

4 Write down a non-published, publicly held piece of information that is of interest to you. Which public body holds this information? On what grounds might they not want to release it to you?

3.3.2 Ethical issues

3.3.2.1 Codes of practice

Many organisations will have a code of practice to make it clear what uses can be made of their computing facilities. The main uses will be to support the purpose of the organisation, but a code of practice will often define the extent to which private use of the computer system is permitted. Examples of items included in a code of practice are as follows.

- **Use of email:** Threatening or harassing emails are usually banned, as well as spamming or producing large numbers of unsolicited emails. Limited use of email for private purposes is often allowed.
- **Use of Internet:** Inappropriate classes of website, such as pornography or gambling, are usually banned, either by the code of practice or by filtering software. Limited Internet use for personal purposes is often allowed, as this can be difficult to distinguish from professional research. Where an organisation has its own web server, there are often strict rules as to what can be posted to it. There may be exceptions for clearly identified personal pages.
- **Whistle blowing:** Codes of practice will often protect computer users who draw management's attention to other users' misuse of the system. The codes will certainly protect IT administrators who run the servers and will often be the first to detect misuse.

Activity 3.3

Codes of practice

1 Find examples of computer codes of practice, either from your college or by carrying out Internet research.

2 Produce a code of practice for a top secret military or government establishment.

3 Produce a code of practice for a small web design or computer consultancy company.

4 List the areas in which these codes are similar. List the areas in which they differ significantly. Explain the reasons for the areas where they differ.

3.3.2.2 Organisational policies

An organisation's policies may have a significant effect on how it treats information. An organisation with a strong hierarchy that operates on a need-to-know basis is likely to impose policies restricting access to information. For example, it may keep its databases, files and email servers in a secure central data centre. IT security and data centre staff may put in place tight controls on who can access or update this data.

A decentralised organisation with decentralised computing is also likely to restrict access to information, but this time for more practical reasons. Here there may be few security restrictions on access to files, databases or email. However, there may be limited or no direct connectivity between the organisation's different computers. This could prevent staff at one location accessing information held at another location, even though the company would be happy for them to do so.

3.3.2.3 Information ownership

The department that produced the data should own every field of data in every record. They should have the responsibility for making sure that it is entered into the computer system in a timely way, that it is correct and that it is consistent.

Information ownership is much more complex. Many data owners may have supplied the original data that has been processed to produce this information. The often arbitrary way of allocating ownership is that the department responsible for defining or running the program that produces the information owns it. Except for internal IT information such as computer network performance, it is not a good idea to make the IT department responsible for information ownership. They are its guardians rather than its owners.

Test your knowledge

1 What might appear in a code of practice for email usage?

2 What might appear in a code of practice for Internet usage?

3 What are the responsibilities of data ownership?

3.3.3 Operational issues

3.3.3.1 Security of information

System users expect the ICT department to keep its information secure. This means that it is safe from unauthorised or unexpected access, alteration or destruction. It is management's responsibility to specify who can look at and update information. In small organisations with a simple structure, management may decide that anyone in the organisation can look at any information or that people on an authorised list may update information.

Many organisations have much more complex rules. Management may require a log of who has made updates or accessed information. It is usually the responsibility of the IT department to advise on security and to implement the chosen rules.

3.3.3.2 Backups

It is good practice to make frequent backups of information in case of physical or processing problems. This may be a full backup of all information or a partial backup of just the information that has changed since the last full backup. The IT department should occasionally practise a recovery or restore from the full backup of all the information. They should then apply any partial backup.

3.3.3.3 Health and safety

Although information systems are relatively low risk, there are a few health and safety issues that must be addressed. There are regulations that apply to screens and monitors, their positioning and usage. Keyboards, mice, chairs and tables must be appropriately positioned. Computer users are entitled to eye tests. They should have breaks away from the computer. All existing office and other workplace environment laws apply to using information systems.

3.3.3.4 Organisational policies

Many organisations have policies for the use of information systems that their staff should follow. These may range from keeping information confidential within the company to the procedures to follow to correct any information that appears to be wrong.

3.3.3.5 Business continuance plans

IT is at the heart of how many organisations operate. It should therefore be an important part of any **business continuance plan** (BCP) to plan how operations can continue if any major part of an IT system should fail.

Health and safety regulations must be adhered to in any workspace

The IT department should have things set up so that if there is a major failure, they will be able to continue to provide a service, even though a more limited one. A good example is to provide a dual network, attaching alternate terminals to each network. Then, if there is a complete failure of one network, half the terminals will continue to work.

The organisation needs to make decisions regarding their BCP. For example, a retailer may decide to have more tills or point of sale terminals than strictly necessary in order to allow for failure. They may also decide to have two servers in the back office driving the tills, rather than one, in case of server failure. However, do not expect the BCP to cover every eventuality.

Case study

Business continuance plans

A business had its offices in an area that was liable to flooding. It therefore decided to install the servers for its information systems on the fourth floor of the building in case the ground floor or basement ever flooded. One day, the staff arrived to find water cascading through all the floors of the building due to a leak. The building was closed for several weeks while the leak was fixed and the building dried out and cleaned. The BCP planners had not known there was a large air-conditioning water reservoir on the roof of the building and this had burst.

1 What actions might be in the BCP for that building and system?

2 What could have been done to prevent this incident?

3 Once the leak had happened, how could its effects have been minimised?

3.3.3.6 Costs

Whether an organisation is a business with a focus on costs, a government organisation whose aim is to deliver the best possible service within a fixed budget or a not-for-profit charity, it is important to manage the costs of an IT project. The total benefits of an IT project should greatly exceed the total costs. There are two important areas you should consider in the costs part of a business case.

- **Additional resources required:** The introduction of a new system often entails the one-off costs of new equipment purchase and installation, and user testing and training. In the IT department there are often more resources needed and so there will be ongoing costs to run a new system.
- **Cost of development:** This is usually a large part of the budget for a new computer system. There will also be ongoing costs once the system is running for minor changes to keep the system in line with the organisation's needs.

3.3.3.7 Impact of increasing sophistication of systems

Early information systems often just automated existing manual processes. This meant that little user training was needed and the software was relatively simple. Today's computing power means that systems are now becoming increasingly sophisticated. They need the following.

- **More trained personnel:** Users often need training in how to use the equipment, the basic computing features, the processes brought in with a new computer system and the transactions, queries and reports that form the new system.
- **More complex software:** Modern development software hides a lot of complexity from the application builder. This means they can focus on the business problems that the new system will solve and create overall better and more complex systems. However, when there are problems, it may need both a development software expert and a business software expert to work together to fix them.

Activity 3.4

Customer information and constraints

Focus on an organisation that uses customer information. This could be the organisation you studied for Activity 3.2, or another organisation. You should consider at least legal, ethical and operational constraints.

1 What constraints affect the way the organisation uses customer information? **p**₅

2 How does the organisation deal with these constraints? **p**₅

Test your knowledge

1 What security issues might apply to an information system?

2 What health and safety issues might apply to an information system?

3 What costs apply to an information system?

3.4 Features and functions of information systems

3.4.1 Tools

3.4.1.1 Databases

At the heart of each information system is a database. One of the first tasks in developing an information system is to design the data model. A data model (see Figure 3.6) describes every piece of information stored in the system, what it means and how it relates to the rest of the data. It is a business document and could apply just as well to a manual system based on paper stores.

A database (see Figure 3.6) is where all the data described by the data model is actually stored, usually on disk. It has indexes to speed access to frequently used data and pointers from one piece of data to another.

a)

b)

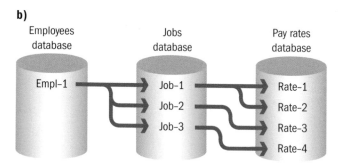

▲ **Figure 3.6 a) Data model b) Database showing linked tables or files**

3.4.1.2 Artificial intelligence (AI) and expert systems

AI and expert systems have rules, which may be changed, to model business actions taken by an expert. A good example of this is an airline fare management system. The business objective is to sell all the seats on a flight for the most money. High demand increases the price of a ticket or fare, while low demand reduces it. This expert system increases the fare each time a ticket is sold. If no seats are sold, it reduces the price as the date of the flight approaches. Rules will say how quickly the price changes and if there is a maximum or minimum fare for the flight.

3.4.1.3 Internet

Most systems today provide Internet access to them. Some may be for general public or subscriber use. Many are restricted to members of the organisation and will be protected, often by a user ID and password. Providing access from the Internet reduces many of the network issues that an organisation may face. Internet access can also reduce development time, as part of the system can be built using one of many easy-to-use Internet development tools.

3.4.1.4 Other tools

An example of another tool is a data mining system. When directed by an expert user, this finds patterns in sets of data. Sometimes these patterns are known, but the greatest value is when they are not. Sometimes they are used to identify groups of customers.

For example, a supermarket may know its total sales and total customers per day. However, this simple statistic hides the fact that a large number of its customers come in to buy just a newspaper and maybe a few low-value items. This means that the average sale per customer will be much less than the value of a weekly shopping trolley.

Activity 3.5

Tools

By searching the Internet, or using information provided by your tutor, research information system tools available.

1 List the types of tool that you find.

2 What does each tool do? Give an example of where it might be used.

3.4.2 Information system examples

Almost all departments of an organisation can make effective use of an information system. Here are some of the more common examples where many businesses have benefited.

3.4.2.1 Marketing systems

Many of the first examples of information systems were in marketing and sales.

- **Sales performance:** If a business could identify where and why its sales were increasing, then it could apply those conditions elsewhere with the same effect. For example, a retail chain might run an advertising campaign or a reduced price offer in one shop or a small number of shops. An information system could identify how successful this was. A chain of shops or hotels could have a programme of refurbishing their properties. An information system could show how successful this programme was in increasing business.

A supermarket needs more than simple statistics to identify its customers' needs

- **competitors:** Typical competitive activities include selling competing products, opening competing stores and reducing prices. As competitors introduce these changes, an information system can show what effect these changes have. A business can also make similar changes specifically to compete and the system could identify the effect of these changes.

3.4.2.2 Financial systems

Once a business has an information system to help manage income or revenue, the next area to address is often expenditure or costs.

- **Financial costs:** Spreadsheets can be used to help manage regular costs. However, information systems will more easily find trends and unusual patterns. Typical questions they could answer are: Do costs regularly surge or drop at the start or end of the year? Which overspends are gradual? Which are caused by one large unexpected or excessive item?
- **Investment returns:** A bank or investment company wants to understand its portfolio of investments. Some investments are high risk but potentially high return. Some are low risk but with low return. Some offer no return at all, but increase the capital value of the investment. An information system will help identify the investments that fall into each category.

3.4.2.3 Human resources (HR) systems

Human resources departments often produce a lot of analyses and so may have an information system to help them.

- **Staffing:** One of the goals of an organisation may be to have the right number of people doing the right work with the right skills. An information system can identify staff and skill shortages and excesses. It can also identify staff turnover, age, gender and experience profiles.
- **Professional development:** This is an extension from staffing – it covers the organisation's needs, staff training, and skills and experience for professional development. Analysis of this can identify suitable candidates for jobs and potential training opportunities for staff.

Test your knowledge

1. How might a marketing department use an information system?
2. How might a finance department use an information system?
3. How might a human resources or personnel department use an information system?

3.4.3 Management information systems (MIS)

3.4.3.1 Features

An MIS is a decision support system in which the form of input query and response is predetermined. It is often summarised from an information system. It is used where management want to ask the same question frequently, though perhaps about different subjects. Here are two typical questions:

- List the top ten stores for sales this month, by product type, together with last month's data and the percentage change. (This would help management review their flagship stores.)
- For a particular store, list this month's average sales by day of week and by product type. (This would help store management plan the staff needed at different times. It could also help them understand their sales – for example, it might show that groceries sell best on Fridays, wines, beers and spirits on Saturdays and home improvement items on Sundays.)

3.4.3.2 Benefits

A benefit of an MIS is that it is easy to use by senior management, as much of the complexity is hidden from them. The answers are often provided as both tables and graphics and for import into a spreadsheet for flexibility. An MIS also typically provides answers very quickly.

For an MIS to be effective it must meet these criteria.

- **Accuracy:** It must be as accurate as any other source of this information.
- **Sustainability:** The information must be reliably available, week by week and month by month.
- **Consistent timelines:** Where information is displayed by time period, then these times must be consistent. For example, for a store that is open 24 hours a day, it needs to be decided when the day's sales start (e.g. at midnight or at 04:00 when the till system is backed up and reset). For a UK-based international operation, is the time based on UK local time or is it based on the local time in each country?
- **Confidence:** The users must have confidence in the MIS for it to be used. This means that any faults found with the data, processes or computer system must be quickly put right. The users need to be informed of the upgrade and reassured that it has improved the quality of the system.

STOP Test your knowledge

1. What are the typical benefits of an MIS?

2. What are the four effectiveness criteria of an MIS?

3. List questions that a manufacturer might want its MIS to answer.

3.4.4 Key elements of information systems

An information system has five parts: data, people, hardware, software and telecommunications. We will look at each of these in turn.

3.4.4.1 Data

The data input to the system must be as accurate as it can be, subject to its cost and timescales for capture. It should then be stored in the most logical way.

This often differs from how the data is input. The data then needs to be summarised to create information in a way that best meets the needs of the system's users – this may not necessarily be the most logical way or the easiest or cheapest for the IT team.

3.4.4.2 People

People are involved both in capturing the data and in exploiting the information. It is important to motivate those who capture the data by highlighting the value that the exploited data brings to the organisation.

3.4.4.3 Hardware

In a small organisation, the MIS may run on just the sales or finance director's PC. In larger businesses, it

Case study

Where in the world are we?

An international organisation reduced its sales management overheads by merging its African sales division into the UK division. ICT had to change their MIS to attribute all African sales to the UK. The operations department then decided that part of their New York operation should be allocated to the European division. This was more complex as all New York sales and some operations remained with the New York division.

Geographic changes often happen with information systems. One of the best ways to cope with this is to have supporting data that relates divisions with their names and what forms them. It is then easier to add or take away the parts that change and to rename the divisions.

1. What are the advantages of summarising data, for example, by division, before making it available to the users?

2. What are the advantages of every query going to the detailed data to produce the information?

3. What could the IT department do to reduce the effect of such changes?

usually runs on a server, shared or dedicated, with Internet or intranet access for those who need it. It is unusual to require specialised hardware.

3.4.4.4 Software

The simplest MIS can be built using standard software. However, most MIS use specialised software, which has the most common features of an MIS already built in. The developer configures this by describing the database and its structure, where the data comes from, how to summarise the data and what standard queries will be required. The cost of this software varies widely. The cheapest offers limited functions for one PC. The most expensive is highly functional, providing high performance and many features for hundreds or thousands of users and vast amounts of data.

Activity 3.6

MIS and Tools

Again select an organisation that you know.

1 Describe the features and key elements of a management information system (MIS). **p**₄

2 Show how and where it supports the functional areas of your chosen organisation. **p**₄

3 For your chosen organisation compare, with examples, how useful different tools might be for processing information to support effective business decision making. **m**₂

4 Evaluate a range of these tools noted in question 3 with respect to their support in decision making. **d**₂

5 Explain the purpose and operation of data mining and predictive modelling. **m**₃

3.4.4.5 Telecommunications

An MIS may be delivered across the Internet, though this sometimes brings difficult security questions. Many MIS are delivered across an intranet within a company's firewall for protection from competitors and others

seeking this valuable management information. Occasionally, a dedicated telecommunications network is used to provide the utmost security.

3.4.5 Information systems functions

An information system has four functions: input, storage, processing, output. There is often also a control or feedback loop so that system output can affect future input, as shown in Figure 3.7.

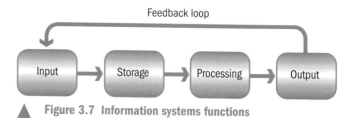

▲ Figure 3.7 Information systems functions

3.4.5.1 Input

Input to an information system has two parts. There is the detailed data described in section 3.4.4.1. This is stored and processed and forms the basis for the output from the system. Then the user must also tell the system what sort of analyses they are expecting from the system. Sometimes this is hidden from the user and the IT department sets up this input in advance of users using the system.

3.4.5.2 Storage

The data should be stored at the most detailed level possible. The IT department may also choose to store various summaries of data for ease of use and consistency. The IT department should take regular **backups** of the data. Some of these should be kept in a different location in case of a disaster.

What does it mean?

A **backup** of data is a copy of the data that is kept in case anything should happen to the original.

3.4.5.3 Processing

Processing is what turns data into information. At its simplest, it may just be adding up all of the individual items sold by a supermarket and producing totals by store, by product, by time of day or by any other classification. At its most complex, a computer program or the user will perform complex calculations, make assumptions about missing data and select criteria to include or exclude. For example, a complex mathematical model might be used as part of a stock control system – as well as looking at sales, this might consider lead times, cost of being out of stock, the effect of the weather and expected future demands.

3.4.5.4 Output

Output can be in two formats: **graphical** and **textual**. Graphical output is often the best for seeing the big picture, understanding trends and presenting the information to management. Textual output is best where it is important to analyse the detail and to know exact values. A common way of using both formats is to use graphical output to identify areas of interest, then to use graphical again to focus in on the details and to switch to textual output to see the lowest level of detail.

Output is best presented in the form that each user wants. For example, for supermarket sales, a product manager mainly wants to see sales by product or product group. The store managers are mainly interested in what is happening in their own store. A regional manager wants to see what is happening across all stores in their region. The default output for each of these users should be the one that they are interested in.

3.4.5.5 Control and feedback loops

A control or feedback loop is what happens in the organisation as a result of the output from an information system. It should have some effect, direct or not, on future inputs to the information system.

An automated example is a data feed of actual sales data to a computerised stock control system. This could note which products have increasing sales and reorder these products from suppliers in order to reduce the likelihood of being out of stock. A similar example is management looking at the sales reports to see which products are selling well and which are not. To maximise profit, they might choose to increase the price of the products that are selling well and reduce the price or offer a promotion on those that are not selling well.

3.4.5.6 Closed and open systems

In a **closed** system, the user may have some choice about what to report on, but they are limited to predefined output formats. These are often easy to use. They mainly use graphical formats and are often aimed at management.

In an **open** system, there is often great flexibility on what to report on and the format in which the information is output. This powerfulness may mean that significant training is needed before the systems can be effectively used. Open systems are aimed more at analysts. They typically use both graphical and textual formats.

What does it mean?

Graphical output is information that is presented as charts, diagrams, graphs or pictures.

Textual output is information that is presented as characters, numbers or text.

A **closed** information system is where the outputs are fixed.

An **open** information system is where the user has a wide choice in how to present the output.

Preparation for assessment

The assessment tasks in this unit are based on the following scenario.

You are the newly recruited Head of Information Systems for a nationwide restaurant chain. The Chief Executive and the Operations Director have asked you to prepare a strategy report for the company on how they could benefit from and should develop their information systems. The company already has good systems to run the day-to-day business, but little to help with decision making.

Task 1 (P1, P2, P3)

The company has a powerful till (point of sale) system, a purchase order system for ordering goods and services from their suppliers and delivering them to their outlets, and the usual administrative systems such as human resources, payroll and finance.

The till system works independently in each store. Each night every till system can transmit to head office details of that day's sales in great detail.

The rest of the company's systems are run at head office. Personnel data and hours worked for payroll are entered at each store directly into the head office system. You will need to make assumptions about how other systems might work.

1 Describe the existing systems and what information they might provide.
2 Describe which parts of the company might want to use this information and why.
3 Describe how these systems might link together and how this information might flow across departments.

Task 2 (P4, P5, M1, D1)

You need to describe, propose and justify a new information system to your company's senior management. You are not required to put costs and timescales in this report.

1 Produce a proposal for your company's new MIS, describing its features, key elements and how the company would use it.
2 Describe the benefits to your company of collecting and using this information.
3 Suggest various options for the system to improve business information. Justify your suggestions.
4 Record the constraints on your company's use of customer information and the impact this may have.

Task 3 (M2, M3, D2)

Your company's policy is to select ICT tools by competitive tender. However, your colleagues want to know the types of tool that may form part of the new information system.

1 Compare, with examples, the usefulness of various types of tool for your new system.
2 Describe data mining and predictive modelling.
3 Evaluate for your company a range of these tools.

IT Systems Analysis and Design

Introduction

Designing a new or revised system is a complex process and it is remarkably easy to produce systems that do not match the needs of the clients or users. Systems analysis provides structured processes that help give reliability to designs so that they meet the requirements.

In completing this unit, you will gain an understanding of the principles and stages involved in IT systems analysis and of the documentation involved. Perhaps the most important early task facing you is the production of the requirements specification document. This is essential to ensuring that an appropriate solution is designed and created. In addition, it will provide the basis for later testing and evaluation.

This unit also covers the reasons why organisations undertake systems analyses as well as the benefits of engaging in such a formal process.

Different organisations will adopt their own approaches to systems analysis that meet their needs. Here, you will consider a range of life cycle models and methodologies. The practical activities focus particularly on two particular models: the waterfall life cycle and Structured Systems Analysis and Design methodology (SSADM).

After completing this unit, you should be able to achieve these outcomes:

- Understand the principles of systems analysis and design
- Be able to investigate, analyse and document requirements
- Be able to create a system design
- Be able to design a test plan.

Thinking points

It is generally accepted that to make an effective systems analyst, experience and perspective are required as well as technical skills, so it is rare for new entrants to the profession to be considered for such posts. This requirement reflects the fact that systems analysis is a complex activity requiring a broad base of skills. What do you think some of these skills might be? Why do you think a new IT professional might not have all of these skills?

A particular requirement of effective systems analysts is the need to work in a methodical way. The whole process can often take a long time and involve a number of people, which creates lots of opportunities for misunderstandings and miscommunications. Many people are keen to get started on the actual programming or practical development work and so may make assumptions about what is needed. Why do you think this can be counterproductive?

It is important for systems analysts to work in a methodical way and to formally document each stage of the process before moving on to the next stage. Why do you think that this is important?

Here are three different definitions of systems analysis:

- the study of a business problem in order to recommend improvements and to specify the requirements for a solution
- a phase in which the current system is studied and alternative replacement systems are proposed
- a detailed analysis of the components and requirements of a system, the information needs of an organisation, the characteristics and components of current systems, and the functional requirements of the proposed system.

There are many more possible definitions but there will be ideas common within all of them – in particular, the study of the current system if there is one, understanding and specifying the requirements, and the design of new or replacement systems.

Fundamentally, systems analysis is a **process** and, although different companies describe and operate the process in different ways, the key purpose is always the same, as is the need for a structured and organised approach.

This unit will help you to gain an understanding of the principles of systems analysis and the documentation involved. Although all stages are important, it is crucial to capture the requirements fully in order to ensure that the new system is fit for purpose. Remember also that the later testing and review should be based on these requirements.

7.1.1 Development life cycle models

To structure the systems analysis process, a number of particular models have been developed. One very common model is the **waterfall model** – so named because it cascades from one activity to the next. Another popular model is **rapid applications development** (RAD).

7.1.1.1 Waterfall life cycle model

The waterfall life cycle model has been modified in different ways over time and is often described in slightly different ways, but the essential 'no turning back' feature remains at its core. Just as with real waterfalls, water never goes back up to the top! In the classic version of this model the key stages are as shown in Figure 7.1.

The waterfall life cycle model is a very popular approach. The advantages of this model are that it is simple and sequential – the processes are compartmentalised in order to give good control and the development process moves from one phase to another like a car in a car wash. There are no repeated steps which could slow up the process and so deadlines set can often be met.

The key disadvantage of waterfall development is that, because of the 'no turning back' structure, once a phase of development has been completed, it will never be visited again. So, it does not allow for revision or reflection. If one of the stages is not completed well (for example, the requirements are not fully captured or the testing not undertaken rigorously), then the final product may not be fit for purpose. If, of course, each phase is completed with care and the outputs can be relied upon, then the waterfall method can work very well.

Alternatives to the classic waterfall model include modified waterfall models and the **spiral** model.

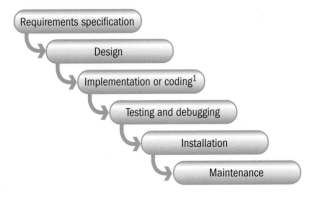

[1] The implementation phase often requires some integration where different parts of the new system that were created separately are brought together into the complete system.

Figure 7.1 Classic waterfall life cycle ▶

Activity 7.1

Exploring variations of the waterfall method

1 Research some of the modified waterfall models.

2 For each of these models, find out how the waterfall method has been modified and why.

7.1.1.2 Rapid applications development (RAD)

RAD (see Figure 7.2) is a development model that was devised as a response to the inflexible processes developed in the 1970s, such as the waterfall model. As well as the disadvantages of the waterfall method already described, using it (and other similar models) to build a system could take so long that requirements had often changed before the system was complete. This often resulted in unusable systems.

RAD is a software development methodology that focuses on building applications fast – it involves **iterative development**.

The speed is achieved by using specialist tools such as **CASE** tools that focus on converting requirements to code very quickly. It achieves this using **prototypes** that are iteratively developed into a full system.

The initial prototype serves as a proof of concept for the client, but more importantly it also serves to focus discussions to help define and refine requirements.

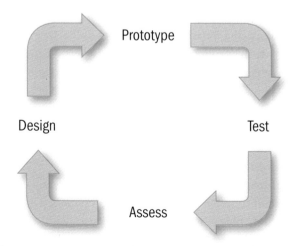

▲ **Figure 7.2 Rapid applications development (RAD)**

What does it mean?

Iterative development means repeating the development process until all the required functionality has been developed. It can be used to produce increasingly sophisticated and functional versions of a system in short development cycles.

A **prototype** is a restricted version of the finished product that can be produced in as short an amount of time as possible, preferably days.

CASE stands for **computer-aided software engineering** and describes the use of software tools to assist in the development and maintenance of software. Tools used to assist in this way are known as CASE tools.

The quality of the finished product is improved because there are many opportunities to review the emerging system and adapt it to meet the requirements.

A disadvantage of RAD is that the speed can compromise the features available in the final system. Also, it may not be easy to expand or scale up the system later because it was developed specifically to meet a particular need.

Remember!

Getting the requirements specification right is one key to success.

7.1.2 Developmental methodologies

Working within a particular life cycle model does not guarantee an effective development. Additional rigor can be added using a methodology that provides more detail about how each stage is performed.

In many cases, the development methodology works best within a particular life cycle model. This is the case with the **structured systems analysis and design method** (**SSADM**), which works best within a waterfall type life cycle.

Other developmental methodologies, such as the object-oriented **unified modelling language** (**UML**), work best within other life cycle models such as RAD. In an object-oriented methodology, the whole system is broken into a number of objects that are designed to interact with each other to produce a working system. Object-oriented methods are becoming more popular and are particularly useful in large and complex systems.

Every methodology does have the same basic characteristics – particularly in terms of having a notation (often using diagrams and charts) that details in consistent ways the process, the working of the system or the design of a new system. Also each methodology will use a series of tools and techniques that are used at different stages of the development.

7.1.2.1 Structured Systems Analysis and Design

Although SSADM is certainly a waterfall type method, some of the terminology used is different from that used in the classic waterfall. In addition, SSADM focuses mainly on the early stages of this model, the capturing of the requirements and the design of the new system.

The whole system development process can be broken down into six stages:

- project initiation and feasibility
- investigation and analysis
- design
- implementation
- testing
- maintenance.

The last three stages are not covered in this unit.

Test your knowledge

1   Why is a structured approach necessary?

2   What are the main advantages and disadvantages of the classic waterfall life cycle model?

3   What are the main advantages and disadvantages of the rapid applications development model?

7.1.2.2 Project initiation and feasibility

At the start, there must be a trigger that *initiates*, or starts, the whole process of development. Typically this will be one of the *business drivers* as described in the later part of this unit (see section 7.1.3). At this early stage, the implications and costs of the development will not be fully known and so a feasibility study is undertaken.

The key questions that a feasibility study aims to answer are:

- Should this project be undertaken?
- Can this project be justified?

These are difficult questions to answer without going through all the stages of systems analysis. However, it is necessary to undertake a limited feasibility study in order to avoid committing to a potentially costly system that is not feasible. It is possible that an outcome of the feasibility study will be a decision *not* to proceed.

A feasibility study will normally be broken into sections, as follows.

- **Purpose of the system:** This will be often be a relatively short section. If the project is to replace or upgrade an existing system, then the purpose might include something about what the existing system does, as well as the aspirations of what the new system will do.
- **System scope:** This section identifies what areas and aspects of the system are to be considered in the development. Also stating what is not in scope is often a good way of ensuring clarity. As the project develops, the impact on other parts of the system outside the original scope may be discovered and it is important to revisit the scope from time to time and possibly question the decision to proceed. It is important to note that most IT systems cannot be developed in isolation and so the scope may well include changes to connected administration procedures and job functions.
- **Problems and requirements:** This section can be difficult to write without a full investigation. This might involve a limited set of interviews with some key people and a review of any documents that have led to the project being initiated in the first place.

If possible, the analyst should interview people who actually use the system as well as meet the managers of the organisation or department. Capturing things that work well, as well as those that do not, is also important. At an early stage, these requirements will often be in the form of prioritised lists. The requirements may then be translated into what it means for the system and documented using similar techniques to those used when undertaking the more in-depth investigation if the project goes ahead. A typical method will use data flow diagrams, identifying how the inputs are processed into outputs. Later on, these diagrams will be reused and refined.

- **Constraints:** At this stage, it will be necessary to consider what the constraints might be. Although it may not be possible to fully explore the constraints at this stage, key aspects should be identified.
- **Recommendations:** As noted earlier, one possible recommendation might be not to proceed with the development. Alternatively, a cost-benefit analysis might suggest that there is reason to proceed but with recommendations to restrict or extend the scope of the development. It is important to note that this section might identify a number of possible solutions or variations of solutions, each one with sufficient information to allow managers to make a decision.

Test your knowledge

STOP

1 Why might people be optimistic about the costs of projects?

2 Identify the problems that could develop if the system scope is not sufficiently clarified at the start of a project.

■ Feasibility as an iterative process

Although the SSADM methodology is a type of (no turning back) waterfall method, it is likely that a discussion of the recommendations made in the feasibility study might raise more questions. So the analyst could be asked to revisit some of the work undertaken in the earlier parts of the feasibility study in order to clarify some of the detail.

At the end of this part of the activity, there would normally be a 'sign off' of the final feasibility report and a documented acceptance of the requirements of the new system. It is also possible that, at this stage, the analyst will need to make commitments about such things as timescale for the full analysis process, costs (whether they are internal or external to the organisation), reporting and interim reporting arrangements.

7.1.3 Key drivers

Given that the development of new systems can be fraught with problems and delays, what drives organisations to develop systems? These drivers will be very different in different organisations.

The most important drivers come directly from the needs of the business and are often not related to technology, but require technological solutions. Examples could include:

- the organisational needs to grow or acquire other companies in order to extend their market share
- a change in legislation that requires organisations to develop new or adapt new systems and processes
- the need to reduce staffing costs.

Activity 7.2

Identifying key drivers

1 From the information in the feasibility study in the following Gibbons case study, what do you think are the key drivers for Gibbons Books?

2 What other drivers might exist that are not mentioned in the feasibility study?

Case study

Gibbons Books Ltd

Gibbons Books Ltd is a small company that publishes fiction and non-fiction books. The books are written by freelance (self-employed) writers who are paid a royalty (a percentage of the sale price) for each copy of the book sold. Currently, the accounts department manually calculates how much royalty money to pay each writer but, as the number of books the company sells has increased, this system is time-consuming to use and needs to be automated.

Gibbons Books has asked Pat Jones, a systems analyst, to produce a feasibility report for the development of their royalty payment system. Pat has spoken to the managing director of the company, as well as some of the staff in the accounts department who use the current royalty system. Using the information she obtained, Pat has produced her report which is shown below.

Feasibility Study – Gibbons Books Ltd.

System: Royalty payment system
Analyst: Pat Jones

Purpose of the system
- To record details of writers in a database (contact details, book or unit writing history, specialisms, etc.). This database is to be linked with existing databases, e.g. sales database, accounts database.
- To record for each book what royalties are due to whom and when.
- To calculate royalties due on a yearly cycle.
- To produce standard reports on demand.

System scope
- Needs to run on a networked PC in accounts department.
- Volume of book sales data for the system to be provided by existing sales recording system.
- System to provide data to the accounting system.

Out of scope
- Networking aspects of linked databases (this will be undertaken in-house).
- Tax calculations related to writers (they will do this themselves).

Current deficiencies
- Current system requires manual input of data and the process of producing the royalty payments takes too long which irritates the writers.
- Mistakes are not easily identified.
- Royalty payments reports sent to writers do not provide sufficient detail.
- Details of payments made have to be manually entered into the accounting system.

User requirements
- Reduced need for manual calculations.
- Faster processing and ability to scale upwards as the business expands.
- Improved accuracy.
- Improved detail on reports.
- Automatic collection of sales data and output of accounting data.

Potential benefits
- The new system will reduce the need for overtime payments in the accounts department, possibly also allowing staff reductions or to cope with expansion without increasing staff.
- Fewer complaints from writers – potentially improving retention of good writers.
- Easier and more accurate reporting of payments made.
- Side effect of creating an electronic database for writers means that other tasks will be easier to manage.

Constraints
- Approximate budget of £8000 for purchase of software and development costs.
- System must be tested and in place by 1 April (for next cycle of payments).

Conclusion and recommendations
Alternative systems could be:
a) A customised database package using macros and some VBA. This would provide reliability and also relative ease of future maintenance. This could be developed within the estimated budget and would take approximately six weeks.
b) A fully bespoke programmed solution. This system provides the greatest potential for flexibility and additional functions could be easily added into the system. However, the costs would exceed the budget and maintenance would require specialist expertise.
c) A simple spreadsheet that was not linked to the other databases in the network. This solution could be developed in-house and, although it could not link with the existing databases, the data entry could be made efficient and it would achieve some of the requirements identified.

Recommendation
It is recommended that option a) is taken forward.
Note: the database to be created would need to be linked to the existing networked database. The costs are not estimated here. However, it is estimated that 'one developer day' would be needed to establish and test these links.

Case study tasks

1 An initial comment from a manager queries the need for the accounts system to be networked. Outline briefly the arguments that might be used to justify a networked system.

2 The IT manager has critised the feasibility study because no mention of backups is made. Consider the importance of this issue and add appropriate statement(s) to the user requirements list.

3 Identify what the implications on the staff in the accounts department might be and how you would approach managing their concerns and requirements

4 Explain the disadvantages of adopting alternative systems b) and c)

7.1.4 Benefits of effective systems analysis procedures

During the process of designing and producing a new system, it can be very tempting to cut corners to save time or maybe to skip aspects that seem obvious. Experienced professionals will always advise against this and quote a number of benefits of keeping rigorously to the process.

Those benefits include:

- reduced risk of projects running over budget or over time
- good-quality systems that are more likely to meet requirements
- manageable projects
- maintainable systems
- resilient systems.

7.2 Investigation and analysis

Assuming that the feasibility report has been discussed and a decision has been made to commit to a new system, the next stage is to perform a more in-depth **investigation**.

7.2.1 Investigation techniques

There are a variety of techniques that can be used to gather information about both the current system and the required system. The four basic techniques are below:

- observation
- interview
- document analysis
- questionnaire.

Normally, an analyst would not depend on one technique only and would choose the techniques appropriate to the situation.

Interviews can be an excellent way of collecting detailed information and also allow an open dialogue in which the interviewee has the opportunity to bring up issues that the analyst had not considered. Typically, the analyst will start by interviewing or meeting with the managers and decision makers in order to get an overall picture of the issues. They will also gain an understanding of the organisation structures, the people involved and any areas of sensitivity.

Interviews can be an excellent way of collecting detailed information

Questionnaires can be used to obtain information more quickly and cheaply from a larger selection of people.

Observations need to be undertaken carefully and with some sensitivity, as they could result in employees becoming worried about what is happening and how it might affect them. In addition, the employees observed may not be typical of other employees. A good systems analyst will engage with the individuals within the organisation and explain what is happening and why.

Document analysis might be undertaken early in the investigation. The issues identified in the documentation can be used to construct questions for questionnaires or interviews. A wide range of documentation should be looked at, including possibly: procedure manuals (to compare with observed practice), complaints files, paper records or files, etc.

STOP Test your knowledge

1   What might be the impact of an investigation on the people who find themselves in the middle of a systems analysis activity?

2   How might they react? How would you react if you thought that what you did at work was about to change?

Method	Advantages	Disadvantages
Observation	• Workloads, methods of working, delays and bottlenecks can be identified.	• Can be time-consuming and therefore costly. • Users may put on a performance while under observation. • Problems may not occur during observation. • Employees may not co-operate.
Interview	• A rapport can be developed between interviewer and interviewee. • You can adjust questions as the interview proceeds. • Interviewees may identify issues, problems or requirements that have not already been identified. • You can add more in-depth questions to find more information.	• Can be time-consuming and therefore costly. • Poor interviewing skills can lead to misleading or insufficient information. • May not be feasible for a large organisation; it is important to identify key people to be interviewed in depth.
Document analysis	• Good for obtaining factual information, e.g. data stored, procedures, volume of sales, inputs and outputs of the system.	• Not all aspects will be documented and employees may not always follow the defined procedures. • Manuals and paperwork may not be up to date.
Questionnaire	• Many people can be asked the same questions – this is a relatively cheap way of accessing large numbers of people. • Anonymity may encourage honest answers. • Questionnaires can be processed electronically.	• Questions need careful design, e.g. tick boxes are simple and easy to answer but do not allow shades of responses. • Need to avoid ambiguity. Questions may require interpretation. • Cannot guarantee return rate and the people who do respond may not be typical of all involved.

Table 7.1 Investigative techniques

Case study

Investigating the Gibbons Books Ltd royalty system

The feasibility study has been presented and a decision to go ahead with a more detailed investigation has been agreed. Pat Jones, a system analyst, has been asked to carry out the investigation stage.

It is felt that the people involved should include:

- the managing director of Gibbons, who will be paying for the system development
- the administrator who currently does all the royalty calculations manually and sends the royalty cheques to the writers
- the IT technician
- the office manager and other administration staff.

Initial thoughts are that at least the following information should be collected.

- **Data types, sources and flows:** Where does the information come from about how many copies of each book have been sold? How does the administrator know what percentage to pay each writer? Does all the data come from the same place or does it come from different sources? What other databases are used in the company – and what are their structures, field names, key fields, etc.? Are any backups made of previous amounts paid and to whom?

- **Decisions taken and types of processing:** What equations are used – does everyone get the same percentage? How often are the payments made?
- **Storage methods:** How does the administrator store the data used? Where is it kept? Is historic data kept?
- **Documents:** Are there any procedure manuals available? Are past records, letters, reports, etc. available of what has been done before?
- **Types of output:** What are the outputs of the system? How is the money paid to the writers? Does anyone want any new reports? If so, what do the required reports look like? Is any other output needed?
- **Technology:** What is the specification of the existing PC and the network that it is connected to? What storage and backup facilities are available? What are the existing skill levels of the employees?

1 For each area above, identify which investigative method or combinations of methods you think would work best.

2 List the order in which you think the individual activities should take place and who should be involved.

7.2.2 Requirements specification

As the investigation develops and additional information is collected and analysed, it is likely that the original statement of requirements as identified in the feasibility study will need some modification. The end of the investigation phase is likely to be a key decision point in the whole systems analysis activity. It is also likely to be marked with some further detailed dialogue with the customers resulting in an agreement or 'sign off' of the requirements.

7.2.3 Analysis tools

As the investigation progresses, the information collected, including a more detailed understanding of the requirements, is analysed and documented.

Several modelling and structured analysis tools are available within SSADM. Other methodologies provide alternative tools and methods. These tools can be used at various stages of the process and might include:

- data flow diagrams (DFDs)
- process descriptors
- entity relationship diagrams (ERDs).

These tools are described in section 7.3.

7.3.1 Documentation

This phase of the process begins to draw together the various outputs from the analysis phase and gives details of how a solution that meets the requirements can now be put together. There are a number of key parts to this design – the input and output specifications and the processes that transform the input into the required output. Some of this detail will have been explored in the earlier phases of the process, including the feasibility study. We will look at each of the three elements in turn:

- input specification
- output specification
- process descriptors.

7.3.1.1 Input specification

The method by which the input data is captured needs to be decided and specified. For example, the system's users may enter some data manually, while other information may be retrieved automatically from another computer system.

Bar-codes are one example of a data capture method

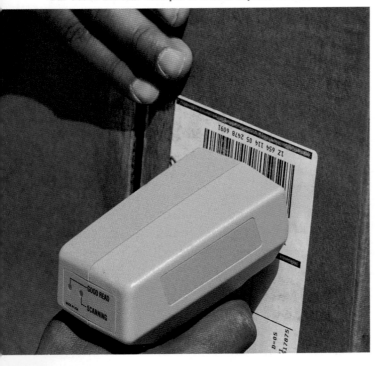

There are other data capture methods, such as bar-codes and magnetic strips, and it is important that the best method is chosen to suit the system requirements, taking into account factors such as accuracy of input and costs. A focus on ensuring that accurate data is input into the system is crucial. Where data is entered manually, it is essential that **validation** and **verification** controls are used effectively. Specific techniques such as drop-down menus or range checks should be employed wherever possible.

■ Verification methods

Verification methods include requesting the operator to enter important data twice and then checking to see whether both entries are the same. This method is usually needed for high volumes of numeric data that are very difficult to read. Another method is to re-display entered information and request the operator to check it and confirm that it is correct.

■ Validation methods

If it is known, for example, that customer references are always one character and three numeric digits, then this format can be checked on input. Dates are often a problem because there are different ways of representing them – however, in most situations where dates are involved, the system will have built-in validation routines. A very effective technique is to cross-reference input data with an existing database. For example, customer references that are input on orders can be referenced to the customer database and check fields, such as the customer's name, can be displayed as a visual check for the data entry operator.

What does it mean?

Verification is the method of checking that the data entered on to the system is the same as that on the original source.

Validation is the process of checking that data entered into a system is reasonable and in the correct format.

Remember!

The maxim **GIGO** stands for Garbage In = Garbage Out.

Where data is input using a screen, the layout of the screen should be clearly specified. The use of prototype screens that can be easily and quickly put together (but do not actually work) are useful in helping the customer understand and comment on the design.

Screen design would normally include:

- a title for the screen
- purpose
- data items that will be collected using the screen
- screen layout and tab order of items
- any fixed data items that are sourced elsewhere and displayed on the screen, plus where these data items are obtained from
- user instructions
- error messages.

A similar list can be constructed if the data is to be collected using a printed form.

7.3.1.2 Output specification

There may be a variety of output, including screen outputs, printed reports or files. The specification for the screen or print output may include information such as:

- a title for the screen or report
- purpose
- data items that will be output on the screen or report
- screen or report layout design.
- source of data items to be displayed on the screen or report.

7.3.1.3 Process descriptors

There are different techniques for defining processes, each having different strengths that may be suitable for different situations. Choosing the best way of describing a process is important.

Having identified the processes needed within the investigation phase, it is necessary to define each process so precisely that there is no ambiguity. A variety of different methods can be used to create process specifications:

- structured English
- flow charts
- decision tables.

Typically, you would choose one of these techniques to describe a particular process, rather than using all three.

Structured English describes processes in an informal way using English words. It might be particularly useful in the early stages when you are providing overview descriptions of processes without providing the detail. Also, if it is known that the solution is to be programmed, then perhaps this technique can be used that almost starts the process of coding. Sometimes this technique is called **pseudocode**.

Flow charts are diagrams which show processes linked in a systematic way, with branches according to a number of decision choices. It is important, for clarity, to use the right shapes for each part:

- diamonds for decisions
- rectangles for processes
- ovals or circles for start and stop.

All process boxes should have active verbs: e.g. send, calculate. All decision boxes should contain questions. You should avoid flow lines crossing each other.

Decision tables are useful when there are a lot of different options to choose from and you want to identify what happens in each circumstance. They are used when the equivalent flow chart would be too complex to draw.

7.3.1.3.1 Process descriptor examples – structured English

Here is an example of a process descriptor for paying royalties, written in structured English.

```
Open writers database
Open books database and get details of first book
   Get number of books sold
   Calculate royalty payment
   Add payment to be made to writer in writers database
   Move to next book and repeat process until end of books
Close databases
Arrange for payment of writer
```

Note the use of indents to structure sections of the text – this is used in a very similar way in some programming languages. If necessary, individual sub-processes, such as 'Calculate royalty payment', may need additional detail – perhaps using a different type of process descriptor.

7.3.1.3.2 Process descriptor examples – flow charts

The royalty calculation flow chart shown in Figure 7.3 assumes that there is a different royalty percentage for fiction books (1%) and non-fiction books (1.5%).

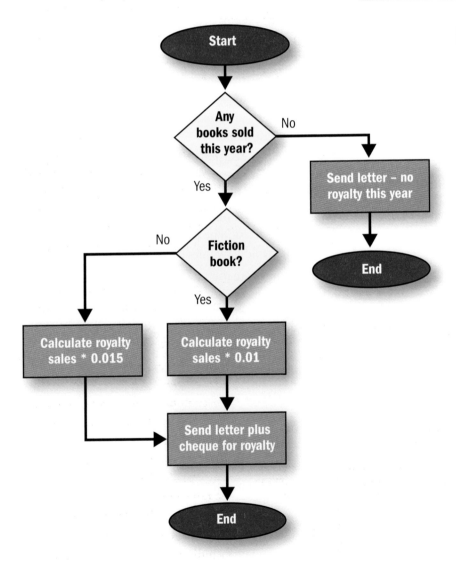

Figure 7.3 Flow chart – calculation of royalty payment

Activity 7.3

Working with flow charts

Adapt the flow chart shown in Figure 7.3 to take account of the following new criteria.

1 For fiction books only, if the book is hardback then the royalty is reduced to 0.9% (i.e. a multiplier of 0.009).

2 For non-fiction, the royalty multiplier is 0.015 for sales in the UK. For any international sales, the multiplier is 0.012.

7.3.1.3.3 Process descriptor examples – decision tables

Decision tables are used mostly for more complex processes. They represent these processes in two-dimensional tables showing the decisions to be taken based on the variety of inputs. If, for example, we wanted to represent the flow chart in Figure 7.3 as a decision table it would be as shown in Table 7.2.

The X in each column identifies the action that should be taken based on the input conditions in the top half of the table.

Activity 7.4

Decision tables

1 Adapt the decision table on the basis of the following additional criterion. For all books: if the price of the book is more than £50, then the royalty percentage is 0.8%.

Hint: first work out what additional condition and action need to be added to the table.

Books sold this year	Y	Y	N	N	
Fiction book	Y	N	Y	N	conditions
Non-fiction	N	Y	N	Y	
No payment			X	X	
Calculate royalty at 1.5%		X			actions
Calculate royalty at 1%	X				

Table 7.2 Decision table – calculation of royalty payment

7.3.1.4 Data flow diagrams

In most cases, a number of data flow diagrams at different levels of detail are needed to describe how systems operate.

At the highest level, the system within scope is shown as a single rectangle and the only data flows shown are those that link outside the system with external entities. Sometimes this highest level diagram is described as **Level 0** or the **context diagram** (see Figure 7.4).

The main point of a context diagram is to clarify the links with external entities.

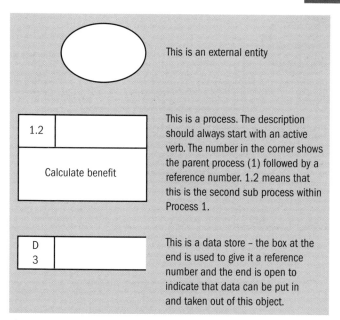

Figure 7.5 Elements of data flow diagrams

Note that every arrow must have a direction and must be labelled to show what information is transferring. Where necessary, the detail of the information being transferred should be clarified. For example, the label 'Details' on the information flow leading from 'Writers' does not give sufficient information – the analyst would need to provide supporting information that explains exactly what it is.

The next step is to break up the one process into a number of processes and to add further data flows that show internal data transfers. The next level of detail is called a **Level 1** data flow diagram (see Figure 7.6).

The symbols used in these data flow diagrams are always the same to assist people in understanding a diagram that was created by someone else. This is part of the **notation** of a particular methodology (see Figure 7.5).

Data stores need further detail, including field names, key fields, field types and sizes, etc. All of the details for all of the data stores will be stored in the **data dictionary.**

Figure 7.4 Context diagram for royalty payments system

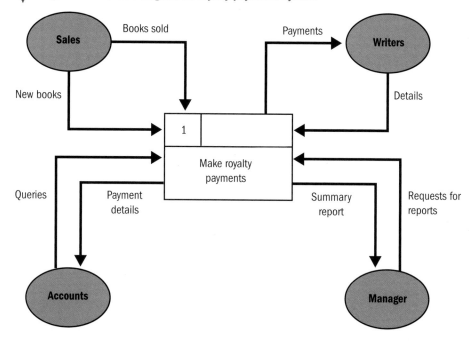

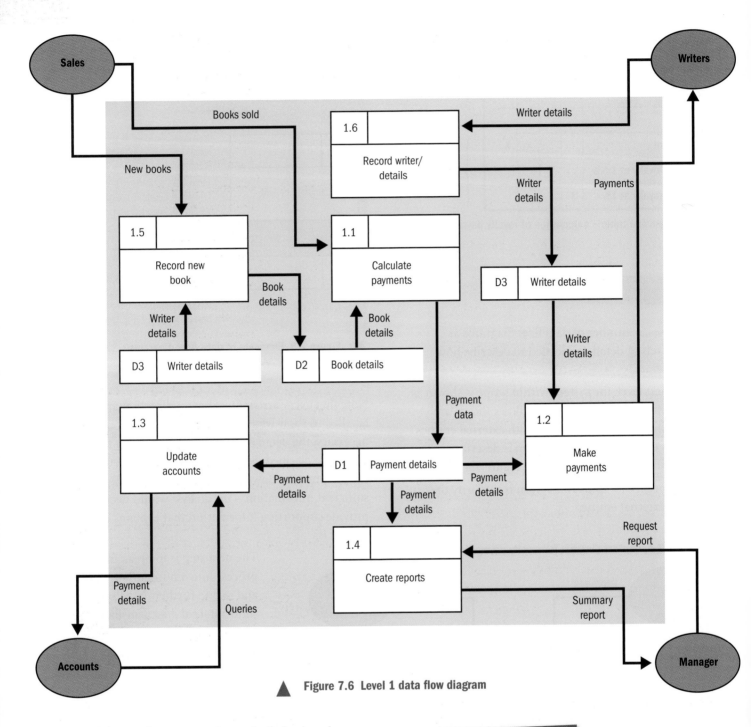

Figure 7.6 Level 1 data flow diagram

If one of these sub-processes is particularly complex, it too will need breaking up into further detail. For example, if this was the case for 'Update accounts' (shown in Figure 7.6), the further sub-processes would be numbered 1.3.1, 1.3.2, 1.3.3, etc. All of the data flows must match up when moving from one level to another.

7.3.1.5 Data dictionaries

In large or complex systems, it can be very difficult to keep track of all of the different tables and data items. If different tables are constructed over time or by different people, then different or inconsistent naming conventions can cause errors and confusion. A data dictionary is a centralised store of information about all the data in a database. The expectations of particular employers and methodologies are likely to vary but there will be a core set of details that will always be necessary, as follows:

- table names and descriptions
- relationships between tables (i.e. entities) – often shown using ERDs (see section 7.3.1.6)
- field names (attributes) and the table(s) in which they appear
- field definitions, including field types and lengths and meanings, if not self-evident
- additional properties for each field, including format and validation controls
- aliases or alternative names for the same field as used in different tables.

7.3.1.6 Entity relationship diagrams (ERDs)

Entities are the real world things that are part of the system under investigation and need representing in the data flow diagrams. Examples are products, customers and orders information. **Attributes** are the qualities that are of interest and hence worth storing in a database. The attributes for a product might be its product code and the current stock level. For a customer, the attributes would include contact data. For orders, the attributes would include the date of a sale and its monetary value. When stored in a database, it makes sense to use the attribute names for the field names. Most entities will be implemented in a practical way as tables, as shown in Table 7.3.

One (or more) of the attributes of a particular entity has to be defined as the primary key. This uniquely identifies a particular occurrence of an entity. For example, in the customer entity, the primary key 'Customer reference' uniquely identifies a customer. (The primary key for each entity is shown in bold italics in Table 7.3.)

Most systems have a number of entities within them, and entities are often related to each other. For example, the entity 'Customers' and the entity 'Orders' are related, because every order a company receives comes from a customer.

This relationship can be shown as in Figure 7.7 and can also be represented in words.

Entity	Possible attributes
Products	***Product reference*** Stock reference Product name Minimum stock level Price Stock level
Customers	***Customer reference*** Customer contact Telephone Customer address Customer name
Orders	***Order reference*** Date of order Date of despatch Salesperson

Table 7.3 Entities and their attributes

Each customer will have placed at least one and possibly many more orders. So, for one customer, there will be many occurrences of the orders entity. This type of relationship is therefore called a **one-to-many relationship**. In an ERD, this is shown by a fork at the 'many' end of the line that joins the two entities (see Figure 7.7).

One-to-many relationships are the most common type of relationship between entities, but are not the only type.

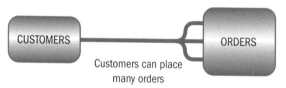
CUSTOMERS — ORDERS
Customers can place many orders

▲ **Figure 7.7 Entity relationship diagram**

Activity 7.5

Creating an ERD

1 Draw an ERD to show the relationship between the order entity and the product entity. Assume in this case that when a customer makes an order, they can order a number of products at the same time. For example, think of an order made by a customer to a supermarket.

Most of the detail about the process descriptors will already have been documented at the investigation and analysis phase. However, some additional detail may be necessary.

Proper design documentation is vital if all of the hard work in the earlier stages is to be converted into a new system that is fit for purpose. At this point the customers of the system formally review the design and 'sign it off' before the implementation phase – this is likely to be another key point in the larger development life cycle.

Much of the raw material for the final report will be available and although there are many ways of structuring it, it is likely to have the following sections:

- summary of the requirements
- overview of the whole system, including details of interfaces with other systems or procedures
- input specifications
- output specifications
- process descriptors
- test strategy and plans.

Although it is hoped that such a document will never need to be revised, it is however likely that some issues would arise in the implementation phase that might impact some of the original design work. In such cases, further versions of the design documentation will need to be produced, each one given a new version number.

The document is likely to be long and, in most situations, readers will not want to read it all from the start but will want to jump to particular sections as needed. For this reason, the document needs to have a contents page and to be well indexed and referenced.

7.3.2 Constraints

One of the most important constraints on a new system is money and, at this stage, some estimation of the costs of the project will be balanced against the potential benefits. The costs are often difficult to estimate accurately and, in many real life situations, people are often overly optimistic.

The costs need to include such things as hardware, software and development costs. In addition to these obvious costs, the analyst must think more widely and consider perhaps the cost of training users in the new system, any changes in employee costs, and so on. The benefits may also be complex to identify. Some may be easy, such as financial savings in linked employee redundancy. But less tangible benefits that might have been stated in the requirements, such as 'improved customer service' or 'increased sales', are particularly difficult to quantify.

Other constraints might be organisational policies, timescale, the need to integrate with existing systems, the available hardware systems or staff expertise in the company.

Training users is one of many costs that may arise on a project

Although this unit deals only with the early phases of the whole systems development cycle and testing happens at a later stage, considerations of how the final system should be tested would be made during these early stages. If systems developers are to be sure that the product is fit for purpose, they need to make decisions about what test strategy to adopt and begin to develop the criteria for the testing itself.

Planning for testing should begin when the requirements specification is being developed and should continue as the project moves towards the design stage. Planning for testing includes deciding which aspects of the system can and should be tested, as well as considering how they can be tested.

7.4.1 Testing strategies

This section considers two types of testing: **white box testing** and **black box testing**.

7.4.1.1 White box testing

The white box testing strategy deals with the internal workings, logic and detail of the system – particularly any programming code that has been developed. White box testing is also called **glass**, **open box** or **clear box testing**.

It is, however, almost impossible to look at and test every individual aspect of a system and this type of testing requires skilled testers who can understand such detail – potentially including the programming language used to develop the system.

7.4.1.2 Black box testing

Black box testing involves testing without knowledge of the internal workings of the system being tested.

The only type of testing that can be planned for during the development phase of a system is black box testing as the detail of the system operation and implementation will not by then have been decided.

Activity 7.6

Exploring different testing models

1 Find out about V model testing.

2 Explain the benefits of this model as compared to black box and white box testing.

7.4.2 Testing purposes

There are two major aspects to testing:

- testing functionality
- user acceptance.

Advantages	Disadvantages
• More effective on larger systems. • Tester needs no knowledge of the detail by which the system was constructed. • Tester and developer are independent of each other. • Tests are done from a user's point of view. • Black box testing can expose any ambiguities or inconsistencies not previously seen. • Test cases can be designed as soon as the specifications are complete.	• Only a few possible inputs can be tested. • Testing every combination would be impossible. • Test cases are hard to design without clear specifications. • Black box testing can be hard to focus on particularly complex parts of the system.

Table 7.4 Advantages and disadvantages of black box testing

Testing the functionality can be a relatively mechanical activity as long as it is designed carefully and the detail in the requirements specification is used to construct a series of test cases. In theory, if the requirements specification has been constructed well, then it ought to be the case that user acceptance can be taken for granted – as the needs of the users are exactly what should have been met by the system. This is, however, frequently not the case!

Functionality testing is most readily implemented through a combination of appropriate testing strategies and test plans and could include testing any interfaces between the new system and other systems.

However, the reality may be more complex. Occasionally when the user tests the system, issues are identified that show that it does not fully meet the user's need(s). Potential issues might be the user interface or the speed of the system – potentially areas that were not defined well enough in the early investigation. Whether issues found at this stage are rectified or not may depend on their seriousness and impact. Who has responsibility for the cost of any changes will depend on the nature of the contract agreed and what was included in the detail of the requirements specification when it was 'signed off' by the customer.

7.4.3 Components of a test plan

Test plans typically involve:

- how the testing will be done
- who will do it
- what will be tested
- how long it will take
- what the test coverage will be, i.e. what quality level is required.

At the heart of the test plan will be the test log and this will typically include:

- inputs
- expected outputs
- actual outputs
- test data.

Additional detail will include who carried out each particular test and when.

Activity 7.7

Testing standards

1 Find out about the IEEE 829-1998 standard for testing.

2 Describe the advantages and disadvantages of adopting a standards-based approach to testing.

Preparation for assessment

The assessment tasks in this unit are based on the following scenario.

A large building services company currently employs a team of IT technicians to manage their IT infrastructure and support the IT users. Recently, the company has taken over a similar but smaller company which also employs technical support staff in the same way.

The number of IT technicians is different in both the companies, but the general structure of both IT departments is the same (see Figure 7.8).

Other staff involved in the IT support provision include staff representatives from different departments who constitute an IT user group. This group meets with the IT manager monthly to discuss IT developments and other issues. In addition, other managers, e.g. Finance, Sales, etc, have staff that need IT support on specialist software.

The company feels that it needs a centralised IT-based support system that will track, monitor and report on the progress of problems identified by users across the two sites – generally improving the IT support service. To progress this, they have decided to employ an external consultant to undertake an analysis and design.

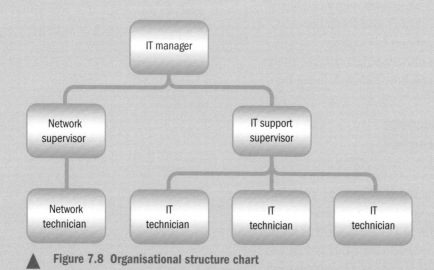

▲ **Figure 7.8 Organisational structure chart**

Task 1 (P1)

As preparation prior to the development of detailed plans for meetings with employees, an initial question and answer session took place with the manager and this has been transcribed as shown in Table 7.5.

Using the responses given, describe what key drivers the company had for commissioning an analysis that might lead to a centralised IT support facility across the two companies. Explain the advantages that might result from the development of such a system.

Task 2 (P2, P3, D2)

It is felt that the existing IT manager is averse to adopting a structured approach to the proposed work. Given that the provision of IT support is a crucial function, the company needs to be sure that the final solution will be fit for purpose.

Provide three presentations with supporting notes that describe the following:

1 two different development life cycle models, with examples of why and when each might be chosen
2 the features, advantages and disadvantages of a particular developmental methodology
3 the potential risks in undertaking a systems analysis and design activity, and how each risk might be minimised.

Task 3 (P4, M1, M2, M3, P6)

a) Devise and document a strategy for further investigating the system. Identify the people you need to get information from and the techniques you would use to get information from each person or group.
b) Ask your tutor to respond to the strategy that you have identified in task a) and use the information provided to produce a requirements specification.
c) In order for you to fulfil criterion M2, your tutor may be able to provide a witness statement that confirms that you have worked independently on tasks a) and b).
d) Meet with your tutor to confirm and agree the requirements specification.

e) Once the requirements specification has been agreed, design a test plan and explain your choice of overall test strategy.
f) Identify two different solutions that will meet the requirements specification and explain any not yet known circumstances that might cause one or the other to be chosen.

Task 4 (P5)

Design and document the system based on the agreed requirements specification. Use any appropriate tools based on the methodology you have chosen.

Task 5 (D1)

Revisit the process you followed in the systems analysis. Make reasoned judgements for each stage as to whether:

- the decisions you made were appropriate
- the tools and techniques you chose were appropriate and used to good effect.

Finally, recommend any improvements to the systems analysis procedure that you would make the next time you undertake such an activity.

Question	Response
When did the merger of the two companies take place?	Two months ago
Where is the other company based?	About two miles away in an industrial estate.
Why did you decide to take over the other company in the first place?	A few reasons, I suppose. We were a little concerned that if that company got bigger they might start to threaten us and take our business. We felt that there would be economies of scale in terms of purchases, maintenance contracts, etc. I am not sure what will happen in the future in this area, but potentially if one of the bigger national chains came to our area, then the bigger we are the more easily we might fight them off.
And why start thinking now about developing a centralised support function?	We knew that one of the IT departments had a particularly successful and innovative network manager and we hoped to use her skills – we know that she has some useful ideas about how a new support service might be constructed. We used an in-house questionnaire in the parent company last year to see how the users felt about IT support and there were a number of problems raised. We think that if we centralise, this will improve the consistency of responses to IT queries, share specialist expertise, etc.
Do you intend that the two IT departments will work relatively independently on a day-to-day basis?	Initially yes, but over the next three months, I want all of the jobs to come into a central place so that they can be prioritised and allocated out to balance the workloads and keep everyone productive. In the longer term, we may choose to shut down one of the technical support areas completely and rely on technology that monitors the networks at a distance. We would ask technicians to travel as and when necessary. Even at the beginning, I expect that if we have a particular problem at one site, then technicians will come from the other one to help with the work. I guess that if we log all of the problems centrally on a database then we should be able to see trends and common problems – maybe even start to go back to suppliers with fault records to negotiate special deals.
At this stage, are you thinking of any redundancies in the IT support section?	Too early to say, but it is possible that we might promote one of the network managers and ask her to play a more strategic role in running the networks. Then, over time, we may only need a network technician at the smaller site, if we need one at all. At the moment, anyone who is available in technical support answers the phone and responds to emails, but we may want to appoint someone to be on the help desk full time so users get immediate responses to problems.
What about supporting the users – any changes to how you manage that?	I want them to have a single point of access for their queries. At the moment, they either call or sometimes come to the technicians' area and ask them to fix it there and then, which can be disruptive to other work. Over time, we can analyse the questions and problems, and maybe our human resources department can arrange some special training events for common problems.

Table 7.5 Transcribed record of meeting

Communication Technologies

Introduction

With the explosion of Internet technologies – such as voice over IP, Skype, podcasting, cable television, Internet gaming, email and chat – communication technologies are now at the core of everyday life. Each component of this unit reveals different technologies and explores their operation and impact. In completing this unit you should develop an understanding of the technologies used to connect, control and manage network and Internet communications.

After completing this unit, you should be able to achieve these outcomes:

- Know the main elements of data communications systems
- Understand the communication principles of computer networks
- Understand transmission protocols and models
- Understand Internet communications.

Thinking points

Communications has become the cornerstone of all networked systems; no communications means that computers cannot communicate with each other across a local network, across a wider network or across the Internet.

You will discover:

- what technologies are used
- how wireless systems compare to wired systems
- how the data is managed
- what devices enable this to occur
- the security issues
- quality issues and how they affect communication on our networks

Many technologies provide Internet communication. To use a computer at home or work requires a complex interconnection of equipment, technologies and systems which often remain invisible to the user.

8.1.1 Communication devices

To access the Internet and use a network to communicate with others (such as your learning centre or a mobile phone service provider), the technology uses data terminal equipment (DTE) and data circuit-terminating equipment (DCE).

8.1.1.1 Data terminal equipment (DTE)

DTE is a historical term for the device at the end of the line – this could be a mobile phone, a **modem** within a computer, the cable modem, Bluetooth or a network card.

There are different types of DTE according to the communication method used. With Bluetooth the size and range are important issues, while with mobile phones the quality and **bandwidth** are more important. Modems and network cards exist in many formats and are configured for a wide range of transmission speeds.

Each computer has a DTE with a network card and the same applies to laptops with wireless cards.

8.1.1.2 Data circuit-terminating equipment (DCE)

DCE works together with DTE. A DTE connects to the Internet or network service offered by the DCE. DCE is network equipment which controls communication. Many examples exist, including:

- the wireless **router** in your home, to which you connect your laptop or other devices
- the **switch** in a communications room at work or college, which connects all the classroom computers to the LAN (local area network) and the Internet

- the Bluetooth dongle on your PC, used to synchronise your mobile phone or **PDA**
- equipment at the other end of the broadband service which is connected to your cable modem
- a central router which connects many other local routers in a WAN (wide area network).

8.1.1.3 Wireless devices

Over the last ten years, mobile communications have become commonplace, with wireless devices such as third and fourth generation (3G, 3.5G 3. 75G and 4G) cellular phones, wireless PDAs and wireless laptops being used by many people.

The use of mobile communications has also been accelerated by the blurring of technology boundaries – there are now mobile phones with PDAs and wireless laptops that connect to the mobile phone network.

Wireless networks use the 802.11x standard (see page 140), which defines the speed and range of the network communication. The mobile phone network is an

What does it mean?

Modem is two words combined and abbreviated: **mod**ulator + **dem**odulator = modem. Modulation and demodulation are processes used to convert the computer's digital signal to the method used to transmit the data (such as a phone line) and then back again.

Bandwidth is the measure of how much data can be sent across a given communication method per second. It is almost impossible to use the full bandwidth of any system.

A **router** is a networking device used to connect multiple networks together; see page 148.

A **switch** is a networking device used to connect multiple computers together; see page 148.

A **PDA (personal digital assistant)** is a handheld computer.

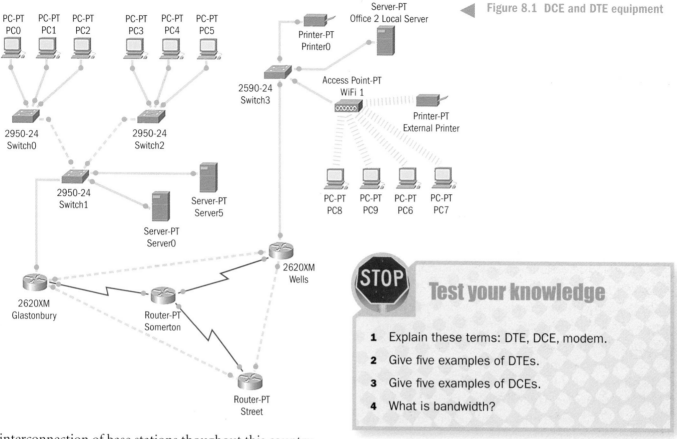

Figure 8.1 DCE and DTE equipment

interconnection of base stations thoughout this country and internationally which allows subscribers to communicate via a low bandwidth voice system. Data services have improved on mobile phones with better video and audio services as well as download speeds for data.

Figure 8.2 A PDA

Test your knowledge

STOP

1 Explain these terms: DTE, DCE, modem.

2 Give five examples of DTEs.

3 Give five examples of DCEs.

4 What is bandwidth?

8.1.2 Signal theory

This section looks at how data is sent across a network from one computer system to another. All computers communicate using a variety of media (light, radio, electrical and microwave). The principles used are based on electronics and physics.

8.1.2.1 Digital signalling methods

Figure 8.3 shows the properties of a data transmission being sent from one computer system to another.

The sine wave has two properties of interest: amplitude and frequency.

A represents **amplitude** or strength of the signal, and can be explained simply as volume or loudness. The higher the amplitude of the signal, the louder and stronger it is; the lower the amplitude, the quieter and weaker it becomes. With any transmission, higher amplitude signals will travel greater distances.

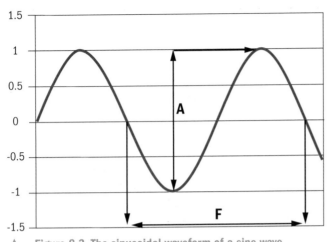

Figure 8.3 The sinusoidal waveform of a sine wave

For different systems, amplitude has different meanings, as follows.

- Radio and microwave both use the same method of transmission: radio waves. For all radio waves, the amplitude of the waveform is measured in metric terms (metres or millimetres).
- All cables rely on electrical current, the strength of which is measured in volts. The current in a normal data cable will be $+/- 5V$ – any higher a voltage may damage the sensitive computer equipment. A telephone cable can carry up to $+/- 50V$. The range of the signal switches from positive voltage to negative voltage and is referred to as **AC (alternating current)**.
- With light, the brighter the light source, the stronger the signal. Most fibre optic cables use infrared or laser-generated light; the difference between these two light sources affects the distance the signal can travel and the speed of the line.

F represents the **frequency** of the signal. The frequency is the rise and fall of the waveform from zero to bottom, then to the top and back to zero (shaped like a rollercoaster ride). This is called a **cycle** and is measured in hertz (Hz). A low frequency signal has a small number of cycles per second; a higher frequency signal can have billions of cycles per second (such as GHz or MHz).

■ HOW TO CREATE A SINE WAVE

1 Creating a sine wave without a signal generator can be a challenge. Using Excel, create a sine wave using the chart wizard.
2 In cell A1 enter [0.1]; in cell A2 enter [=A1+0.1] and drag the cell down to row 100.
3 In cell B2 enter [=SIN(A1)] and also drag down to row 100.
4 Select all of column B and start the chart wizard, using the line chart to create a sine wave.
5 What happens if you multiply the contents of the cells in column B?

Visit http://scope.teraknor.co.uk and try some of the simple scope demonstrations.

8.1.2.2 Representing data electronically

Based on the technology used for a sine wave, data is transmitted as a square (or digital) wave. All computers use binary in which each bit of information is represented as 0 (zero) for the off state and 1 (one) for the on state. The binary is organised in chains of bits, called bytes or words according to the system that is going to use it. For example, 01001100 is a single byte that represents the decimal value of 76 or the **ASCII** value of 'v'.

Sending data from one computer to another is called **encoding** and various formats exist according to the system used (wireless, fibre or electrical cable). Common formats are Manchester encoding or Huffman coding.

Encoding is not a new concept: it is more than 160 years since Samuel Morse developed Morse code to be used on the new electric telegraph (see Table 8.1). He created a system of combinations of two signals (a short pulse called a dot and a long pulse called a dash), similar to the binary zero and one. This system was invented so that a telegraph operator could key messages in any language at a relatively fast speed.

Encoding that is used to send data across a computer network is based on a digital 'square' wave, which is an adaptation of the sine wave shown in Figure 8.3.

What does it mean?

ASCII (American standard code for information interchange) is the format for storing letters, numbers and symbols in documents.

Letter	Morse	Letter	Morse	Digit	Morse
A	.-	N	-.	0	-----
B	-...	O	---	1	.----
C	-.-.	P	.--.	2	..---
D	-..	Q	--.-	3	...--
E	.	R	.-.	4	....-
F	..-.	S	...	5	.....
G	--.	T	-	6	-....
H	....	U	..-	7	--...
I	..	V	...-	8	---..
J	.---	W	.--	9	----.
K	-.-	X	-..-		
L	.-..	Y	-.--		
M	--	Z	--..		

Table 8.1 Morse code, which is still used by enthusiasts

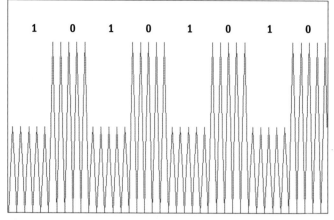

Figure 8.4 A square wave

Remember!

A bit is the smallest unit of information and is represented as a binary digit (1 or 0).

In order to avoid data being lost or the computer system being confused (which would cause an error), there are two simple rules when sending data:

1 All binary zeros (off) are sent at high amplitude so that there is no confusion with the 'power off' of no signal being sent. This is like the Morse code dash.

2 All binary ones (on) are sent at a mid-range amplitude to contrast with the rule for the binary zero. This is like the Morse code dot.

Figure 8.4 shows that the frequency of the signal is fixed (although this value will vary according to the speed of the transmission medium), but the amplitude is varied and based on a zero or a one coming through the line.

To ensure data is successfully transmitted, an agreed common method is used for sending the data, one that can be managed by all computer systems. Representing data electronically, computers use **bits, bytes** and **data packet** structures.

A byte is the unit of storage made from 8 bits; it has 2^8 (i.e. 256) possible combinations. Units of storage in computer systems operate in powers of 2 because binary has two states (0 and 1).

Because transmission media can be unreliable, transmitting or downloading a file which is over

kilobyte	megabyte	gigabyte	terabyte
2^{10} bytes	2^{10} kilobytes	2^{10} megabytes	2^{10} gigabytes
1024 bytes	1024 kilobytes	1,048,576 megabytes	1,048,576 gigabytes
	1,048,576 bytes	1,073,741,824 kilobytes	1,073,741,824 megabytes
		1,099,511,627,776 bytes	1,099,511,627,776 kilobytes
			1,125,899,906,842,624 bytes

Table 8.2 Relative sizes of bytes, kilobytes, megabytes, gigabytes and terabytes

5 or 6 kilobytes in size is also unreliable. To make data transmission more reliable, a large quantity of data is divided into smaller packets; and these can easily be re-sent if the data is found to be damaged.

Different methods are used for structuring packets. Each packet normally has information to identify it and its content:

- the number of the packet in a sequence of packets
- the address of the computer or network to which it is being sent
- the address of the computer or network it has come from.

As well as whatever data the packet contains, there are also start and stop bits to indicate the start and end of the packet.

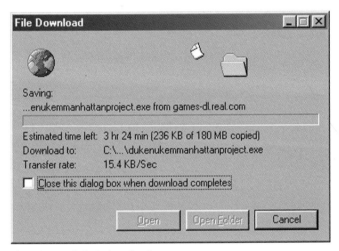

▲ Figure 8.5 A download

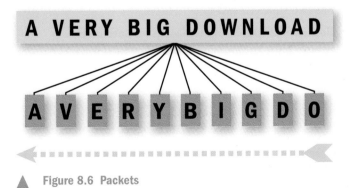

▲ Figure 8.6 Packets

8.1.2.3 Synchronous and asynchronous transmission

On a network, synchronous transmission and asynchronous transmission are the methods used to regulate the sending of data. For two devices to communicate, there needs to be a signal which synchronises the transmission on receipt of data; this is called the clocking signal. When both devices send and receive the same clocking signal, they are able to communicate in tandem and successfully transfer data.

The DCE in a networked system normally sends the clocking (or synchronising) signal. This may be a router, WAP or switch. The clock rate is a bit rate set by the network administrator on some systems but may be automatic on others.

Asynchronous means 'without clocking' and is used to refer to systems which will communicate one way on demand. Examples include computer to printer communication, and computer to keyboard and mouse. While this type of transmission may be local to a computer, the technology used is the same for a network connection. (See also Unit 2 page 60.)

```
SanFrancisco(config-if)#
SanFrancisco(config-if)#int s0/0
SanFrancisco(config-if)#clock rate 56000
SanFrancisco(config-if)#
```

▲ Figure 8.7 Setting a clock rate

8.1.2.4 Error correction and detection

Error correction and detection are managed by techniques such as **parity** checking and the cyclic redundancy check (see also section 8.1.3.1 on page 134).

In the transmission of data across networks, it is important to check the integrity (quality) of data, as error, failure and interference are always likely. To do this, the data is sent with a small checksum: a unique mathematical value obtained from a simple calculation taken on the data.

Figure 8.8 shows how interference can corrupt data. If no parity checking takes place, the computer receiving the data is unaware that the data received is now erroneous, so it will still process the data, possibly causing a serious error (Figure 8.8a).

To prevent this type of problem, parity checking is applied: all the binary 1s are counted. If there is an even number of bits set as on, then a binary 1 is used as the

checksum. If there are an odd number of bits set as on, then a binary 0 is used as the checksum (Figure 8.8b).

Parity checking is very simple and involves the counting of odd or even numbers of binary digits (called odd and even parity). However, it is also susceptible to error (Figure 8.8c).

Parity checking is normally applied to small groups of data, or to every byte, where the system can afford the memory overhead of checking every byte. However, most systems are 'best effort' systems and economics dictate that it is ideal to apply one check to a packet of data up to 1514 bytes in size – Ethernet frames (see page 134) provide a good example of this.

What does it mean?

Parity means equality (e.g. equal amounts, equal status or equal value).

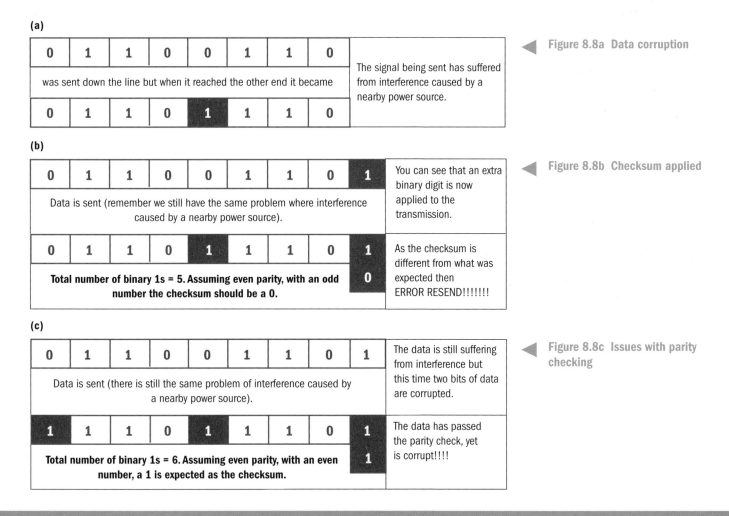

(a)

The signal being sent has suffered from interference caused by a nearby power source.

◀ Figure 8.8a Data corruption

(b)

You can see that an extra binary digit is now applied to the transmission.

As the checksum is different from what was expected then ERROR RESEND!!!!!!!

◀ Figure 8.8b Checksum applied

(c)

The data is still suffering from interference but this time two bits of data are corrupted.

The data has passed the parity check, yet is corrupt!!!!

◀ Figure 8.8c Issues with parity checking

The solution used in LANs is called the cyclic redundancy check (CRC); this is a formula that is applied by using a **polynomial**.

The computer that receives the data looks at the **co-efficient** and completes the same calculation. If the receiving computer calculates the same result of 18108, then the data packet is accepted; otherwise, it is rejected.

The probability of a different set of data giving the same polynomial with the same co-efficient is incredibly low, so this error checking mechanism is extremely reliable.

Test your knowledge

1 Define parity checking and the cyclic redundancy check.

2 What is a checksum?

3 Define polynomial and co-efficient.

What does it mean?

A **polynomial** is the result of a series of smaller formulae all with the same **co-efficient**.

A **co-efficient** means a co-related value, which is any number.

VoIP (**voice over Internet protocol**) is the method used to allow voice telecommunications to take place over a computer data network.

Activity 8.1

Cyclic redundancy check

1 Visit the ASCII Table website (go to www.heinemann. co.uk/hotlinks and entering the express code 2315P). Convert each letter of the phrase 'the cat sat on the mat' from ASCII to its decimal equivalent. (Remember that you have spaces in the phrase and the space character has a value.)

2 Take the result and then create a CRC where each value can be computed with the formula 4*ASCII where 4 is the co-efficient used to create the polynomial.

8.1.2.5 Bandwidth limitation and noise

Bandwidth limitation and noise have a considerable impact on the quality of the data being transmitted. In many cases, the quality requirement and volume of the data being downloaded is now greater than some systems can handle. With lower bandwidth systems like wireless networks, there are limits on how much data can be successfully sent at any given moment.

For bandwidth-sensitive services such as **VoIP** and Video on Demand, the central network technology has to be configured to ensure that these services have priority over any email or chat traffic.

This means that sensitive traffic will always be sent, ensuring no delays or loss in transmission. Less sensitive traffic may be stored (queued) until there is an ideal

A data packet being sent from one computer to another									
Data	Byte 1	Byte 2	Byte 3	Byte 4	Byte 5	Byte 6	Byte 7	Byte 8	The co-efficient is 2, which is the first half of the CRC.
	21	34	56	34	34	43	12	4	
Formulae with same co-efficient	$2*21^2$	$2*34^2$	$2*56^2$	$2*34^2$	$2*34^2$	$2*43^2$	$2*12^2$	$2*4^2$	
Result	882	2312	6272	2312	2312	3698	288	32	The polynomial (18108) is the second half of the CRC.

The polynomial is the addition of all the results which equals **18108**.
So **2:18108** is sent with the packet of data.

Table 8.3 A simplified example of a CRC

opportunity to send this data. This happens in terms of microseconds on a network device, so the user will notice this happening when chatting using MSM or watching a video across a network.

Noise is any external or internal interference that has an effect on the quality of the data being sent. External noise may be caused by electrical equipment or local physical features; internal noise is often caused by poor-quality cabling or connections.

Depending on the communications media selected, the effect of noise differs.

- Wireless networks rely on high-frequency radio transmissions, which are normally limited to a range of no more than 100 metres. Noise can be caused by metal-framed buildings (causing reflection and acting like a Faraday cage), as well as any powerful unshielded electrical equipment. Wireless networks tend to suffer from external interference.
- Copper cabling, as used for most data networks, is limited to a range of 100 metres for data networks. This is very susceptible to noise from external power sources, even something as simple as a power cable run. Also, with the electro-magnetic nature of the cables and the fact that many cables are run together, the cables have to be twisted to reduce internal noise (called crosstalk) and the connectors have to be 'terminated' professionally to improve the quality of the communication. Otherwise, internal reflection and crosstalk can occur, which add to the noise. In practice, both unshielded and shielded twisted pair cable are used.
- Fibre optic networks are a self-contained method of transmitting data using light. Except on low-quality connections, there is only a small chance of internal interference and no risk of external interference.

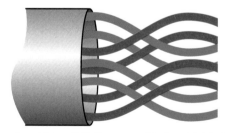

▲ **Figure 8.9 Copper cable (unshielded twisted pair)**

Test your knowledge

1. What is VoIP?
2. What is noise in the context of data transmission? What effect does it have on the data?

8.1.2.6 Channel types

The transmission of data is also reliant on the channel type: the medium used to transmit the data across considerable distances. Wireless, fibre and copper have distance limitations. The following common communications channels are in frequent use.

- **Telephone links**, often referred to as POTS (pretty old telephone system), are still used in developing nations and remote parts of the UK, as well as a backup method for accessing core networking equipment in case of a primary communications failure.
- **ISDN** (**integrated services digital network**) is a slightly dated but still used digital network connection for 'higher-speed' communications. This has now been largely superseded by ADSL and broadband.
- Transmissions sent by Bluetooth and wireless networks are defined as microwave as they operate on the 2.4 GHz band of the electro-magnetic spectrum. High-powered microwave transmission is still used in line of sight communications for high-speed network communications in large cities.
- **Radio** transmission, at lower frequencies, is used by a wide range of services to exchange data. Services such as the police, ambulance and fire use radio transmission to communicate critical information.
- **Satellite** data transmission and reception have been used for some considerable time as a method of core high-speed data transmission between countries. This facility is becoming more accessible to the individual user and small business as costs drop. Satellite transmission is reliant on atmospheric conditions as well as line of sight communication with the satellite. However, communication with a satellite in a geo-stationary orbit can increase the distance around the globe that a network can reach.

- **ADSL (asymmetric digital subscriber service)** and **broadband** are an extension of the type of technology used in a network at work or college. ADSL and broadband use an unbalanced bandwidth to improve performance. You may be able to download at a rate of two megabits per second, but your upload speed is likely to be one-tenth of this. ADSL accesses unused bandwidth on telecommunications systems and is limited to a two-kilometre reach from the telephone company relay. Newer ADSL technologies are extending this range.

8.1.2.7 Data compression

Data compression is required on low bandwidth services to improve the rate of data transmission. Compression of applications, games, images, videos and audio also still takes place; for example, the JPEG image is a compression format.

There are many formats used on different systems. A common format used in data transmission and compression of files is **Huffman coding**.

Huffman coding applies a binary sequence to characters (letters of the alphabet, digits and symbols) according to how often they are used. Therefore, if a letter is used more than others, it is given a small sequence; if a letter is uncommon, it is given a longer sequence (see Table 8.4).

E	0
A	1
I	10
O	11
U	100
S	101
T	110
D	111
....	....
X	11010
And so on, including characters such as 1234567890 and !'£$%^&*(){}[]@~'#,.<>?/	

Table 8.4 Huffman coding, based on the English language

Huffman coding thus allows data compression in the transmission of information from one system to another. Huffman coding requires a small overhead in the use of processor resources for the sending and receiving devices.

STOP

Test your knowledge

1 Name five common types of communication channel and give one property of each.

2 What is Huffman coding used for and how does it work?

8.1.3 Data elements

To transmit a packet of data from one network device to another requires that the data is constructed into a set of data elements; the principle is based on the theoretical OSI model, which is explored in greater detail on page 157.

8.1.3.1 CRC (cyclic redundancy check)

As described in section 8.1.2.4 on page 131 the cyclic redundancy check is a method used for error correction and detection in the transmission of data across any network system. The check bits are appended to the packet when it is sent by the computer.

8.1.3.2 Frames

Independent of the communication method, a frame is the data sent from one device to another. A large download will not be transferred as one item but will be divided into smaller units, and the frame is based on the **WAN** or **LAN** technology used. A common type of frame is the Ethernet frame, which is used on all LANs.

The Ethernet frame comprises seven elements:

- In the preamble, the start bits are used to identify an oncoming valid frame of data from any background noise on the cable.

OSI Layer	Data Element	Data being transmitted			
4	Datagram using the UDP or TCP protocols	Sequence number			
3	Packet of data being sent	Sequence number	IP (or logical) addresses		
2	Frame, transmitted across a WAN or LAN	Sequence number	IP (or logical) addresses	MAC address for an Ethernet LAN, interface identifier for a WAN connection	
1	Start and stop bits as well as a checksum	Sequence number	IP (or logical) addresses	MAC address for an Ethernet LAN, interface identifier for a WAN connection	Polynomial from cyclic redundancy check

Table 8.5 Data elements and their relationship to each other

Figure 8.10 The Ethernet frame ▶

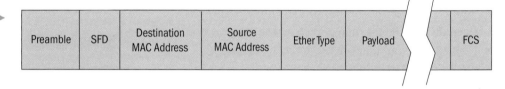

- The **SFD** (**start frame delimiter**) is the 8-bit value marking the end of the preamble. The SFD is always 101010112.
- The destination address, called the **MAC** (**media access control**) address, is a unique 48-bit physical identifier hardcoded into a computer's network card; most network devices also have one. It identifies the device to which the data is being sent.
- The source MAC address, similar to the destination MAC address, identifies the device from which the data is being transmitted.

- The **EtherType** declares what higher-level packet is being transported in the Ethernet frame. Each type has an identifier in hexadecimal which is recognised by the receiving system. Common identifiers include: 0x0800 Internet Protocol version 4 (IPv4); 0x0806 Address Resolution Protocol (ARP); 0x86DD Internet Protocol version 6 (IPv6).
- **Payload** is the term used to describe the data that is being sent.
- The **FCS** (**frame check sequence**) contains space for the CRC.

What does it mean?

WAN (**wide area network**) is a system where more than one network is connected across a distance. The Internet is an example of a complex WAN infrastructure.

LAN (**local area network**) is a self-contained network in a local geographic area. A LAN may be connected to a WAN which may, in turn, be connected to the Internet.

In networking, a **protocol** is a common method of communication, following a set of rules.

IP (Internet protocol) is used by most computers and all systems which access the Internet.

8.1.3.3 Packets

A packet of data can be a collection of frames; it will normally be sent by **protocols** such as **IP**. Unlike an Ethernet frame, which is limited to 1518 bytes, a packet can be up to 65536 bytes in size (64 kilobytes).

Figure 8.11
The computer's MAC address

When sent across an Ethernet LAN, the packet will be broken down into smaller frames. A frame may contain the payload from multiple packets. Each packet has a header, payload and trailer.

IP is now offered in two versions: version 4 and version 6. Version 4 systems can handle up to 4,294,967,296 devices, whereas version 6 systems can manage over 340,282,366,920,938,463,463,374,607,431,770,000,000 devices.

An IP packet will contain these bits of information:

- 4 bits indicate whether it is an IP version 4 or an IP version 6 packet
- 4 bits describe the header size (as this can vary)
- 8 bits are used for quality of service – this is used to prioritise traffic such as voice or video over email
- 16 bits describe the size of the entire packet
- 16 bits have identification numbers if the packet has been divided across many Ethernet frames
- 3 bits contain an identifier to indicate whether this packet is part of a divided packet
- 13 bits contain the order of packets to which this one belongs
- 8 bits are used to record the time to live: in networking, packets are sent through many devices and each one will increase the time to live – then, if the number is too high, the packet is lost and is therefore discarded

- 8 bits contain the protocol being sent: TCP, UDP, ICMP, etc.
- 16 bits contain a checksum
- 32 bits contain the source IP address
- 32 bits contain the destination IP address.

8.1.3.4 Datagrams

A datagram is the less reliable counterpart of the packet. Packets are sent via **TCP** and IP, which is designed to ensure the data reaches its destination. A datagram, however, is sent via **UDP** and IP, and this is designed to be 'best effort' – it does not matter whether the packet successfully reaches its destination.

What does it mean?

TCP (**transmission control protocol**) is used for the transfer of data which is connection-oriented and must be sent via a reliable system.

UDP (**user datagram protocol**) is used on connectionless systems; this means that the data may travel different routes and reliability is not a primary concern.

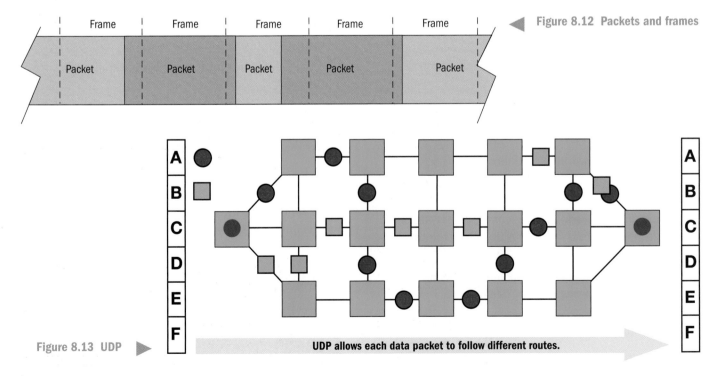

Figure 8.12 Packets and frames

Figure 8.13 UDP ▶   **UDP allows each data packet to follow different routes.**

Datagrams are used for services where the data is broadcast and no response is required from the device receiving the data. The best example of datagrams in use is web radio. With this best effort service, losing some data and missing a small part of the transmission is irritating but has no impact on the overall service.

8.1.3.5 Addresses

All networking systems use addresses. Like the postal system, it is an essential mechanism used in ensuring the data is sent to the correct destination. Table 8.6 shows the two principal types of addresses already mentioned in this unit.

8.1.3.6 Sequence numbers

When packets and datagrams are sent, they form part of a larger set of data. To ensure the data is 'reassembled' in

the correct order, each packet or datagram requires an identifier, known as a sequence number.

Consider an image being downloaded from a website. If the packets arrive in the wrong order, because some are re-sent while others travel down a faster route, the result may be a very confusing image. The sequence number ensures that the data will be reassembled exactly as it was sent.

Sequence Number	Packet Size
0	1340
1341	1290
2632	999
3631	etc

Table 8.7 Sequence number and offset

Type	Description	Example
Physical address	Can be hardcoded into a device like a network card or configured on a WAN connection.	MAC address
Logical address	Is configured by the network administrator or issued by a server and may follow a scheme.	IP address

Table 8.6 Types of addresses

Figure 8.14 UDP data stream

The sequence number is an 'offset in bytes' based on the size of the packet or datagram being sent. Figure 8.15 shows a download from a website; as each packet is added, the offset moves by 1 and the sequence number increases.

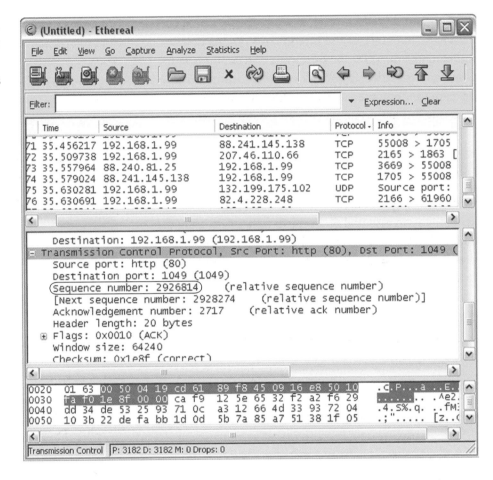

Figure 8.15 Sequence numbers

STOP Test your knowledge

1 Define frame, packet and datagram.

2 What are the seven elements of the Ethernet frame?

3 Define these terms: WAN, LAN, protocol, IP, TCP and UDP.

4 What is a sequence number used for?

8.1.4 Methods of electronic communication

When network devices communicate with each other, they use a variety of communications techniques.

8.1.4.1 Simplex, duplex and half-duplex transmission

In many systems, there are three common methods of electronic communication used: simplex, half-duplex and duplex.

- Simplex is one-way communication, with no response allowed. FM radio and keyboards are prime examples of simplex communication.
- Half-duplex is two-way communication, but only one device can transmit at a time. Most Ethernet and wireless systems use half-duplex to maximise the bandwidth; they use synchronisation and signalling to control whose turn it is to transmit.

- Full duplex is also two-way communication, but both devices can communicate simultaneously. More advanced Ethernet systems use full duplex and will only work on compatible devices. This is accomplished by the fact that most network cables are groups of eight cables and some are unused by most systems.

8.1.4.2 Parallel transmission

Parallel transmission is a rapidly diminishing technology. While it was designed to transfer data in tandem (each bit on a separate line), it was limited by distance and speed; 9 to 15 feet was the maximum reach.

Parallel has been superseded by **USB** (**universal serial bus**) among other systems. USB operates at 4 megabits per second (and higher). Each USB port on your PC can be cabled to manage up to 128 devices and so some users choose to install a USB hub.

USB offers power to some devices as well as the ability to connect a wide range of devices. Typically you can expect to connect storage devices, cameras, printers, scanners, keyboards, mice, joysticks and external network devices. In fact, the range of devices that can be connected is almost endless.

8.1.4.3 Serial transmission

While USB has superseded parallel communications, this is not necessarily the case with the **serial RS-232** (or EIA/TIA-232) standard. Some manufacturers

have started removing serial interfaces from their PC motherboards, but since all network devices require a serial connection to configure them at an advanced level, this is of some concern to their customers.

The RS-232 standard uses synchronous as well as asynchronous communication, and it is used on DCE as well as DTE devices. 25-pin, 9-pin and 8-pin connectors can be used for RS-232, each pin having a specific purpose. These are commonly identified as shown in Table 8.8.

Figure 8.17 ▶
USB

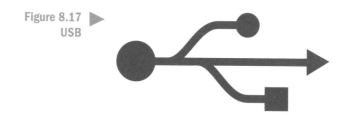

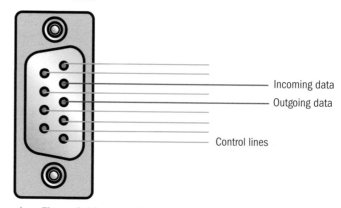

A serial connector

Incoming data
Outgoing data

Control lines

Figure 8.18 A serial connector

Figure 8.16 Parallel communication ▶

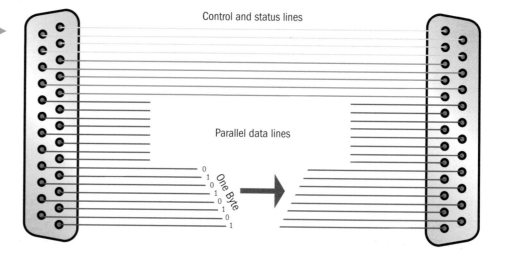

Control and status lines

Parallel data lines

0
1
0
1
0
1
One Byte

Transmitted Data (TxD)	Data sent from DTE to DCE
Received Data (RxD)	Data sent from DCE to DTE.
Request To Send (RTS)	Is it OK to transmit?
Clear To Send (CTS)	It is OK to send.
Data Terminal Ready (DTR)	I am online and ready.
Data Set Ready (DSR)	This connection is active.
Carrier Detect (CD)	Is there a signal?
Ring Indicator (RI)	Used on older telephone systems (a modem would need this)

Table 8.8 RS-232 standard

Test your knowledge

1 What are simplex, duplex and half-duplex transmission?

2 What is a USB?

3 What is the serial RS-232 standard?

8.1.4.4 Infrared, Bluetooth and WiFi

Infrared interfaces and communication are used by mobile phones, PDAs, printers and laptops as a method of local peer communication. Bluetooth has, for many systems, superseded infrared, due to its improved speed and lack of line of sight limitations.

Infrared is on the electromagnetic spectrum, slightly below visible light. For two devices to communicate with each other, they needed to have direct line of sight of each communication port (which was often on the side of the device).

Bluetooth is available in many systems. It uses an ultra high-frequency spread spectrum signal (this means that the wavelength is over 2.4 GHz). Bluetooth uses a range of frequencies and techniques to send the data. The purpose of Bluetooth is to create mobile short range networking for all small devices. So far, several benefits of Bluetooth have been identified:

- the inclusion of Bluetooth in 3G and later mobile phones allows pictures and files to be sent from one subscriber to another on a one-to-one basis
- laptop computers can be connected to a small personal area network
- it is possible to connect a PDA to a computer or a mobile phone without any cables or installation of additional software.

Most Bluetooth systems operate at a range of 10 metres; a Bluetooth **transceiver** can be used to increase the range to 100 metres.

What does it mean?

A **transceiver** is both a transmitter and a receiver, a device which may therefore act as a communications relay.

WiFi comprises wireless network cards and access points. These devices operate by radio transmission and use the IEEE (Institute of Electrical and Electronics Engineers) 802.11 standard, which is closely associated with Ethernet LAN technology. IEEE 802.11 has a set of four specifications in the family: 802.11, 802.11a, 802.11b and 802.11g. Each operates at a different frequency and speed:

- **802.11** and **802.11a** operate at speeds up to 6 megabits per second
- **802.11b** is the version commonly used for wireless networking at home, school, college or in small enterprises – it can operate at up to 11 megabits per second.
- **802.11g** operates in the 2.4 GHz range like Bluetooth but, with greater power, can offer up to 54 megabits per second.

Wireless adapters use **spread spectrum** and **narrowband** transmission techniques:

- spread spectrum uses a range of frequencies and techniques
- narrowband sends a signal over a limited frequency range.

Common practice is for an organisation that is managing a LAN to offer a wireless network infrastructure, which:

- serves to increase the range of the network into unreachable areas where it may be too costly or impractical to run a cable
- allows users to connect to the system with a laptop or PDA without being tied to a wall socket
- creates portable network centres that can be taken anywhere, hence the popularity of public wireless hotspots.

The implementation of a wireless network is based on geographic coverage. So, the area covered by the radio signal generated by the devices on the system has to be considered. Figure 8.19 gives an example of wireless coverage.

Wireless networking requires two pieces of networking equipment:

- A **wireless adapter** is a network card that, instead of connecting to a copper cable, will send a radio transmission. Computers with wireless adapters can communicate directly with each other on a **peer** basis.
- The **wireless access point** (**WAP**) (also called a **wireless bridge**) is essentially a network hub. This is connected by a copper or fibre cable to the main network. The purpose of a WAP is to share and distribute network communications.

What does it mean?

A **peer** is someone (or something) which is an equal to yourself or others (e.g. your friend is a peer). Peer devices are devices which have equal 'rights' on a networked system.

 Figure 8.19 Wireless coverage

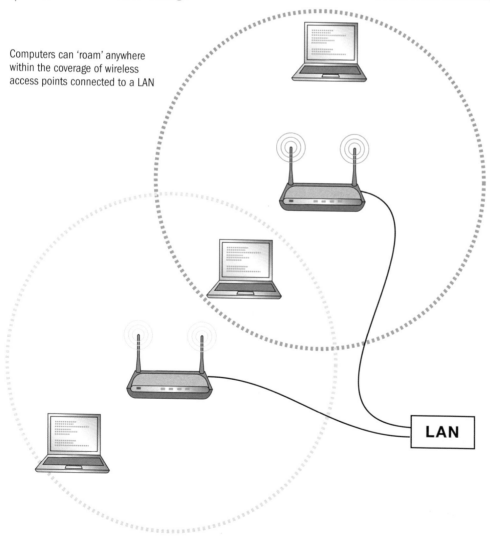

Computers can 'roam' anywhere within the coverage of wireless access points connected to a LAN

LAN

Case study

A college has recently installed an Internet café in an outbuilding that is not connected to the LAN.

1 Visit various networking retailers on the Internet and produce a spreadsheet showing how, and at what cost, 20 computers could be connected to a WAP. (You are looking only at the cost of the communications equipment; you already own the computers.)

2 Look up the term 'wardriving' on the Internet and devise an action plan to prevent this happening at the college.

Wireless network technology uses spread spectrum radio transmissions to gain the maximum bandwidth through the radio frequencies available. A spread spectrum signal is automatically varied, which gives the transmission four advantages:

- if there is interference on one frequency, the data can be successfully sent on another frequency
- the data can be shared across many frequencies
- the system can adapt if there is more than one communication taking place
- there is scope for multiple stations to operate in the same location.

Test your knowledge

1 Describe the properties of infrared interfaces, Bluetooth and WiFi.

2 Define the following terms: transceiver, wireless adapter, WAP.

8.1.5 Transmission media

A transmission medium is the technology used to carry the signal from one device to another across the network. The choice of media depends on cost, quality, speed and the range of data travel.

8.1.5.1 Coaxial cabling

Coaxial is an older method of cabling networks. Although it was the networking medium of choice during the late 1980s and early 1990s, it was rapidly replaced by UTP (unshielded twisted pair). However, more recently, coaxial cabling has made a comeback with home broadband/ADSL services and has always had a place with terrestrial TV (in a rooftop aerial).

Coaxial is so named because it has a copper core surrounded by a plastic sheath and then another copper braid (see Figure 8.20). The inner cable is used to transmit the data and the outer cable (usually an interlaced braid of copper wires) is used as a ground (connects to earth).

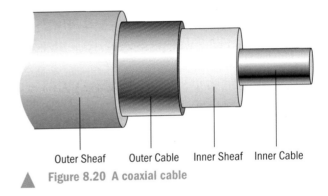

Outer Sheaf   Outer Cable   Inner Sheaf   Inner Cable

▲ Figure 8.20 A coaxial cable

8.1.5.2 UTP (unshielded twisted pair) and STP (shielded twisted pair)

UTP is the most popular cable type in use on academic and commercial networks throughout the world. UTP and STP originated during a change in phone technology in the 1980s and have endured many revisions. UTP and STP are still in use for several reasons: they are low cost in comparison to fibre optic and coaxial cabling; they are versatile and can be adapted to many uses; they can adapt to changing speeds and standards.

UTP comes in a long roll that contains eight cables inside one jacket; these cables come as coloured pairs (see Figure 8.21).

Each cable generates a small magnetic field which will create interference for the neighbouring cables. Each

Advantages of coaxial cable	Disadvantages of coaxial cable
• Can run up to 185 metres before the signal becomes weak and unreliable • Can handle high bandwidth signals, such as multiple video channels (i.e. television) • Flexible and reliable	• Susceptible to external interference and noise • Costly to install as the higher quality cable costs more to produce • Less adaptable than its UTP counterpart (see section 8.1.5.2)

Table 8.9 Advantages and disadvantages of coaxial cable

pair is twisted around each other to reduce an effect called **cancellation**, which occurs because of the close proximity of the cables – hence the term twisted pair. Four pairs are used.

UTP is susceptible to external interference and noise. With no protection, external sources such as power supplies or cables can also corrupt the data sent along the media. To overcome this, the more expensive STP cable can be used. It operates on the same principles as UTP, but has an extra foil wrapping around the cables for protection.

UTP is rated in categories – current LAN standards include categories 5, 5e, 6 and 7. Categories 1, 2, 3 and 4 (these included coaxial) are no longer used for LANs and are found solely in the domain of WAN technology (as WANs often use slower connections between buildings). Each category (see Table 8.10) is related to the quality of the cable, its connectors and the speed at which data can be sent reliably.

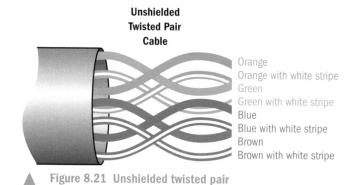

Unshielded Twisted Pair Cable

Orange
Orange with white stripe
Green
Green with white stripe
Blue
Blue with white stripe
Brown
Brown with white stripe

Figure 8.21 Unshielded twisted pair

What does it mean?

ISDN (**integrated services digital network**) is a digital telephone line that shares voice and data communications.

Mbps (**million bits per second**) is a higher measure of bps (bits per second).

Category	Maximum data rate	Usual application
1	Less than 1 Mbps	Voice cabling IDSN
2	4 Mbps	IBM token ring networks
3	16 Mbps	The original category for coaxial cable on Ethernet systems
4	20 Mbps	Short lived
5	10 Mbps	Still in use on small office, home office networks and older legacy networks
5e	100 Mbps 1000 Mbps	Ideal LAN cabling standard – will handle a guaranteed 1000 Mbps in ideal cabling circumstances
6	1000 Mbps	Higher-quality termination (wiring) allows this cable to manage continuous higher data rates
7	1000 Mbps and above	

Table 8.10 Categories of UTP

With category 6 and 7 cables, all the termination (wiring) is done within the factory or with specialist equipment. Category 5e cabling is normally terminated with an **RJ45** (see Figure 8.22) plug or socket and can easily be done in class with low-cost equipment.

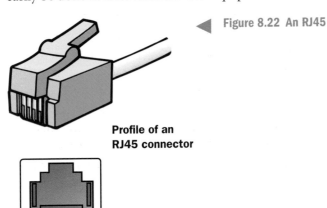

◄ **Figure 8.22 An RJ45**

**Profile of an
RJ45 connector**

8.1.5.3 Fibre optic cabling

Both coaxial and UTP rely on the transmission of data using electrical pulses down a copper cable. Fibre optic cables use light to transmit the data and so can achieve greater speeds and distances than their copper counterparts.

There are two types of cable in common use: **single-mode**, which is 8 microns in diameter, and **multi-mode**, which is 125 microns in diameter (with an inner core of 62.5 **microns**).

Figure 8.23 shows an example of a **multi-mode** fibre optic cable. The light source is a light emitting diode (LED), which sends frequent pulses of light down the cable (no pulse equals a digital 0, a pulse equals a digital 1). The light will travel around the cable based on the different densities of the medium it is travelling through.

What does it mean?

RJ (**registered jack**) is an American term for the type of plug used on a connector that has been recognised by a standards organisation.

A **micron** is a thousandth of a millimetre.

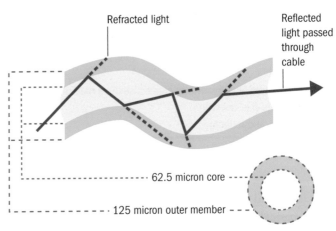

▲ **Figure 8.23 Reflection inside a fibre optic cable**

As it reaches the denser material, most of the light will be reflected and will continue its path down the cable. Some of the light will be refracted (absorbed) into the denser outer coating.

Overall this allows the light to travel up to three kilometres before it becomes too weak. On a LAN, normally the cable is run less than 285 metres, guaranteeing a signal that can carry data of one gigabit per second.

Single-mode fibre optic cable (see Figure 8.24) is thinner (8 microns) and uses a Class 3 laser to send the data. The smaller diameter reduces the angle of reflection and therefore minimises refraction and loss. A Class 3 laser is dangerous and is outside of the visible light spectrum. If you accidentally look into a Class 3 enabled fibre optic cable, you will not see any light but will burn the cells at the back of your eye. This will cause a permanent blind spot in your vision.

The fibre optic cable is surrounded by Kevlar fibre, an ultra strong resin that is used in the manufacture of bullet-proof clothing. This gives the cable strength – important when it has to be bent to fit into cable ducts.

Fibre optic cable is more costly than its copper counterparts; the termination of the cable has to be done under exacting and clean conditions.

Single-mode fibre offers less refraction

▲ **Figure 8.24 Single-mode fibre optic cable**

Test your knowledge

1 List the types of cabling available. Give the advantages and disadvantages of each.

2 Define these terms: ISDN, Mbps, RJ, micron.

8.1.5.4 Infrared, radio, microwave and satellite communications

Infrared, as mentioned in section 8.1.4.4 on page 140, is a technology which uses line of sight communication between PDSs, mobile phones and laptops. The limitation of this technology is proximity and speed, with an accepted maximum of 4 megabits per second.

Figure 8.25 Satellite communication between the UK and South Africa

Radio and **microwave** operate in similar bands on the electro-magnetic spectrum, with microwave being at the upper end of the radio wave frequencies. These communication systems are used in Bluetooth and WiFi, as described on page 140.

Satellite communications rely on the satellite being in a geosynchronous orbit, with receiving stations being positioned to communicate with these satellites. In the UK, due to our latitude (position in relation to the equator), dishes used for satellite communication have to point to a position low on the horizon towards the south. Major international satellite communications follow this rule, with the Goonhilly Satellite Earth Station being located in Cornwall, the most southerly county.

Activity 8.2

Communication for mobile workers

Communication for mobile workers has evolved considerably since the 1980s:

1 Identify what key communication technologies exist to enable a worker with a laptop to move from office to office and communicate with others.

2 If a worker wants to work from home, what technologies are available and how do they operate?

3 The worker is dropped in the middle of an uninhabited region and has suitable power from the 4x4 they are driving to power communication devices. What technologies exist to enable communication with others via the worker's laptop?

4 Can you answer the following?
   a) Why are data checking systems such as parity and CRC used?
   b) Which is the best communication medium for a LAN?
   c) What communication media are used for long distance communication?
   d) How is a signal generated?

Networked systems have become increasingly complex over the last 30 years. This section describes many of the common systems used to implement and manage a computer-based network.

8.2.1 Features of networks

8.2.1.1 Types of network

In networking, the type of network is defined by its geographic reach. The term **LAN** (**local area network**) normally describes a system contained on one site and running as a self-contained network with a connection to a **WAN** (**wide area network**) or the **Internet**. The term WAN usually describes a distance-based system which may connect many sites or organisations.

With networking speeds always increasing, these terms have become blurred. With current technology, a LAN may be spread across many locations and WANs may be international in nature. Some LANs and WANs use secure connections across the Internet to maintain their communication; for example, a home user can connect to a corporate WAN or LAN and become part of the system.

Some regions have **MANs** (**metropolitan area networks**) so that organisations with a common goal can share data and services. MANs are often found in local authorities, education and finance (for example, the City of London).

Bluetooth has defined a new technology with the **PAN** (**personal area network**) connection of laptop, PDA and mobile phone.

8.2.1.2 Network topologies

Each LAN, WAN or MAN requires a structure; this is called its **topology**. Common topologies include bus, star, ring, mesh and tree (or hierarchical) – see Table 8.11.

Some topologies are **logical** – this means the design does not reflect the actual system. An excellent example of this is the star topology. To have a central point of failure is a considerable risk, and this is overcome by having a switched network which interconnects using the bus topology (see Figure 8.26). Therefore, a network can have multiple connections in a tree or extended star using the bus infrastructure on the switches. A specialist protocol, **STP** (**spanning tree protocol**), will configure the switches to stop loops occurring and watch for any lost devices or connections on the system.

STOP Test your knowledge

1 What type of network is each of the following: LAN, WAN, MAN, PAN?

2 What is a topology?

3 Give five examples of topologies, how they work and the advantages and disadvantages of each.

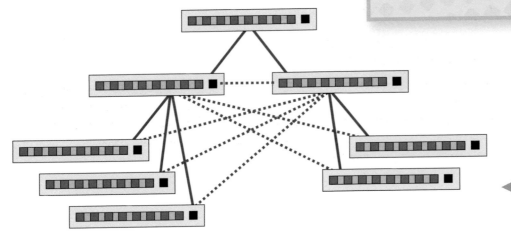

Figure 8.26 Star and bus topologies combined

Topology		Operation	Advantages	Disadvantages
Bus		A historical system centred around one cable which runs as a core. The term bus comes from the language used in describing the system bus on the motherboard. In modern networking the bus is still in use, but condensed to the circuitry of a network switch. This enables many physical and logical bus networks to be created in a process called micro-segmentation. Two computers communicating with each other on this bus have private and almost error-free communication.	It is easy to add new devices to the bus.	If cut or dislocated, one half of the system will be unable to communicate to the other. If a switch is disconnected from other switches, the local bus network is still operational but cannot communicate with the rest of the network.
Ring		Like the children's party game pass the parcel, the ring network works on an equal share, where everyone gets to communicate in turn. Used in fibre systems.	Easy to manage and everyone has equal share of the bandwidth.	Limited security as everyone can see the traffic of others. Is not ideal if the system has big talkers like file servers.
Star		With a central core to the system, all the nodes (components) of the network are directly connected. The star also comes as an extended star where one of the nodes acts as the core of another star. As a logical structure, it is closely related to the switch structure on a bus network.	Easy to add new nodes. If one node fails then the network is not affected.	If the core of the system (the hub) fails, then the whole network will fail.
Tree (or Hierarchical)		A centrally controlled and managed system in which the network can be designed to reflect an organisation structure from HQ to each branch office. (It is worth noting that the hierarchical network is a logical hybrid of the star.)	Easy to add more components.	Like the star, if the centre fails the whole system fails.
Mesh		This system enjoys multiple redundancies, where there are multiple connections and multiple routes for the data. The Internet is a large-scale version of the mesh network structure.	If more than one line fails a node can continue to communicate.	The management of this topology is very complicated as it involves circular routes, split trees and repeated information.

Table 8.11 Common topologies of networks

When transferring data across distances, across a WAN, via broadband or through wireless, a variety of network services have to be used. Common examples include packet switched, circuit switched, multiplexed, ADSL and broadband and WAP.

There are many **packet switched** WANs in operation. Popular examples include MPLS (multi-protocol label switching), ATM (asynchronous transfer mode) and frame relay.

Packet switching operates by ensuring that there is a group of **routers** or WAN switches interconnected, all communicating which connections are active and the speed and reliability of each connection.

A packet switched system can direct the traffic via a variety of routes (like the mesh topology). These can be logical **permanent virtual circuits** (**PVC**s) defined by the communications expert. One system or one connection may contain many PVCs, each oblivious to the communication of the other. Large telecommunications providers use this technology to separate the traffic of their different customers, even though they may be using the same lines across part of the network (see Figure 8.27).

To identify each PVC, different technologies use mapping or labelling techniques. This equates to each device having an identity set for each connection and directed to the connection across the system. The physical WAN topology will then differ from the logical network topology created with the PVCs (see Figure 8.28).

Circuit switched systems like ISDN create a physical wired circuit during the period of communication. This is not necessarily logical or adaptive, as the communications line has to be in place for this to happen.

For historical reasons, standards for ISDN differ in Japan, Europe and the US, so if you look up this communications standard on the Internet you may be perplexed.

ISDN was the first solution to attempt to bypass limitations set by the public telephone system to data transmission in the 1980s. ISDN is different from a public telephone line in several respects: it has the capacity to have a separate channel for data, the capability to send voice and data simultaneously and can be used for 'other signals'.

An ISDN line can be provided in one of two ways:

- **BRI** (**basic rate interface**) is used for connections to remote sites, or customers such as small business or home users
- **PRI** (**primary rate interface**) is the core circuit switched system for medium to large organisations to connect their BRI-based sites.

What does it mean?

Packet switching is a mechanism which sends network traffic in small manageable data units across the system.

A **router** is a device which connects networks and makes traffic forwarding decisions based on information learnt via its connections or a routing protocol (see page 155).

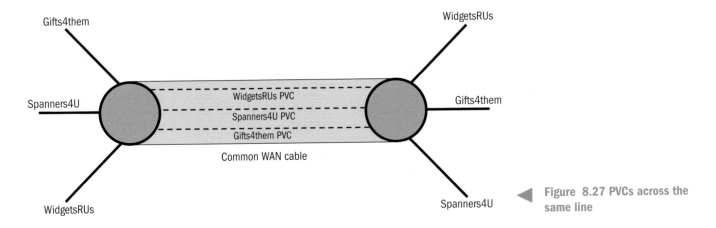

Gifts4them · WidgetsRUs · Spanners4U · WidgetsRUs PVC · Spanners4U PVC · Gifts4them PVC · Common WAN cable · Gifts4them · Spanners4U · WidgetsRUs

Figure 8.27 PVCs across the same line

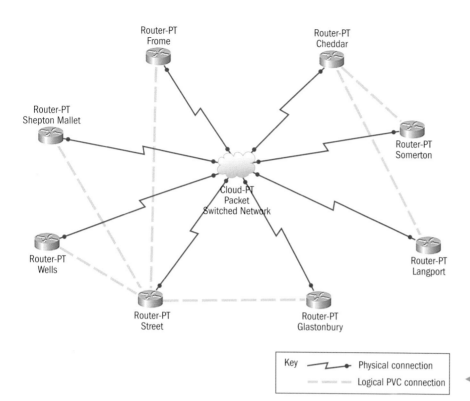

Key — Physical connection
--- Logical PVC connection

Figure 8.28 PVCs: logical versus physical topology

Each interface is divided into channels:

- A BRI can have two 64K B channels, each of which can carry voice or data, and one 16K D channel for control signals. So, you could have one voice line and one data line on a shared connection, or you could have a data line of up to 128K.
- A PRI can have up to 30 B channels of 64K and one D channel of 64K. This allows for up to 30 voice lines or data lines. If all the data lines were in use, then the PRI would have a data carrying capacity of over 1.9 megabits.

With **multiplexed communication** across a WAN, multiple communications have to use the same single channel (or communications line). Multiplexed communications is managed by a **MUX** (a term for multiplexer), which rapidly switches from one communication to another. Unlike packet switched networks, the MUX is part of a complex circuit switched system which allows more than one circuit to occur on the same line.

ADSL (**asymmetric digital subscriber line**) is a technology for transmitting digital information at higher speeds on existing phone lines to homes and businesses.

ADSL can provide a continuous connection. It is asymmetric (having no balance or symmetry) – it uses

Figure 8.29 The operation of a MUX

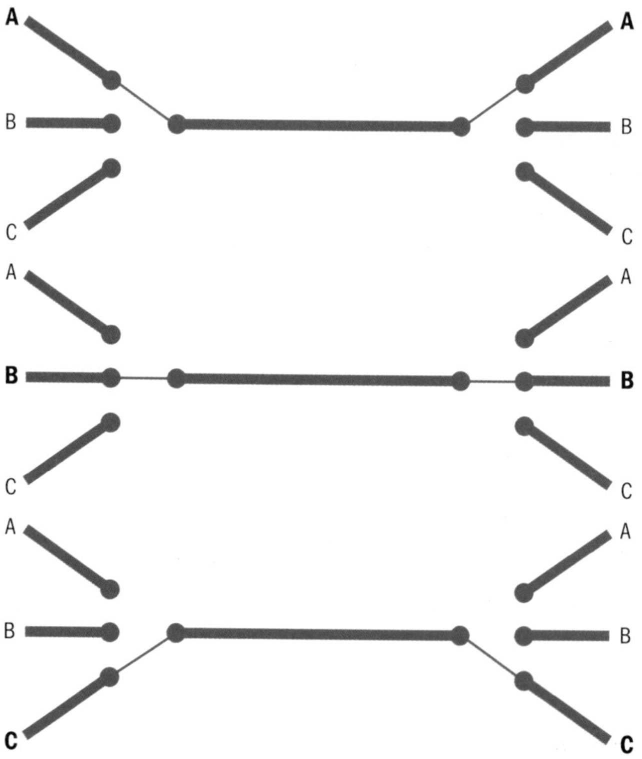

most of the transmission line to transmit downstream to the user and only a small part to receive information from the user. ADSL simultaneously accommodates analogue (voice) information on the same communications line. Some systems will transmit from 512Kbps to 10Mbps down to the user. Also, on some business ADSL systems, the company can purchase a specific 'upload' bandwidth so that they can maintain successful two-way communications with other sites or with their web server.

ADSL is designed to exploit the one-way nature of most web-based communication in which large amounts of data (web pages, etc.) are downloaded and only a small amount of control information is ever returned.

ADSL relies on the local telephone exchange being enabled for ADSL. It is also distance-to-speed limited where a modern exchange can serve homes and businesses in a two kilometre radius. **RADSL** (**remote ADSL**) has been developed to serve wider communities and is currently available in some phone exchanges in the UK.

Broadband is a general heading for a variety of technologies which include ADSL. For some ISPs, broadband is provided by sharing a range of frequencies unused by other services.

Cable TV providers offer the best example of broadband. The local cable junction which is fed into the subscriber's home offers three services: phone communication, TV and high-speed Internet. This is accomplished by multiplexing the frequencies at a core location.

Wireless access points (**WAP**) offer a hive communications medium for LAN and WAN systems. With the positioning of WAPs in crossed over fields of influence, a mesh can be created (see Figure 8.30), which ensures the roaming device always has communication and provides a method of increasing bandwidth by sharing multiple communication channels.

▼ Figure 8.30 A WAP mesh

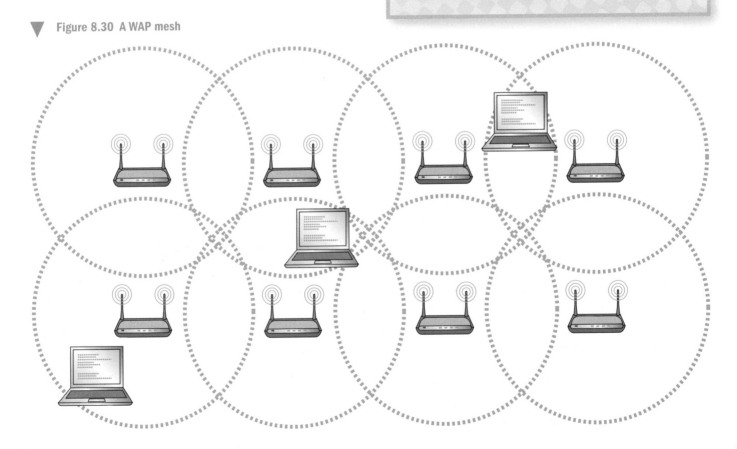

8.2.1.4 Network software

The **network operating system** (**NOS**) often resides on a server. The purpose of the NOS is to provide controlled access to common services on a network. Examples of NOS products include the current Microsoft Windows range, Linux, Unix and the IBM 'System i' platform.

A NOS is normally on a specialist computer platform with greater processor, storage, communications bandwidth and memory to handle the task. A NOS may offer a variety of services such as: printer control and management, access privileges for services and files, file management, database management, web servers, **proxy** and content management systems for Internet access, email servers, directory and **domain** control (for large systems and the Internet), Messenger and chat relay and voice traffic relay.

In the world of open-source and licence-free technologies, with some research it is possible to convert a home computer into a server and effectively turn ordinary client-based operating systems such as Windows XP or Vista into a NOS.

8.2.1.5 Network connection software

Network connection software is often referred to as a client – this software allows a system to access the services provided by a NOS and the server it is managing. The client will vary according to the service offered, such as in the examples below.

- Printer control and management clients are part of the printer wizards in Windows XP and previous Windows operating systems.
- Access privileges for services and files will be controlled centrally by the server and will be based on the login used to start the operating system profile.
- File management is accessed by Windows Explorer or FTP (file transfer protocol) clients.
- Web servers are available via Internet Explorer or Firefox.
- Proxy and content management systems for Internet access will be invisible to the user and will be contacted by Internet Explorer or Firefox.

- Email servers can be accessed via a web-based client or using applications such as Outlook.
- Messenger and chat relay are available via GAIM, Windows Live Messenger (see Figure 8.31), etc.
- Voice traffic relay is available via the Skype client.

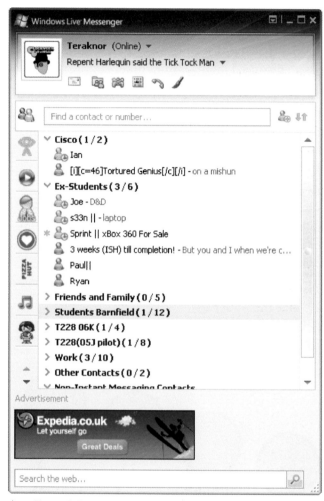

▲ **Figure 8.31 Windows Live Messenger client**

What does it mean?

A **proxy** is a person or system which acts as a go-between.

A **domain** is a group of networked computers and devices that are treated as a unit and have the same communications address.

On a LAN, devices cannot communicate whenever they feel like it. To ensure order, an **access control method** controls who has the 'next turn' for network communication. Token ring networks make each device on the system wait its turn as in the party game pass the parcel. Problems arise when there are **big talkers** on the system that need more network time.

Ethernet overcomes this problem with a best effort solution: each device on the system can send data as and when it sees fit. The problem with this solution occurs when two devices contest for the same service and a **collision** occurs (see Figure 8.32).

Each device has to wait and resend, where another collision may occur, in which case the devices have to wait and then resend the data – and so on. To overcome the collision issue, Ethernet has a solution called **CSMA/CD** which works by following five steps.

1 Check if local data line has any traffic on it (the power level will be higher).
2 If no traffic, then send data.
3 Wait for recipient to send acknowledgement.

What does it mean?

A **big talker** is a network device that communicates more than the others, normally a server.

CSMA/CD stands for **carrier sense multiple access/collision detection**. It is a method employed by Ethernet to detect and avoid continuous collisions of network data.

4 If no acknowledgement, wait for a random period of time.
5 Go back to step 1 and resend data.

CSMA/CD is commonly referred to as the **backoff algorithm** and is applied by all devices on the system. Unless the network is too busy, the reattempt is normally successful.

CSMA/CA (collision avoidance) on LAN systems is a less common variation of CSMA/CD. It is based on the detection of the signal before any data is sent. CSMA/CA is used in 802.15 (which is known as Wireless PANs or Bluetooth). It is used to stop Bluetooth devices contending with existing communications. It would be useful if you were sending a MP3 ring tone to a classmate and someone else with a Bluetooth-enabled mobile phone wandered by and unwittingly disrupted the transfer.

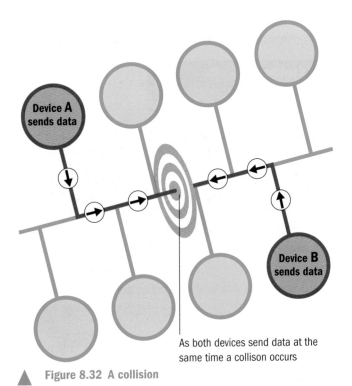

Device **A** sends data

Device **B** sends data

As both devices send data at the same time a collison occurs

▲ **Figure 8.32 A collision**

STOP Test your knowledge

1 Define the following: NOS, proxy, domain, PAN.

2 What types of service might be provided by the NOS?

3 What is a big talker? How does CSMA/CD solve the problem caused by big talkers?

4 What are the five steps followed in CSMA/CD?

8.2.2 Network components

In a network infrastructure, two devices form the 'fabric' of the network: servers and workstations. These are connected to the network via different network cards.

8.2.2.1 Servers

Servers offer many different services on a network. Each system is different and these are examples of common uses.

- Servers offer printer control and management, regulating who can print to what printer and in some cases how much they can print.
- With directory and domain control, servers manage a user's levels of access and can control their privileges for networked services and files.
- File management is achieved by ensuring the data is backed up – this involves placing files somewhere where they can be accessed by specific users or groups of users.
- Database management is achieved by controlling the integrity of the data and how the information is accessed.
- Web servers are both information services and 'retail outlets'.
- Servers used to manage common proxy and content management systems for Internet access can prevent certain users from accessing inappropriate website material.
- Email servers, Messenger and chat relay enable communication between users and customers.
- Voice traffic relay, a relatively recent development, is used to direct and manage voice communication across a network that has many users.

8.2.2.2 Workstations

The definition of a workstation has become more ambiguous over the last ten years. At one time, the term described a personal computer or terminal with access to a network. Since then, technology has advanced considerably. Nowadays, a workstation is considered to be any device which accesses services offered by the network, for example:

- a personal PC, with Windows or a similar operating system accessing the Internet at home or the network at school/college through regular phone links
- a laptop, at home, work, school/college on a regular phone link, or roaming on a wireless system like those provided at an airport or in some fast food outlets
- a PDA, anywhere with wireless roaming facilities
- an XDA (extended digital assistant), which is a PDA kitted out with mobile phone technology
- a mobile phone
- some set top boxes for cable and satellite TV, which act as clients, especially when you select on-demand TV.

8.2.2.3 Network cards

To enable workstations and servers to connect to a network infrastructure, they need a network card. For smaller devices, this may be a chip hidden on the main circuit board.

The type of network interface used depends on the communication medium available: wireless interfaces are used for Bluetooth as well as conventional wireless; for a standard Ethernet LAN, the network interface is via an RJ45 connector (see page 144).

Some network cards are specialised in the speed of service they offer with 10Mbps, 100Mbps and 1000Mbps autodetecting cards (or chips) available.

Some specialist systems have fibre optic network cards or cards for token ring systems.

▲ Figure 8.33 A network interface card for an Ethernet LAN

8.2.3 Interconnection devices

The fabric of a network is managed by a range of complex communications devices. Each has a purpose in enabling access and connectivity to the network infrastructure. This section explains more about these devices: hubs and repeaters, switches and bridges, routers, gateways and wireless devices.

8.2.3.1 Hubs and repeaters

Repeaters and hubs still exist. While they are rapidly dying out in LAN technology, their counterparts in the wireless technology community are continuously developing.

A **repeater** was used to extend the reach of a network cable (or segment) beyond the normal range of network cabling (see section 8.1.2.5 on pages 132–133). This is now considered to be an unacceptable practice as fibre optics offer a considerably superior alternative and the noise (unacceptable background interference) generated by boosting the signal renders higher-speed network connections useless.

The **hub**, which you may have seen in use over the last ten years at some centres, is a multi-port repeater. It has many connections which repeat the incoming signal to all outgoing **ports**.

The hub is part of the Ethernet bus topology and it has usage limits:

- as the data is broadcast (repeated) to all outgoing ports, there is more traffic and therefore a greater risk of collision (see page 152)
- there is no security, as everyone can see the traffic of everyone else
- speed and bandwidth are limited with greater quantity of traffic.

8.2.3.2 Switches and bridges

Bridges and switches are closely related.

The **bridge** is a simple technology formerly used in networking. Its purpose was to separate segments of a

What does it mean?

Port is a technical term for a socket or connection.

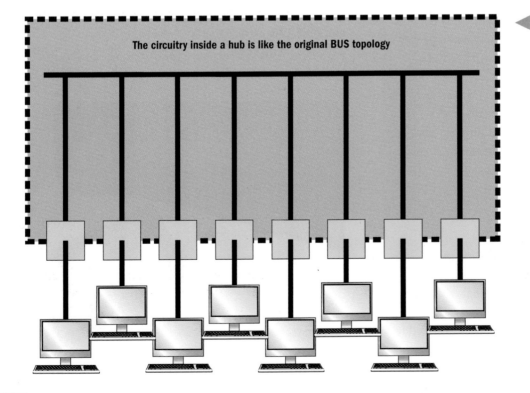

The circuitry inside a hub is like the original BUS topology

Figure 8.34 The hub device as a bus network

network and reduce the number of network broadcasts. The bridge has enjoyed a minor renaissance – some commercial VoIP (Voice over Internet Protocol) phones have internal bridges so a PC can be connected to the phone and the phone to the single outlet on the wall.

A **switch** is a complex array of bridges which has developed as networking technology becomes more complex. The switch increases the speed of communication as it creates unique mini-networks (circuits).

Switches can be implemented on a LAN to:

- increase the speed of the connection – most network systems are 100 Megabit or 1000 Megabit to the computer; you can purchase specialised or auto-sensing switches that will remotely detect the speed of the NIC
- aid control and security of the network via managed switches that can be divided into **VLAN**s
- control some large systems, which require a core switch to manage all the other switches on the system.

Switches come in a variety of specifications – you can purchase very small switches with four ports up to commercial switches with 96 ports.

The switch creates virtual circuits between each device communicating on the system, thus increasing bandwidth, improving security and reducing collisions. This is achieved by the switch storing in memory the MAC address of all devices attached to each port. This allows the forwarding decisions to be made as each MAC has to be unique.

▲ Figure 8.35 Interconnected switches

8.2.3.3 Routers

A router is actually a 'bridge with attitude'. Instead of connecting LAN segments the router will connect multiple networks, i.e. WANs. A router is a device which connects your network to the Internet, connects your network to a greater WAN, forwards traffic coming into the networks and directs outgoing traffic.

A corporate may have many switches, but only one router. So this device has to be efficient in order to move a considerable quantity of network traffic. Routers are often combined with other systems – they can provide access control and firewalls, and manage connections between different sections of a company LAN.

To operate, most routers have to be programmed and joined to a WAN using a routing protocol. The routing protocol is a limited form of artificial intelligence as it learns what devices are connected in the WAN infrastructure.

8.2.3.4 Gateways

A gateway is a device on a network which acts as an entrance point to another network, this is often referred to as the **default gateway** or the 'way out'; naturally, this is also the way in. A gateway may be a router, a switch with routing capabilities, a firewall and/or a proxy server.

A suitably advanced network will have multiple default gateways, each available if any fail. This is derived from a routing technology called **HSRP** (**hot standby routing protocol**) as shown in Figure 8.37.

What does it mean?

VLAN stands for **virtual local area network** – it is a method used to divide a LAN into smaller logical structures.

A **default gateway** is a device, which may be a router or switch, that will enable your device to connect to another network, such as the Internet.

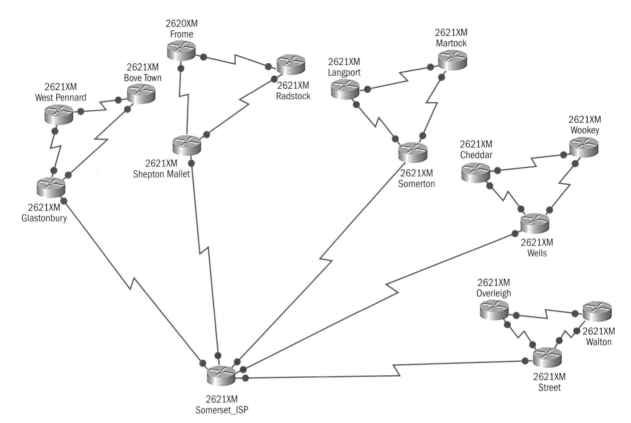

▲ Figure 8.36 An infrastructure of routers

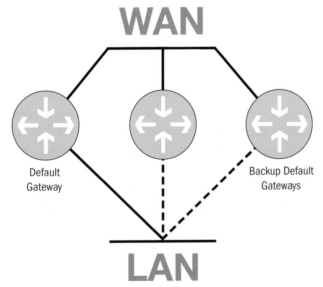

▲ Figure 8.37 HSRP for managing default gateways

Like access points, these devices are also hubs but with a different technology and differing sensibility. Devices can be connected together on a peer or ad hoc basis. There may also be a hub (WAP) to control and direct traffic, often to a cabled network infrastructure.

▼ Figure 8.38 WAPs

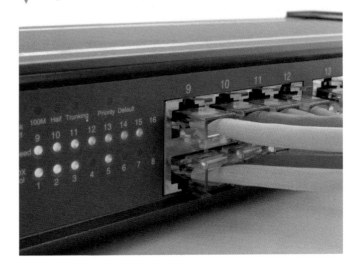

Test your knowledge

1 Define the following terms: repeater, hub, port, switch, bridge, router.

2 What is a VLAN?

3 What is a gateway and a default gateway?

Activity 8.3

Topologies

1 Compare the different topologies and describe the advantages each offers.

2 Visit a well-known networking retailer's website and complete a price comparison for all the different devices described in section 8.2.3. Explain why some devices are 'better' than others and how they may enhance the network at your centre.

3 Can you explain:
   a) why different topologies exist?
   b) why there are differing standards of ISDN?
   c) the purpose of a router?
   d) how a server supports a network?

8.3 Transmission protocols and models

Protocols offer different methods of communication between devices on a networked system. To ensure that the communication devices operate fairly and in a controlled fashion, models are used to describe the controls in place. One of the most commonly used models is the OSI model.

8.3.1 The OSI Model

The OSI (open systems interconnection) model is a logical ideology which describes network communication between network devices. Because of the variety of manufacturers and technologies, the ISO (International Standards Organisation) agreed the OSI model to ensure that differing computer systems could communicate effectively with each other.

The benefit of the OSI model is that it makes no difference if you are on a Windows-based system at home and the website you are visiting is on a Linux platform – it ensures that all devices concerned in this communication act equally and effectively.

The OSI model (Table 8.12) is represented by seven layers, with 7 being the top (nearer the user, who is considered to be layer 8 by some experts) and 1 at the bottom for the communication medium (the data leaving the computer).

8.3.2 Communication protocols

For systems to communicate physically and to ensure information is successfully transferred, a communications **protocol** standard has to be agreed.

Layer	OSI role	Component
7	Application	Used for applications such as email and web browsers, this layer has many protocols associated with its operation.
6	Presentation	Is responsible for the organisation of the data into a format usable by humans. There are as many presentation layer entities as there are media types. Common examples include: ASCII (American Standard Code for Information Interchange), which is the plain text used for HTML (web page) documents Doc, for word documents JPG (Joint Photographic Engineers Group) for images MP3 (Multimedia Players Engineers Group, format 3) for audio media etc.
5	Session	This allows you to have multiple browser, chat and email windows open simultaneously without any conflicts in the data transmitted.
4	Transport	Devices such as firewalls and layer 4 switches operate at this layer; here the traffic providing security and prioritisation is controlled. This is essential when VoIP (Voice over Internet Protocol) operates, as it needs to have the greater share of any bandwidth. Protocols such as TCP and UDP exist at this layer; each network communication channel is called a port.
3	Network	The logical address for the server or workstation is managed on this layer. The most common protocol in use is TCP/IP (Transmission Control Protocol/Internet Protocol) where a dotted decimal IP address is allocated to the network card (e.g. 10.189.12.3). Routing (the movement of data between networks) takes place at this layer and is completed by routers.
2	Data link	On a LAN, the data link layer has a physical address (called a media access control (MAC) address) which is used to identify each device (normally hardwired into a chip on the network card). Some WANs have a similar addressing scheme, which is simpler. At the data link layer you will find network cards and Ethernet switches, as well as specialist WAN connections such as ATM, ISDN, frame relay and the lower part of MPLS.
1	Physical	This is principally the media, cables or wireless. The physical layer concentrates on the transmission and encoding of the bits of data (010101010111). A wireless access point operates at this level, but uses layer 2 to maintain control.

Table 8.12 The OSI model

Test your knowledge

1 What does the acronym OSI stand for?

2 What is the OSI model used for?

3 What are the seven levels of the OSI model?

8.3.2.1 Standards

The **IEEE** regulate the standards agreed for different communications systems to operate – see Table 8.13.

By acting as the regulator, they ensure that everyone creates a system that will communicate with other systems.

The **Infrared Data Association** (**IrDA**) defines the standards for PAN communication with infrared receivers and transmitters. IrDA standards follow the principles set by the OSI model.

What does it mean?

Protocol is a common method of communication and information exchange.

802.1	Higher layer LAN protocols	Used for LAN control, such as MAC security, VLANs and the Spanning Tree Protocol
802.2	Logical link control	Defines whether a system is connectionless or connection-oriented
802.3	Ethernet	A collection of standards which define the operation of Ethernet across multiple systems
802.5	Token ring	Defines the operation of token ring networks
802.11	Wireless LAN (WiFi certification)	Defines the 802.11a, b, g and n standards; each definition looks at distance and speed
802.15	Wireless PAN	Definition for low-power short-range networking devices; ZigBee is a standard being developed at the time of writing for devices requiring lower processing payloads than those demanded of Bluetooth
802.15.1 802.15.4	Bluetooth certification ZigBee certification	
802.16	Broadband Wireless Access (WiMAX certification)	Definition of a standard for Mesh
802.16e	(Mobile) Broadband Wireless Access	
802.17	Resilient packet ring	Used for fibre optic communication systems

Table 8.13 IEEE standards

The lowest levels of control ensure the physical layer with range of 0.2–1 metres, angle of +-15°, speed of 2.4 Kbit per second to 16 Mbit per second, modulation (how the signal is sent) and the infrared window. The data link or access control establishes the discovery of potential communication partners, a reliable connection in both directions and the negotiation of device roles.

Cellular radio enables mobile phone technology: the UK and other developed regions have a 'cellular' coverage of base stations to ensure continuous mobile telecommunications. In the UK, however, cellular coverage is not complete, with remote areas lacking mobile communications for some networks.

GSM (**global system for mobile communications**) is the set of standards used to define how communication is managed on a cellular radio network. GSM technologies are described according to their generation (see Table 8.14), with most phones in current use being 2G (2nd generation) or later.

TCP/IP is a complex suite of protocols that operate on four layers to enable LANS, PANs and WANs to intercommunicate. The standards for TCP/IP are long standing and are under constant review and development. TCP/IP and its logical model are explored on page 161.

▼ Figure 8.39 Cellular coverage

0G	The first cellular communications systems date from the 1980s.
1G	The first common analogue phones were in use from the mid-1980s to no later than 1998. 1G was used as the method for communication, but was insecure and subject to hijacking and listening scandals.
2G	This first digital standard used less power than its analogue counterpart and led the way for smaller phones. It suffered issues around distance from base stations which was not a primary concern for its analogue counterpart. 2.5G was a revision which allowed data exchange, such as **WAP** for mobile phone web pages via **WML (wireless mark-up language)** and the downloading of ring tones.
3G	Provides the ability to communicate via voice and data simultaneously and has the bandwidth capacity to offer mobiles video phone services. In the transfer of data, 3G uses **UMTS (universal mobile telecommunications system)** as a standard to ensure different phones on different networks and in different regions are all compatible in the transfer of data.
4G	Conceptual and under development at the time of writing, this system offers technology closer to wireless networks.

Table 8.14 Development of GSM technologies

One of the greatest issues with wireless networks is wireless security, or the lack of it. The standards for wireless systems dictates that, when a user first plugs in a WAP and connects using a wireless network card, there must be no security to ensure connectivity.

This means that many home and commercial wireless networks are insecure, thus enabling others to steal bandwidth or snoop on the system.

Many standards for wireless security are designed to overcome this problem. Protocols such as **WEP** (**wired equivalent privacy**) ensure that the devices exchange a common key, which is set by the user, and encrypt every packet sent via this key. WEP is available in two forms: the 64-bit version has a 10 hexadecimal digit key; the 128-bit version has a 26 hexadecimal digit key.

The wireless connection on a computer, PDA or laptop will also need to be configured for WEP.

STOP

Test your knowledge

1 What is a protocol?
2 Which types of standards are defined by the following: IEEE, IrDA, GSM and TCP/IP?
3 What is WEP?

Figure 8.40 WEP configuration

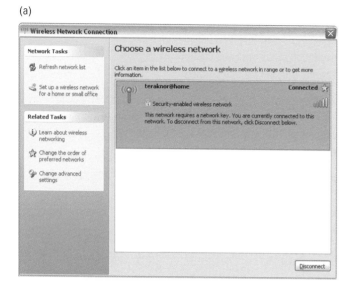

(a)

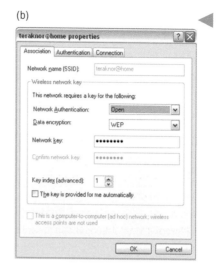

(b)

Figure 8.41 Wireless network configuration

8.3.3 TCP/IP model

The Internet development was based on the standards of the TCP/IP four-layer model and gained credibility because of its various protocols. While the OSI model is not generally used to build networks, it is often used as a guide for those who need to understand network communication.

The OSI and TCP/IP models are similar in that both use layers to distinguish tasks; they also have very similar transport and network layers. Networking professionals need to know both models and their differences.

The TCP/IP protocol suite has an extensive range of protocols working at each layer of the OSI model (and the TCP/IP model).

OSI model		TCP/IP model	
Application	Application layers	Application	Protocols
Presentation			
Session			
Transport	Data Flow layers	Transport	
Network		Internet	Internet
Data Link		Data Flow (or Network Access layer)	
Physical			

Table 8.15 OSI and TCP/IP models

- **FTP** (file transfer protocol) is used for file exchange and storage.
- **Telnet** is used for remote access and control of servers and networking equipment such as routers.
- **HTTP** (hyper text transfer protocol) is used for the distribution of web pages.
- **HTTPS** (hypertext transfer protocol secure) is used in credit card and other secure web transactions.
- **POP3** (Post Office Protocol version 3) is used to collect email from an ISP.
- **SMTP** (simple mail transfer protocol) is used for sending emails.
- **TFTP** (trivial file transfer protocol) is used by network devices to back up critical data, simply and quickly.
- **DNS** (domain name system) is used to match easy-to-remember domains, such as www.bbc.co.uk, to IP addresses like 82.165.26.58 (which are not so easy to remember).
- **TCP** (transmission control protocol) is used for connection-oriented systems.
- **UDP** (user datagram protocol) is used for connectionless systems.
- **IP** (Internet protocol) is used to identify a computer and all devices on a network.
- **ICMP** (Internet control messaging protocol) is used by a variety of management applications, including Ping, to test communication.

4. Application layer In TCP/IP the application layer also includes the OSI Presentation layer and Session layer. This layer includes all of the processes that involve user interaction. The application determines the presentation of the data and controls the session (which is true for the Windows operating system). In TCP/IP the terms socket and port are used to describe communications routes.	**Protocols**
3. Transport layer In TCP/IP there are two transport layer protocols. The Transmission Control Protocol (TCP) guarantees that information is received as it was sent. The User Datagram Protocol (UDP) does not perform end-to-end reliability checks (see page 136) and so is faster but less reliable than TCP.	
2. Internet layer The Internet Protocol (IP) is the TCP/IP Network layer. Because of the inter-networking emphasis of TCP/IP this is commonly referred to as the Internet layer. All upper and lower layer communications travel through IP as they are passed through the TCP/IP protocol suite.	**Internet**
1. Data Flow or Network Access layer In TCP/IP the Data Link layer and Physical layer are normally grouped together. TCP/IP makes use of existing data link and physical layer technologies (i.e. LANS and WANS) rather than defining its own. This ensures that TCP/IP is adaptable and can work across a multitude of different systems.	

Table 8.16 TCP/IP model layers

OSI Layers	Some TCP/IP protocols							
7 Application	FTP	Telnet	HTTP	POP3	SMTP	HTTPS	TFTP	
6 Presentation								
5 Session	DNS							
4 Transport	TCP	UDP						
3 Network	IP	ICMP	EIGRP	OSPF	BGP	RIP	HSRP	DHCP
2 Data Link	ARP	RARP						
1 Physical								

Table 8.17 Some TCP/IP protocols

- **EIGRP** (extended interior gateway routing protocol), **OSPF** (open shortest path first), **RIP** (router information protocol) and **BGP** (border gateway protocol) are all used by routers to manage communication and connectivity between different network infrastructures.
- **HSRP** (hot standby routing protocol) enables a LAN to have multiple default gateways for extra reliability.
- **DHCP** (dynamic host configuration protocol) is used to issue IP addresses to devices during the login process for a network.
- **ARP** (address resolution protocol) and **RARP** (reverse address resolution protocol) are used to match IP addresses to MAC addresses on a computer.

Test your knowledge

1 What are the four layers of the TCP/IP model?

2 Give ten examples of TCP/IP protocols. What does each acronym stand for and what is each protocol used for?

Activity 8.4

Protocols and models

1 Compare the OSI and TCP/IP models. What advantages do each offer and how are they implemented at your centre?

2 Many protocols are mentioned in this section, the majority of which will be used in your centre's network. Carry out a survey of protocol use at your centre and establish which are the most commonly used.

3 Thinking points:
   a) Why do the TCP/IP and OSI models exist?
   b) Why are there differing standards in networking and what are their benefits?
   c) What is the purpose of the TCP/IP suite individual protocols?

8.4 Internet communications

With the scale of the Internet constantly expanding, different technologies and protocols have to be employed to enable access across our planet and potentially beyond.

8.4.1 Internet communication

Internet communications rely on TCP/IP to operate (see page 161). The Internet is a massive network of interconnected networks and can continuously grow because of its ability to allow new systems to connect to the edge of the existing Internet.

The Internet is not one single technology, but a heterogeneous (all mixed together) combination of technologies. During daily use of the Internet, a user probably only experiences around one-tenth of the technology in use.

8.4.1.1 Internet terminology

The term **worldwide web** (**www**) describes the interconnection of web servers and search engines via HTML (hypertext mark-up language). The single anchor tag creates a hyperlink from one page to another on a website. It can also create a link from one website to another. For example:

<a href='http://www.teraknor.co.uk'>Please Visit Me</a>

To transfer a web page, a web server uses **HTTP** and **HTTPS**. These protocols deal with the delivery of a web page (called a 'get') and the submission of data from web page forms (called a 'put').

FTP (**file transfer protocol**) does very much as its name suggests. Basic file and data transfer can be accomplished using HTTP, but for large collections of files, uploading websites and common information exchange FTP is still the preferred technology.

Internet Explorer can be used as an FTP client. There are many applications such as CuteFTP which offer more complex services.

SMTP (**simple mail transfer protocol**) is a language used to transfer email from a client to a mail server; this is often the protocol exploited by Internet worms and junk email scams.

SMTP is a 'command language' which can be used within other programming languages such as Java. The code shown in Figure 8.42 could be used to send an email if the name of the mail server is correct.

```java
import java.io.*;
import java.net.*;
public class SMTP
{
public static void main(String[] args) throws IOException
{
Socket echoSocket = null;
PrintWriter out = null;
            String host = "mail.mycollege.ac.uk";
try
{
echoSocket = new Socket(host, 25);
out = new PrintWriter(echoSocket.getOutputStream(), true);
}
catch (UnknownHostException e)
{
System.err.println("Don't know about host");
System.exit(1);
}
catch (IOException e)
{
System.err.println("Couldn't get I/O for the connection");
System.exit(1);
}
            String userInput = "";
            userInput="helo";out.println(userInput);
            userInput="mail from: me@mycollege.ac.uk";out.println(userInput);
            userInput="rcpt to: webmaster@mycollege.ac.uk";out.println(userInput);
            userInput="data";out.println(userInput);
            userInput=" Too Much Too Little Too Late";out.println(userInput);
            userInput="";out.println(userInput);
            userInput=".";out.println(userInput);
            userInput="";out.println(userInput);
            out.close();
            echoSocket.close();
}
}
```

▲ Figure 8.42 Java script incorporating SMTP code

http:// www.teraknor.co.uk :8080 /genres/startrek ?series=DS9   ◄ Figure 8.43 Dissection of the URI

scheme   host   port   path   query

Scheme the protocol used such as ftp or http
Host the DNS (domain name system) entry for the website you wish to visit
Port the TCP or UDP channel you wish to transfer the data (8080 is often used by proxy servers)
Path the directory and subdirectory used to store the web page or service
Query a web form entry set of information sent to the web server
Fragment additional information sent to the web server

8.4.1.2 URL

The URL (Uniform Resource Locator) is a popular synonym (similar term or word) for the URI (Uniform Resource Identifier). The URI can be dissected into six sections as shown in Figure 8.43.

8.4.1.3 Internet technologies and services

The Internet and WWW are used for an immense range of technologies and services including **wikis**, which are online encyclopaedias, guides and information services (e.g. Wikipedia), **blogs** (short for web logs) and the video equivalent **vlogs** (see the VlogMap Community website). (To visit the Wikipedia and VlogMap Community websites, go to www.heinemann.co.uk/hotlinks and enter the express code 2315P.)

Video conferencing can be easily accomplished with a low cost webcam. Software providing this service is now freely available, with Windows Live Messenger and Skype offering competing alternatives. These applications offer **direct communication** via voice, video and text (chat). (See also section 8.4.3.2 on page 167.)

Email offers long-term storage of conversations as well as the exchange of files, information and ideas. Together with the Internet, email is one of the main causes of improved global communication, mainly because it is

not dependent on time barriers. Although email now seems indispensable, it has only become commonly used in the last ten years. (See also section 8.4.3.3 on page 168.)

Test your knowledge

1 What are URL and URI?

2 Give an example of a URL and name each section of the URL.

3 Define these terms: wiki, blog and vlog.

8.4.2 System requirements

When setting up a computer system for Internet communication, you need to consider the different technologies available:

- wired systems, like UTP network cards or fibre connections
- mobile systems such as Bluetooth or Wireless for an Internet connection
- hardware with the specification of the computer system, PDA or laptop as well as the specification of the network card (type and speed) and the communication media type (fibre, wired or wireless)
- the communication services you intend to use, such as email, video, voice, chat or Internet gaming
- software such as Internet Explorer or Firefox for web access, as well as the operating system to use on the computer system, such as Windows XP or Vista, Linux or Windows Mobile.

What does it mean?

Blogs are online journals describing everyday personal occurrences of Internet users.

HOW TO CONFIGURE YOUR INTERNET CONNECTION

Figure 8.44 Network connections

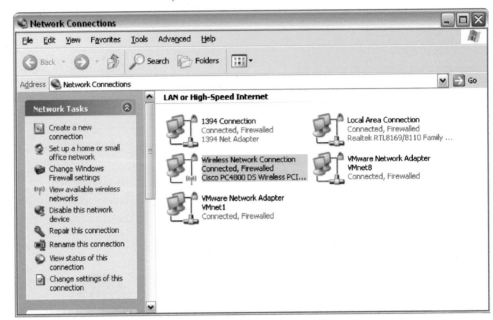

1 Using Windows XP, Internet configuration and communications set up is a very straightforward process provided you have essential information to hand in advance:

- the IP address of the default gateway
- the IP address of the DNS server(s)
- the IP addressing scheme (or whether the system uses DHCP to issue IP addresses).

For this example, the following addresses are used:

- the IP address of the default gateway is 192.168.1.1
- the DNS server IP address is 194.168.8.100
- the IP address being given to the computer is 192.168.1.99 with a subnet mask of 255.255.255.0

2 Make sure that the network card is correctly installed and the connection is valid to the switch or WAP.

3 Right click on the **My Network Places** icon on the desktop or from the **Start** menu to open the **Network Connections** dialogue box. Alternatively, select **Start/Control Panel/Network Connections**.

4 You will be able to see in the **Status** column if a connection is connected or disconnected. Click on the connection you are using to connect to the Internet.

5 Right click and select **Properties**. On the **Networking** tab select **Internet Protocol (TCP/IP)**.

6 Click on **Properties** and change the settings to those recommended at the start of this example.

7 To test if your connection has worked you could open the browser and visit a website.

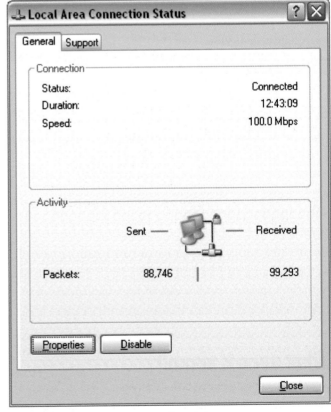

Figure 8.45a LAN connection status

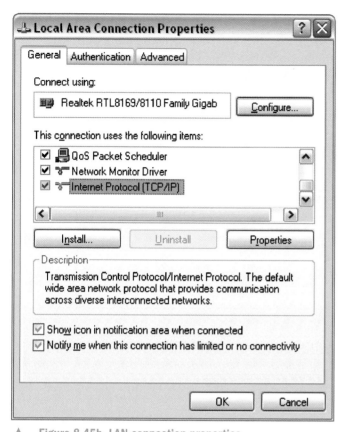

Figure 8.45b LAN connection properties

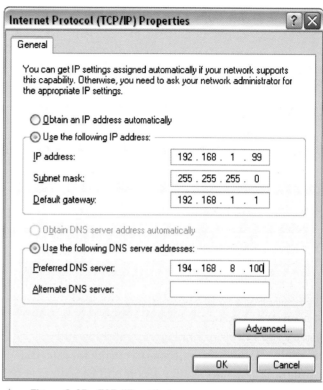

Figure 8.45c TCP/IP settings

8 If it is not working, follow these steps.
  • Check the cable or connection.
  • Check that your settings are correct.
  • Check whether the operating system has recognised the network card correctly.
  • Check whether the switch or WAP is working correctly and is connected to the Internet.
  • Check that you have used the correct addresses when configuring the local IP address, default gateway, subnet mask and DNS server.

8.4.3 Direct communication

8.4.3.1 Chat

Chat is a simple one-to-one or one-to-many text-based communication system which relies on a central relay server to pass the conversation between all the clients. Systems such as IRC, Skype, AOL Instant Messenger and Microsoft Messenger all support text-based chat.

8.4.3.2 Video communication

Video communication is bandwidth intensive and was once used only by commercial organisations to reduce the cost of transatlantic trips for essential meetings. With the development of lower-quality (in comparison) webcams and an increase in speed with broadband communications, the average Internet user can easily obtain a webcam at low cost and already has the software installed to support this.

Video communication can take place using the same applications described in section 8.4.3.1 on chat and can support voice as well as text-based communication.

8.4.3.3 Email

Email has been available on networked systems since the early 1970s and the technology has changed little since, with a few minor improvements in security.

Email relies on a server acting as a post office, relaying the messages across the Internet to other mail servers in each domain (using DNS as the method for locating these servers).

Your email client could be an application such as Outlook or Eudora, or a web page such as Hotmail or GMail. Currently email use accounts for over half of all Internet traffic.

8.4.3.4 Web phone

Voice communication over the Internet differs from communication via mobile phones and land-based phone systems that we use every day. This is an emerging technology and is still improving as you read this section. Web phones are classed as VoIP (Voice over Internet Protocol) technology. Establishing and managing a voice conversation across the Internet is a complex process as the lines of communication must be reliable and the conversation must not be affected by any interference (delay in delivery of the data).

Protocols such as **SIP** (**Session Initiation Protocol**) are used to establish and manage web phone calls, with applications such as SipGate using this protocol to enable free or low cost calls to your home computer.

Activity 8.5

Internet communications

1 Identify how different domain names and URLs are constructed. Compare URLs of different types of organisations: for example, educational establishments, charities, commercial websites, etc.

2 Compare different email, chat and video/voice communication systems and identify how their integration is leading to a single common method of communication.

3 Thinking points:
   a) What protocols are in common use on the Internet?
   b) What technologies are used on the Internet and how is this set to evolve?

Preparation for assessment

Task 1 (P1, P2, P4, M1, M2)

Identify and explain the different types of communication devices in use. Using the modem as an example, create a diagram to explain the principles of signal theory and annotate this diagram with information on the techniques that can be used to reduce errors in transmissions.

Wireless, fibre and copper transmission media are chosen in particular situations. Explain why this is the case and how they operate.

Task 2 (P3, D1)

Critically compare the OSI seven-layer model and the TCP/IP model, looking in detail at what operates at each layer of these models. Describe the communication protocols used at each layer and explain why they are important.

Task 3 (P5, P6, P7, M3, D3)

For this task, you need to set up communication between two networked devices which must connect to a LAN and may also connect to the Internet. To complete this you must:

- identify common network components and describe their roles and how they are interconnected
- describe the features of networks and the communication services offered
- describe Internet communication and what is required to enable a computer to connect to the Internet.

Keep a photo/screenshot diary of your task, ensuring you have explained each stage completed.

Compare and evaluate data transfer over both wireless and wired networks. What advantages does each type of network offer and why?

Task 4 (D2)

What access control methods are employed by wireless and wired networks? Which do you think is the best method? Justify your choice.

Organisational Systems Security

Introduction

In the management of any networked computer system, ICT professionals need to consider every aspect of the system's security to protect the corporate interests of the organisation it supports.

This unit describes threats, methods of securing systems and their impact on various organisations. As you read this, please consider that there are already more threats to your system than are mentioned here, be it at home, college or work.

WATCH OUT!

This unit covers 'hacking technologies'. Carrying out some of the techniques explored in this chapter on a network without the direct permission of the network manager is a criminal offence; see the section on the Computer Misuse Act on page 202.

After completing this unit, you should be able to achieve these outcomes:

- Know potential threats to ICT systems and organisations
- Understand how to keep systems and data secure
- Understand the organisational issues affecting the use of ICT systems.

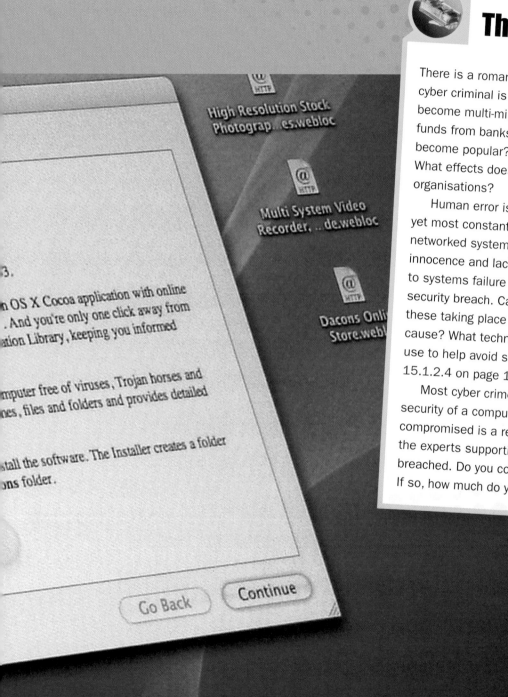

Partial text visible on the installer screen:

3.

n OS X Cocoa application with online
. And you're only one click away from
ation Library, keeping you informed

mputer free of viruses, Trojan horses and
nes, files and folders and provides detailed

stall the software. The Installer creates a folder
ons folder.

Go Back   Continue

Desktop icons:

High Resolution Stock
Photograp...es.webloc

Multi System Video
Recorder, ...de.webloc

Dacons Onli
Store.webl

Virex 7.2.pkg

Thinking points

There is a romantic notion that the intent of the cyber criminal is to subvert governments or to become multi-millionaires through the redirection of funds from banks. Why do you think this notion has become popular? Do you think that this is true? What effects does cyber crime have on organisations?

Human error is probably the most unpredictable yet most constant cause of security issues in any networked system. Forgetfulness, ignorance, innocence and lack of knowledge can all contribute to systems failure and the increased potential of a security breach. Can you think of any examples of these taking place and the problems that they cause? What techniques could a network manager use to help avoid such problems? (See also section 15.1.2.4 on page 180.)

Most cyber crime and situations where the security of a computer system has been compromised is a result of ignorance on the part of the experts supporting the system which has been breached. Do you consider yourself to be an expert? If so, how much do you (or don't you) know?

The landscape of threats to an organisation and the ICT which supports it is constantly changing with new, imaginative and often destructive ideas being inflicted on the world at large all the time. This section looks at potential threats and their impact on organisations. These include: methods for gaining unauthorised access, damage and destruction of systems and information, information security, e-commerce threats, counterfeit goods and the overall impact of threats on organisations.

15.1.1 Unauthorised access

Gaining unauthorised access is the desire of all hackers and budding cyber criminals. Ensuring they do not achieve their heart's desire is one of the many roles of the ICT professional.

15.1.1.1 Internal and external threats

To appreciate the types of threats posed to any system, you need to identify the different internal and external threats in existence.

Unfortunately, you cannot rely on all the people using your network to be entirely trustworthy. Internal threats and external threats may include those shown in Table 15.1.

Internal threats from within your system	External threats from outside the network infrastructure
Use of scanners	Virus attacks
Man in the middle attacks	Trojans
Magic disk tactics	Worms
Key logging	Hacking with piggybacking, tunnels and probes
	Forging data
	Phishing and identity theft

Table 15.1 Internal and external threats

Scanners

Scanners enable unscrupulous people to establish what methods may be used to 'attack' a system. They range from very simple to advanced, depending on the tactics used. On the Internet in the public domain it is possible to download scanners to scan a range of addresses, identifying whether they are active and learning what TCP ports (see Unit 8, page 136) are visible. Some scanners use DNS to map the discovered IP address to a domain name. This tactic is used by hackers to establish what systems are active and therefore available to hack.

Scanning does have a legitimate use in allowing network professionals to check computers and other network devices remotely.

There are a range of scanners for legitimate purposes which can be obtained easily, each serving a different specialist purpose, including: looking at a range of addresses, conducting a deep probe of one system and scanning a wireless system.

Range of addresses: A simple, visual and fast scanner which looks at a range of addresses is the Angry IP Scanner, which can be downloaded from the Angryziber Software website (go to www.heinemann.co.uk/hotlinks and enter the express code 2315P). This can be used to

What does it mean?

Scanners are software utilities used to analyse vulnerabilities in a network.

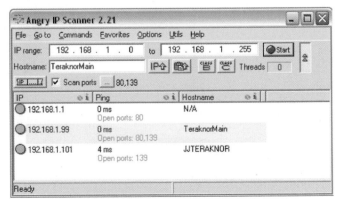

Figure 15.1 Angry IP scanner

scan a large range of IP addresses at high speed and can be used to check TCP ports during the scanning process.

Deep probe: Completing a deep probe can reveal useful information about a device, and can be used when there is a remote fault as well as to gain illicit information. Considered by many to be the best at this is Nmap, which can be downloaded from the Insecure website (go to www.heinemann.co.uk/hotlinks and enter the express code 2315P).

Nmap is a command-based tool, which offers many scanning options.

Scanning a wireless system: Wireless systems are especially vulnerable if there is no encryption (see page 190 in this unit and Unit 8, page 160). But in mobile networking, there is a need to establish where the wireless access points are and how they can be accessed if you are to connect your laptop, PDA or mobile phone.

Windows offers a simple tool which can be found when you click on the network icon for your wireless network connection.

Many 'scanning' tools for wireless networks are available via the Internet, many to gain illicit access. Tools such as the Retina Network Security Scanner (which can be downloaded from the eEye Digital Security website – accessed via www.heinemann.co.uk/hotlinks, express code 2315P) allow professionals the legitimate opportunity to find access points within range of the mobile device.

Figure 15.2 Nmap scan result ▶

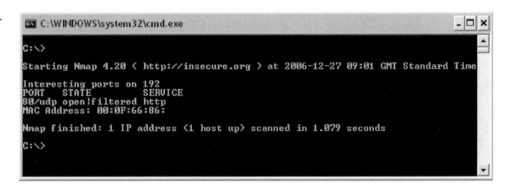

◀ **Figure 15.3 Windows Wireless Networking**

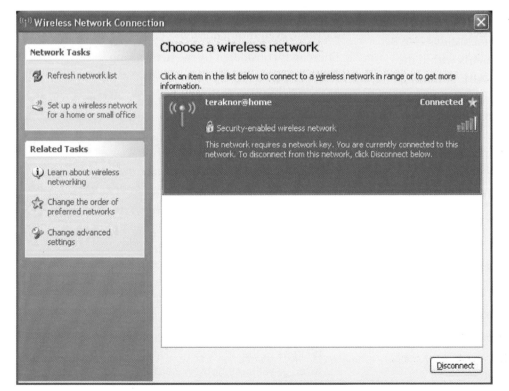

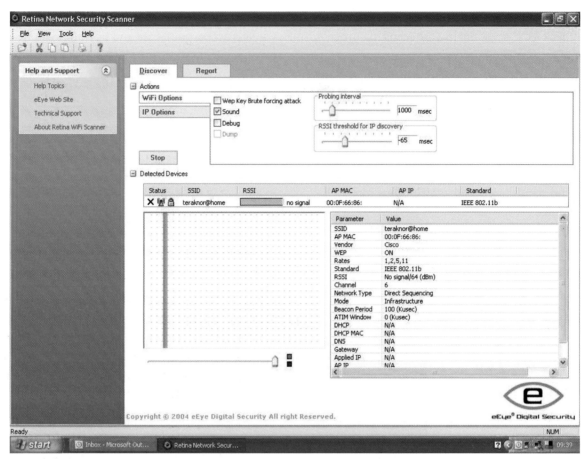

Figure 15.4 The Retina Network Security Scanner, finding a local access point

■ ARP poisoning

Switch-based networks have long been considered to be very secure as they create **micro-segments** within the system. However, techniques such as '**ARP** poisoning' have rendered this idea useless, with the **man in the middle attack** being an issue on many corporate networks. To overcome this threat, a network manager has to monitor the memory of any network switch, to check if any **MAC** address appears in more than one location, even momentarily.

Ettercap is considered by the networking industry to be the primary ARP poisoning tool and can be used to generate as well as prevent attacks.

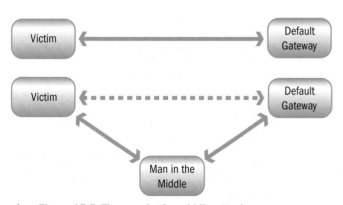

Figure 15.5 The man in the middle attack

What does it mean?

Micro-segments are a method of dividing network traffic into a 'network per cable' system to increase speed and reliability.

ARP stands for **address resolution protocol**. It is used to match IP addresses to MAC addresses.

A computer using **man in the middle attack** tricks the victim into thinking it is the default gateway, and tricks the default gateway into thinking it is the victim computer.

MAC stands for **media access control**. The MAC address is the address hardcoded into your computer's wired or wireless network card.

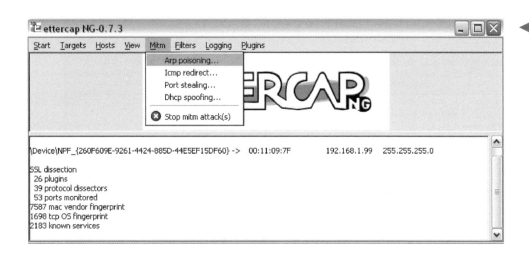

Figure 15.6 Ettercap

■ Magic disks

'Magic disk' is a collective term for all the boot disks which can be downloaded from the Internet to restart a computer and subvert the operating system. Some magic disks like the 'ultimate boot CD' are useful in resolving issues with viruses and trojans as well as drive, hardware and operating system failures.

When you start a computer, your system can boot from the USB, CD/DVD or a floppy disk. As your operating system (Windows) is resident on the hard drive, anyone with a basic knowledge of BIOS configuration can select any of the other boot options (in fact, in many systems the default is the CD/DVD, which saves the hacker considerable effort).

Some magic disks are used to scan your hard drive for SAM files; these contain usernames and **password hashes**. Once found, the magic disk will use analysis techniques such as **rainbow tables** to find the administrator password for the computer.

To prevent anyone from using a magic disk, it is prudent to password lock the BIOS and prevent anyone from being able to use USB sticks, floppy disks and CD/DVDs as boot devices.

■ Key loggers

A key logger is an application which will record all key strokes (and in some cases mouse activity) and send the information to a file or, in many cases, to a remote network location. Most key loggers are hidden applications and can be 'found' using the latest **definitions** on an anti-virus application.

If you suspect there is an undetected key logger running on your system, an alternative technique to discover activity is to run a protocol scanner, which looks at the contents of each data packet. Applications like Wireshark (formerly called Ethereal) can 'watch' all outgoing traffic from your computer, which may reveal some interesting activity from many applications.

15.1.1.2 Access causing damage to data or jamming resources

In gaining unauthorised access the software used may cause damage to data or jamming (restricting) resources. Some attacks may have the intent of accessing systems or data without damage, and the impact may initially go unnoticed.

Whatever the intent, an intrusion always has an impact on the system.

What does it mean?

A **password hash** is a mathematical representation of a password, not the password itself.

A **rainbow table** is a list of all possible hashes, often compressed and indexed for fast searching.

In the context of an anti-virus application, a **definition** is a database entry about applications which are not trusted, trojans, worms or viruses.

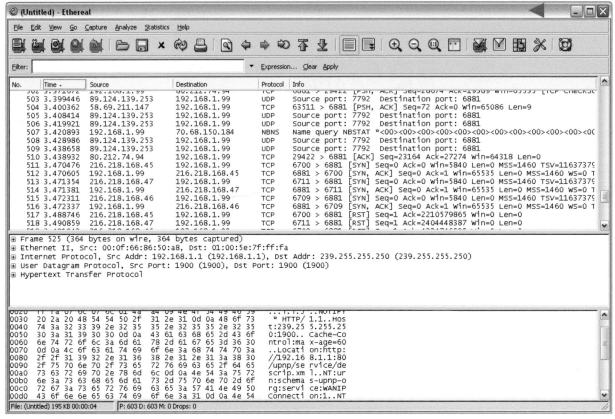

Figure 15.7 Ethereal analysing outgoing network traffic

■ Virus attacks

Virus attacks occur when rogue code has entered the system; a virus will hide itself inside ordinary executable code and can: be a nuisance by opening/closing the CD/DVD door, swapping key responses (£ for @, etc.); self-reproduce, spreading itself from application to application to evade detection and elimination; cause serious damage to data and cause critical damage to the hard drive.

Viruses are concealed by a simple deception. They will embed themselves inside an application, redirecting its commands and code around itself while running as a separate task.

Most virus scanners will detect a virus by opening the file and scanning the code, looking for this type of redirection. Ironically, students who create code in languages such as Pascal, C++ or Java can fall foul of their college's virus scanner because their programming style is treated as suspect.

Many anti-virus applications will create a hash (known as an MD5, see Unit 27 page 265) for each application.

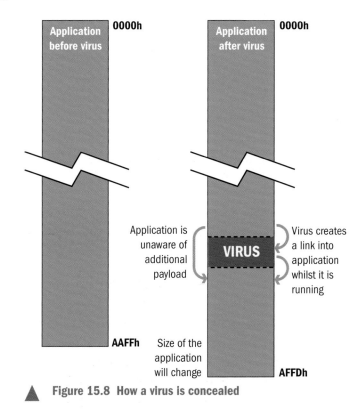

Figure 15.8 How a virus is concealed

If the MD5 changes, this may be treated as a virus attack (or an application update).

Once found, the anti-virus application offers the option to remove or isolate the virus (in a quarantine zone).

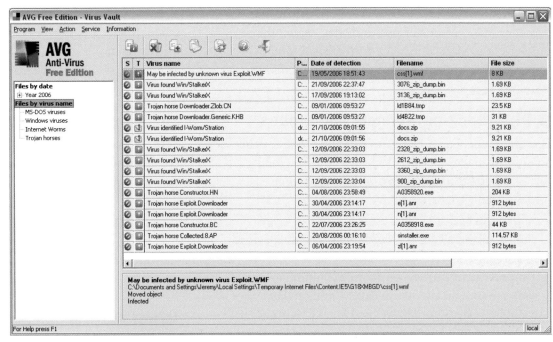

▲ **Figure 15.9 A virus quarantine**

■ Trojans

Trojans are stealth applications which are designed to allow others to access your system. Transported via infected email attachments, infected downloads, infected CD/DVDs or worms which use vulnerabilities in your operating system, trojans have the potential to cause the most damage. The most famous trojan is Sub-7, which has been used for key logging, pranks, remote attacks (controlling your computer to start the real attack) and **distributed denial of service** attacks.

■ Worms

Worms are self-transporting applications which carry an active payload such as a trojan or a virus. Worms are active or passive: active worms self-transport without human intervention, while passive worms rely on the user's innocence to transport themselves from one location to another.

Active worms use email, vulnerabilities in your operating system, the web and DNS servers, as well as other alternative 'traffic' systems, to move their payload around a network infrastructure.

▲ **Figure 15.10 Sub-7 being used for pranks**

What does it mean?

Distributed denial of service is an attack where multiple systems will flood a single system with traffic, intending to block the network or device from being able to access the Internet.

While many system weaknesses have been patched up over the years, worms still exist and often exploit the unsuspecting. Many worms are currently attempting to exploit VoIP systems like Skype or chat systems like Windows Live Messenger.

■ Piggybacking, tunnels and probes

Hacking using piggybacking, tunnels and probes can be accomplished with a level of expertise (not the 'good' sort of expertise) and attacks can be formed when network traffic is 'corrupted'.

- With **piggyback** attacks, a normal, safe communication carries an additional harmful payload of a trojan or covert application.
- **Tunnels** can be formed via existing communication channels to send alternative data. Common data channels such as port 80 are used for HTTP. Someone with a level of network expertise could send any data they wish via this port and create a wide range of applications running underneath one innocent communication channel.
- A **probe** can use an open, and therefore available, port to start an in-depth analysis of a network or computer system. Once the open hole is found, it will start digging into the system.

■ Forging data

Forging, or spoofing, data requires knowledge of programming in networking languages such as Java, C++ or VB.NET. A hacker could 'hand craft' a data packet to: force an application or server to give away information, cause a denial of service attack or piggyback/tunnel into a system via an 'acceptable' protocol.

The code needed to accomplish this is on the Internet and is openly available on many non-hacking websites.

15.1.1.3 Phishing and identity theft

Phishing and identity theft are relatively recent developments in methods for unauthorised access. The purpose of a phish (pronounced fish!) is to lure you into revealing personal information; it does this by **social engineering**, i.e. using something or someone trusted by you. Phishing employs many tactics, which are evolving all the time. For example:

- an email purporting to be from a long forgotten school friend, looking for contact details; this leads to identity theft
- an email that claims to be from your bank, ISP, etc., asking you to follow a link to their site to update your details – the email looks authentic and when you follow the link, the site looks very much like the site of the bank/ISP, except the protocol is unlikely to be HTTPS, and some links on the page may be inoperational.

Phishing may also exploit **homographs** and our detailed reading skills by directing us to domain names with similar spellings. (Have you ever mistyped a domain name with surprising results?)

What does it mean?

Homographs are words with the same spelling but with different meanings, e.g. fluke means both a parasite and a stroke of luck (as well as a networking company).

Activity 15.1

Phishing

To test your phishing detection skills, which of these is an incorrect domain?

- www.heinemann.com
- www.heinemann.co.uk
- www.heinneman.co.uk

The impact of phishing is that it results in unauthorised access to personal data, commercial data and financial information via deception (the legal term for which is fraud).

▲ Figure 15.11 Java code to send 'hand crafted' packets

```java
import java.io.*;
import java.net.*;
public class forgeData
{
    private static void delay(int duration)
    {
        try{
            new Thread().sleep(duration*1000);
        }
        catch(InterruptedException e)
        {
        }
    }
public static void main(String[] args) throws IOException
{
    System.out.println('Forge Data');
    Socket echoSocket = null;
PrintWriter out = null;
String host = 'dodgywebsite.org.uk';
        int ping = 100;
        int port = 80;
        String userInput = 'blah!';
try
{
echoSocket = new Socket(host, port);
}
catch (UnknownHostException e)
{
System.err.println('Don't know about host');
System.exit(1);
}
catch (IOException e)
{
System.err.println('Couldn't get I/O for the connection');
System.exit(1);
}
out = new PrintWriter(echoSocket.getOutputStream(), true);
        for (int loop=1;loop<=ping;loop++)
        {
        out.println(userInput);
        System.out.print('!');
        delay(1);
        }
        out.close();
        echoSocket.close();
        System.out.println('');
        System.out.println('.... Finished');
    }
}
```

15.1.2 Damage or destruction of systems or information

A major threat to any system is the damage or destruction of systems or information on a networked computer system. Threats include loss of files or data, natural disasters (flood or fire), malicious damage (through internal and external causes), technical failures, human error and theft.

In the management of a network, a network manager should complete a robust schedule of daily, weekly and monthly backups to overcome the impact of any loss of files or data on a system (see Unit 8 page 160 and Unit 27 page 273, as well as section 15.3.1 of this unit on page 199).

While data may be recoverable, the greatest risk to any organisation lies in:

- the time taken to recover files or data
- distributed systems where users store mission-critical data on local/home computers or laptops and do not maintain a robust backup policy
- versions of files or data held at different locations not being synchronised, which could cause the recovery process to revive an older version.

15.1.2.1 Natural disasters

Natural disasters cause issues for anyone and any system. Natural disasters range from power outage to flood or fire, which can cause considerable damage. Organisational security requires the management of any networked computer system to have a series of measures in place to cope with extreme issues. Depending on the critical dependency of the system (of which an air traffic control system has among the highest critical dependency), technology should be employed in order to provide resilience.

As part of a disaster recovery policy, a network manager may wish to implement the following:

- remote storage of all data acquired in the daily backup
- remote mirroring (duplication) of all critical servers
- maintaining a contract with alternative data centres to transfer control at times of serious emergency (many organisations offer this).

15.1.2.2 Malicious damage

Sadly, the threat of malicious damage (through internal and external causes) to a system is constant. Malicious damage can be caused by the archetypal external hacker hacking into and attacking systems or by a disgruntled employee seeking revenge against management for, say, an unsatisfactory pay rise. While there are many security techniques available to limit access, dedicated and devious hackers will always find a way to cause damage.

Activity 15.2

Cyber damage

1 Complete a search on well-known search engines for 'cyber damage'.

2 Find out how many insurance companies now offer cover for this possibility.

15.1.2.3 Technical failure

While networking and computing technology has become increasingly reliable over the last 20 years, the complex nature of the systems being used means that technical failure is still always a risk. The loss of a server, storage devices or an Internet connection can cause considerable disruption to any individual worker as well as to an organisation as a whole.

With our increased dependence on networked technology, with voice-, video- and CCTV-based systems being transmitted across many systems, technical failure can cause commercial damage as well as inhibit the security of the system.

15.1.2.4 Human errors

'To err is human, to forgive divine.'

Alexander Pope

Human error is probably the most unpredictable yet most constant cause of security issues in any networked system. Forgetfulness, ignorance, innocence and lack of knowledge can all contribute to systems failure and the increased potential of a security breach.

Forgetting to back up data, to place data in a secure location, to erase a hard drive before a computer is disposed of or to close a port on a firewall when installed can all cause serious problems on a networked system.

Ignorance and the lack of appreciation of the need for network and general systems security have been the most common cause of network intrusion and virus infection. With the increase in use of broadband/ADSL connections over the last few years, there has been a noted increase in 'hack attacks' and virus/worm/trojan transmission. As a result, firewalls are now common on most operating systems, with many home and commercial users more aware of the issues.

However, many otherwise intelligent and well-informed individuals have succumbed to social engineering and phishing attacks. Innocent misunderstanding can lead to the best people being deceived. Avoiding such attacks comes through learning from experience, both good and bad. For many, forgetting once and seeing the effects means it will not happen again.

15.1.2.5 Theft

Theft of data and technical property can have a long-lasting impact on an organisation or an individual. Theft can take place in the 'cyber' sense in the case of hacking, or in the physical sense, with data being removed on CD/DVDs or memory sticks. Discarded printouts which have not been shredded might be stolen and the theft of computers is also a possibility. Theft of data can have many serious consequences, including: long-term commercial damage, a competitor gaining an advantage (even if it is not they who have stolen the data), loss of goodwill with customers, financial ruin through loss of fiscal control, the inability to track current business, loss of employment (often for the employee whose error has allowed the theft to occur) and legal action.

Theft of technical property can have the same impact as the theft of data. Laptops that are used outside the office as well as external hard drives can constitute a major theft risk.

15.1.3 Information security

Wherever data is stored, the overall security of the data must be controlled. This area is covered by three principles: confidentiality, integrity and availability.

15.1.3.1 Confidentiality

In managing the confidentiality of information, the system manager has to consider these points:

- Who can see the information?
- Who can update the information?
- For how long is the information to be stored?
- How often must the information be reviewed for currency?
- What information can be stored?
- What systems are available to store the information?

Regularly reviewing who can access this confidential information and what information is stored is essential. Systems storing personal information such as bank details, credit records or medical records must be accurate and managed in a confidential manner.

15.1.3.2 Integrity and completeness of data

The integrity and therefore completeness of data is critical; having incorrect data on any matter can cause considerable personal as well as commercial damage. The wrong information on a medical record, credit report or police system can cause an individual considerable distress, as well as possibly lead to legal action.

Checking the data is correct may involve asking appropriate people to review the information. In the case of customer or personnel details, asking the customer or colleague to check the data is correct and up to date enhances the integrity of the data stored.

15.1.3.3 Availability of data as needed

Who can access what data and when controls the overall availability of data. It is important to review regularly who has access to data and when they have access, because:

- those who have access may no longer need it
- when someone may access the data may be driven by a legal protocol – for example, a credit report may be requested by a lender only when someone applies for credit.

15.1.4 E-commerce threats

Since the use of e-commerce has increased dramatically since 1996, this area has become another battle ground in the war against hacking and other criminal activities.

15.1.4.1 Website defacement

Website defacement is an incredibly common nuisance attack. It involves a brand of hackers called **crackers** looking for script or version vulnerabilities in web servers and website code. Once crackers have found the vulnerability they can 'edit' the **HTML** and/or the **script** on the website to display their own version of the site. For example, they might change the website to show: sexually explicit or other inappropriate images; their personal tag to impress other crackers and prove it was them; political or religious statements, depending on the site attacked; or random statements of a childish nature.

While such attacks are seldom financially motivated, there have been some cases of organised criminals trying to use this technique for their own gain by writing in **meta-refresh** tags to forward victims to their own 'spoofed' site (which comes under the domain of phishing).

For an e-commerce system, any form of website defacement is an issue. Apart from the time and income lost as the website is recovered, there is the potential loss of goodwill with customers who may stop trusting the site. They might ask the question: If hackers can change the web page, can they get into my account?

15.1.4.2 Denial of service attacks

There have been many distributed **denial of service** attacks over the years, with worms being devised to leave trojans that will send traffic from multiple devices. While firewalls can be configured to prevent most uninvited traffic from entering the system, traffic can be 'crafted' to evade many systems as well as flood a firewall and cause problems at the entry point to the system.

For an e-commerce system, any denial of service is a denial of income. While the denial of service attack may only last for a few minutes, with the loss of service and the recovery time, an organisation stands to lose a considerable amount of income.

Some e-commerce sites use **third party** suppliers to enhance the services they offer. Instead of directly stocking and selling the service or product, they act as an agent (or outlet) for the third party supplier. This approach is common on sites such as eBay and Amazon. eBay offers its services to private retailers who set up an 'eBay shop'. Amazon cannot feasibly stock all the products and services it offers and so extends its portfolio by acting as a go-between for many other sites.

The principal weakness of working with third party suppliers is the threat to the commercial security of an organisation as well as the personal security of the customer because of the need to exchange personal information in the transaction.

eBay overcame the financial transaction issue by creating the PayPal system, which acts as a level of obscurity in hiding the financial information of the third party supplier and the customer from each other. Amazon approaches the problem by taking the income directly and then sending the supplier an agreed fee.

The risk remains when sending the goods, as the third party supplier has to obtain the address details of the customer. This allows the supplier to collect customer details which, in turn, increases their customer base and potentially enables them to set up shop alone.

An additional issue is the matter of trust. While e-commerce sites work with third party suppliers, they ensure that the exchange of data, especially financial data, is carefully managed. Some third party retailers never deliver on their goods, which has an adverse impact on the good name of the e-commerce site. To combat this, eBay and Amazon manage a fraud and complaints section to remove any rogue suppliers.

What does it mean?

HTML stands for **Hyper Text Mark-up Language** – it is the tag language used to create websites.

A **script** is a programming code, often short and used as part of another system. The most common web script language is JavaScript.

Meta-refresh is an HTML tag which redirects the website visitor to another web page.

A **denial of service** attack is when a service (such as a web server) is sent so much traffic that it slows down to the point of failure, either through the lack of bandwidth or through an increased load for its processor to handle.

In the context of retail and e-commerce, a **third party** is an additional organisation that is involved in the commercial transaction. It is called a third party because it is additional to the supplier and the customer.

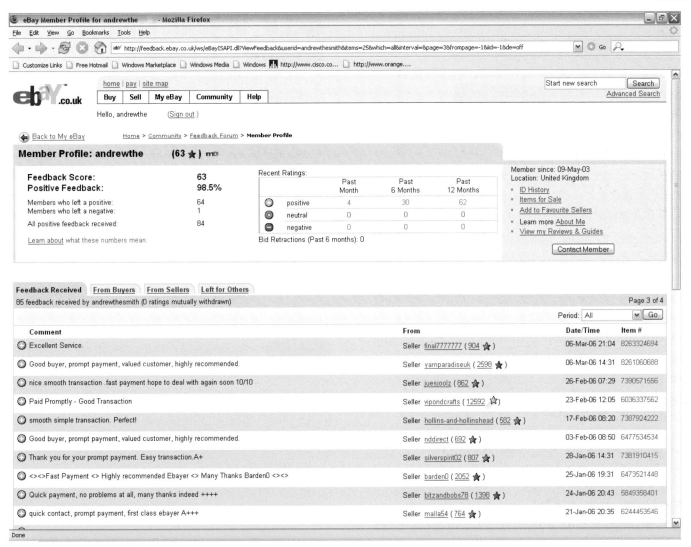

▲ Figure 15.12 eBay supplier transaction record

15.1.5 Counterfeit goods

The trade and exchange of counterfeit goods has a two-fold impact:

- it affects the creator of the software, game, movie or music as there is a direct loss of potential income
- it places the recipient in a legal position where they could endure a heavy fine, be sued for damages and have all their equipment seized.

With the technology to duplicate all media formats using a computer system readily available, the avid pirate can create a comprehensive collection of illicit media, placing many products at risk.

Software and games can be easily copied using CD/DVD duplication software, and software now exists to create images of the CD/DVD and load these as a virtual CD/DVD drive. With DVD cloning software, any commercial DVD movie can be easily 'ripped' from its original media, and many versions can be created, including compressed versions for **MP4** devices.

What does it mean?

MP4 is a coding format for highly compressed movies to be played on portable media players.

With the many available music formats and media players, creating files of favourite songs and albums has been commonplace for over ten years.

15.1.5.2 Distribution mechanisms

Distribution of pirated media is rife; as soon as one system is closed, another appears. The first system to offer this service was Napster, which has been famously pursued through the legal system by the music industry and now offers a fully legitimate service.

Napster, like its many clones, used a peer-based file sharing system, with each member keeping a collection of their favourite music in a folder; this is then distributed via the peer software which advertises what you have to a central server.

Since Napster, there have been many peer systems, with the current popular system being BitTorrent.

Illegally downloading any software or media is an offence which may result in a heavy fine, litigation (being sued) and the loss of your computer system. Because of the way networked technology operates, each data packet sent and received has to have the destination IP address. This means that network professionals with suitable technical knowledge can identify where the download is heading and work with the music, film or software industries to prove who is downloading what and when.

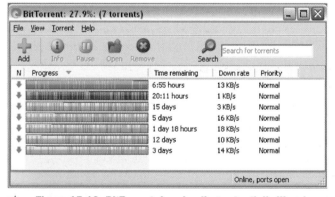

▲ **Figure 15.13 BitTorrent downloading potentially illegal software**

15.1.6 Organisational impact

Already, in describing each area of unauthorised access, you have seen how they might impact on an organisation or an individual. To summarise, an organisation may suffer the impact in a variety of ways. A potential loss of service for the customer or to the Internet can impede the organisation's ability to operate. There may be loss of business or income through the loss of essential data. In the long term, increased costs are caused by the replacement technology and the need for increased insurance. It is likely the increased cost will be passed on to the customer. Damage is caused by the potentially poor public and commercial image.

Test your knowledge

1 What are the various types of threats to organisations, systems and data?

2 What is the impact of these threats?

3 What are the most common threats?

4 How can the risk of threats be reduced?

Activity 15.3

E-commerce attacks

1 What examples of e-commerce attacks can you find in the media?

2 Try to find out how the organisations involved combated these attacks.

The previous section of this unit investigated many of the attacks, scams and issues which impact on the systems security of any organisation or individual.

Preventing a security incursion, like the attacks themselves, is a constantly evolving process. The security measures described in this section are a sample of those in use and are an introduction to what you may have to manage in the ICT industry.

15.2.1 Physical security

While no one would wish to live in a society with a 'Big Brother' figure watching every move, it is natural for people to desire the assurance that the working environment and all systems are safe.

The system may be secured with the latest anti-virus system and firewall technology but this will be useless if anyone can pop into the server room and copy all the critical data to a USB memory stick.

In the management of a secure system, these features should be present: lock and key security, equipment identification, CCTV, intrusion detection systems, staff and visitor identification, access control (sign in/out) systems, security personnel, cable and communication shielding and port lockdown.

15.2.1.1 Lock and key security

There is a need to secure mobile devices such as laptops – if you look closely at a laptop, you will see a small slot, into which you can fit a padlocked chain. Fitting a chain ensures mobile technology is not so mobile.

Many lock and key systems in buildings operate on a master/submaster system. There are a series of keys for individual doors, groups of doors and for the whole building. The network manager may have a submaster key for all of the server and communication rooms.

When they issue keys to employees, most organisations keep a journal of who has what key and what access it offers.

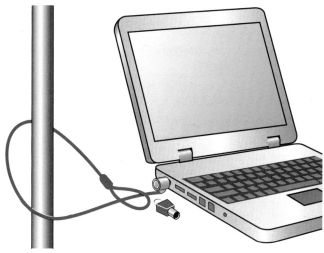

▲ Figure 15.14 Laptop security

Household and car keys can be reproduced at high street key cutters. However, the lock and key systems used by many organisations are unique, often with only one set for the building in question.

Digital keypads may reduce the cost of the reproduction of keys and can be reprogrammed at regular intervals, but these cannot prevent access by observation – when the key code is observed – or by colleagues passing on the code to others.

While having a high-quality lock and key system is essential, it has no value if the surrounding environment is vulnerable. Unauthorised access can be gained through unlocked windows (even on upper floors), via unmanned side doors, through walls (most interior walls are plaster, which is not difficult to penetrate), over ceilings (in a building with suspended ceilings, security is an issue) or by damaging the door and/or breaking the lock.

So, lock and key security relies on the quality of the environment it is supporting. In some critical areas, it may be necessary for the walls, doors, windows and ceiling space to be reinforced and possibly alarmed.

What does it mean?

Lock and key security is when essential systems are held in rooms and buildings which are secured under lock and key.

▲ A digital keypad

15.2.1.2 Equipment identification

Equipment identification assists in prevention as well as identification of stolen property. Equipment which is clearly marked (for example, as 'property of Northingham College') acts as a deterrent for the majority of petty thefts. When stolen computer equipment is found, such marking assists in the prosecution and recovery when there is clear proof of its origin and ownership. Identification can be achieved by using indelible ink to label clearly all equipment as 'property of . . .', marking property with invisible and **ultra-violet** sensitive ink or covertly marking property with a 'DNA' compound which has been uniquely created for your organisation.

What does it mean?

Ultra-violet light is at the high end of the visible light range.

15.2.1.3 CCTV (closed circuit television)

The use of CCTV is prevalent in the UK, with a reported 1.2 million cameras in operation at the time of writing. While many people take the view that this is an invasion of reasonable privacy, the counter argument that CCTV enhances security and offers a localised deterrent is also valid. CCTV offers three immediate advantages:

- the ability for a centralised control centre to monitor remote locations
- a comprehensive record of events 24/7 is maintained
- announcing the presence of CCTV in the locality causes behaviour to change and may act as an appropriate deterrent.

CCTV images are admissible as evidence in most legal cases and the technology and image quality are continually improving. Most CCTV systems can move (pan/tilt) and can enhance any given area in their field of vision (zoom); some include a directional microphone to supplement their use.

Some locations may have 'covert surveillance' with hidden CCTV. If you cannot see a camera, that does not mean one is not in operation covering a sensitive area.

15.2.1.4 Intrusion detection systems

Many organisations use complex intrusion detection systems, which can sense a human presence in a variety of complex ways. Common detection technologies include:

- passive infrared which detects body heat
- microphones which detect any movement and enable the remote control centre to listen in on the environment
- circuit breakers, for doors, windows and access hatches
- pressure-sensitive pads for floor areas
- low-power laser beams, which if broken will activate an alarm (some lifts use these to detect if anyone is still in the doorway).

▲ CCTV cameras are increasingly commonplace

15.2.1.5 Staff and visitor identification

Most medium to large organisations maintain a system of staff and visitor identification – your college may have a system which identifies staff, students and visitors. This system offers immediate authority for those who should be there to challenge unknown people's rights to be there.

In many environments, identification only has value if the culture supports it – there is no point issuing identification cards if no one wears them. Many organisations use the identification card as a method of entry, with security and reception personnel checking identification on entry. Many identification card systems are used in combination with access control systems (see next section), where the identification card also acts a key.

With current technology, the identification card can form part of the personnel database. Together, with photographic identification from a personnel record, many organisations also use a colour-coding system on their cards to indicate, for example: if you are a contractor; which department, site or partner company you work for; the level of access allowed; the floor(s) you may access; and your position in the company.

Visitor cards are by their nature temporary and indicate that the visitor has limited access rights: most organisations have a policy of escorting all visitors from entry (sign in) to exit (sign out).

15.2.1.6 Access control (sign in/out) systems

These are a variation on lock and key systems and are often used in conjunction with staff and visitor identification systems. Instead of using keys to access areas of a building, the system relies on personnel using swipe cards or dongles as keys. There are several advantages of access control systems:

- the system can log personnel entering and exiting buildings (which means they can also be used to monitor the time-keeping and attendance of employees)
- each key can be programmed, which means personnel can be allowed/denied access to any area on a 'door by door' level
- records can be maintained on who has used what door, with secure and critical areas open to scrutiny
- when an employee leaves the organisation, if they do not return their key, it can be disabled
- the keys can be reprogrammed when an employee changes role within the organisation.

Barnfield COLLEGE ✳

Terak
Nor

Student 07/08

▲ Figure 15.15 An identification card with colour coding

Most swipe cards and dongle systems contain no information, only a unique ID (like a MAC address on a network card). The access information is kept on a central server which manages the access control system. Naturally, if these keys fall into the wrong hands, before anyone becomes aware of this, they can be used to gain access. To overcome this, some systems work in partnership with CCTV or key code systems, which record who has entered the area as well as creating a secondary security mechanism.

15.2.1.7 Security personnel

Security personnel offer an essential service in managing the security of an organisation and the system on which critical data is stored. In many cases they will not offer a technical role, but in a large organisation they are likely to be among the few who know everyone in the company (or building) and will be able to identify 'suspicious' behaviour or someone who does not belong.

Out of normal working hours, security personnel often monitor a variety of safety systems, as well as monitoring the building and its environment. They play an essential role in theft prevention and may be the first to discover if any 'technology' is out of place.

15.2.1.8 Shielding network cables and wireless communication systems

Any data which is transmitted using electromagnetic or radio transmission is open to being remotely monitored. The signal travelling along a copper data cable emits a magnetic field, which can be analysed to discover what data is travelling along the line. This may seem the stuff of fiction, but the technology does exist to access data covertly. Only data sent via fibre optic cannot be 'tapped into' without considerable effort and possible damage. Some cable systems are shielded, partly to protect the cable from external magnetic interference (power sources, etc.), but also to dampen the external noise generated by the cable.

Wireless systems are by their nature less secure, and so a system which uses WEP encryption has been developed (see section 15.2.3.1 on page 190 and Unit 8 page 160 and Unit 27 page 273). To maintain total trust, the

▲ A swipe card reader

devices which can join a wireless system need to be pre-configured, so that the wireless system does not allow just any device to join the system.

15.2.1.9 Port lockdown

One type of port is the wall socket into which the computer's network cable connects. If the port is inactive then port lockdown should take place in the central communications room. This can be done by remotely accessing the switch and disabling the port or, in some cases, unplugging the cable from the opposite end of the cable leading to the port. This will prevent additional devices from joining your system.

15.2.2 Biometrics

The technology of **biometrics** is constantly being developed and refined. Common technologies in current use are fingerprint recognition, retinal scans and voice recognition.

What does it mean?

Biometrics is the implementation of technology to use biological information about ourselves as a method of unique identification. It comes from the ancient Greek: **bios**, meaning life, and **metron**, meaning measure.

15.2.2.1 Fingerprint recognition

This form of biometrics has been used in crime detection over the last 100 years and no two prints have yet been found to be identical. Our fingers secrete a fine watery solution from the ridges, which allows detection and fingerprint scanners to operate. Some scanners use a rapid laser to detect the ridges in our fingers; others have an electro-statically sensitive pad which detects the current formed by the small quantities of water in our fingerprint.

Fingerprint scanners are often used in conjunction with an additional identification system. For example, international travel requires a passport, visa and, in some countries, additional recognition using fingerprint identification from more than one finger.

Case study

Biometrics

A well-known resort and theme park uses biometric fingerprint scanners to prevent fraudulent sharing of multi-day passes among visiting families.

1 What is the cost implication of using such a system and what impracticalities may be involved?

2 What are the benefits to the resort?

3 What are the potential legal implications?

15.2.2.2 Retinal scans

The retina is the rear of the eye and, like a fingerprint, everyone's has a biologically unique configuration. Unlike fingerprints, which can be changed (as the skin can be cut or burnt), retinal scans rely on the biological fact that it is almost impossible to change the retina without considerable damage (so it is unlikely that anyone would let someone tamper with their eyeball) and the retina remains the same from birth, acting as a constant and reliable method of identification.

Retina scans take about two seconds to complete, but require the close proximity of the recipient.

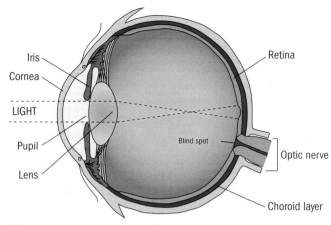

▲ **Figure 15.16 Diagram of an eyeball**

15.2.2.3 Iris scanning

Another eye feature which is unique is the iris; unlike retina scanning, iris scanning can be accomplished when the recipient is wearing glasses or contact lenses. Like the retina, the chances of the iris changing are incredibly remote, allowing for a reliable source of biometric information. Iris scanning is already in use at some international destinations and may increase in popularity through time.

Activity 15.4

Retina/iris scans

1 With the consent of your classmates, look closely at each other's eyes with a pen light and notice the differences.

2 There is a well-known science fiction film that shows iris scanning in use. Do you know which it is? If not, use the Internet to find out.

15.2.2.4 Voice recognition

Voice recognition as a method of biometric access control has considerable limitations because voices can change in different circumstances – for example, when we are stressed, excited, tired or ill (say with a throat infection) and, more importantly, as we age (for example, the inability of young men to control their voices during puberty).

Voice-based security systems can also be 'circumvented' by a mobile phone on speaker mode or a voice recording, therefore requiring the voice recognition system to be used in conjunction with other access control systems (such as CCTV, swipe cards and dongles). In many other situations, however, voice recognition has improved considerably and has an important use in speech to text systems for people with disabilities and in handheld games consoles.

15.2.2.5 Other biometric technologies

Other biometric systems are being developed and deployed: facial recognition systems, for example, have been developed which can be used to scan groups of people via live CCTV footage. Alongside facial recognition systems, technology has now been developed to identify individuals who may be behaving in a suspicious manner by their actions and posture.

Activity 15.5

Biometrics

1 What biometric systems have you encountered?

2 How do you think biometric systems will evolve?

15.2.3 Software and network security

To combat intrusion and subversion of a networked computer system and commonplace accidental damage to data and resources, all ICT systems need to employ an extensive range of security and data management techniques and technologies. The following examples are covered in this section: **encryption** techniques, call back, handshaking, diskless networks, the backup and restoration of data and redundancy, audit logs, firewall configuration and management, virus management and control, virtual private networks (VPNs), intrusion

detection systems and traffic control technologies, passwords, levels of access to data and software updating.

15.2.3.1 Encryption

Many simple ciphers exist, such as the Caesar cipher, which relies on a simple key of changing one letter with the letter a fixed number of places down the alphabet. So, using a shift of four places, A becomes E, B becomes F, etc.

Ciphers such as **DES** (**Data Encryption Standard**) use a key which is 56 bits in length. Using simple mathematics, this means there are 2^{56} (72,057,594,037,927,936) possible combinations. With the increasing power of computers, this cipher is now obsolete as it is possible to crack the cipher in a short time.

RSA encryption uses a **public/private key** exchange – the security certificate issued by a website is a common example. The certificate is a public key part of the exchange and a private key is also created. The private key is based on a 1024-bit value (2^{1024} which is 1.797693134862315907729305190789e+308 – the e means you move the decimal point to the right by 308 digits) and is a **prime number**.

What does it mean?

Encryption is a method of converting normal information such as text, images and media into a format which is unintelligible unless you are in possession of the key that is the basis of the conversion.

RSA encryption comes from Ron **Rivest**, Adi **Shamir** and Len **Adleman**, the mathematicians who devised the principle for public/private key encryption using prime numbers.

Public/private keys are mathematically related. The public key can be widely distributed and is used to encrypt data. The private key *only* can decrypt the data and is kept secret. It is not technically practical to derive the private key from the public key.

A **prime number** is a number that can only be divided by itself and 1. This means that by no matter what number you try to divide this number, it will never return a whole value. Prime numbers are mathematically interesting as no one has yet managed to predict the next prime number – they appear to follow no pattern. This property is invaluable in network security.

For many secure WAN connections, routing protocols exchange their updates using a MD5 hash (see page 265), which is a formula that provides the result of a complex calculation based on a large dataset, with the hash being the result from each calculation. This is used across common communication systems to ensure that no one attempts to add unauthorised equipment to join the system, as well as by anti-virus systems to check if an application has been changed by the insertion of a virus.

For wireless systems, **WEP** (**wireless equivalence protocol**) allows all members of a wireless system to share a common private key which is used to encrypt all the data transmitted. The wireless device cannot join the system unless the WEP key is directly entered into the wireless settings for the mobile device.

Two WEP key standards are in use, offering 64-bit (18,446,744,073,709,551,616) and 128-bit (3.402823669209384 6346337460743177e+38) keys.

As WEP keys are in binary, they can be entered in hexadecimal, as this has a direct mathematical relationship and is a more understandable format.

15.2.3.2 Call back

Call back is used on dial-up systems where remote workers or network administrators can dial into a network or a network device and it will call them back. The call back number is pre-configured, which means

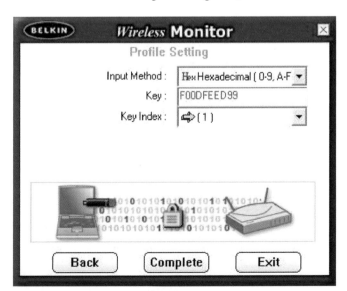

Figure 15.17 A 64-bit WEP key

that the user cannot connect from any location, only a trusted, registered line.

While dial-up systems using modems (see Unit 8 page 126) may seem out of date, many remote areas and developing regions still use this reliable technology. Modems are still used as a backup connection to gain direct access into the network router in the case of major failure of the main incoming line (which may be caused by a hacker attack).

15.2.3.3 Handshaking

On WAN systems, data may be sent across a medium which is not trusted (a public communications line). To improve the trust, each device completes a challenge (which may be random and carries a remote username and password) to establish the identity of the opposite device (CHAP – Challenge Handshake Authentication Protocol).

15.2.3.4 Diskless networks

One of the greatest risks of data being stolen is caused by the ability to easily transfer data from a computer to a mobile storage device.

In diskless networks workstations do not have CD/DVD drives, USB ports (or Windows is prevented from recognising new USB devices) or floppy disk drives. In most cases of diskless networking, the BIOS must also be configured and secured to prevent more astute individuals from adding new devices.

Some systems also prevent local hard drive access, either by applying local restrictions so the user cannot view, add or remove files, or by having no local hard drive, with the workstation booting from a remote location into memory, using terminal services technology.

What does it mean?

Handshaking is a process where two communication devices continuously agree a method of data communication.

Various versions exist, including: Remote Desktop with Windows XP and Vista; VNC (Virtual Network Computing), which can be used on a diverse range of systems; Linux X-Windows, which offers similar facilities.

15.2.3.5 Backups

The use of backups and the restoration of data are critical in ensuring that data is safe and secure. Having a centrally managed backup system, where all the data is safely copied in case of system failure, with everyone following the same standards, is essential.

Backing up and restoring disks and data are considered to be a critical role of a network administrator. Depending on the size, type and nature of the organisation, it is expected that the network administrator completes at least one backup per day. Some systems employ **incremental backups**, while others use **differential backups**. (For definitions, see Unit 27, page 274.)

An effective backup relies on defining the exact quantity of data that requires backing up, deciding on what appropriate media needs to be used in the backup process, the frequency of backups and a copy of the data needs being stored off-site.

Some organisations complete a backup every eight hours as the data is undergoing continuous change. It is normal for most companies to complete an overnight backup and, once a week, a copy is taken to another location (off-site).

To ensure redundancy, most server systems storage is managed by **RAID**. The benefits of RAID are that if one hard drive fails the system can be rebuilt from the existing images or the system can continue while a new hard drive is installed.

What does it mean?

RAID stands for **redundant array of independent disks**. It is used as a live backup mechanism with multiple hard disks maintaining multiple images of the data.

Systems such as RAID and **mirroring** provide companies with quicker recovery times. RAID allows data to be recovered from 'duplicated' hard drives. Mirroring requires a second, duplicate server to be in operation at the same time as the primary server.

15.2.3.6 Audit logs

Audit logs are used to keep a record of network and database activity, recording who has done what, where they did it and when. The audit log may contain a simple reference to the service accessed along with the system identity of the user.

The majority of database and network activities will go unnoticed, but the purpose of the audit log is to:

- maintain a detailed record of how any system has been used
- on recognition of an issue, enable system administrators to track the possible cause (or infringement)
- work with monitoring systems to enable alarms to be placed on a system, alerting system administrators to potentially suspicious activity.

Syslog is one of the most common systems in use to maintain simple, auditable records of system activity across a networked system. The syslog server stores all access records for the network administrator to review as appropriate.

15.2.3.7 Firewall configurations

Most simple firewall systems in use at home are automatic and seldom require user intervention and configuration. For a commercial environment, firewall configuration is essential to ensure the efficient and effective transit of data.

As the purpose of a firewall is to block unwanted traffic from entering the network, configuration must be done with care. In many systems where traffic has to enter to reach servers (such as email or web servers), two or more firewalls may be installed to offer zones of security. This allows different security levels depending on the direction of traffic – data intended for externally accessible devices is managed differently to data for internal devices.

```
2006-12-30 17:32:35    192.168.1.101    www.hellochristmas.co.uk
2006-12-30 17:32:38    192.168.1.101    images.shopping.msn.co.uk
2006-12-30 17:32:39    192.168.1.101    www.maketheworldabetterspace.com
2006-12-30 17:33:30    192.168.1.101    download.windowsupdate.com
2006-12-30 17:33:36    192.168.1.101    update.microsoft.com
2006-12-30 17:54:53    192.168.1.99     www.googleadservices.com
2006-12-30 17:54:53    192.168.1.99     www.orient-express.com
2006-12-30 17:54:55    192.168.1.99     orient-express.lbwa.verio.net
2006-12-30 17:54:56    192.168.1.99     oe.nucleus.co.uk
2006-12-30 17:59:16    192.168.1.99     download.windowsupdate.com
2006-12-30 18:53:13    192.168.1.100    rad.msn.com
2006-12-30 08:53:02    192.168.1.99     phobos.apple.com
2006-12-30 08:53:04    192.168.1.99     ax.phobos.apple.com.edgesuite.net
```

Figure 15.18 A Syslog record list

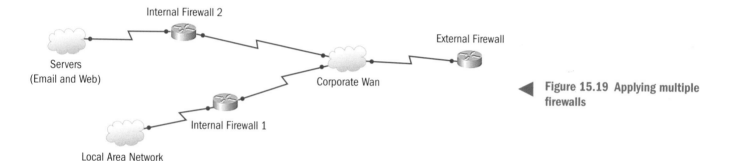

Figure 15.19 Applying multiple firewalls

Many systems will not allow internal traffic to exit the system unless it has been sent from a computer and user that has been 'authenticated' using the internal directory system. Therefore, if the traffic is coming from a computer that is not logged in, then the traffic will not exit.

Many firewalls work in conjunction with **NAT** (**Network Address Translation**) systems, with the internal devices all hidden behind one (or a small number of) external IP address.

There are 65536 UDP ports and 65536 TCP ports, as well as ICMP, IP and other protocol traffic.

WATCH OUT!

Be very careful to find out what ports you may open, as you do not want to open up your network to attack.

■ HOW TO CHECK YOUR FIREWALL SETTINGS

1 Typically with Windows XP you can find a resource by many avenues. The easiest way to find the Windows Firewall is to open the Control Panel.
2 Select the Exceptions tab and you will see a list of automatically configured exceptions.
3 Select the Add Port option and create a port to open. Hint: to test this, you will need to have software which will respond to the port you have opened.

Security Center — Software Explorers — Sound Effect Manager — User Accounts — Windows Firewall — Wireless Network Set...

Figure 15.20 The Windows Firewall icon

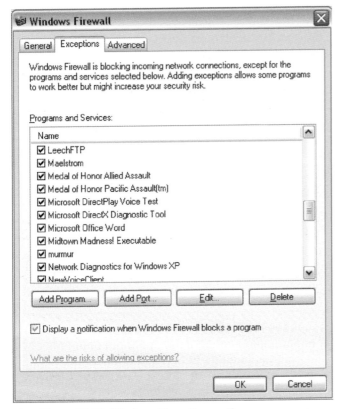

Figure 15.21 Windows Firewall exceptions

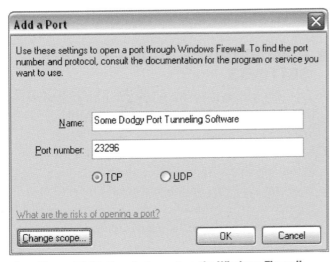

Figure 15.22 Opening a port on the Windows Firewall

4 It is worth looking at all of the configuration options with the Windows Firewall. You can create a scope, which defines from which IP addresses the rule will allow traffic to enter.

In the home environment, virus checking software comes in many shapes and sizes, from those which only cover viruses, trojans and worms to comprehensive integrated security suites that interact with a firewall and the operating system to maintain the welfare of the system.

All virus checking systems are only as good as the databases (called dictionaries) they maintain on the latest attacks. So, it is essential to ensure that the anti-virus software goes daily to download the latest virus definitions.

Anti-virus software always runs in the background of any system; on your computer you may see its icon in the system tray. The anti-virus software will scan each file as it is being opened for any 'fingerprints' which match the virus definitions. It will also attempt to identify any 'suspicious' activity from a program while it is running.

Corporate anti-virus systems must be deployed centrally as well as on each local computer system. Many medium to large organisations will:

- have a server which downloads the latest virus definitions and distributes them to each computer daily
- monitor all incoming and outgoing traffic for potential threats; this may be via the router, proxy server or firewall
- monitor all incoming and outgoing email traffic for potential threats; it will look at all attachments
- use the anti-virus application in partnership with local computer administrative policies to prevent the local system from running unacceptable software (a tactic used to stop employees using well-known hacking software and games by finding the MD5 hash for each application).

■ HOW TO INSTALL FREE ANTI-VIRUS SOFTWARE

Running a computer without anti-virus software installed is a recipe for disaster, so don't do it. AVG offer their anti-virus software in a free version, which will:

- update its anti-virus definitions daily
- run a comprehensive scan of your entire system on demand, or scheduled daily

- check all running programs
- check all emails, incoming and outgoing
- check for 'script' attacks from websites
- carry out a **heuristic** analysis.

To download and install the software, visit the Grisoft website (a link to this website has been made available at www.heinemann.co.uk/hotlinks – enter the express code 2315P).

For anti-virus applications, a heuristic analysis suggests there may be a virus infection inside a file; it does not declare absolutely there is an infection. Heuristic analysis is used to discover new viruses or when a virus has managed to replicate itself in a unique manner.

Computer systems cannot run with anti-virus software only; they must also run with **anti-spyware** tools. Spyware deploys many tactics used by worms, viruses and trojans and often comes as part of a welcomed application (like a free download or website you have visited).

What does it mean?

Heuristic: in computer science this is a method of arriving at a good solution that works, rather than a perfect solution.

The primary risk from spyware is the information it will send out about your activities – the sites you have visited and possibly the keystrokes used.

Available to download for Windows XP and part of the Vista suite of operating systems is Windows Defender, which is designed to replace the Microsoft Anti-Spyware application and monitor your system continuously.

15.2.3.9 Virtual private networks (VPNs)

The use of VPNs allows organisations to communicate from site to site across a public system (like the Internet) via a tunnel, which is an agreed route for all encrypted traffic. Many home workers can connect directly to the corporate network via local VPN tunnels.

Therefore, VPNs create a trusted connection on a system which is not trusted.

There are many protocols and methods used in the management of VPNs; the primary purpose of these is to prevent snooping (packet sniffing) and fraudulent authentication.

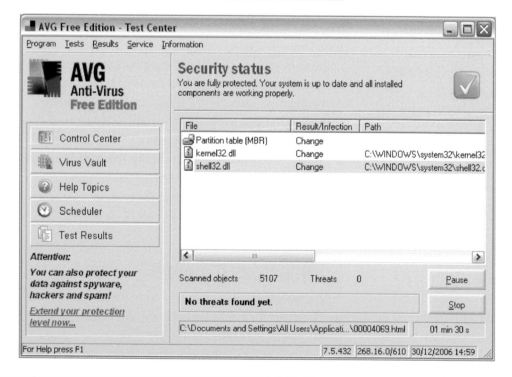

Figure 15.23 A comprehensive virus scan

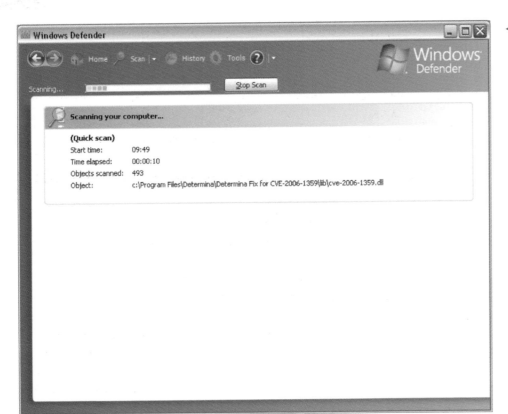

Figure 15.24 Windows Defender in action

15.2.3.10 Intrusion detection systems

Intrusion detection systems go beyond the role of the firewall and will monitor traffic for undesirable manipulations from hackers and the tools they may use. Some systems are **passive**, which means they will record the attempts for the network administrator to decide what is to be done. Others are **reactive** (called **intrusion prevention systems**) – on identifying an intrusion attempt, the system will reconfigure the firewall to block the intrusion.

Traffic control is accomplished on many networks by the use of **access-control lists** (**ACL**) and routing protocols.

- An ACL may be applied to routers and servers alike. They can be used to create traffic-based permit or deny rules for whole networks, individual devices or a specified range of devices.
- Routing protocols: a routing protocol enables routers to make decisions about which way and to whom network traffic can be sent.

Some ACLs can be used in a temporal (time-based) context, allowing or denying access to networks at certain times.

While many different systems use ACLs, the common rule may look like the one shown in Table 15.2.

15.2.3.11 Passwords

The management of passwords is essential. This tried and tested authentication technique is still the most commonly used in all areas of organisational systems security. To ensure that passwords are suitable and secure, many organisations adopt a policy that will encourage common practice. In an example policy, users must:

- not write down their password
- change their password periodically, from 90 days (three months) to as little as every seven days
- use a **strong password** with eight or more characters

What does it mean?

A **strong password** uses letters (upper and lower case), numbers and symbols, e.g. JacOb_$m1th instead of jacobsmith.

access-list	101	Permit	TCP	192.168.0.0	0.0.0.255	172.16.10.16	0.0.0.15	eq	80
This is the rule which has a unique number		Can be permit or deny	This could be TCP, UDP or IP	This identifies the source network, device or range of devices	This is a wildcard mask*	This identifies the source network, device or range of devices	This is a wildcard mask*		Is equal to TCP port 80 for HTTP traffic

Rules are in lists (or collections) and are executed in order. When a rule with a condition matching the incoming or outgoing traffic is met, the rule is executed. If you have a 'deny FTP' before a 'permit FTP', then FTP traffic will never be allowed.

ACLs have a default 'deny all' rule at the end. If you only write permits, all other traffic is automatically denied, which is a subtle and useful security feature.

* Wildcard masks are used as matching rules and are: binary 0 = must match, binary 1 = does not care.

Table 15.2 An access list to allow one network to access a small collection of web servers, but prevent web access by any other system

- choose a password which is nonsense, to evade casual attempts at social engineering while remaining memorable.

■ HOW TO THINK OF A NONSENSE PASSWORD

Picking the name of a family member, pop star, football team or town you were born in is susceptible to discovery through social engineering.

Trying to devise a word which has no meaning but can be easily remembered is also a challenge. Lewis Carroll managed to create a whole new vocabulary with considerable skill in his poem The Jabberwocky (Jabberwocky is one example of a nonsense word).

1 Try mixing nouns (names) and adjectives (something which modifies a noun). For example:

Adjective	Noun
Red	Chicken
Atomic	Snail
Hyper	Cucumber
Micro	Titan

Many systems will log failed attempts when users forget their password, with their username being locked out after three failed attempts; the hapless user then has to visit the network manager to explain why the password has been forgotten and to provide suitable proof of identity. (In some cases, it may have been an unauthorised user who tried to enter the system using the legitimate user's identity.)

15.2.3.12 Levels of access

All centrally managed network systems, servers and many client-based operating systems offer control over the levels of access to data. This may be accomplished by controlling a user's access to files, directories (folders) and data:

- read privilege allows the user to see selected information
- write privilege allows the user to change selected information
- execute privilege allows the user to create new files, folders or data sets.

These privileges may be issued via a user group, as a direct privilege or as part of a domain a user belongs to. The level of privilege may also roam with the user as they use a range of systems or may be specific to one computer system.

Membership of user groups and the privileges offered to each employee must be reviewed at regular intervals. It is essential that someone who no longer needs access to certain files or data has their privilege level amended.

15.2.3.13 Software updating

Ensuring that software updating takes place guarantees the system is safe from possible faults and vulnerabilities. For many applications, the update process is automatic, removing the need for the user to worry about how up to date their system is.

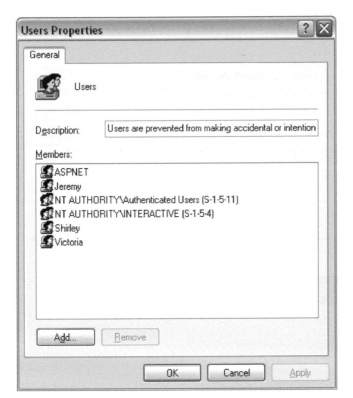

Figure 15.25 Members of a user group

Figure 15.26 Automatic updates for the Windows operating system

Operating systems such as Windows use automatic updating to maintain the security and quality of the operating system. Linux systems use the apt-get tool, which accomplishes a similar function.

Activity 15.6

Security check

1 Check what security is on your home computer, assess the threats and complete a comprehensive audit of your system.

2 Use your audit to improve security as you proceed.

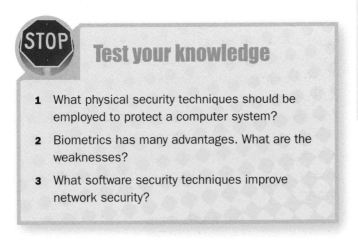

Test your knowledge

1 What physical security techniques should be employed to protect a computer system?

2 Biometrics has many advantages. What are the weaknesses?

3 What software security techniques improve network security?

To ensure that the ICT system is secure is essential, and the security measures have an impact on organisations as well as individuals. Security issues affect the daily lives of many people and are covered by legislation in many cases.

15.3.1 Security policies

Many organisations will agree, maintain and operate a range of policies in the management of security in their organisation's ICT environment. The purpose of these policies is to ensure that all employees, departments, suppliers and customers adhere to a common principle which will ensure their welfare as well as that of the system.

Common policies agreed by most organisation include: budget setting; disaster recovery; predetermined updates and reviews of security procedures and scheduling of security audits; codes of conduct, including email usage, Internet usage and software acquisition and installation; how surveillance and monitoring may occur; risk management.

15.3.1.1 Budget setting

Annual budget setting and the management of finances to ensure organisational systems security is maintained at an acceptable level are essential. Effective security is not free and requires continual investment to maintain control. In budgeting annually for organisational systems security, you may need to consider:

- the replacement cost of redundant equipment and software versions
- the cost of each audit
- the training of staff
- software licensing
- the procurement of external consultation and support
- staff wages relating to organisational systems security.

15.3.1.2 Disaster recovery

A disaster recovery policy details what actions are to be taken in the event of a human-based or natural disaster which may befall an organisation. Disasters may include: natural disasters, fire, power failure, terrorist attacks, organised or deliberate disruptions, system and/or equipment failures, human error, computer viruses, legal issues, worker strikes and loss of key personnel.

The disaster recovery policy may include procedures for data relocation, use of alternative sites, the hiring of additional personnel and equipment, and will be supported by appropriate levels of insurance to fund the immediate aftermath and recovery process.

See also section 15.1.2.1 on page 180.

15.3.1.3 Updating security procedures and scheduling security audits

Predetermined updates and reviews of security procedures need to be carried out on a periodic basis. A security review is only as good as the knowledge acquired at that time. It is essential to check security policies for currency and to compare the policy against current knowledge and new threats. While security and computer systems need regular updating, the update may have an impact on established systems. Often updates need to be trialled before a planned roll out occurs.

Security audits of physical and networked systems need to take place at regular intervals; these are often done without informing the employees of the organisation, to prove the authentic effectiveness of the systems.

In network management, an audit of database and network logs may occur, with detailed analysis to look for recurring issues, which may represent an existing threat. This audit is often combined with penetration testing, simulating a hacker or denial of service attack to establish the validity of existing systems.

While breaking into a building may seem an extreme way of testing physical security, some organisations will employ covert personnel to attempt to circumvent their physical security systems.

15.3.1.4 Codes of conduct

Many employees, contractors, customers and suppliers may use your organisation's systems. To allow them complete freedom is inadvisable. Creating codes of conduct which are signed by the individuals who need access to your system places the legal responsibility on them. Many organisations operate codes of conduct including those listed in Table 15.3 on page 202.

15.3.1.5 Surveillance and monitoring policies

Placing a CCTV or covert surveillance camera in any organisation may cause considerable distress among the workforce and could be the prelude to union action. How surveillance and monitoring may occur has to be clearly defined and agreed with employees, including describing the reasons for using surveillance, where it will be used and the type of surveillance equipment.

15.3.1.6 Risk management

Risk management involves the measurement and prediction of possible issues, together with a strategy for dealing with each risk if it arises. Depending on the severity and the type of threat, an organisation may elect to:

- **tolerate** the risk and 'ride the storm' – for example, a change in the economic climate or a competitor attempting to undermine the product
- **treat** the risk, by investing in an upgrade or an alternative approach
- **terminate** the risk by attacking it head on, stopping the hacker or the virus
- **transfer** the risk by adapting the approach of the organisation.

Activity 15.7

AuditsRUs

Imagine you are a security auditor with AuditsRUs and have been asked to review the network security policies of BigCity College.

1 Using your own place of study, identify what email and Internet usage policies exist.

2 Compare these policies to others which may be in operation (search the Internet).

3 Create a comprehensive policy that would protect the network as well as maintain the academic interests of future students and staff.

15.3.2 Employment contracts and security

15.3.2.1 Hiring policy

When recruiting new employees or promoting existing personnel, organisations need to establish a positive hiring policy which does not conflict with national employment law. It is essential to look at the background of the employee, their previous employment record and criminal record, to check their references and to set an assessment task.

Many organisations have a probationary period for new personnel and, in some cases, when internally

▲ **A CCTV camera**

promoting staff. This enables the organisation to carefully establish trust with the new recruit and allow them responsibility one stage at a time. It is foolish to give the new recruit full access to all systems straight away before they have proved their trustworthiness.

15.3.2.2 Separation of duties

To ensure that there is not complete reliance on one individual to maintain the overall systems security of the organisation, a separation of duties is often established. This involves having many team members who each have one critical duty to manage, and a deputy who is also experienced in that area to cover in the case of absence or departure.

15.3.2.3 Disciplinary and investigation procedures

While organisational systems security is paramount, infringement by any employee or business partner has to be dealt with in a fair, confidential and legally acceptable manner, ensuring compliance with established disciplinary and investigation procedures.

There is always the possibility that the suspected employee might not be the one who has caused the infringement, so to falsely accuse someone could lead to a very damaging legal action. If an infringement has occurred, appropriate steps may include:

- suspension (with pay) of the employee involved
- an independent party recruited to investigate the matter fairly and impartially
- the immediate involvement of the police if it appears to be a criminal matter.

15.3.2.4 Training and communication

While ignorance is no defence in law, it is reasonable to expect any employer to ensure that staff receive necessary training, as well as maintaining regular communication with staff to ensure they are aware of their responsibilities.

Test your knowledge

1 Managing various policies is complex. What policies are needed in the security of a typical system?

2 How should any issue with an employee be handled?

15.3.3 Code of conduct

A verbal assurance from an employee (and therefore user of the system) that they will 'behave' is not quite enough assurance for most employers and systems managers. Instead, employees are expected to sign, agree and adhere to a variety of policies (see Table 15.3), each of which ensures that the system users will abide by rules that suit the organisation and its security needs.

Activity 15.8

Security policies

1 Find out what the user area usage policy is for your centre.

2 How is software acquisition and installation managed at your centre?

15.3.4 Legislation

With improvements in computer technology came the ability to subvert the rights and intellectual property of others. In the management of organisational systems security, the ICT professional needs to be aware of four primary laws:

- Computer Misuse Act 1990
- Copyright, Designs and Patents Act 1988
- The Data Protection Acts of 1984, 1998, 2000
- Freedom of Information Act 2000.

Email usage policy	Governs what subjects are unacceptable in the sending of emails. Often the policy will define the acceptable size of attachments to be sent, as well as the types of attachments and how to manage the mailbox contents. Gives details of unacceptable activities such as stalking, harassment, spamming and the deliberate exchange of corporate information to external parties. Many email usage policies will declare the network management's right to monitor all emails.
Internet usage policy	Details which sites cannot be visited and what cannot be downloaded. Like the email policy, the network management normally declare their right to monitor network traffic.
Software acquisition and installation policy	The purpose of a software acquisition and installation policy is to prevent personal and unlicensed software from being installed on the system, as well as ensuring that there is no duplication of software – this prevents compatibility issues as well as the transmission of worms, viruses and trojans.
User area usage policy	In systems with a large number of users (such as your educational centre), storage space is at a premium. To ensure that copyright is not infringed and that decency is maintained, many organisations will define what users cannot store, as well as the limit you may have on your user area. Naturally, storage needs will vary according to role; for example, software developers may need more space when working on a complex application.
Account management policy	An account management policy operates at two levels, and will define: ● the responsibilities of the network management in maintaining a level of service ● the responsibilities of the user to ensure that their password is current and that they do not share their details with anyone else.

Table 15.3 Security policies to be agreed by employees

Remember!

Outside England and Wales, some legal authorities have slightly differing dates and definitions; it may be worth checking how the law is implemented in your part of the UK.

15.3.4.1 Computer Misuse Act 1990

The Computer Misuse Act 1990 is criminal law (involving penalties such as imprisonment) and deals with three areas:

1 unauthorised access to computer material, such as:
   a) the use of another person's username and password in order to access a computer system, use data or run a program
   b) altering, deleting, copying or moving a program or data or simply obtaining a printout without authority
   c) laying a trap to obtain a password.

2 unauthorised access to a computer system with intent to commit or facilitate the commission of a further offence – for example, creating a backdoor or trojan, or allowing a covert user administrator privileges

3 unauthorised modification of computer material, including the distribution of viruses, as well as the amendment of data to gain personal advantage (such as bank account details).

The terms of the Computer Misuse Act are comprehensive and cover all known instances of hacking, system access and network use.

15.3.4.2 Copyright, Designs and Patents Act 1988

The Copyright, Designs and Patents Act 1988 gives the creators of unique works the right to retain the intellectual property and seek action for damages against those who distribute copies of their work or steal the work in order to pass it off as their own.

The act covers:

- music such as CDs, MP3s and podcasting
- visual media such as DVDs, video streaming and AVI files
- written material such as unique work submitted in an assignment (this is why your tutors don't allow plagiarism) or any other written material, including text from a website
- designs which have been used to create a unique system, application, structure or machine, which impacts on the duplication of some computer hardware technologies
- software in its many forms – for example, if a piece of game software has been created for a hand-held console and it is 'ported' across to a PC **emulator**, this is considered copyright theft
- unique images such as works of art – artists have been known to sue websites and publications for use of their images without the appropriate permission and licence agreement.

When using the intellectual property of others, there are two ways to ensure you are not the subject of legal action:

- explicitly quote the source, who it is, when it was created, etc.
- get their permission, in writing.

15.3.4.3 The Data Protection Acts of 1984, 1998, 2000

The Data Protection Acts of 1984, 1998, 2000 are governed by eight principles:

1 All data stored is fairly and lawfully processed.
2 Any data is processed for limited and clearly declared purposes.
3 The data is adequate, relevant and not excessive.
4 All data is accurate and is maintained as such.
5 No data is kept longer than necessary.
6 Data about a person is processed in accordance with the individual's rights.
7 All data is kept secure.
8 Data is not transferred abroad without adequate protection.

The Act covers how personal information can be used and accessed. The Data Protection Act is not limited to computer-based information and also covers most paper records. In the UK the Information Commissioner regulates the Act and can be contacted by anyone concerned about data held about them. (A link to the Information Commissioner's Office website has been made available via www.heinemann.co.uk/hotlinks – enter express code 2315P.)

15.3.4.4 The Freedom of Information Act 2000

The Freedom of Information Act 2000 is unlike the Data Protection Act, which allows you to see data only about yourself. The Freedom of Information Act allows you to request a copy of any official information or communication, whether electronic, paper-based or published by other means.

The Freedom of Information Act applies to information published by public authorities such as central and local government, the National Health Service, schools, colleges and universities, the police and a variety of other public bodies, committees and advisory bodies.

As a private individual you can apply for a copy of information on a huge range of subjects – this could be problematic for an organisation's system security as the information could be used as a tool to engineer knowledge.

The Act allows an organisation to refuse disclosure in many circumstances, including:

- if the information is already accessible by other means
- if the information is to be publicly published
- information that was supplied by or relates to an organisation dealing with security matters – e.g. if the information applies to an organisation's system security
- if it would be against the interests of national security and defence

What does it mean?

An **emulator** is a software application which behaves like another system.

- information that regards international relations and relations within the United Kingdom
- information that could affect the economy
- current investigations and proceedings conducted by public authorities
- law enforcement and court records and information for the legal professional
- audit functions
- parliamentary privilege and the formulation of government policy, along with the conduct of public affairs
- communications with the monarch and the management of honours
- health and safety and environmental information
- personal information and information provided in confidence
- commercial interests – this applies to an organisation's system security
- prohibitions on disclosure in line with official secrets.

Test your knowledge

1. What laws protect the user and how?
2. What is the impact of copyright law if legal action is to be taken?
3. What does the Computer Misuse Act cover?

15.3.5 Copyright

In order to access the copyrighted property of an individual or an organisation, a licence agreement is established. This is the case for music, video, published documents and software.

The complexity of software, its uses and who may benefit from it has lead to an extensive range of licence agreements being developed (see Table 15.4).

Licence type	Explanation
Individual	A commercial licence for the user or computer only. Duplication of software on to any other computer system can invalidate the licence and incur potential legal action.
Concurrent	A commercial licence where a user may have many computers but only use one at a time, as in the case of home, office and laptop computers. A concurrent licence will add to the cost of the software.
Site/Campus	A commercial licence for all computers in the offices of one specific organisation. This may be a regional or national branch or the site of your school/college.
Corporate	A commercial licence for the entire organisation, including all sites.
Freeware	There are many definitions for this type of licence. Common etiquette implies that this software is free to use, but you cannot distribute it or sell copies of it without making some financial concession to the owner.
Shareware	Shareware is like freeware, but the expectation is that if you like the software, use it regularly or intend to use it for commercial gain, you have to pay a fee to the creator.
The differences between freeware and shareware are a grey area, as the creator decides the terms.	
Open-source	The code for the software is freely available for you to edit, compile and recommend improvements. Commercial gain is based on an agreement between yourself and the original creator(s).
Educational	A commercial licence with reduced costs for schools, colleges and universities, as well as some charities. The purpose is often to encourage the proliferation of the software.
Student	A commercial licence for the benefit of the student, often an older version or a version at a reduced cost, where you get the software only with no manuals or support.

Table 15.4 Types of software licence agreements

15.3.6 Ethical decision making

Ethics is the study of values and equality and is a subject that has kept philosophers in business for thousands of years.

15.3.6.1 Freedom of information versus personal privacy

The proliferation of the Internet enabling data to be widely accessible has had a positive impact on the freedom of information but a potentially negative impact on one's personal privacy.

It is now possible to sign up to sites in the UK which offer a directory services resource, combining information from the electoral roll, phone directory and postcode information to offer services such as street maps and Google Earth. The positive use of such information is that people can find their way to a long lost relative; but the negative impact is that it creates the opportunity for unwanted visits.

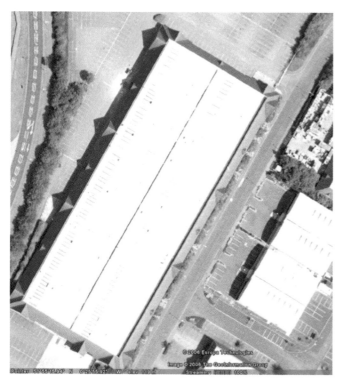

▲ Could this image be used to invade privacy?
Image obtained from Google Earth™ Mapping Service
©Google 2007

15.3.6.2 Permission issues

The use of photographs (images), videos and CCTV footage of others can be emotive; apart from the obvious copyright issue, the possible invasion of privacy needs to be considered. Websites containing user videos and images are very popular (for example, YouTube). However, if there is no permission from the copyright holder or the person(s) who is/are in the video, you may find that – apart from causing them distress – you have a team of ambitious legal professionals looking to relieve you of your bank balance!

As technology becomes increasingly pervasive and the methods used to share information and media become easier, the ethical nature of technology will continue to be questioned.

Many organisations will need to decide what they will allow and what they feel they need to deny in order to maintain their own corporate ethical values.

Activity 15.9

Copyright

1 What copyright exists for operating systems such as Linux?

2 How would you protect your copyright if you created a new application or game?

15.3.7 Professional bodies

There are many professional bodies that have an interest in organisational systems security. Here is a list of those who have a specific impact on legal issues and the overall decision making process.

- **Business Software Alliance (BSA)** work with companies to help them avoid software licensing issues and offer a range of audit tools to check their systems.
- **Federation Against Software Theft (FAST)** is the anti-piracy arm of the software creation industry. They work at an international level to combat 'organised' as well as 'private' piracy.

- **Federation Against Copyright Theft (FACT)** is the anti-piracy arm of the media industry and deals with the illegal duplication and distribution of music, movies and other media.
- **British Computing Society (BCS)** regulates some of the standards set for the computer industry in the UK. Many higher education courses use a framework defined by the BCS. Many ICT professionals, especially in the software sector, are members of the BCS.
- **Institute of Electronic Engineers (IEE)** – as part of the IEEE, the IEE has set many networking standards, with wireless and Ethernet being notable examples. Many ICT professional are members, the largest membership being within the systems development and networking sectors.
- **Association of Computing Machinery (ACM)** is the international equivalent of BCS.

Preparation for assessment

Task 1 (P1, P2, M1, M2, D1)

Describe the various types of threats to an organisation, a system and data. Explore the direct security issues that may be encountered within an academic network, identifying the likelihood of each threat (you must identify at least four) and describing their potential impact. Propose acceptable steps to counter these issues.

Take two of the threats identified and explain their operation of security issues and how they could enable illegal access to data without causing any damage.

Task 2 (P3, P4, M3)

Describe the countermeasures available to an organisation that will reduce the risk of damage to information and physical systems. Encryption is used to prevent unauthorised access to information. Explain the operation and use of an encryption technique in ensuring security of transmitted information.

Task 3 (P5, P6, D2)

Disaster recovery is critical to the management of a secure system. Following common practices, describe different methods of recovering from a disaster.

Using your study centre as an example, describe the tools and policies your organisation can adopt in managing organisational issues in relation to ICT security. Justify the security policies used at your centre.

Principles of Software Design and Development

Introduction

Computer **programs** can be written to carry out a wide range of tasks, from writing letters to guiding a space rocket. Programs are particularly good for repetitive tasks, since computers can work very fast; they do not become bored or tired and they can do tasks involving calculations with 100 per cent accuracy. However, computers have no in-built intelligence and are incapable of independent thinking – they can only follow the instructions within a program.

Whatever function you want a computer to perform, all you have to do is write the program.

A program is a little like a recipe for cooking a meal. A recipe lists, in detail, the steps you must follow to make the meal. Recipes are written in English, to be understood by humans and assume a level of common sense from the cook.

Computers, on the other hand, do not have common sense and require a very precise set of instructions.

After completing this unit, you should be able to achieve these outcomes:

- Know the nature and features of programming languages
- Be able to use software design and development tools
- Be able to design and create a program
- Be able to document, test, debug and review a programmed solution.

> ## What does it mean?
>
> A **program** is a set of instructions that tells the computer what to do.

Thinking points

Programming is the key to everything about ICT. Without programs a computer is useless, but a program can make a computer do almost anything. While writing programs can be difficult and challenging, it can also be exciting and rewarding. Many people feel a real sense of achievement when they get a complex program to work and programming gives an opportunity for you to be creative and provides limitless opportunities to further your knowledge.

What programs do you most enjoy using? Why do you find them enjoyable? How complex do you think they were to create?

Even if you don't intend to become a programmer, a basic understanding of how programs work is useful for anyone who is planning a career in IT. Why do you think this might be?

The microprocessor or chip at the heart of a computer can only understand instructions in the form of binary codes (made up of 1s and 0s), but as binary codes are very difficult for humans to understand, all modern programming is done using **symbolic languages** with English-like statements. This section looks at the nature and features of programming languages:

- the types of language
- the reasons why an organisation might choose one language in preference to another
- how data can be categorised into data types, ready for processing.

18.1.1 Types of language

Over the years, many different programming languages have been developed, each with their own set of features. As well as individual languages such as Cobol or Visual Basic, there are also broad categories into which programming languages fall, as follows.

- **Procedural programming languages** break up the programming task into a number of procedures (also called subroutines or functions). Each procedure carries out a specific task and is called from the main program (see section 18.2.2).
- **Object-orientated programming** (OOP) takes a different approach to the structure of a complex program. OOP was developed in response to the difficulties that were experienced in creating highly complex systems using the procedural approach. With OOP, a program is broken down into **objects** rather than procedures.
- Rather than being a different way of structuring a program (like procedural and OO programs), a **visual programming language** is simply one that is designed to work in a Windows environment. It has features which support the creation of Windows objects such as menus, dialogue boxes and buttons.
- **Mark-up languages** are not true programming languages, as they do not contain instructions to control the flow of the program, such as decision structures or loops. Instead, mark-up languages

give instructions to control the format and layout of a computer file. The best known mark-up language is **HTML**, which is used to create web pages.

- Where web pages need to carry out programming functions like making decisions, the code for this has to be included within the HTML using **script languages**.

Table 18.1 summarises the different types of languages.

It's worth bearing in mind that these different categories are not necessarily mutually exclusive. Many modern programming languages combine features of the different types. For example, although Visual Basic was originally thought of as a procedural language, the latest versions have included facilities which allow programs to be written in a way that follows the object-oriented approach – and, of course, Visual Basic is also a visual programming language.

Types	Examples
Procedural languages	Cobol Basic
Object-oriented	Java
Visual	Visual Basic
Scripting	JavaScript
Mark-up	HTML

Table 18.1 Types of programming languages

What does it mean?

Objects are different from procedures in that they group program instructions and data together. Objects represent real world entities, such as a student in a college database or a book in a library system.

HTML stands for Hypertext Mark-up Language

Scripts are small pieces of code which are included in web pages to provide additional functionality and interactivity that cannot be provided by HTML.

Activity 18.1

Types of languages

1 See if you can find examples of code written in different languages.

2 What differences and similarities can you find between the languages?

18.1.2 Choosing a language

The choice of which program language to use is often a complex one. A number of different factors will influence the choice, and each of these factors will now be considered.

18.1.2.1 Organisational policy

Some companies (particularly larger ones) have an organisational policy as to what computer hardware and software is to be used. For example, a company might have a policy to use only Microsoft software because of the level of support that may be provided by such a large software vendor. Another company might have chosen to use Mac machines, while another might have a policy to use open-source software such as Linux.

A company's organisational policy may decide what type of computers are to be used

18.1.2.2 Suitability in terms of features

Two questions have to be answered when deciding on the suitability of a programming language.

- Will it work on the platform, i.e. the hardware?
- Does it have appropriate features to suit the type of applications that have to be written?

Some programming languages were specifically designed for particular types of applications. They have features and tools which support those types of applications. For example, military application software such as missile guidance tends to be written in languages such as Ada, while Windows programming is well supported by languages such as Microsoft Visual Basic. Languages such as Java are well suited to programming for the Internet and mobile phones. **PHP** is an open-source, server-side scripting language used to create dynamic web pages and is thus well suited to web server programming.

Some programming languages only work with particular hardware and software. The Visual Basic programming language, for example, will only work on PC hardware, running the Windows operating system. Other programming languages, such as Java, are hardware and software platform independent.

What does it mean?

PHP is a shortened form of **PHP Hypertext Preprocessor**. The initials come from the earliest version of the program, which was called Personal Home Page Tools.

18.1.2.3 Availability of skilled staff

In a commercial programming environment, the programmers who work for a particular company may already be skilled in using a particular language, so that language may be the natural choice for a new project.

For a project where staff need to be recruited to complete the programming, it should prove easier to recruit staff for a popular language rather than a less widely used one. So, this may also be a factor to be considered when deciding which language to use.

18.1.2.4 Reliability

Some programming languages have features built into them which help to make the programs more reliable and less likely to crash. The best example of this is the Ada language – it was designed from the outset to include features which make it reliable. Ada is often used for safety-critical systems such as the fly-by-wire control system of the Boeing 777 aircraft.

18.1.2.5 Development and maintenance costs

Clearly, the cost of developing and maintaining programs is an important consideration when embarking on a software development project. Some languages have a reputation for cutting development costs by making it easy and quick to develop and maintain (update) programs. For example, in the 1980s, RPG (report program generator) was specifically designed to allow the speedy creation of reports.

18.1.2.6 Expandability

While most of the programs you will write for this unit will only be used by one person at a time, some software systems have to support hundreds or even thousands of simultaneous users. Systems written for interactive websites, for example, may need to support a very large number of users – without crashing.

Some languages expand or scale better than others and have features which support large systems. Such languages would be the choice for a project where this is an important consideration. For example, programming languages such as PHP support computer clusters, where a number of high-performance computers can work closely together to support very large number of users.

Activity 18.2

Availability of skilled staff

1 Which programming skills are in the most demand? Take a look at some computing job websites to see what skills appear in job adverts. The jobs section of www.computing.co.uk is a good place to start.

2 Ada and PHP are popular languages but are not often used for teaching programming. Use the Internet to research the history of these languages. Where does the name **Ada** come from?

18.1.3 Features of programming languages

All programming languages have a number of common features. These enable the programmer to handle data (through variables), to structure a program (through loops, conditional statements and case statements involving logical operators) and to write the individual lines of code that set up the data and allow input and output to take place.

18.1.3.1 Variables

All the data that is input into a program must be stored somewhere. Programs store this data in defined memory areas called **variables**. Variables are also used as temporary storage areas for data needed during processing and the data output by a program would normally come from program variables as well.

The contents of variables are lost when a program ends. For more permanent storage, programs must save (output) the data to files.

Variables have two important attributes:

● a **name** is allocated by the programmer to identify the variable within the program.
● a **data type** defines the sort of data that the variable can store (see page 217).

Naming conventions for variables expect the name to start with a letter and consist of any combination of numbers and letters (but not spaces). A name can be up to 255 characters long but you cannot use any symbols (except the underscore symbol). You cannot use any of the **reserved words** in a language either.

You could name variables by simply using single letters of the alphabet, such as a, b or c. However, this is not recommended because it gives no clue as to the variable's use. A better approach is to give variables meaningful names such as 'counter' or 'student_age'.

Remember!

Note the use of underscore in 'student_age' to separate the words and create visually a more meaningful name.

Variables are normally declared or created at the beginning of a program. In Visual Basic, for example, there is a **Dim** instruction, which takes the general form:

Dim variable_name As data_type

So, to declare a variable called student_age with an integer data type, your instruction would be:

Dim student_age As Integer

You could declare more variables with additional Dim instructions but it is more efficient to list variables with the same data type in the same instruction:

Dim student_age, counter As Integer

18.1.3.2 Local and global variables

The 'scope' of a variable is an important concept.

Most programs are split into a number of different sections (usually called procedures, subroutines or modules, depending on the language). Variables are normally declared within a section and can only be accessed and used within that section, not throughout the whole program. These are known as **local variables**. You can, however, declare variables which can be accessed and used across all the sections of a program – these are known as **global variables**.

In Visual Basic, global variables are declared at the top of the program before all the different subroutines. Instead of using the Dim key word, the variable name is preceded by 'Public shared':

Public Shared Grand_Total as Integer

Although there are occasions when you cannot avoid using global variables, they are not considered good practice. Problems can arise with global variables, especially in large and complex systems which are written by a team of programmers. There may be misunderstandings about how the global variables are used and different procedures may use them in different ways.

18.1.3.3 Arrays

Variables normally only store a single value but, in some situations, it is useful to have a variable that can store a series of related values – using an **array**. For example, suppose a program is required that will calculate the average age among a group of six students. The ages of the students could be stored in six integer variables:

Dim age1 as integer
Dim age2 as integer
Dim age3 as integer
. . .

However, a better solution would be to declare a six-element array:

Dim Age(5) as integer

This creates a six-element array, age(0) through to age(5). Note that arrays are numbered from zero.

18.1.3.4 Loops

Loops are used where instructions need to be repeated either a certain number of times or until some criterion is met.

What does it mean?

A **reserved word** is one used within a programming language as part of a command, e.g. PRINT.

A **loop** is a part of a program that is repeated.

For example, if you wanted a program that printed out a times table from 1 to 12, the most efficient way to write the program would be with a section of code that repeats (loops) 12 times.

Remember!

A loop is also called an **iteration construct**.

There are various types of loops. The main two are:
- **fixed loops**, which execute a fixed number of times
- **conditional loops**, which execute repeatedly until some condition is met.

■ Fixed loops

In Visual Basic (and many other programming languages), the fixed loop is implemented using the **For** statement, which takes the general form:

```
For counter_variable = start_value to end_value
    Statements to be executed inside the loop
Next
```

The counter variable (called counter_variable in the example) is a counter which is set to the start_value at the start of the loop. The statements inside the loop are executed and, when the Next statement is reached, the counter_variable is **incremented** and the loop is executed again.

This continues until the value in the counter variable reaches the end value. Then the loop stops and the statement following the next statement is executed.

This example shows how a For loop could be used to create a 4 times table:

```
Dim result(12) As integer
Dim counter As Integer
For counter = 1 To 12
    Result(counter) = 4 * counter
Next
```

What does it mean?

When a variable is **incremented** 1 is added to it, so it 'counts'.

■ Conditional loops

Conditional loops, as the name suggests, continue to loop until some condition is met. In Visual Basic, these loops are implemented using the **Do…Loop Until** statement. Conditional loops can have the condition placed at the end of the loop, in which case they are known as **post-check loops**, and have the general format:

```
Do
    Statements to be executed inside loop
Loop Until condition
```

Alternatively, they can have the condition at the beginning, in which case they are known as **pre-check loops**:

```
Do Until condition
    Statements to be executed inside loop
Loop
```

The only difference is that with a post-check loop, the code within the loop is always executed at least once. With a pre-check loop, if the condition is met at the start of the loop, the code within the loop will not be executed at all. Therefore, the choice of which to use depends on the application.

The following piece of code will work out the average of the numbers entered. The user stops entering numbers by inputting an X (note that it must be a capital X):

```
Dim numbers As String
Dim total As Integer
Dim counter As Integer = 0
numbers = InputBox('Enter number, X to exit')
Do Until (numbers = 'X')
    total = total + numbers
    counter = counter + 1
    numbers = InputBox('Enter number, X to exit')
Loop
MsgBox('average is ' & total \ counter)
```

In this example the condition is placed at the beginning of the loop (pre-check) since if the user inputs an X the loop must be exited before the rest of the loop is executed, otherwise an error will result when trying to add the X to the total.

18.1.3.5 Conditional statements

Conditional statements allow a choice to be made as to which set of statements are to be carried out next. The choice is made based on a criterion such as the value of a variable, and this may depend, for example, on an option that the user has selected. In most programming languages, selection is done with conditional statements using the **If** key word.

Generally, selection constructs take the form:

```
If (condition) then
    statements to be executed if the condition is true
else
    statements to be executed if the condition is false
end if
```

For example, the following simple If statement adds £2.50 postage and packing only if the total order is under £15:

```
If (ordertotal < 15) then
    ordertotal = ordertotal + 2.5
End if
```

The comparison operator < is used, which means 'less than'. A list of the comparison operators you can use is shown in Table 18.2.

In the previous example there is no **Else** section to the statement, but you can use this to select which one of two sets of code statements are executed. This is shown in the next example which adds a discount of 5 per cent if the total order is over £50 or 10 per cent if it is over £100, but no discount for orders of £50 or less.

```
Dim discount As Single = 0
If (ordertotal >100) Then
    discount = 0.1
ElseIf (ordertotal >50) Then
    discount = 0.05
End If
```

18.1.3.6 Case statements

The **If… Else …** constructs can become quite complex, especially where there are many different conditions to be tested. An alternative to using multiple If statements is to use a **Select case** statement. This takes the form:

```
Select case Variable_used_as_condition
    Case Is Condition
        Statements to be executed if condition is true
    Case Is Condition
        Statements to be executed if condition is true
    Etc.
End Select
```

The example code shown below gives an extension of the discount example – now there are four different discount levels:

```
Select Case ordertotal
    Case Is >1000
        discount = 0.25
    Case Is >500
        discount = 0.15
    Case Is >100
        discount = 0.1
    Case Is >50
        discount = 0.05
End Select
```

18.1.3.7 Logical operators

The conditional statements used in both If statements and in Do Until loops can use **logical operators** to combine two or more conditions. The logical operators are shown in Table 18.3.

The following example shows how a logical operator can be used in an If statement. It is another version of the code used to select the correct discount. In this case, some

Operator	Meaning
>	Greater than
<	Less than
=	Equal to
>=	Greater than or equal to
<=	Less than or equal to
<>	Not equal to

Table 18.2 Comparison operators

Operator	Meaning	Example
AND	Produces true if both sides are true	Age >18 AND Gender = 'F' Will only produce true if BOTH are true (over 18 and female)
OR	Produces true if either side is true	Age >18 OR Gender = 'F' Will produce true if EITHER the age is over 18 OR the gender is female
NOT	Produces the opposite result	NOT(UserInput = 'Y') Will produce false if the user input is 'Y', otherwise it will produce true

Table 18.3 Logical operators

customers are 'Gold' customers, as they have ordered over a certain amount in the past. 'Gold' customers automatically get the 25 per cent discount no matter how much they order. A variable called 'level' is used to record the fact that a customer is a 'Gold' customer.

    If (ordertotal >1000 Or level = 'Gold') Then
        discount = 0.25
    ElseIf (ordertotal >500) Then
        discount = 0.05
    End If

In this example an **Or** logical operator is used to give the 25 per cent discount to any order that is over £1000 or is made by a 'Gold' customer.

Remember!

In some languages, the assignment sign is an equals sign preceded by a colon as in **var := 0**.

18.1.3.8 Assignment statements

Assignment statements are used to assign values to variables. The equals sign is the assignment operator, and the value is assigned from right to left. So, in the following example, a value of 20 is assigned to the variable.

    myVariable = 20

Assignments can also be done in combination with mathematical operators. For example:

    myVariable = 20 + subtotal

This will take the value in the variable subtotal, add 20 to it and place the result in myVariable. The full list of mathematical operators is shown in Table 18.4.

Where operators are combined, the order in which they are executed is not left to right. Instead it is based on the order of mathematical precedence (as shown in Table 18.4). For example:

    myVariable = 10 + 2 * 3

In this instruction the answer is not 36 but 16, as the multiplication is done first. Parentheses (brackets) can be used to modify the order – anything in parentheses will be done first:

    myVariable = (10 + 2) * 3

This will produce a result of 36.

Operator	Meaning	Example	Order of precedence
^	Exponentiation (raise to the power of)	2 ^ 3 = 8	1
*	Multiply	3 * 2 = 6	2
/	Integer division	5 / 2 = 2	3
Mod	Remainder part of division	5 mod 2 = 1	4
+	Add	4 + 5 = 9	5
-	Subtract	3 - 2 = 1	6

Table 18.4 Mathematical operators

In a visual programming language such as Visual Basic, input and output are usually done via **controls**: text boxes, list boxes and buttons are placed on the form or web page that is displayed to the user.

Visual Basic is an event-driven language, so subroutines are written to respond to user events such as clicking a button. The subroutine can collect values that the user has entered in text boxes by assigning the text property of the text box to a variable. For example:

MyText = txtMyInput.text

This statement assigns the value entered in a text box called txtMyInput to a variable called MyText.

In a similar way, you can output a value to a text box or label simply by writing the assignment statement the other way around. So, to output text to a label called lblMyLabel, you would use the statement:

lblMyLabel.text = "Hello"

In this case, a string value has been used (note that it must be in double quotes), but a value contained in a variable could just as easily have been used. For example:

lblMyLabel.text = MyText

What does it mean?

A **control** is an object on a form such as a text box, label or drop-down box. Controls have attributes which decide how they look (such as their colour and font) and behave.

18.1.4 Data types

Every variable has a data type. This sets the type of data that will be stored and the range of values that the variable can accept. It can also define how the data will be formatted when displayed. The data types supported by Visual Basic and the range of data they can accommodate are listed in Table 18.5.

Choosing the right data type for a variable is important. Inappropriate choices could result in excessive amounts of storage space being set aside. If too little space is allocated, a problem could arise during data entry, or the system might crash when, for example, a table becomes full.

If a data item needs to be used in more than one part of a program, then it is important that the data type is consistent.

Data that you need to do calculations with must be placed in a numeric data type such as Integer or Single. However, you must ensure that only numeric data gets placed in these variables, as otherwise the program will crash.

Type	Used for	Range of values
Boolean	Values that can be true or false	True or false
Byte	Whole numbers	0 to 255
Integer	Whole numbers	–32,768 to +32,767
Long	Very large whole numbers	Approx. plus or minus 2 billion
Currency	Decimal numbers with 2 digits after the decimal	
Single	Floating point numbers	Up to 7 significant digits
Double	Large floating point numbers	Up to 14 significant digits
Date	Date and time	
Variant	Any type of data	
String	Any type of text	

Table 18.5 Data types supported by Visual Basic

Activity 18.3

Programming languages

1 What programming language will be used at your college or school for this course? Find out from your teacher why this choice was made. Were any other languages considered? What languages have been used in the past and on other courses? Are there any web development courses or modules at your school or college? If there are, what programming languages do they use? See if you can get some examples of code written in other languages from these courses or modules. You could meet up with students who are learning these languages and compare the program you have written. This will provide useful evidence for D1, which will be covered towards the end of the unit.

2 Based on the research you have done, write up a report explaining why different programming languages have been developed.

3 By now you should have written a number of example programs to learn how to use some of the features of the language you are using. Write an explanation (which can largely consist of annotated program listings) of the programs you have written, including:
   - what the benefits are of having a variety of data types available
   - what features the language has and how they work.

STOP

Test your knowledge

1 Explain what the following instructions are used for: If, ElseIf, End If, Select case, Dim, Do, MsgBox, Public shared.

2 Explain the difference between local and global variables.

3 What is an array?

4 Explain the meaning of these terms: loop, increment, condition, data type.

18.2 Software design and development tools

You will need an understanding of the basic features of programming languages before you can start to write a program. Before that, though, you need to consider how to design programs. Writing all but the simplest of programs is a complex process that requires planning. Just as an architect needs to design a new house, the first step in creating software is to produce a detailed design.

Much of the work done at the design stage is done by a systems analyst rather than a programmer. Systems analysts are often people who were previously programmers and who use the experience gained in developing software to help them plan and design how complete systems will work.

18.2.1 Software development life cycle

Developing a complex piece of software is a process involving a number of steps. Generally these steps are:

- understanding the scope of the project
- identifying requirements
- designing the system
- writing (coding) the programs
- testing the programs work properly
- maintaining the system once it has begun to be used.

This section looks at the first three of these steps. Section 18.3 (on page 223) looks at an actual example of designing and writing a program. In section 18.4 (on page 237), testing and documenting software systems are explained.

18.2.1.1 Understanding the scope of the project

The question being asked here is really, 'What will the system do, and what won't it do?' This may sound like an obvious question, but it is an important one to consider. It is also important to decide what is to be included and what is to be left out.

Computers are very powerful machines and there are many facilities you could include in the software you are developing if you had endless time and money. However, resources are likely to be limited. So, in some cases, you may want to decide on the most important features and to develop the first version of the software with those features. You would then put the remaining features on the 'wish list' for future versions.

18.2.1.2 Identifying requirements

The next step in software development is to obtain a statement of the **user requirements**: what do they want the program to do? This may also sound like a simple question but, for a number of reasons, it is often difficult to answer.

- The user may not clearly understand what is required or they may not be able to give sufficient detail.

- The user requirements may be stated in terms which relate to their business and which the programmer may not be familiar with. For example, a user in the banking world will tend to state their requirements in banking and financial terms, but the programmer is an expert in programming, not banking.
- The user may not understand what is (and is not) possible when writing the software.

The user requirement may therefore need to be the subject of some discussion and negotiation between the user and the programmer.

There are a number of key questions that need to be asked.

- What are the primary **aims** of the system you are going to develop? This is one of the first things that need to be defined and will probably be in terms of the problem that the system is intended to solve or some opportunity it will provide. It is important to clarify this at the start because, sometimes, during the process of developing the software, people can lose track of the original reason for which the software was required.
- How does the **current system** work? In many cases, the software to be developed will replace an existing system. It may be a manual system (i.e. using people rather than computers) or it may be an old computer system that has outlived its usefulness. In any case, it is important to understand the current system thoroughly so that the new software can preserve its essential elements and its good features and avoid the problems from which it now suffers.
- What other systems does it need to **interface** with? No system works in isolation. All systems take input, from the user or another computer system. They also produce some kind of output. Part of understanding the system to be developed involves defining these inputs and outputs. At this stage, there is no need to go into great detail; that will come later.

18.2.1.3 Design

Once the scope and requirements have been defined, you need to consider how the program will achieve what is required. You will need to draw up a design for the program which defines:

- the user interface that will be provided – this might include designs for the screens that users will use to input data and the reports that will be output from the system
- the general structure of the program, including how it will be broken up into procedures and how those procedures will relate to each other
- the detailed design, showing how each of the procedures will carry out their required tasks
- how data will be stored by the system, including the variables that will be used and the file structures required.

A number of techniques can be used to produce this design, some of which are described in section 18.2.2.

18.2.1.4 Code

Once the design is complete, the task of coding the program can begin. In a large development project, this may involve a number of programmers, each of whom works on a different aspect of the system.

18.2.1.5 Test

As each part of the system is completed, it needs to be tested. Testing involves checking that the program works as it should and that all the functions and features of the program work correctly.

Testing is important to ensure the quality of the finished product and to ensure the program does not contain any **bugs**. It is also important to ensure that what has been produced matches the requirement outlined at the start of the project.

What does it mean?

A **bug** is a fault or error in a program which causes it to crash (end unexpectedly) or produce unexpected results.

18.2.1.6 Maintain

Once the program has been completed and is in use, the process is not over. Even with careful testing, it would be very unusual for a program not to experience problems when it is used for real. Such problems need to be corrected and there may also be improvements or additions to the program that are required. These issues are dealt with during the maintenance phase of the development cycle.

STOP Test your knowledge

1 What do you understand by the phrase 'scope of the project'?
2 What key questions should be asked at the requirements stage?
3 What sort of things need to be defined at the design stage?

18.2.2 Design tools

Developing programs is a complex process and, over the years, a number of different tools have been developed to model the way a software system will work. Most of the techniques involve creating diagrams, often starting with simple ones and then building up to more complex ones as the understanding of the system develops.

As Visual Basic is an event-driven system, any system developed with it naturally breaks down into the procedures that run as the various events occur. In simple programs, most of these event procedures are associated with command buttons. Therefore, creating the design for the user interface will often identify the main procedures in the program.

The design tools used are often chosen to match the language that is to be used at the coding stage, but this is not essential. Instead, they can serve to bridge the gap between the original problem and the solution that will, eventually, be coded. The diagrams produced clarify the problem and provide a way of communicating it to all concerned.

One device that can be used to define the steps that are required within a procedure is a **structure diagram**.

Structure diagrams define how the system will be broken down into procedures. They can also be used to model the working of individual procedures by showing how they can be split into decision structures and loops.

Case study

Northgate College

Northgate College requires a program that will keep track of students, including their personal details and the course(s) on which they have enrolled. The system needs to provide the following functions:

- enter new students on the system
- search for an individual student
- produce class lists of students by course.

This list is used to create the first simple structure chart, which breaks the system down into the three functions, as shown in Figure 18.1.

Having created one level of structure chart, more detailed structure charts can be created for the individual modules within the system.

The 'Enter new students' module needs to validate the details entered by the user (such as the student's age and postcode) to check they are correct. This requires a decision structure, because if the details are valid they can be saved, but if they are invalid an error message should be displayed. When drawing a structure chart, a decision structure is shown as a box with a circle in the corner, as in Figure 18.2.

The 'Produce class list' module requires a loop. First the course for which the class list is required must be identified. Then records of the student details on file

What does it mean?

A **structure diagram** is a simple diagram that shows how a program will be split into procedures.

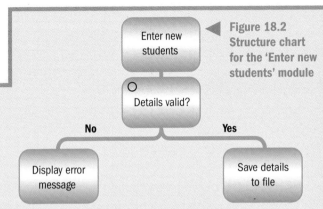

Figure 18.2 Structure chart for the 'Enter new students' module

need to be read off one by one until the end of the file is reached, using a loop. The records of the students who are enrolled on the course in question need to be displayed. Records for students on other courses can be ignored. The structure chart for this module is shown in Figure 18.3. A loop structure is shown as a box with an asterisk (*) in it.

1 Is the box process 'Input class required' (Figure 18.2) all that is required? Does the class number or name need validating? What would happen if the class entered did not exist? Add more detail to this part of the chart.

2 Produce a structure chart of the 'Search for an individual student' process shown in Figure 18.1.

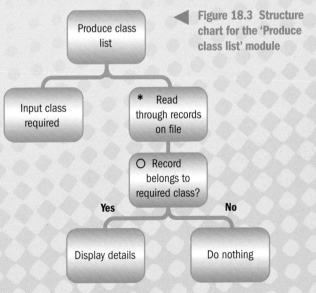

Figure 18.3 Structure chart for the 'Produce class list' module

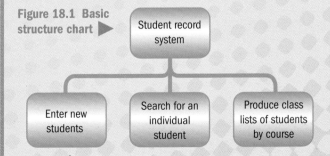

Figure 18.1 Basic structure chart

A **data flow diagram** (DFD) is concerned with how data flows into and out of the system, how it flows between the procedures inside the system and how it is stored inside the system.

Entity relationship diagrams (ERDs) show the relationships between data items.

■ Data flow diagrams (DFDs)

It is normal to create a series of DFDs, starting with the highest level, which gives a general overview of the information flow, and then progressing to more detailed and complex diagrams (low-level DFDs).

To draw DFDs correctly you must follow certain rules about the boxes, circles and arrows that make up the DFD.

A **high-level DFD** (sometimes called a **context diagram**) shows how the system interacts with the outside world. To construct a high-level DFD, first identify all the sources and recipients (input and outputs) of data that are external to the system. These are called the **external entities**. These external entities may be people or they may be other systems.

The high-level DFD then needs to be broken down into more detail (decomposed) to produce a **low-level DFD**. To do this, the single process in the centre of the diagram is divided into several, more detailed processes. The systems analyst refers to the information obtained during the investigation stage – the decisions made and the processing carried out should allow him/her to break down the single process into several steps.

As a rule of thumb, there should be a single process dealing with each data flow attached to an external entity.

Remember!

Don't be tempted to divide the process into too many steps or the diagram will become too complicated. Your low-level DFD needs to fit easily on to a single sheet of A4 paper.

Case study

External entities

For the Northgate College student records system, the external entities are:

- **administration staff** who enter student details and enrol them on the courses – input data flow
- **teachers** who request student lists for their classes – input data flow (to request the particular list) and output data flow (to produce the list).

To draw the high-level DFD for this, take a piece of A4 paper and write each of the external entity names inside an ellipse (an oval shape) around the outside of the paper. In the centre of the page draw a single process box, with the name of the system in it. Now add in arrows indicating the data flows that have been identified. With input data flows, the arrow must point

into the process box. The output arrows must point from the process box to the external entity. Each arrow must be labelled with the data flow name.

The complete high-level DFD for the student records system is shown in Figure 18.4.

1 Are there any other external entities and/or additional data flows in or out of the system that might exist in a real-life student records system?

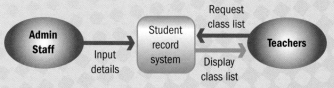

▲ **Figure 18.4 High-level DFD for the student records system**

So far the DFD has used external entities, processes and data flows. A new component is needed for the low-level DFD: the **data store** (see Figure 18.5). This is drawn as an open-ended box and is where data is held or stored in the system. It represents real-world stores of data such as files, lists, tables, etc. When drawing DFDs, only a process can write or read data to or from a data store, and each data store must be written to and read from at least once.

D1	Student Details

◀ Figure 18.5 A data store

Both process boxes and data stores are numbered for identification purposes. The one shown in Figure 18.5 is numbered D1.

The same external entities and the same data flows in and out of the external entities should appear in both the low-level and the high-level DFD. If you realise that you have missed out an external entity and/or data flow, you must redraw your high-level DFD.

You may find it helpful to practise drawing DFDs in small groups so you can discuss different ways of drawing the diagrams.

Case study

Low-level DFD

The single process in the high-level DFD of the student records system can be broken into two processes in the low-level DFD (see Figure 18.6).

Finally a data store is added, along with data flows that write data to the data store and read data from it. The data store is used to hold the student details. The completed low-level DFD is shown in Figure 18.7.

1 Think of a simple application, such as a system for tracking books in your college or school library, then create a high-level and a low-level DFD for the system.

2 Once you have created your DFDs, work in small groups to compare your DFDs. Remember that there is not always one single correct way to draw the DFD for a given system.

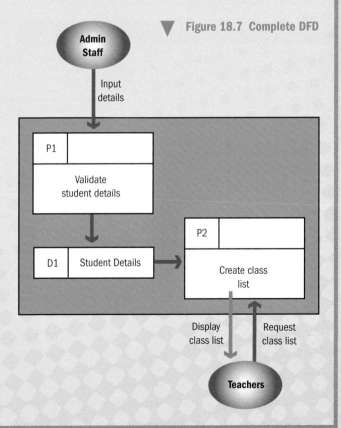

▼ Figure 18.6 Processes added to the low-level DFD

▼ Figure 18.7 Complete DFD

Creating DFDs can be quite difficult and requires practice. It may take several attempts to get a DFD right. Following the rules will help, but there is not necessarily just one correct diagram for a particular system.

Although this course only looks at two levels of DFDs, an analyst may go on decomposing the processes in the DFD to show even more detail.

■ Entity relationship diagrams (ERDs)

When an analyst has used the DFDs to identify the processes and data stores in the system, the entity relationship diagrams (ERD) can be produced (although in some cases the ERDs are produced first, then the DFD). There is no strict order in producing these diagrams; often the design evolves over some time with DFDs, ERDs and other diagrams being refined through several versions. ERDs are used to model the relationships that exist between different entities in the system.

Entities are real world things (customers, products, books) that need to be represented in the system. Entities have **attributes** – these are the elements that define a particular entity. Some simple examples are shown in Table 18.6.

Entity	Possible attributes
Customer	Name
	Address
	Credit limit
Product	Description
	Type
	Price
Book	Title
	Publisher
	Price

Table 18.6 Examples of entities and attributes.

An **occurrence** (sometimes called a **record**) of the entity Customer might be:

Name:	John Smith Office Supplies
Address:	10 Main Street, Watford
Credit limit:	£1,500

■ Primary and foreign keys

One (or more) of the attributes of a particular entity is normally defined as the **primary key** attribute.

The primary key is used to uniquely identify a particular occurrence of an entity. To guarantee uniqueness, numbers are normally used for primary key attributes. So, for example, on a database recording details of the entity Student, the attribute Student number would be the primary key. The system would need to ensure that each student received a unique number.

Most systems have a number of entities within them and entities often have relationships between them. For example, the entity Customers and the entity Orders are related, because every order a company receives comes from a customer. The relationship between two entities can normally be described by a verb. In this example the verb is 'place', because customers place orders – see Figure 18.8.

| CUSTOMERS |——— Place ———| ORDERS |

 Figure 18.8 The ERD showing the relationship 'Customers place orders'

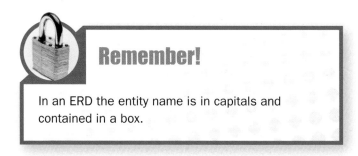

Remember!

In an ERD the entity name is in capitals and contained in a box.

How could you know which orders were placed by a particular customer? One of the attributes of the entity Customer will be the customer number. This unique number identifies each customer and so is the primary key of that entity. When that customer places an order, an occurrence of the orders entity is created. So that it is possible to tell which customer placed the order, the customer number is inserted into that occurrence of the orders entity. This is known as a **foreign key** (foreign because the key value belongs to another entity) – see Figure 18.9.

Note that the fields used to create the relationship between the two entities must have the same data type in both entities. This is one of the reasons why data types must be chosen with care.

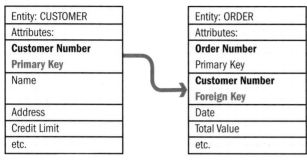

Figure 18.9 Primary and foreign keys

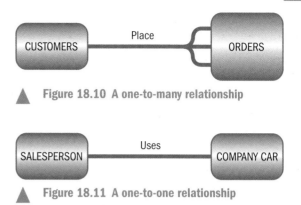

Figure 18.10 A one-to-many relationship

Figure 18.11 A one-to-one relationship

One-to-many relationships

Each customer will have at least one and probably many more orders that they placed. So, for one customer, there will be many occurrences of the orders entity. This type of relationship is therefore called a **one-to-many relationship**. In an entity relationship diagram, this is shown by a fork at the 'many' end of the line that joins the two entities (Figure 18.10).

One-to-one relationships

One-to-many relationships are the most common type of relationship between entities, but they are not the only type. Imagine a company that has a system to store data about its employees. The entity Employee will have attributes such as name, address, salary and the primary key will probably be employee number.

The sales people who work for the company are provided with a company car. That gives us another entity, Company_car, which has attributes such as registration number, make, model, etc. There is a relationship between these two entities, which can be described by the verb 'uses' because a salesperson *uses* a company car. As each salesperson is assigned only one company car at a time, this is not a one-to-many relationship, but a **one-to-one relationship**. The ERD for this type of relationship is shown in Figure 18.11.

This example also introduces another concept. A newly employed salesperson may not receive his/her company car until he/she has finished training, so the relationship between the two entities is optional. In other words, a salesperson does not have to have a related record in the company car entity. Likewise, when a salesperson leaves the company his/her car will remain unassigned until it is either sold or assigned to a new salesperson. Therefore, the relationship is optional at both ends.

However, in the case of customers and orders, an order *must* be related to a customer. Otherwise, who could have placed the order? This relationship is mandatory at the 'many' end. But since a new customer could register their details with the company without placing an order, a customer does not have to have a related occurrence on the orders table (although most will) so it is optional at the 'one' end.

Many-to-many relationships

There is a third type of relationship between entities: a **many-to-many relationship**. Imagine that a health centre is investigating a system to keep track of which drugs have been prescribed to patients by the doctors. Two of the entities that would be defined are Patients and Drugs. For each patient, at various times, the doctor may prescribe different drugs. This appears to be a one-to-many relationship as one patient can be prescribed many drugs. However, looking at it from the point of view of the drugs entity, then one drug can also be prescribed to many different patients – it is therefore a many-to-many relationship.

The problem with many-to-many relationships is that, for a given occurrence in one entity, it is not possible to tell which occurrence in the related table it is linked to. It could be linked to many different occurrences so it would not be clear which foreign key should be inserted.

For this reason, many-to-many relationships have to be rethought. To do this a new entity is added to link the two original entities. This link entity contains the foreign keys from both the original entities. The original entities both have one-to-many relationships with the link entity. In this example, Prescription is the link entity (see Figure 18.12).

In an ERD, this would be shown as in Figure 18.13.

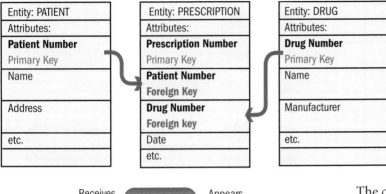

Figure 18.13 Replacing a many-to-many relationship

Figure 18.12 The Prescription entity

Activity 18.4

ERDs

1 Create an ERD design for a doctors' surgery appointments system. The surgery has several doctors and, of course, a lot of patients.

18.2.2.3 Form design

Forms are the part of the program that users will interact with. If the screens are not labelled correctly or clearly or if the order of the fields is inconsistent or illogical, users may find the program confusing and difficult to use. If the form layout is messy and contains spelling errors, users may perceive the software to be of poor quality and be reluctant to use it. Form designs consist of two main parts:

- the form layout showing the position of the various **controls** such as labels, input boxes, etc.
- a table showing the name and other properties of each of the controls.

The form layout can be hand-sketched or drawn using a graphics program. Form layouts must be clearly labelled, with the various controls placed in a neat and consistent way, with proper horizontal spacing and vertical alignment.

The controls should be in a logical order – that is, they should be in the order the user is most likely to use them, from the top of the screen to the bottom, and working from left to right.

18.2.2.4 Flow charts

We have already looked at DFDs, which provide an overview of the interrelationships within the whole system, and structure charts, which identify the structure of particular procedures. Now we will look at **flow charts**, which are used to add yet more detail to the design of a procedure and increase the programmers' understanding of the processing involved.

Flow charts can be used to design all sorts of processes, not just in programming. They use a variety of symbols to indicate the type of step involved at each stage in the process. These symbols are linked by arrows. Flow charts start with a circle containing the word Start, with a single arrow leaving the circle, and end with a circle containing the word Stop, with a single arrow entering.

Normal processing steps such as doing a calculation are contained in a rectangle – a brief description of the step

What does it mean?

A **control** is an object on a form such as a text box, label or drop-down box. Controls have attributes which determine how they look (such as their colour and font) and behave.

A **flow chart** is a diagram that shows the steps which must be taken to carry out some task, the sequence in which they occur and how they are linked.

Case study

Menu screen

The design for the menu screen of the Northgate College student records system (as described on page 221, is shown in Figure 18.14.

1 Can you think of other designs for the main menu that might be easier to use or more visually appealing?

2 Create a screen design for one of the modules in the student records system

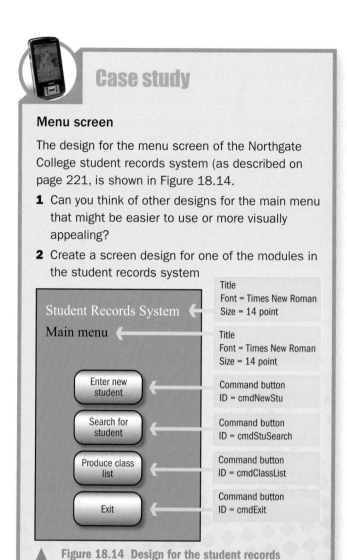

▲ Figure 18.14 Design for the student records system main menu

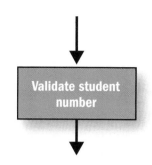

▲ Figure 18.15 Flow chart processing step

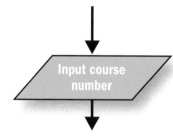

▲ Figure 18.16 Flow chart input box

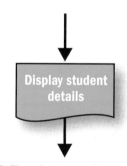

▲ Figure 18.17 Flow chart output box

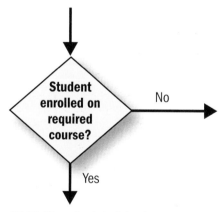

▲ Figure 18.18 Flow chart decision box

is written inside the rectangle (see Figure 18.15). The rectangle has one arrow entering (from the previous step) and one leaving (to the next step).

Processing steps which involve some input are shown in a parallelogram (see Figure 18.16) – also with a brief description of the step written in the box and with one arrow entering and one leaving.

Output steps are shown as a box which is meant to look like a torn off piece of paper (see Figure 18.17).

Where a choice or decision needs to be made (a selection building block) a diamond shape is used, containing a question that describes the choice (see Figure 18.18). One arrow enters the diamond shape and two leave it: one for the route taken if the answer to the question is yes, the other for if it is no.

Case study

Flow charts

One of the process boxes identified in the Northgate College student records system DFD was the 'Produce class list' process. The flow chart for this process is shown in Figure 18.19.

1 The structure chart for this same process is shown in Figure 18.3 on page 221. In groups, take a look at both the flow chart and the structure chart and discuss which gives you a better idea of how the process will work.

2 Create a flow chart for one of the other processes in the student records system.

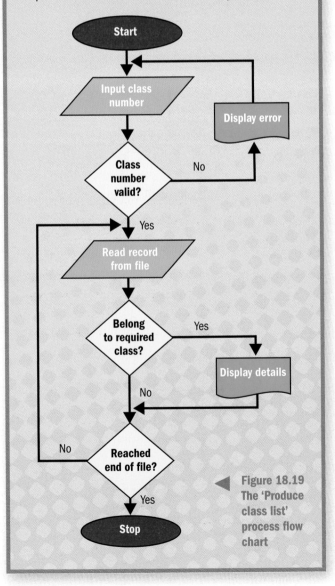

Figure 18.19
The 'Produce class list' process flow chart

One problem with flow charts is that they rarely resemble the actual code that must be written. To move the design closer to the actual code, **pseudocode** can be used.

Pseudocode (or **structured English**) provides a design technique which is very close to the code that will eventually be written. It is a kind of 'halfway house' between the high-level generalised techniques like DFDs and structure charts and the low-level details that are required in the actual code.

The name pseudocode comes from 'pseudo' (which means 'like' or 'a form of') and 'code'. It is an informal version of programming code that uses the structure of a programming language (e.g. decisions, loops, etc.), but does not worry about the strict syntax (rules) of the language. Flow charts can be thought of as diagrammatical pseudocode.

An example of pseudocode is shown in Table 18.7. This pseudocode is for the 'Produce class list' procedure for which we have already created the structure chart (see Figure 18.3) and the flow chart (see Figure 18.19). The pseudocode is shown alongside a simple version of the code written to implement this procedure.

Note that the pseudocode is very similar to the actual code, but the strict syntax rules of the language are not adhered to. With a simple procedure like this it would be unusual to create a structure chart, a flow chart and pseudocode, although you might do this for a very complex piece of code.

Action charts are particularly useful with event-driven Windows programs, as they show what happens when a certain event occurs. In a multi-form program they can also be used to show how the forms are linked together and how the user can move between them. To create action charts you really need to have completed your form design and have decided on all the different events that each form can respond to. An example action chart is shown in Figure 18.20.

Pseudocode	Actual Visual Basic code

Declare variables for:
Name (of student)
Age (of student)
Course (student is on)
Choice (of course to display)
Choice = input from list box
Open file
Do while not end of file
    Input name
    Input age
    Input course
    If choice = course then
        Add name to display list
        Add course to display list
    End if
Loop
Close file
	Dim name As String
	Dim age As Integer
	Dim course As String
	Dim choice As String
	choice = lstChoose.SelectedItem.Text
	lstName.Items.Clear()
	lstdispC.Items.Clear()
	FileOpen(1, 'myfile3.txt', OpenMode.Input)
	Do While Not EOF(1)
	    Input(1, name)
	    Input(1, age)
	    Input(1, course)
	    If choice = course Then
	        lstName.Items.Add(name)
	        lstdispC.Items.Add(course)
	    End If
	Loop
	FileClose(1)

Table 18.7 Pseudocode and Visual Basic code

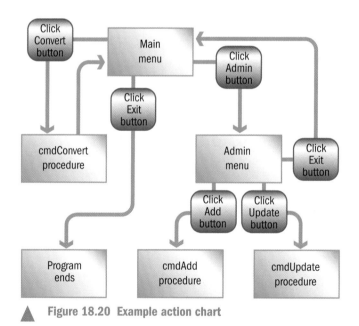

Figure 18.20 Example action chart

There are no strict rules on how to draw action charts. They just need to show clearly what happens when the actions (i.e. events) occur on each form.

18.2.2.7 Data dictionaries

Data dictionaries are used to list all of the data items that a program will use. They should include all the relevant information about the items, including the name of the item, the data type that will be used, the scope of the data item (local or global) and the procedure the item is used in. When the software being developed uses a database system, the data dictionary will relate to the ERDs that have been drawn up and will include information on primary and foreign keys. An example data dictionary is shown in Table 18.8.

STOP Test your knowledge

1 What are the different shapes of boxes used in flow charts and what does each shape mean?

2 Give examples of one-to-many, one-to-one and many-to-many relationships.

3 List the basic rules for creating DFDs.

Variable name	Type (normal or array)	Scope (Local or Global)	Data type	Used for
StudentNo	Normal	Local	Integer	ID number of student
Name	Normal	Local	String	The name of the student
Age	Normal	Local	Integer	The age of the student
Course	Normal	Local	String	The course the student is on
AddrLine1	Normal	Local	String	Address line 1
AddrLine2	Normal	Local	String	Address line 2
Town	Normal	Local	String	Town
Postcode	Normal	Local	String	Postcode

Table 18.8 Example data dictionary

18.2.3 Software structures

The structure of a program depends on the type of programming language you are using. Procedural languages split the system into procedures while object-oriented (OO) languages are based on objects.

18.2.3.1 Code structures

There are three basic structures which can be used to build a program, as follows:

- **Sequence** is when the program statements are followed one after the other. An example might be doing a calculation or accepting some input from the user.
- **Selection** (or a decision) is when a choice is made based on some criterion, and in most programming languages this is implemented using the 'if' instruction.
- **Iteration** (or repetition) is when a section of code is repeated using a loop. The two main types of loop are fixed and conditional loops.

When designing a procedure, a structure diagram can be used to identify which types of structures are required.

18.2.3.2 Functions

Most programming languages have a number of built-in facilities which carry out commonly required tasks for the programmer – these are usually called functions. Visual Basic has two types of function: the built-in ones which

are provided as part of the language and user-defined functions which can be written by the programmer.

An example of a Visual Basic built-in function is the IsNumeric function. This function is passed a value (in the bracket that follow the function name) and returns a value of true if the value it has been passed is numeric or false if it is not numeric. This function can be very useful in validating values entered by the user to check they are numeric. For example, in the student records system one of the student details that needs to be entered is their age – the following code could be used to ensure that the value entered by the user is numeric.

```
If IsNumeric(txtAge.Text) Then
    age = txtAge.Text
Else
    MsgBox('Age must be numeric')
End If
```

There are of course many other built-in functions – some useful ones are shown in Table 18.9.

18.2.3.3 Procedures

Procedures have already been mentioned – Visual Basic programs are mostly made up of event procedures which respond to user events such as clicking a button. These procedures always start with a line of code which Visual Basic creates for you, such as:

Protected Sub cmdCheck_Click(ByVal sender As Object, ByVal e As System.EventArgs) Handles cmdCheck.Click

Function	Purpose	Example
Format()	Used for formatting values	If variable MyNumber contained 27.5 the following would format it as £27.50: format(MyNumber, '£0.00')
Rnd()	Produces a random number between 0 and 1 (useful for games etc.). Multiply it to get a number in a larger range	MyNumber = 10 * rnd() This will produce a random number between 1 and 10
Left$()	Selects characters from a string starting from the left	If variable MyString contained 'BTEC' the following would produce 'BT': left$(MyString, 2)
Right$()	Selects characters from a string starting from the right	If variable MyString contained 'BTEC' the following would produce 'TEC': right$(MyString, 3)
Lcase$()	Converts a string to lower case	If variable MyString contained 'BTEC' the following would produce 'btec': Lcase$(MyString)
Ucase$()	Converts a string to upper case	If variable MyString contained 'btec' the following would produce 'BTEC' Ucase$(MyString)

For more information about the many other functions included in Visual Basic, use Help.

Table 18.9 Useful functions

In this example, 'cmdCheck' is the name of the button that this event procedure responds to. We know it responds to the user clicking the button as it contains the instructions 'Handles cmdCheck.Click'.

Visual Basic event procedures always end with the instruction 'End Sub'. You must ensure you don't change the starting and ending instructions and that all your code for the event is between them.

18.2.3.4 Classes and objects

Object orientation involves linking the data and the functions together in the basic OO building block of the **object**.

Software objects are based on real-world things in the application area that the software is being written for.

- In a library system, the objects might include books, members and loans.
- In a mail order system, the objects might include customers, orders and products.

Objects generally represent either physical things, like customers and books, or conceptual things like an order or a loan.

Closely related to the concept of the object is the **class**. A class is like a template for the objects of that class.

For example, in the class cars, objects of that class might be my Renault, the Queen's Rolls Royce and my neighbour's Ford. These are all **instances** of the class.

Classes have data associated with them, called **attributes**.

- A customer class would have attributes such as name, address, telephone number, etc.
- A book class would have attributes such as title, author, ISBN, publisher, etc.

Attributes are the data that belongs to the class, i.e. the things that describe the class.

Examples of instances of a class might be different types of car

Classes also have functions, called **methods**. Methods are things that the class can do.

- A customer class might have a 'change of address' method.
- A book class in a library system might have a 'go on loan' method.

A class defines the attributes and methods, and all objects of that class have the same attributes and methods.

Classes can be described by using a **class diagram**. This lists the name of the class, the attributes and the methods. Imagine a system that keeps track of the marks students have achieved in various assignments. Figure 18.21 shows the class diagram for the Student class. This simple class has just two attributes (name and marks) and three methods (set name, show marks and update marks).

An OO system is made up of objects (created using the class as a template) which work together by one object requesting a service from another (using the methods of that class). This process of requesting services is known as **message passing**. For example, imagine a Teacher class. An object of the Teacher class might pass a message to the Student class asking it to invoke its showMarks method, and the Student object returns the mark.

Student
StudentName
StudentMarks
setName
showMarks
updateMarks

◀ **Figure 18.21 Class diagram for the Student class**

It is important to understand that the only way in which other objects can gain access to the attributes of a class is by the methods of that class. This is one of the key differences between the earlier approaches to program design and the OO approach. In earlier methods data is passed between functions. In the OO approach data is contained within the object and is accessible only by the object's methods. This concept is known as **encapsulation**.

Test your knowledge

1 List and describe the three main software structures.

2 What are functions? Give an example of how they can be used.

3 Explain what objects, classes and methods are.

What does it mean?

Methods are the functions of a class, i.e. the things that the class can do.

Message passing is the technical name for the process by which one class gets another class to do something by calling one of its methods.

Encapsulation is the technical name for the way in which the attributes (data) and the methods (functions) of a class are packaged together within the class, and the data of the class can be accessed only via the methods.

This section shows how to apply the techniques that have been described so far, using a case study: the Fast Cash Bank currency converter.

18.3.1 Requirements specification

The requirements specification stage of the development process involves identifying the user requirements, not identifying technical requirements – that comes later in the design stage. As previously mentioned this stage and the design stage are often carried out not by a programmer, but by a system analyst.

Clearly, this stage needs to be undertaken in close consultation with the users and there are various ways in which their requirements can be defined. One way is to ask users to make a list of what they require from the new system. Another is for the systems analyst to interview users to identify what they think needs to be achieved by the new system. It is important for the users to prioritise the list of requirements, as not all may be achievable due to constraints on time or money. The end result of the requirements stage is a document which describes in detail what the user requires. This is usually agreed with the users before work on the design of the system begins.

We will look at the various sections of the requirements specification in turn.

18.3.1.1 Inputs

The purpose of this section of the requirements specification is to identify the data that will be input to the system. Because it is important that the data that is input is correct, it should be validated. So, the users will need to identify what would be valid and invalid input for each data item. This might be in terms of ranges of acceptable values if the data is numeric or a list of valid text entries. The information about the input data will be used at the design stage to create the DFDs for the system. It will also be used much later when testing the system to ensure that the validation works as required.

18.3.1.2 Outputs

The purpose of this section is to identify the outputs that the users will expect from the system. As with the input, this information will later be used in the creation of the DFDs.

18.3.1.3 Processing

In this section, the user defines what functions the program will need to have. This should not be thought of as processing in the technical programming sense, but rather the user's explanation of the functions or facilities that the program should have and what they should do from the user's perspective.

18.3.1.4 User interface

This section outlines the type of user interface required, including any special requirements such as touch screens or special methods of input (e.g. bar code scanner). With the user interface being the most obvious point of interaction between the users and the system, the developers may involve the users quite closely in the design of this part of the system, perhaps through the creation of 'prototype' versions of the software so that users can test out the look and feel of the interface.

18.3.1.5 Constraints

Every software development project has a limit on the funds and time available to complete the project, and this budget is normally set by the sponsors of the project. The requirements specification will need to estimate the cost of completing the project, including the cost of hardware and software, manpower for developing new software and training.

The new development will probably also have cost benefits. These might be tangible cost benefits such

Case study

Fast Cash Bank – Inputs, outputs and processing

The people who work behind the counters at the Fast Cash Bank all use PCs. A new application is required which will allow them to carry out foreign currency conversion for customers.

As well as providing a simple calculator, the program will need to allow the list of foreign currencies to be maintained.

The **inputs** to the system will be as follows:

- the names of foreign currencies, the symbols used to represent those currencies and their exchange rates. The names and symbols can be any text value. The rates will be a numeric value ranging from 0 to 5000.
- the amount of sterling (£) that the customer wants to convert. The maximum amount the bank will accept in a single transaction is £10,000.

The **outputs** of the system will be:

- a list of available foreign currencies for the user to choose from
- the amount of foreign currency for a given amount of sterling (input). This can be calculated using the following simple algorithm:

    foreign currency amount = sterling amount * exchange rate

The **functions** of the system will be:

- an exchange rate calculator which will allow the user to enter an amount of sterling, choose the foreign currency from a list and display the resulting amount of currency
- a facility to add new currencies, along with their exchange rates
- a facility to modify the exchange rate of existing currencies.

1 Are there any other functions that might be useful, either to the users or to the customers of the bank?

---

as reduced costs of processing or manpower, increased sales, etc., or they may be intangible benefits such as improved customer service. The systems analyst may have to identify what cost benefits the project sponsors are expecting and to consider these carefully to see if they are achievable. This section is sometimes known as a **cost benefit analysis**.

There will also probably be a timescale for the project so the systems analyst will need to consider if what is required can be achieved within the time available. There may also be other constraints on the new system – for example, it may have to work with a certain type of hardware (for example, using a hand-held computer) or with some existing software.

Case study

Fast Cash Bank

The users require a simple, clear Windows user interface which is split into two separate screens.

- The main screen will allow users to make foreign currency calculations.
- An administrator screen, protected by a password, will allow currency rates to be changed and new currencies added.

1 What sort of constraint do you think might apply to a system like this?

2 What are the constraints that will apply to the software you develop for this unit?

18.3.2 Designing a program

The theory of design is covered in section 18.2 (see page 218). Here we examine the practicalities of design and apply the techniques to the Fast Cash Bank case study.

Case study

Fast Cash Bank

Based on the requirements outlined in the previous section a simple design will be produced which includes a screen design, structure charts and a data dictionary.

The requirements identified that two screens or forms are needed: a main screen and an admin screen (where new currencies can be entered and the rates changed). The design for the main screen is shown in Figure 18.22.

The basic structure chart for the system is shown in Figure 18.23. The 'Load currency rates' process will read in the available currencies and their rates from a file when the program starts.

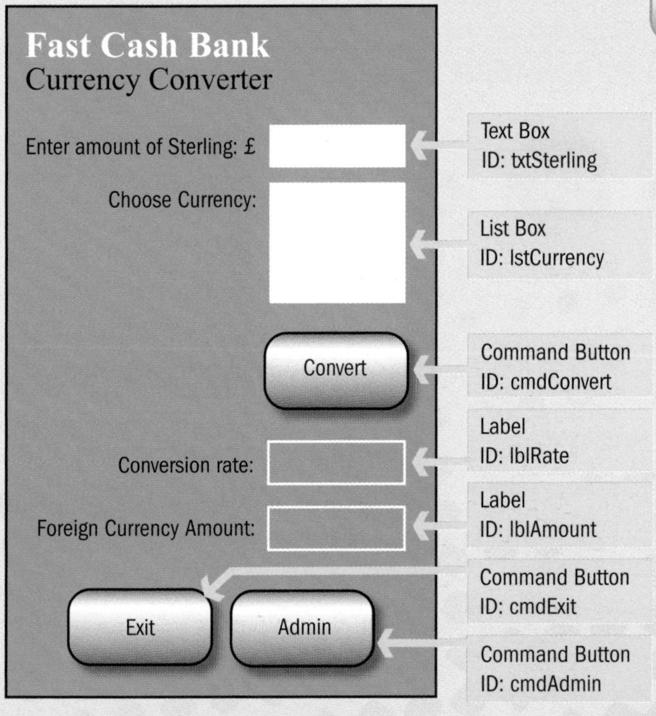

A more detailed structure chart for the 'Convert currencies' process is shown in Figure 18.24.

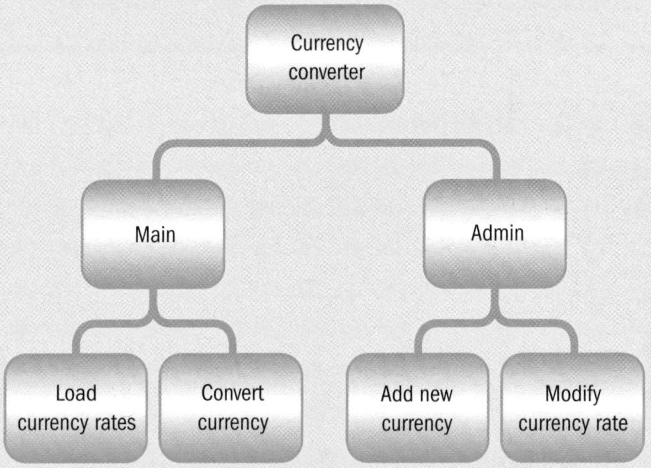

▲ Figure 18.23 Basic structure chart for the Fast Cash Bank

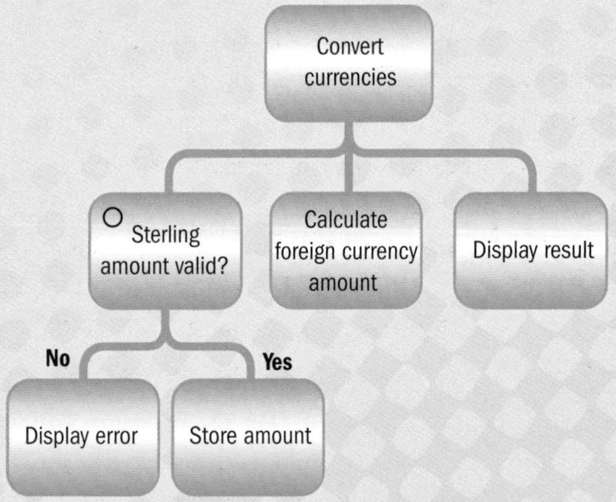

▲ Figure 18.22 Screen design for the Fast Cash Bank

▲ Figure 18.24 Structure chart for the 'Convert currencies' process

continued

The data dictionary for the system is shown in Table 18.10.

Attempt to complete the design by creating the following:

1 a screen design for the admin form
2 structure charts for the 'Add new currency' and 'Modify currency rate' processes.

Variable name	Type	Scope	Data type	Used for
Name(10)	Array	Global	String	Storing the names of currencies
Symbol(10)	Array	Global	String	Storing the currency symbols
Rate(10)	Array	Global	Single	Storing the currency conversion rates
Counter	Normal	Local to cmdConvert	Integer	Used to count number of currencies and as an array index

Table 18.10 Fast Cash Bank data dictionary

18.3.3 Technical documentation

Technical documentation is written for support staff and programmers. Throughout the life of a program changes or improvements may need to be made, and it may be the case that, despite careful testing, some errors only surface after many years of use. The programmers who originally wrote the software will probably have moved on to new projects or different companies. Technical documentation is therefore needed so that the people who need to modify or correct the program can understand how it works.

The technical documentation for each procedure in the program should include:

- the original requirements specification
- the design documentation produced, including form designs, flow charts, pseudocode, etc.
- a listing of the program code
- a print of the form, including the object names
- details of testing carried out, and any modifications made as a result of testing.

The documentation should also include details of the operating system and version that the program will work with, as well as disk space and any other hardware requirements. Instructions on how to install the software should also be included.

When improvements and/or corrections are made to the program, details of these changes should be included in the technical documentation.

Activity 18.5

Fast Cash Bank foreign exchange system

1 Design and write a program which will implement the Fast Cash Bank foreign exchange system. Some of the work has been done for you but you need to complete the design and then write the program. **P**₅

Test your knowledge

1 Why is it important to identify valid and invalid inputs?

2 List what should be included in the technical documentation or a project.

3 List some of the typical costs and benefits of a software development project.

Debugging, testing and documentation are important, if often unpopular, parts of the software development process. The users of the software would not be very impressed if the program produced the wrong answers, nor would they be happy if it kept crashing while they were using it. Therefore the program must be thoroughly tested and debugged, and documentation must be written to instruct users on how to use the program.

18.4.1 Testing and debugging

Testing is the process of checking that all the functions of the program work as they should and give the correct results. The definition of terms like 'work as they should' and 'correct results' needs to come from the original program specification that was agreed by the users and the developers before the program was written.

The programmer who wrote the program is probably not the best person to test the program as he/she is likely to be too forgiving with his/her creation! It is much better to get someone else to test the program, as they are likely to do a more thorough job.

As well as checking that the program works correctly when used as intended, the software developer also needs to check that the program is robust and can withstand being used incorrectly without crashing. The reason why this is important is because the users of the program may misunderstand how the program is supposed to be used. They may make mistakes such as pressing the wrong keys or buttons or making inappropriate entries in a text box (a text entry, for example, rather than numeric).

18.4.1.1 Test strategy

Making sure a program works properly may sound like a fairly simple task but, except for the very simplest of programs, software testing is a complex and involved task which requires planning.

To test a program you first need to produce some test data. This involves choosing some input values and then manually working out what output the program should produce with these chosen inputs (the expected outputs). The program is then run using these input values and the expected outputs are compared with the actual ones the program produces. If there is a difference between the expected outputs and the actual outputs then the program has failed the test and will need to be modified so that the actual and expected values match.

The choice of input values is important. A range of values needs to be chosen in each of the following categories.

- **Normal** values are what would normally be expected as an input value.
- **Extreme** values are, in the case of a numeric input, unusually large or small values. In the case of a text value they might be a very large or small number of characters. For example, in a text box where someone's name is to be entered, two extreme values might be 'Ng' and 'Fotherington-Thomas'.
- **Abnormal** values are incorrect entries – for example, 32/10/02 for a date, 205 for someone's age or a text value where a numeric value is expected.

18.4.1.2 Test plan

The results of testing a program are normally recorded using a document called a test plan. This is created before the testing begins and lists the test data that will be input and the results that are expected. An example template for a test plan is shown in Figure 18.25.

Once the test plan has been created, the test data listed in it is used as input to test the program. The results of each test are recorded on the test plan. If the expected outcome and the actual outcome match, then the program has passed the test, but if they differ then the program has not passed the test and the error messages produced must be entered in the plan.

The completed test plan is then passed back to the programmer to investigate and correct the problems. The corrective actions the programmer takes should be

System name:						Tested by:			
Page no:						Date:			
Test number	Test description		Input	Expected result		Actual result		Error messages	Corrective action taken

 Figure 18.25 Example test plan template

noted in the last column of the test plan. Once this has been done the program should be tested again.

You might imagine that when the program has been corrected and is to be tested again only the tests that it failed need to be done again. However, it is possible that the programmer has inadvertently introduced other faults while making the corrections. So, to be sure the program works properly, the complete set of tests should be done again.

18.4.1.3 Debug

On many occasions when developing a program, errors occur and produce unexpected results or cause the program to crash. Often a careful inspection of the program code will help you identify the error, but on other occasions it may be difficult to identify why the error is happening. On these occasions the debugging facilities built into the program development environment can be used to try to trace the error.

When a program crash occurs, Visual Basic automatically provides quite a lot of useful debugging information. It will show you the line where the program crashed and the reason why it crashed. You can also see the values contained in all the variables at the time of the crash. An example is shown in Figure 18.26.

 Test your knowledge

1 What categories of data should be used in test data?

2 What columns should be included in a test plan?

3 Why is it a bad idea for a program to be tested by its creator?

18.4.2 User documentation

User documentation is written for the program's users, and is sometimes called the **user manual** or **user guide**. There are two main approaches when writing user documentation:

- **reference guide** – each function and feature is described, normally in some logical order
- **tutorial** – teaches the user how to use the program using a step-by-step approach.

Some user manuals combine both approaches. Whichever approach is taken to user documentation, it must be written in a way that the target audience can understand.

Technical jargon needs to be avoided and the manual must be relevant to the way the program will be used in the workplace, for example, by using realistic examples. Annotated screen dumps need to be used rather than long written explanations – these are much easier for the

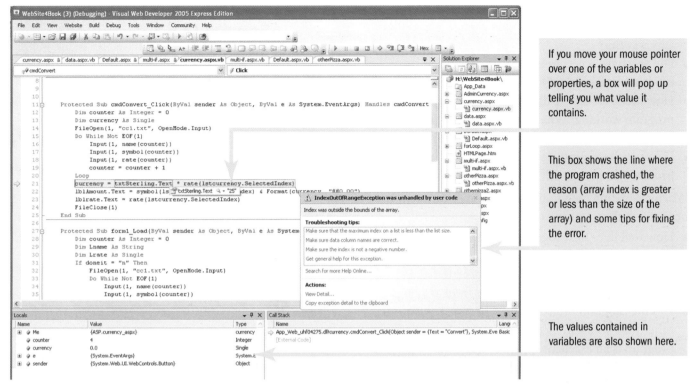

If you move your mouse pointer over one of the variables or properties, a box will pop up telling you what value it contains.

This box shows the line where the program crashed, the reason (array index is greater or less than the size of the array) and some tips for fixing the error.

The values contained in variables are also shown here.

▲ Figure 18.26 Debug example

user to follow, and he/she can compare what appears on the computer when running the program with the screenshot in the manual.

The user documentation needs to contain:

- details of how to start the program (how to find the program icon on the desktop or in the Start menu)
- comprehensive instructions for using each of the program's features – including details of what buttons, text box, list boxes and any other objects should be used for. The instructions should also explain how to use any menus and shortcut keys
- explanations of any error messages that the program displays, including an explanation of what to do to correct the problem and how to avoid the error in future
- details of what to do if something goes wrong or the program crashes, such as whom to contact
- how to exit the program
- frequently asked questions (FAQs) – you may need to use some imagination to decide what questions users may ask. Showing the program to a group of people who are unfamiliar with it and seeing what questions they come up with may help with this.

STOP Test your knowledge

1 What are the different approaches that can be taken to producing user documentation?

2 List the information that should be included in user documentation.

18.4.3 Reviewing

Having completed the development of a software system for this unit, you will need to evaluate or review both the program(s) you have created (the finished product) and the development process that you went through.

When evaluating the development process you need to ask the following questions.

- How accurately did you plan the development process? (You should have drawn up a project plan with identified deadlines for all the major steps in the development process.) Were your timescales realistic? Did you keep to your deadlines? If not, you need to explain why.

- How closely does the finished product match the original design? If you needed to change your design, why was this?
- Did you have access to the resources (such as hardware and software) you needed?
- How much assistance did you need to get your program working? What areas caused particular problems and how did you overcome them?
- If you need to complete a similar development process again, what will you do differently?

When evaluating the program you have produced, you need to ask the following questions.

- How well does the program you have produced match the stated user needs?
- How thoroughly has the program been tested and how confident are you that it is free from any bugs?
- Has the program been evaluated or tested by anyone other than yourself? Getting other people to test your program is an excellent way to evaluate it.
- What are the strengths and weaknesses of the finished product? How would you improve it if you had more time/resources? How does it compare with commercial products?

Rather than leaving all the reviewing and evaluating to the end of the process, you might find it useful to keep a diary or log of the work you do to develop the program and carry out interim reviews every few weeks with your tutor or with a group of your classmates. When carrying out interim reviews you should consider in particular how much time you have got left to complete the work and how far you have got in the development process.

Activity 18.6

Documentation, test plan and review

1. Using examples from the program you have written to implement the foreign exchange system, explain why it is beneficial to have different data types available.

2. Write user and technical documentation for the system you have written. **p**₆

3. Create a test plan for the foreign exchange system and test the system using the plan. **p**₆

4. Review your program and evaluate its effectiveness. Suggest further extensions to its functionality.
p₆ **d**₂

Test your knowledge

1. List the questions you should ask yourself when reviewing your work.

2. What is the purpose of interim reviews?

3. How can keeping a diary help you review your work?

Preparation for assessment

There is no scenario for the assessment tasks in this unit, as the tasks should be applied to your own projects.

Task 1 (P1, M1, D1)

Research and prepare a presentation describing the different types of programming languages, giving examples of each. Describe the main differences between the types of languages and why they have been developed. With two of the languages compare and contrast their approach to programming and the features they have. Choose a language for two different circumstances and justify your choice (one of these could be your creation of the programs in Tasks 3 and 4).

Task 2 (P2)

Create a table listing the different data types that can be used in Visual Basic. Show the type of data and range of values, and give some example of the sort of data the latter might store.

Task 3 (P3, P4)

Write and test a series of example programs which demonstrate the following features:

- local and global variables
- arrays
- pre-check and post-check conditional loops
- fixed loops
- conditional (if and case) statements
- use of logical operators
- assignment statements
- input and output statements.

Add detailed annotations to your programs explaining what each feature does and how it works.

Task 4 (P5, P6)

Design and write a program to be used by an interior decorator to estimate the cost of painting a room. The decorator needs to enter the height of the room (between 2 and 6 metres), then the length of all 4 walls (min. 1 metre, max. 25 metres). The program should then calculate the total area of the room.

The program should allow a choice of three paints:

- luxury quality which costs £1.75 per square metre
- standard quality which costs £1.00 per square metre
- economy quality which costs £0.45 per square metre.

The decorator should also be able to choose to use undercoat paint if required which costs an additional £0.50 per square metre.

The program should display an itemised bill with a total.

Having written the program, create a test plan to fully test the program. Create user and technical documentation and review your experiences in creating the program and the end result.

Task 5 (M2)

Explain and justify your choices of data types for the variables used in the program you wrote for Task 4.

Principles of Computer Networks

Introduction

Network technology is now in nearly everything we do – using satellite or cable television, using the telephone, our mobile phones and e-commerce.

In completing this unit, you should gain a broad understanding of the many technologies used to enable networks to operate and remain usable by you.

As networking is now so pervasive and is essentially part of our everyday lives, even when we consider otherwise, you will discover the many complexities in these systems and how they work together to support the communications, media and technologies we take for granted.

After completing this unit, you should be able to achieve these outcomes:

* Know the types of network systems and related standards

* Understand the hardware and software used in networking

* Know the services provided by network systems

* Understand how networked systems are made secure.

Thinking points

As a networking expert you must consider:

1 The impact of the technology you wish to use and the types of networked systems available

2 The speed of each system and how it affects the performance of the network from the user's perspective

3 How each technology interoperates and works together

4 What is required to ensure each technology operates successfully

5 The security implications and how a well-maintained system may remain secure.

Networking is not one singular skill and combines many disciplines in the management of a successful infrastructure. Depending on the system, you may become a master of many skills and a specialist in some.

For networks to communicate locally as well over considerable distances, different systems operate to ensure effective communication.

27.1.1 Types of network

This section considers the many different types of networks, such as LANs and WANs, their topologies and access methods.

27.1.1.1 LANs

The definition of a **local area network (LAN)** has become increasingly vague over the last ten years. At one time, it was understood to mean a system of interconnected computers at one location such as your school or college. Now, with faster technology and the ability to use LAN devices over greater distances, LANs can span many sites within a town or city, depending on who is using the system.

You may have a wireless router at home – this will allow between five and ten wireless devices and at least four devices connected by cable to share a broadband or ADSL connection.

A LAN can be as small as two computers, connected with one cable, and is only limited by the size of the organisation.

Larger LANs are carefully managed to ensure that network communication is transmitted efficiently. Devices such as switches and routers are used to extend the number of computers connected. The network infrastructure is divided into separate subnetworks to ensure a greater level of control.

27.1.1.2 WANs and WAN technologies

A **wide area network (WAN)** is a complex network system, comprising interconnected LANs. A WAN could be two LANs connected to each other over distance (e.g. the head

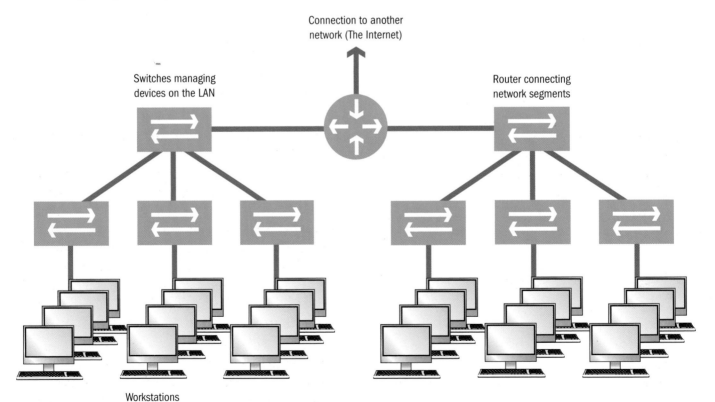

Connection to another network (The Internet)

Switches managing devices on the LAN

Router connecting network segments

Workstations

▲ Figure 27.1 A LAN infrastructure

office of an organisation and the production facility) or it could be many networks in a large organisation.

Your school or college is a member of a WAN infrastructure provided by your local education authority or JANET (Joint Academic Network).

The Internet is also a WAN, although unlike most WANS, which are privately managed by an individual organisation, the Internet is a network of interconnected WANs with the LANs connected at the edge of the system. It enables commercial organisations, academic centres, governmental organisations, telecommunications companies and you, the private user, to communicate via one common system.

Depending on the location and who is offering the WAN connection, there are many WAN technologies that you may encounter, including frame relay, ISDN, ATM and MPLS systems.

Frame relay is used at the core of the WAN, where all traffic is directed from system to system. Frame relay is a **packet switched** network structure and can be configured to enable multiple systems to communicate on the same structure without any direct communication. This is accomplished by ensuring that every connection in the frame relay system is connected in a mesh (see Figure 27.2) and configuring the equipment to create the logical structure required for the customer.

Frame relay can monitor the amount of traffic on the system – if the system gets too busy it can be configured to ensure the system does not overload. This is very useful for telecommunications and video, as these types of system do not cope with delays on the system – when there are delays, voice communications sound terrible and videos keep stopping and starting.

ISDN (integrated switched digital network) is an older **circuit switched** network system. It is still found in older

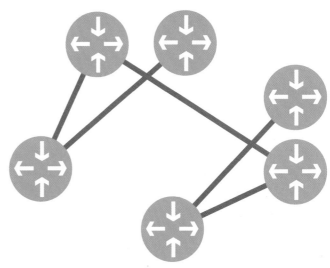

▲ **Figure 27.2 Frame relay**

'legacy' systems, as well as areas not yet accessed by broadband and ADSL technology.

The standards for ISDN differ in Europe and the USA. ISDN was the first solution used to attempt to bypass limitations set by the public telephone system to data transmission in the 1980s. ISDN is different from a public telephone line in several respects: it has the capacity to have a separate channel for data; it has the capability to send voice and data simultaneously; it can be used for 'other signals'.

An ISDN line can be provided in two ways:

- BRI (basic rate interface) for small business or home users
- PRI (primary rate interface) for medium to large organisations.

Each interface is divided into channels. A BRI can have two B channels of 64 Kbps, each of which can carry voice or data, and one D channel of 16 Kbps for control signals. Therefore, you could have one voice line and one data line on a shared connection. Alternatively, you could have one data link of up to 128 Kbps. A PRI can have up to 30 B channels of 64 Kbps and one D channel of 64 Kbps. This allows for up to 30 voice lines or data lines. If all the data lines are in use then the PRI will have a data carrying capacity of over 1.9 Mbps.

ATM (asynchronous transfer mode) has many similarities to frame relay as a WAN-based packet switched network system. Its principal difference is the size of the packets (units of traffic) sent. In ATM, the

What does it mean?

Packet switching is a mechanism which sends network traffic in small manageable data units across the system.

Circuit switching is a mechanism which sends network traffic via physical connections created in the network device.

packets are called cells and the data size is considerable smaller than most systems. This offers the advantage of speed, reliability and reduction in jitter (staggered loss of data), which affects voice communication systems such as Skype.

MPLS (multi-protocol labelled switching) is the most recent successor of frame relay and ATM technologies. ATM and frame relay are systems which operate at layer 2 of the OSI model only (see Unit 8 pages 157–163, particularly Table 8.12 on page 158). In contrast, MPLS is designed to cooperate with routing protocols at layer 3 of the OSI model. Routing protocols are used to enable networks to communicate with each other and ensure that the structure can adapt to changes such as the loss of connections, changes in bandwidth or preferred routes. For MPLS, this ensures that the central WAN structure is highly adaptable when working with the routing protocol to spot changes in the network, follow the network structure and work with corporate or customer needs.

27.1.1.3 VANs

Most commercial systems in use by commercial organisations are an extension of the value added network (VAN), where the customer leases communications lines, bandwidth, data rate or time from a service provider (a telecommunications company).

With your broadband/ADSL connection at home, you or your family are paying for a lease which may include an initial fee to install the line (in many cases), a monthly lease of the line and a monthly bandwidth (speed of the line, like 2 Mbps) rate which may be upgradeable. Some may have a pay-as-you-go service, where you pay extra for exceeding a download limit. There is often a guaranteed contention ratio, with a limit on how many customers access the local relay (as this affects the overall speed of the system).

Test your knowledge

1   What is the difference between a LAN and a WAN?
2   Explain these terms: packet switching and circuit switching.
3   Give four examples of WAN technologies and briefly describe each of them.
4   What is a VAN?

27.1.1.4 Topologies

In the conventional development and operation of a network infrastructure, each system has a physical **topology** as well as a possible logical topology (see Table 8.11 on page 147 of Unit 8).

What does it mean?

In computer terms, **topology** means the structure or layout of the communications network.

Test your knowledge

1   What does topology mean?
2   What are the main characteristics of these types of topology: bus, ring, star, tree (or hierarchical), mesh.
3   What are the main advantages and disadvantages of each type of topology?

27.1.1.5 Network access methods

A network is a highly competitive environment; for a device to send data, it must find an open time slice. Token ring networks solve this problem by each device on the system waiting its turn (as in the game pass the parcel) to communicate fairly. When a device has received the token, it can send data. The problem arises when there are **big talkers** on the system that need more network time.

Ethernet overcomes the big talker problem with a **best effort** solution. Each device on the system can send data as and when it sees fit. The problem with this occurs when two devices contest for the same service. Figure 27.3 shows how, when two devices send data across the same line at the same time, a **collision** occurs. Each device has to wait and resend, where another collision may occur, in which case the devices have to wait and then resend the data – and so on.

To overcome the collision issue, Ethernet has a solution called **CSMA/CD** (see Unit 8, page 152).

What does it mean?

A **big talker** is a network device that communicates more than the others, normally a server.

CSMA/CD stands for **carrier sense multiple access/ collision detection**. It is a method employed by Ethernet to detect and avoid continuous collisions of network data.

CSMA/CD is commonly referred to as the **backoff algorithm** and is applied by all devices on the system. Unless the network is too busy, the reattempt is normally successful.

CSMA/CA (collision avoidance) is a variation of CSMA/CD, which is based on the detection of the signal before any data is sent. CSMA/CA is used in wireless systems. With more homes using wireless, collision is increasingly becoming an issue as each network contends for a channel on the network.

Test your knowledge

1   How does a token ring network work?
2   What is a big talker? Give an example.
3   Explain the terms best effort solution and collision.
4   What do CSMA/CD and CSMA/CA stand for?

27.1.1.6 OSI seven-layer model

The **OSI (Open System Interconnection) model** is a logical ideology which describes network communication between different network devices. The OSI model is a concept that is often used as a tool to describe networking. The benefit of the OSI model is that it makes no difference if you are on a Windows-based system at home and the website you are visiting is on a Linux platform – it ensures that all devices concerned in this communication act equally and effectively.

The OSI model is represented by seven layers, with 7 being the top (nearer the user, who is considered to be layer 8 by some experts) and 1 at the bottom for the communication medium (the data leaving the computer) – see Table 8.12 on page 158 of Unit 8.

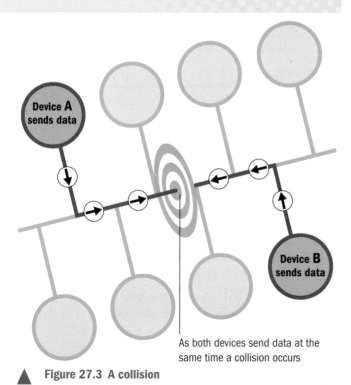

Device A sends data

Device B sends data

As both devices send data at the same time a collision occurs

▲ **Figure 27.3 A collision**

27.1.1.7 Choosing a network to meet a business need

Choosing a network to meet a business need relies on:

- the technical expertise of those who are expected to support the system
- what current technologies are available
- the region where this network is to be implemented; what technologies are commonplace and can be supported
- cost implications – what the customer can afford to implement and support.

Case study

Widgets R Us, the global widget manufacturer, requires a business needs analysis of its system and requires a consultant to:

1 Look at the best WAN structure to support its regional offices in Europe.

2 How broadband/ADSL will support managers who work from home.

3 How the OSI model affects the choice of equipment purchased.

4 Why Ethernet is preferable to Token Ring based networks.

27.1.2 Network protocols and standards

For any device on a network to communicate, the system and each device must use a range of protocols. This ensures that the communication is consistent and reliable; each protocol is used for a different purpose depending on what data is to be transmitted.

This section focuses on a range of protocols and standards. *Unit 8: Communication Technologies* explores wireless technologies in great detail, including 802.11a, b and g, infrared, Bluetooth and the various factors which affect the range and speed of wireless technologies.

27.1.2.1 TCP/IP

Internet development was based on the standards of the **TCP/IP** four-layer model (see Table 8.16 on page 162 of Unit 8) and gained popularity because of its various protocols.

What does it mean?

TCP/IP is a complex suite of protocols which operate on four layers to enable LANS and WANs to intercommunicate.

The TCP/IP protocol suite has an extensive range of protocols in common use on a LAN, as shown in Table 27.1.

OSI Layers		Common TCP/IP protocols			
7	Application	FTP	HTTP	POP3	SMTP
6	Presentation				
5	Session	DNS			
4	Transport	TCP	UDP		
3	Network	IP	ICMP	DHCP	
2	Data Link	ARP	RARP		
1	Physical				

Table 27.1 Common TCP/IP protocols

27.1.2.2 AppleTalk and IPX/SPX

AppleTalk (devised by Apple for the Mac system in the early 80s) and **IPX/SPX** (Internet Packet Exchange/ Sequenced Packet Exchange – supported by Novell) are historical protocol suites which have lost the battle to the more dominant TCP/IP protocol suite. Some old systems may still have to use these protocols for legacy reasons, normally when there is an application or device which requires the use of the older protocol.

What does it mean?

FTP stands for File Transfer Protocol: used for file exchange and storage.

HTTP stands for Hypertext Transfer Protocol: used for the distribution of web pages.

POP3 stands for Post Office Protocol version 3: used to collect mail from an ISP.

SMTP stands for Simple Mail Transfer Protocol: used for sending emails.

DNS stands for Domain Name System: used to match easy-to-remember domains typed in by the user, such as www.bbc.co.uk, to IP address like 82.165.26.58 (which are not so easy to remember).

TCP stands for Transmission Control Protocol: used for connection-oriented systems.

UDP stands for User Datagram Protocol: used for connectionless systems.

IP stands for Internet Protocol: used to identify your computer and all devices on a network.

ICMP stands for Internet Control Messaging Protocol: used by a variety of management applications, including Ping, to test communication.

DHCP stands for Dynamic Host Configuration Protocol: used to issue IP addresses to devices as they log into a network.

ARP (Address Resolution Protocol) and **RARP** (Reverse Address Resolution Protocol): used to match IP addresses to MAC addresses on a computer.

27.1.2.3 LAN standards

The **IEEE** (Institute of Electrical and Electronic Engineers) maintains the LAN standards for communication at layer 2 of the OSI model. These are defined as 802.2, 802.3 and 802.5.

- **IEEE 802.2** manages Ethernet data packets (called **frames**) and the link to the upper and lower layers of the OSI model (called the logical link control).
- **IEEE 802.3** is the definition of the MAC addressing on a network card and data collision detection over a variety of different speeds and media.
- **IEEE 802.5** manages token passing over a ring topology.

FDDI (Fibre-Distributed Data Interface) is a LAN standard using fibre optic technology to extend the distance of a LAN to over 200 kilometres (120 miles). This enables LANs to operate over considerable distances. FDDI uses two connections to enable traffic to travel in both directions. This enables greater speed and efficiency but also adds to the complexity of the system.

STOP Test your knowledge

1. Name the four layers of the TCP/IP model.
2. Give five examples of TCP/IP protocols. Say what they stand for and what they are used for.
3. What do the acronyms IEEE and FDDI stand for?
4. What do the following do: IEEE 802.2, IEEE 802.3 and IEEE 802.5?

27.1.3 Application layer protocols

When you use the Internet or email, different protocols are used to transfer the data; these are commonly referred to as application layer protocols. Common examples of application layer protocols include:

- HTTP – Hypertext Transfer (or Transport) Protocol
- FTP – File Transfer Protocol
- SMTP – Simple Mail Transfer Protocol.

A network is not simply the infrastructure and protocols that move the data around the system. The network offers many services, with specialist devices accessing and supporting the network.

27.2.1 Network devices

27.2.1.1 Workstations

The workstation is the most commonly found device on a network infrastructure, whatever the size. The sole purpose of a network is to enable the user to access its wide range of services via a workstation.

In the last ten years the term workstation has changed its definition, as new technologies are blurring what can be used on a network infrastructure. In its purest form, a workstation is a computer (or terminal) which enables you to access the network and the services it offers. Now, a workstation can also be: a mobile phone; a PDA, Blackberry or any specialist hand-held device; a Gameboy or PSP (PlayStation Portable); a laptop computer; a television set top box; an Internet telephone; a microwave oven (yes, no joking, an Internet-enabled microwave has been released).

27.2.1.2 Servers

A **server** is a specialist computer system that is designed to offer a dedicated service to other workstations (and other servers) on a network. Some of the server types you may encounter are:

- **web** servers for the distribution of data, communication and e-commerce
- **email** communication servers
- servers for the management of shared **printing** services, to centralise control, reduce printer investment and output costs for an organisation
- servers for the central management and storage of **files and data**

▲ Figure 27.4 An example of a more obscure workstation!

- security servers with the use of a **proxy** (go-between) or **firewall** (access control)
- **network addressing** servers, including DNS and DHCP
- **chat**, discussion and conference servers
- **game** clan management servers.

To operate, most servers need to have a better hardware specification than an ordinary desktop computer system. It is considered normal for most servers to have more memory (which now may be in excess of 2 GB), a large hard drive system (which may be in a **RAID** array to cope with any failures) and multi-processor motherboards, to cope with the greater demands.

What does it mean?

RAID stands for **Redundant Array of Integrated Drives**. It is a technology used to connect multiple hard drives together to act as one to ensure that data can be recovered in the event of failure.

STOP Test your knowledge

1 Give five examples of devices that can be workstations.
2 Give five examples of types of server.
3 What does RAID stand for and what is it used for?

27.2.1.3 Network interface cards

To use the services of the network, the workstation will use a **network interface card** (**NIC**) and an operating system (which may be XP, Vista or Linux, or may be a dedicated operating system like those found in some

What does it mean?

A network interface card (NIC) is part of the workstation hardware that allows connection to a network.

mobile phones) to communicate with the network and the protocols in operation.

The NIC's sole purpose is to provide a workstation with network connectivity. The type of NIC will vary with the network topology and media type in use:

- UTP network cards automatically detect the network speed, e.g. as 10 Mbps, 100 Mbps and 1000 Mbps
- wireless adapters for 802.11a, b or g systems
- Bluetooth transceivers
- fibre optic network cards
- external network adapters (which can be plugged in via USB)
- on board (on motherboard) network adapters.

STOP Test your knowledge

1 What is a network interface card (NIC)?
2 What are the steps involved in installing a NIC?
3 What four pieces of information are needed when configuring the NIC?

27.2.1.4 Features and functions

A network is often designed and managed for a purpose; it could be high reliability and bandwidth for telecommunications or video, or robust data lines with backup services for critical data with many servers running backup technologies. How a network is implemented depends on the business needs of the organisation supporting it.

27.2.2 Interconnection devices

To enable our computers and networks to communicate with each other, a wide range of interconnection devices are used according to the communication system and whether it is a WAN or LAN connection.

27.2.2.1 Modems

The **modem** is among the oldest interconnection devices, enabling communication over a conventional telephone system. The term modem comes from **mod**ulator, **dem**odulator, which describes the communication task it has to complete (see the five stages of modem transmission below). While seldom used as a primary communication device in the age of broadband and ADSL, the modem is popular as a backup device to gain access to routers (read ahead) on systems which have communication issues. Modems are also popular in remote or underdeveloped locations with older phone exchanges.

The task of sending and receiving a transmission by modem has five stages:

1 Dial the phone number of the receiving computer's modem.
2 The receiving computer's modem will answer and acknowledge.
3 A telephone line carries an analogue voice signal, but the data sent by a computer is digital, using a sequence of 0s and 1s. So the modem converts (modulates) the binary sequence to a carrier wave and the data is transmitted across the telephone line.

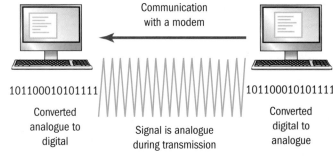

Figure 27.5 Communication between two computers which use a modem

4 The receiving computer accepts the modulated transmission and then converts (demodulates) the transmission into a binary sequence.
5 The receiving computer modulates a reply, and this loop continues until one of the computers is disconnected.

Modems use a variety of technologies to assist and improve their communication. All modems can offer **asynchronous** and **synchronous** communication.

What does it mean?

Asynchronous communication occurs between two devices which do not require a common timing; often the data will come in bursts. This is not to be confused with ADSL, in which the asynchronous elements are the different upload and download speeds.

Synchronous communication is a continuous timed transmission.

For a dial-up Internet connection, the transmission will be a timed and managed synchronised signal, where blocks of data will be sent and received via the Internet service provider. Modems offer asynchronous transmission to remote systems that require a permanent 'immediate' connection. This may be a critical system which is found in some building security products, where the modems will contact a control-room and feed all video, fire and alarm signals.

27.2.2.2 Repeaters and hubs

See section 8.2.3.1 on page 154 of Unit 8.

A modem – one of the earliest interconnection devices

27.2.2.3 Wireless access points

Wireless access points are also hubs but with a different technology and controlled by collision avoidance. Devices can connect together on a peer or ad hoc basis as well as look for a hub (wireless access point) which will control and direct traffic, often to a cabled network infrastructure.

▲ A wireless access point

27.2.2.4 Bridges and switches

Bridges and switches are closely related.

The **bridge** is a simple technology formerly used in networking. Its purpose was to separate segments of a network and reduce the number of network broadcasts. The bridge has enjoyed a minor renaissance – some commercial VoIP (Voice over Internet Protocol) phones have internal bridges so a PC can be connected to the phone and the phone to the single outlet on the wall.

A **switch** is a complex array of bridges which has developed as networking technology becomes more complex. The switch increases the speed of communication as it creates unique mini-networks (circuits).

For more on switches and bridges, see section 8.2.3.2 on page 154 of Unit 8.

27.2.2.5 Routers

See section 8.2.3.3 on page 155 of Unit 8.

27.2.2.6 Gateways

A gateway is a device on a network which acts as an entrance point to another network – this is often referred to as the **default gateway**. The gateway may be a router, a switch with routing capabilities, a firewall or a proxy server. See also section 8.2.3.4 on page 155 of Unit 8.

Activity 27.1

Default gateway

1 To see the default gateway your computer is using, open the Run box and enter 'CMD'. Then enter the command 'ipconfig /all'. Now you will see the default gateway along with other services on the network

27.2.2.7 Purposes, features and functions

To keep a network operational, protocols, gateways, routers, bridges, and switches have to work in unison to ensure successful communication flow. Working with your tutor, look at how all of these are used to connect your academic network to the Internet.

Test your knowledge

1 Where does the term modem come from?

2 What are asynchronous and synchronous communications?

27.2.3 Connectors and cabling

To ensure successful communication different networks use different **media** to ensure connection takes place.

What does it mean?

Media: the material used in communication; this could be wireless, fibre or copper.

Fibre-optic cable

27.2.3.1 Leased lines and dedicated lines

Telecommunications organisations and Internet service providers offering network services to corporate and private customers will offer two levels of service:

1 **leased line**, where the customer leases time, bandwidth or download capacity – this is similar to home broadband/ADSL and will be on a system shared with other customers

2 **dedicated line**, where the customer pays for total ownership of the communication on this line – while more expensive, the service is potentially limitless and more secure as there are no other customers on this system.

27.2.3.2 Media types

Section 8.1.5 of *Unit 8: Communication Technologies* explores in detail the media types and transmission systems involved in the connectors and cabling for STP and UTP, Category 5, coaxial, fibre optic, wireless and microwave and satellite links.

STOP Test your knowledge

1 What is the difference between a leased line and a dedicated line?

27.2.3.3 Wireless

Wireless networks rely on high frequency radio transmissions, normally limited to a range of no more than 100 metres. Wireless networks are susceptible to noise, which can be caused by metal-framed buildings as well as any powerful unshielded electrical equipment. Wireless networks tend to suffer from external interference and can have considerable limitations.

A successful wireless network must have many wireless access points, all offering overlapping coverage to ensure the mobile device (your laptop, mobile phone or PDA) has continuous coverage.

27.2.3.4 Microwave and satellite links

Satellite data transmission and reception has been used for some considerable time as a method of core high-speed data transmission between countries. For the user, or smaller business, this facility is becoming more accessible as costs reduce. Satellite transmission is reliant on atmospheric conditions as well as line-of-sight communication with the satellite, but communication with a satellite in a geostationary orbit can increase the distance around the globe a network can reach.

Satellite communications relies on the satellite being in a geosynchronous orbit, with receiving stations being positioned to communicate with these satellites. In the UK, due to our latitude (position in relation to the equator), dishes used for satellite communication have to point to a position low on the horizon towards the south. Major international satellite communications follow this, with the Goonhilly satellite station being in Cornwall, the UK's southern-most county.

Wireless devices are microwave based and operate in similar bands on the electro-magnetic spectrum, with microwave being on the upper end of the radio wave frequencies. These communication systems are used in WiFi, which has been described in the previous section of this unit.

27.2.3.5 Cable standards

Standards such as **10Base-T** are used to define the signalling, communication rules and speed of a cabled system. The standards defined by the IEEE do not specify the exact length of cable (as there are multiple fibre and copper systems which differ in distance) but rather the rule base used to ensure quality of communication.

27.2.4 Software

A network infrastructure alone offers no purpose; we need software such as application, server and client software to enable users to use the network.

27.2.4.1 Network operating systems

A networking infrastructure is purposeless unless there is software using, maintaining and managing the system. In the normal use of a network infrastructure you may encounter a network operating system, a virus checker on servers and workstations, firewalls (either dedicated or software based) and email clients and servers.

What does it mean?

10Base-T: the **10** represents the bandwidth in Megabits per second, the **Base** is for a baseband signal and the **T** represents twisted pair cables.

IEEE Standard	Description
802.3	10Base5 10 Megabit over thick coaxial
802.3a	10Base2 10 Megabit over thin coaxial (often described as 'thinnet')
802.3b	10Broad36, transmission over a coaxial cable TV system
802.3e	1Base5 or StarLAN, the first standard using RJ45s on a phone system, this only transmitted at 1 Megabit over unshielded twisted pair
802.3i	10Base-T 10 Megabit over twisted pair
802.3j	10Base-F 10 Megabit over fibre optic
802.3u	100Base-TX, 100Base-T4, 100Base-FX Fast Ethernet at 100 Megabit
802.3z	1000Base-X Gigabit Ethernet over fibre optic
802.3ab	1000Base-T Gigabit Ethernet over twisted pair
802.3ae	10 Gigabit Ethernet over fibre optic; 10GBase-SR, 10GBase-LR, 10GBase-ER, 10GBase-SW, 10GBase-LW, 10GBase-EW
802.3af	Power over Ethernet – while not a definition of speed, VoIP phones and wireless access points could be powered via the same cables carrying the data. Reduces the cost of the network, along with the flexibility of the devices on the system
802.3ak	10GBase-CX4 10 Gigabit Ethernet over twin-coaxial cable
802.3an	10GBase-T 10 Gigabit Ethernet over unshielded twisted pair
802.3aq	10GBase-LRM 10 Gigabit Ethernet over multimode fibre, which is used on many LANS

Table 27.2 IEEE cable standards

Network operating systems offer two defined structures: **peer-to-peer** and **client-server**.

A **peer-to-peer network** is an infrastructure which ensures that all devices on the system are treated as equals sharing a wide range of network services between each other. There is no centre to a peer system, but some devices may offer greater services than others. This ensures that users of many different computers systems can join a simple network infrastructure.

Peer networks are found in many situations. Four common examples are:

- a private network created at home to share an Internet connection
- some network gaming clans (teams who play network games together)

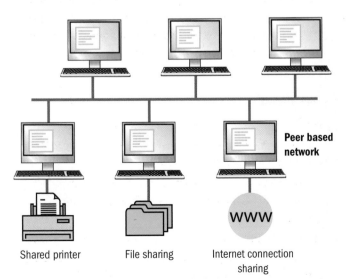

Shared printer   File sharing   Internet connection sharing

Peer based network

▲ **Figure 27.6 Peer to peer networks**

- a small network in a company with less than ten computers
- file and resource sharing systems like BitTorrent, which are applications designed to ensure that file sharing occurs.

The principal advantage of peer-to-peer systems is their technological simplicity – they are easy to install, operate and manage. But their ability to scale (grow larger) is restricted – it is accepted in the networking industry that 20 workstations is the reasonable maximum and 40 is pushing your luck!

File sharing systems overcome the issues of scale by your computer having a client which reports your files to a server which manages the peer connections.

All operating systems since the early 1990s have offered a peer-based element. It is now possible to create peer connections with all operating systems.

As opposed to the peer-to-peer system, a **client-server system** has central control and management, which allows a considerably larger number of devices to become part of the system.

Examples of client-server systems are wide ranging and diverse. Some examples include:

- web server being accessed by many clients (the client being the web browser)
- many online gaming systems
- the file server at work or your centre of learning which is accessed via Windows Explorer
- MSM, Skype and other chat/communication systems
- web radio, with the client being e.g. Windows Media Player, Winamp or RealPlayer.

To operate, a client-server system must have different operating systems and computers for the client and the server. As a rule of thumb, the client can be implemented on most standard operating systems. It can be very small in software terms but must allow network or Internet access. It can run on a lower-specification computer system.

The server must run on a network operating system (or one which supports multiple connections and processes). It may need a system with a higher-specification computer (multiple processors, more memory, larger hard drives, etc.) and it needs a better-quality network/Internet connection as it will be busier.

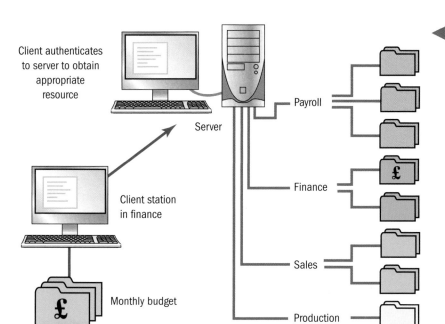

◀ Figure 27.7 Client server systems

Client authenticates to server to obtain appropriate resource

Server

Client station in finance

Payroll

Finance

Sales

Production

£ Monthly budget

Client – Server

■ Anti-virus software

It is essential to ensure that your virus checker is current. As you are reading this paragraph, a new **virus**, **worm** or **trojan** will have been released which may affect your computer system.

What does it mean?

A **virus** is a malicious file which, when inserted into your system, will cause some form of damage. An additional feature of viruses is their ability to reproduce.

A **worm** is a program that can move itself around a computer network and leave a payload, which may be a virus or trojan.

A **trojan** is an application which, when left in your system, will provide 'back door' access to your hard drive and data.

The terms virus, worm and trojan are often simplistic as most attacks will be hybrids of two or more of them. (For more on viruses, worms and trojans, see section 27.4.3.2 on page 276.)

Activity 27.2

Installing anti-virus software

1 Visit the Grisoft website (you can access this by going to www.heinemann.co.uk/hotlinks and entering the express code 2315P), where you can download a free and updateable anti-virus application called AVG Anti-Virus Free.

2 With the permission of your tutor, install this application and ensure you are connected to the Internet to update the anti-virus database. Run a comprehensive scan of your hard drive and any other storage devices.

■ Firewalls

Firewalls, either dedicated or software-based, are essential for all networks and network devices. The best implementation of a firewall is to:

- ensure you are running one on your workstation – the Windows XP or Vista internal software firewall is suitable for this
- ensure you are also running one on the edge of your network – this may be an external hardware firewall running as part of the wireless/wired ADSL/broadband router at home

- have a firewall at the edge of each network segment of a corporate network to ensure multiple layers of security.

Firewalls filter traffic using TCP and UCP ports at layer 4 of the OSI model (see Table 8.12 on page 158 of Unit 8). In principle all ports are blocked and a network administrator will open only those that are needed.

Ports open on some systems may include:

21   File Transfer Protocol
25   Simple Mail Transfer Protocol
53   Domain Name Service
80   Hypertext Transfer Protocol
139 NetBIOS name resolution (used for Windows file share naming)
443 Hypertext Transfer Protocol Secure (used for secure e-commerce)

This is a very small number of the 65536 ports available on a computer.

Strong firewalls use 'reflective' rules – this means that traffic is only allowed in if a device or application on the inside of the firewall has originated the network conversation. To test if your firewall is secure, use the Nmap application which can be obtained from www. insecure.org (access this website via www.heinemann. co.uk/hotlinks, express code 2315P).

■ Email

Email client and server systems have been operational since the early 1970s. Email uses protocols such as SMTP (Simple Mail Transfer Protocol), IMAP (Internet Message Access Protocol) and POP3 (Post Office Protocol version 3).

To send an email requires SMTP. To receive (or pull) an email requires POP3. SMTP is a 'plaintext' language, which can be typed in via applications such as telnet or HyperTerminal. Figure 27.8 gives an example of an SMTP command conversation when sending an email.

Email has contributed to the boom and popularity of the Internet. The popularity of email has enabled organisations, workers and educators to become more flexible in their communication, with location and time zones becoming irrelevant. Email can be accessed via many systems, with websites, mobile phones and television set top boxes all offering this service.

```
Client: HELLO teraknor.co.uk
Server: 250 Hello teraknor.co.uk
Client: MAIL FROM:webmaster@teraknor.co.uk
Server: 250 Ok
Client: RCPT TO:student@teraknor.co.uk
Server: 250 Ok
Client: DATA
Server: 354 End data with<CR><LF>.<CR><LF>
Client: Subject: test message
Client: From: webmaster@teraknor.co.uk
Client: To: student@teraknor.co.uk
Client:
Client: Hello,
Client: .
Server: 250 Ok: queued as 23296
Client: QUIT
Server: 221 Bye
```

▲ **Figure 27.8 An email SMTP command conversation**

27.2.4.2 Virus checker

Virus checkers are covered in detail later in this unit. Since the 1980s, the growth in malicious software which affects the operation of computer systems has become especially prevalent. Ensuring your computer system has the latest anti-virus software is essential.

(For more on malware, see section 27.4.3.1 on page 276.)

27.2.4.3 Firewalls

With hacking and various malicious programs being used to probe your network and computers on a daily basis, a robust firewall ensures a level of invisibility and prevents the most common attacks.

27.2.4.4 Others

Since the early 1970s email has proved to be one of the most common uses of networks and the internet.

Test your knowledge

1 Distinguish between a client and a server.

2 Explain the terms peer-to-peer and client-server.

3 Give three examples of a peer-based system.

4 What is the difference between a virus, worm and trojan?

5 How does a firewall work?

6 What are SMTP, IMAP and POP3?

27.2.5 Commercial systems

Examples of network operating systems are various versions of Linux, Novell Netware, AppleShare, Windows 2000 and 2003 and IBM iSeries OS. Desktop systems such as Windows XP and Vista can offer this resource but in a more limited format as they are not specifically designed for the task.

A network operating system is multifaceted and serves many purposes for many organisations. Unlike the client operating system you are used to (e.g. Windows XP or Vista), the network operating system will reside on a dedicated computer system.

The network operating system manages the server that provides a network service accessed by many other computers and users on the network. The services offered by network operating systems are wide and varied – common services include:

- web servers, to provide e-commerce and information portals
- file servers to share common resources
- database servers which manage large quantities of information
- print servers, to manage access to network printers which are used by many users
- domain name servers (DNS), which keep a log of all web addresses and IP addresses, so you can find your favourite website no matter where it is on the planet
- firewalls, which control corporate security and protect entire systems from unwanted intrusion

- proxy servers, which regulate access for many devices to the Internet
- content management systems, which will control what websites users may visit
- dynamic host configuration protocol (DHCP) servers, used by many organisations and ISPs (Internet service providers) to ensure your computer has an address which will enable your computer to access the network or Internet
- mail servers to manage email.

All of these services are available using Windows 2000/2003 and Novell NetWare. Linux and Unix also offer these services according to the needs of a particular organisation, allowing network managers to configure them to specific requirements.

Activity 27.3

Setting up a small server

Setting up a simple server is not difficult. In fact, you can run one from your own home computer, without placing any unreasonable demands on your computer system. In the Linux community there is a movement for 'small = good', so you can find operating systems that will run in less than 50 MB of storage (small enough to fit on a small memory stick).

1 You can download a copy of DSL, which is a small version of the Linux operation system from www.teraknor. co.uk/dsl.zip. The readme file includes instructions on how to start the operating system while you are running Windows (it uses a simple PC emulator).

2 Follow the instructions included and you can set up a simple web server using this system.

Test your knowledge

1 Give three examples of network operating systems.

2 List at least five services offered by network operating systems.

On the top of the network infrastructure, networked systems provide a variety of services which enable you, the user, to interact with other users, systems and applications. The services covered in this section are directory services, telecommunication services, file services and application services.

27.3.1 Directory services

When a network has only ten devices or less, it is easy to remember the IP address or the device name for a printer or file server on the system. But what happens when the system grows?

When a network increases beyond ten devices there needs to be a way of managing user's **rights** on the network and ensuring that each device is easy to identify.

To offer comprehensive directory services, a network operating system must offer:

- **domain** control (which may also be called 'active directory' or 'directory services')
- account management for groups and users
- **authentication** management.

What does it mean?

On a network, the term **rights** means what systems and services you are allowed to access and not allowed to access.

A **domain** is a group of networked computers and devices that are treated as a unit and have the same communications address.

Authentication involves security measures like password protection or chip and pin, used to check that the user is who they claim to be.

27.3.1.1 Domain control

On a networked system a domain is either:

- a system that is provided by major networking operating systems that provides control over computers, servers and services, or

- an Internet system that consists of a set of network addresses. This type of domain is organised in levels. The top level identifies the geographic location or the purpose of the domain (for example, the nation that the domain covers or a category such as 'commercial'). The second level identifies a unique place within the top level domain and is equivalent to a unique IP address on the Internet.

In Windows, each domain is managed by a **domain controller**. To support this, the system requires additional domain controllers to ensure resilience (to act as a backup if the main domain controller fails).

What does it mean?

A **domain controller** is a server which is used to manage printers, servers and communications resources across the network.

Users may authenticate (log in) to the domain controller to obtain access to the network's services. If the domain controller is too busy or the server has failed, then the user can continue their work by authenticating to additional domain controllers. A large system will have multiple domain controllers to ensure that all users can always access the system.

The domain controller is a complex database with details of all users' accounts, all servers and services, printers, files system and permissions, backup systems, any specialist services and the addressing scheme. This is called the active directory (as the directory is constantly being changed). At regular intervals the domain controller will send an update of this database to all additional domain controllers. This allows all users seamless access to the system.

If any of the servers are switched off or are unavailable for a considerable period of time (e.g. while repairs take place), an engineer has to ensure that the latest image of the database has been loaded onto the server. Otherwise the system becomes fragmented and users may not be able to gain access to system resources.

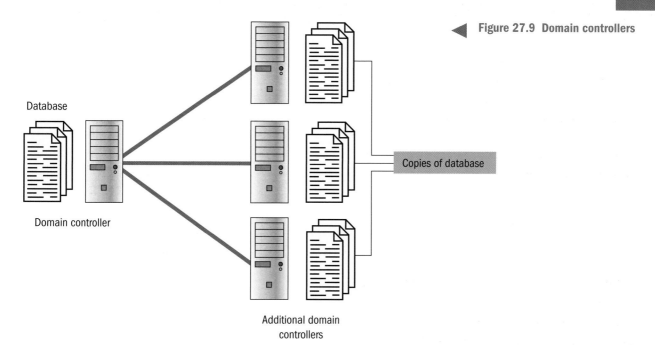

Database

Domain controller

Copies of database

Additional domain controllers

Servers that are part of the domain, but do not provide access to the directory, are **member servers**. They rely on the domain controllers to manage access to their resources. A common example of this is an Internet proxy server. This server is the gateway to a shared Internet connection – not all users may be allowed to use this service, so the domain controllers will manage access according to directory permissions.

A simple network system will have one domain controller and may have one additional supporting domain controller. This will work for a small to medium enterprise that is situated on one site. Large organisations will have multiple domains according to region, department or business need. Figure 27.10 shows how multiple domain controllers can operate in a tree structure across the world to manage the network.

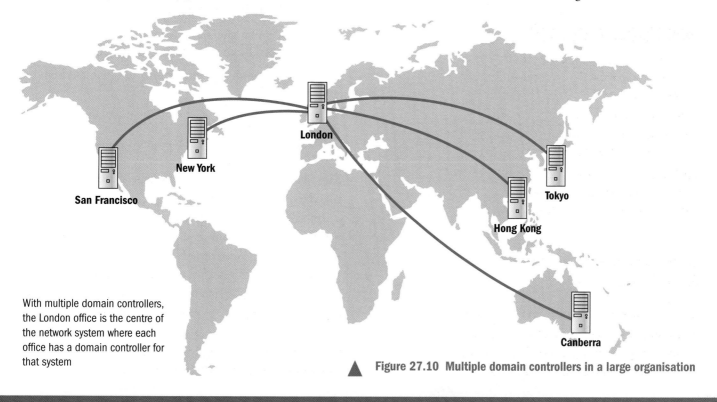

San Francisco

New York

London

Hong Kong

Tokyo

Canberra

With multiple domain controllers, the London office is the centre of the network system where each office has a domain controller for that system

▲ **Figure 27.10 Multiple domain controllers in a large organisation**

A team of network administrators often manages the database. The database allows a hierarchy of management – this means that there are administrators who can control the whole system as well as local administrators who only have responsibility for part of the database.

■ Domain names

Each domain is named according to the infrastructure of the organisation and the network administrator will issue names using a common sense principle. Figure 27.11 shows the likely domain names for the company Widgets R Us, which has offices in Seattle, San Francisco and Madrid. The office at each site has three departments: finance, production and sales.

The advantages of using a directory services structure are:

- each section can be managed according to a specific business need
- localised management means that the system can adapt without the management of the whole network being too cumbersome
- local management also allows part of the system to be backed up and restored separately – any failure will have only a local impact
- new branches of an organisation may be added at any time – the network does not have to be redesigned to adapt to a changing business climate.

The top of the domain tree:

```
\\WidgetsRUs
The domain entry for each location:
\\WidgetsRUs\Seattle
\\WidgetsRUs\San_Francisco
\\WidgetsRUs\Madrid
The domain entry for each department:
\\WidgetsRUs\Seattle\finance
\\WidgetsRUs\Seattle\sales
\\WidgetsRUs\Seattle\production
\\WidgetsRUs\San_Francisco\finance
\\WidgetsRUs\San_Francisco\sales
\\WidgetsRUs\San_Francisco\production
\\WidgetsRUs\Madrid\finance
\\WidgetsRUs\Madrid\sales
\\WidgetsRUs\Madrid\production
```

▲ **Figure 27.11 An example of domain naming**

Activity 27.4

Domain structures

You may be considering applying to UCAS for a university place. Each university (a domain) is part of the UCAS system. Each university has a directory of courses that is subdivided into faculties (areas of study, which are also domains). Each faculty will then have its own course listing (database or directory).

1 Using the same convention as Widgets R Us, take a course directory for your intended university and create the domain structure that will describe each course. Tip: The convention may be \\university\faculty\ section\course.

The Internet and the majority of network infrastructures use a domain management system called the **DNS**. This is based on the **UNIX** domain system. The domain name architecture is managed in a tree structure by **registrars**. In control is the organisation InterNIC who control the issue of any Internet address. They manage a group of local registrars who in turn manage a range of domains.

What does it mean?

DNS stands for **domain naming system** and is currently a web-based system for naming network domains.

UNIX is a centralised server operating system from the 1970s.

A **registrar** is an organisation that manages Internet domain names.

The web address of www.yourcollege.ac.uk is therefore managed by:

- InterNIC, who manage all Internet addresses
- Nominet, who manage all .uk addresses
- JANET (Joint Academic Network), who manage all .ac and .gov addresses
- your college, who manage their own domain (yourcollege) and any subordinate domains (www).

(You can access the InterNIC, Nominet and JANET websites by going to www.heinemann.co.uk/hotlinks, express code 2315P.)

InterNIC controls all address naming conventions to the right-hand site of the Internet address. Once you have control of your own domain it is your choice – for example, the following names are allowed:

- www.yourcollege.ac.uk for the web server
- mail.yourcollege.ac.uk for the mail server
- technology.yourcollege.ac.uk for the technology campus
- cappuccino.yourcollege.ac.uk for the online coffee machine!

Each network that connects to the Internet must have a DNS server. This server contains a database (like active directory or DNS) of all Internet domains. This database will map the Internet address to an OSI model layer 3 IP address. For example:

- www.yourcollege.ac.uk could map to 80.10.55.1
- mail.yourcollege.ac.uk could map to 80.10.55.2
- technology.yourcollege.ac.uk could map to 80.10.55.3
- cappuccino.yourcollege.ac.uk could map to 80.10.55.4

Like active directory, the DNS needs to have a primary and secondary domain controller (called servers in DNS terminology). Figure 27.12 shows that you can find an example of a DNS system on your home computer.

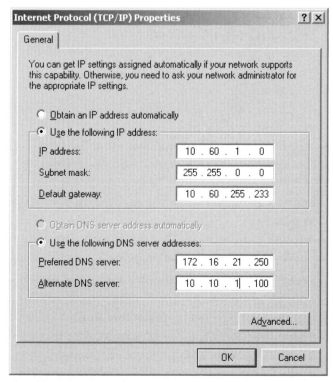

▲ Figure 27.12 DNS system

The Internet is an ever-growing system, where all domain servers point to a controlling server higher up the domain tree, each leading to the core server run by InterNIC. Therefore, all domain servers point to each other in a mesh structure, where any update that takes place on the Internet (a new domain name) is distributed from one domain server to another up the tree until it reaches the core, and then it is distributed to all systems across the Internet.

For your college, the domain structure will be:

- all computers in your college will point to the network domain server
- your college's domain server will point to the .ac domain server at JANET
- JANET's domain server will point to Nominet's domain server
- Nominet's domain server points to the InterNIC core server.

Domains with Window 2000/2003 and Linux are based on the UNIX DNS. If you create a network at home, you can point your DNS server to the service provided by your **ISP**, where the Internet allows for further connections at the edge. If you purchase and register a domain name, it may take up to five hours for the registration to propagate to all DNS servers on the Internet.

What does it mean?

ISP stands for **Internet service provider**, an organisation that provides access to the Internet.

 ## Test your knowledge

1. Define these terms: rights, domain, authentication, domain controller.

2. How are domain names structured? Give an example.

3. Define these terms: DNS, UNIX, registrar.

4. What is the function of InterNIC, Nominet and JANET?

Activity 27.5

Registering a domain name

1. Visit the InterNIC website and complete a 'Whois' search for the following websites: www.bbc.co.uk, www.ic.ac.uk, www.microsoft.com, www.ja.net and www.google.com. (You can access the InterNIC website by going to www.heinemann.co.uk/hotlinks and entering express code 2315P.)

2. Search the Internet for the best price to register www.yourname.co.uk (yes, your name!). How many domains are there? You may be aware of .com, .co.uk and .net. What else can be used as a top level domain?

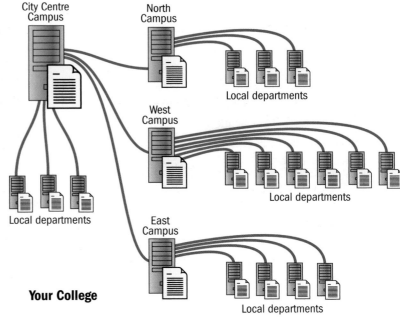

 Figure 27.13 A networked system

27.3.1.2 Account management

With the directory structure intact, each network administrator has to ensure that there is appropriate account management for groups and users.

■ User groups

Networked systems with domains will allow personnel within a company to be managed by associating them with a variety of user groups. Each group may provide the user with access to different resources, such as files, directories, printers or servers. User groups can also be associated with the allocation of privileges: some users may only have read access, while other users have read and write access.

The advantage of user groups is that a company employee can be mobile (moving from computer to computer, or from site to site) and their network privileges follow them.

■ User accounts

In order to visualise user accounts, you are a user on the network at your centre, as are your teacher and the network technician. With current technology, devices such as other servers, printers and workstations are also allocated 'user' privileges and are treated in a similar fashion. Each of you will have an account on the network directory, which will contain a variety of important information:

- personal details
- login or account name (e.g. you are Jacob Smith and your account is jsmith01)
- your password (encrypted of course)
- a date for when you need to be reminded to change your password
- groups that you are a member of
- directories and files that you have access to, along with your rights to those files
- servers and printers that you may access
- times that you may (or may not) be able to login
- computers that you can or cannot use (newer systems can lock a user to a range of computers based on their IP address)
- websites you may or may not be able to access
- email address (e.g. jsmith01@yourcollege.ac.uk).

User accounts are added to the directory as and when people join an organisation. Your centre may create a large number of accounts in September when the new academic year starts. You also need to be aware that user accounts can be removed or suspended from the system. You may have experienced this if your centre has a policy of disabling user accounts for misuse of the network.

27.3.1.3 Authentication management

Combining domains, groups and users, the networked system can implement comprehensive authentication management. This is used to ensure that only those who are allowed to use the system have access to it.

Authentication management occurs at many levels and is not simply focused on the user. Some examples of where authentication takes place follow.

■ Internet e-commerce and secure web pages

For secure web pages, authentication is by the use of **SSL**. This requires a website to issue a security certificate, which is checked by the browser as part of the exchange. The certificate is the **public key** part of the exchange and a private key is also created. The **private key** is based on a 1024-bit value (2^{1024} which is 1.7976931348623159077293 05190789e+308 – the e means you move the decimal point to the right by 308 digits) and is a **prime number**. This is commonly referred to as **RSA encryption**.

■ Secure WAN connections

For secure WAN connections, routers use authentication methods such as CHAP (Challenge Handshake Application Protocol) or exchange updates using a MD5 hash (Message Digest) – this is a formula which provides the result of a complex calculation based on a large data set, with the hash being the common key result from each calculation. This is used across common communication systems to ensure that no one attempts to add unauthorised equipment to join the system.

■ Devices such as routers, servers, switches and proxies

To manage many devices can be an issue for network administrators as this requires the creation and

What does it mean?

SSL stands for **secure sockets layer** – it requires a website to issue a security certificate.

Public/private keys are mathematically related. The public key can be widely distributed and is used to encrypt data. The private key *only* can decrypt the data and is kept secret. It is not technically practical to derive the private key from the public key.

A **prime number** is a number that can only be divided by itself and 1. This means that by no matter what number you try to divide this number, it will never return a whole value. Prime numbers are mathematically interesting as no one has yet managed to predict the next prime number – they appear to follow no pattern. This property is invaluable in network security.

RSA encryption comes from Ron **Rivest**, Adi **Shamir** and Len **Adleman**, the mathematicians who devised the principle for public/private key encryption using prime numbers.

management of a large number of usernames and passwords. To coordinate this task, many systems have centralised authentication servers, known as TACACS+ (Terminal Access Controller Access-Control System) or RADIUS (Remote Authentication Dial In User Service).

■ Wireless systems

For wireless systems, WEP (wireless equivalence protocol) allows all members of a wireless system to share a common private key. The wireless device cannot join the system unless the WEP key is directly entered into the wireless settings for the mobile device.

27.3.2 Telecommunication services

The primary use of the Internet is as a means of communicating with other people. As such, the use of the Internet is becoming increasingly prevalent in our lives. This section will look at the many technologies in use on the Internet and how they have enabled low-cost and effective communication to take place.

27.3.2.1 Communication

Common and popular methods of communication include email, Internet relay chat (IRC), VoIP (Voice over IP), SMS (short message service) and discussion boards. We will look at these in more detail in this subsection.

Email has been explored earlier in this chapter (see section 27.2.4 on page 258).

Internet relay chat (IRC) is an older term for the various forms of chat used by many on the Internet. Popular chat services include Windows Live Messenger, Yahoo! Messenger and Skype.

Chat operates using a server which acts as a relay for all conversations. Each member logs in and allows (or refuses) other users to create private conversations. Chat can be one to one, or many to many, depending on the type of conversation taking place.

Many of the chat systems available also offer application sharing, video conferencing and remote assistance tools. These features enable professionals from many geographic locations to work together and offer each other support.

VoIP usage is on the rapid increase, with Skype, SIP (Session Initiation Protocol) and H.323-based telecommunication systems across the Internet. Skype is a proprietary service, which means that the technology used by Skype to communicate with other Skype systems is incompatible with any other VoIP technology – this is considered to be a downside to Skype by many people.

All Skype conversations are secure, and are relayed via the many Skype hosts as well as central servers. You can now easily obtain a personal number for Skype, which

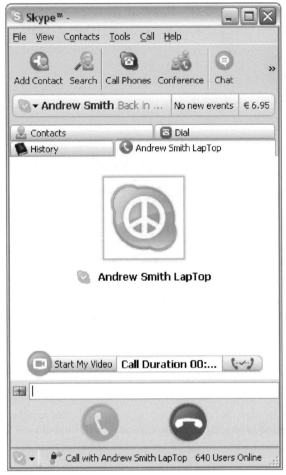

▲ **Figure 27.14** Skype

means that landlines can phone your computer. Alternatively you can use Skype to buy credit to telephone mobile phones and landlines in almost any country – this is a considerable benefit for people involved in international travel and business. Skype is free for Internet-only conversations. You can find out more about Skype by visiting the website (access this by going to www.heinemann.co.uk/hotlinks and entering express code 2315P).

Many alternative systems exist using SIP and H.323 as these are **open source**, allowing organisations to work together to create common communication systems.

What does it mean?

Open source: software code (or related technologies) which are free and open to anyone to use or improve.

A popular server which can be used on Windows and Linux is Trixbox. This can be connected to traditional phone systems as well as a conventional networked system and can be used to control communication between them.

Trixbox works like any client-server system, offering telephone communication to as many users as there is server power to handle them. For example, an old 700 MHz PC with Trixbox would be able to manage 20 phones, while a modern server with a 4 GHz multi-process system would be able to manage 200+ phones.

Trixbox is free and can be obtained from the Trixbox website, www.trixbox.org. Many clients are also available for free download (for example, X-Lite from CounterPath). (For both of these websites, go to www. heinemann.co.uk/hotlinks and enter express code 2315P.)

With VoIP and web interaction, many system offer free or versatile **SMS** solutions. For example, those who have already installed Skype can use their SMS tool (at a small cost) to send SMS to any mobile phone and tag the return number with their mobile phone number.

Figure 27.15 Skype SMS

SMS can also be sent via many websites and mobile phone providers may also offer this service to customers. Independent, free or low-cost providers offer web servers with SMS capability (for example, CardBoardFish from CBFSMS – access this via www.heinemann.co.uk/ hotlinks, express code 2315P).

Discussion boards, **news groups** and **bulletin board**s are among the earliest methods of common communication and information sharing. Email clients are able to manage bulletin board services via the news group feature.

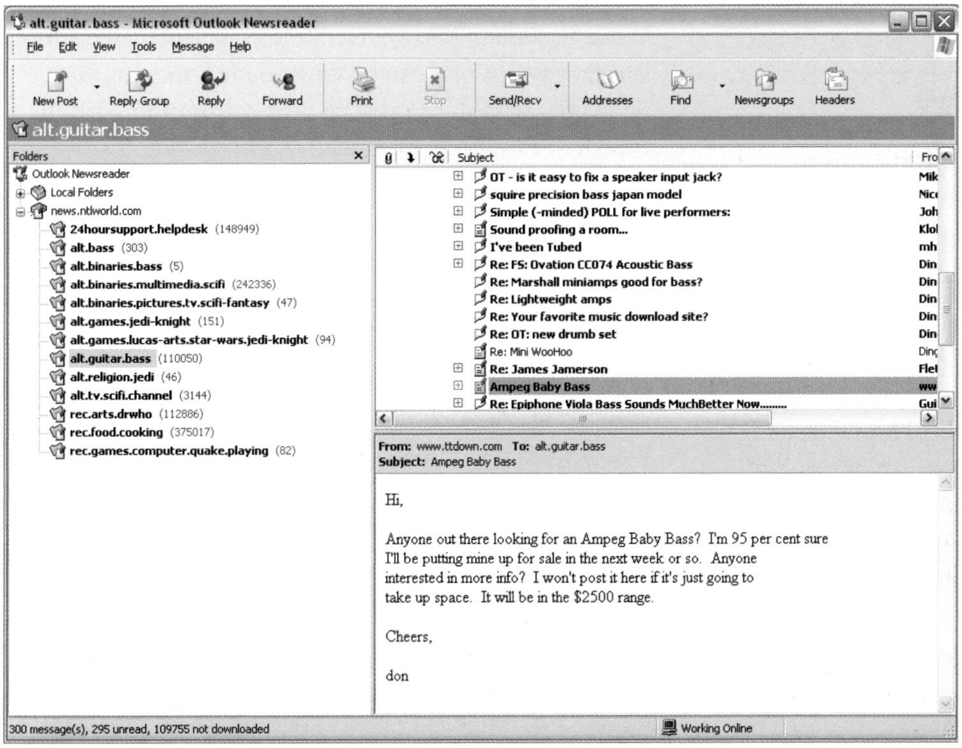

Figure 27.16 Outlook newsgroup reader

STOP Test your knowledge

1 What do the acronyms IRC, VoIP and SMS stand for?

2 Give three examples of types of VoIP.

27.3.2.2 Remote access

As mobile devices have evolved, it is possible to access your primary computer system remotely via small GUI (Graphical User Interface) applications such as Microsoft Terminal Services, Remote Desktop and VNC (Virtual Network Computing). These allow a limited system to use Internet technology to access a fully enabled system.

STOP Test your knowledge

1 What do the acronyms GUI and VNC stand for?

2 What is a limited system?

27.3.3 File services

Networked systems allow users to share files, from documents to media files, and applications. This functionality has been a feature of the Internet and networked systems since the early 1970s, with UUCP (Unix to Unix CoPy).

Many systems exist to enable file transfer and file sharing, including:

- FTP, which is the file transfer protocol for dedicated servers and clients. Internet Explorer can be used to access a FTP site. Many Internet domains have FTP. Anonymous FTP exists to enable the open sharing of files without the need to create usernames or passwords
- peer-to-peer systems which use file sharing applications such as BitTorrent, Kazaa and Blubster to enable common storage for all users

▲ Figure 27.17 File transfer

- direct, with Windows Messenger and other chat applications allowing users to send each other files
- HTTP websites which allow the download (and also upload) of files
- email which can be used to send files as attachments.

While broadband/ADSL technology has increased the speed at which files can be downloaded, moving large quantities of data can still be time consuming. Also the transfer of multiple files can be cumbersome. To overcome this, files are often collected together and compressed.

Depending on the operating system, files can be compressed as ZIP, TAR (Tape ARchive), JAR (Java ARchive) or RAR (Roshal ARchive) files. Windows XP and Vista support file compression and Office 2007 compresses all documents automatically.

File sharing can also be accomplished with many operating systems, where a user or network administrator can enable a folder (or collection of folders) to be accessible.

In Windows, to share a folder is simple: find the folder you wish to be shared, right click on the folder icon and select the Sharing and Security option. Decide on the name of the share and if the other users are allowed to

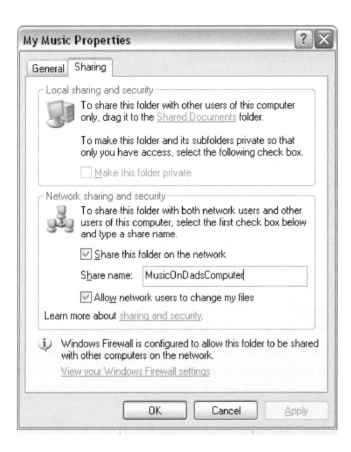

My Music

▲ Figure 27.18 Folder sharing

alter the files (in which case, you are enabling write and execute file privileges instead of read only). On your local computer, the shared folder will have an open hand icon. Across the network, you will be able to find the folder via the My Network Places icon.

27.3.4 Application services

There are many applications used on networked systems, from servers to printing, from storage to email.

27.3.4.1 Application software

Many servers on a networked system are purpose specific; within large organisations, servers are installed to offer single services to their customers or employees.

Database servers normally run in the background, managing large quantities of data. Applications run from web servers or clients to access and manage this large data set. Common systems include Microsoft SQL and Oracle 9i.

Web servers were originally designed to act as information sharing tools. Although this original purpose has not changed, the level and complexity of the information and applications available from web servers has extended their use to become the most common type of server in current use.

Web servers can be used for the following purposes: e-commerce and trade tools, email portals, chat and discussion boards, educational environments, gaming systems, VoIP management portals, device management and configuration portals, CCTV portals, video and entertainment systems, and web radio relays and servers.

Proxy servers manage Internet access on a large networked system (see earlier in this unit, page 259). Proxy servers enable network administrators to: time control users' access to the Internet; log and record when, where and on whose computer users have visited the Internet; control who can and cannot visit the Internet; control what websites users can and cannot see;

keep a local cache of some popular sites, to speed up local access as well as reduce Internet traffic (this has some weaknesses, as some sites are continuously updated).

Test your knowledge

1 Name three types of server.
2 What is a proxy server and what is it used for?

27.3.4.2 Shared resources printing

Printing is still considered a costly resource. Even though the cost of printers has reduced dramatically over the last 20 years, a network administrator still needs to consider: the cost of printers for hundreds of users; the replacement cost of printers, as they are subject to wear and tear; the cost of toner or ink per printer (this is also based on use); the cost of paper; the need to reduce waste and encourage limits on printing to reduce the ecological impact of paper use.

Print servers can manage many printers simultaneously. This enables control over how much a user can print and who can print to which printer (for example, to avoid everyone printing to the same printer – see also page 259).

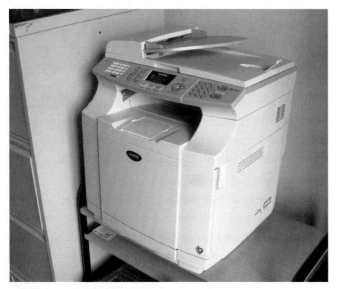

Standard modern office printer

27.3.4.3 Storage space

Many of you will have a network drive (storage space) on your college network; this is a small part of a larger storage (file server) system held at your study centre. Protocols such as FTP deal in the large-scale storage and transfer of data from remote servers.

With FTP you could easily configure your home computer with suitable free software to act as remote storage space and enable you to have continuous access to your work from anywhere.

Test your knowledge

1 Distinguish between database and web servers.
2 Explain shared resources printing.
3 Explain storage space.

27.3.4.4 VOIP

Voice over IP (VoIP) has been explored in section 27.3.2.1 on page 266. This is a developing technology with many interesting servers and services available. With the competition between Skype and open source systems it is likely that the many different systems will continue to exist but will be developed so that each will have a 'gateway' allowing that system to work with others.

27.3.4.5 Mobile working

Mobile working has given the Internet and related technologies their greatest push. As commerce becomes increasingly international, being able to work with customers irrespective of location offers considerable benefits. Laptops, PDAs and mobile phones offer professionals the chance to take their office with them when they are on the move. Many hotels, coffee bars and airports now offer wireless Internet access.

27.3.4.6 Authentication

Authentication (checking you are who you say you are) is a feature of many networked application services. With computer crime being a constant risk, every system you encounter will have a system to check your identity and prevent misuse. Software authentication may take place by: ensuring you have exchanged a 'trust' certificate; checking a password and username, and/or using a key personal identifier, like your mother's maiden name.

Hardware authentication systems tend to work in partnership with software systems and may include: chip and pin; biometrics (fingerprint and retina scanners); dongles (specially programmed USB sticks) and cards inside selected computers. Using such a device adds an additional layer of application security, as the device has to be security compliant as well as the user. (For more on authentication, see section 27.3.1.3 on page 265.)

27.4 Network security and resilience

Network security is now an everyday part of our lives, at home, work and college, and when out shopping. Ensuring that the networks we all use are secured is paramount. Apart from the issues surrounding personal data, the impact of network failure or a system being compromised could be financially costly.

27.4.1 Business issues

The majority of networks support business. Business in this context may mean a trader on the Internet, a larger corporation, your college (as its business purpose is to provide your education), a government department, a charity or a sole worker using their computer at home.

27.4.1.1 Risk to business

A networked system has many advantages, but with many organisations now dependent on their network and its connection to the Internet for the majority of their business functions, the network is considered as a primary risk to business.

For many companies the loss of Internet connectivity or the use of primary networked services may have many adverse effects. It might lose them essential income from customers or prevent them from being able to carry out their core business. It could mean the loss of essential data which is irreplaceable or could cause loss of goodwill with trading partners and suppliers.

See section 15.1.2 (page 179) for further information on this topic.

27.4.1.2 Costs

Unless an organisation relocates or acquires a new site, it is uncommon for a network to be built from scratch. To ensure the network is viable it has to be maintained and each year of operation brings new costs and new opportunities.

When managing any system, a network manager has to consider the cost of ensuring that:

- the size of the system increases in line with the size of organisational growth
- there is enough bandwidth on inter-network WAN connections
- there is enough bandwidth on the Internet connection
- the core network devices can handle all the services required of the network
- the servers are fit for purpose.

27.4.1.3 Responsibilities

Because of the security risks involved in running networks, the administrators of many large network systems are responsible for ensuring that resilience is part of their infrastructure. They do this by:

- carrying out regular backups of critical data
- using multiple connections to the Internet and other networked locations
- using multiple systems such as routers to ensure that if one fails another will take its place automatically
- load balancing data on more than one server, to ensure that the system will cope if one server fails or in times of increased load, such as the pre-Christmas rush on e-commerce sites.

27.4.1.4 Systems and procedures

The management of the network requires that there are systems and procedures in place to ensure standards and common practices in the use and control of the network password policies.

Many organisations will not openly reveal their password policies. It is considered common practice on networked systems that all users must:

- not write down their password
- change their password periodically, from 90 days (three months) to as little as every seven days.
- use a **strong password** with eight or more characters.
- sign an agreement before they are issued their first username, which binds them to corporate policy and requires them to acknowledge laws such as the Computer Misuse Act and the Data Protection Act.

What does it mean?

A **strong password** uses letters (upper and lower case), numbers and symbols, e.g. JacOb_$m1th instead of jacobsmith.

Many systems will log failed attempts when users forget their password, with their username being locked out after three failed attempts.

27.4.1.5 Disaster recovery

In order to have a disaster recovery process means that an organisation's network management needs to have clear policies and processes in place in case of disasters such as fire or flood (when the networked services may need relocation), server failure, loss of Internet connectivity or attempted intrusion.

The policy may involve using alternative technologies, relocation plans or ensuring the data is safe while the organisation rides out the issues that have caused the network loss.

Documenting the network is key to survival: listing addressing schemes, domain structures, cable runs and technologies in use. As well as customers, business partners on the system and users are an essential tool for change management.

In most organisations there are regular changes in the professionals who run different parts of the networked system. Detailed and up-to-date documentation is therefore essential in order to ensure the equilibrium of the system – it enables each network professional to learn from their predecessors and record any changes which may occur.

Test your knowledge

1 Give three examples of risks to business from network loss.

2 What four procedures must network administrators carry out to ensure network resilience?

3 What is involved in a typical organisation's network policy?

4 Why is documenting the network essential in an organisation's disaster recovery process?

Managing your systems security is paramount. As a network administrator you must ensure:

- all security software is up to date
- firewalls are checked regularly
- who has what privileges and why is checked
- no business decision will compromise the network and vice versa.

27.4.2 Securing data

Any data which is compromised or accessed without authority is open to abuse and can lead to fraud, corruption and compromise. To ensure data and networked systems are secure, many technologies and techniques are employed.

In the management of a network and working in the ICT profession you may encounter: authorisation techniques, permissions and access control lists; backup and restoration of data; encryption; biometrics; vetting and control of personnel; CCTV; and lock and key security.

As described in section 27.3 of this unit (see page 265), networked systems use many authentication techniques, which range from the exchange of certificates, secure WAN links, WEP encryption of wireless systems, password control and strong usernames.

In authorising a user, the system must be assured that the person using the system is the person to whom the authority has been issued. Ensuring that fraudulent use does not take place is critical, as it often leads to financial loss or damage to commercial reputations.

- To authorise a user, checks need to be made before they join the system. Creation of an online account with a bank, insurer or credit broker is dependent on this. Often such systems will: check the user's place on the electoral roll; send an email to which the user must reply within a time limit; ask for a phone number, which an operator will use to contact the user; book an appointment at a local branch of the business for a face-to-face meeting to which the user must bring along a passport and additional identification documents; check the user's credit history; confirm previous addresses.
- In a corporate setting, authorising a user follows a similar pattern. Network management will not issue a network username unless: the person has been employed by the company; the supporting line manager has made a suitable application for permissions; the details of the terms of the individual's contract have been submitted, with details of contract expiration if they are working for the organisation on a short-term basis; a contract (commonly called an acceptable use policy) has been signed by the individual, indicating their acknowledgement of the terms under which they can use the networked system.
- When a user name is issued on any networked system, specific permissions are allocated. Personnel are seldom given complete authority over the entire system unless they are the network manager. Permissions issued for a user may define: where their home drive is located; the storage capacity they may use; times they may access the system; locations they may access the system from (which allows some professionals to work from home); areas with read only permissions; areas with read and write permissions; printers, servers and databases they may access; groups they may belong to; whether they can grant local permissions to other users (some systems have the concept of a super user); websites they can and cannot visit.

An **access control list** (**ACL**) is a tool used in network traffic management and may be applied to routers and servers alike. ACLs can be used to create permit or deny rules for networks, devices or a specific range of devices based on specific traffic.

ACLs are applied to firewalls and can be used in a temporal (time-based) context, allowing or denying access to networks at certain times. While many different systems use ACLs, the common rule may look like the one shown in Table 15.2 (see Unit 15, page 197).

The backup and restoration of data is a critical factor in all networked systems in order to maintain the management and reliability of the system. Having a centrally managed backup, where all the data is safely copied in case of system failure and with everyone following the same standards, is essential. Many organisations have fallen into the trap of not managing local backups using the same standards or frequency, so when there is a system failure the site loses essential data. Another common error is to have differing levels of support, which means that many employees are missing out on potentially essential assistance.

Backing up and restoring disks and data are considered to be a critical role of a network administrator. Depending on the size, type and nature of the organisation, it is expected that the network administrator completes at least one backup per day. Some systems employ **incremental backups**, while others use **differential backups**.

What does it mean?

An **incremental backup** involves storing only changed data since the last backup of any type.

A **differential backup** involves storing only changed data since the last **full backup**.

When considering the backup requirements of a system, you must identify the exact quantity of data that requires backing up, the appropriate media that needs to be used in the backup process, the frequency of backups and where a copy of the data needs to be stored off-site.

While it is desirable to back up and recover all information on the network, there is data that is not critical to the running of the organisation, such as system logs, applications that can be re-installed, etc. You need to ensure that the media (tape, network storage server, DVD-RW or CD-RW) can hold the required volume of information, and the frequency of backups take place according to the changeability of the data.

Some organisations complete a backup every eight hours, as the data is undergoing continuous change. It is normal for most companies to complete an overnight backup, where once a week a copy is taken to another location (off-site).

The backup disaster recovery procedure is based on what is critical to the running of the system and is based on the following considerations:

- how quickly data that has been deleted or altered can be recovered
- how effectively a 'downed' server can be restarted
- how soon a damaged or stolen server can be replaced and the data accessed.

On most server systems the storage is managed by **RAID** (see Unit 15, page 192). Currently there are nine different RAID systems. The benefits of using RAID are that if one hard drive fails the system can be rebuilt from the existing images or the system can continue while a new hard drive is installed.

Systems such as RAID and **mirroring** provide companies with fast recovery times. RAID allows data to be recovered from 'duplicated' hard drives. Mirroring requires a second, duplicate server to be in operation at the same time as the primary server.

The amount spent on backup and recovery will be based on the critical nature of the network in respect to the main business of a company. For example, an office cleaning company may be able to manage for 48 hours without their computers, whereas a City bank could be struggling after five minutes of computer loss.

STOP Test your knowledge

1 Give two examples of problems that arise when systems are not properly backed up.

2 Explain these terms: incremental backup and differential backup.

3 What is RAID?

27.4.2.3 Encrypting

Encryption has been explored in section 27.3.1.3 of this unit (see page 265). The main characteristics of data encryption are obscuring the data in transit and ensuring the sender and receiver trust each other in the process of sending the data.

27.4.2.4 Other methods of securing data

■ Biometrics

Biometrics is still evolving as a method of secure authentication, although the technology already exists. Limitations are based on cost and reliability. Some PDAs and USB dongles have single finger scanners, while advanced systems use retina scanners.

What does it mean?

Biometrics is the use of methods of authentication based on unique physical characteristics, such as fingerprints, retina and iris scans and signatures.

With the changes in airport security, you may have been on a long-haul flight to a country where you were required to offer a forefinger scan from each hand as a method of tracking your entry and exit from the country.

■ Vetting and control of personnel

An essential part of maintaining the security of systems is the initial vetting of personnel. Vetting involves checking the background and personality profile of someone who will enter a position of trust and is crucial for personnel who will be involved in using or managing systems with highly sensitive data.

Once permissions have been issued, it is also prudent to check continually whether the individual still needs them. For example, the project they were working on may have ended, so they may no longer need the same level of permissions.

■ CCTV

In the popular press, much is made of the increasing CCTV culture of the UK (and many other nations). While we are all entitled to our view in this matter, for the management of network security it offers an additional advantage. The use of CCTV in key locations can: monitor access to server and communications rooms; allow an independent check of the identity of personnel; limit the potential for theft; authenticate that the person at a computer is the authorised user.

■ Lock and key security

Lock and key security has been with us for hundreds of years and is still a proven technique in maintaining the overall security of many computer systems. The technology may have advanced, with swipe cards, proximity dongles and chip and pin systems all in use.

A security manager can work in partnership with the network management to control physical access to sensitive resources. They can control who has access to what, where and when, as well as keep a record of all personnel entering and exiting some areas.

STOP Test your knowledge

1 What is biometrics? Give two examples.
2 What are the advantages of using CCTV?
3 Give three examples of current types of lock and key security.

27.4.3 Software used in securing a networked system

Protecting a networked system is of paramount importance. Ensuring your system is protected with a firewall as well as protected from malware is essential.

27.4.3.1 Malware

As the technology of networks advances, with more users being able to access them from a wider range of locations, the problem of **malware** has become an increasing problem, including **viruses**, **trojans**, **worms**, **phishing** and **spam** scams.

What does it mean?

Malware is a hostile, intrusive or annoying piece of software or program code.

Definitions of **virus**, **worm** and **trojan** can be found in section 27.2.5 on page 257.

Phishing involves criminals sending out fraudulent emails that claim to be from a legitimate company, with the aim of obtaining the recipients' personal details and committing identity theft.

Spam is unsolicited bulk email used for advertising purposes.

Phishing is a mailing technique, usually used to deceive individuals into revealing their bank password and login details or parting with their money for dubious deals. Some phish emails will direct you to a phoney website that looks the real website (e.g. a bank's website). Even if you do not fall for the deception and do not enter your details, visiting the site could enable the site's web server to download a trojan. As you click on the hyperlink in the email, you will have activated a server-side script which could cause you many problems.

Most **spam** sent today is a form of low-level advertising often for dubious medical or commercial offers. As with phishing, avoid clicking on links to any sites or opening attachments, as it is very likely the web server will attempt to download a trojan.

Spyware is a type of malware that may have been downloaded willingly by the user. The information collected by spyware can range from the sites visited by the user to, more dangerously, the passwords and usernames they use.

In some contexts spyware is used as a tool to enable commercial organisations to direct their marketing and product development, while others use spyware to commit fraud.

Some free applications come with 'legitimate' spyware, using the creators of the spyware to sponsor the development of their applications.

There are some excellent free anti-spyware applications available, but be careful as some of these may themselves be a form of spyware. Microsoft have released Windows Defender as part of Vista, with free downloads for older versions of Windows.

Adware is not normally considered malicious, just annoying. Many free applications (often referred to as shareware) are supported by the fees generated from the advertising that is included in the application as a banner or a separate window.

Many adware systems, such as Gator, Gain and HotBar, will impose advertising on you even when you are not using the offending application.

Some adware systems, especially ones downloaded from dubious sites, border on the spyware and malware category and are considered problematic.

What does it mean?

Spyware collects information about a user's various activities without their consent and reports it back to a central server.

27.4.3.2 Levels of security risk of different malware

Protecting your computer with anti-virus software is essential. (See section 27.2.5, particularly Activity 27.2, which describes how to download a free anti-virus application.)

Each virus, worm, trojan, spam or phishing email will carry a different level of risk – in most cases those which cause the greatest damage entail the greatest risk. If a worm or trojan is involved, it can be safely assumed the risk is high as someone is looking to gain access to your computer system.

Organisations such as McAfee profile each new malware they learn of and monitor its effect across the world. McAfee categorise each malware according to the level

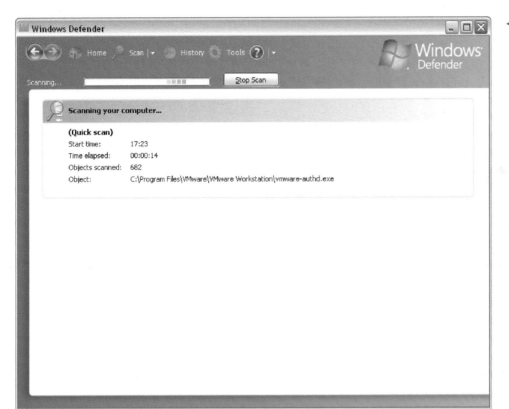

Figure 27.19 Windows Defender

of threat, using the following categories: High-Outbreak, High, Medium-On Watch, Medium, Low Profiled and Low. Visit the McAfee website to discover the current malware issues (go to www.heinemann.co.uk/hotlinks and enter express code 2315P).

27.4.3.3 Firewalls and intrusion detection systems

As discussed in section 27.2.5 on page 257 of this unit, firewalls control access to the network by opening only the TCP or UDP ports that are needed for network traffic. Most firewalls will prevent incoming traffic unless it was requested by a device on the inside of the network.

With many firewall systems, you may also find **intrusion detection systems**. Some of these are passive and simply

warn the network manager of a possible incursion, while others are active and can be configured to disable the offending data stream.

With applications such as Snort, AirSnort and Wireshark (formerly Ethereal), it is easy to create a **span port** on a network switch and attach a PC to monitor the traffic for the entire system. This is surprisingly efficient and can be used to trap many users' illegitimate activities.

What does it mean?

A **span port** is a port on to which all the data on the network is copied.

What does it mean?

An **intrusion detection system** is used to monitor network traffic and analyse if an incursion has taken place.

STOP Test your knowledge

1 What is malware?

2 Name five types of malware.

3 Define intrusion detection system and span port.

Preparation for assessment

The assessment tasks in this unit are based on the following scenario.

Scenario

The Widgets R Us data centre is up and running. The chair of the board, pleased with this new development, wants to declare its praises to the board of directors. Whilst the chair is a captain of industry and responsible for the exponential growth of Widgets R Us over the last 10 years, their technical ability when it comes to networks is somewhat lacking. This means you are going to have to produce a set of 'technical' documents which explain the technology in terms understood by the chair, whilst refraining from language which will insult their intelligence.

Task 1 (P1, P2, P6)

Produce a chart which describes the types of networks available and how they relate to the network standards and protocols. Add examples as to why different network standards and protocols are necessary as well as typical services provided by networks.

1 Describe the types of networks available and how they relate to the network standards and protocols.
2 Describe, using examples, why different network standards and protocols are necessary.
3 Describe typical services provided by networks.

Task 2 (P3, P4, P5, M4)

Create a PowerPoint presentation which:
- describes the functions of a logical set of interconnection devices

- describes the key components required for client workstations to connect to a network and access network resources
- gives an outline description of the OSI 7-layer model and explains the importance of each layer
- compares the benefits and disadvantages of peer-to-peer network or a client/server network.

1 Describe the functions of a logical set of interconnection devices.
2 Describe the key components required for client workstations to connect to a network and access network resources.
3 Give an outline description of the OSI 7-layer model.
4 Explain the importance of the OSI 7-layer model.

Task 3 (P7, M2, M3, D1, D2)

Panic stations – it has all gone wrong; the network for the new data centre was designed and implemented by Bodgers R Us who have done a 'runner' when the network did not meet the required standards. Based on the network in Figure 27.20:
- suggest improvements and justify the design and choice of components used
- complete a new design for this network, ensuring it has at least two connections to the Internet and double connections on all core WAN links
- describe the business risks of insecure networks and suggest how they can be minimised
- evaluate the value of typical services available from using DNS or active directory for server naming
- compare and explain the differences in data transfer rates between typical LANs, WANs and mobile networks.

1 Describe the business risks of insecure networks and how they can be minimised.
2 Design a networked solution to meet a particular situation with specific requirements.
3 Compare and explain the differences in data transfer rates between typical LANs, WANs and mobile networks.

4 Justify the design and choice of components used in a particular networked solution.
5 Evaluate the value of typical services available from a network operating system directory service.

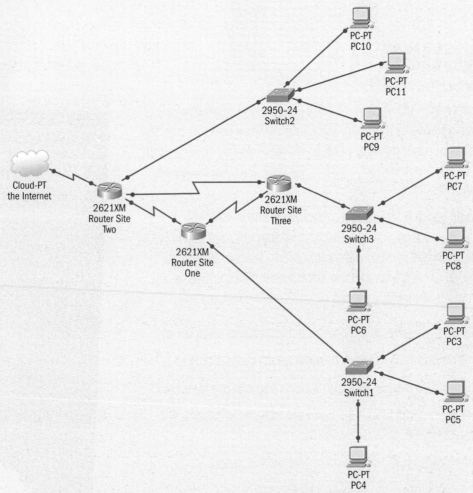

▲ Figure 27.20 Data centre network

IT Technical Support

Introduction

Technical support personnel offer support for individuals and organisations in a variety of ways. This unit focuses on help desk and desktop support but also includes an awareness of other options, such as remote support (connecting to the client machine and attempting to resolve the problem), field support and call centre support.

In completing this unit, you will increase your technical knowledge. You will be expected to develop your research skills and to show that you can select relevant and reliable information from different sources. You will learn how to apply this knowledge to help end users to resolve technical problems and improve the performance of their IT systems.

After completing this unit, you should be able to achieve these outcomes:

- Be able to gather information in order to provide advice and guidance
- Be able to communicate advice and guidance in appropriate formats
- Understand how the organisational environment influences technical support
- Understand technologies and tools used in technical support.

Thinking points

This unit provides you with an introduction to the world of IT support. You will learn about the role of help desk staff. This should help you to understand what is expected of the people who provide guidance and support to users who are having difficulty with a computer system.

Help desks are the first point of contact for a user who is experiencing difficulty with a computer system. Teams of support staff are on hand, often 24 hours a day and 7 days a week, to answer telephone calls and process them. How do you think the teams are managed? What training would each member of the support team need to be in a position to provide useful help to a caller? How could the calls be filtered so that each member of the help desk support team receives only those calls that they are trained to handle? These and other questions are addressed in this unit.

Anger management is a topic which may be new to you. It is included in this unit for a good reason; it is now seen as important for many people, including IT support workers. However, it is a sensitive topic and one which may make you feel uncomfortable. Thinking about what makes you angry and uncovering causes of anger, or doing activities to learn how to cope with angry feelings, may alarm you. However, your teacher will guide you through this topic and, hopefully, it will help you to become more successful in your dealings with others.

Although you will be studying IT, many of the skills you learn in this unit would apply to customer support in other industries, such as retail or banking. This is because the way you handle people is important, whatever job you do.

The staff in a **call centre** are employed to service telephone calls from customers, and to record the details of all such calls on a **call logging system**.

Some call centres provide help desk support to IT users. Before the staff in the call centre can provide advice and guidance, they need to identify the problem. This will involve information gathering from a variety of sources. The end user who is having the problem should prove to be a valuable source of information, but help desk staff also need to consider other sources, such as a **fault log** or **diagnostic software**, and they may need to consult some technical documentation.

This section focuses on a range of information sources and how best to gather that information.

28.1.1 Information gathering

Information gathering requires a variety of skills, plus a strategy for success and a method of documenting your findings.

- Information can be gathered from a number of sources, such as direct questions to the client, consulting a fault log or using diagnostic and monitoring tools. Each of these requires different skills on your part: communication, research and analysis.
- There will be constraints on your time and pressure to find a solution quickly, so you will need to identify priorities. Having a clear idea of what you are looking for and where to look will help you to prioritise, so you need a strategy for success.
- Faults fall into broad categories – such as loss of service or poor performance. The ability to recognise patterns will help you to solve problems more quickly. So keeping accurate and detailed records forms an essential part of information gathering.

Each of these aspects of information gathering will now be considered in turn.

28.1.1.1 Direct questioning

An end user has a problem and wants you, the support technician, to fix it. He/she contacts you and starts to tell you what he/she thinks is wrong. During the conversation that follows – either face-to-face or on the telephone – you need to find out as much as possible, so that you can start to make decisions as to where the fault lies, and how you might resolve the problem.

However, before you can accept the call from the end user, you may need to check that he/she is entitled to your support services. This may include asking for a user name and password, or maybe an account number and password. This personal data may allow you access to information about the end user that you can bring up on your screen:

- What level of service is the user entitled to expect from you? If there is a **service level agreement (SLA)** you will need to make sure you meet the expectations of the end user in full.

What does it mean?

A **call centre** is a place where customer and other telephone calls are handled by an organisation, usually with some amount of computer automation.

A **call logging system** is a computerised system which is linked to a database of customers' details and keeps a record of any communication with them.

A **fault log** is a record of events that occurred, and may include information about how the fault was fixed.

Diagnostic software attempts to diagnose a problem; it identifies possible faults and offers solutions.

A **service level agreement (SLA)** sets out what level of support is expected – for example, the speed of response for particular types of problem. See also page 304.

- When did this user last contact the help desk? The user's attitude may be affected by how often he/she runs into difficulty and how effective the support has been previously. Often, end users are frustrated by problems they are experiencing and may be angry. Having as much background information to hand as possible may help you to cope with their anger. This topic is considered in greater detail on page 300.

- What action has been taken previously? Since help desks (and call centres) are often staffed on a shift basis, it might be rare for an end user to talk to the same support technician two times running. The end user would appreciate not having to start all over again each time he/she rings. It is therefore important that records – such as a fault log – are kept of each conversation and what action was taken.

Case study

Support service providers

FastHosts provide hosting services to individuals and organisations who want an Internet presence. Their support technicians are trained to advise the end user in processes essential to the maintenance of a website, such as uploading web pages. Before offering support, the support technicians at FastHosts ask for an account number and password. Only then can a client be given help.

1 Identify a support service that you can contact. This might be the IT support team at your college or place of work, or a service provider such as your telephone company.

2 Contact a support help desk and note what information is requested to establish your right to assistance. Compare this with the checks done by FastHosts and any other organisations that others in your group have contacted.

3 If you cannot remember vital information, such as a password, how can you prove to the support team that you are indeed entitled to help?

Once you have established that the end user is entitled to your support services, and have been informed of what has happened to date, you are ready to talk to the end user. However, before you ask, 'What seems to be the problem?', there are a number of important facts that you will need to know and record, or confirm with the end user. As well as the name of the end user (or the person who is reporting the fault), it is essential to record other contact details.

Case study

Essential contact information

The BT help desk for broadband enquiries asks for a mobile phone number. Many of their broadband customers have to telephone from the number that would normally be used to connect to the Internet, and this is the number on which there would appear to be a fault. Any test on that line can cause the connection to fail and the caller to be cut off. For the customer to locate the same help desk person is almost impossible. BT therefore have to contact the customer if the support is to continue at all – for this, another telephone number, such as a mobile number, is needed.

1 Compile a list of details that you might collect from the end user, so that you could contact them again if need be.

2 Compare your list with others in your group and, between you, devise a form to record this information.

Most problems relate to faults in the hardware and software being used or, often, the way in which they are being operated by the end user.

- If the problem appears to be a hardware fault, you need to know the make and model of the hardware (such as 'Hewlett-Packard printer, model PSC 1210' or a 'SpeedTouch modem, model 330'). This may enable you to access the relevant technical information, for example, on the manufacturer's website, so that you can talk the end user through a sequence of steps towards identifying the precise fault and resolving the problem.

- It may also be relevant to know the software platform (such as Windows XP) and/or the software applications (such as Word) that they are running. Part of your training will be to become familiar with how the software works. In fact, you ought to be an expert in using any software that an end user might have installed on their computer.

Table 28.1 lists the questions that need to be answered and recorded at some point during the processing of a fault.

Table 28.2 shows the data fields that might be needed to record the information so that it can be analysed. The items in the first three rows of Tables 28.1 and 28.2 are relevant for this unit. The data in the remaining rows is essential for a complete picture of the incident and how it was resolved, but relates more to the content of *Unit 29: IT Systems Troubleshooting and Repair.*

Question	What needs to be recorded
Who reported the fault?	Name and contact details
When was it reported?	The exact time as well as the date
Has someone been assigned to deal with this problem?	Who was assigned, and at what time it happened
Has anyone decided on a course of action?	What action was decided upon, when this took place and who made the decision
What was the actual problem?	Categorise as: End user error/Faulty hardware/Faulty software, etc.
Has the problem been fixed?	How it was fixed
How much did it cost to repair?	Time spent doing the repair, cost of replacement parts

Table 28.1 Questions that a call logging system should answer

Data field	Notes
Call ID	A unique reference number to identify this particular call and all subsequent action taken to resolve the fault.
Date and time of initial call	It is important to record the time as well as the date. Some faults will be reported and solved within the space of a couple of hours. Others may take longer.
Who initiated the call?	The person who called may be noted by their name and department, or maybe an employee ID code, linked to other databases held by the company. This may allow the HR (human resources) department to identify employees who regularly call for IT support, and may need to be given extra training.
Technician allocated to supervise the solution	The help desk assistant will need to make an initial decision as to who can help the caller best. This will be based on information given by the caller, and the call assistant may have a questionnaire to complete which also helps to decide whether the fault is mostly hardware related or mostly software related.
Data and time of passing information to technician	A delay in passing details of the problem on to a technician will mean the end user might be waiting longer than he or she needs to. Keeping track of this data will ensure more efficient processing by the help desk assistant.
Report from technician(s)	This may include information such as what equipment was repaired on-site, what equipment was removed for repair, what loan equipment was given to the user as a temporary fix or what replacement equipment was given to the user as a permanent fix. Each event needs a date and time of action so that progress can be monitored.
Error diagnosis	Details of exactly what went wrong and how it was fixed will help if other users call in with similar problems.
Costs (money)	Equipment that is supplied to replace faulty equipment can be charged to a particular reported fault.
Costs (time)	Time spent repairing equipment or just on-site with an end user, trying to diagnose the problem, needs to be accounted for, and charged against each call.
Recommendations	Lessons learnt in solving a problem should be recorded and considered when making decisions about staffing levels within the support team, the equipment that is to be purchased in future and training needs of support staff and end users.

Table 28.2 Data stored in a call logging system

Sometimes, lack of knowledge on the part of the end user is the root cause of the problem, and it may prove necessary to recommend training for individuals.

If several end users ask the same questions, one solution (that may save on time spent providing one-to-one support) is to set up a web page (on the Internet or within a company's intranet) listing **FAQs** and their answers – see page 294.

Case study

FAQs

FastHosts' FAQs answer the questions that are often asked, such as 'What is broadband?', 'How can I check that broadband is available in my area?' and 'What spec PC do I need to run broadband?'

1 Visit the site of one of your service providers and read the FAQs.

2 Compile a list of five FAQs that a novice user of one particular software package or one item of hardware might ask. Swap these with a partner and provide the answers for your partner's FAQs.

 (partial evidence)

Activity 28.1

Data collection forms

1 A novice computer user is trying to connect to the Internet, without success. List the details you would expect this user to provide when calling the **ISP**'s help desk.

2 An experienced web designer is trying to upload a new page from Dreamweaver, and is having problems. List the details you would expect this user to provide to the host company's help desk.

3 Design a form to collect relevant data when recording one call to a help desk.

What does it mean?

FAQ stands for frequently asked questions.

ISP stands for Internet service provider.

How you communicate with the end user – your manner and attitude towards the caller – and how to extract relevant information are covered in more detail in section 28.2.2 (see page 296). But at this stage of the call you simply have to collect facts and your direct questioning needs to be done courteously and efficiently, using a manner and tone that will not inflame an end user who may already be angry.

You may be provided with a script to help you through this initial stage, so that you do not forget to ask for particular information. When reading from a script, it is easy to sound bored because your conversations become very repetitive. The end user quickly realises you are using a script and might view this negatively. Therefore, it helps if you can develop some personality to your voice so that your end user feels better served by you.

You need to communicate courteously and efficiently during a call

Activity 28.2

Help desk scripts

1 Call a help desk and note precisely the conversation that took place. Could you tell that a script was being used?

2 Compare the conversations that you and others have recorded. Check how similar the questions were, and the order in which they were asked. From this, devise the script that might have been used.

3 Working in pairs, role-play the process of calling a help desk, using your script. As the help desk technician experiments with ways of making the end user feel more like an individual receiving the level of attention he/she might expect. **p**₂

28.1.1.2 Fault log

Remember!

A **fault log** is a record of events that occurred, and may include information about how the fault was fixed.

A log should be maintained for each computer system: when the equipment was obtained, and when software was installed, what settings have been used and so on. If the system breaks down, this information may be needed. When the system breaks down, the same log may be used to record what went wrong and how it was fixed, or a separate fault log may be set up just to record the problems and how they were overcome.

A fault log may be kept manually, or it may be created automatically by software. The fault log can prove useful if a problem keeps happening, and the cause is unknown. Noting the date and circumstances each time something 'goes wrong' may throw light on the source of the problem.

Electronically generated fault logs may be created by software tools such as Dumprep.exe. If a serious error

occurs, this Windows XP fault-logging program writes the error details to a text file. The user is then prompted to send the error information to Microsoft (see Figure 28.1).

The software manufacturer can then collate information about problems that users are experiencing and use this data to help them to track down the cause of the fault.

Unit 29: IT Systems Troubleshooting and Repair also considers fault logs; see page 320.

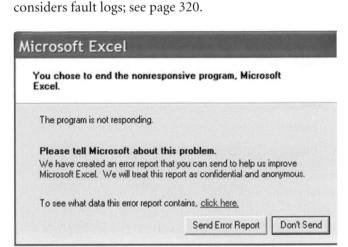

▲ **Figure 28.1 The prompt to send details of a fault to Microsoft**

28.1.1.3 Diagnostics and monitoring tools

As each new operating system is introduced, so too are diagnostic and monitoring tools aimed to help the user – and support technicians – track down faults and improve the running of the computer system.

When you turn on a computer, the **POST** checks the hardware to make sure everything is functioning correctly before the operating system is loaded and run.

What does it mean?

POST stands for 'power on self test'.

If there are problems and these are found before the screen is operational, a sequence of beeps is used to indicate the nature of the fault. Once the screen is operational, an error code is given on-screen instead, showing which device is not functioning properly.

Unit 29: IT Systems Troubleshooting and Repair looks at the value of the POST diagnostic information (see page 00).

Once the computer is up and running satisfactorily, in a Windows environment, the **Control Panel** offers the Systems Properties route to information about how the computer is functioning; see page 289.

What does it mean?

The **Control Panel** is a folder which offers routes to files that can be used to manage the computer system.

Event Viewer is one example of a monitoring tool that is supplied with an operating system (Figure 28.2). Windows XP logs major events such as the boot-up sequence, the start-up and closing down of applications, and any errors that are reported. These are recorded in the Application, Security and System logs. The Event Viewer tool can be used to manage and view these events and therefore to track security events and identify possible software, hardware and system problems.

Unit 29: IT Systems Troubleshooting and Repair (page 336) explains how Event Viewer might be used to predict and identify the sources of system problems.

There are other tools available from third-party suppliers, such as Dr Watson for Windows (see Unit 29, page 336). These utility programs exist to aid the end

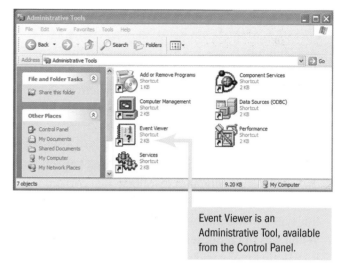

Event Viewer is an Administrative Tool, available from the Control Panel.

Figure 28.2 Route to Event Viewer

user or support technician in maintaining the system and, typically, promise to maximise a machine's performance (Figure 28.3).

28.1.1.4 Identification of priorities

It is possible to filter incoming calls to a help desk and to answer those that are considered more important first. However, the end users who are kept waiting in a queue are likely to be angry by the time their call is answered. This could mean that it takes longer to take the details of their fault and so this approach can prove counter-productive. It is not only fairer but also more efficient to accept calls in the order in which they arrive.

Prioritising can then be applied on follow-up action, for example, in arranging for a support technician to visit the end user. There are three main ways of prioritising requests for support, although a combination of these may also apply.

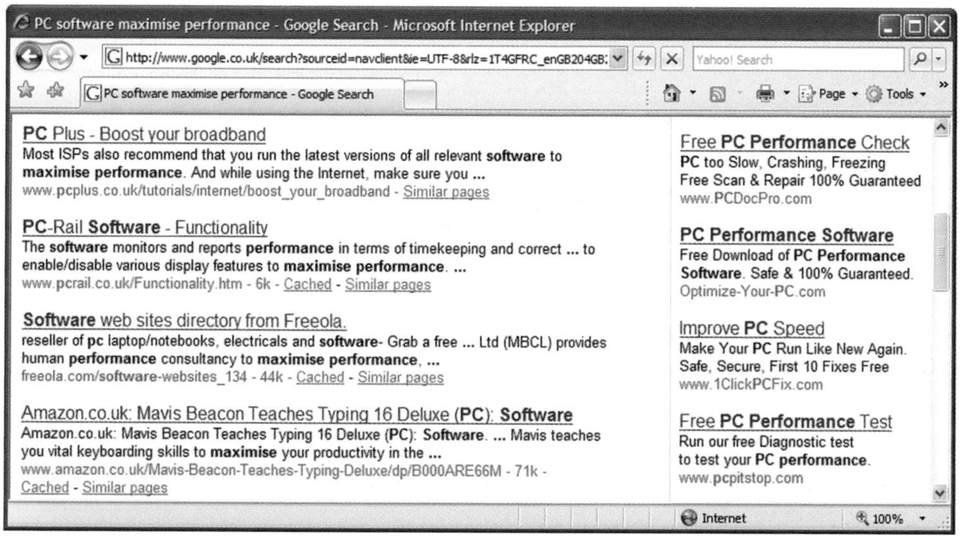

Figure 28.3 Software offering to maximise performance

- **How critical is the problem to the continued operation of the business?** Who is experiencing problems and how essential to his/her job function is his/her access to IT services? Some staff can continue with other work, so fixing their IT problem is not as crucial as for staff who spend all their working time at the computer.
- **How severe is the fault?** Will it cause more problems if it is not fixed immediately? For example, a problem that involves a faulty hard drive may well corrupt data. Even if the end user did not have a high priority, this type of fault may warrant speedier treatment.
- **When was the request for support made?** How long is *too* long for any end user to wait for a problem to be resolved? Even users with the least important problems deserve to be paid attention. If it seems to take forever to receive support, this reflects badly on the help desk team so all requests ought to be processed within a reasonable time.

One way of deciding what is and what is not acceptable is to draw up a **service level agreement** (SLA); this is discussed in more detail on page 304.

Case study

Service levels

BT has a two-tier system of support: residential customers versus business customers. Business customers pay more for telephone connections than residential customers and are entitled to compensation if BT fail to provide the service that has been promised. Because the service is costly to BT if there is a problem, business customers therefore receive a speedier support response. And since the resources available to BT are limited, this can mean that residential customers have to wait longer to have their problems resolved.

1 For a service provider, establish how the calls are prioritised. Is the system fair?

2 Find out the details of a service level agreement that has been set up with a service provider at your college or place of work.

28.1.1.5 Fault type

Although the root cause of a problem might be hardware or software – or inefficient use of the computer by the end user – the fault, as perceived by the user, is either loss of service or poor performance.

Loss of service includes:
- a crash – when the whole system goes down
- the system has 'hung up' – moving the mouse no longer results in a movement of the cursor and there is no response to a key being pressed
- a peripheral that no longer works: e.g. the printer or the screen or the hard drive
- failure to connect to the Internet – an error message reports that there is a fault: no dial tone, or failure to connect at the server end.

Poor performance relates to the slowing down of the system. It may take a long time for a web page to load, or for material to be sent to the printer. Either way, the system is not operating in a way that is satisfactory for the end user and he/she puts in a call to the help desk.

This unit focuses on the role of the help desk staff in fielding complaints. Tracking down what is causing a problem is the subject of *Unit 29: IT Systems Trouble Shooting and Repair* (page 316).

28.1.2 Validation of information

Some sources of information are more reliable than others. So, in the process of gathering detailed information, you need to make sure that the information is valid. Invalid information will get in the way of you arriving at a speedy solution to the problem.

28.1.2.1 Cross reference checks with user

While talking to an end user about the problem, you may be able to call up data on your computer system, including the current configuration of the end user's computer. However, this information may be out of date; the end user may have upgraded the equipment or installed a more modern operating system. So, it makes sense to confirm this information with the user during the initial conversation.

Simple direct questioning will ensure you are basing your judgements on correct information.

- Which operating system are you using? Windows? Which version?
- Which make of printer is it? Hewlett-Packard? Which model?
- Which modem are you using? The internal one or an external modem? If an external one, how is it connected to your PC?
- What software are you using? Word processing? Which package? Which version of that software are you using?

Some users may not be able to answer these questions and you may have to direct them to how they can find out.

For example, to discover which operating system is being used, you may need to guide the end user to press Start, click on Control Panel and select System. The General tab window will then reveal the information you need to confirm (see Figure 28.4).

▲ Figure 28.4 System Properties: General tab

Activity 28.3

Questions, questions, questions

1 Compile a series of questions that you could ask to confirm details about the end user's PC – for example, the configuration of their PC.

2 Working in pairs, try out your questions on your partner. Discuss the answers and refine your questions so that a novice user could answer them.

28.1.2.2 Problem reproduction

So far, the conversation with the end user has related to simple direct questioning to establish who the end user is, how you might contact them and what configuration they are working on. Now you need to find out exactly what is wrong – and what needs to be done to fix the fault. However, the end user may jump to conclusions and suggest things that are wrong with the PC, rather than just giving you the facts.

As part of your problem-solving strategy, encourage the user to describe the problem as they see it, but ignore – or at least set aside – the interpretation that they give as to what is causing the problem. Problem reproduction is a useful strategy – asking the end user to talk you through what went wrong can reveal important information that the user might not otherwise have told you.

One important fact is the date when the problem was first noticed. If new hardware or software was installed immediately before the fault appeared, this might be to blame. Take the end user back to a time when the PC was working – this will help him/her to think through the events that led up to the problem, in the right order and exactly as it happened. This may reveal vital clues, but it will still be important to keep an open mind and to consider alternative sources of the problem.

The goal of problem reproduction is that, if you can recreate the same situation, you could be halfway to solving it.

Having gathered as much information as possible from the end user, you can start to form a picture as to what might be the cause of the end user's problem.

You may also find some other sources of information helpful.

- Manufacturers' websites are a valuable source of information (see Figure 28.5). If an application fails to work, you can search the manufacturer's website for the latest information about known bugs in the system.

- Open user forums (see Figure 28.6) can also prove useful, although the advice given may not be tried and tested, so you ought to be cautious before following it.

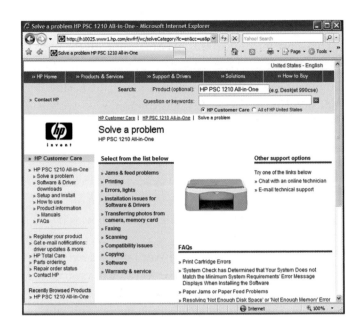

▲ Figure 28.5 A sample manufacturer's website: Hewlett-Packard

◀ Figure 28.6 A sample open user forum site: Tiscali

Each posting on a forum is called a **tile**. A string of tiles is called a **thread**.

Open forum sites are moderated, i.e. someone has the job of checking every posting to make sure the site rules are followed. On this forum, Chris is the **moderator**.

You might also consult with colleagues. They may have met a similar problem before and be able to advise you. If good records have been kept of previously reported problems and the ways in which they were solved, this too can prove to be an invaluable source of information. Both of these sources are considered next.

28.1.3 Technical knowledge

Before you can hope to solve a problem which involves the breakdown of hardware or software, you need to have a good understanding of how the system works normally, and the kinds of problems that can occur. This technical knowledge includes lots of facts and figures – and knowledge and experience can be built up over a period of time.

However, to share this expertise and help people with less experience, written records such as product specifications, manuals and fault records are provided as a reliable source of documentation. Colleagues can also prove to be a useful resource, as well as software-oriented sources such as knowledge bases and those found on the Internet.

28.1.3.1 Product specifications and manuals

The **product specification** is written by the manufacturer of the product. It contains details of the technical aspects of a product, for example: its dimensions, the correct voltage to use and details of any consumables that are recommended. Failure to comply with the recommendations in the product specification may result in the product not working as intended.

For example, some PCs have a voltage switch (see Figure 28.7) so that they may be used in more than one location. In the UK, the normal mains power supply is 240 volts; elsewhere, it may only be 110 volts. The switch needs to be set for the correct voltage. Otherwise, the power supply unit may not be fed sufficient power to operate the equipment. This may result in the screen not functioning, for example.

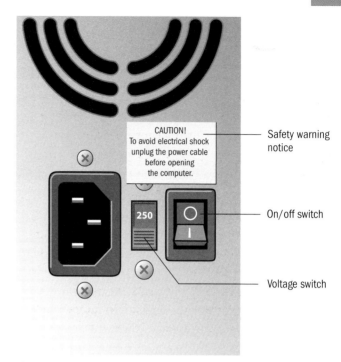

▲ Figure 28.7 Voltage switch on PC

A **manual** explains how to make the best use of a hardware or software product. It is also usually written by the manufacturer, but is addressed more to the end user rather than to a technician. *Unit 29: IT Systems Troubleshooting and Repair* (see page 318) explains how these manuals might be used to assist a user who is having problems, e.g. to create a particular effect with a software package. Some effects are more complicated to achieve, and greater experience in using the software is needed. Some manufacturers provide tutorials to introduce the end user to a particular concept (see Figure 28.8).

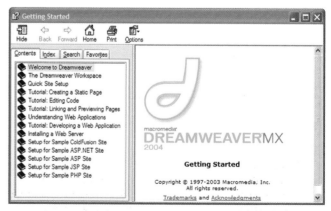

▲ Figure 28.8 Tutorial in Dreamweaver

A manual explains how to make the best use of a hardware or software product

Some users need to be led through tutorials and would benefit from one-to-one tuition. These users are likely to call the help desk to ask for support. However, while you may have the skills to help these end users, it may not be the most efficient use of your time, so the organisation's policy may be to refer the end user for extra training elsewhere; see page 296.

28.1.3.2 Colleagues with specialist expertise

Technical information can often be gleaned from the people around you. Colleagues at work, and friends outside work, can offer their experience in solving problems that you have just encountered. Knowing the right person to ask is the key to success. Sometimes, you may need to call on specialists: someone who is technically competent at a higher level. Such specialists may work within your organisation or you might be able to contact them via a telephone help line (Figure 28.9).

28.1.3.3 Knowledge bases

Expert systems rely on knowledge bases. Support technicians can draw on a knowledge base to help them to decide on a course of action.

The Microsoft Office Online knowledge base underpins the help options offered on all Microsoft applications (see Figure 28.10).

Using a knowledge base like this one involves searching for information that is relevant to the problem you are trying to solve. *Unit 29: IT Systems Troubleshooting and Repair* explores this aspect of using a knowledge base; see page 318.

What does it mean?

A **knowledge base** is a database of key facts.

50/50   ASK THE AUDIENCE   PHONE A FRIEND

Figure 28.9
'I think I'll phone a friend.'

Pressing F1 (or selecting Help/ Microsoft Office Word Help) opens a Search panel.

Figure 28.10 Accessing the Microsoft Office Online knowledge base

Having entered a key term and clicked on the green arrow, the Search Results are listed...

... and you are given the option to search the knowledge base.

Or, you can go to Microsoft Office Online from the drop down Help menu.

Activity 28.4

Knowledge bases

1 Bob is trying to print an Excel worksheet for an important meeting. He needs to present a one-page report, but the last column of his spreadsheet goes on to a second page. Bob rings the help desk and asks: 'Is there a way to fit all the data on one page?' Access the Microsoft Office Online knowledge base to locate information that you could use to help Bob, and find a tutorial on printing techniques for Bob to watch.

2 Bob does not have time to learn how to solve his printing problems. Suggest other ways that he could present his information to the meeting. What other communication routes could he use? Compare these options with the original plan to present a worksheet.

 (partial evidence)

3 Search the Internet for more examples of knowledge bases. Pool your findings with those of others in your group.

28.1.3.4 Fault records showing previously found solutions

A fault log is most useful when it lists not only the problems that were encountered but also the way in which they were solved. There is no point in trying to reinvent the wheel – referring to these records can save a lot of time and energy. A fault log that includes the name of the technician who solved a particular fault will allow you to contact him/her if you have encountered a similar fault and need specialist help.

28.1.3.5 Internet sources

There are two main sources of help on the Internet: FAQs and technical forums.

Remember!

FAQs stands for frequently asked questions.

Online help often supplies a list of **FAQs**. Providing answers to these FAQs, in this way, can solve the most common problems for users, with minimal effort for the help desk staff.

Technical forums (see Figure 29.2 on page 320) provide a talking space for users experiencing problems with their hardware or software. Faults are often discovered after software has been released and will affect all users. As soon as such a fault is noticed and reported, the manufacturer can start to try to fix the fault. Meanwhile, technical forums provide other users with warnings of what does and does not work. This can save a lot of time wondering if a particular fault lies with the user rather than with the system.

Activity 28.5

Sources of information

1 For a software package that you use regularly, find out what it has to offer in the way of FAQs. What other guidance does it provide for the novice user? Make a list of 10 top tips. **p**₁

2 For a given problem, such as a peripheral not working, identify three sources of information that you could use to solve the problem. Describe the validity of and evaluate each source. **p**₁ **m**₁

3 Discuss with your friends: Whose advice do you value the most? Which of you is most expert – and can therefore help others – for a particular application? Make a note of your areas of expertise for future reference. **m**₁ (partial evidence)

Test your knowledge

1 What is an FAQ?

2 Where might you find hints and tips?

3 What other source of technical support – apart from hard copy resources and electronic help – might prove useful?

Communication is an essential part of problem-solving.

- The end user may be experienced and know what is wrong, whereas a complete novice might have no ideas to offer. Your skills in communicating with all types of user will help you to discover as much as possible in the shortest time, and to keep the end user calm and happy in the process.
- Once you have arrived at a solution, you need to choose an appropriate way of offering advice or giving guidance. For example, if the root of the problem is the end user you may need to suggest tactfully that they have some training.
- Forms of communication range from a face-to-face discussion with the end user to placing a guidance note on a website for all interested users to see. You will need to choose the most appropriate form for the situation.
- Communication is a two-way activity. It is not enough to tell the user how to resolve a problem and then leave him or her to it. You need to check that your instructions were clear enough to be followed and that your advice proved to be useful. Only then can you be sure that you provided support in a way that suited the end user. Some evaluative feedback is therefore needed.

Each of these aspects is now considered.

28.2.1 End users

The end user is the person who has the problem, and your problem is to solve his or her problem.

Your skills in communicating with the end user are needed to help you to find out as much as possible about the problem in the shortest possible time. With the appropriate skills, you can also keep the end user calm and happy during what might be a time-consuming process of finding the source of the problem, and fixing it.

How you communicate – the vocabulary that you use and your manner of speaking – should be matched to the needs of the person with whom you are communicating.

- The end user may have little experience of the hardware and software that he/she is using. If you use

technical terms which sound like jargon to the novice, you will create a communication barrier. Instead, use the correct terms but add guidance to talk the user through the steps involved. For example, you might say 'I need you to open the Control Panel. To do this, click on the Start Button. Yes, the one at the bottom left of your screen. Yes, a left-click. Now, can you see the Control Panel listed as an option? . . .'

- The end user may be more experienced – a **power user** even – and have a good idea of the problem and how to communicate it to you. With this type of user, you may use more technical terms and expect the user to understand them. However, at each step, check that the user is still with you! So, you might say 'I need you to go to the Control Panel. OK?' If the user replies 'Yes. Now what do I do?', you can continue. If not, you may need to give more guidance, similar to that given to a novice.
- The end user may be a technician like yourself. You would expect to be able to give high-level commands such as 'Go to the Control Panel' and be understood. You should not need to give additional instructions, nor check that the technician has carried out your command correctly. How the conversation continues will confirm that you are working in tandem.

What does it mean?

A **power user** tends to use shortcuts and be adept at using the mouse.

To summarise, your choice of vocabulary – the technical terms that you use – and the level of the commands you give need to match the understanding of the end user. Finding out how much the end user knows and their level of competence cannot be done by asking 'Are you a novice?' outright. This could offend the end user. Instead, during the initial stages of your conversation, give reasonably high-level commands but be ready to back them up with more detailed guidance. Then, according to the response of the end user, provide the appropriate level of guidance after that.

Activity 28.6

Giving good guidance

1   Refer back to your answer to Question 1 of Activity 28.4. At what level did you answer Bob? What assumptions did you make about his level of expertise? Compose an email in reply to Bob's problem, attaching a guidance document which presents your advice as if he were a complete novice. Print a copy of the attachment.

2   Revise your email to Bob, assuming he is a power user. Revise the guidance document also, using Track Changes. Print a copy showing the changes that you made. **p₂ m₂**

3   Compare your two versions with those of others in your group.

28.2.2 Types of advice

There are no quick fixes. The advice you give must meet the needs of the user in the long term; otherwise, the problem may occur again very soon.

To provide the right advice and to solve the problem completely, you should consider the problem from all angles and complete sufficient investigations to be sure that you have discovered the cause of it. Only then can you decide how the end user can proceed.

28.2.2.1 Recommendations for repair or replacement

Your recommendation may involve the repair of an item of hardware or the replacement of components. This may involve a visit to the end user's workspace, and you will need to book an appointment that suits both the end user and the technician who will be assigned for the task. *Unit 29: IT Systems Troubleshooting and Repair* (see page 323) considers this type of remedy in more detail.

28.2.2.2 Provision of training or direct instruction

You might decide that part of the solution should involve some additional training for the end user. This might mean your giving some direct instruction on a one-to-one basis, and arranging a suitable time for this to take place, or you may be able to direct the end user to an online tutorial source. Meeting the training needs of end users is considered as a remedy in Unit 29 (page 324).

28.2.2.3 Recommending software solutions

Software is often released for sale under licence before it has been tested enough to find all the bugs. The manufacturer wants the product to reach the market as soon as possible, before a rival company can get in on the action. The organisations that are first to take on a new release often find themselves testing the software for the manufacturer – this is called the beta test distribution stage. Once bugs are found, and the fault identified, a **patch** is one immediate solution that can be provided to users as a download from the software manufacturer's website.

What does it mean?

A **patch** (or 'fix') is a quick repair job for a piece of code which is found to be faulty after its release to the market. It is usually made available as a replacement for, or an insertion in, compiled code (i.e. in a binary file or object module).

The patch is not necessarily the best solution for the problem. However, any better solution has to wait until the next official release date of the software. As time passes, the manufacturer completely debugs the software and may then issue a new release. To acquire the updated versions, the support team need to download them from the Internet and install them on the network or individual computers that are licensed to use that software.

Depending on how recently software was installed, and how 'clean' it is, your recommendation may therefore include some changes to software, such as the installation of a patch. Depending on the skill level of the end user, you may need to arrange for someone to do this, either at the end user's desk or remotely.

Often, after such an installation, the computer has to be restarted – or **rebooted** – before the fix applies (see Figure 28.11).

What does it mean?

Rebooting is another term for restarting the computer.

The manufacturer also leaves data on the user's computer to show which version of the software is installed.

A system reset takes the computer back to its factory settings. Less dramatic is the Windows utility – called System Restore – that allows a user to restore the computer data to a specific former state (called the restore point). Any personal data saved since that time (such as new files created or new email messages, or changes to documents) remains intact, but all system changes are undone. The System Restore utility creates automatic restore points – called system checkpoints – periodically, to protect data from unexpected problems. The user may also be advised to create manual restore points before making any significant changes to the system, such as installing a new program or making a change to the registry. However, for some problems, a system reset may be necessary.

Activity 28.7

Types of advice

1 Bob (from Activity 28.4) is still having problems printing out material from his spreadsheet. Write an email suggesting that you provide one-to-one instruction to help him make the best use of the software. Plan what you might cover as an introduction to printing material from a spreadsheet.

2 Check the availability of software patches for one program that is installed on your computer. Download a patch as directed and then reboot your computer.

3 Anita's computer has crashed for the fourth time this week. She has rung for help. Write down the instructions you would use to talk Anita through the process of rebooting her computer.

▼ Figure 28.11 Instructions to reboot after installation

28.2.3 Communications

As a support technician, you need good interpersonal skills. You must be able to interact with customers and provide technical support in such a way that you arrive at a solution that meets the needs of the end user as quickly and efficiently as possible. There are a variety of methods that you can use to provide support; there are also a variety of ways you can present information to meet your end user's needs. This section considers your options and it looks, in particular, at how you might cope with the best- and worst-case scenarios in your everyday work as a support technician.

28.2.3.1 Direct to user in response to a query

There are three main options as to how you might communicate directly with an end user: by email, by telephone, face-to-face.

Some organisations insist on initial requests for support being sent by email. This allows the support team to prioritise the incidents and to deal with the most important people and/or the highest risk problems first. A standard email can be sent back saying, 'Your request has been noted and someone will be in touch soon.' This can give much needed breathing space, especially if the end user is very angry. Within a team of support technicians, it is also then possible to assign the technician best suited to deal with a particular 'problem' end user.

Email communication provides a written record of the request for help and, since it is written by the end user, it takes no time or effort on the part of the help desk technician, apart from reading the email.

Most organisations also offer a telephone link to the help desk. More information can be gleaned more quickly in a verbal conversation. However, the technician has no visual clues about the end user and he/she cannot use body language to show a caring, sympathetic attitude to the end user. That is why the tone of voice and the words used are so important. Telephone conversations can be recorded – but often, telephone help desks rely on the technician to record incidents, and this takes time.

Face-to-face conversations require that the end user and the technician are located in the same place. This may not be possible: for many organisations, the customers may be spread across the country and the call centres may be overseas. In organisations where face-to-face discussions are possible, the technician should read the body language cues from the end user and respond in a manner which creates a sympathetic and caring atmosphere in which the problem can be solved.

28.2.3.2 Secondary provision of guidance

Sometimes, the support team needs to let everyone know about a change in operations: perhaps all the passwords have to be changed, or the network will be down for 30 minutes for essential maintenance. An email to all concerned is an effective way of broadcasting this information.

If there are more widespread changes coming up – maybe the provision of a new service with effect from the beginning of next month – it may be more appropriate to report this in the organisation's monthly newsletter. This acts as a press release and can be used to improve the image of the support team. Photos of the support team might be included to present a personal image and this might help end users whose only contact is via telephone conversations.

Sometimes, especially after the introduction of new software, there is a flood of calls asking about the same thing. Rather than dealing with every caller individually, as soon as the pattern is noticed, an FAQ can be set up. End users can then be directed to the FAQ; this method works especially well when initial calls are via email.

If there are more complex procedures which require explanation, a technical help sheet can be devised and distributed to all end users. This might be announced in an email and supplied as a PDF attachment; and it might be pinned up on the notice board in the staff canteen.

28.2.3.3 Providing information to relevant people

An FAQ page on the Internet or intranet is accessible to all, but only those that have a problem will take the time to refer to it.

With newsletters, the tendency is to send to all employees, but to catch their attention the layout and general presentation has to be good enough to entice everyone to read it. The same philosophy now applies to regular emails; if it looks like the 'same old stuff', people will not find time to read it.

So, when sending out emails – with or without help sheet attachments – it is important to direct the emails to those for whom the information is relevant. If end users are bombarded with emails, some of which are not relevant, eventually the emails lose their impact and will be ignored.

28.2.3.4 Anger management skills (self and customer)

Nine times out of ten, the calls made to a help desk are from end users under pressure: their workflow may have been interrupted by a system failure or there could have been a loss of data or a communications breakdown. The end user is therefore likely to be upset and is calling you because he/she needs your help.

Anger is a natural response to feeling threatened. If a computer breaks down or fails to behave in the way it should, anger can result from the frustration that this causes the end user. Some users, who can see that they are not able to make best use of a computer, may be angry more with themselves than with the computer.

Anger ranges in intensity from mild irritation to violent rage. It affects the body by increasing adrenalin levels and speeding up the heart rate. If anger is the result of a threat such as imminent disaster, these two physical changes are essential – they prepare your body for fight or flight. If there is no physical threat, anger on a regular basis has adverse effects on the individual, as it raises blood pressure and prevents clear thought.

Anger in the workplace – as generated by malfunctioning computer systems – is therefore potentially damaging to workers and needs to be managed.

If attempts are made to ensure the smooth running of the computer systems, the chances of a malfunction are reduced and the frustration that downtime causes is largely eliminated. In the real world though, things do go wrong, and often a computer system fails at precisely the moment when the end user has no time to spare – 'That report is needed right now!'

So, when the end user calls the support help desk, it is almost certain that you will hear a level of irritation in his/her voice, and if this is the tenth time he/she has had to call this week, the anger level may be high.

Some people can express their anger in a controlled and constructive way, but some can't! If feelings build up, anger can erupt in an uncontrolled fashion. People can say things which would have been better unsaid and relationships can deteriorate.

In your conversations with end users, you need to take into account that any anger that is expressed is a natural – if socially unacceptable – response to frustration. It is your job to remove the cause of the frustration. It is not your job to upset the end user; so you must not take offence at what the end user has to say. It is possible that the user's tone will be aggressive to start off with. A sign of your skills in handling such an end user will be how much the tone has softened by the end of your conversation.

One way of managing anger is to talk things through with someone. At the help desk, you may find that you are the person the end user needs to talk to. He/she may have legitimate concerns about new software or hardware, and you will be the first to hear about these.

If, after a morning of angry callers, you are beginning to feel angry too, how can you control your own anger?

- Calming down is essential. Taking long slow breaths will slow down your heart rate. If you can, leave your workstation and walk around for a few minutes. Go outside and empty your mind of the previous caller. Look at the weather instead.
- Distance can make impossible situations seem not so impossible. Distance can be physical, e.g. walking to the end of the corridor and back. Distance can also be time, e.g. doing something else for ten minutes and then returning to the problem. The problem might sort itself out in your head in the meantime.

Often, anger is not caused by what has just happened. The printer jamming may just be the final straw. Instead, there may be some underlying sense of frustration which is the root cause of a person's anger.

- If you feel angry, ask yourself if there are other factors that are upsetting you. Are you unhappy in your working environment? Do you feel undervalued in your work or in your relationships with your colleagues? Is the behaviour of other team members affecting you adversely? Have you got financial or health worries or other problems outside your workplace?

- If you are faced with what seems like unreasonable anger from an end user, ask yourself what else may have upset this person. Assume that the computer breakdown is just the last straw for this person, and you happen to be in the firing line. Your task is all the harder, but you still have to resolve their computer problem and maintain a good working relationship with them. Most importantly, stay calm.

When angry, the ways in which end users express themselves – and how you might express yourself to colleagues or to your manager – leave a lot to be desired. The tone used and the words that are chosen tend to make matters worse; sarcasm is often used. Suppressing anger does not work either, so saying nothing – or sulking – is not effective.

One way of dealing with anger is to be assertive. Assertiveness involves expressing yourself clearly and calmly, without resorting to anger. Being assertive is not easy, but there are classes you can attend and books you can read on the subject. It takes practice!

Another way you can reduce feelings of anger is to change your lifestyle out of the office environment.

- Regular exercise can help to reduce tension and create a window of time when you stop thinking about work. Taking out your anger on a squash ball is one healthy option. Less vigorous activities can work equally well: yoga or meditation classes teach you how to switch off.

- Your diet, and especially sugar, caffeine or alcohol intake, can affect how you feel. If you eat a bar of chocolate, or have a cup of coffee, you may have a brief surge in energy but feel low later on. If you are

There are many ways to relax your body and mind

feeling angry and then drink alcohol, the alcohol lowers inhibitions and you may say or do something you will regret later.

- Having a more positive view of life can also fend off anger. If you are not happy with something in your life but cannot change it, then focus on other aspects of your life and make sure you have times when you are happy and relaxed. You might vent feelings by talking to friends, or express them through painting or writing. You might also immerse yourself in a hobby like DIY or gardening.

It is not part of your role to suggest how your end user might reduce his/her anger levels but, if you control your own, you will be better placed to cope with outbursts. You may also serve as a role model for those around you.

28.2.3.5 Soft skills

During your training you will have learnt how to use a computer, how to install and customise software, and how to test and fix hardware. You should have a lot of facts at your finger tips and experience in using a variety of equipment. These are 'hard' skills.

'Soft' skills relate to your attitude while carrying out these tasks. When it is just you and the computer, soft skills may not be needed. However, when you are dealing with end users and trying to resolve their problems, these skills are important.

You need to empathise with the end user. You need to try to understand things from his/her viewpoint.

- The novice user may be reluctant to experiment with software and so will not have wandered through the menus to see what can and cannot be done. They may have so little experience of software that even the standard icons for Save and Print are alien to them.
- The more experienced user may be confident in one way of working but a new software package requires a different way for doing the same things. This level of user may find the transition difficult. They may have to slow down as they are learning the new software and can speed up again, and this may irritate them.

One way of showing that you have empathy with the end user is to convey it through what you say. Use phrases such as 'OK' and 'Yes, I see' and 'I am sorry. I appreciate how frustrating this is for you.' If you make sure that your tone confirms that you are indeed in sympathy with the end user, you should be able to placate even the angriest end user.

You also require patience. Give the end user enough time to say whatever he/she has to tell you. Don't interrupt or cut across or use put downs. Apply active listening skills instead.

Figure 28.12 Body language clues

- In a face-to-face discussion, if you can maintain eye contact while the user is speaking, this will show that you are listening – or at least give that impression!
- Repeating what the end user has just said, but rearranging it into a question and asking for confirmation, will convince the user that you have understood the problem. For example: 'So, the printer was turned on, but nothing printed?'

Your body language can reinforce what you are saying. Nodding implies agreement. Head to one side, looking puzzled, shows you are thinking about how to solve a problem. Even if you cannot be seen by the end user, using body language somehow conveys this in your voice.

Activity 28.8

Body language
Body language is a subtle way of communicating. Posture, facial expressions and positioning of hands and feet all tell a story. One researcher claims that what is said only conveys 7 per cent of a message, the tone used conveys another 38 per cent but body language tells 55 per cent of the story!

1 Look at the images in Figure 28.12. Working in pairs, decide what the conversation might be between each pair of people. Each of you assume one of the characters and write down what you might be saying.

2 Compare your notes with other pairs. Did you have a similar understanding of what was being said?

There will be situations when the problem presented to you by an end user is one you cannot solve, and you need to refer the end user to a more senior technician.

Most likely, you will be expected to take as much information as possible and then alert a more senior support team member that you feel you need help. You will advise the end user that 'someone else' will look at the problem and contact the end user shortly.

An end user may request action which is beyond your authority, for example, compensation for lack of service or provision of replacement equipment. In this case, you will either have to direct the end user to the appropriate department or pass on the details for them.

It may happen that the end user demands that he/she speaks to someone with greater authority than you. This may be because they are frustrated with the apparent lack of action and believe that, by insisting on **escalation**, they will be given more preferential treatment. This may well be the case! You will only have the responsibility for certain aspects of support, and if the end user is demanding more than you can offer, you will need to refer them to someone higher up. However, be sure that you have explored all possible avenues first and collected as much information as possible. Your superior's time is more expensive than yours, so if you present all the facts, the end user's problem may be solved very quickly as soon as it is escalated.

An end user faced with a computer system which does not work wants it fixed, but they appreciate that this may take time.

Support is essentially about providing a service, but creating a good impression is important too. If you can give the impression that the end user's problem is being dealt with, and that resolution will happen as soon as possible, the end user will feel reassured. But avoid making a promise that you cannot keep.

What does it mean?

Escalation means the referral of a problem higher up the chain of command.

If you say the problem will be resolved within 6 hours and at the end of the 6 hours it is still not fixed, the end user will complain. So, it is important to give the end user realistic information about response times. If you don't know, don't lie!

Activity 28.9

Bad news week

1 Working in pairs, role-play a scenario in which one person (the end user) reports a fault and the other person (the help desk support technician) knows that, due to understaffing (holidays, sickness or lack of allocation of staff to the help desk), he or she will not have time to look at this problem for a further 24 hours.

2 Discuss how to convey bad news to an angry person without increasing their frustration levels. Make a list of do's and don'ts.

28.2.4 Checking solutions

Having arrived at a solution, you could simply tell the user how to resolve the problem and leave him or her to it. However, you may not have fully understood the problem, or the end user may not have fully understood your solution or may lack the skills to carry out your instructions correctly. They could be back on the phone five minutes later with an even more complicated problem.

So, you need to check that your instructions are clear enough to be understood and then follow up to check that your advice proved to be useful in the form that it was given. Only then can you be sure that support was provided in a way that suited the end user. Evaluative feedback may take time to collect but it can prove helpful in adjusting how you solve similar problems in the future, and save valuable time then.

This subsection focuses on two aspects of checking solutions: testing and user review.

28.2.4.1 Testing

If a change has to be made to an end user's configuration, you should take the end user back through the start-up process and make sure that the changes have worked as planned.

If a new component has to be installed or a peripheral replaced, you should test the computer system before the end user is given access to it again. Then you should ask the user to attempt to replicate the problem that they reported in the first place. Hopefully, your solution will have cleared any problem and the confidence of the end user will be restored.

28.2.4.2 User review

Sometimes the advice of the technician on the help desk is sufficient to solve the problem, but sometimes it is not. An end user may need to refer to other sources of help in order to find a satisfactory solution. If this is the case, the help desk should be told about it, and measures should be taken so that other end users do not have to do the same. If the end user manages to solve the problem more quickly than the support team could, the support team must be willing to learn from them.

A feedback form might be used to collect this type of information.

Activity 28.10

Feedback

1 Explore the Internet to find examples of feedback forms.

2 For one particular problem that has been solved for you by another student, give feedback as to how the help that you needed was provided. Include positive and negative comments.

3 Review the feedback received about one of the problems you solved for another student. What changes could you make to how you interact with users? Set yourself some goals to improve your own performance. **p**₂

4 Considering the types of feedback received and given, design a form that would be suitable to record the feedback. Compare your design with those created by others in your group.

28.3 The influence of organisations on technical support systems

As a support technician, you will work within an organisation, and this organisation will have procedures that you have to follow, and methods that you are expected to adopt. This section explores aspects of how your day-to-day work will be governed by these rules and other constraints such as time and the cost of the resources you use.

28.3.1 Working procedures and policies

As part of your induction training, you will be told how you fit within the organisation, whom you will report to and what is expected of you. You may be working on your own or within a team of support staff, and your 'clients' may be in-house colleagues or end users working for another organisation.

Whatever the terms of your employment, it is important to follow instructions and work within the organisational guidelines set out for you.

28.3.1.1 Organisational guidelines

The organisation will have drawn up policy documents which set out the rules on the reporting of faults, Internet use and security, etc.

For example, it may be organisational policy that all requests for help desk support are emailed to the support team. You may work within a team of similar technicians, sharing the same inbox for these emails. You may be expected to use standard paragraphs in the compilation of the reply to the end user, so that there is consistency in how these emails are processed.

If calls come by telephone, there may be a logging system, and you may need to glean information from the end user about the details of the fault. If it is an operational query, you may be able to talk the end user through a solution. If that is beyond your powers, you may pass the call on to a more senior technician, i.e. escalate the incident. If the fault is a hardware failure, your job may simply be to assign the incident to a queue, and advise the end user that 'it will be looked into soon'. The logging system may give you an idea of how many other jobs are waiting for attention and you may therefore be able to give an estimate as to when a technical engineer might visit the end user's workspace.

You might be expected to access the Internet for technical information – there may be guidelines telling you which sites are to be used. There might be an Internet site or intranet where any FAQs are displayed, so that end users can go there directly for help on common problems. It may be part of your job to generate material for that site.

Help desk technicians will often take calls from end users who have forgotten their passwords. Before revealing a user's password, you will need to check his/her identity by asking suitable questions. You may then reset the password and email the new password to the end user.

28.3.1.2 Service level agreements (SLA)

Remember!

A **service level agreement (SLA)** sets out what level of support is expected – for example, the speed of response for particular types of problem.

An SLA may be an internal document drawn up between the support department and other departments within an organisation, or an SLA may apply between an organisation and an external supplier of support services.

The SLA will specify service obligations, for example: response times, downtimes, schedules for work to be completed and/or security arrangements.

Special terms may be used to describe the problem.

- When a problem is first reported it may be called an **incident**.
- If the incident cannot be resolved within, say, 30 minutes, by the help desk staff, it is escalated to **fault** status and a technician with more specialist skills is assigned to it.
- If the technician cannot resolve the problem, it really *is* a problem!

Within an SLA, the support level in terms of response time may be graded according to the user category.

- An occasional user (i.e. one who needs the IT system working for non-essential tasks or one who is an irregular user) might be promised a response on the next day or later.
- A regular user such as a typist, programmer or graphic designer (i.e. one who cannot do his/her job without a working system) would be promised same-day response.
- Essential users (i.e. people for whom downtime might result in loss of life or be critical to a business – e.g. workers in medical systems, financial systems or process control) would expect a response time measured in minutes rather than hours.

Keeping accurate records provides a measure of the success rate of the support team. Records should include the calls taken, incidents dealt with satisfactorily by the help desk staff, those faults that were escalated to a technician (and how these were resolved). These records also provide valuable information about the types of faults (see page 288) and where they arise. Recognising trends in this data can help in the formulation of plans to provide better (i.e. more reliable) hardware or software, and may also be used to target training for the end users who need it the most.

28.3.1.3 Confidentiality

There are a number of safeguards, both in terms of legislation and in terms of your contract of employment, which exist to protect the confidentiality of personal data, and you will be expected to abide by those rules and regulations.

In particular, the information revealed to you by end users may give you access to their private data. You must not reveal this information to anyone else, nor use it yourself for any purpose other than the one for which it was supplied.

Failure to abide by the given rules could result in disciplinary action and termination of contract. For more serious offences, you might face a fine or a term of imprisonment.

The Data Protection Act and other relevant legislation are considered in *Unit 29: IT Systems Troubleshooting and Repair*, page 340.

28.3.1.4 Sensitivity of information

Some of the information you need to carry out your job may be sensitive. It may relate to future plans for upgrading hardware or software, or relocation plans. As with any job, as an employee, you are expected to respect the sensitivity of such information. To reveal highly sensitive information, for example, to a rival organisation, may well result in dismissal.

If you are working for a government department, you might find that you are bound by the Official Secrets Act. Contravening this Act is a very serious offence and can result in imprisonment.

28.3.1.5 Outsourcing and geosourcing

It is possible for the user support function to be **outsourced**.

What does it mean?

Outsourcing means arranging for an external service provider to carry out, on an ongoing basis, an activity that would normally be performed in-house.

Instead of having an in-house team look after all the IT equipment and maintenance needs, an organisation may decide to place this service with another organisation, which specialises in the field of support. The core competency of these companies lies in their technical expertise – ideal for support services which an organisation may not be able to staff from the in-house staff skills base.

Some service providers host the technology and provide all technical support, such as for desktops, networks, data centres and software applications, while the client retains responsibility for owning and handling the complete business process. For example, a service provider might host and support a company's website, but all data entry and processing of the database on which the site is based continues to be owned and performed by the client.

The aim of **geosourcing** is to locate a business function in a place where costs are minimised and/or to exploit favourable exchange rates across countries. This may be done internally or externally to the organisation – branches may be set up in other countries or the work outsourced. Geosourcing may be applied to a particular business function or type of processing (such as a call centre) based on costs, expertise, technological infrastructure.

What does it mean?

Geosourcing is the process of seeking expert skills in the best geographical location.

28.3.2 Organisational constraints

Organisations have to balance their books. There will be income from products sold or services provided. Out of this, the organisation can allocate funding for purchasing materials and overheads such as office accommodation for staff and capital expenditure on equipment such as computers. The employment of staff to provide support for in-house colleagues is an additional burden on the budget.

This section considers how cost constraints impact on the day-to-day working of support technicians, and how the level of expertise of end users also affects the role of the support technician.

28.3.2.1 Costs of resources required

Although the costs of IT equipment tend to fall over time, they still represent a large capital investment. The person responsible for buying IT equipment will be careful to place orders with manufacturers who have a proven track record and will seek favourable rates through bulk purchases.

It is important to keep records of faults attributed to hardware. If a particular choice of hard drive is found to be unreliable, this will inform the next round of purchasing.

With software, the buyer will need to know exactly how many personnel require access to particular packages and to ensure site licences are purchased accordingly. A record of what software is installed on each computer then needs to be maintained so that it can be shown that the terms of the licence have not been broken.

28.3.2.2 Time

The support team needs to be on hand whenever other employees are on-site. The team also needs to undertake tasks overnight, like backups and essential network maintenance. For this reason, the support technicians tend to have to work on a shift basis. One week, you may be on 'earlies', starting at 8am and finishing at 4pm. The next week, you may be on 'lates', starting at noon and finishing at 8pm. The third week, you may be on nights, working from 8pm till 8am. Since coverage may be needed seven days a week, you might also have to work weekends. The pattern of hours worked can therefore become quite complex, with days off built in to make up for working overtime or at weekends.

When you are at work, you might also have to keep a log of how you spent your time: how long you spent answering calls, processing emails and dealing with faults – as well as giving details of the particular incidents or faults that you dealt with. Analysis can then be made of how the support team is being used, and the cost of particular aspects of the job can be identified. This log keeping will inform management of the needs of the end users, and provide data for future decision making about the deployment of the team.

The level of support needed for a particular organisation depends very much on the level of expertise among the employees.

For example, in a company that specialises in web designing services for other organisations, nearly all the employees will be competent in using computers and languages such as HTML and Java. The level of user support required for these employees is different from that required by an engineering company which has a large sales force, all using laptops, or in a factory where process control is used to create a range of products.

The technicians working in the support team need to be trained to become expert users of the software that the employees have to use, as well as competent in maintaining the hardware. Since there are a variety of software platforms (Windows, Unix, etc.) and lots of versions of any given platform (Windows 95, Windows XP, etc.), a technician needs to accumulate experience over time so that he/she can assist all manner of end users.

Activity 28.11

Organisational constraints

1 You work for an organisation that employs 150 staff, all located in one building on four floors. All employees have access to the company intranet and the Internet via networked workstations. Normal working hours are from 9am to 5pm, Monday to Friday. There are eight full-time employees in the IT support team, each working a 40-hour week. Devise a rota for the support staff in which at least any two members of staff are always working from 7am until 7pm seven days a week.

2 Search for job advertisements for IT support staff. What expertise is expected? What training is offered? What hours are the support staff required to work, and at what salary? Present your findings to others in your group.

3 What might be the effects for staff in your organisation if IT were outsourced? Consider and evaluate both the positive and negative effects. **m d**

28.4 Technologies and tools used in technical support

As a technician, you are expected to make best use of available technologies. This section looks at what is currently available (at the time of writing) and considers what is likely to happen in the future.

28.4.1 Technologies

This subsection covers three of the technologies which IT support technicians may use on a daily basis: email, software diagnostic tools and the Control Panel.

Email correspondence has increased dramatically in recent years. It is rare for an organisation to send a business letter, unless it is a mail shot; and it is rare to receive letters through the post, unless they are junk mail.

- Organisations such as banks, building societies and gas and electric companies offer to provide online bills and statements, rather than mail out a paper version.

- Organisations send remittance advice as attachments to emails, telling suppliers that an amount has been credited to the supplier's bank in payment of an invoice.
- Many airlines provide e-tickets and these are sent by email, far quicker than sending conventional tickets in the post.

When sending an email, it is possible to send to more than one person at a time. The fields To:, Cc: and Bcc: can contain as many email addresses as are necessary. If you regularly send an email to the same group of addresses, it makes sense to set up a **distribution list**.

What does it mean?

A **distribution list** is a collection of email addresses which can be referred to by a single group name.

The method given here selects the addresses from an address book; you might also create a distribution list by copying names from an email. These instructions apply to Microsoft Outlook (see Figure 28.13). If you are using other software, use the help function to find out how to set up a distribution list.

■ How to set up a distribution list

1 Select File / New / Distribution List.
2 In the Name box, type a name that makes sense for this group of email addresses.
3 Press Select Member – this opens a dialogue box.
4 In 'Show Names from the:', click on the down arrow to reveal the available address books. Select the one that contains the addresses of the people you want to include in the group.
5 For each person you want to add, select the name from the list. If you use the CTRL key you can select more than one person at a time from a single address book. When you press OK, any selected addresses are added to your distribution list.
6 To add more members, perhaps from a different address book, repeat steps 3, 4 and 5.
7 The distribution list is saved in your Contacts folder, and can be selected as the addressee for an email.

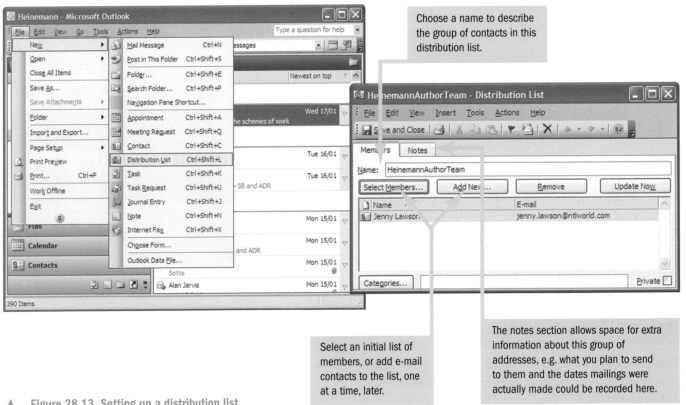

Choose a name to describe the group of contacts in this distribution list.

Select an initial list of members, or add e-mail contacts to the list, one at a time, later.

The notes section allows space for extra information about this group of addresses, e.g. what you plan to send to them and the dates mailings were actually made could be recorded here.

Figure 28.13 Setting up a distribution list

Activity 28.12

Email distribution lists

1 For the email software installed on your computer, check how you might set up a distribution list.

2 Write guidance notes on how to set up a distribution list, including screen grabs of each important step in the process.

3 Set up a distribution list which includes at least six of your friends, and email the guidance notes to them.

4 You will receive emails from friends with details of how to set up a distribution list. Notice where your name appears on the email. Check the attachment and try to follow the instructions given. Write a reply for each set of instructions received, commenting on the usefulness of the guidance.

28.4.1.2 Software diagnostic tools

Remember!

Diagnostic software attempts to diagnose a problem; it identifies possible faults and offers solutions.

Software diagnostic tools are essential when you are troubleshooting. They provide much needed information, and can be used to eliminate what is working, until you are just left with what is not working. *Unit 29: IT Systems Troubleshooting and Repair* considers diagnostic tools, and also tools such as WinVNC, that are available to monitor traffic on a network; see Unit 29, page 336.

28.4.1.3 Control Panel

Remember!

The **Control Panel** is a folder which offers routes to files that can be used to manage the computer system.

The Control Panel provides access to everything needed to control a PC: from adding a new piece of hardware to setting the time, from choosing your Internet options to setting power options. It also provides options to customise the appearance and functionality of a computer. The Control Panel can be accessed through Windows Explorer, My Computer, or by clicking on Start and selecting it (see Figure 28.14).

Figure 28.14 Start menu route to the Control Panel

Within the Control Panel, there are many icons (see Figure 28.15): clicking any of these leads to a separate function.

You should visit every location on the Control Panel to become familiar with every dialogue box, and every option available. However, becoming familiar with every route through the Control Panel is not quite as big a task as you might think. Many of them lead to the same place, so what you need to learn is which route is best for you.

For example, in Windows XP, there are two routes for getting to the **Device Manager**:

- click on the Administrative Tools icon in the Control Panel (see Figure 28.2 on page 287) and then on the Computer Management icon (Figure 28.16(a))

- alternatively, click on System in the Control Panel, then select the Hardware tab on the System Properties panel (see Figure 28.16(b)).

Similarly, here are two ways of locating **Performance Logs and Alerts**:

- Control Panel / Administration Tools / Computer Management / System Tools
- Control Panel / Administration Tools / Performance.

And to get to the **Disk Defragmenter**, you can go via:

- Control Panel / Administration Tools / Computer Management / Storage
- Start / All Programs / Accessories / System Tools.

▼ Figure 28.15 The Control Panel

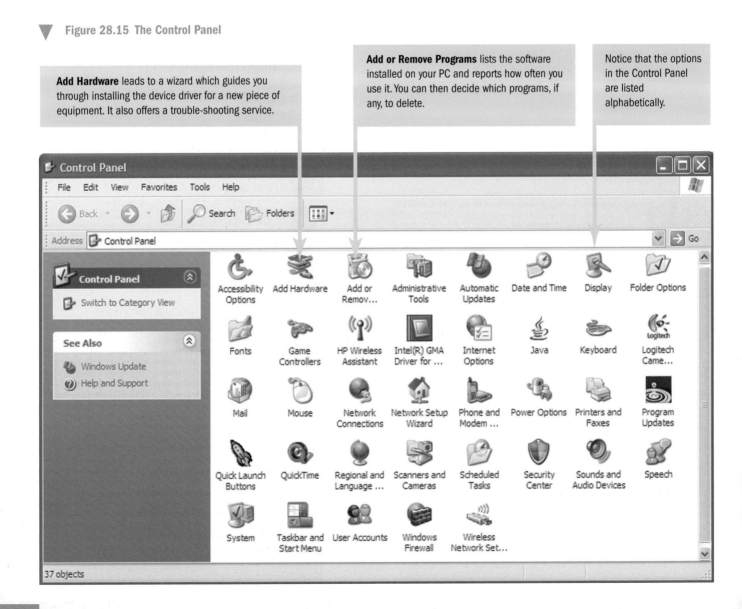

Add Hardware leads to a wizard which guides you through installing the device driver for a new piece of equipment. It also offers a trouble-shooting service.

Add or Remove Programs lists the software installed on your PC and reports how often you use it. You can then decide which programs, if any, to delete.

Notice that the options in the Control Panel are listed alphabetically.

(a)

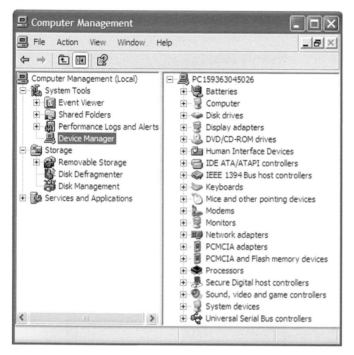

(b)

Figure 28.16 Routes to the Device Manager: (a) through Computer Management and (b) through System Properties

Activity 28.13

The Control Panel

1 Working with two friends, share out the list of icons on the Control Panel. From your share, select two or three that interest you.

2 Explore in detail the effect of clicking on each of your chosen icons. Make notes so that you can remember what you have discovered and will be able to explain it to your two friends.

3 Take it in turns to present your findings to each other.

The settings that you change through the Control Panel are stored in the **Registry**.

What does it mean?

The **Registry** stores settings that Windows makes itself, e.g. the hardware configuration identified during the boot process.

Each time you turn on your PC, the operating system refers to settings in the Registry so that it 'knows' the settings that you want to use:

- the hardware attached to your PC
- the applications that you have installed
- the machine's IP address
- details of your user account
- the colour settings of your desktop.

Test your knowledge

1 Give three examples of settings that can be changed via the Control Panel.

2 What information is stored within the Device Manager?

3 Explain what information is stored within Performance Logs.

4 What is the Registry?

5 Give five examples of settings that are retained within the Registry.

Whenever you make a change to your settings, e.g. using the Control Panel, it is recorded in the Registry. There is no need to use the Registry itself, because settings can be changed more safely within the Control Panel.

28.4.2 Future trends

Of course, it is impossible to predict exactly what will happen in the future. However, close inspection of what has happened in the recent past and of the latest inventions may help you to identify possible future trends.

This subsection focuses on three topics that have been identified by the awarding body. In addition, there may be others that develop as time passes.

28.4.2.1 Increasing reliance on remote support

It is possible to allow a remote user to have control over your screen and to show you, on-screen, how to do something. This can be activated through, for example, Messenger (see Figure 28.17).

The end user has to agree to accept remote control and can cancel it at any time. So, a basic level of control is retained by the end user. However, there are monitoring systems already available which allow monitoring of users without their knowledge and hence without their permission; see WinVNC in *Unit 29: IT Systems Troubleshooting and Repair* (page 336).

Balancing rights and responsibilities, and providing end users with help while still allowing them a level of privacy, is a juggling act which may prove difficult in years to come.

28.4.2.2 Development of systems that analyse and report on faults for other uses such as planning corporate training programmes

Part of the purpose of collecting statistics about incidents is to analyse the data and make decisions based on trends spotted within the data.

- If the same fault involving the failure of a particular component happens often, the person responsible for

Messenger provides an online chat option.

You can build up a list of contacts, all of whom also have Messenger installed on their computer system.

The person from whom you want to request remote assistance must be one of your contacts, and they must be online at the same time as you.

▲ Figure 28.17 Remote control

purchasing IT equipment needs to know, and perhaps a decision will be taken to change supplier.

- If the same end user makes repeated requests for support, perhaps this individual should be directed towards more formal training options.
- If the same questions are being asked by lots of end users, perhaps more training is needed on that particular topic, or perhaps an FAQ or help sheet is needed.

Automatic analysis of the data would speed up the feedback time and allow management to make better decisions. It would also free up the person who currently completes the analysis manually. In the future, therefore, we might expect that all aspects of IT support activities will be monitored and analysed automatically.

28.4.2.3 Development of central infrastructures, contracted out and offshore services

The larger UK organisations, like BT and the major banks, have already set up call centres overseas. If these services prove successful, it may result in smaller organisations following suit and opting to contract out services and consider geosourcing. Over time, this could have an adverse impact on the availability of IT technician vacancies in the UK. It might, however, open up possibilities for suitably qualified technical support staff to take up posts overseas.

Test your knowledge

1 Give examples of recent inventions that have transformed how people communicate with each other.

2 Suggest further developments in technology that may alter the way people work and play.

3 How might the role of the IT support technician alter in the next five to ten years?

Activity 28.14

Predicting the future

1 Research the Internet for news reports on the setting up of call centres by banks and other large organisations. When were they set up? How many staff do they employ? How has this data changed over the past five or ten years? Present your findings as a report.

2 Working with others, search the Internet for call centres located within a 50-mile radius of your home. Extend your search, looking further afield, even overseas. Record contact information for each call centre and plot the locations on a map.

3 Describe three current software tools used by support staff – two should be diagnostic tools and one a monitoring tool. Outline possible future developments in this area. Comprehensively review a recent advance in support systems technology and evaluate the impact it is having on the provision of such support.

Preparation for assessment

The assessment tasks in this unit are based on the following scenario.

ITSMAGIC is a small company which makes props for magicians, such as top hats from which a rabbit can be pulled. ITSMAGIC employs 35 people, most of whom need access to information that is currently held on a number of standalone computers.

Most of the marketing work is done on computers. Customers are contacted by telephone, but the customer details are called up from a large database. Mail shots are sent out on a regular basis to a mailing list held on a computer. Leaflets and questionnaires are designed in-house to be sent in mailshots. The company administration tasks are performed on computer, e.g. the payroll details for all staff.

You are new to ITSMAGIC and your role is to provide IT support to all staff. Your line manager supervises you and two other support technicians.

Task 1 (P1, P3, M1)

Your teacher will give you details of some problems that ITSMAGIC employees might raise and requests that they might make.

- Identify three different sources of technical information and, for each, discuss how useful these sources might be in resolving each of the employees' problems.
- For one of the situations your teacher has provided, explain the techniques that you could use to gather information about the request from an ITSMAGIC employee.

- For another of the situations your teacher provided, use different sources of technical information and evaluate your sources of information.

Task 2 (P6, D1)

Your teacher will provide you with a policy and procedure document, including details such as those regarding setting priorities and any working conditions of the support team.

- Describe how these policies and procedures impact on the provision of technical advice and guidance. Review the organisational policy, and evaluate the impact of this policy on the support service provided to internal customers.

Task 3 (P2, P4, M2)

Your teacher will supply details of some problems that ITSMAGIC employees might raise and requests that they might make. You will work with a partner for this activity and take turns to take the role of the ITSMAGIC employee and support technician.

Your teacher will check that you respond appropriately to questions raised by the employee (your partner) and that you checked that the solutions you proposed were successful.

In relation to the specific technical problem that you addressed in the role play:

- explain the different communication routes you can use to make advice and guidance available to the ITSMAGIC employees
- produce support material that will guide the employees in relation to an appropriate specific area of expertise.

MAGIC is considering disbanding the in-house support team and outsourcing the provision of technical support.

- Explain the advantages and disadvantages to users and organisations for outsourcing the provision of technical support (ignoring the fact that you will be made redundant).

- Identify two current diagnostic tools and one current monitoring software tool that may be used by the ITSMAGIC support staff. Describe these tools and outline possible future developments of these tools that might prove useful for ITSMAGIC.
- On behalf of ITSMAGIC, comprehensively review a recent advance in support systems technology. Prepare a report evaluating the impact it could have on the provision of support within ITSMAGIC.

IT Systems Troubleshooting and Repair

Introduction

To provide support for end users where and when required, technical support staff need to make the best use of the latest technologies. So, one of the challenges for these ICT professionals is to keep abreast of the continuous development of technology.

This unit presents both theoretical and practical knowledge needed for diagnosing and troubleshooting computer hardware and software problems. During your course, you will utilise this technical knowledge and expertise to resolve such problems.

You will also learn about health and safety issues and good working practices that are necessary when rectifying faults on an IT system.

After completing this unit, you should be able to achieve these outcomes:

- Know how to identify and select suitable remedies to repair IT systems

- Be able to apply fault remedies to hardware and software systems

- Understand how organisational policies impact on diagnosis and repair

- Be able to apply good working practices when working on IT systems.

Thinking points

This unit should help you to understand what is involved in the repair of computer systems that fail to work as hoped. You will become a troubleshooter.

How confident are you that you know how computers should work? And what experience do you already have of troubleshooting? Think about situations where your computer has let you down. How have you overcome the problems? Have you had to rely on others? Do others ask you for help?

IT is a fast-moving subject. What courses might you attend in the future to extend your knowledge and keep you up to date with developments?

This unit highlights the health and safety issues involved with working with computers. Are you already safety conscious? What could you do to reduce the risks in your workplace, both for you and those around you?

This unit also promotes good working practices. What tips would you give to a newcomer to the role of troubleshooter?

All support technicians need a range of remedies to apply to the problems presented by users whose computers are not performing as expected. The technician's skill lies in knowing which remedy is best suited to each situation.

29.1.1 Sources of technical know-how

A support technician needs to be able to identify and select remedies by using a variety of sources of technical know-how. Apart from colleagues and any personal fault histories, external sources of technical information can also prove useful for any support technician with a fault to solve. This section considers three such external sources: knowledge databases, technical manuals and the Internet. It then looks at training options.

29.1.1.1 Knowledge databases

Knowledge databases tend to be called **knowledge bases**, even though they are retained within a database.

What does it mean?

A **knowledge base** is a database of key facts.

Microsoft offers a knowledge base via its Search option – the route is shown in Figure 28.10 on page 293 of Unit 28. To make accessing information as simple as possible, most knowledge bases offer a basic search tool. By entering relevant key words, you will be directed to articles which may provide the information that you need.

■ HOW TO ACCESS INFORMATION WITHIN A KNOWLEDGE BASE

1 Select the Microsoft Help option (from the main menu toolbar, or by pressing the F1 function key).
2 A panel appears. Enter the key word(s) in the space provided and click on the right arrow to start the search.

3 The search engine connects to Microsoft Office Online and the results of your search are listed. One or more of these articles may provide the information you require. Click on any link to investigate further. This opens a fresh window, so you can still go back to the results list if the article is not helpful to you.
4 To access the Microsoft knowledge base, scroll down the Search Results panel to reveal the section 'Other places to look'.
5 Click on Knowledge Base Search. This takes you to the basic search option (see Figure 29.1) and lets you search the Support Knowledge Base (KB).
6 For a more advanced search, click on the link 'Switch to Advanced Search'.

Activity 29.1

Accessing a knowledge base

1 Find information about a topic of interest to you from the Microsoft Support knowledge base. Note the route you take to find this information.

2 Consider the effect of your choice of key words. How can you widen your search? How can you narrow your search?

3 Microsoft has a large range of products. It also has a variety of sources of help including 'How to' articles, downloads, guided help and TechNet articles. Find out how to focus your search to extract information from particular sources. Make notes so that you could explain the process to others in your group.

29.1.1.2 Technical manuals

A technical manual or **user guide** – as opposed to a **product specification** (see *Unit 28: IT Technical Support*, page 291) – should explain how to make the best use of a hardware device or software application. A manual is usually written by the hardware manufacturer or software vendor, and is written for the end user rather

You can narrow down your search by deciding where to search.

Advanced search tools are also available.

The search engine offers more precise key words to help you to narrow down your search.

Figure 29.1 Microsoft's knowledge base

than a technician. The user can consult the manual to find out what steps are required to achieve a particular effect.

Manuals may be provided electronically as help files. This makes it easier to find what you want as most manufacturers offer a search option with electronic help files. Keying in a phrase like 'change column width' should lead to the relevant help page within the manual. Following the instructions should solve the problem.

Activity 29.2

Product specifications and manuals

1 Refer to *Unit 28: IT Technical Support* (page 291) to find out the main differences between a product specification and a manual.

2 List the manuals relating to the hardware and software on your computer system. Compare your list with those of others in your group. Locate any other sources of these or additional manuals, e.g. in your college library.

FAQ pages and discussion forums are excellent sources of information

29.1.1.3 Internet sources

The Internet is a rich source of technical information.

- Most sites offer **FAQs** so that users who are experiencing the most common problems can be helped with minimal effort.
- Some sites also provide **discussion forums** so that users with problems can share their experiences and help each other towards a solution. These are referred to in Unit 28 (page 294) as technical forums (see Figure 29.2).

What does it mean?

FAQs stands for frequently asked questions.

Of more direct use to a technician are **manufacturers' websites** (see Figure 28.5 on page 290). The site may provide its own FAQs and a discussion forum, and it will also be the first-stop call for technical information about a product (see Figure 29.3 on page 321).

29.1.1.4 Training options

There are various types of training options: product training by the manufacturer (which may be free), product-based training courses leading to certification, and general courses in the IT support field.

Members need to log in. This gives them options to take part in the forum. Non-members can view discussions, but not take part.

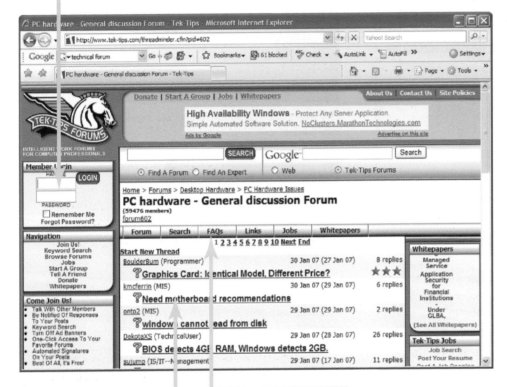

Figure 29.2 A technical forum run by the Tecumseh Group

Each 'conversation' appears on a thread. You can start a new thread asking for advice, or post a comment on an existing thread, adding your own advice to other members.

This site also offers FAQs.

Support technicians should have undertaken training programmes so that they have a level of proficiency in the use of the same hardware and software as that available to the user. The technicians should also have acquired expertise over a period of time, having met and solved a variety of problems.

The methods used to solve a problem may have been documented as a fault log (see *Unit 28: IT Technical Support*, page 286).

Activity 29.3

Online sources of technical information

1 Visit the manufacturer's website for a particular peripheral attached to your PC. Note the information that is available.

2 Visit the website of a software vendor. Check what guidance is offered. Read through the FAQs.

3 Identify some discussion forums that are relevant for the equipment you are using. Read through some threads to discover what is of interest to those who post on these sites.

▼ Figure 29.3 A manufacturer's website: Hewlett-Packard

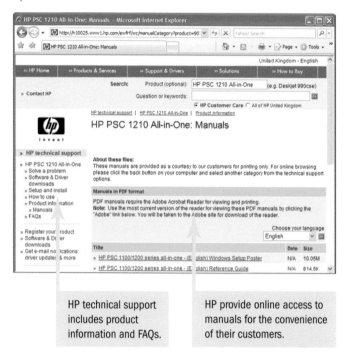

HP technical support includes product information and FAQs.

HP provide online access to manuals for the convenience of their customers.

If the technician recalls having seen something similar to the current problem, the fault log may help to speed up the resolution of the current problem. As discussed in Unit 28 (page 292), colleagues might also prove to be a valuable source of information because, although their training may be the same, their experiences will have been different.

Sharing expertise informally, or formally through the use of fault logs, results in a better-qualified support team who are likely to give a better service to the end users.

Activity 29.4

Training options

1 Compare the training you and others in your group have already undertaken that should be useful for working in a support role. Identify any gaps in the expertise of your group.

2 Use the Internet to discover what training programmes are on offer for Microsoft Windows products.

29.1.2 Types of remedies

The user who is faced with a system that does not work wants the swiftest resolution possible to the problem. As the technician, you will need to be able to identify the type of problem and the type of remedy that could apply.

29.1.2.1 Repair or replace hardware?

If one sector on a hard disk fails to read or write and this fault repeats, this is a sure sign that the hard disk may fail altogether in the near future. It makes sense to replace it before it crashes completely with perhaps loss of important data.

The same goes for any **peripheral**, such as a mouse or printer. The time it takes to replace an item that has failed is downtime for the user. If you can anticipate failures and have spares ready to replace immediately, the inconvenience to the end user is minimised.

Remember!

A **peripheral** device is any device that is an optional extra to a computer which extends its functionality, e.g. for input, secondary storage or output. For a PC, a peripheral is often housed outside the processor case. *See Unit 2: Computer Systems*, page 54 for a full list of peripherals.

Some peripherals give no warning signs. Wear and tear simply results in a sudden failure. So, it is important to have spares of all peripherals and major components, just in case.

Some peripherals are 'throw away' items – the cost of replacing them is minimal and it is not worth investing time trying to work out what is wrong with the equipment and then fixing it. Even if the equipment is expensive and worth trying to repair, the end user might need a replacement item while the repair is being done. So, a stock of spares is needed, and should include all items of equipment which might need to be sent back to the manufacturer for repair.

When equipment such as the **pointing device** is upgraded, the out-of-date equipment need not be thrown away.

What does it mean?

A **pointing device** is used to control the position of the cursor on screen, for example, a mouse, joystick or tracker ball.

For example, the old-fashioned mechanical mouse has moving parts – when the rolling ball gets dirty, it can fail. The more modern optomechanical mouse uses optical sensors, rather than rollers, to detect the motion of the ball and is more reliable. The optical mouse is an even more recent invention which uses a laser to detect the mouse's movement. All of these versions of the mouse are linked to the processor via a cable, and this may fail too.

With a wireless mouse, the data is sent using infrared signals. There is no cable and there are no moving parts, so it is less likely to fail. If the old-style equipment still works, it can be kept to use as a replacement in case of emergency. Similarly, old-style keyboards or monitors may provide an interim solution while waiting for new stock to arrive.

Activity 29.5

Repair or replace?

1 Find out the cost of each peripheral attached to your computer system. Which ones are 'throw away' items?

2 Find out how much stock of spare equipment is held by the IT support section at your college or place of work. Check how often equipment failures necessitate replacement.

3 Find out which items of equipment would need to be sent back to the manufacturer for repair.

Links to an **intranet** or the Internet are dependent on all communication paths working correctly.

What does it mean?

An **intranet** is similar to the Internet, except that the users on this network are confined to a smaller group of people, usually those working for the same organisation.

Wireless technology means you can send emails, for example, using the infrared **port** on a laptop and a mobile phone. Other peripherals need a cable to link them to the port.

Remember!

Ports provide the link between peripherals and the CPU; see Unit 2, page 42.

Infrared ports rely on a clear line of sight between the device sending data and the one receiving it. So, any obstructions in the path of this signal can prevent communication happening.

Devices fall into two groups. Those that are outside the processor (i.e. the peripherals) have a wireless or cable connection to the processor. Others are housed within the processor case and are connected to the motherboard and other components such as the **PSU** – these connections might be through cabling but some devices, such as memory cards, are slotted into place.

What does it mean?

PSU stands for power supply unit; see Unit 2, page 47.

For devices that rely on cabling, faults may occur in the cable or in the connections between the cable and the hardware of a system. Cables can be severed or fail to work if they become submerged in water. Connections can be loosened, especially if equipment is moved. Devices that are cards, arranged in slots within the casing, may not have been properly seated. Unit 2, page 77, shows how to install and maintain such cards.

Software faults may also be responsible for the fault in the communication path. But if a system has worked with a given setting (see Figure 29.4), it should continue to do so unless something else is changed, e.g. the hardware upgraded.

Loose connections for cabling are easy to fix: check every link and make sure both ends fit well into the port. The connectivity of a cable can be checked using a multimeter (see page 327). Using a replacement cable – one that you know works – will identify whether the cabling is at fault. See page 336 for more details on how substitution can be used to identify the source of a fault.

Data about devices is accessible through the Control Panel. Click on the Phone and Modem Options icon and select the Modems tab. Make sure the correct modem is highlighted and select Properties.

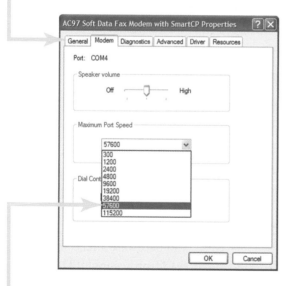

The modem settings include the speed of transfer through the port. For different devices and different connection lines, this has to be set appropriately. Too fast a speed may result in corruption of the data and errors occurring; too slow a time will result in unnecessarily lengthy delays while transmission takes place.

▲ **Figure 29.4 Settings for a modem**

Activity 29.6

Getting to know the hardware on your PC

1 Identify all the ports on the casing of your computer system. Sketch each surface and label each port.

2 Identify each section of cabling joining any two parts of your system: the printer to the PC, the keyboard to the PC, etc. Draw a sketch to show how the component parts of the system are connected, and how these are connected to external links such as the power supply and a telephone link. Label all items of equipment, including cabling and connectors.

3 Examine the inside of a PC. Identify all the main components and draw a sketch to illustrate this. Identify how each device is connected, e.g. to the motherboard and/or the PSU.

29.1.2.3 Software remedies

When software is designed, the vendor targets the needs of a huge market. The bigger the market, the greater the potential sales. To meet the needs of individual users, options are provided for the user to reconfigure the software. The default factory-set settings should suit most purchasers; but the end user is free to change them, i.e. to reconfigure the settings (see Figure 29.5). This job may fall to the IT support team.

When software is released on to the market by the vendor, it should work and will have been tested to a certain extent. However, in this competitive field, release dates are set artificially early. As soon the vendor thinks the software works well enough, it is made available to users who are willing to buy such unproven software. Only when these first purchasers use the software do the remaining faults start to emerge. Software vendors then provide updated versions, in which the faults have been rectified. Sometimes, rather than reissue the entire software product, these updates are provided as **software patches** – correct code is provided to overwrite incorrect code. See *Unit 2: Computer Systems* (page 70) for details of how this is done.

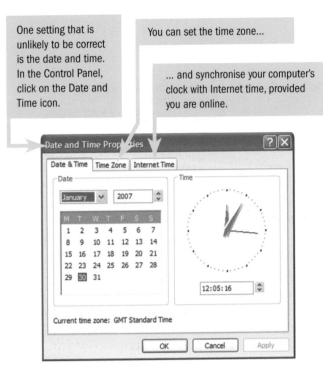

One setting that is unlikely to be correct is the date and time. In the Control Panel, click on the Date and Time icon.

You can set the time zone...

... and synchronise your computer's clock with Internet time, provided you are online.

▲ Figure 29.5 Reconfiguring software settings

For some faults, it can be more effective simply to reissue the product. Users then need to reinstall the software, but the previous version has to be removed first. To delete an application from a PC, it is not sufficient to delete its program files. The installation may have caused changes to other systems files, which also need to be amended. Most software vendors supply an **uninstall program** that allows you to remove all traces of an application. (Figure 29.6 shows an example of this.)

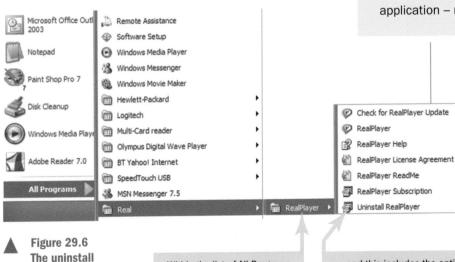

▲ Figure 29.6 The uninstall option for RealPlayer

Within the list of All Programs, RealPlayer has a folder...

... and this includes the option to uninstall this software.

Activity 29.7

Getting to know the software on your PC

1 Identify the default settings on your PC: for example, the mouse settings or which email client software is used for sending an email while on the Internet or where files are stored while using a particular software package. Change one of these settings.

2 Visit the website of a software vendor and locate information about software patches available for software that is installed on your computer. Check the dates of recent fixes. Download any fixes that are on offer that you need to bring your software up to date.

3 Make an inventory of software on your system. Identify applications with an uninstall option. Check that you have a copy of the software, e.g. on CD, so that you could reinstall it if necessary.

4 Look at the systems files (such as the CONFIG.SYS or AUTOEXEC.BAT file) to see what data is contained within these about software and hardware on your PC. Experiment with removing some hardware and/or software to check how these systems files are affected. Reinstall the hardware and/or software to make sure you leave the PC as you found it.

What does it mean?

An **uninstall program** removes all traces of an application – not just the program files.

29.1.2.4 Instructing users

The pace of change in software and hardware affects not only the IT professional. The end user in the workplace may find that the way they've always done things is no longer valid. As a result, the user may use new equipment or software incorrectly. The implication for you is that, having replaced faulty hardware or reinstalled software, you might then have to give on-the-spot instruction as to its correct use, so as to avoid the same problem arising again.

Whenever new hardware or software is installed, there should be provision for staff training. If someone joins an organisation after the changeover training has been delivered, a diagnosis of what this new employee knows and what he/she needs to be taught will reveal the training needs of that individual.

Training may also be necessary on an informal basis. An end user who makes a lot of calls to the help desk may need personal instruction to overcome the problems that he/she is facing.

Activity 29.8

Instructing users

1 Identify one peripheral (such as a mouse, keyboard, monitor or modem) and check that you know how to connect it to a PC. Make notes as to how you might explain this to a novice end user. Plan to demonstrate this to an end user, with you making all the physical connections. Then, plan how you might instruct the user over the telephone so that he/she can make all the connections. Decide how you might check that the user is doing what you want, and how you can test that the peripheral works when the user has completed the installation.

2 Identify one software setting (such as the mouse settings for a left-handed user, or the choice of a default printer). Check that you fully understand the steps involved in changing the setting. Make notes on how you might demonstrate this to a novice end user. Create a script to talk a novice user through the process. Include questions to check that the user has done what you asked.

3 Identify one technical task that you would not expect an end user to do, such as installing additional memory. Make notes as to how to demonstrate this to a newly appointed technician. Complete your demonstration, and then ask your 'trainee' to demonstrate it back to you.

29.1.3 Nature of reported faults

A student doctor has to learn how to identify a disease from a whole range of symptoms, some of which may not even relate to the disease. Similarly, a technician needs to be able to determine the cause of a problem from incomplete information from the end user, some of which may be misleading.

The simplest problems involve a single item of equipment which malfunctions in a systematic way, e.g. a printer which doesn't print a document. The technician can talk the end user though a number of checks:

- Is the printer connected to a power supply? Is the printer turned on? Is there a green light indicating the printer is ready? Or is there an error code showing?
- Is the cable pushed fully into place? Is the cable connected to the correct printer?
- Is the document being sent to the printer that is attached to the PC? The default printer setting can be changed using the Control Panel (see Figure 29.7), or you can choose to send to a different printer using the Print dialogue box (see Figure 29.8).

Having checked the most obvious causes that the end user might be able to fix without you making a site visit, you need to consider failures in the hardware.

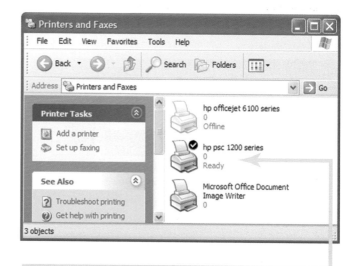

The printer with the tick is the current default printer. This is where documents will be sent, unless you instruct the computer otherwise.

 Figure 29.7 The default printer setting in the Control Panel

- If the print head has jammed within the printer, a replacement printer may be needed.
- The printer cable may have been damaged or the pins within the connector may be broken or bent. A replacement cable may be needed.
- The software may have been corrupted. It may need to be reinstalled.

Any (or a combination) of these might explain the problem. Deciding where the fault lies involves the **substitution** method (see page 336): replacing components that may not be working with those that are known to be working. By a process of elimination, the fault might then be identified. This process might seem quite complicated, but it is actually straightforward provided the end user can point to a particular peripheral or situation that can be replicated.

Complex problems arise when the end user reports faults with non-specific symptoms. The computer may crash without the user apparently doing anything to cause this to happen. The fault may be due, for example, to overheating, which happens within a random length of time from start-up. Intermittent faults often happen prior to a complete breakdown in a component, so all faults need careful investigation and resolution.

To resolve such complex problems, the whole computer system may need to be recalled and the end user provided with a complete replacement. To allow the end user access to data that was on the system prior to the problem, backups must be available or, if on a network, data might be held centrally and be available from any (working) workstation.

Activity 29.9

Identifying reported faults

1 Working in groups of four, split into two teams.

(a) In your team, plan a hardware fault that you will present to the other pair, e.g. disconnected cabling, unseated expansion board. Agree between you the symptoms that your PC would show if this fault were to happen.

(b) Taking turns, act as user pair and technician pair. The technician pair ask questions to try to find out what the problem is. The user pair answers these questions (honestly).

(c) Technician pair: write down what you would do to isolate the fault, and hopefully to fix it.

(d) User pair: with the permission of your teacher, set up a PC with the fault as planned, out of sight of the technician pair.

(e) Technician pair: follow your plan to isolate the fault and then fix it.

(f) Discuss what you found difficult about this process and what you found easy.

(g) Repeat the activity, choosing different hardware faults.

2 Working in groups of four again, split into two teams of two. Repeat the activity of question 1, but this time decide on a software fault, e.g. the wrong setting for a monitor.

3 Repeat the activity, making the problem even more complex for the technician pair. Choose two hardware faults, two software faults, a mix of types or some underlying problem. Note how you (and your partners) eliminate possible sources of faults to arrive at your diagnosis. For each fault, suggest at least two solutions and then explain why you chose the one you did. **p₁ m₁ m₂**

Note: remember that each individual has to provide evidence for themselves.

You can send a document to a printer other than the default printer.

Print

Printer
Name: hp psc 1200 series | Properties
Status: | Find Printer...
Type: hp officejet 6100 series
Where: | Print to file
Comment: hp psc 1200 series | Manual duplex

Page range
○ All | Microsoft Office Document Image Writer
○ Current page
○ Pages: | ☑ Collate

Enter page numbers and/or page ranges separated by commas. For example, 1,3,5–12

Print what: Document | Zoom
Print: All pages in range | Pages per sheet: 1 page
| Scale to paper size: No Scaling

Options... | OK | Cancel

▲ Figure 29.8 Choosing a printer using File/Print

A technician needs to be able to fix faults in hardware and software. Part of the challenge lies in deciding whether the hardware is at fault or whether a software glitch has occurred. This section looks first at how to test hardware, and then at the aids that are available to uncover faults in software settings. Finally, it looks at troubleshooting techniques that can be applied to solve any problem presented by the end user.

29.2.1 Hardware tools and techniques

A technician's tool kit should include conventional tools such as screwdrivers, as well as other types of tools. A bootable floppy disk or CD might be needed to restart a crashed system, diagnostic hardware might help to identify the root cause of the problem and access to the manufacturer's specifications of hardware (online or hard copy manuals) may be needed to check facts and settings.

This section focuses on three particular tools (test instruments, self-test routines and monitoring devices) and then the conventional tools that a technician might need to fix any given fault.

29.2.1.1 Electrical/electronic test instruments

Computers rely on electricity for power, whether battery-operated or plugged into the mains. Ensuring the correct power supply is reaching every component is the role of the **PSU** and if this fails in some way, the computer will not work.

Remember!

PSU stands for power supply unit; see *Unit 2: Computer Systems*, page 47.

Electrical faults can lie within a hardware component, in the cabling that connects these components or in the connectors between the cabling and the component. Within a hardware component, an electrical fault such as a short circuit or broken connection can result in the component not working at all, or not as expected. For successful transfer of data along a cable, continuity of the power supply is necessary; a damaged cable or connector can interrupt the flow of power. A **multimeter** (see Figure 29.9) can be used to check both the condition of cabling and whether power is reaching key hardware components.

What does it mean?

A **multimeter** is three machines in one: a voltmeter (which measures the potential difference between two points in volts), an ammeter (which measures current in amps) and an ohmmeter (which measures resistance in ohms).

Table 29.1 suggests when you might use a multimeter.

The voltage (in volts) and resistance (in ohms) can be measured between two points in a circuit. A multimeter

Symptoms	What might be wrong?	What to measure
A beep code indicating a CPU fault (see self-test routines, page 330)	A defective power supply	Voltage
A peripheral device such as the printer stops working	A defective cable	Voltage and resistance
	A defective cable connector	Voltage and resistance
	Broken/defective shielding of a cable	Resistance

Table 29.1 When to use a multimeter

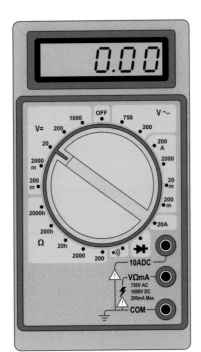

Figure 29.9 A multimeter

What type of current?	AC or DC (or VDC, voltage direct current)
Measurement?	Voltage (volts) OR current (amps) OR resistance (ohms)
Range?	Power supply: 3–12V
	AC wall plug output: 105–125V (USA) or 230 (UK)

Table 29.2 The settings to use

> ## WATCH OUT!
>
> Do not connect a multimeter to the mains, which carries 20KW or more. It will damage the multimeter – and you!

■ HOW TO MEASURE VOLTS (GENERAL PRINCIPLES)

> ## WATCH OUT!
>
> Follow these steps carefully, keeping your fingers clear of any contacts.

1. Set dial to DC.
2. Select voltage rating (see Table 29.2).
3. Hold the black/negative probe to a grounding point (see Figure 29.10).
4. Touch the red/positive probe to a hot point.
5. Note the reading (in volts).

> ## WATCH OUT!
>
> Before you start, check: Are you wearing your **ESD wrist strap**?

has two probes. To test a device or cable, put the red (positive) probe on the 'hot point', i.e. high point of the circuit. Put the black (negative) probe on the 'ground', i.e. low point of the circuit. Table 29.2 shows the settings you might select and Table 29.3 shows what the reading on the multimeter might tell you.

> ## WATCH OUT!
>
> When using an ammeter, the current will flow through the ammeter, so check the rating of the ammeter to make sure it can cope with the flow. More flow than the ammeter is designed to handle may blow a fuse in the meter.

Meter type	Unit	What it measures	What it can be used to test
Voltmeter	volts	Potential difference between two points	
Ammeter	amps	Current	If power is reaching this component
Ohmmeter	ohms	Resistance between two points	If there is continuity between these two points For a cable, if there is a fault between these two points

Table 29.3 What a multimeter measures

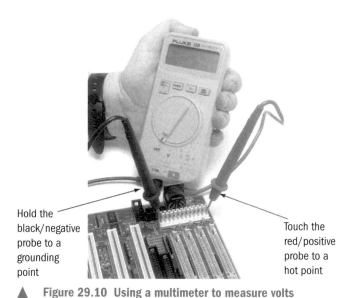

Hold the black/negative probe to a grounding point

Touch the red/positive probe to a hot point

▲ **Figure 29.10 Using a multimeter to measure volts**

What does it mean?

An **ESD (electrostatic discharge) wrist strap** is a safety device used to channel static electricity to a proper ground, such as the computer's chassis or a static ground mat, while the wearer is handling sensitive computer equipment.

■ HOW TO MEASURE VOLTS ON A POWER SUPPLY CONNECTOR

1 Switch off the PC, leaving it connected at the wall socket.
2 Prepare the multimeter: DC, 20V.
3 Open the computer case and remove the cover.
4 Identify one unused power supply connector. (You could remove one, e.g. from a CD-ROM drive or the hard/floppy disk drive.)

5 Turn on the PC.
6 Using the black probe, touch any of the black wires in the unused power supply connector (see Figure 29.11). At the same time, use the red probe to touch the connector's yellow wire.
7 Check that the multimeter shows a reading of +12V. Anything in the range +11.5V to +12.6V is OK. *If your reading is very different (e.g. 5V), check that you are using the correct probes with the correct coloured wires.*
8 Keeping the black probe in place, now move the red probe to touch the connector's red wire.
9 Check that the multimeter shows a reading of +5V. Anything in the range +4.8V to +5.2V is OK.

■ HOW TO MEASURE RESISTANCE (GENERAL PRINCIPLES)

1 Make sure that the circuit has no power running through it. For example, to test circuits inside the PC, turn off the PC.

> ## WATCH OUT!
>
> Using a multimeter to test a circuit which has power running through it can damage the multimeter.

2 Prepare the multimeter to test ohms, with an appropriate range.
3 Using both probes, touch two different metal points in the circuit that are very close to each other. Make sure that the multimeter reading shows zero – adjust it if necessary so that it does show zero.
4 Move the two probes so that they are either side of any suspected source of resistance. Check the multimeter reading. If it still shows zero, there is no resistance. If it shows a value, that is the resistance between the two points.

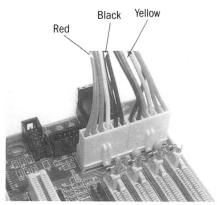

Red   Black   Yellow

(a) AT connector

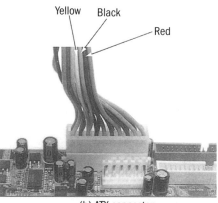

Yellow   Black   Red

(b) ATX connector

◀ **Figure 29.11 The various coloured wires on power supply connectors: (a) AT and (b) ATX**

■ HOW TO MEASURE RESISTANCE IN A CABLE

You can use this test for a cable from any external serial device, and for a null modem cable.

1 Disconnect the cable at both ends.
2 Prepare the multimeter to test ohms, with an appropriate range.
3 Identify Pin 2 of the cable's connectors at each end (see Figure 29.12).
4 Touch one Pin 2 with the black probe and the other Pin 2 with the red probe.
5 Check that the multimeter indicates continuity (by its reading, a beep or a buzzing noise, according to the model of multimeter). *If the multimeter does not indicate continuity, check your connections.* If you are making good connections and there is no reading, then the cable is defective.

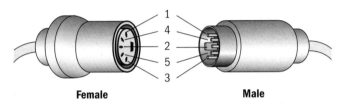

Female   **Male**

If you cannot make a good connection at the female end, poke a wire segment (e.g. a paperclip) into the pin hole

▲   **Figure 29.12 Identifying Pin 2 – the male and female ends**

Activity 29.10

Using a multimeter

1 Practise using a multimeter in each of its modes: as a voltmeter, an ammeter and an ohmmeter.

2 Your teacher should provide you with a selection of cabling, some of which is faulty. Use a multimeter to identify the faulty cabling.

29.2.1.2 Self test routines

When a computer is turned on, the **boot process** commences.

Power is not supplied straightaway to all devices. Instead, the power supply system checks what power supplies are needed for the rest of the PC. This process is called initialising the power supply. For more details on the PSU, see *Unit 2: Computer Systems*, page 47.

If the proper voltages can be supplied, the processor moves on to the next stage of the boot process: loading the **BIOS** into RAM.

When the computer is turned on, its memory is empty, apart from one set of hardwired instructions that are located at an address in the ROM called the **jump address**. These important few instructions, when executed, will load the BIOS into memory.

Remember!

The **BIOS (basic input output system)** is the part of the operating system that handles the input and output of the computer. **RAM (random access memory)** is volatile memory, i.e. it retains its data only while the power is switched on. **ROM (read only memory)** is non-volatile memory and retains its data even when the power is switched off.

So, the computer 'jumps' to the jump address and starts executing instructions, resulting in the BIOS being loaded. The processor then starts executing the BIOS program and the next stage of the boot process begins: the **POST**.

The POST is a hardware diagnostic routine that is run during the boot sequence. It checks configuration settings held in **CMOS** against the actual hardware configuration.

What does it mean?

The **boot process** is an automated process that happens every time you power up.

POST stands for **power-on self test**.

The **CMOS (complementary metal-oxide semiconductor)** is an essential chip located on the motherboard. It holds both the BIOS program and data such as the expected configuration details of the computer. It is powered by a battery so its data is not lost when power is turned off.

The POST ensures the integrity of the computer system and can therefore prove to be the most important diagnostic tool available to you. If there are problems at the earliest stages of the boot process, the system will sound an error beep. The use of sound – available directly from a speaker on the motherboard – is necessary until the monitor is running properly. As soon as the BIOS has loaded the device BIOS of the video adaptor into memory, communication can be on-screen. So, instead of beeps, error codes can be displayed.

The boot process continues, loading relevant software to handle all other peripherals. When the configuration is confirmed, the POST process has ensured that the PC with all its peripherals is ready for use. The POST will also display a message if there is something wrong.

Finally, the BIOS checks the CMOS data to identify from which disk drive the operating system is to be loaded. The operating system, such as Windows, is normally located on the hard drive but, if the hard drive is not functioning properly or you want to avoid it (perhaps because you suspect a virus problem), you can load from another drive using a floppy disk or a CD.

Activity 29.11

Self-test routines – the POST process

1 Find out what error code signifies a problem with your keyboard.

2 Your teacher will present you with a PC that has a fault. Start up the PC and note what happens during the boot process. What is wrong? Try to fix the fault.

29.2.1.3 Monitoring devices

An application that is attached to devices on a network can monitor just about anything you want. It can be as simple as a **ping test** to make sure something is there, or you can request additional detail such as bandwidth use on network links, storage space on servers, etc.

Then, if something goes down, an alert is raised – the format of this depends on the circumstances. An organisation might use a network monitoring tool that

makes, for example, the Star Trek Red Alert sound if something major goes down. For minor problems, the notice might be via an email alert sent through to a service desk.

Any application that monitors the system and alerts the service desk helps IT support technicians to become proactive rather than reactive – they realise something is wrong before the user telephones to say so.

29.2.1.4 Suitable tools

Just like any workman whose job it is to fix equipment, a support technician needs a toolbox. This section considers what might be found in a technician's toolbox.

The most important item is an **ESD wrist strap**. This needs a 1-megaohm resistor, without which it is useless.

Remember!

An ESD wrist strap is a safety device used to channel static electricity to a proper ground, typically the computer's chassis or to a static ground mat, while the wearer is handling sensitive computer equipment. Never remove the ESD's resistor. If it is damaged, dispose of the wrist strap completely, and purchase a new one.

A **torch** or flashlight will help you to spot things in dark corners of a PC. It may also help you to read the small print on some components. **Angled mirrors** (see Figure 29.13), like the kind used by a dentist, can help you to see around corners within a PC.

What does it mean?

A **ping test** is useful to troubleshoot Internet connections. It can determine whether a specific IP address is accessible and works by sending a packet to the specified address and waiting for a reply.

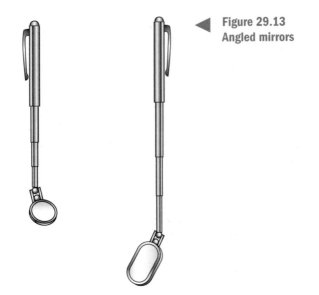

Figure 29.13
Angled mirrors

Needle nose pliers can be used to hold screws and/or connectors, and would be useful for handling wire. They might also have a wire cutter.

WATCH OUT!

Rubber handled pliers are easy to grip but are unlikely to protect you from electrical shock.

Keep a variety of **screwdrivers**: Phillips, slotted, hex head and Torx (see Figure 29.14).

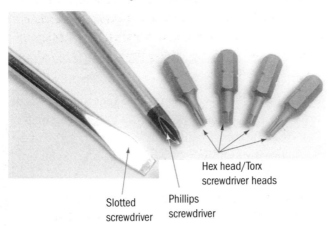

Hex head/Torx
screwdriver heads

Slotted
screwdriver

Phillips
screwdriver

▲ **Figure 29.14 Different types of screwdriver, and parts retriever**

A **multimeter** (see page 327) will let you test and measure the electrical properties of your PC and its components. A **loop-back plug** can be used to isolate a problem with a port. It is constructed so that data that is sent out is immediately sensed on the receiving pins of the port.

WATCH OUT!

Avoid magnetic screwdrivers. The electromagnetic field can damage components within a PC. Instead, use a parts retriever to retrieve things that fall inside the PC case.

A technician should also carry some **cleaning materials**. While a PC case is open, it makes sense to clean away any build-up of dirt or dust. See *Unit 2: Computer Systems*, page 74 for advice on how to clean equipment and the materials you might need for this.

Electrical tape can be used to wrap wire ends and insulating components. There should also be an assortment of **spare parts**: screws, expansion card inserts, etc.

When visiting a site to try to fix a PC, a technician ought to have all relevant **support materials**, including reference disks. A **notepad and pen** will also prove useful, to write down details of components such as the model number and serial number, or to note settings when installing or configuring a system. Sometimes, a diagram is more useful than notes.

Just to be safe, prior to changing anything, a technician should boot the system and write down the system set-up configuration data. Then, if disaster strikes, the relevant details are available to set the system up again.

A **paper clip** can prove very useful when trying to make a connection to a pin on a female connector. Straighten it out and poke it into the hole, leaving a convenient length of wire for attaching a probe from the multimeter (see page 327).

A **wire stripper/cutter** can be used to prepare wires, cutting them to length and stripping back the insulating sheath.

Chip tools are used either to insert or remove **DIPP** chips.

Remember!

DIPP stands for dual in-line pin package. See memory types in *Unit 2: Computer Systems*, page 55.

Some tools, such as a **soldering iron** which might be used to repair a cable, are best left in the workshop. If these tools are needed, the PC probably ought to be in the workshop for mending.

WATCH OUT!

Keep your soldering iron well away from circuit boards.

Test your knowledge

1   Explain these terms: current, resistance, volt, amp, ohm, voltmeter, ammeter, ohmmeter, multimeter.

2   Explain the boot process. Why is it called this?

3   What do these acronyms stand for? POST, CMOS, BIOS, ESD.

4   What is a ping test? What is its purpose?

5   What is a loop-back plug? What is its purpose?

Activity 29.12

Tools for troubleshooting

1   Do a ping test to check an Internet connection.

2   Collect together the tools that you have available for troubleshooting. Check that you know what each tool is called and what is it best used for.

3   Compare notes with others in your groups. Identify the minimum set of tools needed in a technician's tool kit.

29.2.2 Software tools and techniques

Some software tools are supplied with the computer (Table 29.4), while others can be purchased (Table 29.5).

This subsection focuses on a range of software tools: diagnostics (such as virus software), test utilities and monitoring and error logging programs.

Activity 29.13

Software tools

1   Identify the software tools available on your computer system. Categorise the tools according to their uses and draw up a table for reference purposes.

2   Select one tool that you have not used previously. Discover what it does and share your findings with others in your group.

29.2.2.1 Diagnostics

Diagnostic software examines the computer, noting the current settings. It can be used to measure performance or to check for the presence of **viruses**. Unit 2 (page 65) explains how virus protection software can be used to diagnose and fix virus problems.

Remember!

Viruses are so-called because they spread by replicating themselves. They can erase data and corrupt files.

Program	Type of tool	Notes
BIOS POST	Diagnostic tool built into a PC	Runs automatically whenever you power up Checks all the hardware and will report any serious hardware faults
DEFRAG.EXE	Windows utility	Rearranges data on a disk for more efficient input/output; see Unit 2, page 71
SCANDISK.EXE	Available as a systems tool with some Windows systems	Checks and reports problem on the hard disk Includes any corruption of the file system and hard disk read errors Runs automatically if the PC is not shut down properly
SYSEDIT.EXE	Windows tool	An editor that can be used to view and edit systems files, e.g. .INI files, AUTOEXEC.BAT or CONFIG.SYS files
Windows Device Manager	Windows tool	Shows device driver and resource settings, etc. for individual devices Can be used to resolve resource conflicts between two devices, e.g. in their use of **IRQ**, **DMA** channel or **I/O** address
DirectX	Windows tool	Can be used to check hardware faults

Table 29.4 Software diagnostic tools available on a PC

Type of software	Notes
Anti-virus software such as that provided by McAfee and Norton	PCs can be attacked by viruses, arriving with emails or during access to the Internet. Anti-virus software checks for these intruders and zaps them. See Unit 2, page 65
Diagnostic/troubleshooting software	Multi-purpose software utilities offer a range of diagnostic tests and reports on system status: system tune-ups, hardware diagnostics
Uninstaller	An uninstaller can be used to remove software applications that are no longer required It is needed to remove out-of-date software prior to installing an updated version

Table 29.5 Software tools that you can buy

Activity 29.14

Diagnostic software

1 Read the section on virus protection in Unit 2 (page 65) and make sure you understand the distinction between viruses, worms and trojans.

2 Check what anti-virus software you have on your computer system. Make sure you have the most up-to-date DAT files and do a virus check of your hard drive.

3 Look at other diagnostic software available on your computer system and make sure you understand how to use it, and what it has to offer.

4 Look for software that offers to measure the performance of your PC. What recommendations does it make?

What does it mean?

IRQ stands for interrupt request – a memory location that acts as a communication link between the processor and the device.

DMA stands for direct memory access.

I/O stands for input/output.

29.2.2.2 Test utilities

Some utilities, like anti-virus software (see *Unit 2: Computer Systems*, page 65), are supplied by specialist vendors. In Windows, many utilities can be found in the Systems Tools folder (see Figure 29.15).

Unit 2 (page 65) looks in detail at a variety of software utilities such as cleanup tools and those used to defragment and reformat a drive.

29.2.2.3 Monitoring and error logging

Monitoring the performance of a computer can throw light on changes, such as a slowing down of performance, which might suggest a virus attack or the imminent failure of a hardware component.

An **audit trail** provides an opportunity to track potential security problems. It helps to assure user accountability and provides evidence in the event of a security breach.

Using the audit trail options, a network administrator can monitor access to the network. The network access log records who has been using the network and for what purpose. Similarly, a log of who is using which applications, what emails are being sent and what access is being made to the Internet are available.

Within Windows XP, for example, an audit trail option is available as part of the Computer Management option within Administrative Tools in the Control Panel. The first step is to decide the audit policy: the categories of

Activity 29.15

Test utilities

1 Read the section on utility software in Unit 2 (page 65) and make sure you are aware of the range of utility software available to you.

2 Pick one utility and prepare yourself to demonstrate its use to a novice user. Prepare a handout as a reminder of the steps the novice will need to take.

events that are important enough to be audited. When Windows XP Professional is first installed, no categories are selected, and therefore no audit policy is in force. Computer Management lists the event categories that you can audit. For example, you may choose to note each time a user logs on or off a workstation within a network. The next step is to set the size and behaviour of the security log. How much history is to be kept? The longer the history, the greater the size of the space needed for the log.

What does it mean?

Utility programs do the administrative or maintenance tasks needed on a computer system.

An **audit trail** is a record of everything that has happened: all events like users logging on and off, or files being accessed and/or modified.

The Systems Tools are in the Accessories folder.

Disk Cleanup and Disk Defragmenter should be used regularly.

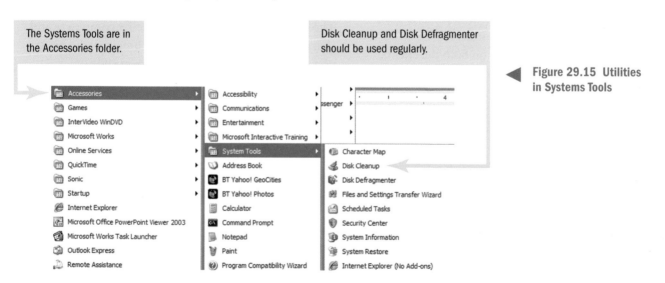

Figure 29.15 Utilities in Systems Tools

You may opt to select the audit directory service access category and/or the audit object access category. For each, you must specify the objects to which you want to monitor access and amend their security descriptors accordingly. For example, if you want to audit any attempts by users to open a particular file, you can set a Success or Failure attribute directly on that file for that particular event.

Event Viewer (available through the Control Panel – see *Unit 28: IT Technical Support*, page 287) may be used to help you to predict and identify the sources of system problems. For example, if a log reports that a disk driver can only write to a sector after several retries, it is likely that this sector will fail completely, and that this may happen quite soon.

Dr Watson is another example of a monitoring and error logging tool. This program error debugger detects information about system and program failure. Whenever an error occurs within a program it records relevant information in a support log file. Once installed, Dr Watson starts automatically in the event of a program error, but you can access it via Start/Run – the program to run is called drwtsn32.

When an error is detected, Dr Watson creates a text file (called Drwtsn32.log). Support technicians can then use this information to diagnose the program error. There is also an option to create a crash dump file, which is a binary file that a programmer can load into a debugger. Although Dr Watson cannot stop errors happening, the information it saves (like memory dumps) might help when trying to work out what went wrong.

WinVNC is a remote display system that allows viewing of a computer desktop environment from anywhere on the Internet. WinVNC can be set up on both the client and server side to allow monitoring of employees' machines remotely.

What does it mean?

WinVNC stands for Windows Virtual Network Computing.

It is possible to modify the original WinVNC program slightly to remove the icon that shows it is running. With the icon removed, employees would not know when they were being monitored.

Activity 29.16

Monitoring and error logging

1 Working with a friend, explore the audit trail options within Windows. In the Help and Support centre, search on 'audit trail' – read about how to set up an audit trail and how it can help to track what is happening on a computer system. Look in particular at any technical articles that show you how to enable Windows security alerting and make notes. Go to the Control Panel and explore the Computer Management option to see how you might set up an audit trail.

2 Working with a friend, explore the facilities offered by Dr Watson. Make notes.

3 Research the Internet for information about WinVNC and other similar remote monitoring tools. Check also the trade press, for example, and look for stories about how spyware might be used to monitor sensitive information, and how hackers might infiltrate a computer system.

29.2.3 Troubleshooting techniques

The more time you spend trying to fix computers and sharing experiences with other technicians, the better you will become at devising your own style of troubleshooting. The techniques suggested here, if applied systematically, should help you to solve problems presented by any end user who has a computer that does not seem to work.

29.2.3.1 Substitution

Imagine you suspect that one item of hardware, such as a printer, is the root cause of a problem. Substituting it with an identical printer – one that you know works –

will confirm whether you have isolated the problem. If the substituted item gives the same problem, then you need to investigate further. If the substituted item solves the problem, then the one you removed is at fault and needs replacing.

You might also try using the suspect item on another system that is known to be working. If the system still works with the suspect item, then there is no fault with it. If the working system develops the same fault, then your substituted item is most likely to be causing the problem.

When substituting equipment, keep notes of which peripherals worked under which circumstances. This will help you to eliminate peripherals that are working and to identify those that are not. See the section on **elimination**, page 338.

29.2.3.2 Test

A computer system comprises many separate hardware components within the processor box, a number of peripherals outside of the processor box, plus the installed software. The various hardware components are linked by connectors and power runs through the entire system. If the system fails to work, it could be because any of the components has developed a fault: a loose connection, a short circuit, overheating or wear and tear. A software setting that controls how the hardware is used could also be causing the problem.

For hardware faults, to identify which component or peripheral is faulty, each one can be tested. For example, you might use a multimeter (see page 327) to check the power supply either side of a component, or the connectivity within a cable (see page 328).

If you believe that the hardware is OK, then you should test the software settings.

- If the modem is not working, has the speed been set appropriately?
- If the printer is not working, is the document being sent to the correct printer?
- If the webcam is not working, has the correct driver been installed?

29.2.3.3 Change settings

Some hardware components, such as a modem or printer, require appropriate settings before they will work as planned. If such a component is not functioning, it may be necessary to change the settings. For example, printers will need to be configured with the correct paper size.

29.2.3.4 Upgrade

When additional or new versions of software are introduced, either these or already installed software may not work on the existing hardware configuration. There may be insufficient RAM, too slow a processor or not enough hard disk space, so a hardware upgrade may be needed.

29.2.3.5 Reinstall software

If a system crashes, damage may be done to the software settings, and it may be necessary to reinstall the software. Any related data files should be backed up before reinstalling software, but before you can reinstall an application, you need to remove all traces of the original version from the computer. This cannot be done simply by deleting program files; instead, an uninstall program is needed – see Figure 29.6 on page 324.

If buying software direct from the vendor via an Internet site, it is important to have a CD copy of the software. Then, if you ever need to reinstall, you can do it from the CD. Trying to download again from the Internet may not be feasible, especially if the vendor has subsequently launched a newer version of the software. The vendor will want you to upgrade (see above) rather than reinstall an older version, so it is not in the vendor's interest to make earlier versions available.

29.2.3.6 Elimination

Finding out which component is the root of a fault sometimes has to be established by a process of elimination. By identifying what does work, you can narrow down the options to a smaller set of likely causes. So, testing components systematically, and noting which ones seem to be functioning correctly, can lead you to the one component that needs attention and that, when fixed, will solve the problem.

29.2.3.7 Applying bug fixes

If the software vendor discovers some time after the software release date that there is a bug in an application, a bug fix may be issued, usually via the vendor's Internet site. Some vendors, such as Microsoft, offer the option for updates to be checked automatically, as soon as a machine goes online, or you can visit Microsoft's website and check what updates are outstanding on your machine (for the operating system or for software such as Office applications).

What does it mean?

A **bug** is a programming error.

29.2.3.8 Generating error codes

Rather than trying to describe a fault, error codes are used as a shorthand. For example, during the POST process, as soon as the screen is operational an error code is displayed. Diagnostic tools such as Event Viewer (see Unit 28, page 287) also refer to errors using a coding system.

Activity 29.17

Troubleshooting techniques

1 Refer back to the notes you made during Activity 29.9 (on page 326). Identify the techniques that you used to solve the various problems presented to you by others in your group. Consider whether your troubleshooting could have been more systematic. Would this have led you to the fault more quickly? Discuss this with others in your group.

2 Repeat Activity 29.9 (page 326) for a complex fault involving both hardware and software, using the troubleshooting techniques described in this section. In your fault report, describe two of the hardware tools and two of the software tools that you used to troubleshoot the problem. Explain why you used the hardware/software tools and why you chose not to use other tools. Make notes on how you identified the root cause of the fault and the steps you then took to fix it. Write a brief report on the potential impact of the faults you discovered on the user, the user's organisation and its external customers. **p₂ p₃ p₄ m₃ d₁**

This section is about making decisions about how and when to repair equipment. It tackles this first from the customer's (that is, the end user's) viewpoint. It then considers the impact of external considerations such as legislation. Finally, the factors influencing an organisation's IT policies are identified.

29.3.1 Customer issues

Providing diagnosis and repair services for end users is the main function of a technical support team. Seeing the problem from the end user's point of view is therefore essential.

29.3.1.1 Communications

The end user will probably initiate communication with the support team by reporting a fault. However, they will do this in the way that has been set up for communications with the support team.

- Some organisations have a help desk with phone lines ready to take incoming calls from end users who are experiencing problems.
- Some organisations require a written notification of a problem, often via email.
- Some – like Hewlett-Packard – provide online help to their customers via chat.

If a fault is reported verbally, the help desk technician has to record the facts of the problem. A form may be used to guide the end user through essential information (location of hardware, contact details) and to ask questions about the type of problem being experienced. The form may be linked to a database – this will help in any subsequent analysis of faults, and provide a way of monitoring performance of the support team.

A record should then be kept, either manually or electronically, showing what action was taken to resolve the problem. This fault history may prove invaluable in solving similar problems or spotting trends (see page 343). It should also help in subsequent communications with the end user – the technician who takes any follow-up call can talk with confidence to the end user, explaining what has been done so far and how long it might take for the repair to be completed.

End users should also be kept fully informed of progress. Instead of adopting a fire-fighting attitude and waiting for users' irate calls, support staff should be proactive in contacting the end user.

29.3.1.2 Understanding the impact of diagnosis and repair on the individual

Technicians need to understand the problems faced by end users and treat them sympathetically. End users whose computer systems fail may be seriously inconvenienced, e.g. with no email access or unable to carry out daily work functions such as report writing. To be left without a computer system for any length of time is unacceptable to most users. So, if the diagnosis of a problem is likely to take some time, the end user would appreciate attempts to provide a replacement service while the repair is being effected.

29.3.1.3 Customer handover and acceptance process following repair

When a fault is repaired, the record for that incident needs to be closed off. The end user may be asked to confirm that the computer system now works satisfactorily. During an on-site visit, the technician could demonstrate that the equipment is working and ask for a signature. If the support is given via a remote call centre, a record can be kept of any telephone call made to the user, checking that everything is OK.

29.3.1.4 Effect of unresolved faults

Unresolved faults can affect the user and, potentially, the service to external clients.

An end user will be inconvenienced by the failure of a computer system, e.g. a deadline might be missed. If the end user provides a service to external customers, e.g. providing quotations or accepting orders over the phone, the customers may also be inconvenienced and might decide to take their custom elsewhere.

Activity 29.18

Customer issues

1 Select one of the faults that you have been required to fix during the activities in this unit. In what way did it inconvenience the end user? What did you do to smooth things for the end user?

2 Repeat Activity 29.9 (on page 326) for a complex fault, making sure that your tone of voice and body language demonstrate due consideration for the 'end users' in your group.

3 Compare notes with others in your group. How can you modify your behaviour to take into consideration the end user and his/her feelings? **P**₆

29.3.2 External considerations

Although organisations can make decisions regarding how and when repairs will take place, there are a number of external considerations which must be taken into account.

29.3.2.1 Relevant legislation

Legislation exists to protect workers and to draw attention to hazards in the workplace. Health and safety legislation (see page 344) in particular has to be taken into account when setting the policy for how and when diagnosis and repair of equipment will be carried out. Proper safety procedures must be followed, e.g. the wearing of ESD wrist straps.

According to separate regulations (the Electrical Equipment (Safety) Regulations 1994), all electrical equipment, not just IT equipment, must be regularly tested, and labelled to show when it was last tested. This should reduce the risk of accidental shocks and fire in the workplace.

There are also regulations governing the safe disposal of materials such as batteries (Hazardous Waste (England and Wales) Regulations 2005). These aim to reduce pollution and possible contamination of water supplies and the environment generally. Any items that are deemed non-repairable and that require special disposal procedures should be kept aside. They must not be put in with other non-hazardous waste.

Legislation also exists to protect privacy (through the Data Protection Act) and ownership of intellectual property (through the Copyright, Designs and Patents Act 1988). While repairing a system, you may need to back up data on another device. Once the system is fixed and the data restored, you should erase any extra copies that you have made of sensitive data.

The Computer Misuse Act 1998 defines electronic vandalism and makes it a criminal activity to write viruses that can cause damage to software and data and disrupt the operation of a computer system. This Act also covers hacking through a firewall and theft of data. During troubleshooting, if you need to disarm the firewall for any reason, you should remember to reinstate it once the problem has been fixed.

29.3.2.2 Service level agreements (SLAs)

An SLA sets out what level of support is expected. For example, it may specify service obligations such as: response times, downtimes, schedules for work to be completed and/or security arrangements. The SLA may be an internal document drawn up between the support department and other departments within an organisation, or it may be agreed between an organisation and an external supplier of support services. See *Unit 28: IT Technical Support* (page 304).

29.3.2.3 Escalation procedures

The decision to escalate an incident lies with the technician who is dealing with the end user at any one time. The manner in which this is done needs to be determined by the organisation. All technicians should be

What does it mean?

Escalation means the referral of a problem higher up the chain of command.

aware of the limits of their own authority and therefore when escalation is necessary. See *Unit 28: IT Technical Support* (page 302) for more information on this topic.

29.3.2.4 Documentation and reporting

Keeping track of faults and how they were fixed is best recorded in a **fault log**.

Remember!

A **fault log** is a record of events that occurred, and may include information on how the fault was fixed. *See* Unit 28, page 382.

A simple manual fault log may be sufficient but an electronic fault log – perhaps a blog – may prove more useful. Perhaps the screen freezes intermittently or the computer system crashes altogether? Details such as what software was running at the time, and what events happened immediately prior to the crash/freeze, can then be used to look for patterns.

- Are two software packages clashing?
- Is a particular feature of the software expecting too much of the hardware that is online?

Noting the date and circumstances each time something goes wrong may throw light on the source of the problem. This may facilitate decision making and allow for more informed consideration of resource allocation and prioritisation of jobs.

Electronically generated fault logs may be created by software tools such as dumprep.exe. If a serious error occurs, this Windows XP fault-logging program writes the error details to a text file.

29.3.2.5 Legal issues

Apart from the legislation that relates to IT (see page 340), you need to uphold legal documents such as:

- contracts that you have signed as an employee (agreeing to maintain confidentiality, for example)

- contracts that your organisation may have signed with a client (which, for example, define the type of support to be provided).

Behaviour contrary to your contract of employment could result in your dismissal. If you act negligently while on client premises and it affects the client adversely, the client may cancel the contract or implement a penalty clause which results in your employer paying compensation. This may also result in your dismissal.

Activity 29.19

External considerations

1 Use the Internet to research legislation that is of relevance to the work of a support technician. List all Acts that you consider necessary and write brief notes on each one.

2 Focusing on one Act, prepare a presentation to explain its main features and how this impacts on the decision making of an organisation with regard to diagnosis and repair of equipment.

3 Review the material given in *Unit 28: IT Technical Support* (page 304) on SLAs. Make notes. Explain the terms incident and fault and how service levels can vary from one user to another.

4 Review the material given in Unit 28 (page 302) on escalation procedures. Make notes. List the circumstances under which you might need to escalate an incident or fault.

29.3.3 Organisational considerations

The management of an organisation are responsible for making decisions about how much time is set aside for maintenance of computer systems and how many support staff are provided to help the workforce. Once the customer issues (see page 339) and external considerations (see page 340) have been taken into account, an organisation has free rein as to how it goes about diagnosing and repairing IT equipment. This section focuses on the issues that arise within organisations that can impact on the support team.

29.3.3.1 Security

Some faults arise because security is lax, allowing hackers to gain access to the system or viruses to attack the data. Security measures are essential and include hardware solutions such as putting equipment under lock and key, and software solutions such as installing a password system. *Unit 15: Organisational Systems Security* explains all the options (see pages 185-198).

29.3.3.2 Costs

The support team provides a service for all employees within an organisation and is therefore an overhead cost. Costs need to be kept to a minimum – the organisation's annual budget will set a fixed cost which limits the cover and maintenance work provided by the IT support team. There may not be enough funds for all employees to have state-of-the-art hardware and the most recent releases of the software, so compromises may be necessary.

If support is provided in-house, the major costs are staff, training and equipment. The support team effort may be split between:

- staffing a help desk
- carrying out regular preventive maintenance
- providing training for end users
- preparing for future upgrades of hardware and software.

How much time and expenditure can be allocated to these various functions will depend on the organisation's needs and the funding available to the support team.

An organisation may choose to outsource part or all of its support needs, such as the care of IT equipment. An SLA (see page 340) may be set up with a third party specifying what cover is provided. The cost of this support will be included in the budget and will be renegotiated yearly.

29.3.3.3 Impact of systems downtime

Websites, such as those offering online banking, need some downtime to make essential changes to the site. During that time, customers cannot access their accounts. This downtime needs to be scheduled to happen when it will affect the fewest number of customers (e.g. in the middle of the night) and to be kept to a minimum. A similar approach is needed within all organisations, especially for unplanned downtime, when the website goes down and there is a delay before anyone within the organisation notices and/or the server can be rebooted.

Employees are adversely affected by the closing down of any computing facilities. Therefore essential maintenance (e.g. to upgrade the system) has to be planned so it causes the minimum amount of inconvenience. This means that support staff may be required to work overtime and/or at antisocial times, while the rest of the workforce is away from the office.

If a fault brings down a network of computers, this can be catastrophic. Some organisations cannot afford for such an event to happen, so they set up a parallel system. This costs more, but if it safeguards the future of the organisation it is worth the expense.

29.3.3.4 Disruption of normal working

Any disruption to normal working can adversely affect the profitability of an organisation. For example, if an insurance company sends out its reminders late, its customers might take out a policy with a competitor that has been quick to contact those in need of cover.

Fully functioning computer systems create an image of efficiency. Any organisation that apologises when you call to place an order or make an enquiry about an expected delivery, saying 'the computer is down just now' loses face – its reputation is tarnished. This problem is particularly acute for online services and retailers. When trying to buy something online, if the website is not functioning, the customer will probably take their custom elsewhere. Online businesses may only have one opportunity to attract new visitors – if the first experience is not a good one, the visitor may never come back and potential sales are lost forever.

29.3.3.5 Contractual requirements

The support team staff may be required to work shifts to provide coverage for employees whenever the offices are officially open, plus extra time in the evenings and weekends to carry out essential maintenance which might involve downtime. The hours worked will be set out in an employment contract. They may also be limited by EU legislation and other regulations such as the Working Time Regulations which provide basic rights and protections as follows:

- A worker can be required to work at most an average of 48 hours a week (though workers can choose to work more if they want to). For night workers there is a limit of an average of 8 hours worked in 24.
- Night workers are entitled to receive free health assessments.
- All staff are entitled to 11 hours of rest a day and to one day off each week. When the working day is longer than 6 hours, workers must have an in-work rest break.
- Workers are entitled to 4 weeks of paid leave per year.

These protections may or may not be in place. You should check your contract to find out any special conditions of service before signing.

There may also be contracts between your organisation and its clients for whom you are to provide a service. The legal implications of such a contract are considered on page 341.

29.3.3.6 Trend analysis of faults reported

The records kept of incidents and how these are dealt with can provide useful data about the success or otherwise of the support team. By careful analysis, trends may be identified which can then help in the formulation of plans to provide better (i.e. more reliable) hardware or software, and may also be used to target training for the end users who need it the most. Trend analysis can be used to re-allocate budgets and resources to identifiable hot spots.

29.3.3.7 Resource allocation

Resources such as equipment and technician time have to be carefully managed. A budget will be set, and purchases carefully researched. For example, if the fault log shows that one particular make of a peripheral breaks down too often, then efforts are needed to find an alternative make that will prove to be more reliable and therefore more economical.

29.3.3.8 Prioritisation of jobs

In an ideal world, all end users' calls would [be answered] instantly and the support team would be wa[iting for the] help desk phone to ring. However, there are c[alls coming] on time, and problems are likely to happen at i[rregular] intervals. So, there will be times when the suppo[rt team] are inundated with calls and some end users will h[ave] to wait for attention. Unit 28 (page 287) looks at ho[w] jobs can be prioritised.

Case study

Fudge-it

Fudge-it is a confectionery company that make sticks of rock, with the name of a seaside resort embedded in the candy. The sales team of four take orders over the telephone all year round, the highest sales being during the summer months. A database of all shops that stock the Fudge-it range is linked to the accounts system, which keeps track of amounts owing to the company. Customers can also place their orders via a website, putting the cost of an order on account or paying using a credit card.

Fudge-it employs one full-time support technician, Jo, who works from 9 to 5, 5 days a week, maintaining the hardware, the software and the website. Jo has 4 weeks' annual leave, taken in May and November.

1 A new member of staff accidentally loosens a vital cable and the network fails the day after Jo has flown out of the UK for her May break. What risks does the organisation face as a result of this mistake? Describe the impact of the organisational policy of Fudge-it on the troubleshooting and repair of this fault. Explain, with examples, what organisational guidelines and procedures might have helped to minimise the impact of such IT faults. **p**₅ **d**₂

2 Search the Internet for examples of organisations which have suffered adverse publicity due to downtime of their IT systems.

3 Research the Internet to find out about legislation related to working hours. Make notes.

...y to conduct
...to a

...d safety

...ty law in Britain is covered
...y at Work Act (1974). This Act
...duties that employers have towards
... and towards members of the public.
...ins the duties that employees have to
...es and to each other. The Act states that these
...s have to be carried out 'so far as is reasonably
practicable'. In other words, the degree of risk in a
particular job or workplace needs to be balanced against
the time, trouble, cost and physical difficulty of taking
measures to avoid or reduce the risk.

The law simply requires what good management and
common sense should lead employers to do anyway:
to look at what the risks are and take sensible measures
to tackle them. The main requirement for employers
is to carry out a risk assessment. This should be
straightforward in a simple workplace such as a typical
office. It only becomes complicated if serious hazards are
involved, such as those found in a nuclear power station,
a chemical plant, laboratory or oil rig.

Technicians should be given adequate training in what is
required by the legislation and in how to protect
themselves and fellow workers from harm. For example,
technicians need to learn the safe handling of
equipment, to avoid back injuries while lifting or
carrying heavy objects – see the section on manual
handling, page 346.

To summarise the requirement of the Health and Safety
Act, employers are required to:

- assess risk to employees and provide risk assessment
- set up emergency procedure provisions as identified
  by the risk assessment
- appoint competent people (often themselves or
  company colleagues) to help them to implement the
  arrangements
- provide employees with clear instructions and give
  training where necessary.

This section considers the hazards that might be faced
while working as a support technician.

Activity 29.20

Health and safety

1 Visit the HSE (Health and Safety Executive) website and
search on 'risk assessment' to discover more about
how organisations need to consider risk in the
workplace.

2 Study the scene in Figure 29.16 and list the hazards.
How could risks be minimised in this office?

▲ Figure 29.16 Hazards in the workplace

3 Working in groups of three or four, carry out a risk
assessment of an area of your college where IT is
used. Present your findings and recommendations.

4 Check with an organisation of your choice. Who is
responsible for health and safety? What do they do to
minimise risks in the workplace?

29.4.1.1 Correct use of tools

Some tools are inherently hazardous.

- Manual tools such as screwdrivers should be handled with care.
- Electrical equipment carries its own risks. When using a multimeter, for example, you need to take precautions with the settings and how you place the probes – see page 328. ESD is also a hazard, and is covered in its own section (see following).

When disks start to become full, files are fragmented when saved, to fill in the gaps left by the deletion of files. Disk space quickly fills, so utility programs should be used to clean disks and to **defragment** the files as part of the regular system maintenance.

What does it mean?

The **defragmentation** process closes up 'gaps' on the disk and puts together fragmented files so that they are saved next to each other on the disk surface; see Unit 2, page 71.

29.4.1.2 ESD and electrical safety

Your safety – and that of the PC – should be top of your priority list when working on a PC.

- Turn off the PC at the power switch and check that the power does go off (e.g. the power light goes out). The mains supply at 230V AC is the most dangerous voltage in the computer. Conventional monitor screens also use high voltages and can be lethal.
- Unplug the PC power cord.
- Place the computer on a flat surface and make sure it is free of metallic objects, electrical cords and power supplies.
- Make sure that you and the PC are not in contact with any other grounded objects. In particular the PC must not touch another PC (or electrical device) which is powered up.

Once the power is turned off and the PC power cord unplugged, there should no risk to you of receiving an electric shock. However, electricity flows from high voltage to low voltage, so if you are carrying a build-up of static electricity, you can give your PC an electrical shock called **ESD**.

What does it mean?

ESD (electrostatic discharge) is an electrical shock caused when two objects of uneven charge make contact. Current flows from high to low potential (from you to the PC) and may damage components.

Therefore, before touching any components you must ensure you are not carrying any static. Discharge any static electricity safely, before risking discharging it on the PC.

- Wear an ESD grounding strap on your wrist (or ankle) and, while working on the inside of the PC, connect this strap either to the chassis of the PC or to a grounding mat.

WATCH OUT!

Never wear a grounding strap when opening a monitor. The capacitor holds an enormous charge, and wearing the strap offers a shortcut – straight through you – to ground.

- Fit a grounded pad beneath the PC. Touching this pad before touching the PC will discharge any build-up of static electricity.

Some techniques for reducing static electricity include applying an anti-static treatment to carpets and storing any electrical components in anti-static bags until needed. Dry air can also cause static electricity, so installing humidifiers which replace moisture in the air and aiming for a humidity level of greater than 50 per cent should reduce the risk of static electricity build-up.

■ HOW TO STAY SAFE WHEN WORKING ON A PC

1 Be prepared: have the right tools to hand.
2 Obey the dress code: wear nothing dangling that could trap you. Wear your ESD wrist strap.

3 Before starting, turn off the PC and disconnect the AC power cord.

4 Read the manual – don't do things from memory. Take your time and think carefully before acting.

5 Ground yourself by touching the chassis to discharge any static electricity that has accumulated.

6 Handle all parts gently, holding components by their edges, not by the connector.

7 Remember that some components may be too hot to touch safely.

8 Have a 'buddy' – someone nearby who can call an ambulance if things do go seriously wrong.

Activity 29.21

Staying safe while troubleshooting

1 Explain, as if addressing a novice end user, how static electricity is a source of harm for a PC.

2 Explain, as if addressing a trainee technician, what can be done to minimise the risk of ESD. **m4**

29.4.1.3 Using correct manual handing procedures

Lifting heavy objects presents a hazard to you. The Manual Handling Operations Regulations 1992 are intended to reduce the incidence of injury caused through manual handling. For example, heavy loads should be labelled (so baggage handlers at an airport may put a 'heavy' tag on your suitcase) and equipment must be used to move heavy or cumbersome loads. If moving heavy PC equipment from one desk to another, you should follow the guidance on posture and use leg muscle power rather than risk damaging your back.

29.4.1.4 Considering fire safety

With any electrical equipment, there is a risk of fire. Power supplies should be turned off at the sockets – and disconnected – when a system is not in use. Adequate testing of all electrical equipment is also necessary, as set out in the regulations (see page 340), as is being aware of the location of the correct fire extinguisher for the fire involved.

Evacuating a building in the event of a fire can be hampered if exits are blocked by obstructions. So when working on site, be sure to keep exit areas free from tools. Even a temporary arrangement (e.g. stacking boxes in a doorway while you work on a computer) could impede your exit – and those of other workers – with disastrous consequences.

29.4.1.5 Ladders to access or lay network cabling

When equipment is being installed, you might need a ladder to access cabling ducts. Climbing a ladder is hazardous. It is important to angle the ladder against the wall and place it correctly so as to provide a stable climb. For the sake of safety, a second person should stand at the bottom of the ladder, adding weight to the lowest rung and making sure it does not slip or topple over.

29.4.1.6 Correct disposal of old parts/equipment

There are ongoing debates as to the safety of various items of technological equipment – for example, mobile phones and other devices which rely on microwave transmission. While a computer is in use and operational, the casing should protect the user from any known risks. However, when a computer is dismantled and broken up for disposal, the materials used to construct the computer may well pose a risk. In recognition of these hazards, regulations (see page 340) cover the safe disposal of items such as monitors and batteries.

Most of the environmental concerns regarding computers are to do with the monitor – specifically its cathode ray tube (CRT) – because each colour monitor contains, on average, four to five pounds of lead.

Computers also contain other hazardous materials, including mercury and hexavalent chromium, which has been shown to cause high blood pressure, iron-poor blood, liver disease and nerve and brain damage in animals. Nickel cadmium (NiCd) batteries represent one of the fastest growing sectors in the battery market, and are used for laptop computers, but nickel cadmium is a known human carcinogen, and therefore needs to be disposed of safely.

29.4.1.7 Considering the health and safety of other people

The Health and Safety Act expects all employees to take care so as to protect fellow workers. Simple acts, like keeping your own work area tidy, can make for a safer environment, not only for you but also for those who work around you. When using laser equipment, it is particularly important to be aware of others near you. Damage can be done very quickly: you might burn or blind someone. Trip hazards are also to be avoided: be careful not to leave equipment on the floor where others might stumble. Cabling that has to run across a pathway temporarily should be taped down to the floor surface to make sure no one can trip on it.

Activity 29.22

Health and safety in the workplace

1 Research on the Internet to find information about correct manual handling procedures.

2 Review the fire escape procedures in force at your place of work or study. Where are the fire extinguishers? What type are they? Do you know how to use them? Which is your route to safety in the event of a fire? Check that all the required documentation is on display and is accurate.

3 Find out what arrangements your local council has on offer for the disposal of batteries.

4 Where is the first aid equipment in your place of work or study? Who is qualified to give first aid?

29.4.1.8 Availability of first aid and supervision

Every workplace is required to have first aid equipment tohand, and to have suitably qualified personnel available to administer first aid in the event of an accident.

29.4.2 Working practices

When providing support services to an end user, you should adopt working practices as specified by your employer. This section considers what might be expected of you.

29.4.2.1 Obtaining permission before repairing

If you are called to fix a computer, before starting to work on it, and certainly before dismantling a computer, you should check that you have permission to do so. The equipment may belong to the organisation that employs you, but you still need to make sure you are entitled to access data on the computer and that you have the blessing of the end user before you start.

This permission may be already understood because the end user called the help desk and your visit is a direct result of the call. However, you need to make sure you have located the correct person and are looking at the computer with the fault.

29.4.2.2 Preparing the worksite

When you arrive on-site, the end user's desk and work area may be so cramped that you need to ask them to clear the desk of paperwork. The end user may need to vacate the area to give you space to pull the computer system away from the wall and perhaps to turn things around. Look for hazards, like a cup of coffee which could cause damage if spilt. There may well be rules against eating or drinking in the vicinity of computers.

When you leave the site, you should return the workspace to its original condition (maybe even a bit tidier and cleaner). While moving equipment, you could remove any dust that has accumulated under or behind each item or built up inside any components.

29.4.2.3 Recording information

An organisation may have many computer systems, with a variety of peripheral equipment. Software may be installed on a network and/or on specific computer systems according to individual employees' needs.

Keeping track of what equipment is being used by whom is essential. Information such as product keys, the licence number for software and installation dates needs to be recorded.

A stock inventory can be checked periodically to make sure equipment has not been stolen.

29.4.2.4 Data backup

Prior to carrying out any maintenance or troubleshooting activity, it makes sense to take a backup of the system, additional to any that would be done as part of the normal maintenance routines. For more information on backup procedures, see Unit 2 (page 78).

29.4.2.5 Maintaining security and confidentiality of data

While working on a computer system, trying to fix it, you may gain access to sensitive and confidential data. Some of this data may relate to individuals within the organisation, such as their payroll data, and you will be bound by legislation (e.g. the Data Protection Act) not to reveal this data to anyone else. Some data may relate to the organisation, e.g. sales figures, plans for expansion or new product designs, and it is likely that any code of conduct specified by your employer in your contract of employment will refer to the sensitivity of this business data, forbidding you to disclose it to others.

Failure to abide by any Act of Parliament may result in a fine or a term of imprisonment. Failure to honour your employer's code of conduct may result in dismissal through breach of contract.

Activity 29.23

Working practices

1 Suggest ways in which you could obtain permission from a user before starting work on the system. How could you check you were working on the correct equipment?

2 List the checks you would make on arrival at a worksite. Compose an instruction sheet for novice support technicians to use prior to their first visit to a worksite. Test it on others in your group.

3 Make an inventory of the equipment and software on your computer system. If your system were to be stolen or destroyed in a fire, check that you have sufficient information to describe it to the police, to specify it for insurance purposes or to replace it.

4 Prepare a presentation explaining the good working practices that you have adopted. Your audience is a small group of new technical support trainees.

Preparation for assessment

The assessment tasks in this unit are based on the following scenario.

Stoneyside is a large college situated on a split-site campus. The college offers a full range of academic courses, together with vocational courses such as those used in the building trade: plumbing, carpentry and so on. It also offers evening and weekend courses as part of its adult education programme.

Networked computers are provided for staff and student use in a number of locations: all four libraries, the staff common room, in laboratories that serve the Maths and Science departments and many other teaching areas.

The support team at Stoneyside work a shift system so that coverage is available while students attend evening classes or weekend courses.

Task 1 (P1, P2, M3)

Your teacher will present you with three complex IT problems that arise at Stoneyside College. Describe the use of two hardware and two software tools to troubleshoot these IT problems. Troubleshoot the problems and identify suitable remedies. Analyse the appropriateness of at least three hardware and software tools when troubleshooting a given IT problem.

Task 2 (P3, P4)

Your teacher will present you with a complex hardware problem that arises at Stoneyside College. Apply a fault remedy safely to this hardware problem.

Your teacher will present you with a complex software problem that arises at Stoneyside College. Apply a fault remedy to this software problem.

Task 3 (M1, M2)

For an identified hardware fault, such as a disk drive that does not seem to be working, define an appropriate remedy from a range of possible solutions, giving reasons for your choice. Then, for an identified software fault, such as the output from a printer not fitting within a page, define an appropriate remedy, from a range of possible solutions, giving reasons for your choice.

Task 4 (P5, M4, D1, D2)

The principal of Stoneyside College asks you to prepare a presentation to describe how organisational policies can impact on the troubleshooting and repair process, and to explain why good working practices are important. In your speaker's notes, include details of the potential impact of two types of faults on a specific user of the system, on the organisation and on any external customers. Explain how good practices may avoid problems arising at all. Prepare a handout to explain to staff and students, with examples, how appropriate organisational guidelines and procedures can help to minimise the impact of IT faults.

Make sure that your material – the presentation, the notes and the handout – all show that you can communicate effectively with users.

e-Commerce

Introduction

One of the most important developments in business in recent years has been the increasing use of e-commerce. It has revolutionised the marketplace and opened up opportunities never before imagined.

Businesses that do not take advantage of this technology are in danger of being overtaken by their competitors who are trading online. They risk losing customers and profit.

After completing this unit, you should be able to achieve these outcomes:

- Know the effects on society of e-commerce

- Understand the technologies involved in e-commerce

- Understand the security issues in e-commerce and the laws and guidelines that regulate it.

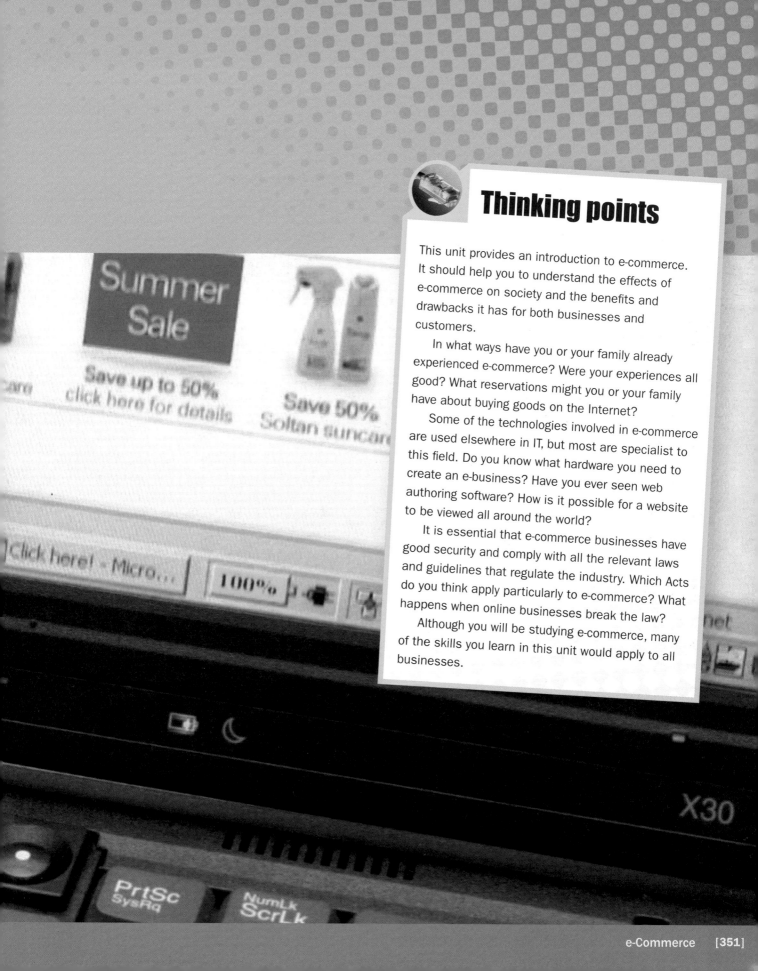

Thinking points

This unit provides an introduction to e-commerce. It should help you to understand the effects of e-commerce on society and the benefits and drawbacks it has for both businesses and customers.

In what ways have you or your family already experienced e-commerce? Were your experiences all good? What reservations might you or your family have about buying goods on the Internet?

Some of the technologies involved in e-commerce are used elsewhere in IT, but most are specialist to this field. Do you know what hardware you need to create an e-business? Have you ever seen web authoring software? How is it possible for a website to be viewed all around the world?

It is essential that e-commerce businesses have good security and comply with all the relevant laws and guidelines that regulate the industry. Which Acts do you think apply particularly to e-commerce? What happens when online businesses break the law?

Although you will be studying e-commerce, many of the skills you learn in this unit would apply to all businesses.

E-commerce is one of the most important developments in business in recent times. It has had a dramatic effect on both commercial industry and society.

This section examines the social implications of e-commerce, the benefits and drawbacks to both business and customers, and the forms that e-commerce can take.

34.1.1 Social implications

E-commerce has several impacts on business, including the need to change business practices and operations so as to take advantage of the benefits of e-commerce. Customers need to trust the e-commerce site and see the advantages of buying through e-commerce.

34.1.1.1 Changing customer perspective

The main issue with e-commerce is the customer's perspective of online trading. Scare stories in the media (see Figure 34.1) warn potential customers about identity theft, items not being delivered and other reasons not to trust buying online.

One of the toughest hurdles that e-commerce businesses have to overcome is to prove that they can be trusted. A site should attract more customers if it promises:

- value – not just offering lower prices than high street stores, but also products that are not available elsewhere
- service – the majority of websites offer a 24-hour delivery time for a small additional cost
- ease – open 24/7 and accessible from home, e-commerce is relatively effortless for the customer; customers may find it is easier to locate products using a website's search facilities rather than searching in a physical store
- security – there are a number of ways to protect customers and websites should ensure that they adopt these to reassure their customers.

Activity 34.1

Customer perspective

1 Conduct a survey with people of different ages. What is their opinion of e-commerce? Do they trust it? Collect relevant data and make notes for future reference.

2 Present your findings graphically to your group, showing any trends that relate to age.

34.1.1.2 Business and society

It is often said that 'the world is getting smaller', and this is mainly due to the advance of technology. Communication is easier and contact can be made to anywhere in the world in seconds. By trading online, businesses open themselves up to the global marketplace. Previously, it might have taken months, even years, to break into foreign or niche markets. E-commerce has allowed instant penetration into all marketplaces.

In contrast, there are challenges raised due to the increase of e-commerce. For example, traditional booksellers are facing huge competition from online booksellers such as Amazon. As pure e-commerce businesses can offer the same products as traditional stores at lower prices, as well as offering other benefits, traditional stores must change their methods of business and advertising to remain competitive and profitable.

With the rise of e-commerce threatening traditional businesses, there is an issue for people who do not have Internet access. More widespread are Internet users who can only use dial-up (56K), as broadband is not available where they live. For these people, e-commerce is not always an effective alternative to traditional shopping. In addition, families on low incomes may not be able to afford to buy a computer or pay a monthly subscription for Internet access or broadband, meaning that they cannot benefit from the lower prices of e-commerce.

◄ **Figure 34.1 Newspaper scare stories about e-commerce**

E-commerce plagued with fraud
Web security breach ignored
Beware of fraud
Internet scams spur charges

Traditional booksellers are facing huge competition from online booksellers

As more businesses begin to trade online, there is an effect on employment opportunities. As traditional stores close, workers cannot gain employment in a similar field. E-commerce favours those with IT training. Additionally, as e-commerce businesses can be run from small locations, shop rent prices may fall due to fewer businesses buying or renting store premises or warehousing. These issues could have a significant effect on the economy.

34.1.1.3 Fast response to economic and social changes

Trading by e-commerce allows businesses to react to changes in the economy and society more quickly than a traditional business.

For example, imagine a competitor is selling more of a certain product so you decide to lower your price for that product. A traditional business would find this time-consuming, especially if it wanted to replicate this action across several products regularly (new price labels for every item in every store, etc.). In comparison, an e-commerce business would merely need to change a figure in a database and the product would be instantly available to customers at the reduced price.

In addition, advertising the new price could be time-consuming and expensive for a traditional business (posters to print, newspaper adverts to update, etc.), whereas an online store could send out an email to all its registered members to advise them instantly of the new, lower price.

34.1.1.4 Bricks and clicks

With the introduction of e-commerce, a range of terminology has evolved to describe the new trading patterns – in particular, to distinguish between traditional retailing and online trading (see Table 34.1).

Activity 34.2

Bricks and clicks

1 Create a mind map for each of these types of business: 'bricks', 'clicks' or 'bricks and clicks'. Write down as many businesses as possible that fit into each category.

2 Examine your three mind maps. What patterns, if any, can you identify?

Bricks	A 'bricks' organisation is one that trades solely using traditional methods. It may have a presence online, perhaps a static website giving the business's contact details, but does not do any business over the Internet.
Bricks and clicks	A 'bricks and clicks' organisation is one that trades using both traditional and online methods. It may have been a 'bricks' organisation originally and developed the business to run online as well, or it may have set up both businesses simultaneously.
Clicks	A 'clicks' organisation is one that trades solely online. It has no physical presence for trading and all business is carried out over the Internet.

Table 34.1 E-commerce terminology

34.1.2 Benefits

This section focuses on the benefits of e-commerce – the drawbacks are considered on page 346.

34.1.2.1 Global marketplace

E-commerce has allowed a global marketplace to develop, in which businesses trading online have access to consumers worldwide. This means that customers now have the opportunity to purchase products from all over the world from the comfort of their own homes. In contrast, traditional stores can only realistically target a local customer base, which is limited to the location of the business premises. If a traditional business wants to attract customers from further afield, it needs to set up another store in that region.

34.1.2.2 24/7 trading

Worldwide trading online means that there is no store needing to be staffed and trading can be carried out at any time, day or night, in all different time zones around the world. Unlike a traditional business, there are no closing times. Because websites can be automated, no staff are required to make sales. All orders and money transactions can be taken and acknowledged automatically.

34.1.2.3 Start-up and running costs

Setting up and maintaining a traditional store involves buying or renting a location, purchasing stock, hiring staff and paying utility costs such as electricity and water. For a brand new business, these costs have to be paid upfront, before any profit has been made, and this means that the start-up costs are high.

An online store does not have such high initial costs. There might be no premises to purchase and generally there will be fewer staff; sometimes only one person runs the whole business. A growing e-commerce business may choose to move to larger premises and employ more staff, but usually not to the extent of a traditional business.

To compare two businesses in the same field of retail (see Table 34.2), the online bookseller Amazon may employ more staff but its turnover is significantly higher than that of the traditional store Waterstones. Waterstones is paying a higher proportion of its revenue to its employees than Amazon, which results in Amazon enjoying considerably higher profitability.

34.1.2.4 Competitive edge

If there are two businesses, equal in all aspects except that one trades online and the other does not, the online business may be more successful, as it has the competitive edge by giving customers more flexibility to purchase.

Amazon	Waterstones
Purely online store	More than 300 stores
12,000 full- and part-time staff	4,500 booksellers
Net annual sales: £4.3 billion	Net annual sales: £414 million
Sources: www.amazon.com and www.waterstones.com – all figures based on financial year 2005–2006	

Table 34.2 Comparison of an online and a traditional business

34.1.2.5 Search facilities

In a traditional large store, if you want to find a product, you might need to search the aisles or ask a shop assistant. No matter how large an e-commerce store is, if it provides a search facility (which most do), it should take just seconds to find the product you want. This is a huge benefit to customers who are shopping online for convenience and speed.

34.1.2.6 Pricing opportunities

For 'bricks and clicks' businesses, generally, there is a price difference between the traditional stores and the online store. There may be online discounts to encourage shoppers to move to that method of purchasing.

Also, online stores can take advantage of **fluid pricing**, which is much more difficult in traditional stores.

For example, when selling airline flight tickets, as more are sold and fewer are available, the tickets could become more expensive as the demand rises. This could make more profit for the business. Alternatively, when selling products such as holidays, as the time draws closer, the price can be reduced to ensure that all places are sold. This can benefit the business as, although they may not earn as much as desired, they are only losing a proportion of the cost of each place, rather than the full cost if it were not sold at all. E-commerce businesses generally have more freedom with pricing as they have lower overheads than traditional businesses.

34.1.2.7 Gathering customer information

Information is the cornerstone of all businesses and learning about the customers can be key to increasing profit. It is difficult to gather information about customers who shop in traditional stores. One method is to use loyalty cards – these allow the business to track what is being purchased by an individual customer.

When shopping online, customers need to register as members to purchase products or services. Businesses can find out a lot about their customers and tailor their services to suit (see Figure 34.2). For example, when someone wants to purchase from Amazon, as soon as he/she logs in he/she is greeted with a personalised message and a list of products he/she might like to buy based on previous purchases.

34.1.2.8 Alternative income sources

Once a business has an e-commerce facility, additional sources of income become available to it. For example, an e-commerce site could have **pay-per-click advertising**. This may navigate the customer away from the site but each click on the advert would still gain money for the business (see the section on banners and pop-ups, page 371).

What does it mean?

Fluid pricing involves increasing or decreasing prices quickly depending on circumstances.

Pay-per-click advertising is where a website hosts an advert and benefits by earning money every time a user clicks the advert.

STOP Test your knowledge

1 Explain these terms: global marketplace, 24/7 trading, competitive edge, fluid pricing, loyalty card, pay-per-click advertising.

2 Give five examples of the benefits of shopping online.

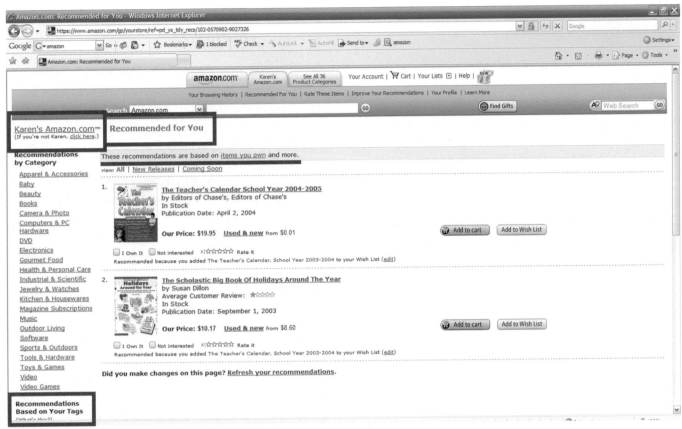

▲ Figure 34.2 A personalised web page from Amazon

34.1.3 Drawbacks

Although e-commerce is a tremendous opportunity for businesses, there are also downsides which need to be explored.

34.1.3.1 Consumer trust

The most difficult issue that online businesses face is customer confidence.

34.1.3.2 Lack of human contact

Some customers are deterred from purchasing online because they cannot speak to anyone from the business. They find this impersonal and prefer instead to shop in traditional stores.

Customers are also wary of buying clothes online because they are unable to try them on before they buy.

34.1.3.3 Delivery issues

When going to a traditional shop, customers have the option to take their purchases home immediately. When shopping online, they have to wait until the purchases are delivered.

34.1.3.4 International legislation

When selling online, businesses are not just subject to legislation in the country of origin, but also to the laws in the countries where the customers live.

Legislation for e-commerce is a very complex area, one that is still being defined. For example, in the UK, you have to be 18 to buy alcohol, but in the United States you must be over 21 in all states. However, it would be quite possible for a business based in the UK to sell a case of wine over the Internet to a customer aged 18 in the United States. Which law should be followed, UK or US?

Case study

Consumer trust

Mrs Jones has heard reports in the news about identity theft and has never purchased items online before. She does not believe suppliers will keep her financial details private or deliver the products requested so she will not purchase from them. She has also heard that e-commerce sites will personalise her online experience, for example, making suggestions of products she may like based on what she has previously purchased. She has had a similar experience of this with store loyalty cards and finds it annoying.

1 Research the Internet to find out which stores offer loyalty cards. Conduct a survey to find out what people think about these loyalty card schemes. Present your findings to others in your group.

2 Conduct a survey of people who buy through sites such as Amazon. How do they feel about the personalisation of the site, based on information gleaned about them?

Case study

Delivery issues

Mr Mahmood has never shopped online. He worries about the cost of postage and packaging and whether the goods will be delivered on time or even at all.

1 What reassurance can you offer Mr Mahmood that his worries are unfounded?

2 If Mr Mahmood does make a purchase online and the goods do not turn up, what can he do?

Activity 34.3

Legislation

1 Research the Internet to find out what laws exist regarding the sale of alcohol to minors in a number of countries. At what age does a person reach majority in these countries? Present your findings as a table.

2 Choose another product for which you think there may be legislation affecting its sale or movement between countries. Research the Internet to find out what legislation exists in the UK and one other country.

34.1.3.5 Product description problems

Some customers worry that what is described on the e-commerce site might not accurately reflect the real product. This is especially difficult for colours, as different computer systems may display colours slightly differently. The quality of the original picture of the product shown on the website is another factor. E-commerce sites can exaggerate their descriptions of products, which may put some people off buying online.

34.1.3.6 Security issues

Perhaps the biggest worry for customers is that their financial details will not be safe: that the business will use them in some unauthorised way or security may be insufficient, resulting in their identity being stolen by criminals (see the section on identity theft – page 377).

Test your knowledge

1 List five drawbacks mentioned by consumers as reasons for not using the Internet to buy products.

2 Name two products for which sale over the Internet could be problematic, depending on where the vendor and/or purchaser live.

34.1.4 E-commerce entities

There are several types of e-commerce entities: manufacturers and retailers, including organisations set up just to trade on the Internet called e-tailers. Some e-commerce sites are consumer-led or primarily offer information or a service, e.g. financial services. A variety of types are considered here.

34.1.4.1 E-tailers

E-tailers are businesses that source products from suppliers and sell them purely online, such as Amazon and ebuyer. Some of these organisations wouldn't have existed without e-commerce. There is a minimal need for warehousing if orders are shipped directly from the supplier to the customer, with the website providing an intermediary service. This is one of several reasons why overheads can be lower. However, as prices must be relentlessly competitive, profit margins can be low. Therefore these businesses must operate at maximum cost-effectiveness. Another reason for lower overheads is that e-tailers do not need shop space, therefore reducing costs of lighting, heating and other utilities. They often employ fewer staff, resulting in lower salary costs.

A relatively recent development in online selling has been the inclusion of second-hand products. For example, Amazon provides both new and used books, games and other goods. This development has been encouraged by eBay, which specialises in customers using the website to sell their own items.

Case study

Amazon

Amazon, originally called Cadabra, was launched by Jeff Bezos in 1995. It was set up during the dotcom boom of the 1990s with an unusual business model – it did not expect to make a profit until after at least four years of business. While other dotcom businesses grew rapidly, Amazon slowly built strong foundations. Finally, at the end of its fourth year, it made a $2.5 million profit. In 2005, it made a profit of $359 million and in 2006, $190 million.

Amazon's most famous for selling books, but the company also sells a wide range of products from CDs to small kitchen appliances such as coffee machines. Sales in books from traditional stores have reduced recently and Amazon has often been blamed for 'stealing' their sales.

Amazon provides an enhanced experience for its customers. For example, when a customer logs in they see a personalised page with suggestions of products they might like. Amazon does not just provide the products, but includes customer reviews, detailed product descriptions and other information to help customers to select the right product for them.

There are facilities to create a wish list and a wedding list: customers create a list of products that they would like and pass this on to family and friends to let them know what to buy for a wedding gift or other occasion such as a birthday.

For more information, visit the Amazon site, especially the About Amazon and Help sections. A link to this website is available at www.heinemann.co.uk/hotlinks. Enter the express code 2315P.

1 Describe Amazon as an e-commerce entity. **p₂** (partial evidence)

2 Why has Amazon become a very successful business? How has the company gained and retained its customers' loyalty? **p₁**

3 How have the lower start-up and running costs of e-commerce affected Amazon? **p₁**

4 Describe the impact Amazon has had on traditional book stores. **p₁**

5 To what extent do you think it is Amazon's responsibility to consider traditional book stores? **p₁**

6 What other factors could explain the decline in book sales?

34.1.4.2 Manufacturers

Some businesses manufacture products themselves and sell them purely online, such as Dell. It is not possible to purchase a Dell computer from a traditional shop such as PC World. However, they do have physical offices in Bracknell, Berkshire, employing over 1500 staff and running a huge call centre. Manufacturers also buy through e-commerce as well as sell. Dell publishes a newsletter which is posted out to all existing customers in the hope that they may upgrade. Dell also uses direct marketing online by emailing adverts at least once a week to existing customers.

Manufacturers like Dell can afford to sell their products at lower prices and have more dramatic special offers because they do not need to pay for retail premises or for as many sales staff to sell the products. They can also provide a much more personalised product, because the computer systems can be made on demand. For example, when purchasing a Dell computer (see Figure 34.3), customers select every component from a range. This means they receive a more precise product to fulfil their requirements. As they are making choices for the product,

a running total is calculated so the customers are always aware of how their decisions are affecting the total price. At any point during the selection process, the order can be cancelled or restarted. Once all selections are made and the product is completely chosen, the customer can then click to process the order and pay online.

34.1.4.3 Existing retailers

Some businesses that exist already in the traditional marketplace with branches all over the country have now converted to selling online as well. This 'bricks and clicks' approach can allow companies to enjoy the best of both worlds. However, it is an expensive process as the business has to be able to keep financing the traditional store and also pay for the initial outlay and maintenance of the new online business. If done proficiently, the profit from the e-commerce branch of the business should offset the costs and therefore the business's profits should increase.

Moving from 'bricks' to 'bricks and clicks' can often only be done by larger, more stable businesses as it can be too risky a strategy for many smaller businesses. However,

▼ **Figure 34.3 Dell purchasing screen halfway through the process**

some small businesses do manage to make the transition from purely traditional to combining traditional and online successfully, usually if they have a unique product for a **niche market**. An example is New Zealand Nature Company, which specialises in silk and sheepskin products and sells worldwide and focuses on a target market of sailors and people who take part in outdoor activities.

What does it mean?

A **niche market** is a small, specialised section of the buying public that is likely to be interested in a certain type of product or service.

34.1.4.4 Consumer-led e-commerce entities

One interesting development of the Internet is the emergence of consumer-led sites, such as eBay, where the public can buy and sell their own items through an auctioning system.

34.1.4.5 Informative e-commerce entities

Many sites provide a wealth of information and, although there are opportunities to make a purchase, this is not in the forefront of the minds of most visitors to these sites. Many travel sites offer tickets, but to support this they also provide details of services and

Case study

Tesco

Tesco is a UK-based international supermarket chain – the core retail area is groceries but Tesco has expanded into other retail areas such as clothing and household goods, as well as finance, insurance and telecommunications. It is the largest retailer in the UK and the third largest worldwide.

Tesco was founded in 1919 at the end of World War I by Jack Cohen, who operated as a one-man trader in London's East End. At that time, food was scarce and Jack bought damaged goods from other businesses and resold them – he learnt the skill of knowing what was in a tin by just shaking it. The first Tesco store was opened in 1929 in Edgeware, London. From these small beginnings, Tesco has gone from strength to strength, with an annual profit of over £3 billion in 2006.

Tesco took advantage of new technology very quickly and began trading on the Internet in 1994. In 2003, Tesco's Chief Executive Officer, John Browett, received an award for the innovative systems which supported Tesco's e-commerce site.

When purchasing online, customers select the products and quantities they want and are given a running total so they know exactly what they will pay, although discounts are only taken off the final bill. Then,

a two-hour delivery slot can be booked. The information is sent to the most local store where, on the appropriate day and time, the products are packed and delivered to the customer's house. If any products could not be included in the delivery, a substitute may be included or an apology will be made at the door. The customer signs to confirm they have received their goods.

As Tesco moves into more areas and becomes a bigger organisation, it has been criticised for trying to create a monopoly (which means it would become the only business providing these products).

For more information visit the Tesco website, especially the Talking Tesco section. A link to this website has been made available at www.heinemann.co.uk/hotlinks. Enter the express code 2315P.

1 Describe Tesco as an e-commerce entity. **p**₂ (partial evidence)

2 How has Tesco managed the transition from 'bricks' to 'bricks and clicks'? **p**₁ **d**₁

3 How has Tesco taken advantage of 24/7 global trading on the Internet? **p**₁

4 Describe the impact Tesco has had on retailing in the UK. **p**₁ **d**₁

Case study

eBay

eBay is an online marketplace which allows users to buy and sell items from each other. It was founded in 1995 when Pierre Omidyar's fiancée (now wife) was having trouble finding people she could trade with for her Pez sweet dispenser collection. He invented the idea of eBay as the solution to her problem and the business has grown exponentially ever since. Recently, it reached the three million listings landmark, which means there are always more than three million items available on eBay. There are more than 10 million registered users and more than 40 per cent of all Internet users in the UK visit eBay. eBay's annual profit was $1.13 billion in 2006.

Because eBay relies on the public to sell and buy products, it has had to put a number of measures in place to ensure that transactions are carried out correctly. For example, the feedback system allows buyers and sellers to leave feedback about each other. This means that if someone does not carry out a transaction properly, the person they were dealing with can let other eBay users know.

A recent issue involved sellers who said they were advertising Xbox 360 Consoles, but the small print stated that they were just selling the console box. Some of these scams were selling for over £300. There have also been instances of sellers buying concert tickets, waiting until the concert was sold out, then reselling the tickets on eBay at an inflated price.

For more information visit the eBay website, particularly The Company section. A link to this website has been made available at www.heinemann.co.uk/hotlinks. Enter the express code 2315P.

1 Describe eBay as an e-commerce entity. **p₂**

2 In what way is eBay different from other e-commerce businesses? **p₂**

3 Can you think of any offline companies that compare with eBay? In what ways do they compare?

4 What social impact has eBay had on the public? **p₁**

5 Which benefits of e-commerce has eBay taken advantage of? **p₁**

6 What effect could unscrupulous sellers or buyers have on the other users of eBay?

---

may offer to help the visitor to plan a journey. For example, the National Rail Enquiries website mainly provides information to train travellers, but also allows them to purchase train tickets.

Many organisations, such as the BBC and the daily newspapers, have websites that are a rich source of information on current affairs, as well as providing learning opportunities and the option to buy products.

The *Daily Telegraph*, for example, ran a series of articles on novel writing and provided a message board for interested people to post their comments and their answers to writing exercises set in the weekly articles. A business aim of this project was to use the Internet to increase sales of the newspaper.

Links to the websites mentioned in this section have been made available at www.heinemann.co.uk/hotlinks. Enter the express code 2315P.

34.1.4.6 Service providers

Not all organisations have a product that can be sent to you through the post. Some, such as easyJet and Lastminute.com, provide a service rather than selling a product. Both specialise in the leisure and transport industry: easyJet provides low-cost air travel and Lastminute.com specialises in selling services at very short notice, for example, flights and holidays close to the time of departure.

Links to the websites mentioned in this section have been made available at www.heinemann.co.uk/hotlinks. Enter the express code 2315P.

Some service providers focus on financial services online. For example, Esure sells insurance, and Egg is a purely online bank.

Online banking is an area which has had a huge hurdle to surmount – trust is much more of an issue with a service such as a bank than a retail business. Egg and Smile have become increasingly popular as alternatives to traditional banking companies (although, at the time of writing, they are backed by established companies: Prudential and the Co-operative Bank respectively). Online banking services are able to offer especially competitive rates due to the lower overheads and running costs.

Insurance is another service that can be sold online and a new business has developed from this: searching a number of businesses for the best deal, such as Confused.com. To use this service, a customer inputs their details for the type of insurance they want and Confused.com searches all registered insurance brokers for the best quote on those specific details. This service is free for customers to use and a number of companies have signed up to be part of it, with the hope that it will increase the number of people applying to buy insurance from them.

Links to the websites mentioned in this section have been made available at www.heinemann.co.uk/hotlinks. Enter the express code 2315P.

STOP Test your knowledge

1   Explain the term niche market.

2   Name six advantages for businesses of using e-commerce.

3   Name four disadvantages for customers of using e-commerce.

4   For each type of e-commerce entity, give an example of a business that has not already been mentioned.

34.2 The technologies of e-commerce

The advent of e-commerce in business was made possible by the introduction of technology such as the Internet and credit cards, and this technology continues to improve. Using a combination of web hardware and software, e-commerce not only gives more functionality to a business but also improves effectiveness. In addition, now that a great number of customers have access to high speed Internet connections, such as broadband, it is even more important that e-commerce is efficient. If a site is slow, a customer is likely to choose to shop elsewhere.

What does it mean?

A **web server** is a server that distributes web pages on to the Internet.

34.2.1 Hardware and software

As with all computer systems, e-commerce consists of a collaboration of hardware and software (see Figure 34.4). The software of both the web developer and the user need to be considered.

34.2.1.1 Web servers

A **web server** holds the live copy of the web page which can be seen by anyone who has access to the Internet.

Figure 34.4 How the Internet is connected together

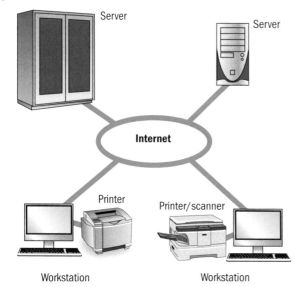

34.2.1.2 **Browsers**

Figure 34.5 Some different browsers: Internet Explorer, Mozilla Firefox

Browsers are installed on a user's computer and convert the data received via the modem into a visual web page.

There are several types of browser available (see Figure 34.5). For Microsoft Windows, the most common is Microsoft Internet Explorer which comes free with the operating system. Others that are becoming more popular are Mozilla Firefox and Opera. The most popular for Apple Macintosh is Konqueror.

When a user first loads a browser, they will be taken to the home page that is set in their browser options. This setting can be changed so a browser automatically opens on your chosen website. This could be the main page of your ISP, a search engine such as Google or, for a business, the organisation's home page.

Browsers store viewed web pages in a **cache** so they can be reloaded quickly if viewed again. This allows you to

What does it mean?

A **browser** is the software that allows the user to view the web page.

A **cache** is a store on a computer hard drive of all the web resources visited by a user. If the user accesses a cached page which has not been updated since the last download, the cached version will be displayed.

view previous pages using the Back button. When you are viewing previous pages, browsers also give an option to reload pages using the Forward button. In addition, they provide a History list of frequently and recently visited sites to allow you to return to them quickly.

Most browsers have a Favourites or Bookmarks list – these are sites that the user has chosen to add to the list, either websites that they access frequently or ones they know they will want to return to in the future. At any time, the user can access this list and select a website. A target of web design is to encourage users to bookmark the site, which usually means they will visit again, hopefully regularly.

By using a cache and the Favourites or Bookmarks list, the user can access sites with a single click.

Browsers provide a visual interpretation of HTML and other web languages. HTML is the generic language in which all web pages are written and understood by all browsers. Web pages are linked together by hyperlinks, which can be presented as menus, buttons or images.

Hyperlinks direct the browser to load a different page, allowing a user to move around the massive selection of web pages on the Internet.

34.2.1.3 Server software

There are several web server software applications, such as Internet Information Services (IIS), which comes bundled with modern versions of the Windows operating system, and Apache HTTP Server. In addition, there is software which makes uploading web pages to the web server easier. This process is called FTP, as it uses the file transfer protocol (FTP). Programs such as CuteFTP are designed to make uploading more user friendly.

34.2.1.4 Web authoring tools

Web authoring tools make it possible for more people to create web pages because they simplify the process and make it less technical. This means that creating and uploading websites on to the Internet is no longer solely the territory of IT experts. There has recently been much debate as to whether this has helped or hindered the Internet, as the quality of content on the Internet has come into question. Suggestions have been made to 'clean up' the Internet, although how that would be carried out is a very difficult question. One response has been to begin to develop Web 2.0, also known as www2. This is a 'new' Internet which has the aim of sharing resources and promoting online collaboration between users.

Activity 34.4

Web 2.0

1 Research Web 2.0 and make notes.

2 Using your research and your own opinion, explain whether you think the Internet needs cleaning up.

All web authoring tools provide the basic facilities to create a web page and upload it to a web server. Microsoft FrontPage, which is part of the Microsoft Office suite, is a good beginner design tool. However, the current industry standard is Adobe Dreamweaver. This is because it has a huge range of tools for web design and includes additional features such as templates, CSS and Flash animations. Although it is more difficult to learn, it gives a wider scope for building sophisticated websites.

34.2.1.5 Database systems

E-commerce websites usually have a database back-end storing the catalogue of products, customer records and other business information. This database should link to the website seamlessly so that the user is unaware of it.

Some organisations outsource the creation of their website but retain control of the content of the database. This means that if any changes need to be made, such as price changes, only the database needs amending and the organisation can do this themselves.

Applications such as Oracle or languages such as **MySQL** can be used to create the database.

34.2.1.6 Programming requirements

Web pages are written in **HTML**.

Within the HTML code, other languages can be used, including **PHP**, **ASP**, **JavaScript** and others which add functionality. HTML itself does not provide e-commerce capabilities, so another language must always be used as well.

What does it mean?

MySQL is a language for creating online databases. It uses an SQL base, which is the language behind most databases.

HTML stands for HyperText Markup Language. All web pages are controlled and structured using HTML, even if they use other languages as well.

In very basic terms, **JavaScript** provides interactivity between the computer and the user.

ASP and **PHP** allow web pages to connect with databases and online payment systems.

HTML uses a system of tags (indicated by angle brackets: < and >) which contain the instructions. Almost all tags use a pair of open and close tags enclosing the content to be affected. For example: <font color='red'>Some text</font> would produce: Some text. Note that American spelling is used in HTML.

HTML pages should start and end with <html> </html> tags to declare the language being used. Each page is divided into a head and body section, each defined by their tags. The head section is unseen by the user and can be thought of as the brains of the page. It contains all the information for the page to function correctly. The body is the part seen by the user and contains all the content of the page. A well designed page should have reusable code in the head and minimal code in the body.

■ HOW TO CREATE A SIMPLE HTML WEBPAGE

1 Open Notepad (or a similar text editor).
2 Enter this code:
```
<html>
<head>
<title>My First Webpage</title>
<bgcolour='white'>
</head>
<body>
<font color='blue'></b>Hello World!</b></font>
<font color=#000000><i>This is my first ever web
page.</i></font>
</body>
</html>
```
3 Click File / Save As.
4 Delete the File name and type **mywebpage.html.**
5 Navigate to where the file is saved using My Computer. Notice how the file icon relates to your browser.
6 Double click your file. It should open in your browser.

The computer acting as the web server needs a large storage area for all the database records, images and other items of the website. The data to be stored is **dynamic** and, if the business is a success, it is likely to grow exponentially.

Activity 34.5

Reading HTML

1 In a browser, open a website which you are familiar with: for example, your school or college website. View the HTML (e.g. in Internet Explorer click View / Source). Examine the code and compare with the visual version in the browser. Make notes.
2 Write down all the tags you recognise and what effect they have on the display of items on the web page when seen in the browser.

It should not be assumed that all users will browse the Internet on a standard PC or laptop. Mobile Internet browsing is also available through technology such as mobile phones using **WAP**. This needs to be taken into account when designing a website. The phone screen is at a much reduced size and is still monochrome on a good proportion of phones, although colour displays are becoming more popular. Due to the WAP interpreting code differently to HTTP, as on computer-accessed web pages, websites need to be written in or dynamically converted to **WML**. Also, not all software will run on all computer systems.

What does it mean?

A **static** website is one with no interactivity and is usually just a presentation of information.

A **dynamic** website can involve any level of interactivity from a simple feedback form to a database which personalises the website for each individual visitor.

WAP stands for Wireless Application Protocol.

WML stands for Wireless Markup Language.

A variety of download speeds are available and a business should never assume that all customers will have the same connection available (see Table 34.3). Internet connection speed is measured in kilobits per

Connection type	Speed
Dial-up (v.92)	56 Kbps
ISDN	60–100 Kbps
DSL/Cable (broadband)	500+ Kbps
Network T-1	1500 Kbps
Network T-2	2000 Kbps
Source: www.mcaffee.com	

Table 34.3 Connection speeds

These days, Internet browsing is available through mobile phones

second (**Kbps**). A kilobit is 1000 bits. This is different to the binary measurement of a kilobyte which is 1024 bits.

There are several ways of minimising the download times of a website. Images are essential to create interest on a web page, but downloading images takes much more time than downloading text. Using smaller image files can be a way of minimising download times. To do this, images should be compressed and conform to the websafe palette. Use the ALT function so that while the image is downloading the user knows what to expect. Text only options need also to work without the images, so great care is needed in designing pages.

Animation can bring a web page to life and demonstrate a product which might help the visitor decide to buy, but uses up a lot of bandwidth (data transmission rates), so animations should be used sparingly.

Tables of information might be the best way to summarise information. However, these also take longer to download, so it makes sense not to include very large tables.

34.2.1.10 Browser and platform compatibility

There are several web browsers available and each renders graphics on a website differently (see Figure 34.6). This is to do with the way the browser interprets the code and must be taken into consideration when designing a website.

In addition, the different computer platforms that users might have should be considered: not just the latest platforms but also older ones that are still being used, such as earlier versions of Internet Explorer and Netscape Navigator. Web developers should design to meet the lowest specifications available, otherwise potential customers may be excluded from purchasing products and so the business will lose potential profit.

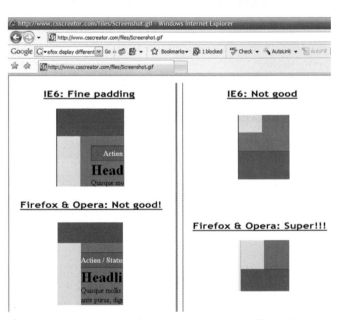

Figure 34.6 The same web page can look different in different browsers

Test your knowledge

1 Explain these terms: web server, browser, cache, IIS, FTP, WWW2, MySQL, HTML.
2 Give three examples of browsers.
3 Explain how to spot a tag. What might it do? Give two examples.
4 How is a dynamic website different from a static website?
5 What is meant by portability?
6 Explain these terms: WAP, WML, Kbps.

34.2.2 Networking

This section focuses on the methods used to connect computers together to create the network. It looks at how individual computers are identified so data can be sent to the correct place, the methods of data transfer across such a massive network and the naming of websites.

34.2.2.1 TCP/IP addresses, ports and protocols

TCP/IP is a **protocol** that is used when transferring data across a network.

If computers do not use the same protocol, it becomes impossible for them to understand the data transmitted between them. This is similar to humans who speak different languages – unless they agree to speak a common language, they will not be able to understand each other.

To make sure the data reaches the right location on a network, each computer is given a unique number, called an **IP** address. It is a set of four numbers, each from 0 to 255. For example, 145.2.78.255 would address a specific computer on a network. The Internet is a large global network and works in the same way as a **WAN (wide area network)**.

What does it mean?

TCP (transmission control protocol) is used for the transfer of data which is correction-orientated and must be sent in a reliable system.

A **protocol** is an agreed way of working, also known as a 'handshake'. If the two computers transmitting data to each other are using the same protocol, the transfer will work.

IP stands for **Internet protocol**.

A **WAN (wide area network)** is a large network, usually covering more than one geographical location and often crossing countries and continents.

The term **resolves** is used when referring to IP addresses changing into domain names.

HTTP stands for Hypertext Transfer Protocol.

WWW stands for World Wide Web.

Ports connect protocols and IP addresses together. Each computer has several ports for data to pass through; they are virtual so they cannot be seen. Ports are like doors: each has a number to identify it and it can be open or closed. There are some default ports; for example, port 25 is usually for email and port 80 is usually for the Internet, although these can be changed. For a web server, it is good practice to close all ports that are not being used; otherwise, hackers can take advantage of open ports to get into the system.

34.2.2.2 Domain names

Every website has an IP address, relating to the server which hosts it. For example, if you were to type 72.14.207.99 into the address bar of a browser, the page for www.google.com should appear. Smaller sites will always use the same IP address. However, large sites like Google have several, because they have many web servers.

Businesses would struggle to entice many customers to their e-commerce sites if the customers had to remember the IP address, so domain names were invented. Each IP address **resolves** to a domain name e.g. 72.14.207.99 resolves to google.com. A domain name is only the core part of the name (google) and the extension (.com).

HTTP and **WWW** are protocols which tell the computer that the data is a web page. This makes sure that the computer interprets the data in the right way.

There are several extensions available (see Figure 34.7).

Each website can be contacted by its universal resource locator (URL) (see Figure 34.8). For example, if www.google.com is entered into the address bar in a browser, Google's website should open at its home page. A URL is any website address, e.g. www.google.com/about/contact/ would also be a URL. However, the domain name is still just google.com.

To make sure they maximise traffic to their sites, businesses usually not only buy the URL they want to use as the main address, e.g. www.google.com, but also other extensions, e.g. www.google.co.uk and www.google.org, and alternative spellings, e.g. www.gogle.com and ww.google.com.

Partial DNS Hierarchy

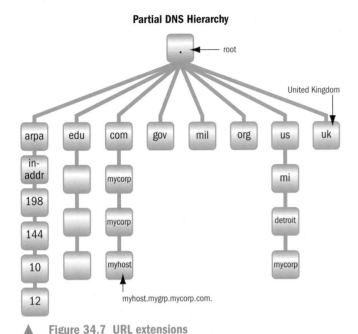

myhost.mygrp.mycorp.com.

▲ Figure 34.7 URL extensions

| protocol | subdomain | domain | extension | page |

▲ Figure 34.8 URL sections

STOP

Test your knowledge

1 What is TCP/IP?

2 Explain these terms: protocol, WAN, HTTP, WWW, URL.

34.2.3 Payment systems

In the early days of e-commerce, online transactions were not possible. Customers could pay by a cheque sent in the post, but this could mean a long delay – waiting for the cheque to be delivered and then to be cleared by the banks before the goods would be dispatched. The other method was credit card, but this would involve either telephoning or emailing the credit card details. Customers were worried about sending their financial details by email, especially as security was not as good then as it is now. Credit card details would be split over several emails, but if one was not received or was in the wrong order, the payment would not go through.

Nowadays, there are several instantaneous payment systems available. Improved technology, such as SSL and HTTPS (see page 377), has also allowed websites to provide better security to reassure customers.

Electronic cheques work in a similar way to paper cheques, although they are instigated digitally. The customer asks their bank to make a payment to a creditor or vendor and the bank can either pay this immediately, if they can accept electronic payment, or produce a paper cheque for the company if they cannot.

When taking payment from a credit card, businesses are protected because the bank will provide the money and invoice the customer. So, the business will always be paid from this type of transaction, whether or not the customer can pay his/her credit card bill. However, as e-commerce becomes more popular and there are more potential customers, businesses have to accept more payment methods, such as debit cards, as not everyone has a credit card. It must be remembered that this is an area where some customers are worried about the safety of their personal financial details and the possibility of someone else being able to access their account and steal their money.

There has recently been an upsurge in digital methods of payment. PayPal is currently the most popular. A user 'uploads' money into the PayPal account from a bank

Payment by credit card protects business financially

Activity 34.6

Payment methods

1 Look at several e-commerce sites. What payment methods does each take? Present your findings in a table.

2 Is there a correlation between the size or type of a website and the amount of payment methods it takes? Make notes for future reference. Present your findings graphically.

account using a digital transfer. That money can then be used to make a safe, instant payment. A number of customers feel happier using this method, as they are not inputting their bank card details into a variety of websites, just the PayPal site. Another similar method available in the UK is NoChex. However, unlike PayPal, NoChex only accepts bank accounts with debit cards.

When making payments online, several details from a card are necessary, including the CV2 security number from the back, which was originally introduced just for e-commerce transactions.

Splash Plastic was devised by PrePay Technologies Ltd, a UK company. This card can be 'loaded' with money at shops such as the Co-op, Post Offices or straight from a bank account. It can then be used instead of a credit or debit card to make online purchases. As this payment method became more popular, in March 2006 a new card was introduced called 360money Splash Plastic. This new card has the Maestro symbol, which means it is accepted in more places. It is available for people aged ten and older (parental consent is needed for under-fourteens) and it can be loaded with a maximum of £1000.

STOP Test your knowledge

1 Give three examples of how you might pay for goods on the Internet.

2 What is a CV2 number? What is its purpose?

34.2.4 Promotion

A business which uses e-commerce to trade online must also advertise. Several traditional methods can be used, such as billboards, television adverts and direct mailshots. However, the Internet provides its own advertising opportunities.

34.2.4.1 Effective use of search engines

If you wanted to find something on the Internet, how would you do it? If you did not know the address of the website, your first thought might be to use a search engine such as Google, AskJeeves or Yahoo. Because of this, e-commerce businesses want to be listed as highly as possible on the search engine results page so that they are one of the first addresses that users see when doing a search (see Figure 34.9).

When a search engine carries out a search on the word(s) keyed in, it does not literally search the whole Internet. Instead, enormous databases are used to store information about all the websites of which the search engine is already aware and it is this database that is searched. To build up and maintain this database, search engines use **spiders** to trawl the Internet.

The spiders examine each web page encountered and send information back to be stored in the database. To ensure these spiders list the web page correctly, the web developer can include **meta tags** in the coding for the web page. These can include a description and/or keywords for the web page. For example:

<meta name='description' content='Board No More – board games from around the world'>
<meta name='keywords' content='board games, dice, Cluedo, Monopoly, chess'>

What does it mean?

A **spider** is a bot (a program that runs on a computer 24/7, automating mundane tasks for the user) which examines websites on behalf of search engines.

Meta tags are words that are put into the HTML code of the web page but are not displayed on the screen.

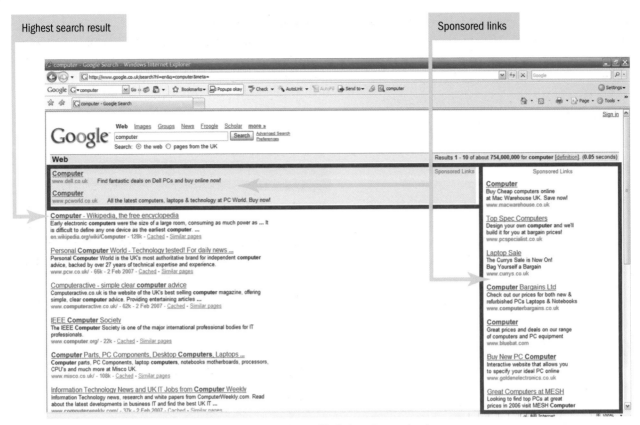

Highest search result

Sponsored links

Figure 34.9 Companies that appear top in a search are likely to get more business

If meta tags are not present, the spiders will read the content of the page and make a best guess as to what it is about. This can result in the page being listed very low in searches, so it is important the meta tags are effective.

With the huge increase of the number of web pages, however, it is no longer sufficient to rely on meta tags. Businesses often pay a search engine to ensure they are listed highly in a related search. These are called sponsored links (see Figure 34.9).

Activity 34.7

Search engines

1 Choose one type of business, e.g. businesses that sell computer hardware. Using a search engine, identify businesses that have paid for sponsored links and those that have managed to obtain high listing positions in searches. Make notes for future reference.

34.2.4.2 Newsgroups and forums

Newsgroups normally use Usenet, a distributed bulletin board system. Newsgroups are separated into very specific topics and there is one for practically every subject. Generally they are text-based only.

Forums are mostly attached to websites and discuss the topic of the site. For example, IMDb (The Internet Movie Database) is a website about films and has a large forum where users can discuss each individual film on the website.

What does it mean?

Newsgroups are a method of posting messages to other Internet users.

Forums are web pages where users can post messages to other users.

Typically, forums are not just text-based. They also allow for graphics, including **avatars** and signatures.

Because they are usually used by people with a particular interest, newsgroups and forums can be used to advertise to specifically targeted groups of people. For example, a website selling computer games may advertise on a gaming forum.

What does it mean?

An **avatar** is an image used to represent a user online. This could be an image of him/herself, something that interests him/her or something completely random.

34.2.4.3 Banners and pop-ups

With pay-per-click advertising, adverts designed by a business are put on to other websites. The host website benefits by earning money every time a user clicks the advert, e.g. £0.02 per click. 100,000 clicks per week would earn £2000 for having the advert on the site. This may seem like a huge number of clicks but it is a very tempting opportunity for a lot of websites. The pay-per-click adverts are often banners, either across the top of the website or in sidebars (see Figure 34.10).

Pop-up adverts open in a new browser window and can be irritating for the user.

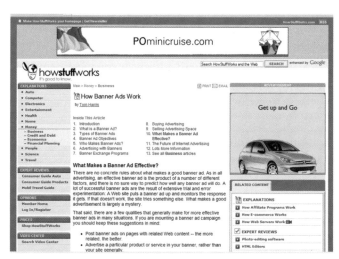

▲ **Figure 34.10 Examples of banner adverts online**

Recently, there has been a rise in centre-screen Flash adverts – the animation activates as soon as the website loads. Often, these will be designed to blend in with the host site and, due to the time and expense of creating them, are usually only used by large businesses.

34.2.4.4 Spam

Spam is the Internet equivalent of a direct mailshot. A business can use its own registered customer list (or buy a mailshot list) and then send an advert out in an email to all the people on the list. In this way the business targets their message straight to the customer. However, there are also disreputable people using spam and now it is seen as a nuisance that email users unfortunately have to accept as an Internet hazard.

What does it mean?

Spam is the term used for junk email.

Spam has also been used to send unsavoury adverts and attached viruses. A number of email services, such as Hotmail and Gmail, have spam filters which are designed to stop these types of emails reaching the user's inbox. Some businesses have set up filters so that spam is immediately deleted as soon as it arrives in the email server, so their employees are not troubled by it.

34.2.4.5 Site names

Businesses try to use memorable domain names so that customers will remember them and return to visit their sites. While short domain names are generally preferable, there are some such as www.iwantoneofthose.com which have proved that longer ones can also be unforgettable.

34.2.4.6 Direct marketing

Businesses wanting to advertise straight to the customer often use direct marketing. This method involves sending emails to existing or potential customers. When a customer registers on the website their email address will be captured in a database, which can be used to generate a list of the email addresses of existing customers. The email addresses of potential customers can be purchased from agencies that operate purely for direct marketing services.

By using direct marketing, businesses can target their marketing precisely. Sometimes, it is also combined with tracking a customer's purchases and tailoring the advertising. For example, if a customer buys science fiction DVDs, they may receive a direct marketing email advertising a new Star Trek box set.

Direct marketing is sometimes considered to be spam (the electronic equivalent of junk mail). It is a matter of perception: if it is unwanted and a nuisance, it is spam. But if the recipient is interested in the content of the direct marketing email, then it is not.

34.2.4.7 Effective user interfaces

The user interface is one of the most important parts of an e-commerce site. There is no point having the most amazing coding and database behind a website if the user interface is unusable. There are several usability paradigms for a good user interface, as discussed on page 355.

34.2.4.8 Establishing customer loyalty in a virtual environment

Due to the lack of human contact and the underlying mistrust a number of customers still have of e-commerce, it can be more difficult to ensure customer loyalty to an e-commerce site than to a traditional retail business.

Loyalty can be encouraged, however, by personalising web pages (see page 355), ensuring customer confidence in the site's security and always delivering on promises.

34.2.5 Customer interface

The customer interface is the first point of contact the user will have with the online business. If visitors are not able to use it easily, it is very likely they will shop elsewhere.

34.2.5.1 Usability issues

Usability issues must be considered when designing an interface (see Figure 34.11).

- Who are the users?
- What do the users already know?
- What do the users want or need to do?
- What is the general background of the users?
- What context is it to be used in?
- What is to be done by the computer?
- What is to be done by the user?

34.2.5.2 Contact information

It is vital that e-commerce sites give customers the opportunity to make contact, especially if they have questions about or problems with their products. Several methods can be used:

- **Email:** Offering an email address is the most common way for businesses to let customers make contact. This is especially important when receiving a high volume of enquiries – the emails can be filtered into the appropriate inboxes and be dealt with as soon as the employees can manage.
- **Telephone:** Some customers will prefer to contact the company by telephone, especially if they need an instant answer or prefer talking to a real person.
- **Frequently asked questions (FAQs):** It is common for websites to have a FAQ, listing commonly asked questions and the answers to those questions. Usually,

Large buttons – easy for children to click.

Theme of primary colours.

Figure 34.11 The Haribo website demonstrates good practice in terms of usability

Pictures rather than writing to make it easier for children to understand. Pictures also mean it can be understood internationally.

Button images have the same design so they are recognisable as clickable elements.

like a telephone call, and allows the employee to explain the situation in writing and also send files. For example, AOL provides a live chat support option. This is not a practical method for contacting the company if the fault is that the Internet connection is not working. This is one reason why several methods of contact are provided.

34.2.5.3 Providing a customer account/profile

For customers to buy products from e-commerce sites, they must register (see Figure 34.12). This usually involves giving full name, date of birth, address and sometimes financial details such as credit card numbers, ready to be used if the customer makes a purchase.

E-commerce businesses can use this data to personalise a website (see page 355).

This can also be used to store a user's purchasing details so they do not have to retype this every time they wish to buy a product. A cookie is stored on the user's computer so when the website is downloaded into the browser or the user logs in to a web page, the cookie is recognised and the customer's information is inserted into their personalised web page. This could be a problem as it makes purchasing from such sites very quick and easy and could encourage irresponsible spending.

34.2.5.4 Order tracking

When buying products online, some customers worry about the delay between paying for goods ordered and receiving those goods. Will the goods arrive? When will they arrive? To allay these fears, some e-commerce

visitors will be directed to it to check if their question has already been answered by the FAQs, before contacting the company.

- **Live chat:** This is becoming more popular, especially due to the proliferation of broadband and other high-speed connections. A visitor can log on to chat with the company's employees and, in a private chat room, they can discuss the issue and hopefully resolve any problems. This gives the visitor the personal experience,

Activity 34.8

Website contact information

1 Look at several e-commerce sites. What contact information is made available?

2 Is there a correlation between the size or type of the website and the number of communication methods on offer? Make notes on ten websites and present your findings graphically.

businesses provide customers with the facility to see where their order is in the delivery chain (see Figure 34.13).

For example, a customer may log on and use the order number to view a particular order and see that the order is being processed. Later, the customer may see that the order has been dispatched and that the products are due for delivery the next day. This reassures customers who might otherwise be contacting the business, worried that they have not yet received their goods.

34.2.5.5 Dealing with complaints

All businesses receive complaints and it is essential that these are dealt with quickly and effectively. This is especially true for e-commerce sites because of the difficulty of earning and maintaining customer trust. An e-commerce business can be unfavourably judged if it fails to handle complaints to a customer's satisfaction. Many e-commerce businesses have staff dedicated to dealing with complaints.

Replies to complaints can take a variety of forms, including letter, email or phone call. Priority is given to replying quickly. Often once a complaint is submitted, a timescale is given for the speed of reply. For example, if a customer complains by email, they will immediately receive an automated response acknowledging receipt of their email and saying they will receive a reply within a certain number of working days.

Case study

Tines (Part 1)

Tines is a company setting up an e-commerce website to sell its handmade cutlery to the public. The company designs and shapes the cutlery from high-quality metal. Because of this the cutlery is beautiful but highly priced. Tines is mainly targeting homeowners with high incomes.

1 Describe the hardware Tines will need. **p**₃

2 Describe the software Tines will need. **p**₃

3 How will the website be uploaded and distributed to the public? Describe the networking technologies that would be involved. **p**₃

4 Which payment methods should the Tines website accept and why?

5 Suggest three methods Tines can use to advertise its e-commerce site and explain why you have chosen these methods.

Test your knowledge

1 Explain the term usability.

2 List two ways that a customer might find out information from a supplier once they are online.

3 What is an account profile? Give three examples of the information it might include.

4 What is order tracking?

Figure 34.12 An online registration form

Figure 34.13 An order tracking page

Any business that operates online is at risk from Internet threats and so security is vital to successful operation. Identity theft can make customers the victims of serious fraud and damage caused by viruses can close companies down. Businesses need to be able to prove that customers' personal details, such as credit card numbers, will be safe.

E-commerce is regulated by laws and guidelines. These aim to ensure that sites operate effectively and that online trading is fair and lawful.

34.3.1 Security

This section focuses on threats to e-commerce sites such as hacking and viruses and the methods that can be used to ensure that websites and data are secure. An e-commerce site that stores customers' personal and financial details needs to be secure. If this is done properly, it can reassure potential customers and widen the potential market.

34.3.1.1 Prevention of hacking

E-commerce sites need to prevent **hacking** so that the running of their business is undisturbed and, more importantly, their customers' details are not stolen.

Specialist software can be used to look at all the ports on a computer and see which are open and which are closed. If a port is open and not being used, that gives a hacker a way in. Therefore, the best way to deter hackers is to make sure unused ports (see page 367) are closed by the firewall (see page 377).

What does it mean?

Hacking is when someone attempts to enter a computer system with the aim of stealing data, damaging the system or just to show that they can.

34.3.1.2 Viruses

'Virus' has become a catch-all term to describe any malicious computer program that can cause an unwanted result when run. There are three main types:

- A **virus** is a manmade program or piece of code that causes an unexpected, usually negative, event and is self-replicating. It is often disguised as a game or image with a clever marketing title, such as officeparty.jpg, and attached to an email or a download file.
- A **worm** is a virus that resides in the active memory of a computer and duplicates itself. It may send copies of itself to other computers, such as through email or Internet Relay Chat (IRC).
- A **trojan** is a malicious program that pretends to be a benign application, but purposely does something the user does not expect. Trojans are technically not viruses since they do not replicate but can be just as destructive.

To try to prevent virus infections, anti-virus software must be installed on the web server and all of an e-commerce business's computers. Not only must it be installed, but it also must be updated regularly, ideally every day. New viruses are developed all the time and anti-virus software must have the latest defences to provide the best protection possible. All computer users must be wary of email attachments, downloading files, floppy disks and any unsolicited communication.

See *Unit 15: Organisational Systems Security* for more on viruses.

Activity 34.9

Viruses

1 Research further into recent viruses and the effects they had on businesses and the public. Make notes for future reference.

2 Categorise each of the viruses as virus, worm or trojan.

34.3.1.3 Identity theft

Identity theft is a new form of crime that has had a recent upsurge and has been highlighted in the media.

Identity theft involves a thief who has stolen the personal details of their victim and uses them to apply for services such as credit cards, loans and mortgages under the guise of their victim. This crime is difficult to detect if the thief has a great deal of information about the victim. The crime is often detected when the victim receives correspondence requesting payment for the thief's spending. Tracing the thief is also difficult, although possible by following the paper trail of all the correspondence received.

The type of customer details stored by e-commerce businesses provides enough information to commit identity theft, so it is very important that all e-commerce businesses protect their customers' data with every method possible, as described below.

34.3.1.4 Firewall impact on site performance

A **firewall** builds a protective virtual barrier around a computer or a network of computers so that only authorised programs can access the data. It sets up a gateway and only allows authorised traffic through the gateway. Incoming data is inspected and only allowed through if it is legitimate. This is done by the opening and closing of ports (see page 376). If ports are left open, a 'back door' becomes available for hackers to enter the system.

When a user views a website that has passed through a firewall, they might not see all of the features on the site. This is because the security policies on the firewall can be set to block certain types of scripts running on the user's computer. This is done to prevent viruses and hackers attacking the system. When a security policy is decided for a firewall, the administrator must balance the need for high security with the possibility of losing functionality from websites.

34.3.1.5 Secure sockets layer (SSL)

SSL is a cryptographic protocol that provides secure communication on the Internet. It provides endpoint authentication, meaning that both the server and the client need to be identified and confirm that they are who they say they are. This is done by **public key encryption** and **certificate-based authentication**.

34.3.1.6 HTTPS

HTTP is the protocol usually used by websites on the Internet. **HTTPS** is a secure version of the protocol, which uses **encryption** to protect the data entered on the site. This protocol is usually used when customers are entering their payment details.

34.3.1.7 RSA certificates

RSA certificates are a method of coding information so that the people at either end are identified by a digital certificate, coupled with a digital signature. These can confirm the identity of the sender or recipient.

What does it mean?

Identity theft occurs when a victim's details are stolen and someone else pretends to be him or her, e.g. applying for financial products and making purchases.

A **firewall** is a piece of software that protects the system from unauthorised access. This is especially important for web servers.

Public key encryption is a method of coding information so that only the people with the right key at both ends of the communication can decode it.

Certificate-based authentication is a method of cryptography which prevents data being read by unauthorised parties.

HTTPS stands for Secure HyperText Transfer Protocol.

Encryption is a method of encoding that is difficult to decipher by unauthorised parties. It uses prime numbers. The higher the prime number, the stronger the encryption.

34.3.1.8 Strong passwords

It is vital for all computer users to use strong passwords. This is especially important for web servers and other e-commerce systems.

A strong password should have:

- both letters and numbers
- both capitals and lowercase
- symbols such as * or #
- more than eight characters.

Hackers can take advantage of weak passwords, especially those which are easy to guess. If a password is personal to the user, e.g. a pet's name, it will not take too much effort for a hacker to guess it. Software programs called password crackers can run through many possible combinations of characters and test whether each one is the chosen password. The stronger the password, the longer this software will take to work it out, and the more likely hackers will be to go on to try a different website. They are not likely to spend time working their way into a well-protected site.

34.3.1.9 Alternative authentication methods

A new authentication method that is slowly becoming more popular is the use of digital signatures. These are the electronic equivalent of the traditional signatures that have been used for hundreds of years as a personal authentication method.

A digital signature allows someone to authenticate a document over the Internet. For example, a customer setting up a direct debit payment would traditionally need to wait for the paperwork to be posted to them, sign it, then return it. Now digital signatures can be used to authenticate the documents immediately anywhere in the world. This benefits both the customers and businesses.

Case study

Tines (Part 2)

Tines is setting up an e-commerce website to sell its handmade cutlery to the public. The website will be taking customers' personal and financial details and therefore needs to have good security.

1 Describe the threats to security that Tines may face. **p**₅

2 For each security issue you mentioned in your answer to question 1, describe a method that can be used to prevent it happening. **p**₅ **m**₃

3 For each prevention method, explain why it would be appropriate. **d**₂

Test your knowledge

1 Explain the term hacking.

2 What are the differences between a virus, a worm and a trojan?

3 What is identity theft?

4 What is the purpose of a firewall?

5 Give three examples of strong passwords.

34.3.2 Legislation

For e-commerce to operate correctly, it needs to adhere to the relevant legislation. These laws protect both the business and the consumer. All the legislation discussed in this section relates to the UK only.

34.3.2.1 Data Protection Act 1998

The Data Protection Act was designed to protect sensitive data held in databases. It was originally passed in 1984, with an update in 1998 which was brought into effect in

2000. It is upheld by the Information Commissioner. Every business that stores data electronically, for example, information about customers, must register and state the data that they plan to hold.

There are eight principles in the Act (see Figure 34.14).

The data subject is the person to whom the data refers. Under the Act, the data subject has several specific rights, including:

- the right to compensation for unauthorised disclosure of data
- the right to compensation for unauthorised inaccurate data
- the right to access data and apply for verification or erasure where it is inaccurate
- the right to compensation for unauthorised access, loss or destruction.

34.3.2.2 Computer Misuse Act 1990

The Data Protection Act was designed to protect sensitive data stored on computers, but there was no legislation to prosecute those who hacked or attacked computer systems with viruses. Towards the end of the 1980s, with the increase of computer use, it was becoming necessary to legislate against these serious problems.

The Computer Misuse Act introduced three new offences:

- unauthorised access to computer programs or data
- unauthorised access with the intent to commit further offences
- unauthorised modification of computer material (e.g. programs or data).

The Act makes a distinction between **computer misuse** and **computer abuse**.

What does it mean?

Computer misuse is an illegal act involving a computer.

Computer abuse is a legal but unethical act involving a computer.

Activity 34.10

Data Protection Act

Visit the website of the Information Commissioner's Office by going to www.heinemann.co.uk/hotlinks and entering the express code 2315P. Find more information on each principle of the Data Protection Act and make notes.

1 What might an e-commerce site do that would contravene the rules of the Data Protection Act?

2 What would happen if they did?

Activity 34.11

Computer Misuse Act

Visit the website of the Information Commissioner's Office by going to www.heinemann.co.uk/hotlinks and entering the express code 2315P. Find more information on each offence defined by the Computer Misuse Act and make notes.

1 What might an e-commerce site do that would contravene the rules of the Computer Misuse Act?

2 What would happen if they did?

▼ **Figure 34.14 The eight principles of the Data Protection Act**

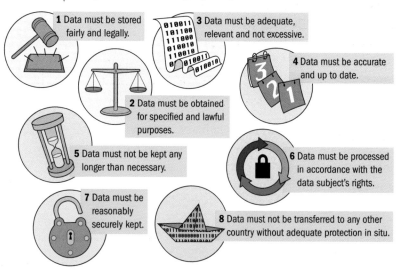

1 Data must be stored fairly and legally.

2 Data must be obtained for specified and lawful purposes.

3 Data must be adequate, relevant and not excessive.

4 Data must be accurate and up to date.

5 Data must not be kept any longer than necessary.

6 Data must be processed in accordance with the data subject's rights.

7 Data must be reasonably securely kept.

8 Data must not be transferred to any other country without adequate protection in situ.

34.3.2.3 Consumer Credit Act 1974

Customers paying by credit card are protected by the Consumer Credit Act for payments up to £25,000. So, if a payment cannot be made by the customer, the business will still receive the money from the bank and can therefore confidently send out the products purchased.

The Act also guarantees a cooling off period during which customers can change their mind about a purchase – for mail order goods the cooling off period is 14 days. This is good for the customer but can be disadvantageous to a company as it means that, even after a purchase has been completed, there is the possibility of the customer asking for a refund.

34.3.2.4 Trading Standards

The Trading Standards Institute works with consumers and businesses to maintain fair trading. It is part of local government and ensures that legislation is enforced, such as:

- the Trades Description Act 1968
- the Consumer Protection Act 1987
- the Price Marking Order 2004

The Trading Standards Institute also deals with issues such as counterfeit goods, the sale of alcohol and tobacco to underage persons and the exploitation of vulnerable consumers from scams and doorstep crime. E-commerce websites must clearly describe their products. This is especially important because customers can only see pictures of the products before purchasing, not the items themselves.

34.3.2.5 Freedom of Information Act 2000

This Act came into effect on 1 January 2005 and gives the public the 'right to know'. The public can request information about public bodies, such as the government, and legal entities, such as businesses.

Activity 34.12

Freedom of Information Act

Visit the website of the Information Commissioner's Office by going to www.heinemann.co.uk/hotlinks and entering the express code 2315P. Find more information about the rights the Freedom of Information Act gives to members of the public. Make notes.

1 Can members of the public obtain any information or are there restrictions?

2 What information can people obtain from e-commerce businesses?

34.3.2.6 Copyright legislation

The Copyright, Designs and Patents Act 1988 protects all works such as music, art, writing and programming code once it is tangible, which means in a fixed form. As the Internet has grown, the question of whether websites are subject to protection under copyright has often been discussed. It is now accepted that a website becomes tangible once it is coded and saved on to storage media, especially if the source code is also printed. Websites are therefore protected by copyright.

Test your knowledge

1 Name the eight principles of the Data Protection Act 1998.

2 Name the three offences defined by the Computer Misuse Act 1990.

3 Explain the difference between computer misuse and computer abuse.

Preparation for assessment

The assessment tasks in this unit are based on the following scenario.

Cuckoo is a small business selling clocks and watches. It currently only exists as a shop in Covent Garden, London. Cuckoo is thinking about starting to trade online and has asked you to compile some information to help the company decide if this is a good idea and, if so, how to go about it.

Complete the following tasks. You are advised to research wherever possible and use correctly referenced sources.

Task 1 (P1, M1, D1)

Prepare a presentation for the staff of Cuckoo explaining the social implications, benefits and drawbacks of trading by e-commerce. Describe the potential risks of committing to an e-commerce system. Evaluate whether it should use a 'bricks and clicks' format for its new venture.

Task 2 (P1, P2)

Create a poster to be displayed in the Cuckoo office describing three current successful e-commerce entities.

Task 3 (P3, P4, M2, D2)

Prepare a report for Cuckoo describing the following:
- the hardware and software needed to build and upload an e-commerce site
- the hardware and software needed to view and use an e-commerce site
- the networking technologies used in e-commerce
- how e-commerce systems can be promoted and marketed

- a comparison of two different payment systems for e-commerce
- the security techniques available, selecting two and justifying your choices.

Task 4 (P5, M3)

Produce a short booklet for Cuckoo about the security issues involved in e-commerce. Describe each of the threats and the methods to overcome them.

Task 5 (P6)

Create a reference booklet for Cuckoo about the relevant legislation for e-commerce. The company should be able to use the booklet initially to learn about the legislation and then later for reference when issues arise. It also needs to know how each law impacts on e-commerce systems in practical terms.

Task 6 (D3)

Is e-commerce the future of business? Having examined the variety of issues of e-commerce, it is appropriate that you also analyse how e-commerce will develop in the future. There are a few possible outcomes, as follows.
- The public mistrust of e-commerce increases and businesses revert to using traditional methods only.
- E-commerce maintains its position of being an alternative to traditional methods, with the norm being that both styles of business are run alongside each other.
- E-commerce becomes the standard business method of the future. All businesses use e-commerce.
- Another technology is developed that overtakes e-commerce and becomes the standard method of business.

No one can know what will happen in the future, but what do you think is most likely to happen?

Prepare a report for Cuckoo describing and predicting the possible future of e-commerce and its impact on Cuckoo's business and on society as a whole.

Impact of the Use of IT on Business Systems

Introduction

This unit explores how hardware, software and systems are forever being developed to improve capacity, sophistication and power.

Keeping up to date with this ever-changing world has a huge impact on businesses and their managers and employees. The latest developments provide collaboration between devices such as **PDAs**, **Blackberries** and mobile phones with cameras, access to the Internet and other multimedia – for example, virtual games such as tennis and golf.

What does it mean?

PDA stands for **palm device accessory** and is a hand-held computer.

Blackberry is the trade name for a mobile phone which combines keyboard and large screen and is used like a PDA.

In this unit you will identify organisational challenges such as the re-engineering of systems, the need for constant upskilling of the workforce and dealing with redundant skills and employees. You will explore the benefits of IT developments, such as reduced business start-up costs, increased opportunities for global companies using e-commerce and access to greater outsourcing and geosourcing.

While working through this unit, you will learn to recognise which IT developments have an impact on organisations. You will report on why and how organisations adapt their activities in response to these developments.

The application and development of your research skills is an essential component of this unit because of the volume, variety and rapid development of IT. You will produce a portfolio of evidence to show how you have achieved the learning outcomes and the journey you took to get there.

After completing this unit, you should be able to achieve these outcomes:

- Know the IT developments that have had an impact on organisations
- Understand why organisations need to change in response to IT developments
- Understand how organisations adapt activities in response to IT developments.

Thinking points

This unit provides you with a greater realisation and understanding of the rate at which IT is developing and how it impacts on the way businesses operate. New businesses are being created to make the hardware and write the software. Some companies such as Adobe, Intel, Cisco Systems and Oracle employ many people in providing the technical infrastructure. Other companies such as Amazon, Google, eBay and Genes Reunited have been created because they are now technically feasible. Other longer-established businesses are changing what and how they operate because of the impact of IT. Many people would say that IT has improved the way organisations operate and increased productivity through efficiency.

As well as looking at the growth in power and range of IT equipment and its impact on organisations, you will be encouraged to give consideration to the human element. You will be provided with opportunities to put yourself in someone else's shoes to help you to appreciate that the rate of change has to be managed appropriately.

This unit will help you to develop an insight into how organisations operate and how many of the devices you might be familiar with are used in different ways. You will be provided with opportunities to carry out research using the Internet, case studies and interviews. Some of the answers might be found among your own family and friends. Although this is an IT unit you will learn about general business infrastructures that will apply to whatever career path you choose.

Before you can measure the impact IT developments have on organisations, you need to identify what developments have taken place – for example, increases in power, performance, capacity of systems and physical size of equipment (see Figure 35.1). For example, there is more computing power in a mobile phone of today than there was in the entire Apollo moon landing mission in 1969.

The world of medicine has benefited greatly from the developments in IT. The identification of illness and injury using equipment such as **MRI** scans enables investigations without surgery. Laser eye surgery and keyhole surgery are widely used. Equipment such as pacemakers and procedures such as kidney dialysis are also made more effective by the use of IT.

What does it mean?

MRI stands for **magnetic resonance imaging** and is used to generate images of living tissues inside the human body.

▼ Figure 35.1 Mainframe computers used to fill a whole room

35.1.1 Hardware and systems

This subsection explores the developments in **hardware** and systems that have evolved because of companies such as Dell, Microsoft and Google.

Activity 35.1

Our technological world

1 List the range of technology you currently own or use.
2 Identify all the devices that you didn't own or use a year ago. Do the same for every device up to five years ago.
3 Identify the computing power in each of the items you have listed (e.g. memory, features, speed).
4 Select two items from your list and search for the nearest comparison available five years ago. Make notes on the differences to each item, such as its features, capacity, memory, speed, size, weight.
5 Identify which items (or features of your items) on your list were not available five years ago.
6 Compare the results with your peers.

Since the founding of Dell in 1984 the organisation has grown to be the world's largest computer firm, selling hardware and systems by mail order. Systems have evolved and are still developing rapidly, while the costs for these systems appear to tumble. The availability of cheaper computers, offering more for the price, has extended access to IT to a wider range of consumers.

The development of Internet search engines as a free tool to find resources using key words has extended the popularity of computers so they are now a must-have commodity worldwide. Google is a particularly popular search engine and has become a hugely profitable organisation.

More recent developments in hardware and systems have led to a greater flexibility (e.g. the ability to use a mobile phone as a camera, access the Internet and emails via phones and PDAs) and compatibility (e.g. use of storage devices such as USB drives). There are still gaps in the

What does it mean?

The term **hardware** describes the parts of the computer you can touch.

Figure 35.2 The Commodore 64 computer

Figure 35.3 The BBC B Micro computer

compatibility of hardware. For example, some storage devices such as memory cards in cameras might only be compatible with a computer of the same make.

Many organisations now rely on their systems in the everyday running of their business to the extent that when the system crashes, operations come to a standstill. Regular updates to computer systems are carried out in an attempt to maintain and increase efficiency, reliability and productivity.

Traditional skills are often replaced with automated systems which are quicker and able to produce a standardised product – e.g. knitwear, embroidery, pottery, artwork and ready meals.

The power supply to the computer (via the **PSU**) is fed to the motherboard and to the peripherals, etc.

Power = speed of processor

Performance = memory of RAM plus operating system capability

35.1.1.1 Increasing power

Due to the increasing power in computers, the speed at which information is processed is faster, so computers can perform more tasks in the same amount of time.

What does it mean?

PSU stands for **power supply unit**. See Unit 2, page 47 for details of how the PSU controls the voltage supplied to an individual component.

Product/model	Year introduced	Approx cost	Power	Performance (main memory)
Commodore 64	1982	£350	1 MHz	64K RAM
BBC B Micro	Early 1980s	£500	2 MHz	32K RAM
Amstrad PCW	1984	£125	4 MHz	64K RAM
Amiga 1000	1985	£900	7.14 MHz	256K RAM
Dell PC	2006	£529	Up to 3 GHz	Up to 4GB (up to 1000GB internal storage)

Table 35.1 Technological developments in relation to specification and cost

Activity 35.2

The quarter of a century change

Table 35.1 compares a few of the early home computers with a typical computer available in 2006. Look at how far computers have advanced over the years. For example, the Commodore 64 with its 64K memory (Figure 35.2) caused quite a sensation back in the early 1980s when home computers started to appear, whereas today computers with 60GB memories are readily available. Notice also the differences in cost.

1 Now extend your spreadsheet to include these additional columns:

   a removable storage device (e.g. floppy disks, tape streamers, CDs, USB drives, memory cards, DVDs)

   b the storage capacity of each of these devices.

2 Share your findings and sources with others in your group.

Remember!

Always label and file the rough notes you make when planning an activity, as evidence of your progress towards your qualification.

35.1.1.2 Computer platforms

With the ever-growing range of software applications, computer **platforms** are also increasing in capacity and sophistication.

The platform could be the processor running the operating system (such as Windows Vista) or it could be a UNIX computer running on an Ethernet network. The introduction of the Apple Macintosh in 1984 with its graphical user interface and Microsoft Windows version 1.0 (see Figure 35.4) in November 1985 revolutionised

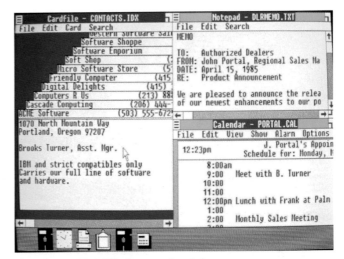

▲ **Figure 35.4 Windows version 1.0**

computer use and set the course for the way computers are used today. Nowadays, almost all software is Windows-based, with Windows and its associated software dominating the market.

Typical platforms include the computer's **architecture**, operating system and programming languages. Computer platforms have evolved due to the need to support applications.

Developments in computer operating systems and collaboration between rival manufacturers have led to software in different versions to run on your chosen platform – for example, Microsoft Office for Mac.

What does it mean?

A **platform** is the foundation around which a system is developed.

Architecture comprises the hardware, firmware, assembler, kernel and operating system, plus applications.

35.1.1.3 New communication technologies

Nowadays, people want and expect to be able to communicate at any time and in any place. A variety of platforms make this possible, including PDAs,

Activity 35.3

Developments to operating systems

1 Carry out research, using the Internet and other sources, to identify developments to operating systems (for example, there have been over 20 versions to Windows since its initiation).

2 Put your findings into a spreadsheet (example shown in Table 35.2). As well as Microsoft systems, also include operating systems from other developers.

3 Share your findings with others in your group.

OPERATING SYSTEMS				
Date first available	Producer	Name & version	Screen shot	Source of information

Table 35.2 Developments to operating systems

Blackberries, CCTV and smart chips in credit card formats. These devices are accessible across networks by wireless or wired methods.

Advancements in devices include networks for backing up data over Ethernet cables and remotely via **Bluetooth,** email and **EDI**.

Bluetooth enables communication between devices such as computers, mobile phones and humans. Data is also transferable between organisations by EDI. EDI uses standard data formats to communicate between businesses, for example, to exchange orders and invoices electronically in a standard format – swiftly, accurately and without using paper (see page 404).

Communication between our planet and satellite is readily available via satellite navigation systems. Satellite navigation (**GPS**) has rapidly become a more widely available and affordable commodity, and is now in common usage by people in their cars.

The ability to forward plan, track and replot a journey has made GPS a vital piece of equipment for drivers who make many journeys, although it is not 100 per cent infallible!

Other communication developments include the use of **CCTV**, and speed cameras to detect speeding drivers. Feeling secure is important for people, hence the widespread use of CCTV. Recent research has identified that there is one CCTV camera to every 14 people in the UK.

What does it mean?

Bluetooth is a wireless device enabling connection and exchange of information.

EDI stands for electronic data interchange.

GPS stands for global positioning system.

CCTV stands for closed circuit television.

Test your knowledge

1 Name at least two companies that have helped IT evolve.

2 What does hardware mean?

3 What does EDI do?

4 What does a computer platform do?

5 What does GPS do?

6 Name at least two devices where Bluetooth can be used.

▲ Figure 35.5 People now expect to be able to communicate anywhere and at any time

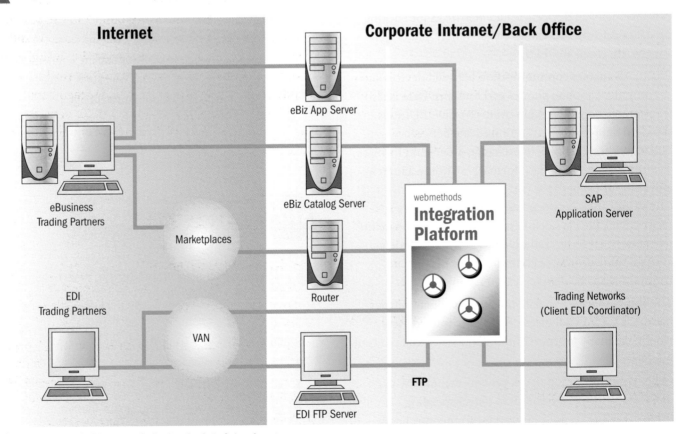

▲ Figure 35.6 Diagram of electronic data interchange

▲ **Figure 35.7 GPS system**

35.1.2 Software

This subsection identifies the developments to software, including its increasing sophistication, and considers the impact of these developments on organisations. As systems become more powerful, a wider range of applications software can be supported. In addition, many companies use bespoke or specialist software to support their business.

- Specialist databases and management information systems (MIS) are used to log sales and purchases, monitor stock levels and manage production.
- **CAD** is a drawing application and an example of sophisticated software. It enables architects, car designers and kitchen designers to produce technical drawings using a computer. These 2D drawings can be manipulated and viewed as if in 3D.

What does it mean?

CAD stands for computer aided design.

Software is becoming increasingly sophisticated. For example, software is now available which allows users to include video clips and background music in presentations, download and mix music and create their own DVDs. Free software such as Picasa from Google and Microsoft Photo Story can be downloaded to turn digital photographs into electronic photo albums with soundtracks, titles and captions.

Some software integrates with other software – for example, some bespoke databases integrate with Microsoft Excel in order to migrate data out of a database into a spreadsheet, perhaps to analyse data further or to produce a graph. However, some bespoke systems such as MIS or databases deliberately avoid integration in order to retain the development rights to generate future business.

As specialist software is developed, it is easy to assume that skilled professionals are a dying breed, as the software can now do their work for them. However, it is still important to have the background knowledge to use software correctly. For example, a draughtsperson still needs to know how to produce a detailed drawing, even though the software now does most of the work. Similarly, an accountant needs to understand how double entry book keeping works in order to get the most out of a computerised accounts package such as Sage or Pegasus.

Activity 35.4

Just how many applications?

1 Make a list of the software applications on your computer system, some of which you might have never used.

2 Identify who makes each application and what it does. Note the version number of each application. Why do you think some computers have different versions from others? List what can be done to update a version.

3 Compare your list with others from your group.

An important question is whether we are becoming too IT dependent. For example, a comparison between the mental arithmetic abilities of people under 20 and people over 40 might have quite different results, showing that young people are no longer learning these skills.

35.1.2.2 Specialist support software

Organisations can select from a range of specialised support software available, e.g. to enable remote access, call logging or to identify network traffic. Some specialist software enables organisations to identify the reasons for increases or decreases in product sales and this information helps them to find out ways to improve performance.

Other specialist support software includes management information systems (Figure 35.8), for collating and analysing data internally, and remote diagnostic software that enables manufacturers of large plant (construction machinery) to monitor the performance of their machinery and very swiftly diagnose the problem and provide a solution.

Car manufacturers such as Mercedes include a service recall in their cars – the software calculates when a service is due based on the way the car is driven. The display in the car shows the driver how many miles are left before the next service and a warning when a service is almost due.

Unfortunately, not all specialist software has proved to be effective. Examples include the databases developed for the National Health Service, the Child Support Agency, the national crime database and the air traffic control computer system.

Activity 35.5

Specialist software case study

1 Identify the types of information systems being installed in two different makes of cars. Visit a garage where you can experience the system in at least one of the cars you have chosen. Find out how the in-car system works, what it does and how it informs the user that, for example, a service is due in 530 miles. How does it do this? Does it speak?

2 What other products use information systems? Find two examples and explain what they do.

3 Keep comprehensive notes of your findings and compare them with others in your group.

Other examples of specialist software include **decision support software** and **expert systems**.

Support systems comprise processes, people and software, whereas decisions support systems (often called business intelligence) are designed to enhance the business decision making process with supporting analyses (reports or graphs).

What does it mean?

Decision support software is designed to help users compile useful information from raw data in order to solve problems and make decisions.

Expert systems are designed to perform tasks that would usually be performed by a human expert. They provide clear answers to questions without any further analysis needed by the user.

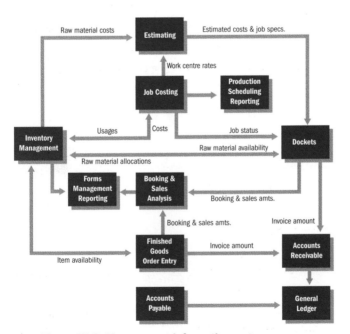

▲ **Figure 35.8 Management information system**

Activity 35.6

Specialist software disasters

1 Research some well-known incidences of when commissioning specialist software has gone badly wrong – for example, for organisations such as the NHS and the Child Support Agency and the new computer systems for the national crime database and air traffic control.

2 In each case, identify what went wrong and why. Was it because the system was too big, staff were not trained well enough or the designers and developers did not identify accurately the needs of the organisation? Maybe the system became larger than ever anticipated and the budget ran out. Perhaps the large sums of money spent gave credibility to the system and so assumptions were made that it must provide the solution.

3 Collate your findings into a report (which can be a presentation or a video) to present to the rest of your group in class.

4 Further your research to find examples of when the failure of specialist software has been blamed for a disaster. Share with other members of your group – how many examples did you find?

Remember!

Also refer to the sections on specialised software in *Unit 3: Information Systems*.

35.1.2.3 Internet and intranets

With the rapid growth of the Internet (for public use) and intranets (for private use), many people now have easy access to a huge resource of information. Both require specialist software to operate them. Search engines are available to locate information, Google being the most popular.

The use of the Internet has enabled organisations to promote their products and services easily, swiftly and relatively cheaply when compared with more traditional methods. Credit card technology has allowed online shopping to grow rapidly from year to year. For example, Tesco introduced online grocery shopping to be delivered to your door in 1996 – since then, other supermarkets have followed suit.

The Internet provides consumers with flexibility such as online repeat prescriptions and electronic voting. Specialist security software (such as Norton and McAfee) offer protection to both software and hardware. Some offer complete Internet security, while others provide a **firewall** and protection against some **viruses**.

The section on **cyber crime** (see page 410) explores the threats to organisations as a result of the development of IT in areas such as cyber crime, as well as the risks if organisations choose not to move with the times.

There might be an over-reliance on information posted on to the Internet and, in particular, its credibility.

What does it mean?

A **firewall** is a software filter which prevents unauthorised access to the computer.

A **virus** is a computer program that is destructive and has the ability to copy and spread itself.

Cyber crime is a crime committed over the Internet or a virtual crime.

Activity 35.7

Protection

1 Find out which organisations provide protection software and what each item of software offers. Identify how much they cost.

2 Share your list with your peers. Which organisation offers the best deals?

Figure 35.9 A computer virus

Activity 35.9

Specialist systems

1 Identify two organisations and investigate the systems and software that they use.

2 Create a questionnaire and use it to collect information about the systems and software used by your two chosen organisations.

3 Following your investigations, collate your results to identify any similarities and differences – what do your findings tell you?

4 Write a short report on your findings, making sure you explain what you did, with whom, why and what you found out.

Activity 35.8

Ignorance is not acceptable

1 Visit a cinema or theatre and check what notices appear regarding copyright regulations. Is capturing part or all of the film on camera (or camera phone) legal? If you record images, what might happen?

2 Research the Internet to find out the rules for downloading music from the Internet. Make notes.

3 Find two more examples where 'ignorance is not acceptable'. Email your list to your peers.

Anyone can put any information they want on the Internet, and just because it appears there doesn't make it true. The easy access to information on the Internet can result in some people believing that they are experts in a field, even though the information they have found there might be inaccurate.

Some organisations use an **extranet** so that staff or other relevant people such as distributors or freelance workers can have exclusive access to files and information

remotely. Staff and other users selected by the organisation are provided with a password and access code to use the extranet.

Throughout this section, we have looked at developments in technology that have occurred over a very short space of time. To get a sense of the rapid pace of change, it is worth looking back over technological developments in the last century and even comparing these with changes over the previous ten centuries.

What does it mean?

An **extranet** is a website that allows restricted access to authorised people only.

Activity 35.10

Today it's here but yesterday it wasn't

1   Ask your grandparents or anyone you know of the older generation (i.e. grandparent or great-grandparent age): 'What technological developments and changes have you experienced in your lifetime?'

2   Make a list of all the technology they had when they were your age and the stages in their lives when new technology became available to them.

3   Compare with the list you made of the range of technology you currently own or use for Activity 35.1 on page 384.

4   Discuss with your peers – what changes did they identify?

Test your knowledge

1   Who might use CAD?

2   What does MIS do?

3   Give three examples of specialist support software and their purpose.

4   What is SAGE?

5   Identify two examples where specialist software has not been successful and why.

6   How is an extranet different from an intranet?

7   What does a firewall do?

35.2   The need to change in response to IT developments

This section explores the changes organisations need to make to cope with rapid IT developments.

35.2.1 Organisational challenges

Organisations face many challenges brought about by change, such as:

- the cost of keeping up to date with developments (changes to equipment and resources)
- changes to the environment (setting, location, culture)
- changes in human resources (number of staff and the skill levels needed).

All of these will impact on organisational structures (see Figures 35.16 and 35.17 on pages 410 and 413 respectively).

35.2.1.1 Re-engineering of systems

Organisations need to have a strategy for dealing with the challenges brought about by IT developments. They can do this by carrying out a cost-benefit analysis of the current IT system. The results of this analysis can be used to inform decisions about how to develop the system. The organisation can compare the cost of updating the system with the cost of discarding and replacing it (**re-engineering the system**).

When deciding on their strategy, the organisation needs to consider the cost, as well as the quality, speed and service of the system. Once a decision is made, the organisation should measure the impact – for example, the increase in productivity which will result in increased profit.

What does it mean?

Re-engineering of systems means starting again with a new system rather than attempting a quick fix.

Activity 35.11

IT strategy

1 The organisation where you are studying this course will most likely have a strategy which plans for updating and upgrading computers and systems. Find out what plans are in place.

2 Find examples of where re-engineering of a system has occurred. Find out whether re-engineering changed productivity and, if so, in what way. (Kodak, IBM and Ford are three examples of organisations that have re-engineered their systems.)

3 Suggest the internal and external challenges facing organisations and the opportunities and threats arising as a result of change.

4 Discuss with your peers what different challenges are faced by small organisations and sole traders (such as a self-employed plumber or electrician).

35.2.1.2 Managers' IT awareness

One of the many challenges faced by organisations is the language and jargon used in IT – this is often unclear and confusing to non-specialists. In organisations where an IT department, technician or systems administrator are employed, it is often difficult for one department to explain to another what is required and why. Managers are the ones who will be making decisions about the system, but they may not fully understand the issues and options.

Issues arise as a result of, for example, trying to justify the size of the budget required to support the system, the time it will take to get the system up and running or the reason why systems need to be updated or re-engineered. The IT specialists need to make sure that they explain and justify all these factors in terms that the management will understand.

They should also identify contingencies to ensure that productivity does not grind to a halt if the existing system is no longer suitable or available. They need to produce a proposal to support the reason for the changes required.

35.2.1.3 Reducing and integrating complex systems

Organisations find that reducing complex (and bespoke) systems for an integrated system (see Figure 35.10) enables their system to talk to other internal and external systems. This may reduce the need for additional systems and processes which take longer to develop and are more expensive to carry out.

35.2.1.4 Payback

Some organisations offer previous customers payback in the form of reimbursements or benefits such as free delivery or a discount for future orders within a short timescale.

▲ **Figure 35.10 An example of an integrated system**

Activity 35.12

That's not what I meant!

1 Produce a list of 20 different IT terms that mean something different in a non-IT context, e.g. **desktop** can mean the screen display or the top of a desk.

2 Try out your list with a non-IT specialist, e.g. a member of your family, by asking them to define each item. How many IT terms did they understand?

3 Compare your list – and your results – with those of your peers.

The introduction of loyalty cards (see page 403), which reward returning customers with points and prizes, has also played its part in increasing sales. For example, the loyalty cards of a supermarket chain encourage customers to patronise its stores or drive out of their way to purchase petrol from its garages. Supermarket loyalty cards have been suggested as a factor in the demise of corner shops – how can the small time grocer or butcher compete with multi-national purchasing power (reduced buying costs) or offer payback in return for loyalty?

Another example of payback is when you make a purchase online and the supplier follows up with a personalised email inviting you to take advantage of a percentage reduction next time you make a purchase. This promotion is exploited further by allocating a limited timescale to the offer, tempting you to buy now in order to take advantage of the offer, whether you want (or can afford) it or not.

What does it mean?

Payback is reward in some form or another for using an organisation's product or service.

Activity 35.13

Payback

1 Identify at least two organisations offering payback. What payback do these organisations offer?

2 Describe examples of payback that you or your family have received. Share these examples with your peers.

35.2.1.5 Technical infrastructures

To cope with the challenges facing organisations and to monitor the effectiveness of the IT system, an organisation should implement a **technical infrastructure**.

A technical infrastructure includes producing reports on the effectiveness of the system, analysing performance and making recommendations for improvements. For example, recommendation might be to provide training on software use for staff and how this should be done – e.g. by internal IT support staff or by external training providers. Other recommendations might be to re-engineer the system and a proposal would need to justify the reasons for this along with the costs and the benefits to the organisation as a whole.

Activity 35.14

My technical infrastructure

Put yourself in the position of an IT support technician within the organisation where you study. Your team has been asked to write a proposal that shows how the organisation should keep up to date with developments, including the cost and justification for any changes.

1 Look at the sorts of challenges that the organisation faces and technical developments they might consider. Research the Internet for details of recent developments and costs of new devices and software. Make notes. TIP: You could build on the costs you produced for Activity 35.2 (page 386). Add in the cost of items such as surge protection, anti-virus software, Internet costs and setting up a new website.

2 Using clear and jargon-free language, present your findings in a short report including details (and images where appropriate) of your proposal (devices, software, costs, preferred suppliers, etc.). Identify the benefits to the organisation for change and the impact of not changing.

Remember!

Don't forget the reasons why you are recommending one supplier or device over another.

What does it mean?

Technical infrastructure means the development of the management's underlying structure.

Test your knowledge

1 How do small organisations manage developments to IT? What are the implications for the sole trader?

2 Why would an organisation choose to re-engineer its system?

3 What is payback?

4 What are the benefits in reducing a complex system?

5 How can IT specialists ensure that non-specialists understand what is required in order to respond to IT developments?

35.2.2 External environment

External environmental factors contribute to the need for change. Some of these factors are **legislative** and some are financial.

This section considers the issues of increasing globalisation, outsourcing and geosourcing.

What does it mean?

Legislative refers to a legal requirement.

35.2.2.1 Increasing globalisation

Developments such as increased access to the Internet, email and video conferencing mean that organisations can very easily and quickly identify other suppliers or distributors of their products located almost anywhere in the world. This is called **globalisation**. However, the same applies to rival organisations, which might result in increased competition and loss of business. So organisations need to ensure that they exploit the benefits of the technology available in the most effective way.

35.2.2.2 Outsourcing and geosourcing

Outsourcing means paying a third party to provide a service that would normally be performed by a member of staff employed directly by the organisation (e.g. an IT technician). When an organisation has to cut costs, perhaps to allocate more of its budget to increasing or updating technology, it might choose to use outsourcing and/or **geosourcing**.

What does it mean?

Geosourcing is the process of seeking expert skills at the best possible price regardless of location.

Outsourcing to provide technical support for an organisation might prove to be more cost-effective than running an IT department. Buying in ongoing specialist support, rather than paying for a full-time member of staff who might require regular training to keep up to date with the changes in technology, could save the organisation money. Small companies often need to outsource. Large companies also outsource, not only in an attempt to cut costs but also to access particular specialist support.

Although outsourcing might appear to be a more expensive option when comparing the hourly rate charged by an external expert as opposed to that of a paid member of staff, it might be a cheaper option in the long run. The reason for this is that the organisation will pay only for the time the outsourced expert is employed on a task – this could be considerably less than the time spent by a full-time employee.

If the organisation can find the expertise needed in a location where labour is cheaper, irrespective of distance, this is called geosourcing. An example of this is when telecommunication links allow call centres to be located in India.

Where customer support staff are employed in other countries, there can be difficulties in understanding other dialects and accents – both for customers and for support staff. Where training is given to overseas call centre staff, some might be as basic as watching British television in the expectation that language and cultural differences will be overcome.

Activity 35.15

Where else can I buy it and for how much?

1 Produce a list of 15–20 different makes of products (e.g. a CD or a particular deodorant) and identify the name of the supplier and their location. Include the cost of the product from the supplier.

2 Present your findings in a spreadsheet, and compare the range of prices located.

35.2.2.3 Regulatory and legal frameworks

This subsection identifies how changing **regulatory** and legal frameworks impacts on organisations and the challenges that they bring.

For example, an organisation might introduce a policy dictating the rules for using the Internet and telephone in office hours – this is likely to define the types of websites that employees are allowed to access and for how long, and will state whether and how often employees can make private telephone calls.

Other policies will be in place for legal reasons, such as ensuring that equipment is regularly tested for safety (**PAT**) and complying with the Data Protection Act (1998).

Other examples of legislation that will have an impact on company policies include the Display Screen

Regulations of 1992 and the Disability Discrimination Act 1995, which requires organisations to supply suitable equipment for employees who have a disability or specific need to help them carry out their jobs (e.g. a tracker ball for a user with arthritis, wrist rests to help prevent **RSI**).

A company may also have a policy to make its website accessible to people with disabilities. In the USA, this is a legal requirement. Research has identified that we are all likely to experience some form or degree of disability within our lifetime so addressing this issue by providing accessible websites makes a lot of sense.

Tools such as Bobby can be used to check and improve on the accessibility of a website.

Accessibility issues include legibility of text, amount of white space, text alternatives for images, etc.

What does it mean?

Regulatory refers to a rule or policy that is not a government law, but is a requirement.

PAT stands for **portable appliance testing**.

RSI stands for **repetitive strain injury** – it is a condition suffered by many PC users.

Activity 35.16

Website accessibility check

1 Carry out a validation check on three websites of your choice using at least two different validation software tools. Write down which websites you checked and what each outcome produced.

2 Compare your findings with those of your peers. How accessible is your college or school website?

▲ **Figure 35.11 A tracker ball for use by people with arthritis**

You will most likely have been introduced to some policies in your school or college. These policies tell you what you can expect from the college and the rules and procedures that you must follow. For example, your organisation should have an assessment policy which sets out the rules for assessment: the maximum length of time that can be taken to mark assessed work and to return it to the learner. This type of policy should also identify the rules regarding late work and the penalties a student will experience if they hand in work late. It will also identify the procedure to follow if you disagree with an assessment outcome: this is called the appeals procedure.

Activity 35.17

What's in a policy?

1 Name three policies that directly affect you. (These could be policies that are in force in your school or college or perhaps in a part-time job or a club or organisation to which you belong.)

2 Select one policy and write, in your own words, what it means. Is the policy based on any legislation?

3 Identify one other policy that is backed up by legislation and identify the legislation (e.g. if it is mentioned in a policy document that you have been given, you can highlight this).

4 Compare your findings with your peers.

35.2.2.4 Costs of business start-ups

Business start-up costs might have been reduced as a result of the developments in information technology. Small businesses are increasing in numbers at a dramatic rate and one reason might be that IT equipment costs less than it used to.

There is now less need to pay for office space, as many businesses can now operate from home – the start-up costs might simply be for a computer, printer and a small amount of office equipment. E-businesses often need only a few staff and therefore only need a small office. Running costs might also be less with the use of email and services such as **Skype** instead of the need for producing and sending out formal letters – this reduces the costs for stationery, postage and telephone.

However, some businesses of varying sizes might find that there is a greater need to have technological equipment available at start-up, whereas historically some resources might have been seen as a luxury item

Remember!

The growth in technology often means a reduction in cost.

and therefore not essential. An example is where computers were not provided for many staff but now are commonplace (in particular for tradespeople such as plumbers, electricians and carpenters).

35.2.2.5 Potential for competition

There is increased potential for competition by global companies at local level using **e-commerce**.

Amazon, eBay and online banking are just a few examples of e-commerce. Increased potential for competition has enabled organisations operating online to acquire business from more traditional traders. For example, online grocery shopping was started by Tesco, which rapidly took business from its competitors. The other supermarkets soon followed suit – if they had not done so, they would have undoubtedly lost more business.

E-commerce allows greater choice that is made readily available to the consumer. For example, specialist websites provide instant price comparisons on products and services such as household goods, insurance and mortgages. Other examples of organisations carrying out business online are airlines, hotels and large warehouses/retailers.

An example of online competition being seen as a particular threat was the introduction of electronic mail (email) and its possible impact on Royal Mail. As yet, email has not resulted in the demise of the traditional postal service.

What does it mean?

Skype is an example of a service offering free or cheap worldwide telephone calls to standard landline numbers using broadband.

E-commerce is trade carried out online.

Activity 35.18

The human element

1 Identify two different organisations: one which mainly uses real, local people to carry out its business and one which uses mainly automated services. Write a report suggesting reasons for these different ways of operating. Explain also the benefits and drawbacks of the two approaches.

2 Make recommendations about how one of these organisations can take advantage of IT developments.

35.2.3 Internal environment

This subsection looks at the human element of implementing change. In order to manage technological change effectively, organisations often have to adapt their ways of working – this will have an effect on staffing structures and job roles.

35.2.3.1 Upskilling of workforce

The fast pace of change brought about by developments in IT requires organisations to recognise the need for upskilling the workforce. Specialist skills are needed to use IT – e.g. the company may need someone who can use Dreamweaver to design web pages.

It is highly unlikely that the workforce (staff and managers) can simply 'pick up and run' with the introduction of new systems, software and even apparently basic or simple devices.

Individuals have preferred ways of studying, learning and working, and also have different levels of ability, understanding and confidence. These factors have an impact on the way that they will adapt to new technology. The workforce is likely to include employees at all levels, irrespective of their previous experiences and qualifications.

Fewer organisations employ secretaries today and so staff and managers are increasingly expected to be

administrators in addition to their main job role (e.g. sales representative, marketing manager, financial director). This will mean that they will need IT skills in using administrative software, such as word processing and spreadsheets. However, the cost of managers carrying out their own administrative tasks may have a greater cost per hour to the organisation than that of employing administrative staff.

Activity 35.19

Training needs analysis

1 Identify a local organisation and look at their organisational structure to identify the roles and responsibilities of the staff.

2 Select three different organisational roles: one director or manager and two administrative or support roles. Identify the skills that each of these employees needs in order to operate the technology that has changed in the last three years.

3 Produce a training plan for each of these employees. For example, an administrator who has been using Windows XP and Office 2000 is likely to require training on the latest operating system and any changes introduced in the latest version of Office. There might be a training need for remote workers or sales representatives to learn how to use PDAs or how to access the organisation's network remotely. The IT technician might require training on new systems or networking.

35.2.3.2 Redundant skills and employees

Changes to the ways in which an organisation operates impact on the number of staff it requires or can afford. Organisations must deal with redundant skills and employees in order to avoid unnecessary costs. For example, if an organisation is considering moving towards a paperless office or outsourcing some of its services, it needs to think carefully about the job role (not the person) being made redundant and whether the salary saved benefits the business sufficiently.

The organisation will have to balance different considerations in order to decide which roles to make redundant. For example, the salary of an administrator might be as much as 80 per cent less than that of a director. In addition, there are the overhead costs to consider such as office space, resources and possibly company cars. The organisation might benefit financially from making a director redundant but also risks losing expertise. The organisation also needs to consider any redundancy payment it will have to offer – the size of this will depend on the length of time the employee has been with the organisation and also the size of their current salary.

Some organisations ask for volunteers to take redundancy.

Activity 35.20

Putting yourself in their shoes

1 Consider how individual employees cope with the fear of redundancy or deciding whether to volunteer for redundancy. Find out the experiences of people you know who have been made redundant. What can an employee do in such circumstances? Make notes.

2 Imagine that you are under threat of redundancy. You have a mortgage, a car to pay for and a family to support. How are you going to manage? Write a diary describing how you feel starting from the time you are advised of the redundancy. In your diary entries, explain the actions you take, the support you seek and what happens subsequently. For example, you will probably need to update your **CV** in order to promote your skills and experiences.

What does it mean?

CV stands for **curriculum vitae** – it is a summary of your education, work experience and skills.

35.2.3.3 Home and remote working

Another way for an organisation to cut costs is to encourage staff to work from home. Some staff (such as sales representatives) benefit from working remotely instead of rushing back to the office after visiting customers to write reports, submit sales orders or attend meetings face to face. With the use of mobile technology such as laptops, mobile phones, intranet, email, video phones and video conferencing, sales and support staff can spend more time with customers and less time in the office.

Some issues might arise with staff working from home – for example, how managers can monitor the productivity of people who are not in the office, and the effect on the individual or the family caused by intrusion into their environment. There are also technical challenges involved in setting up all the necessary equipment at home and maintaining and servicing it.

35.2.3.4 Impact of regular restructuring

Changes in staffing structures and reductions in staff impact on the cost and time taken to carry out changes. Investments by organisations in its staff, such as staff training, accommodation and resources, could be lost. Each member of staff made redundant will take with them a set of skills which another member of staff might not be able to replace.

Those who are working remotely are not easily accessible to discuss and solve problems face to face. Staff who are promoted as a result of the restructuring might not be ready for a higher-level position such as a management role. They might be ill-equipped to manage staff and the employees they are responsible for might resent this promotion and become difficult and uncooperative.

Where new teams are formed they might be less productive than the previous teams. This is because effective teams are made up of people with a range of personality types and job roles who adapt their behaviour in order to accommodate changes.

35.2.3.5 Managing change

All change is challenging to manage. One factor that makes coping with change difficult is the time it takes to put new staff or procedures into place. There is the cost implication too. Then there is the resistance from staff –

Activity 35.21

Changing behaviour

1 Use the Internet to research the behavioural theorist Belbin. What are the main characteristics of Belbin's research? Make notes.

2 What type of behaviour do you think is most effective and why? Do some types hinder productivity? Share your findings with your peers.

Activity 35.22

Out of control?

1 Think of an example when something happened to you which was out of your control, e.g. moving house or changing school. Write a reflective account of how you felt, what you did and whose support you sought to help you cope with this change. How long did it take for you to accept the change?

2 Read again what you wrote for question 1. Identify the different feelings you experienced and the order in which they occurred. What were they? Frustration, anger, anxiety, loss of confidence, unhappiness, confusion, acceptance, or some others? Discuss your experiences with a peer – what would have helped you to be better prepared?

not everyone adapts to change easily. Staff might be moved into jobs they do not particularly want and they might not have the necessary skills to carry out their new jobs efficiently and effectively straight away.

In order to manage change it is helpful to identify why we behave the way we do. It is likely that one of our first reactions to change is to feel upset, shocked, angry or confused. We are likely to experience a number of emotions. One of the reasons for such feelings is the fact that the changes that are happening seem to be out of our control. However, if we are kept informed with clear and honest communication, this will prepare us for the change and make it more likely that we will cope better – even if the reasons are not what we wish to hear and the outcome is undesirable.

35.2.3.6 Balance of core employees with contractors and outsourced staff

When considering staff reductions, changes to job roles and outsourcing of services, a strategy is needed before making any change to the staffing structure. For example, if all the sales staff are made redundant, who will sell the company's products? Devising a suitable strategy will create a delay and therefore has a cost implication.

Consideration of the balance of core employees (those who are employed by the company as a minimum for the organisation to operate effectively) against those who are contracted or outsourced is important.

Core employees are permanently employed by the organisation and receive a regular salary. They are an

ongoing cost to the organisation. Contractors (those who are outsourced) are not on the payroll and therefore are not an ongoing cost (although are likely to cost more per hour). Outsourced staff might include those on temporary contracts – these could be long-term contracts but are not permanent. These staff will not be subject to the same terms and conditions as those on permanent contracts and are likely to be less cost-effective.

Relying on contractors or outsourcing services is not necessarily the most efficient way to run an organisation. Employed staff are likely to be more loyal and generally more available. Organisations might identify that a reasonable number of core employees together with some outsourced staff will provide an efficient and effective working model.

However, changes to the way organisations are staffed might result in the staffing structure being **flattened** (see Figure 35.12).

What does it mean?

Flattening or **delayering** of organisational structures means the reduction in the number of levels of staff and managers.

▲ Figure 35.12 Flattening and delayering of managers!

▼ Figure 35.13 Example of a multi-layered organisational structure

Test your knowledge

1 What does delayering mean?
2 What is the difference between regulatory and legislative policies?
3 Describe geosourcing and how it differs from outsourcing.
4 Give examples of how organisations can cut costs.
5 Give three examples of why staff might require upskilling.
6 What are the benefits of globalisation?
7 What considerations must an organisation take into account when making redundancies?
8 What different emotions are likely to be experienced when faced with change?
9 What strategies can help employees to manage change more effectively?
10 What are the differences between contractors and employed staff?

Figure 35.14 Example of a flattened organisational structure ▶

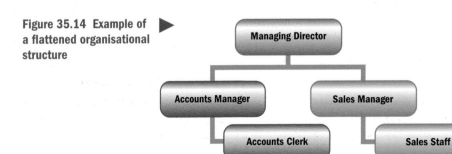

This section aims to help you to understand how organisations adapt their activities to respond to developments in IT.

35.3.1 Activities

This subsection explores the **promotion** (the marketing of products and services) and the **procurement** (acquisition, buying) aspects of an organisation and how to adapt these business activities to accommodate change.

35.3.1.1 Adapting sales and marketing strategies

Organisations are altering the way in which products are marketed and sold to exploit developments in IT. Some examples are included here.

The ability to market an organisation's products on the Internet results in swifter and cheaper global opportunities. Sales representatives can negotiate business deals over the telephone, by email and by conference and video calls, therefore avoiding the delay and cost of lengthy travel. This results in some business deals being closed more quickly and a proportion, if not all, of the cost savings being passed on to the customer – this makes the organisation more competitive.

Another form of online marketing is **viral marketing**, which offers inducements or incentives to pass on the message about a product or service.

What does it mean?

Viral marketing is marketing that relies on social networks passing on product or service information from person to person.

Not all viral marketing campaigns are malicious – some are quite welcome and work well because they build a sense of community among recipients, who actually want to pass on the message. Viral marketing works particularly well among groups with highly developed social networks, such as teenagers.

Many organisations make arrangements with other organisations to promote each others' products or services on their websites. Two examples of when this can be helpful (both for the customer and the organisation) are given here.

- A camera supplier might sell only digital cameras and not printers. It could therefore have a link to another website that sells printers that are compatible with its cameras.
- You might buy a computer from one website and follow a link to another website where you can buy software or peripherals to go with it.

The use of pop-ups is one type of Internet advertising that is not particular popular with consumers, as they appear without the user's permission and have to be closed. The Internet also contains some shocking advertisements that would not be acceptable to television audiences.

Spam emails, such as follow-up emails from an online purchase, are another example of online marketing. This type of marketing is often unscrupulous, with organisations imposing their advertising on consumers without their permission. Some of this marketing can have unsavoury content or be for unsavoury products, and can be very difficult to stop.

The use of specialist software (see page 390) can monitor or log sales. When an organisation monitors sales of a product, it gains a greater understanding of the impact of the product on consumers. It gains better and quicker feedback through the ordering process and therefore can adapt the product range to meet the demands of consumers. This is called **mass customisation**.

One way major organisations can find out what customers want is by using loyalty cards. These are used to track the purchases that individual consumers make and specialist software is used to identify other, similar products that the consumers might be persuaded to buy. In this way, the organisation can tailor the vouchers and offers that are sent to individual consumers, guiding and tempting them to buy more. For the consumers this can feel like Big Brother is watching them and taking note of everything that they do.

35.3.1.2 Adapting new purchasing opportunities

As a result of developments that make it easier for organisations to talk to each other through their systems, automated ordering becomes easier and quicker. One such example is the systems large superstores use to monitor the stock on the shelves – tracking sales and using EDI for automatic reordering before stock runs out. Calculations are carried out in an attempt to avoid stocks running out at critical times based on the likelihood of products selling at peak times. An effective system calculates the optimum level of stock in relation to storage capacity and with the least impact on **cash flow**.

What does it mean?

Cash flow refers to ready funds that are available within a business for spending.

These new purchasing mechanisms are also referred to as channel management as all the different potential channels to market are managed. Organisations decide how to sell their products and services – through catalogues, over the phone, on the Internet, etc. – choosing the method that seems to be the most effective.

Some organisations have been innovative in relaunching existing products to keep up with changing times and make use of the new technology available. One successful example of this is the relaunch of Monopoly, the classic board game that has been around for decades. The new version of the game has no paper money – instead it features calculators and debit cards for buying property around London.

Charitable organisations such as the Poppy Foundation are also keeping up with technology. There is now the opportunity to download the poppy as an icon for display on a mobile phone.

Activity 35.23

What's in a game?

1 Carry out research into board games and identify changes that have taken place through the developments in IT. Which board games have grown with the times and which ones have not? What is the reason for changing or not?

2 Identify your sources and share your findings with the group.

Activity 35.24

Does charity begin at home?

1 Identify other charitable organisations which have adapted or exploited information technology. Carry out your research and remember to identify your sources.

2 Find out when the organisations made the developments and how these developments might benefit the organisations. Share your findings with the group.

35.3.1.3 Using new technology in customer support

Most people have experienced firsthand how new technology has changed the way organisations provide customer support – for example, when asking for guidance on how to use a new mobile phone or a new computer or game console. These developments have enabled access to customer support through a number of channels, such as logging a query on the organisation's website using the 'contact us' section, sending emails or simply searching for an answer on the FAQs page.

However, sometimes technological advancements have resulted in a less satisfactory level of customer service for consumers.

Technology has resulted in many organisations using automated telephone systems to deal with customer transactions and queries. It can be very frustrating to be instructed to 'press 3, press 2, then 5...', and then be told to hold for several minutes, perhaps being cut off without your query being resolved. Such systems tend to be very unpopular with customers.

Some organisations employ support staff who read from a script and are therefore not able to answer questions directly – they simply read back what is on the script. It is likely that some organisations have adopted these approaches because they are cheaper and in some cases so consumers can access support out of usual working hours.

35.3.1.4 Secure funds transfer

With users moving money between bank accounts using online transactions (e-banking), the opportunities for hackers to steal funds has increased. (This is explored further in the section on cyber crime on page 410.) Therefore, software is required to provide security for transfer of funds. A firewall is one method of providing some security (see page 412).

Activity 35.25

'Select an option'

1 Keep a log over the next month of the number of times you, a family member or friends make a phone call and respond to automated instructions. Identify the organisations using these methods. Note any occasions when you are cut off before a resolution is reached. Identify the organisations where an operator communicates via a script and therefore does not supply a satisfactory answer to some of the questions asked – keep a note of the questions you asked. Identify any systems that work particularly efficiently and try to identify which systems.

2 Produce a list of FAQs for using a product of your choice.

3 Discuss your log and FAQS with your peers.

The introduction of chip and pin was intended to provide a secure way of using a credit card. Inserting a personal, private pin number instead of signing for goods is an attempt to prevent signature fraud. Unfortunately, the outcome has not proved to be entirely fraud-free and some would argue that vendors simply shifted the responsibility away from themselves and on to the purchaser. If you let anyone know your pin, you are to blame, as the vendor does not have to check signatures any more.

Activity 35.26

The human element

1 Identify two different organisations: one that uses real customer service people and one that uses automated services.

2 Suggest the benefits and drawbacks of the two approaches and suggest reasons for these different ways of operating.

3 Make comparisons and summarise your findings in a 1000-word report. Note: The report (and all preparation and draft documents) generate evidence towards Communication key skills.

35.3.1.5 Supply chain management

Organisations can manage their processes and services more efficiently with the use of EDI (electronic data interchange – see page 404) and options are extensive with outsourcing (see page 396). For example, with EDI the system can manage and interface with other organisations. The human element (which might be outsourced) supports the system.

Organisations are looking for a combination of effective ways to produce and sell products and services and subsequently to receive payment. The developments in IT allow systems to talk to each other and speed up the process.

35.3.1.6 Logistics

This topic is about adapting to developments and increasing efficiency. For example, an organisation with the ability to effectively track deliveries, sales and production can minimise stock holdings and therefore improve cash flow. It is important to keep an eye on the flow of money. In a family, there needs to be enough money to live on, pay the bills and to put some aside for emergencies. A large stock of tinned or frozen food that sits in the cupboard or freezer and isn't required in the immediate future ties up money so it cannot be spent on other things if needed or desired.

The same principle applies in the world of business. For example, supermarkets do not want to be holding large quantities of stock that will not be purchased in the near future. Likewise, it is important for them not to run out of salad or ice cream when there is a sudden heat wave. Systems such as EDI and MIS enable businesses to react and plan more efficiently.

35.3.1.7 Integration with partner businesses

If organisations use specialist software applications that can talk to each other (e.g. EDI, MIS), they can coordinate their products or services to provide a more customer-focused service. The spin-off here is that partner businesses can then provide a more holistic service – for example, coordinating transport timetables with other transport networks. These other networks might be operated by another company, perhaps even a former competitor, but the result is a transport service that works better for customers, thus encouraging more customers to use the service.

35.3.1.8 Establishing an Internet presence

Many organisations use technology to provide customer support and a website is often an essential part of this. Another essential function of a company's website is to promote its products or services. A custom-built website can be expensive to produce, as it is

Activity 35.27

Time for a break?

1 Carry out research into transport organisations that operate in collaboration with other organisations and what their services include.

2 Can you find any companies that operate a service that is well coordinated with partner organisations? Or do you find that timetables are not planned to coincide with other services?

3 Make notes and compare with other members of your group. Hint: Your first port of call could be to access an Internet website that is designed for planning a journey. Try finding out about companies such as Stagecoach and Virgin Trains.

important for the website to look professional and up to date. A website that has been built on the cheap is not going to create the best of impressions with potential customers. But it is also important to remember that an extremely slick and professional-looking website does not automatically mean that the business is entirely credible.

35.3.1.9 Reducing intermediation

Reducing intermediation is like cutting out the middle man in an attempt to become more efficient. For example, the ability to purchase holidays directly from a travel company removes the need to pay a travel agent. The cost saving is sometimes, but not always, passed on to the consumer (see page 403). Some high street insurance brokers have been put out of business now that insurance can be sourced, compared and purchased over the Internet.

Some examples of Internet-only businesses are eBay, Confused.com and Friends Reunited. Some banks exist only on the Internet, for example, Egg, IF and Smile – these tend to offer better terms for customers because they don't have the high running costs of high street branches.

Intermediation is necessary where there is **asymmetric information**.

What does it mean?

Asymmetric information is information that is known by some people and not others. Usually the seller knows more about the product or service than the customer.

It is usually in a business's interests to make sure it knows more about its products or services than the consumer. It can charge more for something that the consumer knows little about. The Internet has reduced the amount of asymmetric information by allowing consumers to be better informed about products and services and how much they are worth. This has helped to bring down prices.

35.3.1.10 Automating manufacturing processes

There have been tremendous changes in the way we work over the last 20 years. For example, the introduction of the fax machine in the mid-1980s was a major technological advancement to communications. Before this, there had been little development impacting on administrators other than the electric typewriter.

Dedicated word processors and then desktop computers became more prevalent during the early 1990s but, even then, many organisations did not rely on computers for their everyday activities. Early word processors displayed non-printing characters on the screen (such as instructions for italic and bold). This was confusing for novice users, who often deleted these instructions in case they printed out, resulting in unformatted documents.

Now there can hardly be a business in the UK that does not rely on highly sophisticated networked computers, running a range of software applications for performing a variety of tasks.

In the manufacturing industries, the introduction of robots has automated some of the tedious jobs that manual workers used to carry out. For example, the car industry uses robots to build and spray paint cars.

The Formula 1 motor sports industry uses programmable machinery to carry out dangerous and precision tasks in the manufacture of a racing car, such as cutting sheet metal, welding and other precision processes. However, these highly specialist car manufacturers (such as BAR, Benetton and Prodrive) combine both automated and manual processes due to the fine precision engineering used in producing these cars. Other car manufacturers such as Rolls Royce and Aston Martin also prefer to retain a large proportion of the hand-built craftsman approach.

Robots are used for highly dangerous activities such as radioactive areas and drilling undersea for oil.

Robots are not just used for dangerous manufacturing processes. For example, sweet manufacturers use automated machinery to make their confectionery and often to pack the products.

Activity 35.28

Sweet tooth

1 Identify some confectionery organisations that use automated processes in their manufacturing. What manual processes have these replaced?

2 Choose one organisation from the ones you have identified. What can you find out about the organisation's productivity rate? Has it increased since introducing automated processes? If so, why?

3 Write a short report on the benefits of using automated processes in your chosen organisation and identify any disadvantages.

35.3.2 Performance

This subsection considers how organisations need to manage their services in response to IT developments. It considers an organisation's output in relation to meeting demand and how improvements can be made to increase effectiveness. It looks at financial viability and stability and the way in which information is communicated internally and externally.

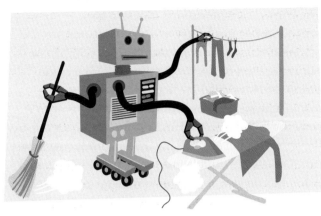

▲ Figure 35.15 A robot at work!

saves the cost of a large camera crew, all the supporting staff and their travel and **subsistence** costs.

Organisations that operate mostly online also benefit from reductions in cost – they generally do not have the high overhead costs of bricks-and-mortar businesses, such as high street premises, large numbers of sales staff, well presented store, etc.

What does it mean?

Subsistence means the living requirements, e.g. accommodation, food, drink.

35.3.2.1 Productivity gains

Productivity gains can be made by using a range of automated manufacturing processes and developments in customer support (see page 404). Although the initial outlay for automating processes in industry can be extremely high, they can result in large productivity gains. Robots and machinery can be operational 24 hours a day, seven days a week.

Machinery doesn't take tea breaks or take lunch breaks. While it may need some time off 'sick' (for essential maintenance or repairs), it never expects to go on holiday. Productivity is usually constant and the organisation can therefore rely on the amount of work the machinery will carry out.

This makes it is easier for an organisation to calculate how many products it will make, how much they will cost to make and the length of time it will take to make them. However, there will be regular maintenance costs to ensure the equipment doesn't break down and costs to keep up to date with new developments and further enhance productivity.

35.3.2.2 Cost reduction

Developments in IT are allowing reduced costs for some services and products. For example, the cost of automated services is often less than the cost of staff. One example of IT being used to reduce costs is the use of video phones by news journalists to make up-to-the-minute reports. This

35.3.2.3 Increased profitability

To identify whether profitability is increased and costs will be reduced by introducing new technology, a cost-benefit analysis can be carried out. When managers make a proposal for purchasing automated or technological equipment or machinery, they will need to justify their suggestions by comparing the cost of the new resources with the cost of staff. In their analysis, they will include the cost savings in time as well as money (see page 409).

Some organisations decide not to pass on these savings, or at least not all of the savings, to the customer – instead they enjoy a greater profit. The risk here is that the desire for profit might result in fewer sales and a drop in sales might then cause a fall in profit. A balancing act is therefore needed to maximise profit – organisations need to pass on enough of the cost savings to protect sales.

35.3.2.4 Efficiency

By introducing more automated processes and exploiting technology in business activities, organisations should become more efficient. Examples include mail order catalogues and stores that use the Internet as another means of selling their products (e.g. clothes, books, CDs, electrical goods, furniture and food). Consumers can make choices about where and how they make purchases.

Organisations become more efficient in servicing orders when they use EDI systems that can process orders, take payment for the product and inform the accounts system. The system identifies whether the item is in stock, reduces the current stock level by the number that is ordered and has the ability to reorder stocks automatically when levels become low.

Some organisations do not physically need to stock a product, in which case the system sends the order direct to the supplier who will despatch the product direct. The customer is usually advised by email almost immediately with a confirmation of the order that has been placed and information about the procedure for delivery. The order is then packed, delivery notes raised and the customer informed by email of precise delivery instructions. The responsibility often lies with the customer to rearrange the delivery if inconvenient. (Also refer to *Unit 34: e-Commerce*.)

35.3.2.5 Improved management information

Through the changes in IT, the development of specialised systems to manage information enables organisations to track and analyse productivity more easily.

Remember!

MIS stands for **management information systems** – see Figure 35.8 on page 390.

The MIS can monitor the stock of components and hence maintain the flow of productivity. Sales invoices can be generated swiftly and accounts reconciled to provide an up-to-date and accurate picture of the state of the organisation. This results in smarter pricing of products and services in attempts to remain competitive.

35.3.2.6 Control

IT systems mean that organisations are likely to have a great deal more control over the performance of their businesses. Improved MIS enable managers to monitor the efficiency and effectiveness of performance. Globalisation enables organisations to locate alternative suppliers who could provide more competitive products and therefore save them money. The use of automated manufacturing processes results in a more consistent and reliable output, contributing to organisations retaining control.

However, organisations still rely on human input – for example, to maintain machinery, to input the programming language that operates the machinery – and these tasks are not without risk (more of this on page 211).

35.3.2.7 Customer service

Some organisations have adapted to provide enhanced customer service and support (see Figure 35.16). However, some consumers are confused by the technology used and have difficulty in coping with new style of customer service. They might lack the level of skill required to access an organisation's website, for example. Where an organisation relies entirely on customers using the Internet – e.g. to refer to FAQ sites – this could be detrimental to the growth of sales for its products or services. So, it is a good idea for organisations to provide alternatives for customers who prefer to use more traditional styles or customer support, such as speaking to an advisor on the telephone.

35.3.2.8 Synergy and integration of systems

The developments that have taken place in IT, how they impact on organisations and how (and if) organisations have adapted their practices accordingly also rely on the **synergy** and integration of systems. In this subsection

What does it mean?

Synergy occurs when two or more elements (in this case computer systems) work together with positive results – the combined effect is greater than the sum of the individual effects.

◀ Figure 35.16 Offshore support

we look at how an organisation can bring together these systems and developments so as to benefit the organisation.

Organisations cannot work effectively when their systems do not work in harmony with each other. One simple example: organisations replace their computers with up-to-date models which include CD/DVD drives but no longer contain floppy disk drives – but if staff have files stored on floppy disks, these files cannot be accessed on the new system.

Effective integrated systems tend to be found in those organisations that opt for EDI or management information systems in order to streamline procedures.

Activity 35.29

Ahead of the times

1 How would you ensure that the desire to have the latest technology does not hinder general working practices? For example, should a business upgrade all its computers every year to the most powerful specification with the latest software? What would be the impact of this on the continuity of the business and effectiveness of its employees?

2 Compile a checklist or flow chart of stages to follow prior to upgrading existing systems. Discuss with another member of your class to test it out.

Remember!

To work towards a merit or distinction, you will need to explore where developments have caused difficulties and what organisations have done to address these difficulties. Difficulties should be seen as opportunities, although they might appear to be barriers at the time!

35.3.3 Managing risk

This subsection explores the risks that accompany developments in IT and ways to manage these risks. Risks are both threats and opportunities. You will need to consider the risks involved both in implementing IT developments and in not making any changes in response to technology developments.

35.3.3.1 Cyber crime

The increase in developments in IT, and in particular the use of the Internet (e-commerce), brings with it the risk of cyber crime. There are cases of Internet fraud where consumers' credit card details are stolen, despite chip and pin which was introduced to increase the security of buying using debit and credit cards. Hackers can also 'break into' bank accounts and steal money by moving it to other bank accounts.

The dark side of e-commerce is that unlawful purchases can be made from undesirable sites and unscrupulous organisations can offer illegal wares to the general public and adult products to under-age consumers. This is a difficult area to police and it is recognised as a major issue.

There is also the risk of share prices being influenced by Internet communications. For example, there are message boards for virtual dialogues about share prices. The information about shares posted on a message board might be nothing more than rumour or gossip, but ultimately it can devalue or increase share values.

Activity 35.30

Preventive measures

1 Investigate and identify what steps could be taken to prevent access to gambling sites. (People have experienced very quick and easy ways to gamble away large sums of money by registering their credit card details online.) Discuss your findings with another member of your group.

2 Identify how some websites have introduced an additional security measure for purchases made by credit card. What does it claim to do, how does it work? Share and discuss your findings.

3 Identify at least five different types of equipment available claimed to help prevent injury when using IT (also known as adaptive or assistive technology). Discuss with your peers.

■ Diverting financial assets

There are several different ways in which financial assets can be diverted. Criminals are able to transfer sums of money ('megabyte money') across the Internet easily and quickly. This illegal activity is made easier due to the high volume of financial transactions made online – it can be difficult to identify and trace individual transactions on a global scale.

■ Sabotage of communications

Deliberate sabotage of communication systems occur through viruses, that might be sent as, for example,

email attachments (see page 391). Software bugs are also a threat and, although non-malicious, the attack is likely to be as of much a risk to software or a system as viruses. Bugs are likely to occur where software is introduced prematurely onto the market with insufficient testing. It can be very tempting for developers to launch their software onto the market too early in an attempt to gain the edge over their competitors.

To protect our technological service against virus attacks, security software should be installed on home and work computers. The computer you use at your school/college or training provider will have at least one form of preventive or blocking device (see the section on firewalls on page 412).

■ Steal intellectual property

There are two main types of business: those that provide a service and those that make and/or sell products. Some organisations have exclusive rights to a design of their product which they have patented. Patented products cannot be copied by anyone else. Many creative works and products are not patented, but are protected by copyright law (e.g. paintings, images, literary articles such as novels, poems).

The owner of the patent or copyright to a the product owns the rights to make or reproduce the product and no one else can do this without permission.

When a person or organisation copies or uses patented or copyright material without the owner's permission, this is called stealing intellectual property. This is a particular problem with copyright material that is made available on the Internet. Many people are tempted to copy and paste information from the Internet and pass it off as their own work – however, this is an illegal activity and is known as plagiarism.

Internet search engines can be used to help combat plagiarism, as they can search vast amounts of text to match plagiarised material very quickly.

What does it mean?

Patented products and products protected by copyright are known as **intellectual property** because they have been thought up by someone and the idea belongs to that person.

Denial of service attacks

Not only are deliberate attacks made on computer systems, but also non-malicious attacks such as the interruption to the operation of a network. Denial of service can happen when a site is bombarded with requests for a page and the site jams. You will find more about denial of service attacks in *Unit 15: Organisational Systems Security*. Strategies for preventing denial of service are identified in the section on preventive technologies.

Activity 35.31

Keep your hands off!

1 Identify an example where stealing of intellectual property has occurred. Explain what happens as a result of this type of theft.

2 Find out the laws that are in place to protect intellectual property.

3 Share your findings with a peer.

4 Discuss with a partner how you would feel if you read someone else's assignment and found that it contained some of your words? Why would you feel this way? What could you do about it?
Hint: A good place to start is by searching for case studies on world news websites. If you have seen the TV programme Dragons' Den you may have picked up some ideas there.

Halt e-commerce transactions

Although there are many benefits of online shopping, together with the ability to geosource products and services, the negative side is the fear of theft over the Internet (see the section on cyber crime on page 410). Some research identifies that this fear is reducing and, in some cases, halting online purchasing. Reasons include the threat of theft of credit card details and the desire not to be bombarded with spam mail.

Furthermore, some countries have experienced massive frauds because of weak Internet regulations, resulting in e-commerce transactions being halted and the loss of customer confidence. Some countries are even being blacklisted from trading over the Internet because their banking systems are inadequate.

35.3.3.2 Preventive technologies

Preventive technologies can aid the management of risks. Preventive measures include systems that monitor compliance with data protection and firewall software that can prevent access to certain undesirable websites.

A simple preventive measure that helps prevent injury such as back conditions and RSI, is to make regular changes in activities when working with IT equipment.

Firewalls

Firewall hardware or software that limits access to and between networks is one method to improve the level of security. Firewalls use filters to block unauthorised material and potentially dangerous attacks such as viruses from entering the system.

Access control methods

Access to computers is usually secured by the need to insert a password to log in. With the use of the Internet and, in particular, the rapid increase in the use of wireless connection, there is a need to security-enable the connection to prevent unauthorised users obtaining access. This is done by selecting the security-enable option during the setup of the connection.

If a wireless connection remains unsecured, an unauthorised user could connect not only without having to pay but could access private information such as emails and bank account details.

One of the ways that criminals gain people's bank details is by **phishing**. This involves sending out spam emails claiming to be from the recipients' bank. These hoax

What does it mean?

Phishing involves criminals sending out fraudulent emails that claim to be from a legitimate company with the aim of obtaining the recipients' personal details and committing identity theft.

emails inform the recipients that they must immediately check their bank details due to a security error. The success of these emails relies on some receivers following a link and entering their bank details (including login and password), which then allows the criminals to access the bank account and withdraw funds. Banks now give warnings to their customers not to act on these emails and to report them to the bank.

▲ Figure 35.17 Phishing for bank details

35.3.3.3 Disaster recovery

A number of risks and threats to personal and business data exist. Organisations and individuals should have a plan for ensuring that information stored electronically is not only secure but also backed up. As individuals, it is important to frequently and regularly back up data. As an organisation, it is necessary to retain such files as financial accounts which should be backed up before and after each month end and annually.

Corporate electronic data retention is a complex area. Decisions have to be made regarding the types of documents to be saved and the information contained within them. The protocols for retention are likely to be identified within a retention policy.

Each organisation should also have a system for backing up everything on the system (including emails) and ensure that backups are not kept on the premises (in case of fire or theft). Data protection does not only apply to file servers but also to PDAs. Remote data centres provide this type of service.

■ Legislative risks

Legislative and regulatory requirements are referred to on page 397. Risks that need to be considered include the risk of an organisation being sued if an employee can prove they have been discriminated against in any way. For example, if an organisation introduced automated services and decided to make all staff over a certain age redundant, they could be prosecuted under the Employment Equality (Age) Regulations 2006, which make it illegal to discriminate against older (and younger) people. Other examples would include discrimination on grounds of race, gender or disability.

Some legislation relates specifically to the use of IT, such as the Display Screen Regulations (see page 397). Organisations are at risk of prosecution unless they abide by the law.

■ Surge protection

One of the risks to data is that of power surges. Power surges can happen at any time, but are more likely during electrical storms. A surge of power can cause considerable damage to electronic equipment. Protection can be bought cheaply and is easily applied. For example, for individual computers, extension sockets with in-built surge protectors are readily available. By plugging into this extension, all leads will be protected and any surge will be channelled away from the electronic device.

More complex solutions are available for networked computers but, essentially, additional equipment is needed to act as a barrier between the power source and the PSU.

■ Environmental risks

Developments in IT have brought with them environmental risks. For example, toxic and dangerous components used in computer systems include printer toner, toxic metals and gases and lithium batteries. Organisations and individuals must make sure that they dispose of obsolete computer equipment responsibly and following environmental guidelines.

■ Opportunities

Risks can also present opportunities, particularly for companies that produce products to help manage risk or provide technical support. Risks become threats only when organisations choose not to move with the times.

Activity 35.32

How green is your organisation?

1 Find out which department writes the policies and procedures for your school/college or an organisation where you have a work placement or part-time job. Who is responsible for the safe disposal of IT equipment? It could be more than one department. Make an appointment to visit each department and find out what preventive measures are in place to protect staff and the environment. You will also need to find out how the policies and procedures are monitored for compliance and how non-compliance is dealt with. Make notes.

2 Evaluate the possible risks and benefits for an organisation of implementing IT-based changes, e.g. disposal of obsolete equipment, upskilling of staff, effect on customers.

3 Investigate ways in which the same organisation could improve their procedures to manage risks when using new IT technology and make some recommendations. Make notes of your suggestions and the reasons for your recommendations.

4 Produce a short report combining your findings in a clear and logical manner.

Test your knowledge

1 What does the term phishing mean?

2 How often should a backup be carried out? How might this differ for different departments within an organisation?

3 How can organisations prevent unwanted or unauthorised access to electronic data?

4 Where should backups be stored? Give two reasons for your answer.

5 Why are some organisations not able to participate in e-commerce?

6 What is the term for when a patented product is copied without permission?

7 What is theft over the Internet known as?

8 Explain what sabotage of communications is.

9 What is 'megabyte money'?

10 Why could using Internet restrict growth of sales for a company?

11 What are the benefits and challenges that customers experience when organisations use technology to provide their customer service?

12 Give an example of an integrated IT system.

13 Give an example of organisation efficiency by use of IT.

14 What is a cost-benefit analysis?

Preparation for assessment

The assessment tasks in this unit are based on the following scenario.

Full of beans

You are the IT manager for a medium-sized family firm employing 50 staff. You manage an IT administrator and two technicians. The firm makes and sells bean bags of all shapes and sizes. You have identified a problem in the organisation – the IT systems and equipment are out of date, slow and often unreliable. As a result, sales have fallen and the company is facing some potentially difficult times ahead.

The business has been slow to move with the times. The accounts clerks and other administrators are using bespoke systems that work in isolation to the sales and buying departments. The production section also has its own system. The delays between departments knowing what each other is doing is also having an impact on the efficiency of the organisation.

The owner has agreed for you to identify a way to improve the current situation. It is your job to try and save the day by carrying out research in order to put a proposal for a new system to your boss.

Task 1 (P1, M1)

As IT manager, you will identify and explain relevant recent developments in IT and the impacts these are having on organisations.

Identify three different types of hardware and systems that might help Full of Beans and, for each, explain how it might benefit the company. Identify the software needed to support these systems.

Your boss will want a report – consider presenting some of the information in a format that will demonstrate the power of using IT.

As this is a really important job, you will want to discuss your preparations with your tutor at each stage. Be prepared to answer questions that identify any gaps or flaws in your proposal.

Task 2 (P2, P5, M3, D1)

Providing examples of where other organisations (small and large) have changed with the times will support your proposal to your boss. Identify the impact that IT has had within three organisations of your choice. Explain how the organisations plan for the internal changes and respond to the external changes generated by IT developments. Make reasoned recommendations about how Full of Beans can take advantage of IT developments and describe the likely impact of IT developments on employees and management. List any risks of using the new IT technology that Full of Beans may encounter and describe ways that they could manage these risks.

Task 3 (P3, P4, M2)

Since presenting your first proposal to the owner and other members of the board, you have been asked to work with the sales and marketing department to meet their IT needs.

Both the sales manager and the marketing manager at Full of Beans are relatives of the owner and somewhat unfamiliar with the power of IT. Marketing is still carried out by leaflet drops and adverts in the paper while sales staff travel long distances, knocking on doors to drum up business.

Identify and explain how other organisations have adapted their sales and marketing activities in response to IT developments. It will be particularly useful to identify the benefits to performance that can arise from adapting organisational activities.

Task 4 (D4)

The owner and other staff and managers are in a position where they can almost see your point of view. Complete your work by presenting an unbiased vision of all the possible consequences for Full of Beans of implementing the IT changes that you have suggested.

Index

encryption 190–1, 275; *see also* RSA encryption; WEP
end users 294–7
entities 117
entity relationship diagrams (ERDs) 111, 117, 224–6
environmental risk 413–14
EPOS (electronic point of sale) 87
EPROM (erasable programmable ROM) 46
equipment marking 186
ERDs (entity relationship diagrams) 111, 117, 224–6
error detection/correction 131–2
escalation 302, 340–1
ESD wrist straps 77, 328, 329, 345–6
Ethernet 134–5; *see also* CSMA/CD
ethical issues 205
Event Viewer 287, 336
expansion slots 57
expert systems 96, 390
extranet 392
eye scanning 189

F

facts 17
fans 48–9
FAQs (frequently asked questions) 239, 285, 298, 372–3
FastHosts 283, 285
FAT (file allocation table) 67–8
fault identification
    electrical 327–30
    general 325–6
    self-test routines 330–1
    troubleshooting techniques 336–8
fault logs 282, 286, 294, 339, 341
feasibility studies 106–7
feedback loops 100
fibre-optic cable 128, 133, 144
file management 77–8; *see also* FAT; network file services
fingerprint recognition 189
fire safety 346
firewalls 66, 192–4, 257–8, 377, 412
firmware 46
fishing *see* phishing
flash memory 59
flow charts 113–14, 226–7
fluid pricing 355
folders 77
form design 226
form factors 44
formatting 66–8
forums 370
frame relay 245
frames 134–6
Freedom of Information Act 91, 203–4, 380; *see also* ethical issues
frequency 128
full-duplex 61, 139
funds transfer systems 405; *see also* payment systems

G

Gantt charts 6
gateways 155, 253
geosourcing 305, 396
GHz (gigahertz) 42–3

globalisation 396
goals 5
Google 384
grammar 22
guard tones 61

H

half-duplex 61, 138
hard drives
    controllers 49–51
    installation 76
hardware
    backing store 58–9
    choosing 41, 62–3
    data transmission 60–2
    development history 384–8
    maintenance 74–7
    system unit components 42–58
HD DVD 58
health and safety 93, 340, 344–7
heat sinks 48–9
Heinemann 9
hertz 42
home working 400
hot swapping 52
HSRP (hot standby routing protocol) 155–6, 162
HTML 208
HTTPS 161, 163, 377
hubs 154
Huffman coding 134

I

I/O (input/output) 54
IDE (integrated drive electronics) 50
identity theft 377
in-trays 9–10
independence 13
information
    business uses 86–8, 96–7
    damage to 179–81
    ethical issues 92
    flows 88–90
    gathering for technical support 282–8
    legal issues 91, 340–1, 343, 356–7, 378–80; *see also* health and safety
    operational issues 93–4
    security 181
    sources 85
information system functions 99–100
infrared connections 51, 140, 145, 322
input specifications 112–13, 233
installation, of peripherals 75–7
integrity 13
intellectual property 411–12; *see also* copyright
internal memory 54–6
Internet 96, 163–7, 391–3; *see also* ethical issues; TCP/IP
Internet cafés 8
Internet Protocol (IP) 135–6, 249
Internet relay chat (IRC) 167, 266
interpersonal skills 19–21
intranets 322
intrusion detection 196

shift work 4
signal theory 127–34
simplex 138
Skype 165, 266–7, 270, 398
SLA (service level agreements) 282, 304, 340
Smileys 19
SMTP (simple mail transfer protocol) 164, 249, 258
soft skills 2, 300–2
software 389–93; *see also* bundled software; decision support software; diagnostic software; email software; presentation software; spreadsheet software
software maintenance 69–73, 323–5
spam 276, 371
spatial locality 56
spell checkers 31
spelling 22
SPI (serial port interface) 61
spiders 369
spoofing 178, 182
spreadsheet software 32
spyware 72–3, 195, 276
SRAM (static RAM) 45–6
SSADM (structured systems analysis and design model) 106
SSL (secure sockets layer) 265, 377
STE (chip select) 61
storage
    in programs 212–13, 217, 230–2
    physical 58
strategy, definitions 5
structure, in writing 22–4
structure diagrams 221
structured English 113–14, 228
Sub-7 (backdoor program) 177
substitution, troubleshooting technique 336–7
supply chain management 405
surge protection 413
swapping 45
switches 126, 155, 253
synchronous transmission 60, 130, 252
synergy 409–10
systems analysis 104

 T

TCP/IP 136, 159, 161–2, 367
team working 10–11, 37
technical infrastructure 395
technical skills 4
technical support
    information gathering 282–8
    information validation 288–91
    knowledge sources 291–4, 318–21
    organisational constraints 306–7
    policies and procedures 303–5
    software tools 307–13
    user communications 295–303
telephone calls, time management 9
telephone communications 267; *see also* VoIP; WAP (wireless application protocol)
telephone lines 133
temporal locality 56
tertiary storage 58
Tesco 360
testing 119–20, 237–8

text readers 32
thermal grease 49
thesaurus 31
time management 7–10; *see also* 'to do' lists
'to do' lists 5–6
tolerance 13
toolkit, for hardware repairs 327, 331–3
traces 71
Trading Standards 380
training
    as part of personal development 35
    for technical knowledge 320–1
    responsibility of employers 201
    upskilling 399
transceivers 140
transmission media 62, 133, 142–5, 254–5
Trixbox 267
trojans 65, 177, 257, 376
troubleshooting *see* fault identification
tunnels 178

 U

UDP (user datagram protocol) 136, 249
URL/URI 165
USB (universal serial bus) 52, 139
user accounts 197
user groups 197, 264
user reviews, in technical support 303
UTP (unshielded twisted pair) 142

 V

validation 112
VANs (value added networks) 246
variables 212–13
verification 112
video cards, installation 77
video conferencing/communications 28, 165, 168
viral marketing 403
virus protection 65, 194–5, 257–8; *see also* spyware
viruses 176–7, 257, 376
visual impairment 30–1, 63; *see also* text readers
VLAN (virtual LAN) 155
vlogs 28–9, 165
voice recognition 189–90
VoIP (voice over IP) 132, 168, 266, 270
volatile memory 44
voltmeters *see* multimeters
VPN (virtual private networks) 195

 W

wait states 56
WAN (wide area network) 135, 146, 244–6
WAP (wireless access points) 150, 156, 253
WAP (wireless application protocol) 365
waterfall model 104
web authoring tools 364
web servers 362, 364
website defacement 181–2
WEP (wired equivalent privacy) 160, 191
white box testing 119
WiFi 133–40

If you liked this book, you won't want to miss out on Book 2!

BTEC National IT Practitioners Book 2
2nd edition

BTEC National IT Practitioners Book 2 covers ten additional option units students will need to complete the Certificate and the Diploma.

◆ Includes case studies of real organisations and people working in the field of IT, so theory is placed into context.

◆ Outcome activities at the end of each section within a unit help towards the collection of evidence for coursework.

◆ Targeted assessment practice helps students get the best possible grades.

Units covered

4: ICT Project	20: Event Driven Programming
5: Advanced Database Skills	21: Website Production and Management
6: Advanced Spreadsheet Skills	22: Network Management
10: Client Side Customisation of Web Pages	24: Digital Graphics and Computers
13: Human Computer Interaction	26: Computer Animation

BTEC National IT Practitioners Book 2, 2nd edition   978 0 435465 50 6   £21.99

Visit your local bookshop or contact our Customer Services Department for more details.

(T) **01865 888118**   (E) **orders@harcourt.co.uk**

(F) **01865 314029**   (W) **www.harcourt.co.uk**